Living Ethnomusicology

Living Ethnomusicology

Paths and Practices

MARGARET SARKISSIAN

TED SOLÍS

Foreword by Bruno Nettl

Afterword by Mark Slobin

UNIVERSITY OF
ILLINOIS PRESS
Urbana, Chicago, and Springfield

Publication of this book is supported by grants from the Quitiplás Foundation, the Provost's Office at Smith College, Arizona State University's Herberger Institute for Design and the Arts, and the Arizona State University School of Music.

Library of Congress Cataloging-in-Publication Data
Names: Sarkissian, Margaret, author. | Solís, Ted, author.
Title: Living ethnomusicology: paths and practices / Margaret Sarkissian, Ted Solís;
    foreword by Bruno Nettl; afterword by Mark Slobin.
Description: Urbana: University of Illinois Press, [2019] | Includes bibliographical
    references and index. |
Identifiers: LCCN 2019001719 (print) | LCCN 2019002613 (ebook) | ISBN 9780252051180
    (ebook) | ISBN 9780252042348 (cloth : alk. paper) | ISBN 9780252084133 (pbk. :
    alk. paper)
Subjects: LCSH: Ethnomusicology.
Classification: LCC ML3798 (ebook) | LCC ML3798 .S27 2019 (print) | DDC 780.89—dc23
LC record available at https://lccn.loc.gov/2019001719

*To our teachers and our many remarkable predecessors
in this field to which we are privileged to belong.*

*And in memory of Elizabeth Travassos Lins,
Judy McCulloh, Clara Henderson, and Barbara Benary.*

Contents

PART 3. SELF-POSITIONING IN AND REFLECTIONS
ON THE FIELD

Foreword

It's an honor to have the opportunity to write a foreword for this interesting and innovative book. Although built on interviews with fifty scholars, it is much more than just interviews, turning out to be an analytical narrative providing a fresh approach to the history of ethnomusicology in the period since the mid-1950s.

The interviews themselves remind me of the questions I am often asked when I'm identified as an ethnomusicologist. The most common of them is, "How did you get into this [rather strange outré] field?" Among the various musical disciplines, people typically think of ethnomusicology as the exotic one, and they are disappointed when I tell them that I simply took a course as an elective and that this, as we say, "turned me on." The second-most-common question is, "Ethnomusicology? What's that?" I may give my two-pronged definition (the study of music in culture, and study of all musics from a comparative perspective), but then quickly I have to add that almost everyone has his or her own definition and probably wouldn't agree with mine. This reply, too, elicits signs of disappointment. The third question is often some version of this: "What are ethnomusicologists like, and what do they spend their time doing?" I'm usually at a loss to do much with this question, but it seems to me to be the one that would characterize my field most authentically, more than academic associations and theoretical stances and formal definitions.

When I've tried to answer this last question or something like it, I've had to admit that in the world of ethnomusicologists—not a very large world at that—their backgrounds, their education, and even their activities of research and teaching are probably more diverse than those of members of other academic endeavors. It's to these

Bruno and Wanda Nettl, Champaign, Illinois, March 2015.

very questions, "Who are the ethnomusicologists?" and "What are they like?" that this book, *Living Ethnomusicology*, provides answers in a unique and comprehensive way. And for this reason it is one of the most important books to have appeared in the literature in a long time—it identifies and defines us in a concrete way.

The authors, Margaret Sarkissian and Ted Solís (both, I am proud to say, are former students of mine), have dealt with their problem in a uniquely effective way. Selecting fifty ethnomusicologists, ranging in age (when interviewed) from around twenty to almost ninety, they deal with a sample representing a number of stages in the short and dynamic history of this field. All of these scholars, teachers, and members of other professions may be said to have succeeded as ethnomusicologists, but this book includes both leaders and, if I may put it this way, followers. Genders are represented equally. This book does not feature major figures (though some are there); instead, we meet a broad cross-section of individuals, with emphasis on North Americans. Otherwise, this sample is truly representative.

Looking at the collective careers from three perspectives—education and formative years, professional career, and personal reflections on the field, and juxtaposing in each section the experiences of all of the interviewees—provides an unusually interesting organization and makes this work, which one might think of as a kind of reference book, actually an interesting "read," something of a page-turner, especially if you know most of the people involved. I found myself surprised at many things these folks reveal about their lives and interests.

Having worked in ethnomusicology all my life, I would have expected to find this book full of the familiar. Indeed, I'm glad to say that my own "take" on the field and its history is substantially supported by Sarkissian's and Solís's interviews. But still, there were moments of the unexpected. For one thing, ethnomusicologists, with their small population, turn out to have more varied backgrounds and to come from a greater diversity of directions than—I would guess—most other academic disciplines. People who ask me "How did you get into this field?" turn out to be amply justified in their curiosity. Ethnomusicologists come from popular music, classical music, anthropology, folklore, Asian and African language study, but also from the Peace Corps, engineering, medicine, elementary school teaching, and the publishing world, to mention just a few from the occupational perspectives. Second, ethnomusicologists, as individuals, have typically changed their interests and the scope of their activities several times in the course of their professional lives, and possibly, as a group, they have been less careerist and more inclined to shift directions—for example, changing from teaching to archiving to government work and back, shifting cultures and genres, avoiding the kind of labeling that exists in the history of some humanistic and social disciplines. And I learned a good bit about the backgrounds, attitudes, and thinking of people I have known (maybe I should say "thought I have known") for many years.

Young readers of this book, students perhaps, will get insight into the stages through which one may move in a scholarly and (usually, but by no means exclusively) academic career, and old hands will read about their colleagues and about the way later generations viewed them. I compliment my friends, the authors of this work, on their innovativeness, on the excellent analytical introductory chapter, and on sticking with this project, as they tell you, for a good many years. Bravo!

Bruno Nettl

Prelude

Living Ethnomusicology was conceived at the fifty-first annual Society for Ethnomusicology (SEM) meeting in Hawai'i in 2006, at a rooftop bar in Waikiki, as we chatted about research projects over cocktails. We hatched the idea, began seeking out interviewees, and never looked back. We never imagined our project, an ethnography of ethnographers, would grow to such proportions or consume the next decade-plus of our lives. It was never intended to be a comprehensive study of the field. Our goal was simply to present a reasonable cross-section of the profession, highlighting the diversity of backgrounds, career paths, and opinions that characterize us. In this spirit, we conversed with ethnomusicologists of many ages, nationalities, and divergent career paths, aiming, to the best of our abilities, toward diversity broadly defined. We hope that this collection will be helpful to those who, hoping to enter the field, are still wondering, "What can I do with a degree in ethnomusicology?" and to those of us already in the field who are fascinated with the lives and careers of other "ethnos."

As we amassed more and more life stories, we began to see generational and career-oriented patterns emerge, so we developed an organizational structure that—we hope—will allow readers to actively make comparisons and follow threads that emerge from their own questions and curiosities.

How to Read This Book

Each individual's life story is divided across three sections, each of which has a different organizing principle. Part 1, which focuses on early lives and education up

The authors hatching the plot at the 51st Annual SEM Conference in Honolulu, Hawai'i, November 2006. (Left to right) Jerry Dennerline, Margaret Sarkissian, Richard Haefer, Ted Solís.

through the start of college, is ordered chronologically, from oldest to youngest, and subdivided by decade of birth. Part 2 focuses on career building and picks up as the speakers begin their graduate studies. In this section conversations are ordered by type and stage of career at the time of the interview. Since we conducted many of our interviews a decade ago or longer, we asked for career updates in 2016 to see how career trajectories had developed. At that moment, we also asked each person to answer two questions in writing. These thoughtful reflections form the content of part 3. In order to emphasize the uniqueness of the responses—and avoid unintended hierarchies—we have organized this final section alphabetically. Thus, instead of reading this book from cover to cover, we urge readers to use the table of contents and the index creatively, whether it be to follow one person's life journey or to explore more actively according to their own personal agendas or interests. In editing the fifty interviews for length and consistency, Margaret has endeavored to retain the individual voices and flow of each conversation. Throughout Ted's introduction, postlude, and framing sections, quotes appear in their original transcribed versions; elsewhere, quotes may have been shortened or (occasionally) omitted due to length restrictions.

Margaret Sarkissian
and Ted Solís

Acknowledgments

We are, of course, infinitely grateful to each of our fifty interlocutors. Some were already friends, and others we knew slightly at the outset, but many were new acquaintances who—with great generosity and trust—agreed to share their lives in conversation with one or both of us. All have been remarkably patient with our slow progress over the ensuing years. We are deeply saddened that three of this group passed away before we finished the project: Elizabeth Travassos Lins (2013), Judy McCulloh (2014), and Clara Henderson (2016). We have retained their conversations, with the blessings of their spouses/family members as a tribute to their lasting impact on our field. In each case, we asked a close friend of the individual to contribute a short postscript. We are very grateful to those colleagues, Anthony Seeger, Margo Chaney, and Alan R. Burdette, respectively.

We owe a great debt to the kind souls who helped get our "two-person" project off the ground. Without the help of some intrepid students, we would still be transcribing interviews in between semesters and during sabbaticals. Margaret would like to thank Smith College student Jaclyn Perreault, who spent a semester transcribing interviews, and Provost Marilyn Schuster for funding Jaclyn's assistantship; Emilie Coakley (then at Mount Holyoke College) and Emily Matz (Smith College) also assisted with transcriptions. Sean Norton, former Hampshire College student and good friend, stepped in toward the end with editorial help that got us over the finish line. Frank Citino (Clark Science Center, Smith College) and Jeff Heath (Center for Media Production, Smith College) provided invaluable technical assistance; colleagues Marianna Ritchey and Kariann Goldschmitt advised us on selecting our final interviewee; and friends Steve Waksman and Ruth Solie provided sage advice over the years. Last, but definitely not least, Margaret would like to thank Ted for being who he is—an exceptionally kind-hearted (if sometimes impish) friend and trusted colleague. Ted would like to thank Katie Palmer and Amy Swietlik, former students and good friends, who offered excellent advice on the book's organization. He would like to express gratitude and deep appreciation for the privilege of working with his patient, compassionate, and inspirational dear friend Margaret during these years; the Yiddish inflection marks his highest tribute: "Everybody should be so lucky!" We are grateful to Tim Cooley and David Harnish for invaluable feedback on earlier versions of this project and, especially, to our institutions for providing sabbatical leaves, travel funding, and other research support.

None of this would have seen the light of day without help from the University of Illinois Press. Laurie Matheson, in particular, took an early interest in our project and shepherded us through the review process. We are grateful for her encouragement and guidance. We would also like to thank the editorial and production staff at the press, especially Julie Gay, Jennifer Argo, and Dustin Hubbart. We are also grateful to our indexer, Nicole V. Gagné.

We will always be grateful to our principal academic teachers in ethnomusicology: in Ted's case, Barbara B. Smith and Bruno Nettl; in Margaret's, Bruno Nettl, Clark Cunningham, Charles Capwell, and the late David Stigberg, who taught us so much about ethnomusicology, fieldwork, and ethnographic writing. We are honored that Bruno Nettl agreed to write the foreword for this project and warmly thank Mark Slobin for his thoughts in the afterword.

Publication has been made possible by subventions from the Quitiplás Foundation, Smith College Provost's Office, Arizona State University's Herberger Institute for Design and the Arts, and the Arizona State University School of Music. We are extraordinarily grateful for this financial assistance.

We would like to thank our partners Julie Codell and Jerry Dennerline for sticking with us through the whole process, for their constant support, sage advice, and limitless patience. Finally, our book includes only fifty out of more than two thousand active ethnomusicologists; we wish we could have included everyone in this community we revere.

Living Ethnomusicology

Where shall we adventure, today that we're afloat,
Wary of the weather and steering by a star?
Shall it be to Africa, a-steering of the boat,
To Providence, or Babylon, or off to Malabar?

—Robert Louis Stevenson, "Pirate Story,"
from *A Child's Garden of Verses*, 1885

MAPS AND GRASS SKIRTS: DREAMING BEFORE PROFESSING

Ethnomusicologists may love or hate the word "ethnomusicology," and outsiders may find it humorously "academic," along the lines of classical music humorist Peter Schickele's "Musicalology" or NPR's *Car Talk* guys' "AutoMusicology,"[1] but we never find the field dull or quotidian. We Ethnos, or Ethnoids, as some of our amiably tolerant colleagues like to call us, never tire of obsessing about it; the late Alan P. Merriam (1964, 3) claimed that ethnomusicology is "caught up in a fascination with itself." Ethnomusicologists are, in the words of Bruno Nettl (2013, 28), "almost inordinately or obsessively interested in the history of their own field." Belonging to one of the youngest of academic disciplines, ethnomusicologists seldom live within their own department, most typically rather finding themselves in slots within music history/musicology areas, as well as outside of music units, in such departments as folklore, anthropology, cultural studies, African American studies, and others. Ethnomusicology was born of musicology and anthropology, but with an arguably more relaxed and more consciously familial relationship with the latter than the former. One oft-noted reason for this difference in comfort level was a widespread perception that musicologists/music historians were ethnocentric high priests of a "pantheon" (Nettl 1995, 12) of dead, white, male European composers, icons of a notation-bound, canonic, and unassailable Western Art music tradition, more interested in abstracted stylistic features than people. Certainly much has changed in this regard;[2] nevertheless, ethnomusicologists both personally and in print often think of themselves as a group apart, drawn to the exotic (Mohd. Anis Md. Nor's early "image of the adventurer traveling all over"[3]), The Other, and/or deep questions about their compatriots and themselves.[4]

Anthropologist Clifford Geertz (1973, 13) claims that "we [he is of course referring to anthropologists rather than ethnomusicologists] are not, or at least I am not, seeking either to become natives (a compromised word in any case) or to mimic them. Only romantics or spies would seem to find point in that." However much this may or may not be true, it seems pretty clear, if we look at what they study, that those who eventually become ethnomusicologists are almost certainly drawn to other cultures and The Other more than are most academics. This still seems to be the case, notwithstanding the increased prominence of more local studies, including a great interest in media and popular musics. This change is due partly to the perception that more "exotic" research niches have become depleted, as well as to the rise of "virtual fieldwork" (see Cooley, Meisel, and Syed 2008).[5] The fascination with *people* is an attraction at least as much as is *sound*—perhaps counterintuitive, historically speaking—for a "–musicology." Note anthropologist-ethnomusicologist Adrienne Kaeppler's comment that she likes "the 'ethno' part of it," but is bored with the "non-'ethno' [music analysis] part." Aspiring opera singer Jon Dueck became aware of his ethnomusicological leanings partly because, he says, "In music theory papers, I'd analyze the structure of a pop song and then contact the guy and do an interview with him. Right from the start, I wanted to talk to people." Pure sound, on the other hand, certainly attracted some of our interviewees: composer-ethnomusicologist Michael Tenzer fell for the disembodied excitement of his first Balinese gamelan recording, before he knew much about either Bali or gamelans. Be it people or sound, the attraction was for the new, distant, exotic. Note Ellen Koskoff's (2008) field notes in Bali, her first extensive overseas fieldwork sojourn after years of fruitful and esteemed work with Judaic music in US venues:

> I am sort of tickled that I have malaria. It seems to give me some ethno "street cred." This whole trip, I've realized, has been a sort of re-entry into ethnomusicology—the older, traditional way: a faraway, exotic culture, traipsing around in a "village" with "traditional" performers, etc. The romance of all of those early ethnographies must have tapped into my imagination more than I realized (thanks Jaap Kunst and Mantle Hood, etc.) And, on top of it all—malaria! How cool is that?!

Does our field attract romantics, seeking the exotic, "faraway places," languages? How typical is Alex Dea, who reports that, as a child, with an old map on his wall, "[I would] close my eyes almost every morning, put my finger somewhere on the map, and open them to see where it was. I suppose I wanted to go to other places"? And Gini Gorlinski, inspired by her military father's home movies of Vietnamese women washing clothes in a river, and proceeding to wash her new pink coat in a nearby creek: "performing The Other" at age five? Does ethnomusicology provide a way for us to continue the sort of make believe we all have indulged in as children, to keep on navigating in our own Pirate Stories, even playing "dressup"—like Adrienne Kaeppler with her newspaper strip grass skirts in Milwaukee?[6]

The notoriously evocative and emotionally entwining nature of music itself may render us more vulnerable to romantic entrapment by and with our subject matter and subjects. Many in this volume made their first conscious steps toward the ethnomusicologist identity as a result of having heard some snippet of sound from this or that tradition.

Those outside or new to academia may more easily grasp the concept of performing music and dance than other, more conventionally academic aspects of the music field. Most relate more readily to the general idea of teaching, which they have all experienced in public education, than to the more abstract and apparently less utilitarian idea of "publishing." Typical questions: "Publish what?" "Publish why?" "What do you mean, 'give a paper'?" Many, not surprisingly, seem to think that performing is the crux of what we in music all do. I have more than once, after answering a question about what I did for a living, gotten in response: "You're an ethnomusicologist? Wow, that must be great, playing all that fun stuff!"[7] Note Alex Dea's first encounter with the word "ethnomusicology," in which friends described the Wesleyan doctoral program as one in which "you can get a PhD to do this [play in gamelan], and it's called 'ethnomusicology.'"[8]

Among the other immediate and profoundly deep aesthetic attractions of music, the exhilaration of performing culture can affect us in a particularly potent way. Mantle Hood, interviewed near the end of his life by Ricardo Trimillos: "I guess the big lesson that I've tried to pull out of all this is: know the culture by becoming part of it to the best of your ability. You know it through music; you know it through dance; you know it through rituals. In these ways you know it better than people who struggle with language" (Hood 2004, 287).

All these things bond—music probably most strongly—in a sort of witches' brew, with other salient aspects of culture: smells, colors, tastes, intensive and extensive academic and intimately applied language training and experience, and close relationships with other informants/research collaborators.[9]

In the words of James Clifford (1988, 24), "Participant observation obliges its practitioners to experience, at a bodily as well as an intellectual level, the vicissitudes of translation. It requires arduous language learning, some degree of direct involvement and conversation, and often a derangement of personal and cultural expectations."

Indeed, many ethnomusicologists identify so strongly either before or during the process of their research involving extended fieldwork, acquired language facility, and shared musical and other deep experiences with their chosen cultures that they resemble "halfies," Lila Abu-Lughod's (1991, 137) term for "people whose national or cultural identity is mixed by virtue of migration, overseas education, or parentage." Conversely, some, like Michael Tenzer, work to avoid this: "I didn't want to give up my identity; I didn't want to be Balinese; I wanted to be an outsider. . . . I felt that if I gave up my Western identity, they would never respect me as much." Many, knowing how seductive altered identities can be, keep them at arm's length. The resistance to "going native," expressed above by anthropologist Geertz, also reflects a similar tendency among some ethnomusicologists to refer to our field as some sort of science, with its presumably greater objectivity and gravitas. At any rate, tenure, promotion, and advancement in ethnomusicology have generally been based on what some might consider the more conventional academic content of one's curriculum vitae, rather than the perhaps more distinctive aesthetic and "romantic," as well as personal aspects.[10]

A Gaseous Coalescence: Our Paths to Ethnomusicology

In the words of author Baroness "Emmuska" Orczy (1947), writing in her autobiography *Links in the Chain of Life*: "How often have I been asked . . . 'do tell me how *The Scarlet Pimpernel* came to be written. How did you think of him?' . . . Ah, well! such is destiny. . . . If this had not happened . . . or that. . . . if . . . if . . . if . . . well, if all those things had not happened *The Scarlet Pimpernel* would not have been written" (1–2). Ethnomusicologists have found their ways into the field through paths numerous and often unlikely. The younger among those we interviewed were generally more aware of ethnomusicology and its employment possibilities than had been their older colleagues at comparable early stages of their careers. Aspiring ethnomusicologists in the 1970s also had many more sonic and literary resources at their disposal than did their immediate predecessors.[11] Note, for example, Judith Becker's account of her first world music exposure, in the late 1950s:

> I was a piano major. And, my husband got a Fulbright to go to Burma. . . . Here I was in Burma, surrounded by this amazing music that I couldn't make head nor tail of. . . . I mean . . . no Nonesuch records, you know. I guess there were a few Folkways [records] at that time, but I sure didn't know about them. World, other musical traditions were just beyond my horizon. I just didn't know about anything. We never had touring groups; we had nothing, none of that.

Compare this with the experiences of Michael Tenzer (born around the time Judith Becker was having her epiphany), who experienced (in New York) cultural exotica such as Indian art exhibitions, restaurants, and an LP of early world music icon and Yoruba performer Babatunde Olatunji. Younger ethnomusicologists were entering a field with a name now generally accepted throughout musical academia, with designated faculty lines and increasingly specific ("Africanist" or "Asianist," or even "South Asianist," for example) job searches.

Regardless of their attractions to cultural exploration, diversity, and the exotic, incoming undergraduate students are even today seldom initially aware of ethnomusicology as a possible major or interest until they happen to stumble upon it. For many music majors this may come about only after they have finished their normally very traditional and extensive "music core" requirements and are finally free to explore an elective or two. Gini Gorlinski, although raised in multicultural communities in Washington, DC, California, and other places in the 1960s and 1970s, and then majoring in music at the cosmopolitan University of Michigan in the early 1980s, was still not aware of such places' long-established ethnomusicology and Javanese gamelan programs, which she soon found very much to her taste, as a nexus of her passions, until tipped off by a Californian friend: "It's getting a little better now, but at that time, if you went into music in higher education, the only option you knew about was performance; you didn't know that anything else existed, except perhaps music education, but that's what pretty much everybody did. It's still like that to a large extent." Ethnomusicologists approach their careers from many directions, in terms of their own backgrounds and disciplinary methodologies—Bruno Nettl (2010, 88) states that "ethnomusicologists have begun to change their approaches, looking less at musical cultures at large . . . and more at specific cases: events, genres, individuals, institutions, pieces."

Even this broad statement does not quite do justice to the variety of our activities. Ethnomusicologists seem to have coalesced, like gasses around a central galactic core, around a term which may imply more unity or cohesion than actually exists—in Ken Gourlay's (1978, 6) words, "a convenient 'shorthand'" for an academic discipline.

Who are ethnomusicologists? How and why did they find their way to this identity? In this volume we aim at a broad view of the field of ethnomusicology through encounters with a diverse variety of those who call themselves ethnomusicologists. Ethnomusicologists, with their widely varied backgrounds and foci, can share close academic interests, theoretical orientations, and professional networks with anthropologists, sociologists, folklorists, historical musicologists, and scholars in the performing arts, cultural studies, performance studies, global and domestic American area studies, and other disciplines.

However diverse their professional origins and preoccupations, ethnomusicologists typically self-identify as such. Can we speak of an "ethnomusicological identity"? Can we find commonalities among those who identify themselves as such in so diverse a field? Is ethnomusicology actually a "field" at all, as opposed to a subset of anthropology or of musicology? Are we motivated by wanting to explore ourselves in exotic contexts?

Do we wish to explore *and* shape the cultures of others? "The ethnographer," according to Geertz (1973, 19), "'inscribes' social discourse; *he writes it down*. In so doing, he turns it from a passing event, which exists only in its own moment of occurrence, into an account, which exists in its inscriptions and can be reconsulted." This shaping, as it applies to ethnomusicology or any other field, constitutes an important form of creativity, in the sense that we are "interpreters, creators, re-creators, and molders of . . . cultures in the academic world" (Solís 2004b, 11). It naturally follows that, because what ethnomusicologists present as scholarship and engage in through their everyday work and the rest of their day is the face of the subjects they mediate, their own personal narratives, experiences, and perspectives are profoundly important and influential in such presentations. This power to present others to the world, in a sense, is a weighty responsibility, with relatively few checks. In the words of Geertz (1988, 5), "Even if, as is now increasingly the case, others are working in the same area or on the same group, so that at least some general checking is possible, it is very difficult to disprove what someone not transparently uninformed has said."

In addition to helping shape and interpret the texts of our research collaborators/informants, we ourselves are often important cultural catalysts.[12] Note Alan Merriam's (1977, 816) reference to himself, in his capacity of investigatory ethnomusicologist, as an agent of change, through his commission of instruments and support for a waning Congolese xylophone tradition, and as a "historic accident," in the sense that (citing Herskovits 1948, 588) he represented "happenings which 'occur outside any sequence of events that might ordinarily have been anticipated' and which are defined as 'abrupt innovations that arise from within a culture or result from the contact of peoples'" (837). It is our fascination with the interplay of these personal and professional origins with the fabrics of their professional lives that has led us to this project.

Ethnomusicologists in the Witness Stand

Living Ethnomusicology is the first extensive and inclusively based ethnography of the field of ethnomusicology, presenting dialogic oral histories as a lens through which to explore the formation, discipline, and professions of ethnomusicologists. Ethnomusicologists have produced fascinating and compelling studies of individuals, including numerous documentary films (see Barret et al. 2005; Zemp 2005; Goldman 1996, and many others). However, apart from some introductions to festschrifts (edited, multi-authored books commonly dedicated to highly respected senior academics), we find even very few short biographies of ethnomusicologists themselves, and very little in the vein of "living dialogue."

As ethnomusicologists, most of us have spent our careers querying others. The older among us may have worked in a sort of subject/object collector mindset that likely evolved into the more recent and preferred "research collaboration." Regardless of methodology, ethnomusicologists are highly aware of the debts we owe to our research collaborators, whom Bruno Nettl (1984) very movingly refers to as our "principal teachers." "In the field, our friends and research collaborators have unselfishly given us gifts we know we cannot repay; we know that whatever fees or presents or help we offered in exchange were nothing compared to the worlds revealed to us" (Solís 2004b, 17). We revere the people who have offered us so much, and often feel guilty asking these things of them. As Bode Omojola says, "At times I feel that we make a lot out of what they give us. So when I'm in front of a class now talking about Yoruba drumming, there are all sorts of information that I didn't know, but were given to me by this man. And that has become an important part of what I teach, what I do. I have built my career on other people's knowledge."

We ethnomusicologists are quite aware that the act of asking the questions, some of which may broach societally or personally inappropriate or sensitive subject matter,[13] may constitute an unwelcome invasion of privacy. Many of us have had to deal with queries such as "Why *are* you asking me these questions?" "Why do you want to know this?" "What *are* you getting out of this?" Heavily indoctrinated in cultural sensitivity, few ethnomusicologists are thick-skinned. This awareness creates a sort of strain that constitutes for some an ongoing occupational hazard.

In the introduction to *Performing Ethnomusicology* (2004c, 8, 9), I stated that

> from the first, I intended that one important contribution of this book be the reflexive examination of ethnomusicologists' personal learning and teaching continua, including their formative influences before succumbing to the blandishments of ethnomusicology as a field per se.
>
> . . .
>
> Inducing contributors to engage in this sort of autobiographical revelation was, however, not always easy; some equated self-revelation with egotism and even exhibitionism. This, although certainly none believed themselves born fully formed, like Athena from the head of Zeus, as world music ensemble directors.

Low-key frustration from not having quite fulfilled that goal, then, was at least one source of this current book. Switching roles and putting ourselves in the position of interviewee/provider of insights might seem a healthy and refreshing break from the role of importunist/opportunist; however, ethnomusicologists are not always comfortable sitting in the witness stand of direct interview, especially by others "in the biz."[14] One most commonly finds such items, in highly edited and often rather distorted form, in "Faculty Doings" sections of university/collegiate house organs and alumni magazines.[15]

Suppression of Self was of course part of the positivist attitude to scholarly research that was dominant until the 1970s. In the words of historian William H. McNeil,

> Historians have usually been very cautious about self-revelation, but the self behind the opus is always interesting, if the works themselves are interesting; and the interplay between

personal experiences and the writing of history is a dimension of our craft which has usually been suppressed or even, in an earlier age, denied. In the late nineteenth century, academic historians thought that history could be made into a science that would establish truths that would be accessible to all reasonable human beings for ever and ever, and that the personality and the biographical element in anybody's contribution to this temple of learning were irrelevant. All that mattered was the careful criticism of sources. This ideal prevailed for fifty or sixty years, but has now, I think, been very generally abandoned. (Adelson 1997, 165)

Ethnomusicologists strongly emphasize and value the centrality (as in our parent discipline of anthropology) of their direct individual communication with their subjects (rather than via their highly edited, translated, reprinted written words). We authors of this volume feel that it is appropriate for us to engage ethnomusicologists in this way.

We agree with McNeil (above) that the "interplay of experiences" and our work is critical, but we are less concerned with the "interest," however gauged, of the "works themselves" produced by our participants. We are more concerned here with the stories, the fabric of their lives and careers. We feel that all oral histories are by definition "interesting"; our only qualification has been the attempt to present as wide a variety of such stories as possible. Our aims thus more closely emulate those of the great popular oral historian Louis "Studs" Terkel who, in such projects as *Division Street* (2006/1993), *Working* (1972), and other classics, helped us view the self-assessment, strictures, and compensatory pleasures in the interplay of careers and daily lives.

In contrast to Studs's quite catholic approach, most oral histories of academics have focused on particular categories of subjects. Roger Adelson (1997, ix), editor of *Speaking of History: Conversations with Historians*, states that he selected "historians who reflect the increased diversity among those who have been teaching, editing, and writing history . . . since the Second World War. . . . [and that while he] sought variety in age, background, culture, and education," he nonetheless sought out "individuals with innovative and global approaches to the past."

The title of Paul A. Samuelson and William A. Barnett's *Inside the Economist's Mind: Conversations with Eminent Economists* (2007) proclaims its own delimitation to "leading lights" of the field, and this is entirely typical of such volumes.

What Do We Want to Know?

All of us in and around the field of ethnomusicology, assertive or shy, whether working abroad or within the neighborhood, are intensely interested in the stories of others. What is it we want to learn from them? The focus of our questions can vary according to the particular project, but virtually all have in common question A: "How do you do what you do?"; and B: "Why do you do what you do?" Probably B is the most fundamental question of all; scholars have usually framed this in the context of identity. It is in great measure the professional component of these identities that serves as the link between questions A and B.

In this volume, we address ways the personal and professional interact organically with one another to create identity. We explore whether an "ethnomusicological identity" actually exists and how ethnomusicologists construct this identity. We seek links between people's upbringing, early influences, and predilections both musical and nonmusical on the one hand, and deliberate and formal education channeling these influences and interests into vocation and careers on the other. This, then, refers us back to question A, "How do you do what you do?"

We attempt to engage ethnomusicologists as they do with their own subjects/informants/research collaborators. This engagement is dialogic (although the finished, edited interviews inevitably can't show *all* the underlying dialogue). That said, and with the focus of a few basic questions we pose, our interlocutors for the most part lead us where they will. Like Nicole Beaudry (in Gregory Barz and Timothy J. Cooley's fieldwork classic *Shadows in the Field*, 1997/2008), we try to be "as receptive as possible, [and] leave it to informants to choose the manner in which they wish to instruct [us] and to decide in which directions they will channel [us]" (Beaudry 2008, 230).

This is largely owing to our great interest in searching for the "ethnomusicological type"; we feel that what some might dismiss as trivialities are indeed the stuff of which we are constructed—the dark matter or dark energy we hardly see but of which we mostly consist—the kind of world in which if you make a right turn one day instead of a left, your life will never be the same thereafter (Solís 2008).

Childhood may or may not be one of the "trivialities" available at a given time and place to people in particular circumstances. As with everything in our accounts, and as is typical of virtually all kinds of investigation in ethnomusicology, we are as much concerned with understanding circumstances and contexts as we are with what ethnomusicologists do per se. Childhood issues are a cultural history of the kinds of experiences that were available at a given time and place. Are our lives created in childhood? Do we seek other cultures because we, like Jonathan Dueck as a child, "have problems placing [ourselves] in a social space"? How are choices and avenues opened to us before we actually have choices? What would we have become if we were not ethnomusicologists? Can we find strong currents of commonality among those who shared their stories with us? To what extent may these contextual commonalities have shaped the field and its main thrusts? These and other questions, we feel, give strong support to our preoccupations and lines of inquiry in this volume.

Reconciling Our "Life's Work" with our "Working Life"

For ethnomusicologists in the academy, the institutions employing them are themselves sites of field work; all academics bring with them background skills and attitudes they must then negotiate with the physical and imagined "place" they spend most of their time working. "Work"—as in "my work," and "I work with . . ."—often means something quite different for ethnomusicologists than for others. As with many academics in postsecondary education, ethnomusicologists are prey to the academic malady of finding it difficult to leave their "work" at the office.[16] Indeed, many (if not most) academics do much of their research, or their research writing, at home. Like most academics, they long for semester breaks and summers so they can pursue this work more intensely and single-mindedly. Like most academics, they are absorbed in their areas of study, especially the most current.

They must reconcile this work that has so absorbed them emotionally with the realistic demands of "the workplace." Ethnomusicologists, like other academics in fields that emphasize ethnography, identify themselves with their informants and the cultural contexts of those informants. David McAllester (1986, 210), in reference to his relationship to Navajo ritual specialist Frank Mitchell, to whom he referred as his "Navajo father and teacher" (1986, 212), expresses sentiments common to many: "My acquaintance with the Mitchell family deepened into a closeness that precipitated the question in my own mind as to whether I was their friend or their scientific observer."

Often, they feel obligations to continue the teachings and traditions, or carry the banners of the *ryu*, *gharana*, *dalang*, and so forth, with whom they may have immersed themselves during the exquisite vicissitudes of field study, arguably our most distinguishing rite of passage, one that indelibly marks us for life. Some have been willing or eager to create traditional spiritual and/or formalized professional bonds, with formalized reciprocal expectations, such as the Hindustani *ustad/śagird* (*guru/śisya*) relationship (Kippen 2008; Slawek 2000), or initiation into *Santería/Regla de Ocha* (Hagedorn 2001, 2002). Many others expect that, in return for entrée into the teacher's world, students will promote a teacher's prestige (Nettl 2014) or that of the lineage, or help enhance the teacher's career (Locke 2004, 172). This is as true for "insider/outsiders" as it is for "outsiders": Bode Omojola, himself a Yoruba (albeit more oriented toward the world of European than traditional music), speaks of "my Yoruba master drummer, for example, [who] is always, always asking me, 'Do it for us, too. We, too, want to travel.'"

Such experiences emphasize the deep asymmetries endemic to the lives of anthropologists, ethnomusicologists, and other fieldworkers. We who are thus engaged are always deeply aware of the imbalances between the worlds revealed to us—worlds that become anchors of our lives and careers—and with what relatively little we can reciprocate. These imbalances are rooted in colonial history and have greatly influenced the methodologies and products of our research. The pervading colonial mindset, whether imperial (most of Africa, Asia, and the Pacific consisted of subject peoples) or the internal-national type (despised, marginalized and/or patronized aboriginal groups who served as "internal colonials"), created a sociocultural barrier that most investigators of the nineteenth century and much of the twentieth could not conceive of breaching. Cooley and Barz (2008, 7), in the sweeping introduction to *Shadows in the Field*, encapsulate this sociopolitical context:

> The asymmetrical relationships of fieldwork in colonial contexts make it unlikely that a fieldworker would understand or even be interested in, for example, the inner life of an Indian or Chinese musician. Asymmetrical relationships may have excluded the possibility of [early observers/scholars] Amiot or Jones submitting themselves as apprentices to master musicians.

Among other things, this barrier greatly influenced the course of music and dance performance as an ethnomusicological research methodology and subject of scholarship in its own right. To enter into formalized "master/student" relationships, referring to those one interviewed, observed, recorded, or studied with as "our teachers in the field" (Nettl 2013) or "our research collaborators" and other such recently embraced terms purporting to eliminate social distance, would have been unthinkable for most ethnomusicological pioneers. To record, interview, and analyze results is one thing; placing oneself in the hands of another in the way one does with a formal teacher is quite something else: it is a reversal of power dynamics that would have been largely out of the question.

This "colonial footprint" extends, in the opinion of many ethnomusicologists, to the post-fieldwork academic setting. As Regula Qureshi puts it:

> [I]t seems to me that for many years I could count African American colleagues on one hand. I look at ethnomusicology and it's so damn white! Why is that so? Maybe it has something to do with privilege, and maybe we have to do something special to make sure everyone has equal access.

Although this is steadily changing, the field has historically been Caucasian dominated. The efforts by many ethnomusicologists to give equal weight to the voices of their research subjects and/or to engage in dialogic presentation (see, for example, Kisliuk and Gross 2004) are meant to mitigate this demographic imbalance, which is of course shared by many other academic disciplines.

We can and do rationalize speaking for and presenting The Other by affirming that "*some*one has to do it, so I'm doing it!" In David Harnish's (2004, 117) words, "[T]hose of us . . . in geographic areas of little diversity [in his case, a small town in northern Ohio] are charged with—*or charge ourselves with*—the task of presenting the music and culture of the ensemble [Balinese gamelan, in his case]."

The responsibility (sometimes verging on guilt) weighing on ethnomusicologists to faithfully and respectfully represent their esteemed fieldwork cultures can somewhat paradoxically coexist with a view that *privileges* the paradigm of researchers representing cultures other than their own. Interestingly, this may have little to do with research integrity or accuracy. J. Lawrence Witzleben (1997, 223) refers to a "bias in favor of cross-cultural fieldwork in a distant and difficult environment." He goes on to state that "colleagues and friends from Asia and elsewhere who have studied ethnomusicology in the United States have mentioned that many American students of ethnomusicology tend to look down on those doing fieldwork in their indigenous cultures, presumably because this type of research is not exotic or difficult enough to serve as a 'rite of passage.'"

In response to my query as to whether he considered the many non-Indonesians teaching gamelan to be "colonizing" or [inappropriately] "appropriating," the late Hardja Susilo, dean of "native" artists-in-residence in America, brought to UCLA by Mantle Hood in 1958 to teach Javanese gamelan and dance, replied,

> To me that is all political talk. I am frankly honored that you guys are studying the gamelan, that you think it is a worthy subject. A lot of Indonesians don't think so, you know.[17] So, appropriate all you want. You see, it isn't like "if you take it then I don't have it anymore." This is a case where if you take it then we have two, you see. . . . [I]t isn't like a flute; if you take it, [then] I don't have it. (Susilo 2004, 66)

So how do we translate profound and life-changing fieldwork experiences into making a living, paid and otherwise supported by those with whom we share few, if any, of those experiences, loyalties, attitudes? First, we must modulate and refocus the competencies we have acquired as intake in classwork, graduate library research, and fieldwork into output in jobs large and small. We commonly have the opportunities to do this incrementally while still students, in work-study situations, whether as teaching assistants with teaching responsibilities either minimal ("All I had to do was take attendance and grade quizzes using a key") or major ("I had to give lectures, work with discussion and lab groups, and grade all the essays"), or more abruptly during or after formal degree studies, as faculty associates or adjuncts at college, university, community college, paid (poorly) by the course.

Nearly all in this book have experienced some degree of such academic scurrying, gigging, hustling about, patching together a usually minimal living, before landing a better-paid, full-time position—if they have indeed succeeded in doing so, and assuming that was their goal. In places like New England and the Los Angeles area, with dense concentrations of institutions, this kind of piecework can become a career, albeit often without benefits. Julie Strand exemplifies this sort of lifestyle, moving among New England institutions as, variously: adjunct, lecturer, faculty associate, postdoctoral researcher, SAT tutor, gamelan performance gigger, steel band teacher, and other capacities, teaching a wide variety of lecture and performance classes. Though somewhat more peripatetic than the average, she is by no means atypical, as we will see.

"Of Course I'm the Person for the Job": Securing and Keeping the Position

Peter O'Toole, in the title role of David Lean's epic 1962 film *Lawrence of Arabia*, assures Foreign Office functionary Claude Rains, "Of course I'm the man for the job! What *is* the job, by the way?" Ethnomusicologists *are*, rather more than many other music academics, "the [person] for the job." In the words of Ginny Danielson, "There is no better skill for anything you do, any career that you're going to pursue, than ethnographic fieldwork. The ability to talk to people who don't necessarily know what you're talking about, to try to make yourself clear, to elicit information, to elicit points of view—those are skills that generalize to every walk of life. I think that's *incredibly* valuable training." Umi Hsu rather poetically opines that "being an ethnomusicologist is a way of life: a way of living and engaging in the world that is driven by curious, critical, and deep listening to the world." In doing this, ethnomusicologists benefit from their exceptionally broad and rich backgrounds in applied social sciences and humanities, as well as music. In addition to the typical academic skills of "close reading, historical inquiry, [and] written argumentation" (Tuhus-Dubrow 2013), ethnomusicologists benefit from intercultural and transcultural ear-training, eye-ear transfer "audiolizing," analysis skills, and the self-motivation, self-discipline, and collaborative habits that have become rather a cliché of the US national education "benefits of music participation" narrative.[18] Training may include language study of the conventional graduate-school "pass the reading exam in French and/or German before proceeding to comps" variety, as well as the more intensely personal, mutually communicative kind necessary for field research—and, increasingly, aspects of science.

In seeking ways to open an essay, desperate students sometimes resort to such hoary jump-starters as "The Merriam-Webster dictionary states. . . ." In that vein, it's (only perhaps) somewhat "significant" that, in Merriam-Webster, "ethnomusicology . . . rhymes with anesthesiology, epidemiology, gastroenterology, otolaryngology" (http://www.merriam-webster.com/dictionary/ethnomusicology). We thus see ourselves semi-seriously linked with scientific rigor and method, a perhaps "too-much protested" arm (mentioned earlier) of our self-definition narrative. For some, however, the linkage in recent years may be more substantive than philosophical: note Judith Becker's assertion that "core disciplines [for ethnomusicology, now] include neuroscience and evolutionary biology," while Svanibor Pettan "welcome[s] . . . increased interest . . . in biomusicology, ecomusicology, zoomusicology, and sound studies." These are relatively new, increasingly productive areas of activity, often linked with a great increase in activism both in and outside academia. All these preceding forms of experience, and others, may be in the toolkits of ethnomusicologists, who, at any rate, tend toward interdisciplinarity.

Careers outside "Professorial Academia"/"The Professoriat"

Like anyone else pursuing tertiary education, ethnomusicology students have a variety of motivations, which may include any or all of the following: a passion for or keen interest in a particular topic or general subject matter; powerful personal role models; a particular worldview; a love for the idea of imparting knowledge via their own enthusiasms; and (not least) a desire to make a living in the context of any of the foregoing. In addition, two phrases currently in vogue infuse all: "making a difference" and "giving back" (in other words, to "the Community," however defined).

Gini Gorlinski cites a facile aphorism by Stanley Fish (public intellectual, literary theorist, and academic administrator); in its original form (Fish 1995, 2), it is "If you want to send a message that will be heard beyond the academy, get out of it." Whether this is true or not, the borders and definitions of academia are increasingly porous and difficult to define. Neither "research" nor "teaching" consistently work as a sole criteria for delineating academia; virtually all our interlocutors, whether formally connected to a college or university or not, feel that their careers involve both. Judy McCulloh (for example) notes that some academics initially considered her editorial position to be evidence of an inability to "find a real [read: teaching] job." Her response: "That did bother me, because editors teach one on one; we just have a different venue for our classroom." Maybe it comes down to whether or not we formally "grade" students in some way, in which case we might use the terms "grading" and "non-grading" academics. I suppose the rather unsatisfying terms "Professorial Academia" and "the Professoriat" are as adequate or inadequate as any.

Whether within or without the Professoriat, all our colleagues who shared their stories with us feel they are "making a difference." Some prefer to pursue their particular goals directly, in venues not encumbered (in their view) by regular and organized teaching and/or what one might call "obligatory strategic publishing" (what Umi Hsu considers an unfortunate "professionalism of the field of ethnomusicology," which "leads to a system of credentialism")—both being requisites for academic success.

The trope of "Ivory Tower" detachment from Real World problems (implying that somehow these do not affect the Academy/Professoriat) has long been a political "straw man." Legislators in America have increasingly retreated from funding education, while simultaneously hoping to micromanage curricula, supporting what they consider of primary practical importance: immediate job creation.

"Practicality" exists, of course, in the eye of the beholder. In the words of Jonathan Dueck, "The activity of paying close attention to musical practice is a way of paying close attention to other people, close and embodied attention—and there are few things that I think the world needs more, right now, than that kind of cultural work." Certainly most of this book's readers would consider such work "practical" in the broadest sense. In a world where languages and the cultures (including musics) they anchor are disappearing even faster than biological species, the single-minded act of collecting/documenting (see Dea, Yampolsky) is critically important. Providing venues for the maintenance of these essential and endangered materials, along with contextualization, editing, and wider diffusion through libraries (Danielson), archives (Chaudhuri, Henderson, Sercombe), museums (Kaeppler, Post), publishing (Gorlinski, McCulloh), "digital knowledge transmission" (Hsu), and record companies (Kleikamp, Sonneborn), vitally supports the process of preservation and dissemination. Perpetuating these traditions through performance (Baily, Dally, Doubleday) and adaptive composing (Benary, Dea) are all means (leaving aside thorny questions of "cultural appropriation") of connecting traditions to a wider world, which may help ensure their survival.[19] Many of our colleagues in this book, both within and beyond the Professoriat, participate in a variety of these activities. Clearly the "obligatory strategic publishing" and classroom teaching to which I referred earlier also can and do also serve this preservation and perpetuation. It is noteworthy, and one of the goals of this book, that numerous ways of pursuing these goals offer solid and rewarding careers outside professorial academia. The accounts of these careers vary too widely for me to encapsulate; I invite you to follow and enjoy their richness and variety, as recounted by our participants.

Careers within "The Professoriat"

As diverse as personal research emphases and job descriptions in mainstream ethnomusicological "professorial academia" may be, they offer a certain general degree of consistency in their trajectories and professional contexts. Some receive full-time temporary or tenure-track job offers when they complete or while they are completing their terminal degrees—in ethnomusicology, usually a PhD. As many academics know, some of the most severe personal stress and fracture zones manifest themselves while one is simultaneously dealing with the demands of the dissertation and the major plateau of the first regular tenure-track position. But dissertation aside, the job itself often provides a built-in set of stresses between the deeply relativistic orientations and goals of most ethnomusicologists and the typically more culturally specific ones of their senior colleagues and departmental administration.

Ethnomusicologists' versatility opens them to such stresses, partly because they most typically, even today, discover their field as young adults attracted from other areas in music (often from what we in the academic music world refer to as "performance" areas). It is of course standard academic/graduate student procedure that one responds to as many job advertisements as one can. Most of us have resorted to the slimmest of rationalizations to convince ourselves, or convince those who have advertised the position, that the job description fits us like a glove. Sometimes this "fit," in actuality, means having taken or taught or been a TA for only one course in the "required" or "desirable" categories, and having perhaps once been in such-and-such an ensemble, or only played such-and-such an instrument in high school, and so forth. We've all experienced the intense desire for that first job.[20] But many ethno-musicologists legitimately have such experience, and it is often substantial. Most have come through a conventional core music curriculum: music history/theory sequence; extensive performance experience of all kinds, including studio curricula; large and small Western European art canonic ensembles; often music education instrumental methods classes.[21] They consider this their nuclear musical background, which they rather take for granted as music academicians. The background and orientation of Regula Qureshi, *née* a cellist, is by no means atypical: "I'm just a person whose head is full of Western classical music, because at home my dad always played the piano repertoire and my mother sang, so I belonged in the world of Western music. I have always had great relationships with Western musicians because that's my music, right?"

This "nuclear musical background" forms the platform upon which they later build their dearest ethnomusicology chops: performance and language skills, geographi-cal area studies, fieldwork experience, knowledge of anthropological, cultural, social theory, and so forth. Thus, the common experience—especially in smaller programs with fewer faculty and less division of labor—of teaching music history, theory, analy-sis, composition, studio instrumental or vocal performance, and other subjects. We often hear "I used to teach all that stuff before we got another line." Some relish this variety; others yearn for more focus, in research and teaching, on what they consider their *real* "work." They also often find themselves viewed as cultural generalists. In the words of Gini Gorlinski, who was in fact hired for one position specifically to "re-form the core [general studies] curriculum," "in many departments, ethnomusicologists are often the ones expected to have material that is accessible to the general student. So we're often asked, I think more than a music theorist, for instance, to do classes for the general students."

However versatile they may be, ethnomusicologists most commonly find themselves working within a music history or musicology area.[22] Their "performance" faculty colleagues and the advising staff often include music history/musicology—along with music education, theory, and somewhat less often composition—in what many refer to as the "academic" wing of a music department or school. (Note the absurdity of the terms "academic" and "non-academic" within the "academy.") *Academic* has often implied "talker" rather than "doer" (note the hoary waggism "Words without Song") by supposed comparison with the activities of ensemble directors and performance studio faculty. Nettl (1995, 57) lays out a sort of –emic view of this hierarchy in his classic *Heartland Excursions*:

> Within the Music Building, the center, the people who do, is largely comprised of the performing faculty and student majors, and the periphery consists of those who—broadly speaking—teach without performing, ordinarily faculty and students of music education, musicology, and music theory. Composers are in a somewhat anomalous position. They obviously do [in other words, "do" as opposed to "merely" "teach"], but they work, like

teachers and scholars, on paper; unlike performers, they are not expected to undertake the risks that exposure to an audience constantly demands.

This sort of dichotomy between "academics" and "performers" does not comfortably fit many ethnomusicologists (and of course many others in the above list). Many have extensive and intensive performance experience in the traditions in which they specialize, as well as in others in which they may have participated along the way, and teaching an ensemble based in one of them is frequently a condition of employment or an added enhancement to one's vitae. In such cases, because the students upon whom they draw to fill these ensembles usually have little or no experience, nor the required instruments, the ethnomusicologist must assume the role both of studio instructor and ensemble "conductor" (Solís 2004b, 6). She thus often de facto finds herself astride not just two but three of the traditional music school divisions: musicology/music history, ensemble, and studio.

While relationships with one's departmental colleagues are by no means always contentious, colleagues sometimes don't quite "get it": "What is it that these folks really *do*? Where do they fit?" One of my own performance faculty colleagues says she thinks of me as a sort of exotic creature who has traveled, lived, and done strange things among far-off peoples with peculiar, fascinating cultures. Victoria Lindsey Levine relates this story:

> In 1997, I convened a panel of six ethnomusicologists at the annual meetings of the College Music Society to discuss teaching at liberal arts colleges. One member of the group was Katherine Hagedorn (1961–2013), who invited us to a follow-up workshop at Pomona College a few years later under the auspices of a Mellon grant. One topic at the workshop was our often-perplexing relationships with Music Department colleagues. Katherine quipped that a senior colleague always greeted her by striking a flamenco dancer's pose and snapping his fingers. We appreciated the fact that he found a way to acknowledge her musical interests, but chuckled at the flamenco reference because Katherine was a specialist in Cuban Santería music, not flamenco. Nevertheless, we adopted the finger-snapping flamenco pose as a "secret handshake" whenever our paths cross at SEM conferences to remind us of the bond we share. We still use that greeting, but now it reminds us of Katherine, with whom we enjoyed many happy and productive hours and who left us far too early. (E-mail message, July 21, 2016)

Thus, ethnomusicologists, who typically take for granted a reasonably conventional musical background *plus* all that is required for the skill-diverse ethnomusicological complex, are more richly equipped for a wider variety of academic employment than many others within the broad "musicology/music history" umbrella.

Achieving the tenure-track position is, however, only the first of the two brims of the grail most academically directed graduate students seek; the second, of course, is being granted tenure. It is in this very versatility (which, as I have stated, also comes with a certain amount of divided disciplinary loyalty) that lie some possible hurdles along the tenure route. Senior colleagues—in effect, *all* of one's colleagues at the time of the job offer—support the hiring of an ethnomusicologist for assorted reasons. They, or more typically one or two of them, may be passionately convinced that the departmental music curriculum is too narrow, too ethnocentric, too antiquated to reflect contemporary musical realities. This, of all those I note here, is probably the rationale most ethnomusicologists themselves would most strongly support.[23] Such influential figures may themselves belong to completely mainstream traditional areas. A noteworthy example was choral conductor/composer Richard Winslow's vital support for Wesleyan University's renowned World Music Program (Sumarsam 2004, 89–90). Other reasons for the hire may include pressures from proximate or university student identity-politics populations. In the Southwest, we often find demands for an Amerindian or Mexican/Chicano/Borderlands specialist; in southern Florida, a Latin Americanist or specifically Caribbean or Cuban music scholar; in Pittsburgh or another Rust Belt urban area, a Slavic or Balkan specialist. Pressures from NASM (National Association of Schools of Music, an influential evaluative body) to improve diversity in curricula and/or the faculty spectrum are behind other searches. Interface with already existing university or college area-studies emphases provides another reason; some examples are Yale and China; University of California–Santa Barbara and the Middle East; Earlham College and Japan; University of Wisconsin and South/Southeast Asia; and University of Texas and Latin America.[24] Some of those in this book (Salwa El-Shawan Castelo-Branco in Portugal, Renata Pasternak-Mazur in Poland, and Svanibor Pettan in Slovenia are examples) found their research paths determined or limited by the nationalist ideologies of their countries, to the extent that funding agencies deemed support for research not concerned with these countries to be "irrelevant." Mohd. Anis Md. Nor found that even in his own country, Malaysia, in order "to survive and make a niche for yourself . . . I make them feel that I am providing the missing link. . . . To create and to impart that element of indispensability, you have to invent it."

In all these cases one's primary affiliation or disciplinary, collegial connections, or emotional attachment maybe be elsewhere than the official musical area of one's job description. Ethnomusicologists are not alone in this; Music Department medievalists, for example, typically have strong links with Romance or Germanic Language, Classics, Art History, or Religious Studies Departments. Their musical contributions, however, are usually considered more mainstream than those of ethnomusicologists. Their colleagues typically see their research areas, ensembles, values, repertoire, instruments, history, theory, and performance practices as part of a traditional historical and cultural continuum with bread and butter seventeenth- to twentieth-century Western Art Music repertoire and practices.

The newly hired ethnomusicologist, on the other hand, may represent something very different, even to those kindly disposed to her. How to make one's position relevant? How to seamlessly fit in with one's colleagues? Feeling themselves, in the words of Roger Vetter (2004), the "square peg" in the "round hole" of an otherwise traditional music department or school is part of many ethnomusicologists' narratives. Some—whether through preexisting unit circumstances or in spite of them; whether through their own manipulation of or adaptation to contexts—navigate the road to acceptance, make what may be a temporary or visiting line permanent, and gain tenure more easily than others.

ORAL HISTORY AS METHODOLOGY

American oral history chronicler Studs Terkel (2006, xxi) described himself as "one man, equipped with a tape recorder and badgered by the imp of curiosity." His interviews for the most part speak for themselves, they themselves being the "text." Oral history as a goal in and of itself has not necessarily been at the center of ethnomusicological inquiry; ethnomusicologists have typically used oral history, in the form of interview questions, as a methodology—data and leavening to either begin or support their own cultural analyses. The words of others may contribute substantively to their conclusions, but investigators naturally emphasize their own voices.

Two ethnomusicological monographs consisting largely of primary oral history provide a contrast in approach: *Navajo Blessingway Singer: Frank Mitchell, 1881–1967*, edited by Charlotte Frisbie and David McAllester (1978), and Judith Vander's *Songprints* (1988). Frisbie and McAllester's work consists almost entirely of oral narrative, with selected editorial footnotes and a brief introduction;[25] the editors appear to consider their main task to have been conducting the interviews, effecting their translations (by assorted translators), editing the interviews, and putting them in order as a source of raw data. Vander, on the other hand, organizes according to musical categories, with short oral history passages overshadowed by extensive editorial comment.

First-person history is most typically self-generated and self-edited, as with David McAllester's short "Autobiographical Sketch," connected to his festschrift *Explorations in Ethnomusicology* (1986), edited by Charlotte Frisbie; or Bruno Nettl's monograph *Encounters in Ethnomusicology* (2002), autobiography in the service of disciplinary history (or vice versa). Our project most resembles the latter, in that we employ first-person testimony and editorial analysis in more or less equal proportions, with the oral history itself as much of a *raison d'être* as the analysis.

It appears to be as much *de rigeur* for a legitimate academic discipline to possess at least one "major figures in the field" volume as it is for a proper sovereign country to possess a national airline—to paraphrase Ricardo D. Trimillos's (2004, 52n) comments apropos of a "proper" university ethnomusicology program's acquisition of a gamelan. Mervyn McLean's *Pioneers of Ethnomusicology* (2006) is a historical survey of the field, featuring a supporting section containing very brief sketches of the careers of about a hundred prominent, mostly (all but two) deceased "pioneers."[26]

Introduction

19

Relatively few disciplinary biographies in any field whatever include the voices of their subjects. Some exceptions include *Inside the Economist's Mind: Conversations with Eminent Economists* (2007), edited by Paul A. Samuelson and William A. Barnett, and *Speaking of History: Conversations with Historians* (1997), edited by Roger Adelson. In the field of ethnomusicology, we hitherto find one only one such project: the distinguished *Garland Encyclopedia of World Music* vol. 10, "The Ethnomusicologist at Work" (Stone 2001). The thirteen illuminating short (auto)biographies are self-written, each in response to a set of questions furnished beforehand, over which the subjects have had a chance to ruminate and, of course, edit considerably. As with similar volumes such as those mentioned earlier, the editors were highly selective in whom they approached. All are senior scholars and perceived luminaries of the field; nearly all are in academic positions at major research universities. They describe how they entered the profession and how they carry out their teaching, research, and publication. Unlike *Living Ethnomusicology*, in which we spend substantial time on formation and formative years, the Garland autobiographies move fairly quickly from their early lives to the time during which "ethnomusicology" and "ethnomusicologist" as their conscious field and identity became apparent: the years of their university educations and beyond. In our project, we are in some ways as fascinated with how early rivulets—childhood interests, opportunities and the lack thereof, family influences—converge into broader streams, as we are with the broader streams themselves. We work from the assumption that lives and careers are of a piece, and of a continuum.

LIVING ETHNOMUSICOLOGY: A UNIQUE CONTRIBUTION

Living Ethnomusicology is fundamentally different from anything that has appeared heretofore in or about our field. First: the autobiographies themselves reflect the actual real-time, dialogic, and collaborative textures of ethnomusicology's most salient feature: interview-generated fieldwork. This human, face-to-face contact and interaction most strongly differentiates us from our parent/sister discipline, historical musicology/music history, whose adherents have by and large not embraced that methodology. The live human aspect—the lure of "Foreign Lands and Peoples" (to cite the evocative title of Robert Schumann's first *Scenes from Childhood/Kinderscenen*)—is indeed, as we show in our book, still one of the most important reasons people with such a variety of backgrounds are attracted to or somehow find their way into ethnomusicology.

After the introduction, we present life stories in three broad sections—early life and influences, career trajectories, and reflections on the field—with editorial introductions preceding and mediating each section. We divide each interview according to this tripartite schema and group all corresponding parts of interviews together to facilitate comparisons. We explore how people were drawn to their fields, how they satisfy their intellectual and creative inclinations while striving to make a living, and how they reconcile their training with what they actually do on a daily basis and throughout their careers. Using the table of contents and index to navigate back and forth, readers may, depending on their particular interest: follow a single life through the book; begin with a particular type of career path and work outward from that; or compare people's experiences and/or reflections at roughly comparable stages of lives and careers.

Our book differs from most disciplinary ethnographies also in its search for a broad and representative cross-section, in which, however, we have perforce included remarkable people. In seeking the "typical," we have deliberately targeted a rich variety of participants—fifty from all across the ethnomusicological galaxy, representing some eighteen countries, with ages ranging from those born in the 1920s to those of the 1980s. Their professional trajectories and career strategies differ, but all are in some way connected to, trained in, and/or self-identified with the field. We include junior scholars, graduate students and undergraduate students (at the times of their interviews), junior academics and tenured senior professors, some who have been on the margins of academia, or who have left academia (by choice or not), or who have never been in academia. They include freelance performers and teachers; scholars in anthropology, music, dance, and area studies departments and special institutes; composers, editors, librarians, and administrators; graduate and undergraduate students. About one-third of our participants come from Australia, Azerbaijan, Brazil, Canada, the Czech Republic, Egypt, Hong Kong, India, Italy, Malaysia, the Netherlands, Nigeria, Poland, Slovenia, Switzerland, and the United Kingdom; the rest are American. We have placed special emphasis on those who have found alternative careers outside the academy, either through choice or after having tried to attain or failed to keep academic positions.

Some are "insiders" to the traditions with which they have involved themselves; some began as unequivocal "outsiders"; and still others are "outsider/insiders," having discovered traditions within the broader societies of their origin that were nearly as exotic to them as they would have been to "outsiders." Note Salwa El-Shawan Castelo-Branco's somewhat tortuous outsider/insider professional journey as an Egyptian who was, however, raised in the Western musical tradition, vis-à-vis the Egyptian classical system—

> (We): It must have been very difficult for you to go back to Cairo, being well known as a Western musician and then to have to persuade all those people that you were interested in Arabic music? (She): Yes, it was very difficult.

—following which she was obliged to turn her energies to re-tooling herself in the Portuguese language, culture, and folk music research in initiating an ethnomusicology program at the New University of Lisbon. Hong Kong native and eventual China specialist Frederick Lau was initially quite repelled by Chinese music ("old people's stuff"), and even as an undergraduate music major in Hong Kong was dismissive, by comparison with outsider American classmate J. Lawrence Witzleben, "who copied every note [in the compulsory Chinese music history class]." Mohd. Anis Md. Nor, a Malay, was raised in multicultural Malaysia without, however, feelings "about art having to be demarcated according to ethnic lines," thinking "it was joyous to do everything" and developing his more specifically Malay focus much later.

Points of entry and sources of initial attraction to ethnomusicology likewise vary widely. Participants' principal backgrounds include music composition, music theory, rock performance, Western classical concert performance, jazz performance, languages, linguistics, musical analysis, dance, religious ritual, library studies, publishing, psychology, art history, area studies, historical musicology, sociology, anthropology, world music performance and entrepreneurship, commercial recording, NGO archiving, and other pursuits.

Unlike Ruth Stone (2001) with the *Garland* volume and most other disciplinary biographers, we have not specifically or exclusively sought out the Big Names, although a good number of our participants arguably fall into this category. Thus, our work reflects the prevailing ethnomusicological philosophy that one probably learns more about a society or societies (or in this case, a discipline) from an interesting cross-section—"the typical"—than from the "unique," sui generis. This is, of course, another way ethnomusicology differs from historical musicology and its search for the inspired exceptional.

To us, our subjects ARE all "exceptional." They have all engaged in significant, admirable, fascinating work. The things they do for a living and the processes by which they relate to their institutions, whether in or out of academia, often seem to strain the credulity even of their colleagues, let alone the ken of the general public. Most of their work transcends the quotidian in nearly every regard: the places they go, the people with whom they interact, their apparent competencies—cultural savoir faire, including linguistic skills (especially impressive to many in the largely monolingual American mainstream) and seemingly esoteric performance interests and abilities. As we have seen, this rich and diverse background ethnomusicologists acquire in the course of their journey equips them for a remarkably wide array of possible careers. To quote Gini Gorlinski, who, after leaving the academic track, became an editor at Encyclopedia Britannica:

> I have always firmly believed, since I was a graduate student, that we have skills that are needed and marketable in areas outside the academy. I've always believed that, but our programs deny it. We are systematically tracked [in other words, through the traditional, pre-music professional curriculum]. We're tracked into the university faculty position as the only legitimate position to come out of this sort of training, which I think is sad.

Martha Davis (1992, 362–63) strongly echoes this sentiment. In considering a colleague's rhetorical question as to "why we are graduating so many people [in ethnomusicology] [considering the fact that] there are no jobs," she replies,

> There are jobs, interesting and meaningful jobs, though many of them are outside of academia.
> . . .
> I . . . want to encourage younger colleagues to consider the many ways, in addition to academic employment, in which they can utilize their studies in the professional practice of ethnomusicology. And finally, I would like to suggest that even we ethnomusicologists who consider our main professional domain to be academic should contemplate the ethical obligations implied by our research. So, in response to Merriam's query about whether "the ultimate aim of any study of man . . . [involves] . . . the question of whether one is searching out knowledge for its own sake, or is attempting to provide solutions to applied practical problems" (1964:42–43), I would say that it involves both.

No one has thus far engaged in a project comparable to this book in our field. We believe this will provide unique perspectives on what ethnomusicological training offers, on the fascinating intertwining of the personal and professional, and will serve as a professional career resource of vital utility and interest to anyone in or contemplating entry into the field or the related fields enumerated above. We are confident that *Living Ethnomusicology* will provide an important and unequalled picture not only of the discipline of ethnomusicology but also of the richly textured and fascinating ecology of academic professional life, as well as the many other fields in which ethnomusicologists live and work.

We co-authors have led reasonably varied, multicultural, plurocontinental lives, "living ethnomusicology," doing interesting work with fascinating people. That we are ourselves so fascinated with the people we have interviewed for our book is tribute both to these subjects and to the freshness and always growing potential of our field. And yet, we could have quite easily found a different list of fifty, or many more, just as varied and just as fascinating! We are confident that readers will agree with us.

Ted Solís

NOTES

1. The Society for Ethnomusicology e-mail listserv for a while carried an initially serious "re-naming" thread devoted to alternatives to the "Ethno" part of "Ethnomusicology." It soon devolved into such mock-serious Yiddish-influenced offerings as "'Kvell[to be extraordinarily proud]oMusicology,' signifying our collective pride in what we do"; and "'Schwitz[sweat]oMusicology,' since so many of us have done fieldwork in hot, sweaty places."

2. In my own music unit, colleagues with formal "musicology" doctorates investigate (among other things) music and wellness; black gospel music; nineteenth-century French coach-horn street music; ecomusicology of the Southwest; Greek nationalism in art music; 1940s and 1950s bebop dancing.

3. I cite this book's interviewees (as here with Mohd. Anis) without formal citation.

4. Nicholas Cook (2008, 66) rightly points out, apropos of this supposed "oppositional relationship" between musicology and ethnomusicology, that "many ethnomusicologists have originally trained in musicology, and thus have an informed if outdated view of what they are rejecting—by comparison to musicologists, many of whom are simply ignorant of ethnomusicology." Beverley Diamond (2006) argues that we ethnomusicologists should recognize "that our ethnography is invariably strongest where it has historical dimensions" (329). She maintains, furthermore, that "[we have] been good at simultaneously doing history while challenging its very premises. . . . We've challenged what music history might be by questioning the nature of past and present, the nature of memory, and the nature of who and what counts as a legitimate way to know the past" (331).

5. Cooley and Barz (2008, 12) enumerate other reasons for the relative decline of traditional fieldwork: "[F]unds for long-term overseas fieldwork appear to be diminishing, and international travel is becoming less attractive due to a series of wars and direct anti-American sentiment. Ideologically, the paradigm of 'area studies' that encouraged location-specific research is directly challenged by issue-driven projects that focus on musical change, transnational and intranational musical fusions, polymorphic rather than circumscribed theories of identity, and ubiquitous commentaries on globalization."

6. Note the now-common term "ethnodrag" (Averill 2004, 100), used specifically to reference the practice of wearing "native" costumes while performing, and more generally to denote the broader idea of musical role-playing—under the cover of an academic career?

7. Sure, it's fun, but elsewhere (Solís 2014b) I note how small a role performance played in the early history of ethnomusicology. It is, even today, seldom the main focus of our job descriptions and the reality of our work days.

8. Mantle Hood most famously articulated the general concept of "bi-musicality" in his article "The Challenge of Bi-musicality" (1960), although he had begun structurally implementing the methodology at UCLA at least six years before that (Hood 2004, 284); David McAllester and others had also earlier discussed and embraced the idea. Harold Powers (1958, iii) acknowledged the utility of personal performance study as an analytical tool in his 1952–54 study of the South Indian classical musical system, with George Herzog (1945, 221) making what is perhaps the earliest published statement supporting that idea, in his African music research.

9. Carol Babiracki's (2008) account of her Indian fieldwork in the context of such a relationship limns a sort of narrative familiar to many of us in ethnomusicology but seldom treated in such perceptive and eloquent detail.

10. Adelaida Reyes (2009, 15, 14) reconciles both aspects in arguing for "Ethnomusicology's recognizabilty as a discipline" in our embrace of expressive culture in "collective experience and associations from which members of the culture draw for meaning."

11. One example was the Nonesuch Explorer LP series initiated in 1967. These recordings were often of fine auditory and performance quality, were relatively mainstream, affordable, and provided for many their first access to "exotic" music.

12. I detail local repercussions of a field recording project in Solís 2014a, one of numerous such ethnomusicological examples.

13. Note, for example, what some might consider uncomfortable truths Margaret Sarkissian (2000) examines in her study of a Portuguese performing tradition that Portuguese Eurasians in Malaysia believed to be unbroken since the sixteenth century.

14. Youssefzadeh (2010), an interview of Stephen Blum by another ethnomusicologist, is one relatively rare example. The ongoing SEM newsletter interview series is another.

15. I will discuss herewith, and differentiate this project from, the excellent "Ethnomusicologists at Work," *Garland Encyclopedia* vol. 10 (Stone 2001).

16. This is, of course, also true for many in K–12 public education, although usually under very different, considerably more constrained and less flexible circumstances.

17. Note Fred Lau's realization that his dismissive attitude toward "his" Chinese music was "embarrassingly colonial."

18. Ricardo Trimillos, describing his early piano experience as his school choir's accompanist, notes, "I was very involved with ensemble performance, not so much training as a soloist, but working with ensembles and other people. Again, if you think about ethnomusicology, that's a skill we learn very early—how to interact with other people."

19. Note also Barbara Smith's University of Hawai'i ethnomusicology program, initiated in the 1950s, pioneering in its emphasis on the rich variety of local traditions. Her motivation was the recognition of music's "potential to validate cultural identity" (Trimillos 2004, 25) [local identities, in this instance] and "its relationship to a person's sense of self-identity" (Smith 1987, 20). See also Feltz 1977.

20. Note the excellent *SEM Student News* online issue, "Finding Paths on the Job Market" (2016).

21. Having embarked as an undergrad Music Ed major, I soon found myself faced with numerous "methods" classes, and the intimidating challenge of reading multiple clefs, and of acquiring highly diverse teaching, playing, directing, and instrument maintenance competencies. I fled to "Music History and Literature" (being naturally attracted, at any rate, to the "cultural" side of things). Turns out, ironically, that, by necessity, the performance aspects of my career in ethnomusicology have drawn on competencies (playing, teaching, singing, directing, maintaining assorted instruments) closer to those of the public-school band director than I would have imagined—plus the whole "dancing thing." This at least partly compensates for those long-ago feelings of incompetency in the face of public-school music teaching, a profession I respect and revere.

22. I use these terms in their most traditional but highly vexed and contested sense, to refer to Western Art Music and its specialist musicologists.

23. This quest for more diversity, globalism, and multiculturalism can actually sometimes be an obstacle to some jobseekers; note Jonathan Dueck's perception that search committees tend to find that his interdisciplinary research on music in transnational Christianity "does not fit very well into a rubric of area studies" and may "not [be] exotic enough."

24. Positions shared between music and other departments, while often in many ways rich and rewarding for all concerned, can pose particular tenure complications, as in the case of our contributor Barbara Benary.

25. Alan Lomax's classic *Mister Jelly Roll* (1993/1950), the oral history of early New Orleans jazz icon Jelly Roll Morton, largely adheres to this formula.

26. See Rice (2007) for a review of this work.

PART I
Early Life and Influences

Mantle Hood stated that "if ethnomusicology is what an ethnomusicologist does, then what he does must somehow relate to what he is" (1971, 9). In this rather intuitive spirit we began our interviews by asking our contributors what might have led them in the direction of ethnomusicology. People from strikingly different backgrounds converge on ethnomusicology, pointing perhaps as much to the multiple possible paths one may pursue in ethnomusicology as to the multifarious origins of its practitioners. Not surprisingly, the backgrounds of those from abroad vary widely; our American narratives, however, are also richly diverse. Both Michael Tenzer (born in highly cosmopolitan multiethnic New York in the 1950s, exposed to many available varieties of exoticism) and William P. Malm (born at the end of the 1920s in monochromatic Chicago suburbs) found, embraced, and emphasized the analytic, sound-oriented aspect of ethnomusicology. Both Judith Becker, who had never been out of the state of Michigan or seen an "exotic" performance, and Sean Williams, born in superhip Berkeley and having been taken to a Ravi Shankar performance at age four, found themselves attracted to what Adrienne Kaeppler referred to as the "ethnic" aspect of ethnomusicology. Our participants come from many corners of the earth, from many disciplines, and have embraced many different aspects of the field. Nearly all come from urban or suburban rather than rural areas; nearly all were, in one way or another, introduced rather early to music as an activity. The birth chronologies of our contributors by decade clearly show how rapidly cultural and professional opportunities and resources increased for all of them—a difference as wide as that gulf between the "Yankee Clipper" flying boat and the internet.

Late Nineteen Twenties and Nineteen Thirties

Our older contributors are in or about to begin public school.

The Depression is worldwide. Prohibition is in force in America from 1920 to 1933. The non-European world is largely a colonial one. Global tourism is relatively undeveloped. Richard Halliburton's numerous volumes, such as *New Worlds to Conquer* (1929), *The Flying Carpet* (1932) and others, documenting his intrepid travel adventures in exotic places, are popular, as are movie shorts presenting such exotic tidbits as "the curious customs of the people of X." Travel abroad is largely via leisurely ocean liners, themselves colonial symbols of romance; the great time required to cover distances between worlds also reinforces the "here/there" separation (even a "Yankee Clipper" flying boat one-way trip from San Francisco to Hong Kong takes six days). Radio, notably stimulating and evocative to the imagination, is universal in the West. The Motion Picture Production Code, in full sway by 1934, enforces a highly repressed and influential American onscreen morality. American college and university music schools and departments overwhelmingly emphasize "performance." Record companies worldwide have been engaged in "ethnic" recording since the early 1900s; American record companies belatedly begin seeking out "race" (read: "black") performers.

Early Big Band pre-swing, swing, "jump bands," and R&B bands are touring and recording widely. Jitterbug dancing exemplifies mainstream American adaptation of a black aesthetic in popular culture.

William P. Malm

In conversation with Ted Solís and Margaret Sarkissian, March 12, 2016, Ann Arbor, Michigan

Early Life

WM: I was born in March 1928, in La Grange, Illinois, a town outside Chicago. I had a standard Midwestern childhood; my father worked and my mother was a homemaker. My father was born in Cleveland, one of five sons and two daughters by a good Swedish family. I never met my grandfather, who died before I was born; he was the first generation, the immigrant. My father graduated from Case Western in 1910, I think, in engineering. He was a traveling salesman, a kind of Willy Loman—clean suit and a car. His territory was the Midwest. He was always on the road, driving or taking trains. At home, he sang in the Episcopal Church choir. The church had a men's and boys' choir and my older brother found out that if he joined, he'd get 50 cents a month. So we both joined. I can still remember taking solfège lessons from the choirmaster. We took piano lessons from a teacher who came to the house. My brother didn't last long but I did. In grade school they showed us instruments. I liked the trumpet but didn't think it was good for my teeth, so I ended up playing the clarinet. I played clarinet and alto saxophone in the high-school band and learned to play jazz piano and swing bass.

TS: Speaking of the Swedish heritage, did you grow up with foreign languages around you?

WM: No. I asked my father whether he ever learned any Swedish or whether his parents spoke Swedish. He said only when they didn't want the children to understand.

TS: You mentioned playing jazz piano. Was improvising something that interested you? Were you drawn toward popular music and dance music?

WM: Yes. If I was playing a pop tune and knew the chord progression, it was like all the notes of the next chord turned green on the keyboard. I knew where they were; I just had to reach for them. I loved Art Tatum. His music really thrilled me—still does. He was a fantastic pianist; so original! It was his harmonization that intrigued me, not just the playing. He redesigned chords; I couldn't believe how he got those structures. I also liked Woody Herman and Stan Kenton.

College Life

I was 1-A draftable through the last half of the war but still in high school, so I decided I'd better get a little college before I got drafted. I started at Northwestern University in 1945 and three months later the war was over. There weren't many male students; they were all still in the Army. I was thinking of majoring in geology because my father and I used to do paleontology. We'd hunt for trilobites and fossils in the sand dunes of Michigan. I wasn't taking any music courses yet. At the end of my first year the geology lab TA mentioned a summer job surveying a mine in Colorado. I asked my father how to do it and applied for the job. I had decided to go to Colorado, but in June I got a letter from the employer, who had found somebody local to do the job. Suddenly, here was summer and I had no job. So I thought I'd take a summer music course at Northwestern. I tried that, but I didn't play piano or read music well enough. The only option was to be a composition major. That was great—you don't have to be talented, you're a genius! I ended up majoring in composition at Northwestern. I soon realized that if you wrote a string quartet, who's going to play it? No one. But because I liked dancing, I had started working with the Dance Department. I composed some music for dance and that got performed. It was the usual college show: "Music by William Malm and lyrics by Sheldon Harnick."

TS: Sheldon Harnick—who did *Fiddler on the Roof*?

WM: Yes, he was another student there. We also did a swimming show together for the Physical Education Department's female aquatic choreography and diving group. Sheldon played in the band and I conducted. The trouble with that show was that I had to conduct while standing on the lip of the pool. It was hard not to fall in the water!

TS: So your education at Northwestern was pretty much a straight Western music curriculum?

WM: Yes, and for my master's degree I wrote an oratorio, text and all. I was freelancing with dance and dance music; that was my interest. I began to ask myself, what music is going to motivate people to dance? So I decided to take dance lessons.

TS: Ballroom dance?

WM: No, ballet! With tights and all that. Back then I couldn't possibly go to a studio in Evanston, Illinois, and take ballet lessons. So I found out about a thing called Jacob's Pillow [in Becket, Massachusetts] and in 1947 I got a summer job playing piano in a barn for dance classes. One perk of the job was free dance lessons. I had exercise every morning with a short, white-haired teacher, Joe Pilates, and ballet with the corps of Ballet Theater. The program included summer stock—every night something had to be performed. Well, one particular night, the show was "Devi Dja and her Java-Bali Dancers." I didn't know where Bali was, for Pete's sake, much less what its music was like. But I was so lucky! She showed up, her dancers showed up, but her musicians were on strike at the Dutch Embassy because the Indonesian Revolution was going on. I don't know for sure, but they didn't show. So this woman comes in with two dancers and no orchestra. There were two pianists—myself and a guy from Juilliard. To this day I don't know what we played, because neither one of us had any idea that Java even had a music. Never heard of it. She had a gong, drum, and *gendèr* (metallophone). I have no idea how we faked the show. That's showbiz—the show must go on!

TS: Were you trying to play something Orientalist?

WM: Probably pentatonic, but I honestly have no idea, because there were two of us. Two pianos trying to sound like a gamelan but not knowing how to spell the word. I had not seen or heard a single gamelan instrument in my life. I didn't even know where Indonesia was. I was strictly from the Midwest; Jacob's Pillow was my first time away from home! After Jacob's Pillow, Devi Dja was going on the road with her dancers. She needed a musician and I was bored at Northwestern. I had a very bad composition teacher, but a good piano teacher. So after the season, with fifty dollars from my father, I took a train to New York, got a fifth-floor walkup, and Devi Dja taught me how to play the gendèr, hit the gong, and fake Indonesian drumming. I debuted at the Natural History Museum in New York. My contract read, "Devi Dja, November 13th–November 26th, 1947. Eighty dollars per week, plus transportation."

TS: That was pretty good money back then!

WM: Yes, and it was a great troupe. Devi Dja was actually from Indonesia. Her manager, so to speak, was her husband, an American Indian called Blue Eagle. The male dancer was from Canada and there were two female dancers, one Filipina and the other a Japanese-American *Nisei*. The only musician was the one-man gamelan: me, "Mas Malm." My 6′1″ body was squatted behind the instruments. I wore a sarong, Javanese jacket, and turban. My hair was red, so I was made to blacken the side burns. One of the hotels on the road billed me for my pillowcase because I forgot to wash off the makeup. I was usually exhausted after each performance.

TS: Look at that photograph—you're playing gendèr with two hands. You actually played that? You played gendèr and gong and, every once in a while, whacked the drum?

WM: That's exactly right. I was a busy man.

MS: Here's a clipping from the San Francisco newspaper: "The group is tiny, consisting only of Devi Dja, her dancing colleagues, and a barefooted turbaned musician that plays very light little wisps of melody endlessly repeated on the bells with a booming gong for punctuation and sometimes only beats out the insistent rhythm with palm and fingers on the drum."

WM: After the tour, I went back to Northwestern totally intrigued by all this other music I never knew existed. The music courses there were so incredibly conventional. One day, I was on the campus, walking out toward the lake and noticed the Anthropology Department. I saw a door marked "Comparative Musicology Lab," so I went in to see what it was. I met the famous ethnomusicologist, [Melville J.] Herskovitz, who said, "You must learn German." It scared the hell out of me, so I never took a class there. He had two lab assistants: Alan Merriam and Richard Waterman. They had a jazz band; I forget what they called themselves. We were in school at the same time, but I only met them that once.

I graduated in 1949 and then did a master's degree in composition in '49–50. My thesis was a giant oratorio, *The Centurion*. I was heavy into the Episcopal Church at that time. The centurion was standing at the cross, he saw Christ die, and was one of the first converts. I destroyed it; it was pretty second rate.

MS: Where did you go from there?

WM: I got a job at the University of Illinois teaching two-thirds music theory and one-third physical education for women. I was the only man with an office in the women's gym! I arrived in September 1950 and right on my new desk was a letter that said, "Greetings from the President, you have been selected for duty in the United States Army." I finally got drafted, so I only taught at Illinois for one semester before I had to report to the Army. I went to Camp Breckinridge, Kentucky, for basic training and learned all about rifles, machine guns, and how to crawl under barbed wire.

When I went to "classification and assignment," I never said I had a master's degree. I just said I played clarinet. So I ended up in the 101st Airborne Division Band. And then I was lucky: I saw a notice on a board about a job teaching music theory for the Army Unit in the Navy School of Music in Washington, DC. I applied for it and got it. They put me right back into my civilian job, except that I had no women in the class and had to wear a uniform. Staff Sergeant Malm. The school was on the Potomac River, across from the Naval Gun Factory. I took Wednesday afternoons off and went to the Library of Congress to read things about Asia. I was trying to find more about where Devi Dja came from, but the only music I found explained was Indian. I couldn't understand raga and couldn't find anything that would tell me how the music actually worked. So one weekend I got on a train and went to Paragon Bookstore in New York. I came back with a copy of Jaap Kunst's *Music of Java* (1949/1973) and a whole pile of other books that I put in my footlocker in the barracks. I bought all those books, but they didn't tell me what I wanted to know. They told you what the instruments were, but they didn't talk about the structure of the pieces.

After two years and one day, I was discharged. I got on a train and went down to New York. I was going to be a composer for dance. I went to the Dance Department at Juilliard and said—true story—"I just got out of the Army yesterday, I'm looking for jobs playing for dance classes. Do you have any openings?" You know what they said? "Come back in an hour." All those Juilliard students were so busy with their concerto contests that they didn't have time to play for the dancers. I got a job playing for dance classes at Juilliard. Next, I went to the housing office at Juilliard to see if they had any places for musicians to live. They listed places not by location or price but by instrument. I found one that had a piano. So I called up, went over to look at it, and took it. That was my apartment—it had a garden looking over the edge of the marquee of the Metropolitan Opera House. You could look down on Times Square to see what time it was. I don't remember how much it cost, but the tenants kept the management from changing the rugs because those were the rugs Caruso walked on.

I was trying to be a piano composer. After a short time it was obvious to me that I wasn't a very good pianist and I wasn't a very good composer. Summer came along and what do you do in summer? You go to summer stock. I got a job as a pianist at the American Dance Festival program in Connecticut. That was great. I was playing for Martha Graham, José Limon, and Doris Humphrey. The only real composition lessons I ever had were there, playing piano for Doris Humphrey. The way she talked about composition was just perfect.

Judith Becker

In conversation with Ted Solís and Margaret Sarkissian, October 25, 2007, Columbus, Ohio

Early Life

JB: I was born in Bay City, Michigan, in 1932. There's nothing in my early life that suggests the path I took, but one thing that was pointed out to me some years ago is the huge number of people from the Midwest who end up in Asian studies. I think it's the shock of discovering the wider world. That's really the only thing I can think of to account for this peculiar phenomenon. You have to remember that in those days people didn't travel. My family didn't travel. We didn't go anywhere. My mother was an English teacher and my father was a high-school principal. They were upper middle class, but we didn't have a lot of money. I had rarely been outside the state of Michigan before I went to Burma.

TS: Imagine that! How did music come into your life—piano lessons like everybody else?

JB: Yes, that's what little girls did.

College Life

I was a piano major as an undergraduate. My husband got a Fulbright to go to Burma and I found myself in Burma, four hundred miles from the nearest piano. We're talking about the late '50s. There were no Nonesuch or world music recordings back then, except for a few on Folkways.

MS: Why did your husband choose Burma for his Fulbright?

JB: He had a weird uncle who was a Vedantist and used to go to India all the time. He had a view of a larger world that I didn't have. I think he probably would have liked to go to India, but apparently they weren't offering Fulbrights to India that year. So, you know, Burma, India, it was all the same! But he fell in love with Burma, so that's why we stayed three years. Fulbrights are usually yearlong, but he renewed for two successive years. I was delighted—I was having a ball! Our second son was born there and our third child was conceived there. I just backed into ethnomusicology; there wasn't any forethought. Very often my graduate students used to say, "I can't decide whether I should get married? Should I postpone marriage? Should I postpone having a family?" And I'd say, "Don't ask me about life decisions. I never made one in my life. I just followed the accidents of my life!"

There I was in Burma, surrounded by this amazing music that I couldn't make head or tail of, so I got interested in what was going on around me. We were way up in the Shan Hills, but it just happened that a harpist who had recently graduated from the Mandalay School of Fine Arts was out in the provinces making his reputation, so I started taking lessons on the Burmese harp. Before we went to Burma I did actually get hold of a Folkways record of Burmese harp and *hsaing waing* (percussive ensemble) music [Courlander and Muang Than Myint 1953]. I thought the harp was beautiful and the hsaing waing was an abomination! It wasn't till I got there that I found out that they were both playing much the same repertoire! Gradually I began to make sense of what was going on. And then there was the *hne*, the really raucous oboe—well, I was brought up in a conservatory—I didn't know how to cope with music that made you jump out of your skin! By the time our three years were up, I'd lost my piano chops, but I didn't care. I had become so interested in this incredible music system, had no idea how it related to anything else in the world, and was determined to find out.

Adrienne Kaeppler

In conversation with Ted Solís and Margaret Sarkissian, October 28, 2007, Columbus, Ohio

Early Life

AK: I was born in the last century, in Milwaukee, Wisconsin. My parents were not ethnomusicologists; however, I was interested in dance from the time I was a very small child. I took my first class in modern dance when I was about five and then went into various other kinds of dance, including tap dance, acrobatic, ballet, and so forth. I was a dance person from the start. When I was in third grade, I started violin. I studied violin for some time and played in the orchestra. In high school I was a baton twirler, part of the marching band.

I went to the University of Wisconsin, Milwaukee, in the late '50s and majored in English. I was interested in literatures besides English, which fed into my anthropological leanings. I took Greek, Japanese, and Chinese literature, all in translation, because I didn't speak any of those languages. One day in my junior year, as I was walking down a street when it was twenty degrees below zero, I decided, "I'm outta here." I completed my junior year and went to University of Hawai'i for my senior year.

TS: Why Hawai'i? Did you have some kind of "hula and lei" image that drew you there?

AK: Not really. It was just about picking a place that was warm, any place that was warm! I don't know how I knew about hula, but I knew that people who did hula wore skirts made out of strips. I remember making my own hula skirt out of newspaper when I was a quite small child, perhaps eight or nine years old. I also made a head lei with long strips of white flowers.

TS: Did you ever hear *Hawaii Calls*? It was a program on the radio, broadcast from the beach in Waikiki. You could hear the surf.

AK: Actually, it probably was *Hawaii Calls*; I can't imagine what else it could have been. We had a phonograph, of course, but I don't remember ever having any records. It must've been the '40s and '50s. I probably heard this music and must've seen advertisements or something. It was somewhere in the back of my consciousness, but it was, shall we say, not in the foreground when I decided to go to Hawai'i! I knew about the University of Hawai'i and the Anthropology Department, but I do things on whims—it was just a cold winter day, and I said, "I'm outta here." So, that's where I went. I stopped the English major and took as many classes as I needed in order to get a BA in anthropology.

Judith (Judy) McCulloh

In conversation with Margaret Sarkissian, March 24, 2009, Urbana, Illinois

Early Life

JMcC: I was born in Spring Valley, Illinois, in August 1935. We lived in town in Peoria for a while and then, in third grade, we moved out to a small apple orchard, maybe three acres, on the outskirts of Peoria. I grew up pretty much in the country. My folks tried various things to make a living, but nothing quite worked out. We raised baby chickens one year, but they got all over the house. We tried to raise Christmas trees, but there was a drought. When I started seventh grade, we moved to a larger orchard, twenty-one acres, farther outside Peoria. I got a ride into the city high school, which was much better than the country high school I was supposed to attend. I think that helped me get to college, because I'm not sure I would have had the credentials otherwise.

There was no music-making at home. My mother sang a couple of songs, but that was about it. The most music I heard was in church—fairly slow, foursquare, Amish-Mennonite unaccompanied singing. In terms of editing, I always read a lot, but I never thought I'd be an editor. We had no writing assignments in school. When I got to college and somebody referred to an essay, I wondered, "What do those initials S. A. stand for?"

MS: At what point did music come into your life aside from church?

JMcC: I would say the first time I became aware of other kinds of music was on Saturday afternoons listening to the Met on the radio and taking piano lessons, as most everybody did at some point. I started piano somewhere between eight and twelve years old. I took lessons for several years and enjoyed it but was not outstanding.

When I went to the city high school, I'd get a ride [there] in the morning but couldn't get a ride back after school, so I'd go to my grandparent's home. They had retired from farming and moved into Peoria. My dad, who was still working the 3–11 shift at Caterpillar Tractor, would pick me up on his way home. Sometimes, I'd stay over at my grandparents' place and walk to school next morning. I'd sleep on the couch in the living room. My grandfather would get up very early and turn the radio on. He listened to the "Chuck Wagon Gang," a country group that sang gospel songs. I remember putting all that down. I'd say, "Oh those religious hillbillies, I can't stand it!" I was more into classical music as an uplifting sort of thing and a way out of being countrified, so I didn't think too much about that kind of music. Now I wish I'd listened to it.

College Life

Eventually I went off to Cottey, a women's junior college in Nevada, Missouri. It's spelled like Nevada, but they pronounced it "Neveda." It was near the Kansas line, just south of Kansas City. Cottey College was sponsored by the PEO [Philanthropic Educational Organization] Sisterhood.[1]

MS: How did you get there from Peoria?

JMcC: A neighbor who lived maybe a mile or so away had taken an interest in me because I was in school with her daughter. She was a PEO recruiter and arranged for a small scholarship, which was exceedingly welcome. So off I went in 1952. I had an English composition teacher named Joan Mueller, who was interested in the folk music revival and had some recordings of Burl Ives. She had a little guitar and sang the way people sang in the revival back in those days. During that period Richard

Dyer-Bennet came through to give a program. Before he started, he said, "Now I need to make a distinction. There are folk singers and there are singers of folk songs; I am a singer of folk songs." That was an eye-opening moment. I thought, "My goodness, what does he mean by that?" I started poking around and found that the songs he and Joan Mueller sang were interpretations of something else. That was when I started tracking down other kinds of music that we would now call "traditional."

MS: Were you tracking down recordings or what?

JMcC: Recordings were all we had. There was nothing in the library. Nobody had a car, so there was no way to do anything approximating fieldwork. We were pretty much stuck on campus. Joan called it "that place of Babylonian captivity." It was too restrictive for her and she left after a year or so. After she left, a bunch of us drove over to St. Louis, on the far side of the state, to the National Folk Festival, which Sarah Gertrude Knott was still putting on. Somehow, we got backstage and met a fellow named Booth Campbell, an old singer from the Ozarks, and a washtub band from Minnesota. They were singing and playing music like I'd never heard before, certainly not live. So I whipped out a piece of paper, found a pencil, and started writing a staff, the tune, and the words. I was collecting and I didn't know it. I just thought, "These are really neat pieces," so I made a little collection of stuff I heard backstage at the National Folk Festival. I don't know where that wound up.

MS: You knew staff notation from playing piano, and you had a good enough ear that you could write down what you heard on the spot?

JMcC: Yes, it was no big deal. It's like another language. You hear the pitch, you hear the rhythm, and you write it down. I didn't do harmony, because I wasn't fast enough. It's hard enough to get pitch and rhythm down and I'd never done it before. I remember furiously writing, making up the staffs and doing the treble clef real fast, just writing things down.

MS: Did you sing them back later?

JMcC: No, I'm not a singer. I just enjoyed listening, both musically and textually. It was so varied. It wasn't the Anglo-American stuff that you got in the folk song revival; it was different languages, different cultures. I never thought I'd carry on in anything like that area, but that had to be formative in some way.

MS: What year was that?

JMcC: That would have been the spring of '54. I was at Cottey from '52 to '54, and I think it was toward the end of that period. It would have been after Dyer-Bennet came, because I was already aware that there were two ways to get at traditional music; either go to the source or go to an interpreter. I already knew the difference when I went to St. Louis; these were sources and, somehow, they had a special value. After junior college, I went to Ohio Wesleyan because Joan Mueller had graduated from there and had talked about it. I was there for two years as an English major.

Regula Burckhardt Qureshi

In conversation with Ted Solís, begun April 21, 2008, Savoy, Illinois; completed February 25, 2017, via Skype

Early Life

RQ: I was born in Basel, Switzerland, in July 1939, at the start of World War II. My family was one of Basel's old patrician families. The historian Jacob Burckhardt [1818–1897] and Sheikh Ibrahim [Johann Ludwig Burckhardt, 1784–1817], the man who discovered Petra and Abu Simbel in 1812 and '13, were part of my family. Both my grandfathers were theologians. Two of my paternal grandfather's brothers became artists, one a painter and the other a sculptor. The son of my grandfather's sculptor brother was Titus Burckhardt [1908–1984]. As a young man, Titus went to Morocco, became a Sufi, and lived in the old city. The French police evicted him because they thought he was a spy—Morocco was still a French colony then—so he became an aesthetic Sufi art historian. He wrote wonderful books—his *Introduction to Sufism* [Burckhardt 1951] has been translated into English and is still being republished.

There was a general sense that our family was intellectually oriented; there were books, literature, and talk about literature in the house. My dad was into cultural politics. He was seen as the black sheep of an otherwise conservative family because he was a socialist. He made a pilgrimage to meet Gandhi and wanted to learn Russian so he could read Lenin in the original, at which point his father—who funded his studies—put his foot down and said, "You cannot learn Russian, it's too Communist." He became a labor lawyer and a civil servant and, later, a diplomat. He was chosen by the Unions to represent them in the Swiss Embassy in Washington, DC. My mother was a feminist, although in actual life she couldn't practice it very much. At that time women didn't have the right to vote in Switzerland. My sisters and I were embarrassed by our parents' activities and beliefs. We grew up politically very conservative.

TS: What was your home language as a child?

RQ: We spoke our own old-fashioned Basel Deutsch (Swiss German) at home. It was a special dialect that belonged to the older families. There were many different dialects in those days, so local identity was very strong. Our written language was German. In the first years of primary school the teacher spoke dialect but soon switched to speaking High German. I started French and Latin in grade 5 or 6 and English around grade 7 or 8.

TS: Was there music in your early life?

RQ: I'm told that I was singing before I was talking. Music was part of what we did in our family. I learned how to play the recorder by solfège and later had piano lessons. My dad loved Schumann and played the piano every day, so I grew up hearing the amateur repertoire and played four hands with him. My maternal grandfather played the cello and I inherited his cello at age fourteen and started studying seriously. Everyone thought I should go to university because I was smart, but I was besotted with music and wanted to be a musician. The only way you could do that on the Continent was to study in a conservatory, not at a university. I felt musicology was dry as dust and didn't want anything to do with it. This was the moment when I moved to the US with my parents. We knew the Busch family, who had also moved to the States. Adolph and his youngest brother, Hermann, a cellist, had founded the Marlboro Festival in Vermont. Because of our connection, my mother was able to get me a spot in their wonderful summer school.

College Life

We moved to Washington, DC, in 1958, and I went to the summer school at Marlboro. One of the other students said, "Why don't you audition for Mr. Rose and come to Curtis?" So I took a train down to Great Neck, New York. I didn't know anything and my English wasn't very good, but I went with my cello, played for him, and he said, "OK, you're accepted."

I studied with Leonard Rose at Curtis Institute of Music from 1958 to 1960. I only spent two years there and didn't graduate. Curtis was fabulous, but I realized that my brain was starving. The people there were good musicians but not particularly well educated. I had never interacted with people who were not educated and realized it was going to be a problem. In addition, I had to work too hard on my technical ability. I wasn't one of those talents who could play without practicing. While this was happening, my roommate set me up on a blind date with a housemate of an Indian friend of hers, a PhD student in political science who was also from India. I was totally ticked off because we went to *The Ice Capades*. I had never seen anything so vulgar. Despite that, we got acquainted. That student was Saleem, who became my husband.

Saleem and I would spend hours and hours talking. He was someone who knew history and poetry. What really hooked me was the poetry, because here was someone who knew Urdu poetry intimately. I was totally intrigued, so we went to New York and found a German *Grammar of Urdu* in a used bookstore. That opened up a whole new world. Saleem also had tapes of Indian music—film songs, old songs, *ghazals*—I did not like the music at all. He had a Ravi Shankar tape and it never modulated! I couldn't stand it. It was so boring. The music did not attract me, but the poetry did.

When Saleem finished his PhD, he had to go back because he was a college lecturer. So we decided to get married in 1959. Before we left, I did a master's degree at Penn in German language and literature, because clearly, I wasn't going to be a cellist in either India or Pakistan. I was allowed into the master's program without a bachelor's degree because the faculty were all émigrés and knew my Gymnasium education was as good as any undergraduate education. I did two semesters of coursework and wrote the thesis later (on a nineteenth-century literary topic) when we were in Pakistan.

We went to Pakistan in 1960. Saleem was hired as a government officer because of his public administration PhD. It was a good job and freed him from his teaching bond. Within a half a year, though, the democratic government was overthrown by Ayub Khan. That became a real problem in terms of politics, so we decided to emigrate at that point. We were there for less than a year. It was very hard to emigrate at that time, and I didn't have the smarts to realize I could've been the immigrant. But I doubt Saleem could have come, even as my husband—the US only allowed one hundred emigrants a *year* from Asia. So we went to India for the rest of the year, and Saleem got a job as a college professor, but the living was measly.

We applied to Canada and the US, but Canada was the better prospect. Saleem connected with the Institute of Islamic Studies at McGill University, and they gave him a research-associate post in 1961. He taught political science while he was a researcher there. After that, he got a job teaching political science at the University of Saskatchewan, so we moved out west and I joined the Saskatoon Orchestra. A year later, in '63, he got a job at the University of Alberta. By then we'd been moving around a lot and I'd had a second child. We had a daughter and a son and wanted to be somewhere where we had a life. I joined the Edmonton Symphony and loved it. They were happy to get someone who could really play the cello.

TS: And you haven't mentioned ethnomusicology yet!

RQ: I didn't know what it was yet! In 1965 we took the summer off and went to his home in Lucknow. It was a hot summer, and I thought, "I've got to connect with this place somehow." I asked my father-in-law to take me to the Bhatkhande College of Hindustani Music to see the instruments. I saw the sitar and other instruments, but they were all plucked. I asked, "Don't you have any bowed instruments?" That's when I saw an old man with a big shock of white hair, sitting on the floor, sawing away on a type of cello. I said, "That's the one I want to learn." I didn't know anything about the *sarangi* or its associations with courtesans, and my family didn't let on! "She's our daughter-in-law, she wants to play music, and she can have what she wants." Luckily I married into a very tolerant and accepting family.

I started sarangi lessons with that old man, Mirza Mahmud Ali, who had been at the college since it was founded in 1928. He taught me an easy tune in *Bilawal*, a melody from the Bhatkhande College syllabus. He sang it for me and taught me how to hold the bow like an old double bass bow [German grip]. And so I sang: "Ni, Sa, Ga, Re, Sa, Ni, Dha, Dha, Sa—Re, Sa." And he said, "Ni, Sa . . ." bow, bow, bow, back and forth. And then he said, "Not like that. It should be . . ." and he played, "Ni, Sa . . . ah . . . ah . . . ah . . . ah . . . ah . . . ah. Dha . . . Dha . . . Sa." And I said, "What? Slurring the notes?" It was a pivotal experience for me. I had spent all my years on the cello learning how to *not* slur, except when you wanted to. It sounded bad to me, and I said, "Why do I have to do *that*?" And he looked at me with piercing eyes and said, "Because it's beautiful." It was such a compelling thing. My ears didn't tell me it was beautiful, but his face told me. His eyes. I knew there was something there. Eventually, I realized I could develop that sensibility. I learned to trust another person rather than my ears. It's not really "the sound," it's what it means to other people, and I could learn to feel that meaning.

Later that summer, we stopped in Karachi and I got a teacher there who became my first *ustad*. As a child, he grew up with his grandfather, who was at the court of Rampur. He was a sweet man who came to our house and started teaching me something real. He asked me to play what I had just learned in front of his other students: it was *Bageshri*. I played it, and one of the students said, "Um, was that Indian?" When I told him it was *Bageshri*, he said, "Oh, I thought that was Western music." I played it so un-idiomatically that he didn't even realize it was Indian music. That shocked me. So I spent the rest of the summer taking lessons and could not stop practicing. When we visited my family in Switzerland, they said, "Oh, just close her up in a room—it sounds like two cats are dying!"

Back in Edmonton, I looked around for someone to teach me, because I needed to learn the music. It wasn't the technique that was on my mind, so I found a woman who was the wife of a professor from Maharashtra. She sang a very rigid style, but she knew it all.

TS: You learned singing?

RQ: I played, she sang. Even my sarangi teacher would often teach me through singing. When he didn't bother opening the instrument, I'd get annoyed and say, "I want to see. Show me how you're doing it." He said, "That's not important. Learn the music."

RUBY ORNSTEIN

In conversation with Ted Solís, October 24, 2008, Greenwich Village, New York

Early Life

RO: I was born in the Bronx, New York City, in early 1939. There was absolutely nothing in my childhood that pointed me toward ethnomusicology. It was a complete accident. I studied the piano as a child; everyone played the piano. I enjoyed music theory very much and had an excellent ear. I could play anything. I was good at languages as well, studying French and a little German. My father was originally from Poland, but his parents thought it was a good idea to move to Germany. My mother was also from Germany. They came here in 1928, and my sister was born in that same year. I went to the High School of Music and Art in Manhattan. It was a very prestigious school—hard to get into—and a good experience. I was good at music theory, so I passed through those classes very quickly and took voice as a second instrument. I loved singing in choruses. It was not a neighborhood school, but drew students from all over the city, so it was the first time that I met people who were different from my childhood friends.

College Life

I wasn't particularly interested in other cultures when I started at Queens College in New York City, in 1955. I majored in music and minored in education. I was their best music student and won all the prizes. When I graduated in 1959 my mentor said, "You really should go to graduate school," so I did.

NOTE

1. The Philanthropic Educational Organization, an International Sisterhood, was founded in 1869 and is now based in Des Moines, Iowa.

Nineteen Forties

The members of the group born in the late 1920s and 1930s are in high school or are undergraduates.

World War II, like The Great War, has the effect of exposing Americans (perennially the most insular of "Westerners") to cultures from Western Europe to North Africa and South, West, Southeast, and East Asia. Servicemen further spread American popular culture throughout both European and Pacific theaters of war, and later return with wives from abroad. The 1944 GI Bill helps make broader intercultural knowledge accessible to millions. These openings are partly offset by a "tightening" born of the Cold War's "East vs. West" realignment. President Truman's 1948 order to desegregate the US armed forces is an early, substantive step toward civil rights. Dutch and French colonies move toward independence. The British Empire begins its twenty-year process of divestiture (excluding Hong Kong, returned to China in 1997) with the independence of India in 1947. Refugees, including prominent European composers, conductors, and musicologists, have been settling in America since the 1930s, an influx which after World War II "rapidly transformed the world of higher education in America from looking to Europe for leadership to being the world's intellectual powerhouse" (Nettl 2009, 22). The prestige and position of musicology within music departments begins to increase. The International Folk Music Council (IFMC) is initiated in 1947; Moses Asch forms Folkways Records in 1948, the same year both the audio tape recorder and vinyl LPs appear.

Ricardo Trimillos

In conversation with Margaret Sarkissian, August 1, 2016, Penang, Malaysia

Early Life

RT: I was born in San Jose, California, in March 1941. My parents emigrated from the Philippines in 1934, so I'm first-generation American born. Both were active in Philippine cultural events in the San Jose area. My parents were from an educated class, so they had a slightly different vision than most of the farmers and unskilled workers who formed the majority of the Filipino community. With four or five similarly educated families, they organized a cultural group called the Filipino Family Club, which taught Filipino dances and music and helped Filipinos adjust to American life. Looking back on it, [I see] it was a class thing where the *ilustrados*, the upper class, organized things for the lower class. It sounds terribly colonial, but that's really what it was.

The Filipino Family Club's dance group participated in intercultural festivals around San Jose with other immigrant groups like Italians, Portuguese, and Japanese. My brother is two years older than me, so when we first started singing and dancing in the troupe, he was six and I was four. Through all this, my introduction to Filipino identity was a very positive thing, whereas in the case of many other Filipinos it was negative. There was a lot of discrimination, particularly if you were from a lower class or a blue-collar family background.

Another unusual aspect of my early life is that we were raised Protestant. My parents had both converted from Catholicism; my mother was Baptist and my father was Presbyterian. Part of our cultural activity included performing at churches. We got invited to interesting places and met interesting people, and the presentational part of being Filipino was very much part of our growing up.

MS: Why did your parents come to California, and what did they do?

RT: My father visited San Francisco as an adventuresome single man in 1931 or '32. At the time, the Philippines was still a colony of America, so it was fairly easy to travel. You didn't need a visa; you just got on a boat and went. He went back to the Philippines in '34 and met my mother. After—according to them—two weeks of courting, they married, got on a ship, and returned to California. My father had studied psychology/psychiatry at Silliman University, a Presbyterian university in Dumaguete. My mother trained as a public schoolteacher at the Baptist College in Iloilo. They resumed those kinds of jobs in California and were thus in a better position than a lot of Filipino immigrants who had come as farm workers.

MS: Was there music in their background?

RT: Yes, my mother was a singer and came from a musical family. Her father was a musician. Of course, with Filipinos, almost everybody played something. There were relatives who were part of the traditional *sarsuwela*. Originally introduced during the Spanish period, sarsuwelas were like light opera with Filipino stories in local vernacular languages. My parents are from the area called Iloilo, so their local language was Ilonggo.

Also on my mother's side, an uncle and his family were part of the big Visayan film industry. Everybody thinks of the film industry as only being Tagalog, but there were other film industries before the war that produced films in Visayan languages, Ilonggo and Cebuano. After the war, most of the vernacular film industries died out because there was a push to use the national language, Tagalog. My uncle's family was part of a company called Sampaguita Films. Sampaguita is a fragrant flower—jasmine. That particular studio lasted into the '50s before dying out.

MS: In addition to singing and dancing, did you play any instrument as a child?

RT: Singing and dancing was the Filipino thing—I never thought it would amount to anything. It had no real relevance for my everyday life. It was only later, when I was about to graduate from college and this ethnomusicology thing came into my awareness, that suddenly there was capital in having all that experience. Aside from that, our family was also part of the American assimilationist project, so both my brother and I studied piano and became quite active in all kinds of Western music. My mother had trained as a singer of light popular music and also played piano, so my first instrument was piano. I started lessons when I was four years old. I went to public school all my life and was very active musically. I played cello in orchestra and baritone horn in band from junior high school onward. At grammar school chorus was required, so I was a singer and, because I studied piano, I was also the choir's accompanist. I was always more involved with ensemble performance than training as a soloist. If you think about it, that's a skill ethnomusicologists learn very early—how to interact with other people.

MS: It sounds like you were already identifying as a musician in high school.

RT: Yes, I was a band geek! I enjoyed the traveling part because in band we were always getting on a bus and going someplace. Again, if you think of ethnomusicology, it's that whole business of going elsewhere, working with other people, and discovering new things.

College Life

Given our family situation, it was a foregone conclusion that we were going to college. My brother did political science and I was a double major in music (piano) and English lit. We both went to school locally, to San Jose State College (now San Jose

State University). At San Jose State there were two of us, myself and a Chinese boy, who had grown up together and taken lessons from the same piano teacher since we were eight years old. We were these cute little oriental kids who played duo piano. We both did solo stuff but stayed together as duo pianists through our undergraduate years and even played the Saint-Saëns double piano concerto in our senior year. We both applied to Juilliard and were accepted, but I didn't want to do duo piano as a career. I wanted to study with Madam [Rosina] Lhévinne, who was the biggie at the time.

That was our plan at the beginning of our senior year. But in January or February 1962, the East-West Center opened at the University of Hawai'i. It was a State Department initiative, the United States' answer to the Patrice Lumumba University, which brought Third World students to the Soviet Union. The East-West Center brought students from Pacific Asia and America together to cement relations. It was a big deal, but also—looking back on it—political pork barrel, because it was a way for Hawai'i, the fiftieth state, to get money for development. The chair of the Music Department at Hawai'i—essentially a Western conservatory at the time—came through to recruit students. They were starting up ethnomusicology, which I'd never heard of, and the East-West Center was providing full scholarships. They paid for everything, plus travel to Asia for Americans or one semester in an American mainland institution for Asian and Pacific students. It was the travel thing again! That was attractive to me so I thought, well, this might be better than becoming yet another concert pianist.

MS: Had you been outside of California at that point?

RT: Yes, I'd been to other places in the United States and spent the summer of '61 (between my junior and senior years of college) as an exchange student in Neckarelz (in Baden-Württemberg, near Heidelberg), Germany. My host family had seven children, which was an extra perk for me. I came from a Filipino family with only two kids, which was very unusual because most Filipino families had six or seven kids. It was a fantasy for me to be in a family with a lot of kids! We all got along very well, and I've kept the relationship with them for over fifty years now. That was my first international experience. It was not only the travel but also the discovery that I was good at this kind of cross-cultural stuff. It was easy, I enjoyed it, and I was good at languages.

Stephen Blum

In conversation with Ted Solís, October 28, 2007, Columbus, Ohio

Early Life

SB: I was born in East Cleveland in March 1942. My mother trained as a teacher, but only started teaching high-school English after my brother, who was two years younger, started high school. My father had a lot of jobs; we weren't wealthy. His younger brother, my uncle, was an amateur cellist whose interests in literature and music were closer to mine than anyone else in the family. My mother liked to sing, and her father, who had retired to a farm, was also very musical and sang hymns as he did his farm work. He sang in a quartet in a country church and took me to tent revival meetings in southern Indiana, which were very exciting and intense. The performance venue was very different from anything I'd experienced and left a strong impression. Later, as a graduate student, I became very interested in shape-note music after Charles Hamm took some students down to Benton, Kentucky.

TS: What was your childhood like?

SB: Music was a huge interest. Cleveland was a good place for a young music student. I started taking piano lessons when I was eight with the organist of my family's church. His wife was a singer, a student of Marie Kraft, head of the Voice Department at the Cleveland Institute of Music. I became very close to them and learned a lot. I also accompanied a lot of her students, so there were a lot of *Lieder* in my high school years. When I was in ninth grade they arranged for a theorist to come to their small music school, so I could take theory lessons, which I did for the next four years. I also liked learning languages and wanted to study literature and history.

TS: What contact with languages did you have in Cleveland?

SB: I remember a high-school English teacher in my junior year playing a record of Brecht reading in German. I didn't understand anything but realized that I liked the musicality of languages. I still do. I like listening to languages for the rhythms and the contours. I took two years of Latin, and then changed to French.

My piano teacher was a student of Leonard Shure, who was then head of the piano division of the Cleveland Music School Settlement. He wanted me to study with Shure at the end of my high-school years, but Shure left just as I arrived at the Settlement School, so I studied with his successor, Theodore Lettvin. I went there for one year. It was funded by the Community Chest, but I lived outside the area that the Community Chest served, so the teachers kindly gave me a fellowship. My theory teacher, with whom I'd been studying for three years already, was head of the theory division. I was lucky to have those four years of theory. When I went to Oberlin I placed out of the first three semesters of theory courses for that reason.

College Life

I went to Oberlin College in 1960 with the thought that I'd do a five-year double major in French literature and piano. In the end, I decided I didn't want to stay at Oberlin College for five years, so I only took the piano degree. I was also taking organ at the same time, as I thought of being an organist.

TS: While you were at Oberlin, did you have any contact with non-Western subjects?

SB: In my last year I took East Asian history and wrote a paper on Chinese Buddhist sculpture for extra credit. Another advantage of Cleveland besides its musical life (and remember, the orchestra was at its peak under Szell) was the art museum, which is strong in East Asian art.

John Baily

In conversation with Margaret Sarkissian, March 5, 2010, Amherst, Massachusetts

Early Life

JB: I was born in July 1943, in Glastonbury, Somerset. Glastonbury has long been a Mecca for people seeking spiritual enlightenment. In the eleventh century, the monks of Glastonbury Abbey spread the rumor that King Arthur was buried there, so it became a site of pilgrimage for many hundreds of years. Like Romeo and Juliet, my parents came from two rival families. They had sheepskin tanneries next door to each other and, until their marriage, were deadly enemies. My father was a solicitor, as was his father before him. My mother came from a highly educated Quaker family. Both maternal grandparents had been at Oxford University during World War I and then had six children, five of whom also went to Oxford. Four girls went to Somerville College, including my mother. Later, my sister went to Somerville, as did my son Thomas—by this time it was co-ed—so we have four generations of Somervillians. Academic work was not central to the family but was always very highly respected.

MS: When you reflect on your childhood, do you see the roots of an ethnomusicologist?

JB: When I was four we moved to Chichester in Sussex. In those days Chichester was a small Georgian cathedral city; for about four years we lived in the Cathedral Close. My father was tremendously interested in music. Sadly, his dream that I would become a Cathedral chorister came to nothing. I discovered, many years later, that after World War II he had enrolled as a part-time music student at Durham University. I have some letters from Delius's amanuensis with critical comments on his compositions. He was also mad about musical instruments. We always had lots of them around the house, and he was always learning something new. He went through an interesting progression in life. When he was young, he was a great admirer of J. S. Bach (I was christened John Sebastian in honor of the great man), and we had a grand piano in the house. By the end of his life, he had graduated from grand piano to concertina, via a whole lot of other instruments. We even had one or two African instruments, including a drum that he got from a friend in the colonial service.

When my mother was at university, her tutor in ancient Greek was Isobel Henderson, a great authority on ancient Greek music. She was my godmother—when you look back on your life you see certain omens! Another omen was that my paternal grandmother visited Morocco when she was young and brought back a *gunbri*, its body made out of a coconut. I still have that, hanging on the wall.

MS: How about your own musical beginnings?

JB: I went to Sidcot, a Quaker boarding school in Somerset, where a Canadian boy introduced Elvis Presley into my life when I was about twelve or thirteen. It was the time of the trad jazz revival and the skiffle era, a very interesting period in postwar British music because it was homemade music. My father had taught me the rudiments of playing the guitar, and my first band was a skiffle group at Sidcot. Our repertoire was largely American folksongs and a lot of blues stuff. Even as a boy of about thirteen or fourteen, I'd discovered this really wonderful black American singer called Huddie Ledbetter, Leadbelly.

I went on to Midhurst Grammar School (about twelve miles north of Chichester) for the Sixth Form. It was a radical school with an inspirational headmaster who turned his little country grammar school into a left-wing intellectual powerhouse. The school's Young Communist League members were very much in touch with the music of people like Ewan MacColl and Bert Lloyd. There was nobody around in those days to teach you; you had to be self-taught. I went on the Aldermaston [anti-nuclear] March in 1961 and observed one guy playing a particular Big Bill Broonzy piece that I simply couldn't work out. As soon as I saw what he was doing, I realized how it was done. That showed me how important seeing what other people do is in this kind of self-taught mode of learning.

College Life

I went up to Oxford University to study geology in 1962 but was encouraged by my college to switch to psychology and physiology. I formed a band with a couple of guys who played tenor saxophone: Bernie Greenwood, a medical student who later became a very close friend, and another guy who worked for Maxwell Publishing. I took up piano because, being rather small and playing in these college gigs where there was no stage or anything, I got rather knocked about at the front of the band. I was a self-taught blues pianist. Our officially registered name was Funkenstein et al., but outside the university we were known as King Cobra and the Rattlesnakes. We met a small-time record businessman, who paid for us to make a demonstration record. On one side we recorded a song that Bernie Greenwood and I had composed, called "Buzz with the Fuzz." It later became a hit for Chris Farlowe. We also won a competition run by the *News of the World*. The prize was a recording session with George Martin at Abbey Road Studios. Unfortunately, we'd just got a new drummer, a very nice Jamaican guy, who went to pieces in the studio. After three takes when nothing worked, we were booted out. That was the end of my career in Abbey Road.

So, back to my studies in Oxford, and eventually I graduated. Bernie and I concocted a mad scheme to take a blues band across Asia to Australia. It was when people were just beginning to travel and get away from their boring British middle-class backgrounds. We put together a band called The Glands that included Eric Clapton, who gave up playing in John Mayall's Bluesbreakers Band to join us, and went off together to Athens. I was the singer. Of course, it was a totally unrealistic plan. We'd never heard of work permits or anything like that, so it was a complete disaster.

At the end of the month, Eric and the others went back to England, but Bernie and I continued from Athens to Karachi in our battered old car. It was a formative experience. Just to travel through all those countries: Turkey, Lebanon, Syria, Iraq, Iran, Afghanistan, and Pakistan! It was late autumn, and we slept out in the open every night—you wouldn't dream of doing that sort of thing today, but we had no trouble. We spent several weeks in Karachi, flew to Sri Lanka (the war between India and Pakistan made it impossible to continue overland), and spent a month there. I loved it, especially all the Buddhist sites. Then we went by ship to Freemantle, Australia, and hitchhiked across the great Nullarbor Plain to Adelaide and eventually to Sydney.

I was lucky to get a job as a research assistant to Professor George Singer in the Psychology Department of Sydney University. My first publication, in the *Australian Journal of Psychology*, dates from that period (Baily and Singer 1967). After several months Bernie and I took a small Italian vessel to Panama—three weeks of misery— and went by bus to El Paso, Texas. We bought another old wreck and drove all over the States, sleeping under the stars every night and cooking our food on campfires. The high point was a wonderful evening with Howling Wolf and his band in a small Chicago blues club. Then we drove to New York, where the car died, so we sold it for five dollars and flew back to the UK. I was away for a year, and I'm sure I came back a different person.

Philip Yampolsky

In conversation with Ted Solís, March 23, 2008, Seattle, Washington

Early Life

PY: I was born in April 1945, in Walter Reed Hospital, Washington, DC, five days before President Roosevelt died there. My father's side of the family was academic. My uncle was a Zen scholar who taught at Columbia. He had the same name as I have, so people always got us confused. My father was a high-school teacher, typographer, and, later, a librarian and rare-books bibliographer. The generation before that were husband-and-wife botanists. And the generation before that was Franz Boas, the anthropologist—I'm his great grandson. The other side of the family was engineers. My mother had a master's in psychology from Columbia, but, being a single mother in wartime and just after, she was never able to use it and became an executive secretary, which was a waste.

TS: What was your childhood like?

PY: The basic background was leftist intellectual. It was a literary but not particularly musical family, though there was recorded music in the house. From the start I loved records. There's a picture of me, aged four, in short pants, standing by the record player, getting ready to listen to something, probably Jelly Roll Morton. I was crazy about old jazz. My parents recognized that I had musical leanings, so I was given piano lessons at age five. Apparently, I got so frustrated because I couldn't sound like Jelly Roll Morton that the teacher thought it would be better if I stopped piano lessons!

My parents divorced when I was five; my mother remarried when I was nine, and we moved to Old Greenwich, Connecticut. Greenwich had a wonderful public-school music program. In junior high I became really involved with music and started singing a lot. It amazes people who know me now that I sang and danced in musical theater back then.

Coming from an academic family, I believed the achievements of the mind were by far the most important thing and nothing else mattered. I believed that the best thing one could be in life was an artist, preferably a novelist or a poet, and if one couldn't do that, the next best thing was to be a scholar of something. This may account for why I've never made much money in my life! I was deeply involved in literature and crazy about music. I used to bicycle to school and would strap my transistor radio onto the bicycle basket and listen to whatever classical music was being played.

I went to a prep school where I was very unhappy but got two things out of it: a lifelong friend and the ability to sing hymn harmony. It may sound strange, but by learning hymn harmony I felt I had mastered a musical language, even though I didn't play an instrument and was not skilled in reading music. My harmonic sense was all by ear, yet it gave me the feeling that I belonged in the Western musical tradition. Of course, I wasn't aware of any other traditions at that time.

College Life

I went to Columbia University in 1962, determined to be an English major and study literature. But music was equally important to me, so in my sophomore year I decided to take a harmony class. This was a determining moment in my life. I showed up as a rather prissy teacher was fussing around, complaining that the class was too large. Suddenly there was a thundering noise as someone came pounding up the stairs and burst into the room. It was Nicholas England. He was so vibrant and alive! He announced, "Well, this is great! Look how many students are here! Tell you what we'll do, everybody whose name starts with A through L come with me; everybody whose name goes from M through Z, stay here."

I went and stood with the A through Ls, and that changed my life. Nick invited us to an extra-curricular African drumming class that he was starting. I became devoted to Nick. He had so much to talk about, about everything in the world. Eventually I became his RA and helped him organize the ethnomusicology archive at Columbia.

Meanwhile, I was floundering as a literature student, so I put more and more energy into the African music group, which, at some point—certainly by the second year—was taught by an Ewe musician, Kobla Ladzekpo, the first of the Ladzekpos to come here. Somewhere along the line, I began to think I wanted to be an ethnomusicologist, but I was struggling in college, partly because I was a perfectionist and didn't want to turn in a paper if it wasn't a terrific paper. When it wasn't terrific, I didn't turn it in. I got F's in a lot of classes and it took me six years to get through Columbia. I graduated in 1968.

TS: Do you remember when you first heard the word "ethnomusicology?"

PY: From Nick. He had just come back from fieldwork in the Kalahari and was writing his dissertation. I must have asked him what discipline allows you to study !Kung music and West African drumming. He said, "Ethnomusicology—it's a very awkward word." I wasn't sure I could be a scholar, but I was beginning to think that I wanted to be an ethnomusicologist. When I graduated, Nick found me a job with Lorna Marshall. She was the anthropologist who, with her husband Laurence, had sponsored the "Marshall Expeditions" to the !Kung in the 1950s and had invited Nick to go with them. Lorna was writing the first volume of *The !Kung of Nyae Nyae* [Marshall 1976] and needed a secretary and editor. I was a good writer, so Nick sent me to Cambridge, Massachusetts, to work for Lorna for a couple of years.

I kept up my involvement with the Ladzekpos and Nick's African group. Whenever they needed a player, I joined them. In the summer of '69, Nick took a group of high-school music teachers to Senegal, Ivory Coast, Ghana, and Nigeria, and I went along as his assistant. It was brief, only six weeks, but it was my first trip to Africa and a key moment for me.

In 1970, Nick was invited to run the World Music Program at California Institute of the Arts. He invited the Ladzekpos to CalArts to teach Ewe music and dance, and he invited me along as his program assistant. I was thinking about going into ethnomusicology but needed to get up my courage before I went back to an academic program. I had somehow acquired a belief that an ethnomusicologist or anthropologist ought to have two areas that were as disparate as possible. I considered Ewe music my first area and was searching for something else. Bob Brown had just moved his Javanese gamelan to CalArts from Wesleyan. I wandered into the gamelan room, not knowing anything, and saw all these pretty, shiny instruments. Bob said, "Sit here. Hit this thing every eight beats. Count to eight and go 'Bong.'" So I sat down, counted to eight, and went "Bong." And while I was engaged in going "Bong," a pretty girl walked into the room and sat down. That seemed a good conjunction of things, so I stayed, and that was that. I continued with gamelan, feeling that it could be my second area. Bob brought with him not just his instruments and teachers but a lot of his best students from Wesleyan, people who were devoted to gamelan. One of the attractions of gamelan for me was that it was a social group. They were all interesting people—not to mention the pretty girl—and I was very much in need of a social group.

The next summer, '71, Brown organized a field trip to Indonesia to play Javanese gamelan. Somewhat to CalArts's displeasure, the school paid most of the expenses. Each student paid only three hundred dollars for a four-and-a-half-month trip. Many of the participants became Indonesian scholars, one way or another: Andy Toth, John Pemberton (anthropology), Nancy Florida (Javanese literature and history), Alan Feinstein, Jody Diamond, Richard Wallis, Susan Walton, and me! Bob loved Javanese music more than Balinese music, but he liked Bali more than Java. So he ended up buying a Javanese gamelan, carting it to Bali, and installing it in Walter Spies's old estate, which had been turned into a hotel. We practiced there every day. Andy Toth and I both felt that we really should start learning something about Bali too, so we connected with Balinese groups and started playing with them as well. I fell absolutely in love with Madé Lebah, the great musician in Peliatan, who had been Colin McPhee's guide in the 1930s. It was a moment—I've only had this feeling a couple of times in my life—when I felt that every cylinder of my brain was firing and it was all focused on one thing. Everything Madé Lebah taught me went straight in and came out through my hands. He said, "You'll know you're a drummer when you start dreaming about drumming." I started having dreams about home and people from home, but the soundtrack was Balinese drum patterns!

By the time we got back, Bob Brown was already planning to leave CalArts and had made a connection with the American Society for Eastern Arts (ASEA). I went into the CalArts degree program and became a student. I was the assistant for the African music group and did some work for Nick, but basically, I was now a graduate student instead of an administrator. When I graduated with an MFA in 1972, Bob told me he was going to take over ASEA and asked if I would be his office manager. I was important to Bob because I could type and was skilled in proofreading and editing. So, after a strange period of being a temporary, a "Kelly Girl," in San Fernando Valley, I followed Bob to ASEA. One of the privileges of the job was that I could continue studying Javanese gamelan. During the school year, I led the Balinese gamelan: I wasn't happy with teaching because I didn't feel I knew enough, even though I had learned a lot from Madé Lebah. I told Bob I could introduce people to the instruments and show them where the notes were, as long as the real teaching was done by the Balinese over the summer. This continued for the next couple years, including the glory years of the Center for World Music, when we were based at the Julia Morgan Church in Berkeley.

When I arrived, the ASEA offices were on Bush Street in San Francisco. Bob was trying to set up a performance school, but at that time ASEA was mainly a concert organization underwritten by Sam and Luise Scripps. From San Francisco we organized an ASEA summer program in Seattle in 1973, which was followed by the formal opening of the year-round school, the Center for World Music, at Berkeley in 1973. ASEA became "The Center for World Music," and later "The Center for World Music and Related Arts."

So 1974 was the great summer of the Center for World Music in Berkeley, with goodness knows how many artists teaching music and dance from South India, North India, Java, Bali, Japan, and Ghana. There was even a medieval music ensemble. Steve Reich came out from New York to teach his music, and Laura Dean taught dance. What a wild summer that was! Somewhere along the line Robert Garfias, a classmate of Bob Brown's, showed up to see what was going on. I was interested in going into ethnomusicology, and eventually Garfias said, "Why don't you think about coming to Seattle?" I applied to graduate schools for the fall of '76. By then Bob Brown had blown up the Center by spending too much money on that big summer. I applied to two schools—Wesleyan and UW Seattle—but Garfias was persuasive and made me feel that it was a choice between doing something I already knew at Wesleyan (gamelan and Ghanaian drumming) or going to Seattle to learn a million things I had no understanding of at all, which appealed to some encyclopedic part of my brain.

Barbara Benary

Skype conversation with Ted Solís, August 24, 2010

Early Life

BB: I was born in Bay Shore on Long Island, New York, in April 1946. My mother became an elementary teacher after raising her children. My father had a wholesale business in tires. He died when I was nineteen; my mother picked up the reins and sustained the family after that. I began violin when I was six. In first grade, I joined the orchestra and started taking private lessons. I've played ever since. I also did visual art until I left high school and went over to music full time. In high school, I discovered Joan Baez and taught myself to play guitar and sing along. I loved folk music. That's probably my connection to ethnomusicology right there. Another big influence through high school was string quartet playing. I fell in love with chamber music when I was about fourteen or fifteen. I think of gamelan as chamber music, quite honestly.

I guess my mother hoped I would become a violinist, but I had an influential experience in the summer of my eighteenth year. I went to the summer music school at Tanglewood, run by Boston Symphony Orchestra members. I had taken lessons the previous year in New York with Raphael Bronstein, one of the founders of the

Manhattan School of Music. Everyone thought I would take the conservatory track, but that summer was decisive for me *not* to go that route. I was turned off by the lives people led who were following that track: very competitive, no social lives, nothing but "practice, practice, practice" and "beat out the other guys."

TS: Did you study any foreign languages at school?

BB: I studied French in high school for four years. I did pretty well, but it was obvious to me that I wasn't as brilliant in languages as I was in music. I could learn music so much faster than language. Later, in graduate school, I specialized in South India, so I attempted to learn Tamil. I took several classes and a summer course, but never got much beyond the basics. I had to learn some Sanskrit too, because my dissertation involved researching music terminology and tying it to religious concepts.

College Life

After my experience at Tanglewood, I thought there had to be other things interesting to me, so I decided to go to a liberal arts school, Sarah Lawrence College. I was impressed by their hype about realizing yourself as an individual. But at freshman orientation in 1964, assembled on the lawn listening to speeches about our individuality, I looked around and realized every single person was wearing jeans and had long hair. They were so damn conformist! I didn't go there [just] because it was a women's college. I missed men but solved that problem in my junior year, when I started taking classes at Wesleyan.

I took violin lessons in my first year at Sarah Lawrence and then threw it out. I got sick of the romantic repertoire that seemed to be the mainstay of the violin. I drifted off in other directions. I played baroque music and whatever I could find that was twentieth century. Several years later, when I met my husband (who played early music), I moved further back to the pre-violin period. I still like doing that. Eventually, I met Philip Glass and other active contemporary composers, and got involved with what was called the "Downtown Movement" in New York.

After my first year at Sarah Lawrence I got involved with John Braswell, a theater teacher who was also a playwright and set designer; he encouraged me to write music for school theater productions. It was a practical way to learn composition—finding out what would work for the situation, the resources, and the story you had. I wrote two operas and was involved with that through the rest of my college career.

TS: Were you using what one might have called "exotic influences" at the time?

BB: No, it was more contemporary classical. I liked Kurt Weill, Debussy, and everything impressionist. It was a mishmash of those styles.

TS: Why did you go to Wesleyan?

BB: I wanted to find new ideas for composing besides what was offered, which was very little. The department had Meyer Kupferman, a die-hard serialist, but no electronic music. Nobody had heard of ethnomusicology. I hadn't either until I talked to the dean about Indian music. I had just returned, very enthused, from a Ravi Shankar concert at the Town Hall in New York. I wanted to buy a sitar and learn to play it and asked if they would hire someone to teach me. The dean mentioned "ethnomusicology" and suggested I check out exchange courses at Wesleyan. Of course, it was much cheaper for them to farm me out for a couple of courses than to hire a faculty person. But Wesleyan didn't have a sitar teacher the first year I went there. So I thought, "I already know violin. That might be an easier way into the music." I studied violin at Wesleyan and was very fond of my teacher, Tyagarajan.

MARCELLO SORCE KELLER

In conversation with Ted Solís and Margaret Sarkissian, October 25, 2007, Columbus, Ohio

Early Life

MSK: I was born in Milan in July 1947. When I reached the age of reason, or just about, I was told that, as soon as my parents noticed my resemblance to Mussolini (which has luckily evaporated) coupled with a somewhat unpredictable behavior, they decided there and then I would remain an only child. My parents were amateur musicians, but of a very different kind. My father used to play violin, my mother the piano. Somehow, they never made music together. My father really was a music lover. Mother, on the contrary, used to say she only learned to play the piano to impress her friends. Astonishingly, however, although she studied only about a year, she gained considerable technical facility and could sight-read almost anything. Neither of my parents ever considered a professional career. It came as a surprise to them when, at about age sixteen, I expressed my intention to become a professional arranger-composer—of all things.

TS: And what did they do for a living?

MSK: My father worked for an Italian bank. My mother was a high-school teacher of German. She was a German-Swiss, while my father was truly Italian, from Sicily.

TS: Do you think this family background might have contributed to your interest in other cultures?

MSK: Quite possibly. I grew up in Italy. Nonetheless, without ever saying it explicitly, my mother put the idea into my head that I was not only Italian but also Swiss. Every summer we spent an extended vacation in Switzerland, so I got some early exposure to German and French. Frequently, family conversation would elaborate upon cultural diversity between Italy and Switzerland, or among different regions in both countries. I learned quite early that patterns of behavior that may be the norm in one context could be unwelcome and frowned upon in another.

My youth was also rich in "field experience," because my father's job required resettling in a new city almost every other year, sometimes in the deep south of Italy, sometimes in the far north. Wherever we settled, as the school year started, my new classmates would unfailingly make fun of my strange accent and vernacular expressions that marked the region I was coming from. Native speakers of English may not realize how dramatic cultural and dialect differences are in Italy between north and south. You do not live in Milan as you do in Rome or Palermo. Dinnertime is different, food is different, even bread is differently shaped—not to mention people's mentality! That's why transitions were always challenging and my parents were constantly concerned I might commit social blunders. But the bright side of such wanderings consisted in always occupying the privileged position of the outsider. In small places, where most people had known each other for a lifetime, outsiders were usually the object of interest and curiosity, often held in higher esteem simply because they came from the outer world. It did happen at times that girls in my class would take an interest in me because of my different accent rather than because of my "superior mind."

TS: So, in a way, you started doing fieldwork long before you knew such an activity was practiced by social scientists?

MSK: Indeed. Many years went by before I discovered what "fieldwork" meant in the social sciences and what "participant observation" was.

TS: Did you speak German and/or French as a child?

MSK: Not as much as would have been desirable. My mother originally spoke German to me but progressively phased it out. Later in life, as I understood its importance in music studies, I reactivated it through reading. Later still, once I moved to Switzerland, where German is the majority language, I finally gained the opportunity of using it rather often, although I live in the Italian-speaking Canton. Both my parents spoke French, and there were occasional exchanges in that language between them. That is how I started learning French. Unfortunately, French is not especially useful in music studies, unless you deal with French music specifically. French literature, however, has been my companion all along.

TS: Can you trace the roots of how and why you became an ethnomusicologist? What led you in that particular direction?

MSK: Oh, this part of my story is easy to tell. At the outset, I intended to become an arranger-composer of popular music. I took private lessons in piano, harmony, and counterpoint while attending high school, and soon began to get occasional jobs helping professional arrangers complete their scores.

College Life

After high school, I became a student at the Milan Conservatory. My parents were quite concerned, as they felt my future would be economically uncertain. While pledging their support, they convinced me to get a college degree in something that might open other doors in case of need. So I enrolled as a sociology major, something I felt attracted to—and that was the unexpected turning point.

TS: So you were attending two different institutions in the same city?

MSK: Yes, I attended both the University of Milan and the Conservatory. It was at the university that Angelo Pagani, a sociology professor who knew about my musical interests, triggered my curiosity toward music studies. One day he gave me a stack of books to read by Max Weber, Theodor Adorno, John Müller, and Kurt Blaukopf. I quickly realized that, however defined, the "sociology of music" was part of the larger continent of music studies. My discovery of musicologies (the plural is deliberate) coincided with the realization that I was not cut out for writing music under constant pressure. That was when I decided I might be better equipped to become a music scholar, and that my double background in music and the social sciences could help me get into ethnomusicology. Once I discovered that ethnomusicology was developed in North America like nowhere else, I decided to apply for a PhD at a major American university and, at the same time, for a Fulbright grant.

TS: Where did you hear the term "ethnomusicology" for the first time?

MSK: I believe it was in 1973, when I read Ivan Vandor's review of Mantle Hood's *The Ethnomusicologist* [1971] in the *Nuova Rivista Musicale Italiana* [Vandor 1973]. Vandor, a Hungarian-Italian who taught at Wesleyan University for some time, then at the University of Hawai'i, and finally in Rome, was a true cosmopolitan, a polyglot, composer, and jazz sax player. Regretfully, few people remember him today. His review helped me realize how fascinating the study of ethnomusicology could be. I even contacted him, and he gave me some useful tips on how to apply to an American institution.

VERONICA DOUBLEDAY

In conversation with Margaret Sarkissian, March 5, 2010, Amherst, Massachusetts.

Early Life

VD: I was born in Rodmersham, Kent, in February 1948. I come from a sort of upper-middle-class landed gentry. That sounds a bit grand, doesn't it? My father is a landowner, and we all lived in a big house. I'm the eldest of six; I have two sisters and three brothers. We all went to a local school, the Convent of the Nativity, in Sittingbourne, Kent. The whole gang of us used to go to school with some other families. We went by car in the mornings and came back together by bus and walked back through the fields. It was a comfortable country upbringing. We had a piano in the house, and all the girls had piano lessons, which I enjoyed. One of my brothers is a blues musician who plays good keyboard and guitar. He was always a bit annoyed that he never had piano lessons. But he made up for it because he learned in a traditional way. He taught himself and then linked up with a Chicago black blues community and married into that.

My mother enjoyed music, too. After leaving school she went to Paris to study the piano and lived with a family of Georgian émigrés. That was a real breakaway for her, as she had lived a very sheltered life in rural Wales and at boarding school. She remained interested in the piano, but my father was not keen on hearing music, so she gave up. And then she had six children, all in close succession, and was probably a bit submerged in motherhood and being a good wife. She kept in touch with a French family she got to know while living in Paris with the Georgians and, much later, arranged that I should have exchanges with a girl who was about my age in the extended family. So I went to France, five years running, for a month or so, to learn French.

MS: Looking back on your early life, growing up on the farm in Kent, can you see the seeds of the person you've become?

VD: I don't know how significant this is, but my father served in the Middle East during the war. He was in Cairo for some time and liked going to the cabarets. I suppose they had belly dancing and stuff like that. He especially liked a singer called Madame Badi'ah Masabni and used to sing two phrases of Egyptian music, imitating her melody. Perhaps that was the seeds of performing an ornamented "Oriental" style. Much later, I found a performance by Madame Badi'ah from that time, released by the British National Sound Archive on one of their recordings.

MS: Did you do anything musical at school?

VD: Nothing in particular. I liked the intimacy of piano lessons, one-to-one with a teacher. It was a contrast with always being in a class. When I was eleven, I went to Prior's Field, a private boarding school in Surrey. I continued piano lessons but didn't particularly shine. I took up the clarinet to avoid having to go to geography classes, which were very dull. I had a wonderful clarinet teacher called Mr. Draper, who was fun; I loved hearing him play the clarinet. I was quite inspired, really. After O-Levels [General Certificate of Education, Ordinary Level, UK national subject-based exams], my parents sent me to Benenden, a strict boarding school in Kent, for two years to do A-Levels [GCE, Advanced Level]. The education was good, but I hated having to wear a uniform and got quite rebellious. I still studied, but I was in a grumpy mood the whole time. My friend and I used to listen to Bob Dylan records, read poetry, and try to create another universe of experience.

After A-Levels I had what they now call a "gap year." I went on a pre-university course and lived in Italy for a couple of months. I liked the idea of being in Venice, even though it had a slightly depressing atmosphere of crumbling decay. I enjoyed the course, which was a mix of art history, introduction to philosophy, and Italian language. After Venice, I wanted to travel more, so I went to Paris and landed up with the family I had spent summers with. After a while, the mother said, "It's OK having you here, but you ought to pay your way a bit." So I got a job in a boutique, read existential books—Camus and that kind of thing—in French, and enjoyed being with friends. That's more or less how I spent my year. Sometimes the family would play music and we'd listen to it. I hadn't ever done that in my family. After supper, the mother would say, "Oh, shall we listen to some Chopin?" It was nice. We'd sit outside, in the moonlight, enjoying the music and drinking wine or something. I have very happy, fond memories of listening to recorded music with that family. I quite enjoyed French music at that time, too, Jacques Brel and people like that.

College Life

After my "gap year" I went to the University of Sussex and studied English in the School of English and American Studies, a flagship interdisciplinary program. A lot of the people who founded the program came from Balliol in Oxford. I think they wanted a new approach to education. We did courses that not only covered English and American literature but also other cultures. It was a three-year degree. I wanted to stay in Brighton, so I did a one-year master's after that. I wanted to read Proust in French, but I couldn't do a master's in French, because French was a four-year degree course, with one year spent abroad. Instead, they advised me to do a master's in English, comparing Proust with an English author. So, I wrote about Proust and Dickens. I wasn't that bothered about what I wrote my thesis on. It's strange looking back on it. I was interested in the style and the reflection of memory, those aspects of Proust. I wanted to immerse myself in his style of writing, creating a remembrance of time past.

ALEX DEA

In conversation with Margaret Sarkissian, June 13, 2010, Singapore

Early Life

AD: I was born in San Francisco, California, in November 1948. When I was in fourth grade, I had a world map tacked to my bedroom wall. I knew *nothing* about the names of the places or where they were. I saw France, and said, "Sure, France, I heard about that." England too, maybe, although it was smaller and harder to see. But the thing that was right in the middle, in bright red, was India. On a map like that, India's pretty big, but the word is very small, so it's hard to spot. Almost every morning I would close my eyes, put my finger somewhere on the map, and open them to see where it was. I suppose I wanted to go to other places. Eventually—I don't know how long it took—I learned to spot India with my eyes closed. So I would say, "Where am I going today?" I knew I was going to India, but I closed my eyes and pointed anyway. In fact, that was one of the first places I ever went.

MS: That's a wonderful story. Can you tell me more about your childhood?

AD: My family is Chinese American. I was the first to be born in America, although my great-grandfather, maybe both of them, came to America during the Gold Rush. Subsequently, my grandfather and my father also came to America, but they were born in Toisan in the Province of Guangdong. I had no pictures of the place; I just knew it as "the homeland." I knew it was not as modern as San Francisco and that there were villages, but it didn't seem very attractive. I went there a couple of years ago; now it's really modernized and very rich. Not as clean or fancy as Singapore, but bigger. The most amazing thing is the weather and the food: it's a little humid and they grow rice. The surprise for me was that the place I had shunned as a child was just like Bali and Java! I think there was something subconscious that led me eventually to Java. I've lived there since 1992.

MS: What did your parents do for a living?

AD: My mother came from a somewhat well-to-do family. They had servants, a big house, and some land. Her grandfather was very rich; he had four wives and a huge house. My father came to the US at age six or eight. He served in the US Army, so he automatically became a citizen. When it was time for him to marry, his father sent him to Toisan to meet the woman the parents had agreed on. It was an arranged marriage. It all worked by clans. Certain clans always marry into certain other clans. He brought my mother to San Francisco at the age of about seventeen, or maybe younger, because I think she was seventeen or eighteen when I was born. When I was young, my father went to UC Berkeley on the GI Bill, and my Mom stayed at home. We lived in my paternal grandfather's house on Russian Hill. Dad ended up working for the US Postal Service but gave up to start his own business. He had various jobs, including teaching Chinese people how to drive. I have three younger siblings, two sisters and a brother.

MS: Were you interested in music as a young child?

AD: We didn't have any training, but my Dad loved music. He used to hang out with Filipinos, because they also came to America in great numbers—men only, just like the Chinese—to work and be in the Army. Some of his friends were barbers on Kearny Street in the Filipino area. They all had instruments—a mandolin, a guitar or two, maybe even a violin—and played nostalgic, piquant music. I imagine it must be very much like *kroncong*, a sweet harmonic thing. That's one of my early memories of music and one of my first encounters with live music.

It was only much later, when I was in third or fourth grade, that I had the opportunity to take music lessons. In San Francisco, music teachers came to the schools. Lessons meant you'd get out of class for a half hour, so I told my parents I wanted to play an instrument. I wanted to play trumpet, but they said, "No, trumpet's bad for you, because you have to use a lot of energy and the pressure's too high," and they didn't have the money for it. But they were OK with violin. I gave it a shot, but I hated the violin. Eventually, when I was eleven, I convinced them to let me play trumpet. I had a King Cleveland, a nice student marching-band instrument. I played trumpet all through junior high and high school. I was pretty good; I could play all the scales and the hard keys, but I didn't know much about music.

We had an AM radio, but back then you didn't hear much on the radio, only what we called "The Hit Parade"—very boring music. You couldn't hear jazz or blues or anything exciting. By the time I went to high school, the Beatles were coming up and I was getting interested in music. I joined the big band. We played "String of Pearls," "Caravan," "The A-Train," and things like that. Around fifteen, I discovered Drum and Bugle Corps. Back then it was still an East Coast thing; on the West Coast there were fewer than a dozen groups. I got into one of them, a Chinese drum and bugle corps at the American Legion, Cathay Post. I got very serious about it. We played more jazzy things, like "Cherry Pink and Apple Blossom White."

College Life

After high school I went to UC Berkeley. I studied theory of classical music, not because I loved classical music; I never knew that. I was into the Beatles and all those fey ones, like Herman's Hermits and Dave Clark. I fell in love with the Beatles because their music was so interesting, the harmonies and arrangements were unusual. That's when I first heard Ravi Shankar. That got me interested in Indian music. Around then Bill Graham started bringing Chicago black blues players to San Francisco. I heard Otis Redding, the Isley Brothers, people that we *never* would have a chance to hear otherwise. Graham also brought Paul Butterfield, a white guy who could play blues, and Mike Bloomfield, who subsequently played with Bob Dylan, another of my heroes. Butterfield opened the door to all the black players he'd learned with. I heard Muddy Waters, Otis Spann, Fred Below, and Willie Dixon—all the people who *created* modern blues.

MS: Were you still an undergrad at Berkeley at this point?

AD: Yes, and I immediately started to dislike everything that sounded like Bach and Beethoven!

MS: How did you get through school, then?

AD: By being very smart! By being very canny about selecting the classes that did not require being present. For a year, I got straight As by writing the right paper and taking the right exam. Meanwhile, all the hippies were moving out to Humboldt County in Northern California. I lived up there with a band. We called ourselves "The Moonshine Blues Band" because there's a beach called Moonshine Beach where the rock formations looked like they came from Mars. That's where we learned to play very bad blues. Somewhere along the line, I discovered how to play the trumpet in a real way. I remember one full moon, walking on the beach at night, holding my trumpet. I was interested in Miles Davis, so I started to "channel" him. I decided to play something that I thought sounded and felt like Miles Davis. From that moment, ever after, I could play music, not notes.

I had been singing and composing rock 'n' roll for a couple of years, even before college, but now I wanted to really sing. A friend told me about an Indian vocal master who was coming from New York, Pandit Pran Nath. Two of his disciples, La Monte Young and Terry Riley, were pioneers of minimalist music. I called the phone number and the voice on the phone said, "Yes, you can take lessons here." I said, "Where?" It was Terry's home, one block from my mother's house, right in the middle of my neighborhood! That's where I went to study Indian singing.

During my last two years of college, the National Guard and the Berkeley police were on campus every day to prevent us from having strikes and speaking against the government. I didn't stand in those lines, but it was part of my space and I got tired of it. I quit school two weeks before graduation, partly as a protest, but mostly because I was fed up that the Music Department was so conservative that they could not make a statement against the Vietnam War.

I came back a year later to finish, took a summer program, and went to Africa. The first time I left the state of California was to go to Africa—that's how I *really* got into overseas. We learned drumming and dancing, took some lessons, and saw a lot of different kinds of ceremonial arts and what I called "performative ceremonies." After Africa, I finally went to India to hear Indian music for real. I was probably twenty-one or twenty-two and went to where my master, Pandit Pran Nath, is from. He's one of the great vocalists, somewhat unsung because he wasn't fancy, but the old masters came to *him* for corrections.

MS: Do you remember the first time you heard the word "ethnomusicology"?

AD: Yes, indeed, because when I came back from India, I was a little confused. My eyes had been opened but I didn't have very good teachers until I met my Indian teacher.

I was walking around in Chinatown wondering what to do next and saw a yellow piece of paper on a post that said something like "World Music Summer Program" sponsored by ASEA (the American Society for Eastern Arts). It said "Javanese" or "Balinese" something strange—just strange enough that I went all the way to Mills College by bus to check it out and heard my first gamelan. On the second or third day of classes, Pak Cokro (a.k.a. K. R. T. Wasitodiningrat, a.k.a. K. P. H. Notoprojo) showed up. Everybody was like, "God is here!" I looked at him and he was not God—he was a short guy with a round face and black hair. My Indian teacher was a real god—he had long silver hair! I talked to the students who were already able to play, Alan Feinstein, John Pemberton, Nancy Florida, and David Locke—Bob Brown's gang from Wesleyan—and they told me, "At Wesleyan we have a program where you can get a PhD doing this; it's called ethnomusicology."

MS: Did you have a sense of what ethnomusicology was at that point? It seems to be where you were headed without knowing it.

AD: I really didn't know, because I'd come from a public-school system—we got just enough school to get into college. We were not really Americans—I didn't speak English until I was five. Most Chinese in San Francisco were the same. All I knew was that you went to college and you got a job. I didn't even know what to study, except I liked music. My mother didn't want me to go into music. She wanted me to be a doctor or a dentist. I didn't know there was such a thing as a PhD or "musicology." When I started the program, all I knew was that you had to go to classes.

Virginia (Ginny) Danielson

In conversation with Margaret Sarkissian, September 22, 2010, Northampton, Massachusetts

Early Life

GD: I was born in Milwaukee, Wisconsin, in April 1949. There was a lot of music in my childhood, and although I was raised in a Norwegian community, there wasn't much folk music around our house. My parents were interested in classical music and musical theater. We moved to the suburbs of Milwaukee—for the school system—when I started school, so I was raised in white suburbia. For much of my life my mother was a stay-at-home mom, but when I went to high school, she went back to work. My dad, of course, always worked. He was a sales manager for a couple of farm-implement companies. He was raised on a farm where he was the younger son. The farm went to the older son and the college education went to my father. He came to Milwaukee to find work, and the way he did that was to find a Norwegian Lutheran Church and rent a room from a church lady! That's how it was—one was passed from hand to hand in the ethnic communities. Milwaukee is generally very colorful that way. My parents met in the choir of the Norwegian Lutheran Church. They both sang para-professionally in Gilbert and Sullivan and other kinds of musical productions in Milwaukee until World War II came along and my dad was deployed. That more or less stopped their musical activity, except that after I was born my mother played the piano quite a lot. Often at night they would play the piano and sing together.

My mother had been an executive secretary when she married my father and joked that she made more money than he did. When she went back to work, she continued as a secretary, but in the school system. The ethos in suburbia was that women *should* stay home, and men *should* work and *should* be successful. I thought my father did OK during those years, but I had friends whose fathers broke down if they were fired or didn't get a promotion. The women weren't any better off, because so many of them were bored. My mother liked her friends at the high school and it was a nice working environment, but it certainly didn't challenge her. Whatever people say about childcare issues now, I think *that* situation was equally bad.

MS: Did you have any early musical experience yourself?

GD: I was probably about four when my mother showed me how to play the piano. She made a cardboard cutout for the piano that had the letters and the colors of an old toy called "Melody Bells." The Melody Bells were different colors, so if you were small and couldn't read, you could play a song by coordinating the colors. She made the cardboard cutout so that I could use the Melody Bells songs, but play them on the piano. I was six when I got the piano teacher who carried me through to college; she wouldn't take students until they could read.

MS: Did your mother teach you to read music?

GD: I think she must have. It must be the same for lots of musically trained people, but I can't remember not being able to read music. I don't know how I learned. The piano was something I was good at. I won some contests, and that gave me an identity during adolescence. It was a way to get some respect in that volatile junior-high-school environment.

College Life

My parents were wary of my going to a conservatory for college, so they insisted on a liberal arts college and that I come out with something useful, like a teaching certificate. So I went to Lawrence University, got a degree in piano and music education, and when I came out, I was certified to teach. I was immediately offered a job in the school system where I'd done my practice teaching. I started teaching and—this will sound silly—for the first time in my life, I came nose to nose with the idea that other families didn't listen to classical music. They had musical lives of their own that were different. I think my first ethnomusicological question was, "All right, so what music is that?" Students in the junior high would bring in Jethro Tull and everything that was popular at the time. I also became interested in Jewish music after a student's family took me to the Reform Synagogue where I heard music and learned some Hebrew. When I went to graduate school, one of my first interests was Jewish music.

MS: How long did you teach before you decided to go to grad school?

GD: Four years. I got the job just as teaching jobs were closing up. It quickly became clear to me that if I ever wanted to relocate, I would need a master's degree, and I didn't want to get it in education. My first thought was, "Well, let's think about piano." I had a wonderful summer with Carroll Chilton, a professor of piano at the University of Wisconsin in Madison. I told him what I was thinking, and at the end of the summer he said, "Ginny, you don't like to practice. That's something you need to take into account." It was hard to hear at the time, but he was absolutely right. I kept up lessons to keep myself able to play accompaniments for the kids in school and to play a bit, but I was moving away from the practice-all-the-time environment. Carroll Chilton was right; I didn't like it.

Lois Wilcken

In conversation with Ted Solís, October 28, 2007, Columbus, Ohio

Early Life

LW: I was born on Staten Island, New York City, in April 1949. My parents were both musical. My father was an auto mechanic but played piano in a wedding band on the side. My mother sang. She had walked into a music store where he worked, looking for some sheet music, and that's how they met. The war interrupted things for a few years. He was drafted, she went down to his boot camp in South Carolina, and they got married. He went overseas and got captured at Anzio. He was a POW for about fourteen months in Germany but came back, and about four years later I was the first of their three children.

Both my parents had grandparents who were immigrants: German, Irish, and Italian. On my mother's side, her father did very well. He established a Ford dealership on Staten Island and built a huge house. My mother grew up in very nice circumstances but didn't get along with her father, so when she met my father, she left home and gave all that up. My father was from a poor, working-class German family, but one that had a lot of music—everybody played something.

I remember holidays when I was a child. We usually went to see my mother's family first, because they did everything early in the day. Then we went over to my father's family, where everybody was having a good time singing. It was all polite on my mother's side but open and loose on my father's side. By the time we arrived, they'd be singing and playing, probably a little tipsy! I'm sure that that helped endear me to music. I wanted nothing more than to take piano lessons, but my mother stood in the way for years. So I acquired a guitar and taught myself how to play. It was initially my sister's; she had asked for it for Christmas. It wasn't a very good guitar, but it was something I could learn something with.

My parents were typical of their generation. They loved big band music; my mother's favorite was Tommy Dorsey. My dad's band had an electric piano in case they went somewhere where there wasn't a piano. At one point during a summer vacation, the bandleader went away, so we set up the piano in our living room. I sat at it all day, every day, trying to teach myself. It should have been clear to my mother that I wanted to study music, but she thought it wasn't a practical career for me.

TS: Was it something about your father's band life that turned her off?

LW: Possibly, though as I said, he was an auto mechanic and had a full-time job in a body shop. Music was for the weekend, and he never went far away, so I'm not sure it was that. Sometimes I think it was because she had wanted to sing or to write poetry. She went through a couple of years of college but had to drop out when her mother got sick and she had to take care of her. After her mother died, my mother never went back to school. She met my father that same year, so her dreams never really happened. Before the war they had both been doing music, and he was trying to be involved full time. He had a day job at the music store owned by his band, but he didn't go back to that band after the war. Instead, when he came back after his POW experience, he took a job as an auto mechanic, and my mother stopped singing, except for occasions like weddings. She had dreamed of a singing career but didn't do it. Sometimes I think that's why she didn't want me to play piano.

TS: Had you heard any music you would consider "exotic" at that point?

LW: Exotic music for me wasn't music from somewhere halfway across the globe—that didn't come until later—but in high school I got interested in atonal and experimental music. In fact, I got up in front of my high-school class and gave a talk about twelve-tone music. Everyone thought it was the weirdest thing! Finally, when I was in high school, we got a piano because I was very persistent about it, and it was clear that I was going to study music no matter what. I got a rather late start, though.

College Life

When I started college and became a music major, most of my classmates had been studying since they were very young. I always had the feeling of having to catch up. Perhaps that's why I went into musicology, not into performing. I did my BA at Hunter

College and thought I wanted to go into theory and composition. I had a teacher, Ruth Anderson, who became my guru and got me very interested in Schenkerian analysis. When I graduated, I wasn't sure what to do next, so I started taking some historical musicology courses at the graduate level. I didn't really want to go in that direction because I had the composition bug. I was very shy about thinking of myself as a composer and making a living as a creative artist.

When I finished my BA in 1971, I moved away from home and went into magazine publishing because I was good with grammar, copyediting, and proofreading. When oil prices hit the roof in the mid-'70s, the price of newsprint paper skyrocketed, the company I worked for folded, and I went on unemployment. I got a little freelance work—proofreading, copyediting—and went back to school, finally going into theory and composition. I went back to Hunter College in 1974 for my master's because Ruth Anderson was still there; she had an electronic music studio by that time.

I became an electronic music composer. I wrote a piece for brass quartet and tape for my thesis and had it performed at the school. It was all analog in those days. I also took a course at Columbia University with Charles Dodge, because I was interested in computer music. Another piece I really loved, called "Voyage in C," was played wherever I submitted it—radio stations, concerts. It was entirely tape that I'd spliced together and mixed. I liked working that way, on my own. Slowly I put together a synthesizer and had it custom made by a company in California. The maker's name was Serge Tcherepnin—his father was the well-known composer Alexander Tcherepnin. Serge had modules available; you'd look in his catalog, order them, and put them in a case, according to what you wanted to do.

Stephen Slawek

In conversation with Ted Solís and Margaret Sarkissian, October 25, 2007, Columbus, Ohio

Early Life

SS: I was born in May 1949, in West Chester, Pennsylvania. I was always somewhat on the periphery, even in school. The time I felt most in with an in-crowd was in grade school, when there was a group of six to eight boys who hung out. I was the best basketball player, the best baseball player, the best left-handed pitcher, and the highest-scoring on academic subjects. I thought, "Hey, I'm somebody special." But once I moved to a large junior high school, we went from a class of thirty to six sections of thirty. I discovered I wasn't the top person but somewhere in the middle, and I wasn't the best on the basketball team, because now there were six people who were 6′2″ and 6′4″. I didn't really fit in with any group, so I became more of a loner from seventh grade on. I did cross-country instead of sports where you had more team playing.

TS: What was your early life like, musically speaking?

SS: My father liked music and listened to a lot of different types of music. He had old 78-rpm recordings of Count Basie and other jazz musicians and listened to opera, string quartets, and such things. I grew up listening to rock 'n' roll. I had guitar lessons for about six years with three different teachers, the last being Joe Sgro, who taught jazz guitar. My lessons with Sgro set me up for studying sitar, because he had a very systematic approach to teaching guitar, systematic exercises and things like that. But going *way* back, I guess the reason I ended up in ethnomusicology is because I liked monkeys.

TS: Monkeys?

SS: Monkeys. I grew up with a fascination for monkeys, and India was a place that had monkeys. This is actually true, really! I owned monkeys for a while. Much later, when I went to Hawai'i, the East-West Center magazine published a story about me with the title "From Monkeys to the Sitar."

College Life

I was a biology major at the University of Pennsylvania and worked at the Monell Chemical Senses Center doing research with Gisela Epple on pheromones produced by marmoset monkeys. It was partly that experience that led me to drop my pursuit of biology. I was not happy dealing with caged monkeys. I liked monkeys who were having fun in the forests, so I started wondering, "Isn't this sort of tantamount to studying prisoners?" Then, in the winter of 1971 a shipment of marmosets came in from Brazil. They arrived on a Friday night, so we weren't told they were at the airport, and they sat in the cold over the weekend. By the time we collected them, they all had pneumonia and about a third to half of the colony were wiped out. I had a traumatic experience trying to save a sick marmoset, which died in my hand as I was giving it an injection.

TS: This turned you away from biology and toward the sitar?

SS: I was already involved with the sitar. My life has been sort of serendipitous. It just so happened that I got a sitar on the same day that Penn announced Harry Powers had brought Lalmani Misra to campus. India was just starting to filter into the culture at large primarily because of Ravi Shankar, George Harrison, and the Beatles. I was playing lead guitar in a rock band and was interested because everybody else was bringing in sitar. I was also lifeguarding at an apartment complex in West Chester where a few Indian families lived, so I asked if someone could bring a sitar for me. An Indian—I think his name was Dinkar Rane—brought me one from Bombay. It wasn't a very good sitar, but it got me started. When it arrived, I learned that I could actually study it the right way, so I never used the sitar for anything popular or non-Indian. I studied for two years with Lalmani Misra as a junior and a senior at Penn from 1969 to 1971.

TS: Have you ever felt that your background was different from other ethnomusicologists? Most come from a Western musical background in some way and are then attracted to other music. You came into it via a direct contact with Indian music and didn't know too much about conventional musicology. Has that made a difference to you?

SS: I don't think it made a tremendous difference. I never heard the word "ethnomusicology" as an undergraduate, in spite of the fact that I took a course in my junior year on Indian music with Harry Powers. I don't recall him ever using the term. At Penn I had a class on music appreciation, a brief introduction to Western music history. It seemed then that the only legitimate musical studies had to do with Western art music. Of course, I was a biology major, but I can't recall any courses on popular music. And the performance part of Harry Powers's program at Penn was done through the South Asia Regional Studies Department. Powers was in the Music Department but affiliated with South Asian Studies. The Music Department, at that time, was dominated by musicology and maybe some composition. Indian music was pretty marginalized. Dr. Misra had an office where he taught sitar, so as his student, I would go there. There was another room with sitars that we could practice on, but it was in the basement of the Music Department. I had very little interaction with the department. All of the concerts took place in association with the South Asian Regional Studies program.

After graduation, I went to India on my own to continue studying with Lalmani Misra at the Banaras Hindu University. I studied there for five years, from '71 to '76, still without ever having been introduced to the term "ethnomusicology" until my last few months when I met Lewis Rowell, who was in Music Theory at the University of Hawai'i at the time.

TS: Didn't you meet your wife when you were studying at BHU with Lalmani?

SS: Yes, he was her local guardian. She sings *khyal* and *thumri*. Her first teacher was a disciple of Amir Khan Sahib in Meerut. She learned a lot from him but then went to Banaras and studied with M. V. Thakar, Balwantrai Bhatt, M. R. Gautam, and Mahadev Prasad Misra.

JENNIFER POST

In conversation with Ted Solís and Margaret Sarkissian, August 12, 2011, Phoenix, Arizona

Early Life

JP: I was born in July 1949 in Columbus, Ohio, but after a few months my family moved to the East Coast. I'm the second of four girls. My father was a minister in the Congregational United Church of Christ and, as a result, we moved a lot from one church to the next. He was an activist during the '50s and '60s and marched with

Martin Luther King and others in support of civil rights. My father felt my mother needed to be at home to support his work. When you are preaching, you need a support system behind you; that's how my parents represented it. It was life shaping for all of us. My mother took the opportunity to go back to school when my younger sisters were still at home, and she became an elementary- and high-school teacher. She went to Sarah Lawrence College because we were living in Scarsdale, New York, at the time.

TS: What kinds of things were you interested in as a child?

JP: I've been involved with music since I was two or three years old. I taught myself how to play the piano and read music at three or four. I started writing music when I was about ten and decided I wanted to be a composer. I started oboe around that time, too. I spent most of my time through high school writing music, studying music theory, and seeking out ways to continue playing and writing music. I'm not sure where this came from because there were no musicians in my family, though my mother was a beautiful singer. We didn't have a piano at home, so I practiced at the church. I hadn't made this connection before, but that must have had an impact on me.

TS: Were you exposed to any foreign languages early on?

JP: From a very young age I was fascinated by Dutch. I must have been around seven when I started studying Dutch. I was completely fascinated by different parts of the world and was always doing massive research projects—"Religions of the World," and that sort of thing. Later, I studied German for a number of years at high school and beyond.

MS: Where did you go to high school?

JP: I didn't fit in at school in Scarsdale. I was involved with music and poetry, while most of my peers were getting the broad-based background that would get them into a good college. So when I was fifteen, I went to Woodstock County School (an alternative high school in Vermont) as a boarder. I think there was some sort of scholarship; I know it was a hardship for my parents, but they made it work somehow.

MS: What musical things did you do at school?

JP: I always played. I didn't have access to ensembles at Woodstock, so that was a bit problematic as an oboist. Before high school I often played percussion or glockenspiel in the marching band, but my primary instruments were piano, harpsichord, and (later) organ. I was also doing a lot of composing. Before I started college I went to Dartmouth for a summer (Aaron Copland was there that year) and studied traditional theory. I remember being about seventeen or eighteen and saying, "I just want to work on this kind of music theory." The instructor just laughed and said, "I want to see you in a few years." I remember him saying that, because, of course, I stepped way outside of that world.

College Life

I went to Eastman in 1967 as a composer. It was the wrong decision, and I left after a year. I arrived as a person who had been involved with music but also with other activities. I did a lot of hiking and was really interested in the poetry of Milton, Robert Lowell, and W. S. Merwin. At Eastman, people wanted to do music, period. It was a big moment for me to realize that there were people who wanted to do music more than I did. I went to Mills College in California the following year. I wanted to study with Milhaud, but I had a bit of a breakdown and had to leave. I didn't even finish the semester. I dropped out and went back to the East Coast. After a couple of other false starts, I ended up visiting my sister, who was in school at Beloit in Wisconsin, and that's where I ended up going to school.

I went to Beloit College from 1969 to 1972 and majored in music. I was able to stay there because Beloit had an independent-study program. I could create my own courses and work one-on-one with the faculty in composition and, ultimately, ethnomusicology. I was taking and making courses that allowed me to find different ways music was connected to other parts of the curriculum. I constructed my own acoustics class and a class on music in education. In the midst of all this I had an opportunity to hear Ravi Shankar perform and became very involved with Indian music as a theorist. I ended up going to Pune, India, on an Associated Colleges of the Midwest program (a trip led by Eleanor Zelliot). We started in the late spring with an intensive, eight-week language-training session at Carleton College, and had more intensive language throughout our time in Pune. We studied Marathi, which became my language (later, I wrote my dissertation on Marathi-speaking musicians). We were supposed to stay for a year, but the war between Pakistan and India broke out, so we had to leave in December. This must have been '71, because I went back to Wisconsin and graduated right away.

DANIEL ATESH SONNEBORN

In conversation with Ted Solís, October 28, 2007, Columbus, Ohio

Early Life

AS: I was born in October 1949 in Chicago, Illinois. My parents were interested in music, so the house was filled with music of all kinds. When people say, "Oh, I like all kinds of music," they often mean some rather narrow, market-defined music, but what I mean ranged from Western classical music to folk traditions from all over the world, particularly via Folkways Records (78s or LPs) and a radio show called *The Midnight Special*. One of my earliest memories is of standing in front of the radio, conducting the stream of music. In my imagination it was like flying: I felt so free. When I was eight years old, my mother brought home a belly-dancing album called *Port Said* [El-Bakkar 1957]. I loved that music and the beautiful image of the dancer on the cover. It opened up an idea of a world that could not be seen in South Chicago. We never encountered any Arabic speakers in daily life, but I learned to lip sync the entire album and performed it whenever possible to anyone who would listen.

I started studying music in the Chicago public schools in the 1950s. When one started first grade, they put an instrument in your hands and put you in the orchestra. I started out on soprano recorder, graduated quickly to clarinet, and was soon playing Haydn's *Surprise Symphony* and loving it. We had a cabinet grand upright in the basement, and one day, when I was six or seven, I picked out a melody I was blowing on clarinet and realized I could play it effortlessly in many octaves. I went running upstairs and said, "I've got to learn how to play the piano." My parents said, "OK," and put me into lessons. I had a straight classical training and continued to play clarinet in the school band and orchestra. There was also a choral program at my school with a wonderful teacher. Through eighth grade, it was glorious. In high school, I played in the band and the orchestra and even conducted while bandleader/conductor (and trumpeter) John Cvejanovich toured with the Chicago Symphony. In the summers, I worked as a wilderness canoe trip guide, and we sang folk songs around the campfire. I loved the feeling of community that comes when people who really don't know each other sing together.

College Life

I graduated from high school in 1967. The following fall I went off to the University of Illinois in Urbana-Champaign to become a psychiatric social worker. One of the key experiences there was seeing the Bread and Puppet Theater in one of its early incarnations. It was very exciting—street theater, political theater. At that time I was very conscious of the war in Vietnam. My brother-in-law had gone off to war, and I started an organization to get holiday gifts for servicemen on both sides. It was controversial. Somewhere in that first semester I realized that I had no interest in becoming a psychiatric social worker. That was a very difficult moment, because that was in direct opposition to the desires of my parents, who were my source of funding.

TS: Your family wanted you to be a psychiatric social worker?

AS: Yes. My sister had already gone through college to a master's in social work and had become a psychiatric social worker. After her first husband was killed in Vietnam by "friendly fire," she realized that she didn't want that career and went back to school in photographic arts. She became a visual artist and went on to direct a 1998 Academy Award–nominated documentary film *Regret to Inform* [Sonneborn 1998].

I had my own epiphany in my first semester and said, "I don't want to do this; this is not me. What do I want to do?" The only thing that had continual meaning in my life was music, so I transferred to the Chicago Musical College, a conservatory associated with Roosevelt University.

I really enjoyed myself, except that I had "curiosities." I would raise my hand and say, "Gosh, it's interesting that Bach was doing this in Lübeck at this time, but what was happening in China?" Most of the teachers would look at me askance; this was not an appropriate question. But one teacher, a harpsichordist named Robert S. Conant, said, "I don't know, but I bet we can figure out how to find out." He turned me on to Curt Sachs's *The Wellsprings of Music* [1962]. It was almost like going back to conducting music in front of the radio—this feeling of "Ah, this could be where music comes from." Where does this incredibly powerful multisensory, spiritual, whole-being experience that I'd never had in any other realm but music come from? The effect of music is extraordinary. *The Wellsprings of Music* was the moment when I said, "You know, it would really make sense to study this." In that book, or somewhere, perhaps in class, around that time—1969 or 1970—I discovered the word "ethnomusicology."

TS: Were there any particular cultures that attracted you at that point?

AS: I had an abiding interest in Middle Eastern music and Indonesian music—you know, the Hood recording?

TS: *Music of the Venerable Dark Cloud* [Hood and Susilo 1967]. My goodness, that recording comes up again and again!

AS: So, Conant took me aside one day and said, "What are you doing here in the conservatory?" By that point I was writing songs and playing alto clarinet and marimba in rock-and-roll bands, rhythm-and-blues bands, big bands, and occasionally accompanying theater productions. He said, "I think you should get your ass out of here and go make your own music." I realized he was right, so in 1970 I dropped out of college, left Chicago, and made a great westward journey in a "drive-away" (where you're driving someone else's car) with two friends. I arrived in Los Angeles on a Tuesday and by Friday I was playing a hit show in a ninety-nine-seat, off-off-Broadway theater called the "Company Theatre." Our most famous work was the "James Joyce Memorial Liquid Theatre."

Liquid Theatre really got the interest of critics, and ultimately a Broadway producer rented the Guggenheim and invited us to New York. Clive Barnes, chief reviewer of the *New York Times*, came and loved it. It was a hit in New York and gave the producer the idea to take it around the world. Before I knew it, Liquid Theatre was going to be produced in Paris with a French cast and I—aged twenty—was to be the musical director. So off I went to Pierre Cardin's Théâtre des Ambassadeurs on the Place de la Concorde in Paris. I hired a French musical ensemble, trained them in the music, and suddenly there I was, in Paris, with a hit show. It really was fun. After Paris we did the same thing in London. But one day the London producer walked in and said, "I'm out of money; you'll all have to go home." I turned to the yoga instructor from the show and said, "So what would your teacher (Swami Satchidananda of integral yoga hatha renown) say now?" She said, "He would say 'Thank God,' because he would say 'Thank God' to *anything*." That thought still resonates. Wow! You know, I was raised to complain often, not so much to be grateful. In the end, the production didn't close and we opened in London.

That was 1971 or '72. After that I created the musical fabric for an Armstrong Award–nominated radio version of a show called *XA: A Vietnam Primer* (*xa* means "village" in Vietnamese), but political theater didn't feel like the thing for me. I applied for a bunch of grants and went off to visit a friend who was hanging out in Mexico City. I played accordion in Chapultepec Park (wearing a poncho), for nickels or pesos, while I waited to see if any of the grants came through. Finally, one did: to study the sound fabric of contemporary American theater practice. I got to travel around for a while. In New York I visited a Ford Foundation entity called "Theatre Communications Group." It helped theater artists all over the world to network. The director (who knew my work) said, "Oh, you'd be interested in a little theater group in Boston that approaches the stage from the silence of meditation." That made sense to me as a musician: If you don't start from silence, how you can get to the music? I boarded the next northbound train. Theatre Workshop Boston's director, Saphira Linden, said their next project was to be a spectacle showing the underlying unity of all the world's religious traditions. It would have a cast of hundreds and they had no money to do it. They asked if I would like to be the producer. I said no, but for reasons I can't remember did it anyway.

That was an interesting experience and led to several years of producing the "Cosmic Mass" and later the "Cosmic Celebration." The biggest one was done for the fortieth anniversary of the United Nations in New York. Spiritual leaders from many world traditions were brought to New York to see if they could come up with a consensus statement. You know, "The world has not done a very good job of being at peace, so how can we get to peace?" We performed the Cosmic Mass in the Cathedral of St. John the Divine. It was around this time, in 1975, that I met composer and instrumentalist Hamza El Din. I ended up being his manager for twenty years, from 1978 to 1998. Hamza is the only person I've met who had a sense of himself that went back five thousand, maybe seven thousand years in one place. That place was no more, because the Aswan Dam drowned Nubia. Hamza was a wonderful human being and became like a brother to me.

TS: How did you meet him?

AS: We needed somebody to do the Islamic Call to Prayer (*adhan*) for the Cosmic Mass at the cathedral, and his name was suggested. I called him up and said, "Can you come and do this?" He said "yes" unhesitatingly, even though there was no money involved. The morning after his arrival, though, he mentioned that he had slept in a telephone booth. I gave him my bed and I slept on the couch. I remember one day soon after that we walked out of a rehearsal, went across the street, and had cold cherry soup at a Hungarian restaurant. It was like falling in love! What a wonderful, wonderful man he was. He died last year, in 2006.

Nineteen Fifties

The late 1920s and 1930s group members are entering graduate school or beginning careers. The 1940s generation are in middle school or high school or entering college.

The French withdraw from Indochina, 1954. Malaya gains independence from Britain, 1957. The Korean War pulls America back toward the Asian/Chinese preoccupation of the conservative political elite. Cold War intensification, 1947–57, leads to the House Un-American Activities Committee and McCarthy investigations of communism in Hollywood and the government, and the lesser-known "Lavender Scare," a crusade against homosexuals in public life. These result in government purges, the notorious Hollywood blacklist, and a profound silencing effect on academia. Externally, the Warsaw Pact serves as a counterweight to the West's creation of NATO in 1949. Armed forces are now completely officially desegregated; the 1954 *Brown v. Board of Education of Topeka* decision is an early desegregation landmark. Radio series have been almost entirely replaced by television counterparts. Radio now becomes a casual listening medium and a powerful vehicle for racial integration, especially through rock and roll, many early examples of which were white covers of black R&B songs and dances. Beatniks are the popular and clichéd face of the introspective, Asian-philosophy-influenced "Beat" movement. Kurosawa's *Rashomon* (1950) is the first Asian film to become prominent in the West. Jaap Kunst coins the term "Ethno-Musicology" in 1950; David McAllester, Alan Merriam, Willard Rhodes, and Charles Seeger meet in 1953 to discuss the possibility of a formal ethnomusicological community, followed by Merriam's launch, that same year, of *Ethnomusicology Newsletter*, which becomes *Ethnomusicology* (journal) in 1958. Hugh Tracey establishes the International Library of

African Music in 1954; the *Columbia World Library of Folk and Primitive Music*, edited by Alan Lomax, is initiated in 1955; Bruno Nettl publishes *Music in Primitive Culture* in 1956; that same year, Mantle Hood begins teaching at UCLA and forms the Institute of Ethnomusicology. A Balinese gamelan from Peliatan tours the United States and Europe in 1952. Ravi Shankar first tours the United States, the United Kingdom, and Europe in 1956, and his score for Satyajit Ray's *Apu Trilogy* (1955–59) brings South Asian music to Western public consciousness on a large scale. The 1959 tour of Guinea's *Les Ballets Africains* exposes Americans to versions of traditional African music, dance, and ritual; Nigerian percussionist Babatunde Olatunji releases his popular *Drums of Passion* album (1960) and begins collaboration with jazz musicians.

LAUREL SERCOMBE

In conversation with Ted Solís, March 22, 2008, Seattle, Washington

Early Life

LS: I was born in Pasadena, California, in April 1950, spent the first nineteen years of my life in Southern California, and then headed north. I come from a musical family: my dad had a nice tenor voice and sang; my mother was, and still is at the age of ninety, a piano teacher. She went to UCLA and took music theory lessons with Arnold Schoenberg, which was a high point for her. She taught piano while she raised her three kids plus my dad's two kids from his first marriage. My dad had a grocery store. In Southern California this wasn't so much a little store as an actual market with a big parking lot. He was not an educated man, but he was very bright. He took care of us by being a grocer and making some good investments, so we lived in an upper-middle-class community. He worked seven days a week for forty years and didn't have much fun, as far as I could tell. I started violin in the fourth grade, like a lot of people did in public schools. I was a violinist all through junior high and high school, even during my Beatles years, which pretty much dominated my life from the middle of eighth grade through high school. I was in all the orchestras. I wasn't good enough to consider being a soloist, so I settled on chamber music. I thought if I could spend my life in a string quartet playing Beethoven, that would be great.

TS: Did certain kinds of music attract you?

LS: We had a lot of Gershwin records at home, because my mother was well educated at UCLA and listened to all kinds of twentieth-century music and musicals. When I was about eight or nine, *West Side Story* came to LA for the first time. I don't remember when it premiered in New York, but the first LA performance was by the LA Civic Opera. I went with my mother and was transfixed by the music. It changed my life. We had recordings of all of the musicals that were popular at the time, but *West Side Story* was the one that got me.

And then the Beatles came. I give a Beatles lecture once every quarter for the American Popular Music class in which I try to convey the impact they had on us. I say, "I don't know what it was for you guys, but for my generation it was February 7, 1964. We heard the Beatles for the first time on the *Ed Sullivan Show*, and everything changed from that night on. We listened to different music, we wore different clothes, we read different books, and we went to different movies. From then on, we grew with their music as they grew politically and culturally." I was the perfect age when they hit: thirteen and a half.

In Southern California you study Spanish in elementary school, but other than that, I was unfortunately fairly cloistered. My mother, being a great humanitarian, felt we should be exposed to other cultures, but I didn't have much opportunity for that until I got active in civil rights when I was in high school (from 1964 to '68). Then there were all kinds of exchanges between Arcadia, a white community where we lived, and Pasadena, which had a much larger black and Mexican population. As I got to be more politically aware and active, music felt more political to me as well. We'd take our quartet out to places where we didn't think people expected string quartets, and we played in the street.

TS: How did that happen?

LS: It was really a part of the times. We were all trying to do something different and unusual; there was so much of the "happening" mentality. You know, "If you expect music to be chamber music in a recital hall, then let's take it out into the streets, let's take it to the park." One Easter Sunday, when I was sixteen or seventeen, we put daffodils in fruit jars, drove up to the mountains, and set up our quartet at a trailhead. It was an exciting time; it seemed like things were changing, shifting.

College Life

By the time I was a senior in high school I was real political. I thought my parents were pretty liberal Democrats, but I was more radical than they were, so they worried about what I would be doing. I had decided not to go to college, thinking, "We're in a pre-revolutionary situation in the US; I have to go out and do something useful—join VISTA or do something for the people." I had this real sense of purpose, but my mother said, "I can't control what you do afterwards, but you are going to register for UCLA and you are going to college."

I was pretty much a radical freak at this point, wearing jeans and army jackets and stuff like that. UCLA was just a big playground to us; we were dropping acid, taking mescaline, running around disrupting ROTC ranks, and going to draft-resister trials in downtown LA. I participated in the university symphony and took tabla lessons for a couple of quarters. I'd never heard the word "ethnomusicology" and didn't have any idea what was going on. I was a lousy tabla student. I was part of the wild, hippie crowd, although they didn't use the word "hippie." I was in the Music Department for two things: I played in the university symphony, which was conducted by Mehli Mehta, Zubin Mehta's father, an incredible fellow, and then I'd go to the basement and take my tabla lessons from Harihar Rao, who was there at the time.

TS: Why were you taking tabla lessons in the first place? How did that happen?

LS: I don't have any idea now! I suspect it was all connected to the Beatles and George Harrison's involvement with Indian music. During high school my best friend and I went to the Hollywood Bowl to see Ravi Shankar. I must have heard that Harihar Rao had played with Ravi Shankar. That's just a conjecture, looking back. I see students wandering into the music building here at the University of Washington, passing our visiting artist studio, and saying, "What's this?" I'm sure that's what I did at UCLA. I'm sure I just said, "Oh, wow!"

TS: Had you thought about other cultures, about the world of travel and languages, or was it all political American stuff?

LS: I was certainly not thinking globally, and my family didn't travel much. I envied people who'd done a lot of traveling as kids, but it wasn't really part of my world. It seemed to me that travel was something you did if you were rich; I wasn't.

I only stayed at UCLA for about a year and a quarter before I decided to leave LA with a girlfriend. I dropped out of the music thing because it seemed like politics—this was 1970—was more important. Everything was happening so fast, culturally speaking. We moved to Northern California to get out of the city and because we had lots of friends at Berkeley. So, after growing up in Arcadia, I spent a number of years in Arcata, Humboldt County. When I went up there, the idea was, "The world is a mess, so we're going to go up there and plant a garden." It was basically a back-to-the-earth kind of impulse.

Coincidentally, Arcata was the location of Humboldt State University and, as soon as anybody at the university found out there was a new violinist in town, they were approached immediately. I was enticed into the Music Department at Humboldt State. It turned out to be a lovely department: small, uncompetitive, and with a focus on chamber music. I got totally hooked on chamber music. As a kid I had looked at Beethoven as the kind of music you had to sit still through, but now I became obsessed with the idea that Beethoven was the most revolutionary music. I felt that if I could be in a quartet and play Beethoven, it would be further enactment of my belief that radical change was what I had to be involved in. Beethoven was a part of that. Suddenly it seemed like it was Beethoven who was breaking down all the barriers.

TS: Did you get back formally into school?

LS: Yes, and graduated in 1974 with a bachelor's degree in music as a violin performance major. During that time I played in a number of music festivals and met the guys in the Kronos Quartet, which was just starting out then. I sat in with them once when their second violinist was off playing golf. We played quartets all afternoon, and David Harrington, who's still their first violinist and a neat guy, said, "You should be playing quartets." It was a real boost to my ego to think that these guys thought I could actually do this, so my fantasy of being a violinist remained intact for a while.

TS: How long did you live in Humboldt County, and how did you get out of there?

LS: I lived in Arcata until 1975. I lived with musicians and knew a lot of people who were orchestral musicians on the West Coast. Most of them were miserable. At that point I got interested in the early music scene, as the man I eventually moved to Seattle with was just starting up a recorder-making business. Another of our roommates started a violin-making workshop. It was a wonderful household of musicians and instrument builders, so I still felt that music had to be the center of my life. It was amazing to have that feeling of community in our early twenties. My partner, David, was one of the best early music musicians. He was a fabulous recorder player; still is. There were early music people in the Bay Area, but I still wasn't looking outside. There was no global thing. In 1975 I continued my northward journey and came up to Seattle to study with a violin teacher I had met at a festival. David came with me, set up his recorder workshop, and got into the community of performers. All kinds of wonderful musicians were here at the time, including Stanley Ritchie, who was doing Baroque violin as well as being the concertmaster of the resident string quartet. He was a big influence. I studied violin for another six months and started doing a little Baroque violin as well.

Salwa El-Shawan Castelo-Branco

In conversation with Ted Solís and Margaret Sarkissian, October 26, 2007, Columbus, Ohio

Early Life

SCB: I was born in Cairo in May 1950. My home was very musical. My father, Aziz El-Shawan [1916–1993], was a composer. He created a nationalist Egyptian style of music that combined Western and Egyptian musical idioms. I studied piano from the age of five. By twelve, I decided that I wanted to be a musician and, of course, my father was a great model. I enrolled at the secondary division of the Cairo National Conservatory at the age of thirteen.

I remained at the Conservatory until the age of twenty, completing my bachelor of music in piano. My piano teacher, Ettore Puglisi, was Italian, an expatriate, like many other Italians, Greeks, French, and English who had moved to Cairo in the second half of the nineteenth century and early twentieth century. Puglisi settled in Cairo in the 1930s and remained there until he died in 1978. My musical training was Western. A wonderful paper session at the Hawai'i SEM meeting [2006] on urban sounds in the Islamic world reminded me of my initial exposure to local musics. Living in my parents' apartment building as well as moving through the streets of Cairo, I listened to and absorbed many kinds of music. I heard the call to prayer and Qur'anic recitation through loudspeakers placed on the outside of mosques. I also heard Umm Kulthum, Abdul Wahab, Abdel Halim Hafez, and all the popular singers in Cairo in the '50s and '60s mainly through the radio.

I left Cairo to study piano at Manhattan School of Music in New York in 1970.

College Life

I had relatives who had immigrated to the US in '63; like them, many people from the Egyptian elite (especially Christians) left during the Nasser regime. I started corresponding with different music schools and got into Manhattan School of Music. I also got a small grant from the PEO [Philanthropic Educational Organization] National Scholarship Fund so I enrolled in the master's of music program in piano. I was a reasonable pianist and returned to Cairo in '72 to play my father's Piano Concerto with the Cairo Symphony Orchestra; it's a quite difficult piece, inspired by Rachmaninov. My piano teacher was Constance Keene, who had studied with Abram Chasins. She actually came to Cairo to attend the concert in which I played my father's concerto, which was a very special moment.

TS: Where did you first come across the term "ethnomusicology"?

SCB: At Manhattan School of Music I took musicology and music history courses. I had a wonderful music history teacher called Ethel Thurston. She was a medievalist and, as part of her course in musicology, she had a module on ethnomusicology and assigned us Bruno Nettl's *Theory and Method* [1964]. I found the book fascinating, so I thought I would like to explore more about ethnomusicology.

MS: What did you think about ethnomusicology at this point?

SCB: I thought of it as the study of non-Western musics. It fascinated me, first of all, because the music was fascinating. I remember looking for and buying a lot of Folkways recordings. Second, it made me think about my future as one more concert pianist—and there are so many good ones—or one more piano teacher. Maybe if I became a scholar I could make some kind of contribution.

I discovered an ethnomusicology program at Hunter College and enrolled as a part-time student in addition to [pursuing] my master's degree in piano. Rose Brandel was the ethnomusicologist there for many years. Rose was a disciple of Curt Sachs and introduced a number of people—who are professionals today—to ethnomusicology. I have an article in the Festschrift published in her honor, *To the Four Corners* [Leichtman 1994]. What fascinated me was the possibility of hearing different musics. This was the first time I ever heard African music or any kind of music outside the Middle East and Western music. I started reading and thought to myself, well, this is something to think about seriously. My master's in piano was a two-year program, but I did it in three years because I was doing this extra course work at Hunter and wanted to have time to make up my mind. I started looking at different graduate programs and applied to a few.

Bernard Kleikamp

In conversation with Ted Solís and Margaret Sarkissian, November 12, 2010, Los Angeles, California

Early Life

BK: I was born in the town of Hoorn, Netherlands, in the province of North Holland (a sub-area called West Friesland), approximately forty kilometers north of Amsterdam in March 1951. My father was born in the town of Sittard in the south of the Netherlands and moved to Hoorn during the Second World War when universities were closed by the German occupation. He got a job with the Ministry of Agriculture in Hoorn, and that's where he eventually bought a pharmacy after he finished his studies. He met my mother there. She came from a small village five kilometers from Hoorn and was a pharmacist's assistant in his competitor's pharmacy across the road, so it was a good move for my father. My mother was a trained choir singer, an alto, and often sang old folk songs from the West Frisian area around the house. I picked those up. She started singing fairly young and was still singing in choirs when she died at the age of sixty. She got that from my grandmother, who was a well-known singer and one of the informants of two Dutch musicologists, Veurman and Bax. They published a book of songs and dances from West Friesland in 1944; I still have the copy my grandmother got from them for her cooperation (Veurman and Bax 1944).

MS: So you grew up singing folk songs?

BK: Yes, as far back as I can remember. During my primary school years, I went to music school two afternoons a week. Regular school would end at 4:00 and music school would start at 4:30 till 6:30. I got four hours of extra musical education and was also a choirboy in the Roman Catholic Church. There was always music in my life. I started piano at ten or eleven and did that for four or five years. During my secondary school years I wasn't practicing music, but I listened a lot. It was the mid-1960s, so we had the Beatles, the Stones, and then the American rock bands, the Byrds and the Eagles. Later there was Joni Mitchell, Joan Baez, and Bob Dylan.

TS: I know that in the Netherlands you study a lot of languages very early on; could you give us a sketch of your own language training?

BK: Although the West Frisian dialect was spoken in the areas surrounding Hoorn, it wasn't spoken in the town. Perhaps because my father came from the south and my mother came from West Friesland, they agreed to speak proper Dutch at home. Our primary school is six years, from the age of six to twelve. In the last two years—so in grades five and six—we learned French, and in grade six we learned English. Or you could go to the Gymnasium and study Latin and classical Greek as extra languages. I had two years of Latin and one year of classical Greek. Later on, the Greek helped me master Russian more easily because the Cyrillic alphabet is similar. At secondary school I had five years of German and six years of English and French, all of which I speak pretty well now. In later life I took courses in Hungarian, Italian, and Tibetan, so I have a basic knowledge of these languages but I'm far from being a fluent speaker.

College Life

My father was a pharmacist and I was the eldest son. It was always assumed that I would be his successor, so I went to university in Leiden to study pharmacy. But it was never my real choice—it wasn't where my heart was. After a couple of years, I decided to stop studying pharmacy. That was one of the most difficult things in my life, to tell my father that it wasn't what I wanted to do. It must've broken his heart, but he seemed quite cool about it and said, "Well, I've never wanted to force you." So I went to the University of Amsterdam to study Dutch language and literature. I continued to live in Leiden, though, because I had gotten married there at the age of twenty-five.

MS: When did you get back to folk music?

BK: I met a couple of students who were musicians at college, and we decided to start a folk club. There was a folk revival in the Netherlands in the early 1970s, and people were starting folk clubs in many university towns. We started the club in Leiden and later organized a yearly festival, which we continued for sixteen or seventeen years, until the early 1990s.

TS: When you say "folk," are you talking about Dutch folk music?

BK: No! That's the funny thing; all the folk clubs were focused on Anglo-Saxon and Celtic music—Irish, Scottish, Breton, and English. I think it had to do with the folk revival in England and Ireland, which was about five to ten years ahead of the Dutch revival. There were so many bands, and they all wanted to travel and make tours.

TS: I find this very interesting, because usually when you talk about a folk revival, it means to revive one's own culture and folk life.

BK: Well, there were folk bands and soloists performing traditional music from the Netherlands, but they were a minority—let's say, 25 percent as opposed to 75 percent Celtic and English. I myself was always a proponent of traditional music from the Netherlands. Later, when I managed a band that performed old-time music from the United States, I kept telling them, "You shouldn't do US music; you should do Netherlands music!" When the band's first LP was released, there was a cartoon of me on the back with a balloon coming out of my mouth that said, "Sing your mother's language!"

T. M. Scruggs

In conversation with Ted Solís and Margaret Sarkissian, October 26, 2007, Columbus, Ohio

Early Life

TMS: I was born in August 1951, in Stockton, California, and took my first steps in Golden Gate Park. I used to think I started playing piano at age six, but my mom said, "No, as soon as you could crawl up on the piano bench, you started banging the keys." So my musical bent goes *all* the way back. I've also thought about what is the Latin connection here (for my later interest in things Latin American). There was quite a bit around when I was growing up in Millbrae, just south of San Francisco. My seventh and eighth grade school was in Mission style, a beautiful building with a big tile dome. When we were in elementary school, we lined up after recess and counted off in Spanish and had a couple of exchange students from Mexico in sixth grade.

I grew up in the Bay Area in the '60s, where there was a lot of experimentation in the air. In high school, I was into the "rock 'n' roll" part of "sex, drugs, and rock 'n' roll." I tried to make up for that when I went to college, but when I was in high school, we had a band. It had drugs in its name, but the idea was totally mercenary. The band was called "Free Beer," so our advertisements would say, "Saturday night at the Recreation Center, 8 pm, Free Beer!" I played piano and bass keyboard. I got the idea of a bass keyboard from seeing the Doors at Mount Tamalpais in 1967. That was the first outdoor rock 'n' roll concert—before Woodstock.

College Life

I went to Lewis & Clark College in Portland, Oregon, and started out as a history major. Lewis & Clark was smaller than my high school but had an amazing overseas program in which students in groups of two dozen, each with a professor, went to live in a foreign country for two quarters. Once they went to Indonesia. I saw gamelan and stuff in the home movies of the music professor who led that group. The black students asked, "How about a trip to Africa?" So they said, "OK, good idea" and sent a group to Tunisia. The black students said, "That's not exactly what we meant!"

They were going to send students to Kenya, but that was changed to Ethiopia, so in my sophomore year, from September 1970 to February '71, I lived in Addis Ababa. That was one of those pivotal moments. Soon after we arrived, there was a concert by the Ethiopian National Orchestra, a concoction of a Peace Corps guy called Charlie Sutton, who was working with musicians to try to get them employment. He created something that could be a folk presentation for government functions. I remember an older man playing the *krar*, a lyre, up on the stage. Usually they strum it and stop the five strings with the fingers on their left hand. But then he took a solo in which he only plucked the strings. I remember thinking, "Now, what is *that*?" He was playing scales or modes with third tones—it just fascinated me.

We had to do a project, so I decided to do mine on music. I learned enough to get in trouble on the *masenqo*, a spike fiddle, which you play by stopping the single string made of horsetail hair with the soft part of your fingers. As I was walking past the marketplace to take lessons from Getamesay Abebe, a master player who's no longer with us, it struck me how the musicians were considered dirt in their country. I saw this even more clearly when I went to another performance put on by Charlie Sutton for a group of German tourists and some Ethiopian officials. The Ethiopians started getting drunk and basically did everything but throw things at the musicians, whereas the Germans wanted to hear the music and were outraged. It was then I realized that to be an *asmari*, a wandering minstrel, is the lowest of the low, but to be a *farengi*, a foreigner, puts you up at the level of royalty. I decided then that there were two things I wanted to do: pursue music more institutionally and learn a language well, because I found myself in situations where I was with Ethiopian musicians who would talk a mile a minute, but I couldn't really follow what they were saying.

On the way back from Ethiopia, I met Jean Jenkins—who had done a lot of work in Ethiopia—at the Horniman Museum in London. When I got back, I decided to major in music because I figured I could do language on my own. My life was a little schizoid at that point: I'd be listening to John Coltrane while fixing my eggs in the morning and then I'd drive to campus and sit in a class where someone with a German accent was trying to analyze Mozart—it would take me half the class to calm down and refocus. That summer I went to UCLA to check out ethnomusicology.

MS: Was that the first time you had heard the word "ethnomusicology"?

TMS: I don't know when I first heard it. I think the Ethiopian experience probably led me that way. I knew people in Seattle who were learning *mbira* from Dumi [Dumisani Maraire]. One of them worked at the University of Washington Press and gave me a copy of John Blacking's *How Musical Is Man?* [1973]. That was the first ethnomusicology book I read. There was another short book by a guy named Powne on Ethiopian instruments [1968], but that was about it.

TS: What did the word "ethnomusicology" mean to you at that point?

TMS: I put it within the cultural context of the '60s (which I really think of as being 1964 to '74)—looking at and listening to music from other cultures. I unwittingly made a connection with anthropology, but I thought of it as anthropologists and ethnomusicologists doing the same things.

I went to UCLA for the summer and took two introductory classes, one of which was by David Morton. On the very first day of class, we looked at some music from India. He gave some introductory information and then said, "Now let's listen to this *alap* from a *rag* played by Ravi Shankar." It was a good six or seven minutes long and I was just transported. It was one of those wonderful pieces that used primal elements of the musical system to really express emotion. And when it finished, Dr. Morton just sat there with his eyes closed, and said, "Ah, well, now we all can come back down to Earth," and then went on to give his presentation. It just clicked. Here was someone who actually *feels* this, a professor who recognizes, deeply, the worth of these other musics. That was *very* refreshing.

I thought about transferring to UCLA to finish my undergraduate, but the department chair, a musicologist, told me I'd have to repeat *all* my history and theory classes to transfer. The ethnomusicologists were livid because this was always happening to them; the musicologists were trying to kill the program. But I did meet someone who was interested in Ethiopia, Cynthia Tse Kimberlin, who had just written a master's thesis. I was just a nineteen-year-old punk, but she asked me if I would read it and see what I thought about it. I said, "Well, sure," but I wasn't totally positive what to make of it. I went back, dropped out of school, and didn't have anything to do with institutional education for the next nine years.

I dropped out without graduating and got into political activism. I wanted to experience a large industrial city and a lot of blues and avant-garde jazz as fast as possible. I had some contacts in Chicago, so I went there. I got lucky and found a job in a tiny record distributorship that carried all the weird record labels no one wanted to deal with. Chuck Nessa had just been hired and put out some recordings. Nessa Records became a kind of boutique jazz label. I was so fascinated by Chicago that I ended up staying there eight long winters, studying Spanish and working.

TS: Why Spanish?

TMS: Spanish has the advantage that there's a country in Europe that speaks it. Then there's all of Latin America, except Brazil, and it's the second language of the United States. When I moved to Chicago, I was around Latinos and Latin Americans. Then, because of my political work, I met refugees from Argentina, Chile, and Uruguay. That was the '70s, when the *salsa* boom was winding down. I learned how to play salsa and was recruited into a Haitian *kompa* band, playing down on the South Side. In Mayor Richard J. Daley's Chicago, you had to be on the South Side if you had a black club. I was the only white guy in the group; there were a couple of other North Americans in the horn section. It was an incredible experience. I was always learning music and doing it on the side; my jobs were just something to keep me afloat.

I joined a volunteer collective that was running a leftist bookstore and center called the New World Resource Center. By that point, my Spanish was getting pretty good, and I noticed how the Puerto Rican and Mexican bookstores in town were terrible—big sections on *Sexología* and *Astrología* and nothing by Gabriel García Márquez. This was in the middle of the big Latin American literature boom. So I started importing Spanish-language books to New World. One thing led to another, and it became half the sales of the store. I had people driving in from Kansas City! They'd come in, fill up their trunks, and go back, wiping me out. Eventually, I got to a point where the weather was beating me down and the lack of nature was starting to get to me, so I started thinking that I should either go back to school and pursue ethnomusicology or start a commercial Spanish-language bookstore.

I looked at Chicago State University, one of the historically black colleges on the far South Side. It had a class on Latin American music and another on jazz improvisation by Bunky Green, a great alto sax player, so I decided to go see what it was like. I walked into the music building and saw a guy who used to play tenor sax in the Haitian band. He said, "Hey, what are *you* doing here?" I said, "Well, I decided to go back to school and take some classes." He started beaming and said "Yeah? Come with me." It was freezing outside—you know, January in Chicago—so I said, "OK." We went up some stairs, toward the [department] chair's office. There were students lined up and a secretary sitting there. The secretary said, "Ah, Professor Whittaker. . . ." He said, "Just tell them to wait. Come on in, T. M." and opened the door. *He* was the chair of the Music Department! He had an office with a view, and he said, "Not bad for a kid from the ghetto, huh?" It was an amazing connection. I thought I was going to know nobody, and it turned out that the sax player was the head of the department!

I took piano lessons with Evangelina Mendoza. After the first semester she asked if I would be interested in learning harpsichord. I said, "Sure!" I loved harpsichord music, so I started learning harpsichord. She even lent me a tiny Dolmetsch clavichord to practice on. All she said was, "Just be real careful with this." I didn't realize what it was worth until a friend came over and gasped, "You have a Dolmetsch?!" After that I was scared to death to touch it. It was worth thousands of dollars.

It was a good education for me. Basically the high schools of the South Side emptied out into Chicago State, so someone like myself, who had just turned thirty and had been around, was able to get to know the professors well. It also raised the prospect of going to graduate school, because I realized I could graduate by the summer. I started asking around. If I want to do ethnomusicology and Latin American things, where should I go? Austin, Texas, was the obvious choice.

Shubha Chaudhuri

In conversation with Margaret Sarkissian, October 28, 2007, Columbus, Ohio

Early Life

SC: I was born in Bombay, India, in January 1952. My ending up in ethnomusicology at the archives is, like a lot of things, an accident. I trained in linguistics, but the only predisposition I had was that I always wanted to be an academic. The academic life appealed to me in some very general sense. I came from a family where there was a lot of interest in music. Both my parents went to *Santiniketan* [spiritual and artistic center founded by Rabindranath Tagore] and had been students of Tagore, so they sang and we had a lot of *Rabindra Sangeet* [songs composed by Tagore] in our home as well. My father sang, not in any serious way, until he was 90. I think he always assumed that his great interest in Hindustani classical music would be reflected in his children. For me, music was another one of the many things my parents were telling me to do. I didn't want to learn classical music or *Bharata Natyam*, both of which I was strongly encouraged to do when I was about six. One of my father's sisters was a very good singer but in those days could not have been professional. There was a stigma attached to women singing, and I think that was why he thought, "How wonderful that this is not the case now and you can at least learn it." I think he spent many frustrated years until I joined the archive, asking, "What *rag* do you think that is?"

MS: What was your earliest musical love?

SC: My father was always singing Hindustani music around the home, but I was listening to the Beatles. I was seriously into rock. It was a lot about standard rebellious behavior. I grew up feeling that my father was a real stick-in-the-mud Hindustani music person who didn't even listen to Karnatak music, let alone Western music. There was a lot of Western classical music in my mother's family, though. She's a Parsee, like Zubin Mehta. I have two cousins who are serious pianists, and so there was musical interest on both sides. My maternal grandmother had trained in Hindustani music. It was all around me, but I guess I didn't want to see it. It was only when I went away to boarding school that I realized my first love was actually the music of *Bharata Natyam*.

I went to the Rishi Valley School, a Krishnamurti Foundation school in the south, out in the country. It was a progressive school, very international, and had a very good *Bharata Natyam* program. I liked the music that they danced to. There was suddenly no pressure—nobody was telling me to do anything, and I could still listen to the Beatles and do what I wanted. I was twelve, thirteen, fourteen—just discovering

Joan Baez, Bob Dylan, and all that. I came to Indian classical music via Karnatak music and then instrumental music. However, going to university in Baroda gave me the opportunity to go to a lot of concerts by famous musicians—and that is when I started listening to Hindustani music more seriously, or perhaps I should say with a greater sense of enjoyment.

What I didn't see—till I joined the ARCE [Archives and Research Centre for Ethnomusicology], actually—was what I'd grown up with. Whenever my father traveled anywhere in the world, he always brought me back a gift of music. In my dying to straitjacket him, I had not seen that as a twelve-year-old I had singles from Yugoslavia, Cyprus, Japan. Wherever he traveled it was important for him to bring me back a bit of music. So I had actually grown up with this exposure without realizing it.

MS: What was your father's job that he traveled so much?

SC: He was an artist, a sculptor. He traveled like most professionals do to conferences, symposiums, and all. My mother is also an artist, a potter. I grew up on the MS [Maharaja Sayajirao] University of Baroda campus where they both taught art. Baroda was an old princely state that had major music patrons, so the city has always been a musical center.

My father was a great collector. I think if we later had a shared interest, it was anthropology. He always felt that if he had his life again, he would have liked to be an anthropologist. He's got a huge collection of artifacts. Much later, after I was at the archives, I took Tony Seeger and Ter Ellingson home for a meal. Tony looked around and said, "You couldn't have been anything but an archivist in an ethnomusicology archive. Look at your home! There are instruments from all over the world all over the walls." And I said, "Yeah, I guess so." It's all part of not realizing how important your early influences are. I always found it funny that I came full circle.

College Life

MS: Did you start out in linguistics as an undergraduate?

SC: No, I have a BA in English literature with linguistics as a minor. I moved to linguistics as a major and studied in Baroda. I took everything very seriously, especially my academic career. I did my MA and worked in publishing for a while during the late '70s. When I finished my master's I came to Delhi, because my parents had moved and that was where my family was. I wanted to do a PhD, but not immediately. I heard of an opening at OUP, so I interviewed and got the job. I spent a year and a half there until there was a national linguistics conference in Delhi. I took a day off to attend the conference and suddenly had this great revelation: I missed classrooms, I missed chalk and blackboards, and I missed the buzz of a campus. So I decided to leave OUP and registered for a PhD.

PETER MANUEL

In conversation with Ted Solís, September 11, 2010, Phoenix, Arizona

Early Life

PM: I was born in Cleveland, Ohio, in June 1952, but came from an upper-middle-class East Side suburban family. My father was in advertising and my mother didn't work. It wasn't a particularly musical family. I had piano lessons for a few years when I was a kid and later picked up rock guitar. I developed a pretty good ear by picking tunes from records. My cultural upbringing and surroundings were completely WASP. I was a maladjusted and not terribly happy adolescent, interested in the Beatles, guitar, smoking pot, listening to music I didn't understand, and the shallow exoticism typical of the times. I played rock guitar in various bands, none of any tremendous distinction. That is to say, nothing in my upbringing would have predisposed me toward music, let alone ethnomusicology. It was more a sense of alienation and exasperation with my whole upbringing that inclined me toward things non-Western. I wanted to get as far away from it as I could, as soon as I could.

TS: How old were you when you began to feel this sense of alienation?

PM: Oh, maybe fourteen or fifteen. My parents were very conservative. My mother is still alive; I enjoy her a lot now, but back then it was a very straitlaced environment, and I rebelled against it in ways that were shallow and provocative. It was the era of the youth counterculture, and there was a real generation gap. I had a desire to break free from it somehow, and my parents, to their credit, supported that. When I told them I wanted to go to India for the summer, or wanted to drop out of school and study sitar, they were essentially supportive. Back then, there was something called the "Putney Experiment," through which you could spend a summer abroad. Putney is a private school in Vermont that ran summer programs. I went to India on this program in 1970, the summer before I went to college. It was fun and interesting and made me want to go back someday.

TS: Why India? Was it because of the Beatles?

PM: That was one thing, but I was also interested in alternative philosophies of life, although I was not, and am not, a religious person. I used to read trendy things of the time—Alan Watts and Khalil Gibran. I was trying to find some sort of peace of mind to transcend my adolescent angst. It never quite worked out, but I developed an interest in Asian philosophies. It was shallow in some ways, and I knew it was, but I wanted to learn more. My sister had done the Putney summer program in India in '68 or '69 and had a good time, so maybe that inspired me. Also, I had somehow got interested in sitar around '68. I traveled to New York to visit a girlfriend and bought a sitar from the Music Inn, a music store in the Village. I don't know what I imagined I would do with it, because there was no one to learn from in Cleveland, but I used to tinker around, listen to Ravi Shankar records, and try to copy licks.

College Life

I started college at Yale. In some ways, it was a continuation of my high-school experience: the academics were good and every class I took was great, but I continued to feel socially alienated. I hated the whole institution and wanted to distance myself from it. I knew from the day I got there that I didn't want to be there for long. I wanted to expand my horizons and get as far away as I could from my WASP-y, narrow upbringing.

I took a World Music survey class from Pandora Hopkins. I really enjoyed it, mostly because of the subject matter. At some point, when Pandora was away, Ruby Ornstein taught a graduate seminar in ethnomusicology on an adjunct basis. I petitioned to get into the seminar. Ruby was a fun and lively person, which made the class very interesting. I'd also drive up to Wesleyan with my little sitar. It was a much cooler place—the performance scene, the "Curry Concerts," and the sense of community were all so arty and creative—and I wished I had gone there. I took sitar lessons at Wesleyan from Krishna Sanyal. I was just a beginner, but it prepared me a little and intensified the India interest.

After three semesters at Yale I decided to go learn sitar in India. It was a cockamamie idea. I didn't know anything about Indian music or what I would do with it, and I had no idea what I would do when I got there. But I had saved up a little money and a friend wanted to travel most of the way with me, so my parents gave me their blessing. We flew from San Francisco, where my sister lived, to Manila and worked our way in progressively smaller boats to progressively smaller islands. We crossed over to Borneo, which was illegal, and had a lot of adventures along the way. We must have taken a ferry to the Malay Peninsula and then worked our way to Thailand by train. At that point he went his direction and I flew to India.

I hadn't the foggiest idea of who I'd learn from; the only name I knew was Ravi Shankar. I arrived in Delhi on a twenty-one-day transit visa. When I look back, I was so clueless and simpleminded! It didn't occur to me that I'd need a visa. Someone gave me the name of Vilayat Khan. Where was Vilayat Khan? Oh, he lives up in Simla. So I went to Simla; Vilayat wasn't there. I went to his house, but he was in the process of moving to Dehradun, a couple hours northeast of Delhi. I met one of his students, who said, "Oh, yes, Vilayat is great; he's the man." So I went back to Delhi, got very sick, recovered, and went to meet Vilayat.

I went up to Dehradun. It was a long way to go without any idea of what to expect, but I was young and adventurous, and if one thing didn't work out, I'd try another.

He was very nice, even though I was a complete simpleton. I asked if he would take me on as a student, and he said, "Sure." He let me sleep in a little side room for a few days, with the understanding that I'd get another place, which I eventually did. By this time, my twenty-one-day transit visa was running out. I really marvel at how clueless I was. I went back to Delhi to try to extend my visa. When they said "no," I made a clumsy attempt to offer a bribe, and the officer laughed at me. Someone said, "Go work it out with the Foreigner's Registration guy in Dehradun." So I went to the office in Dehradun, which back then was one police clerk who was much more flexible. He took me into a side room and said, "Well, this could be worked out if certain expenses are met," and that took care of the problem.

After that I found a place to stay as a paying guest. The family provided my meals and it was all very comfortable, easy, and cheap. I took sitar lessons from Vilayat, together with three or four other students. Vilayat would give us lessons for a week or so, then a month or two would pass while he was off touring, so I'd learn from a couple of his advanced students. I was practicing a lot, trying to get my head together in some way, just sitting in my little room on my floor mat and playing sitar for four or five hours a day. I know people boast about playing twelve and fourteen hours a day, but I did it by the clock, and if you play sitting for five hours solid, by the clock, that's a lot. I would time myself and push myself, playing scales and so on, trying to build up technique.

TS: Did you have a chance to hear live music at all?

PM: No, I wasn't hearing much live music because there was no concert life in Dehradun, and it seemed to me that Vilayat (who was around fifty then) had already lost interest in music. I've seen this with other Hindustani musicians. They reach fifty or so and they've been playing the same ragas over and over again. More power to those, like Nikhil Banerjee, who keep practicing. But I had a radio and I got a bulletin called *Akashvani* that told you, "At eleven o'clock so-and-so will play rag *Brindavani Sarang* [on All India Radio]." I had some books, including Bhatkhande's books, so even though I wasn't hearing a lot of live music, I could look up *Brindavani Sarang* (by this time I was also learning Hindi). Between reading and hearing people play, I could recognize the basic features of the most common ragas.

TS: How long were you in India?

PM: I left on my epic journey in February 1972. I was in India from May '72 until June '73—thirteen months, learning sitar and thinking about the future. I wasn't planning to live in India forever. Having enjoyed the two ethnomusicology courses at Yale and enjoying sitar, I had no aversion to academics. It was something I did reasonably well. At some point in the latter part of '72, I decided to go back to college.

At that time the big programs were UCLA and Wesleyan. I applied to both; UCLA was the one that liked me, I guess. The plan was to stay in India till May or so, learn as much as I could, and then go to UCLA. I was learning from Vilayat, but he wasn't teaching much, and I felt that I needed more material. Another student, Bashir Ahmed, and I defected to Shahid Parvez, a young nephew of Vilayat's. I just told Vilayat that I was leaving. It was a typically tactless and stupid thing to do because, of course, Vilayat found out. It was an insult to go from the great maestro to his lesser nephew and it exacerbated a rift between them. I didn't understand all these protocol things—I was continually clueless. Shahid was young and friendly and easy to get along with. His family was also nice, so it was a very different setup. So when I left in June '73, I was still his student, and I left with the obvious intent of coming back.

I got to UCLA in the fall of '73. I took more general liberal arts classes but also plenty of India and Islamic Studies classes, studied some Persian, and created an Urdu class for myself. By then I was pursuing a music major, which was quite rigorous at UCLA. I had a lot of learning to do because I didn't have a strong Western music background.

TS: Did you continue sitar studies at UCLA?

PM: Yes, I was practicing the material I had learned from Shahid and copying records. I'd drive out to CalArts and practice with John Bergamo, who played tabla. My sister was living at Berkeley, so in the summer of '74 I stayed with her. It was the peak year of the Center for World Music, the Sam Scripps thing. It was just around the corner from where I was living, which was absolutely fantastic because by this time I was enthralled by African music and by Javanese, Sundanese, and Balinese dance. The scene was really happening there, and Nikhil Banerjee was teaching, so I took a summer program of classes from him.

Nazir Jairazbhoy's arrival at UCLA in the fall of '74 was great for me because he was such a wonderful guy, supportive, and a great person to learn from in every way. He became my mentor. He arranged for me to teach sitar and tabla in a performance class, which was unusual because I was still an undergraduate. Steve Loza was doing the same with Latin music, so the department was very open in that way. I continued at UCLA, took a semester off in the winter of '74 or '75 to go back to India and study some more with Shahid. When I came back to UCLA in '76, I met Kalyan Mukherjea, a mathematics professor and fine sarod player with a tremendous knowledge of ragas. That was when I began to realize the limitations of Shahid's command of raga. Kalyan was a great personal mentor and friend as well, and so I defected again from one guru to another. I was really lucky to have this combination of mentors: Nazir on the academic side, Kalyan on the musical side, and both on the personal side. I wasn't in any particular hurry and took a couple semesters off to go back to India, so I finished my BA in '76.

Gage Averill

In conversation with Margaret Sarkissian, October 28, 2007, Columbus, Ohio

Early Life

GA: I was born in Greenwich, Connecticut, in May 1954. Same hospital my daughter was born in four years ago, by total coincidence! I grew up primarily on a hunting, fishing, and game farm in midstate New York, a couple of hours north of the city. I had a very strange upbringing, on my own in the country. My dad was what he described as a "barroom singer." Nice tenor—far nicer voice than mine—and all his life he had sung in duets and casually in bars. He was in the Caribbean throughout the war working for Shell Oil, so I was introduced to Caribbean music fairly early. I had a bongo when I was about five or six and heard my first steel band, the US Navy Steel Band, in Puerto Rico around that time. My parents divorced when I was about five. We stayed at the farm and he resumed travel to the Caribbean for the oil business. He traveled to Puerto Rico and Jamaica pretty regularly. I was probably six or seven the first time I went with him.

MS: Did you have music lessons as a child?

GA: Yes, some piano lessons, some guitar lessons, but I mostly just sang for much of my early life. I was lightly musical but never devoted to it until my twenties. My major interest was drama. I was president of the drama club, I wrote theater, I directed, I acted and built sets. I fell in love with classical music in high school, mostly from hanging out with drama-club types. I jammed a little with random high-school folk and rock-and-roll bands. I was trying to make a decision about going into the arts, but at that point I had the feeling it was maybe not the healthiest direction for me. Drama helped to save me in high school—it gave me close friends, exposed me to older people who took an interest in me and kept me from self-destructing—but I found the production cycle too neurotic. I imagined that if I went off into forest rangering, I would have a rugged outdoorsy kind of life.

College Life

So I went into forestry at the University of Wisconsin. I lived on the aggie side of campus, but the people I was with in the dorms were really not what I was used to. I was used to an arts crowd, so I spent much of my time at the music school. I enrolled in concert choir and went to all the jazz rehearsals, symphony performances, and special events. I lived my social life in and around the arts.

A couple of years later I sensed that I was too restless to stay in school. I was living in co-ops in Madison, and there was a lot I wanted to do politically, so I dropped out of the university. I had a good friend who was also very political, and the two of us would play guitar and write songs on social issues and themes for the co-op and around town. I put together a folk rock group called Arise, essentially to do political activist work. We toured and played everything from picket lines to benefits and rallies. I was also doing community activism at the tenant union, which I came to run for a number of years. I was also an arts journalist for a community rag in Madison called *Free for All*. All of it was connected.

At that point, I was asked to join a new band in town, the Irish Brigade. It was a very political band, focused both on North American politics and on the Irish question. I was recruited because they were trying to get rid of the nonpolitical folks and bring in hardcore folks. I'd just seen the Boys of the Lough and fell in love with the concertina—around '74 or '75—so I started playing concertina and joined the Irish Brigade. We toured the Midwest, Chicago to Minnesota, and did benefits and things. We had a small amateurish, but gigging, career for many years.

From there, someone at the local community radio station, WORT, wanted some world music programming, so I was brought in because they knew I had two things: an attachment to Irish music and I wasn't an ethnomusicologist. They said, "We want you because you're *not* an ethnomusicologist. We could fill the station with all those people down at the university, but they'd do two hours of drumming of the Dan people, and we don't want that."

MS: Was that the first time you heard the word "ethnomusicology"?

GA: I'd probably heard it earlier, because I used to kayak on weekends with a friend who played "some kind of gong thing" as I thought at the time. She was an ethnomusicology student at UW Madison in Nepalese music and gamelan, so she must have used the term. Other than that, it was probably the first time I'd heard the term, and it was used negatively. The station committed to an hour and a half a day of world music and to buying an extensive catalog. This was '75, '76, '77, so it was visionary for the time. The show was called "On the Horizon," and it was the birth of my little radio career. Around then, my buddies in the Irish Brigade had the idea of doing a world music festival in town, so we took over the Capitol and created the Equinox Festival. By the late '70s I was playing Irish music, trying out a little Latin music (not very successfully), doing world music radio, and festival directing in addition to my day job, which was still at the tenant union. I was also writing and doing music journalism for *Free for All*. There were a lot of things that I later talked myself into thinking were applied ethnomusicology.

I was in love with Irish music but had a fairly major crisis in my life around 1980 that resulted in many changes. My sister, whom I was very close to, died; I broke up with someone I was closely involved with; and the Irish Brigade was also breaking up. I was tired of doing tenant organizing work and met someone who wanted to move to Seattle and become a dancer. We started going out, so I quit everything and moved to Seattle. I wanted to study Latin music, so I joined a radio station, KAOS in Seattle, and started doing some programming for them while studying Latin percussion. I drove a tractor and school bus, till I hurt my back really badly and went through a year when I was in intense pain.

I couldn't work and was feeling kind of desperate when I saw a notice in the paper—around August 10 I think—that said the university had a shortfall in admissions and was opening an August admissions for residents, which I was not yet. So I went there, said I was a resident, and got into the university, starting the following week. I had to pick a major, so I looked down the list of majors and saw they had an undergraduate ethnomusicology major. I thought, wow, that's kind of like what I'm doing. So I checked ethnomusicology.

The next week I was sitting in Lorraine Sakata's yearlong introduction to ethnomusicology! The odd thing about that for me was that ethnomusicologists were using the albums I had been assiduously reading notes from for years. I had memorized all that stuff. So Lorraine would put an example on and ask what is this? I would say, "Well, that's called "Buzzing Bees" from the Nonesuch recording of *Inanga Whispered Harp Style of* blah blah blah." I'd gotten a couple of 100s on exams, outdoing the grad students, so she actually called me into her office to ask, "Who are you, and where did you come from?" because no one had told her about the undergraduate student. She and Dan Neuman took me under their wing, and that's how I got into ethnomusicology. I spent the next two years doing nothing but music with a little anthropology and sociology and finished up an undergraduate BA in ethnomusicology. Amazing!

Tan Sooi Beng

In conversation with Margaret Sarkissian, September 1, 2009, Northampton, Massachusetts

Early Life

TSB: I was born in Penang in April 1955. My parents were musical, but they never had the opportunity to learn piano or study singing. So when I was young, they gave my younger sister and me the chance to study piano with our cousin. We went to Convent Light Street, the main convent school in Penang. It was one of the first schools set up by the Holy Infant Jesus nuns in Malaysia in the late nineteenth century and followed the British education system. I was quite a musical child, and the nuns encouraged me to sing and dance. They also taught me to serve society. Back then, Penang people were still influenced by British colonialism and many young people who were doing music studied Western classical music rather than our own local traditions. When I finished my Grade 8 [standardized British music exams administered by the Royal

Schools of Music, Grade 8 being the highest] and my Licentiate (actually I got two licentiates, one from the Royal Schools of Music and the other from Trinity College), I didn't know anything about my own traditions or culture.

MS: Did you ask your parents for lessons, or was it something they thought would be good for you—a kind of colonial mentality?

TSB: My parents thought it was a good thing and that I could earn a living teaching piano later in life. My parents both went to English schools and were impressed with the famous pianists (such as Dennis Lee) that Penang had produced. My father was the main clerk at St. Xavier's Institution, the boy's school opposite my convent school. It was run by the La Salle Brothers and we had quite a close relationship with the Brothers. My mother was a midwife. Both her parents—my grandparents—came from China. My grandfather used to work in the rubber plantations in Kedah. He was always outside of Penang, so my grandmother had to earn a living to support the family. She learned how to deliver babies from the English nurses and became a midwife. My mother followed her footsteps and took a course in midwifery after the war.

MS: You thought your parents were musical; how was that apparent to you?

TSB: They were always singing—singing was free, right! They sang popular songs such as "Rose, Rose, I Love You" and "The Happy Wanderer." They had a group of school friends they used to go out with. They'd go to the swimming club and then go dancing.

MS: Did they go to the Eastern and Oriental Hotel tea dances or anything like that?

TSB: Oh, the E&O was too expensive for them! There was a Chinese swimming club that catered to the Chinese and provided free ballroom dancing lessons (the other swimming club catered only to Europeans). They also went to the Chusan Hotel, near Tanjung Tokong, which was one of the hotels that had a dance floor. That was when they were courting, of course. Once you got married, you settled down and when you had a family, you had to work very hard to earn money to support the family. My dad had two jobs: one during the day at St. Xavier's, then at night he would teach typing in some school. That took up all his time.

College Life

My parents couldn't afford to send me to college, so I had to apply for a scholarship. At that time American colleges were giving scholarships to good students. I applied to a few colleges and was offered a scholarship to Cornell. That's how I ended up there. I was at Cornell from 1974 to 1978, studying piano and Western music history. I wanted to be a pianist, so I was always practicing in the dungeons, the basement practice rooms. It was very lonely, especially in winter.

Marty Hatch ran a gamelan group, and at that point a few researchers who had been doing fieldwork in Indonesia, like Nancy Florida and John Pemberton, came to Cornell. There was new blood and new repertoire so the gamelan was quite exciting. And then they brought in Sumarsam. Slowly I was drawn into the gamelan ensemble and started playing with them. That was when I first heard about ethnomusicology and got interested in it. In my junior year, Bell Yung had a postdoc in the Chinese Department and offered two courses, one on Chinese opera and the other on ethnomusicology. I took both courses from him. That was how I got interested in ethnomusicology.

MS: What was it like as a Malaysian coming to Ithaca, New York, and encountering Indonesian music? Were you surprised?

TSB: It was a bit of a culture shock. I had never heard of gamelan or even seen the instruments before! For me, the world of music was Western classical music. I used to look down on performers doing street opera and all that. I thought it was not very sophisticated. As a result of our colonial upbringing and education, we thought anything Western and European was higher class. We also listened to Western pop songs on the radio, especially groups like the Beatles.

MS: When you took those classes with Bell Yung in your junior year at Cornell, what did "ethnomusicology" mean to you?

TSB: It was the study of non-Western music, an area that had its own methodologies and approaches. One had to go and do fieldwork to learn about people's cultures and conduct ethnographic research objectively. I went through all the standard texts with Bell. I did a reading course with him, so I read Bruno Nettl and Alan Merriam and all that. At that time I was also influenced by the Vietnam War and Southeast Asian politics in general. At Cornell, I took courses from Ben Anderson and David P. Mozingo, who taught me Southeast Asian and Chinese histories, respectively. I began to learn more about what was happening in the world outside the small musical world that I was in. In particular, I realized that music and music research could be employed to bring about change in society.

Elizabeth Travassos Lins

In conversation with Ted Solís, July 11, 2007, Vienna, Austria

Early Life

ETL: I was born in Belo Horizonte, Southeastern Brazil, in July 1955. My father, who was a lawyer, was also in the trading business and played mandolin. I studied piano for five years as a child. It was the dream of my parents to have their children attend the very competitive Colégio de Aplicacão in Rio. This was a high school linked to the

Universidade Federal do Rio de Janeiro, the Federal University of Rio de Janeiro. The entrance examination was very difficult, but I managed to enter the school in 1966. The school had high standards in terms of both intellectual achievement and political discussions. Many leaders from the student movement came from this school, and they began to be persecuted by the police at sixteen or seventeen years of age. This was a time of great political unrest in Brazil.

When I got to the high school, everything was interesting—music, politics—but my interests began to shift to what I understood to be *geographie humaine*: history, geography, philosophy, mathematics, and so on. Authors we were reading in school, like Pierre Georges [a French communist resistance leader better known as Colonel Fabien], were writing about "human geography." We were discussing how part of the globe became dominant, how the north related to the south, what was the position of the communist bloc against the capitalist bloc, everything. One teacher told me, "You should study social science if you like this." So I went over to social science, but that meant I had to make a choice, because I was very happy playing the piano. I had a lot of friends in music, friends who were playing harpsichord, baroque flute, lute, and everything.

TS: They were playing early music?

ETL: Yes, the early music movement was flourishing in Rio de Janeiro. I was singing in choruses and it was very interesting, but I felt I had to make a choice, because piano was very rigorous and I had to study five to six hours a day. At that point I was still enrolled in a technical course in the school of music. I was taking the piano classes in order to go to the school of music at the university, but I was also thinking of going into the social sciences, a different choice.

College Life

I had to make a choice. I thought, "Well, I love my friends in the music school. It's very interesting and I like to play the piano, but the social sciences are more important, because we cannot stay inside a room playing the piano when so many things are happening in the world." The School of Music at the Federal University was completely apolitical. That's what I felt, at least. So, I went into social sciences and decided to play the piano as an amateur, but when I got there, I was very disappointed. It was not a good moment. Many professors were persecuted and forced to retire because the political conditions were very hard, so it wasn't a stimulating place to study. There was a small group of young anthropology and political science teachers coming up. This was when I read Lévi-Strauss and Evans-Pritchard for the first time. That opened a different, broader perspective on the social sciences for me: it was not only about capitalism, domination, and underdevelopment, et cetera, but also about different worldviews, different conceptions of time and space, and different conceptions of persons.

TS: Can you explain your first understanding of what social science was?

ETL: My first understanding was that social science had a response for the world inequalities and the world problems. I had an idea that social sciences meant that intellectuals would plan for a new world.

TS: So you imagined an applied social science?

ETL: Yes, but my early social sciences view was a very ethnocentric view of society. Anthropology proposed something completely different, because it tried to relativize notions of social nature, of person, of individual, and this was very important. I fell in love with anthropology.

INNA NARODITSKAYA

In conversation with Ted Solís, October 26, 2007, Columbus, Ohio

Early Life

IN: I was born in Baku, Azerbaijan, in 1955. My grandmother bought us a big black box—an upright piano—and I trained as a pianist from the age of five. My mother always dreamed that I would become a musician. She was a pediatrician and a Hero of the Second World War. My father was the chief electrical engineer of the Azerbaijani underground system (Metro). I remember being ten years old, coming home, and telling my mother, "I forgot who I am!" I knew I was not Azeri, so I asked her, "Am I Armenian or Jewish?" Well, I'm not Armenian; I'm Jewish with some mix. I hardly know I'm Jewish, though.

TS: Jewish from Azerbaijan? Perhaps there's a sense of "otherness" that feeds into what you do now?

IN: I think "otherness" is a side of us all and how we fill the void; it affects our preferences in a given situation. To tell you that I grew up in anti-Semitic circumstances or that I grew up Jewish, neither would be true. I can't tell any such juicy stories; there was no anti-Semitism. In fact, I was very proud when I learned who I was. In Azerbaijan back then it didn't matter.

TS: What languages did you speak at home?

IN: Mostly Russian. On the street we spoke Azeri, but we went to Russian schools because they provided the best education. I went through traditional musical education in the Soviet Union. I began at a specialized music school that paralleled the public school, then went to music college, and finally to conservatory.

College Life

I studied in Moscow for one year as a pianist, but also got a degree in historical musicology. At that time it was pretty unusual for a person from the Azerbaijan Conservatory to write a thesis on Britten's *Midsummer Night's Dream*. You might think it's Eurocentric, but in the Soviet Union they thought we shouldn't be indiscriminately Eurocentric! We had to study Bach, Mozart, and Beethoven. By studying *Midsummer Night's Dream*, I was doing something different.

TS: You were already moving beyond the canon. Why was it unusual for someone *also* to get a degree in historical musicology?

IN: It was unusual, but not exceptional; my musicology degree was secondary. All good Azerbaijani musicologists are primarily performers. That was the fashion of the place. I can't explain it, but even Azerbaijani composers typically performed their own pieces. That's not always typical of Soviets.

TS: Do you think of yourself more as Soviet or Azerbaijani?

IN: At the time there was no division. It was more a matter of "urban versus rural" not "Soviet versus Azerbaijani." Anyone in the urban environment constituted the intelligentsia, no matter what ethnicity they were. We were all Soviet Azerbaijani because we were essentially the product of a Soviet educational and cultural system. The separation only became apparent in the late 1980s.

I performed for several years until I got married. It was very difficult in Azerbaijan to be married and work, so I got a teaching position in the school of music. I became chair of the Musicology and Theory Department and remained there until ethnic conflict and later war between the Azerbaijanis and Armenians broke out. When the full war began in 1990, I left Azerbaijan with my four-year-old son. We passed through Vienna to Rome and my son, Nick Naroditski, went to an Italian kindergarten. I learned Italian quickly and worked in a clinic as a Russian-Italian interpreter. After ten months, we received permission to come to the United States as refugees. Despite having very limited English, I got a job teaching piano and being an accompanist at the University of Michigan at Flint. My studio grew quickly because I was extremely successful at attracting international students during the four or five years I worked there. The only problem was that I played too much and damaged my hand. By 1994 or '95 I couldn't play anymore; that's how ethnomusicology came into the picture. I was still an adjunct lecturer at the time, not getting paid enough for the amount of work I did, but I had to provide for myself and my son.

The chair of my department, who was also the choir conductor, tried to help me keep my job. She offered to give me a lecture course and gave me three choices: Music Appreciation, a course on Romanticism, or World Music Cultures. I didn't really understand what Music Appreciation was and Romanticism seemed a bit limited, so

I thought, "I've passed through five countries—Azerbaijan, Russia, Austria, Italy, and Georgia—and I know a bit about Muslim cultures, so the World Music Cultures course might be interesting." My chair agreed, and I taught two years of "World Musicology" without actually knowing what "ethnomusicology" was!

TS: What did you do in that World Music Cultures class?

IN: I had to cover the bases with all the creativity I could possibly draw upon. The class was not just for music majors, so I aimed for a broad range of humanity. I covered my lack of English proficiency by basing the course on individual student research. From the start, while studying diverse cultures, each student had to choose a topic and geo-cultural area and do research through the semester that combined the study of music with their own professional area. In my second year, for example, one student worked on an Australian aboriginal tribe. She brought a live baby alligator to the class, which really engaged everyone! The course became incredibly successful.

Clara Henderson

In conversation with Ted Solís, October 28, 2007, Columbus, Ohio

Early Life

CH: I was born in Walkerton, Ontario, Canada, in September 1955. I lived there until I was six, when we moved to Woodstock, Ontario. My father was a Presbyterian minister. My mother trained as a music teacher but was a stay-at-home mom for most of my childhood. She started us off with piano. We also did a lot of singing together as a family. In high school I played in bands and started to learn songs from records. I'd go to the stereo, put the needle on the record, and run to the piano to find out what note it was. I learned pieces that way. I remember being confused in high school and asking, "Are the Rolling Stones musicians?" I was learning from records, but I was also taking classical music and playing things like Mozart, Beethoven, and Bach. I wondered, "What happened to all the music in between?" It was a bit like trying to reconcile the cavemen and the stories in the Bible or something—"What's that gap in between?" At high school I had to choose between music and art. I'd studied music all my life, so I chose art; I really wanted to do both, but I couldn't.

College Life

Everyone was telling me, "Oh, you should study music at university," but in my mind, music was all that Bach and Beethoven, which I liked, but wasn't that intrigued about studying. When it came to choosing a program, I found that I could study music, visual arts, and dance at York University. I could take a general fine-arts program and major in all of them, so I went to York in 1974. I took a lot of music courses; most of the music people thought I was a music major, but I wasn't. I took visual arts studio, I took dance studios, and in my second year I was introduced to South Indian classical singing and drumming through *solkattu*, the rhythmic recitations, in my General Musicianship class.

TS: You learned solkattu in a General Musicianship class in your sophomore year?

CH: Yes, because we had Trichy Sankaran at York. I had walked by a concert and thought Indian music was kind of interesting, but it didn't hook me. When we started solkattu, though, it was something else altogether. I grew up loving rhythm. I always connected it to my Mum rocking me when I was a kid. I would listen to the little clock beside my bed and make rhythms with my teeth. I got hooked by solkattu and decided to take drumming and singing the following year. Jon Higgins was teaching singing. I signed up for both courses, something they didn't normally allow students to do. The singing and drumming students had theory class together with Sankaran, and then they'd break off and have drumming or singing lessons separately. It was all oral tradition, and I found my niche by learning aurally. I worked really hard at both because I knew they'd say "Well, we told you so" if I couldn't keep up. I learned theory well because I knew it counted for both my grades. I loved it and really took off, so much so that I became Sankaran's teaching assistant.

At the same time, Bob Becker from Nexus (a Toronto-based percussion group) was teaching Ghanaian drumming, so I signed up for that. All our courses at York were yearlong, so I took Ghanaian drumming and South Indian classical music at the same time. I also worked with Russell Hartenberg, who had studied at Wesleyan with Abraham Adzenyah for a while. When I started to play Ghanaian music, it was like I found my home. I felt bad in a way, because it was like cheating on South Indian music. I loved it, but somehow the Ghanaian music really spoke to me. I think it was because I could move my body. You can move your body in South Indian classical music, but it's a very controlled movement. With Ghanaian drumming, when you're playing the bell pattern, you can be doing dance steps—it's a whole different interaction with the music—and that really appealed to me.

TS: Was it the difference that appealed or the African style of interaction?

CH: The African style of interaction resonated with me, though I found it odd, because I thought, "Why does this music resonate with me? I've never been to Africa; I don't know any Africans."

TS: When did you get the feeling that this was music and you could study it?

CH: York was very progressive in those days—the 1970s. I still remember when Abraham Adzenyah came and we did concerts in all sorts of places, including the Mariposa Folk Festival. When we played at York, we played in an auditorium, and our final

Highlife piece lasted forty-five minutes. The whole audience was dancing and half of them were up on stage. Then we went to play at the University of Toronto, which at the time was a very disciplined school of music with opera and orchestra, and the students hardly moved! For me, it highlighted the difference between the two schools and the types of music they taught. When I finished school, Sankaran encouraged me to go to Wesleyan to study *mrdangam* and go further with Indian music, but I felt pulled by this African music, too. I knew they taught both at Wesleyan.

TS: Do you remember when you first heard the word "ethnomusicology"?

CH: At York, they called it "World Music." I think there was actually a course that had something to do with ethnomusicology (though it wasn't called "Intro to Ethno"), taught by Bob Witmer or Steve Otto. I never took it; the term seemed too elitist to me. My impression was that it had something to do with studying different musics around the world.

MOHD. ANIS MD. NOR

In conversation with Margaret Sarkissian, March 17, 2009, Northampton, Massachusetts

Early Life

MA: I was born in Penang, Malaysia, in November 1955. As early as six years old, I was encouraged by my late grandaunt to do all kinds of dancing to music from the radio. She said that unlike other children, I moved with the tune. That was about 1961–'62, a period when there was a very interesting shift in Malayan popular music as *bangsawan* film music turned into a newly created Malay nouveau music. I was doing all this even though there was nothing for me to learn from. There was no TV. I was dancing from memories of what I had seen in the movies. When I was in Primary 4 (age ten), I was selected by the school to be a "star performer." From that point onward I realized that I was different from the rest of the kids.

MS: What did being a "star performer" involve?

MA: With a little prodding from the teachers, my talent just came out! We had a British legacy that included a horrendously long Speech Day that exhausted people, followed by an entertainment by the school's best talents. I never missed being a star from Primary 4 to Primary 6. That made me strut! That was what made me feel like going to school, because I wasn't a brilliant kid. It gave me a sense of belonging, pride, and acknowledgment. In my all-boys' school there were plenty of sportsmen and intelligent boys, but there were very few talented boys who could do music and dancing.

MS: What kind of dances did you perform?

MA: They were mixed. Our teachers had graduated from colleges that replicated British teacher training, so you can imagine what they learned: square and folk dancing, clogging, and stuff like that. And then, because it's Malaysia, we would also do Eurasian stuff, Chinese stuff, Indian stuff, and Malay stuff. I never thought about art being demarcated according to ethnic lines. I thought it was joyous to do everything.

MS: Did you have any musical training at that time?

MA: Not formally. I learned what I could in school. I learned the basic rhythmic stuff and a little bit of recorder, but nothing more than that. It was only when I went to high school that I wished I had done music, but I never took music lessons because it was costly. Everything came from the gramophone that my mother and father played in the house for all of us. That's when I got training from my parents, because they both taught dancing in school. That was a fun part. We were very musical in a way; we could hum tunes very well, but we never picked up any instruments.

MS: You said your parents taught dance. Were they schoolteachers?

MA: Yes, they were primary schoolteachers. My dad was a graduate of Sultan Idris Training College in Tanjung Malim, and my mum went to Malacca Women's Teachers' College. These were the best places men and women could study in pre-Independence Malaya. They came back to teach in primary schools. Both parents were sports people and thus taught dance, because dance was part of physical education. They would even spend time, fortnightly, at the famous Eastern and Oriental Hotel and dance in the ballroom there. When the E&O became less popular, in the mid-to-late '60s, they began to go to proper nightclubs, good nightclubs, which served more than just the ballroom dancing at the E&O. They brought these new dance steps back to us kids in the house and we would dance together. I would pair up with my mum, and my sister paired up with my dad. My parents considered psychomotor ability a crucial part of growing up, because we were not privileged in the way that rich kids were, with proper music lessons and so on. In lieu of that, they gave us dance.

College Life

The transition to university was a nightmare for me. I had spent fourteen years in English-medium schools and then suddenly, overnight, ended up in a Malay-medium college, Universiti Malaya. I survived because I was very interested in literature and had been an orator and debater in school, so I was versatile in both languages.

MS: Why Universiti Malaya?

MA: I went there because I had no choice. I wanted to be a law student. I got a place to study law in England but no scholarship. My dad said to me, "Since you'd love to go to England and do your law degree, you can go, but I'll have to mortgage the only brick house that we have, so you will have to study hard and come back so that you can help me put your two sisters through college." That house meant a lot to him, yet he was willing to mortgage it and send me to England. I also had an offer from the government of Malaysia, giving me a full scholarship to go to Universiti Malaya and do a degree in the arts and social sciences. I had very mixed feelings.

I decided to let go of my law dreams and ended up majoring in Southeast Asian studies. I took French and some law courses, because they would help me get into international studies. I was aiming to become a diplomat, because at least I could still travel. But in my second year I met Krishen Jit, who became my mentor and opened up a completely new world for me: the world of the performing arts, the world of theater, music, and dance. It was under him that I embarked on an intensive study of the *boria* dance theater of Penang for my BA thesis. That was a real stepping-stone in my scholarship. It made me question everything that I had taken for granted. Before I took my final exam, I decided that I wasn't going to be a diplomat, but that I would be the first Malaysian to do something that nobody had done before in the performing arts. I remained one more year as a teaching assistant and finally got a scholarship to Hawai'i.

MS: What did your parents think about your desire to become a diplomat? Were they supportive when you changed your mind?

MA: My father had no problem. He was willing to let me be whatever I wanted. He knew that I sacrificed my dream of doing law in England because I didn't want to jeopardize the family property. My mum was different. She was protective because I'm the only son and the firstborn. She said, "I will not stop you from doing anything you wish, but please, not the diplomatic services." So I thought, well, I can do music or dance without her being angry with me! When I told her about the scholarship and the place in Hawai'i, she was very supportive because she felt safe.

MS: So how does a boy from Penang end up at the University of Hawai'i?

MA: Through Krishen Jit. I said, "Look Krishen, I want to do something that is scholarly, but fun." He pondered, looked at me, and asked if I was ready to go to Hawai'i or Michigan. He said, "Hawai'i will offer you the best of both worlds. You will do East and West at the same time and you will have good people to work with." In Michigan, he said, I'd work with Judith Becker, "a rare scholar who will benefit someone like you, because she doesn't straddle a conservative, one-tracked mindset. I like Michigan because it's a very good university, but it's cold." Both places accepted me. When I got their offers, I went back to Krishen and asked what to do. He said, "I think you should check out Hawai'i. It's a smaller university, and it will prepare you better. You can do your doctorate at Michigan." So he lined it all up.

At that very moment, Ric Trimillos found out I had applied to Hawai'i. He was in Malaysia as a consultant to the MARA Institute of Technology, Music Department.

He made a point of seeing me and took me out to lunch. He said, "Anis, these are the things we provide, these are things you will learn; it is a small university, you will get to know your professors better and they will have more time for you." He was very convincing and friendly. I knew he was from the music school and did ethnomusicology, but I had very little knowledge of what ethnomusicology or dance ethnology were.

MS: Do you remember the first time you heard the word "ethnomusicology"?

MA: Yes: it came out of Krishen's mouth. I was doing a lot of work with theater production at the time. I was the choreographer, did some arranging, and played a lot of percussion. Krishen looked at me and said, "You're so talented, Anis, it's a shame you don't have formal training in this. I think you should go and get your knowledge in ethnomusicology." I asked him what the hell it was.

MS: What was your perception of the field at that point?

MA: When he said "ethnomusicology," I had a romantic notion of ethnomusicology as something to do with traveling—the adventurer traveling all over. I had a picture of an anthropologist, carrying heavy gear to record stuff and then going off to have fun. Then Krishen gave me Judith Becker's *Traditional Music in Modern Java* [1980] and Victor Turner's *From Ritual to Theater* [1982] and said, "I want you to read these two books. Don't ask me why, just read them. If you cannot finish, never mind, but you have to read them." It was hard because I never realized fun was difficult, but then, when I began to get into the whole notion of time, frame, and all that, suddenly I was in the conversation with him. That was what he wanted. He wanted me to be curious, to ask him questions. He confessed he had no answers and was only ahead of me by a few paragraphs!

That was when I realized that there was no book on dancing; there were books about ethnomusicology and ritual and theater. I said, "What about dancing?" He said, "Well, you just cannot go and dance and come back with a degree. You say you want to be fun and scholarly, right? These are fun guys. Look at what they have done with the knowledge and scholarship. You want to be as invisible as Becker is, but you have a sense that she's there in the book. You want to be as invisible as Turner is, but you know Turner's spirit is in it."

That put me on a completely different trajectory. I said, "Oh my God, this is serious stuff." And Krishen said, "Yes, Hawai'i is like that. It's like being on a sandy beach, you just choose the pebbles that you want." I thought that sounded fun. And Ric Trimillos convinced me. He said, "Our program is good. It's the only music department in America where the dance ethnology program is kept together with the ethnomusicology program. So in other words, you'll get the best training in both worlds." That sealed my decision. I wrote to Judith Becker and told her that I was sorry to decline her offer and would go to UH, but hoped that when I could come back for my doctorate, she would still accept me. Judith wrote me a wonderful letter. She was very supportive and said, "Finish your degree at UH; any UH graduate is our first priority at U of M." I felt so good. So that's how it was.

Frederick C. Lau

In conversation with Ted Solís and Margaret Sarkissian, October 26, 2008, Middletown, Connecticut

Early Life

FL: I was born in February 1957 in the former British colony of Hong Kong, which is now part of PRC China, SAR. We lived on a small island called Cheung Chau, an hour by ferry from the main city. It had about twenty-five thousand to thirty thousand people, but no cars. I went to a normal Chinese-language primary school. The only music we had was a once-a-week class with singing—regular folk and school songs usually accompanied by a small, portable, one-rank reed organ. I came from an average family. My parents didn't go to college or do anything musical. My dad worked in an office in town. My mom was a housewife. I grew up in an extended family with twenty-two people in the house—my great grandmother, grandparents, aunts, uncles, and cousins. Four generations in one house. Typically we just ran around the mountain and the beach, like rural kids. I remember one time when I was a kid, my uncle came home from Catholic English boarding school with a Beatles album. We thought, "Wow, this is cool stuff!" My cousins and I imitated the Beatles with badminton rackets and upside-down tin cans.

MS: Did you have a record player in the house?

FL: Yes. We didn't have TV, so the prize things in the house were the radio and record player. My grandma from time to time would listen to Teochew opera on her own.

MS: Did you see any street opera or music at the temple?

FL: There was Cantonese street opera and festivals, but when I was growing up, those weren't things that kids wanted to do. That was old people's stuff. When I heard the Beatles—*that* was really fascinating. It was what the people in town had, the people who grew up speaking English or had access to English stuff.

TS: When did you start learning English?

FL: We had English language in primary school, but beginning junior high, everything switched to English. If you got caught speaking Chinese, they fined you. We took exams, and then the government sent us to a high school, depending on the results.

I flunked the first time. The second time I got into a British technical school run by the government. Everything was in English except the subject of Chinese. The school trained us to be civil or mechanical engineers.

Some of the upperclassmen played guitar, which I thought was really cool. I bought myself a cheap guitar and said, "I can learn this—you just place your fingers." I bought a book to learn the chords and taught myself to play guitar and sing along. I was really into Peter, Paul, and Mary, and Joan Baez, so I copied them and figured out the picking, just by listening. The school also had a free violin class. My teacher said, "Oh you like music? You should sign up." So I joined the class, played up to third position, and then said, "This is no fun, I like Peter, Paul, and Mary better." I hooked up with another guy from my island who knew a Portuguese-Chinese girl, Anne Marie Gutierrez, from his sister's convent school; she had a beautiful voice. She said, "Maybe we should form a group and imitate Peter, Paul, and Mary." I said, "Why not?" I was the guitarist, so my job was to figure out all the chords, the picking, and everything. And then we figured out the harmonies and stuff like that together. All by ear from records because we couldn't read music. We entered a local competition run by the Catholic Association. We won, singing Peter, Paul, and Mary, and then got invited to do concerts.

Then a couple of guys on the island knew I played guitar and invited me to join their rock band. They were doing The Who, Deep Purple, that kind of stuff. I said, "OK, I'm game." So we did the same thing, sat together and figured out licks from recordings. I remember borrowing an electric guitar and a drum set and bringing them home. I was practicing drums and my grandpa came down and chewed me out. He was mad because playing band had a really bad image. This was just when we had GCE O-Levels in high school and I flunked, big time. My grandpa chewed out my dad, "Your son is supposed to be engineer. What is he doing? He's flunking out and playing bad music." My dad was mad because his father was scolding him. So he scolded me, too, and made me take the exams again. The second time I passed. I was still singing in the group and playing in the rock band, though I was getting bored with the band. I had seen a picture of a Filipino band that used a flute—this was the time of Sergio Mendes and the Brasil 66. I saw a cheap metal flute in the music store; it was on sale, made in China, and cost about 250 Hong Kong dollars. I thought since I taught myself to play guitar, I could play this thing. So I bought the flute and a book, *A Tune a Day*. I opened the book and saw there was fingering. It looked easier than guitar because you simply push the fingering, blow, and get sound. So I took it home and started practicing. After a few months, my sister said, "Why there's no sound coming out? It just says *pfffft*." I said, "I don't know why." I bought another book. It didn't help!

All this was in contrast to other kinds of music going on in Hong Kong and on the island that I deliberately distanced myself from—Chinese music—Chinese opera on the radio, street opera performances, and all that. This is the stuff I'm writing about now, but then I felt it was backward stuff that was not cool. Sometimes my older sister would sing Cantonese opera and I would say, "That's junk, that's not music." That was the context. I had a flute but couldn't make any sound or read music. I was playing in a rock band where you just chart everything. Finally I decided, "OK, I'm going to ask someone to teach me how to play this thing." I looked in the newspaper but it was really expensive to take lessons.

At that time the Hong Kong Philharmonic was trying to popularize classical music, so they advertised really cheap instrumental classes in the newspaper. Ten people in a class; you pay twenty Hong Kong dollars a month and get four lessons. My sister said, "Hey, there's something cheap, you should go and learn how to play this thing properly." So I went. I was kind of cocky, because I played guitar. I told the teacher—he was American, the principal flutist of the Philharmonic—"I taught myself to play guitar and I know all the fingerings, I just need to get a good sound. There's no sound." He looked at me and said, "Sit down, this is a class." It was a group class and a twelve-year-old kid came out—I was about seventeen—and played, just like that! I asked the teacher, "How do you do that? It's really good. All I want to do is to play like that and I'm cool." And he said, "Well, come to class every week." I learned how to count notes and read music. That was the beginning of my classical music training. I thought, "Wow, this music is very different from rock music and all the stuff I know." So I asked my teacher, "What do you do in your orchestra?" He said, "If you want to know, come to a rehearsal and see." So I went to the rehearsal and there was a lot of yelling. Then he said, "Come to the concert." He gave me a ticket. I went to the concert and in five minutes, I was gone. I slept through the whole thing. That was the beginning of my musical education. And, in the meantime, I flunked my GCE O-Levels.

College Life

My dad said, "One more chance and that's it for your education, you'll have to find a job." I said, "OK." I passed second time, so my dad said, "Well, you passed, but you cannot go to a good school, so your chance of getting into university is close to zero. Why don't you just finish Form 6 and then get a job." So I went to Form 6. At that time, there were two university systems. One was Hong Kong University, British system, three years; the other was the Chinese University of Hong Kong, American system, four years. For the three-year system, you needed Form 6 and 7. At CUHK, you only needed Form 6. So I thought, I'll study one year and take the entrance exam to CUHK.

I flunked, of course. I was still learning how to play the flute and I was still playing in the group. I was not studying, and my grandpa was pretty pissed off. I repeated the year and passed the second time around, but my grades weren't good enough to get into CUHK. There was one last chance, Hong Kong Baptist College, a private university that took all the leftover people. So I said, "Dad, I don't want to repeat again and I can't get into Form 7. This is the last four-year college I could get into. I could get a banker's job or something afterward." My dad said, "OK, if you can get in." So I went there and they said, "You're too late." I said, "I want to study TV, because I'm singing in a group and I've been on TV." They said, "No, it's all full. We only have two vacancies right now, one in Chinese literature and one in English literature. That's it. If you can get into either one, we'll take you." Chinese or English? I had studied English, so at least I had a good background; I had never studied classical Chinese literature. So I became an English major, studying Homer, the Iliad, and literary criticism. I had an old professor from Oxford. I said, "Wow! This is really easy." "Why?" he said. "Well, you read the story and then you go to class and you just bullshit. It's really easy to do!"

Baptist had a music department. The department chair knew that I carried my flute around, so one day he said, "We have an orchestra, if you want to learn how to play flute in orchestra, you can come." I said, "I only have six months of these flute classes. I'll play for you what I can play, but I can play better guitar." He said, "Oh, just sit next to the guy and learn." So I got involved with them. I went to practice all the time. After the first year I was very happy, studying literature and playing flute. Then my friend said, "Hey, since you like music so much and your results are good enough to get into CUHK, where they have a better music department, why don't you apply there?" I had nothing to lose, so I applied. The CUHK Music Department had its own entrance exam—performance exam, written exam, oral exam, and an interview. I played a Grade 4, Royal Schools of Music exam piece, a Bach Minuet, really short and not very good. I knew nothing about theory so I asked, "How do you prepare?" They gave me *The Rudiments*, you know, the little red book? To cut a long story short, the only reason they took me was because they only had one clarinet, one flute, and one violin apply; everybody else was learning piano. I was the only flute. I became a music major and my grandfather refused to talk to me.

After the first semester, the theory teacher said, "I think you need to find a different major for next semester. You have no hope in this department." I was really discouraged but my friend said, "You need to fight this guy. You cannot let him push you around." That was the beginning of my serious engagement with classical music. I started practicing eight hours a day. I studied and slept only three or four hours. At the end of the third year, I came second in the exams and got a DAAD scholarship—a German academic exchange—for cultural study over the summer.

By my final year I was a double major in performance and composition and was playing for the Hong Kong Philharmonic. It was all Western music except for one compulsory class on Chinese music history. My attitude was the same as everyone else's—nobody wanted to go to that class. The teacher was old, and everyone was falling asleep. The only one paying attention was Larry Witzleben, an American exchange student. The rest of us thought, "What is that crap?" At the break, we'd go out to have coffee and only Larry and a few girls came back. But in the exams at the end of the final year, I came first in the class, above all the pianists with their diplomas.

MICHAEL TENZER

In conversation with Ted Solís, October 27, 2007, Columbus, Ohio

Early Life

MT: I was born in Queens, New York, in May 1957. When I was about seven or eight, my mother took a course at the New School with Henry Cowell just before he died. I remember her telling me about Cowell: how he had been imprisoned in California, how he was so crazy for music that he would compose in his imagination in his cell, and about his interest in world musics. I also remember her taking me to Indian restaurants, and to an art exhibit of a young painter my age from India whose work was exhibited at the Asia Society. She played the violin in a community orchestra that was so bad, they had to stop in the middle of movements! When I was about eleven, after my folks divorced and my mother was looking to restart things for herself, she had the orchestra rehearsing in our living room! My dad also loved music, but he didn't play. He was a salesman and a politically liberal New Yorker. I grew up with a lot of that consciousness. I went to Vietnam demonstrations with my parents; I was tear-gassed in Washington when I was ten.

TS: What was your musical background?

MT: I was self-taught. I started playing piano by myself when I was eight and learned Beatles songs and other music I liked. I didn't study formally until I got to college, though I knew I wanted to be a composer by the time I was in high school. I loved composing songs and got together with a friend when I was about thirteen or fourteen to write a rock opera. I was loving jazz, ragtime, and other kinds of music, trying to write for all of them. I became interested in Charles Ives while I was still in high school. I went to the Bronx High School of Science, the partner school of Stuyvesant, in New York City. I was into science, but even there I was the Music Nerd.

TS: Did you teach yourself to read music?

MT: Yes, I was a slow reader, but I knew harmonies and chord structures. I could do jazz voicings and any chord progression at the keyboard and could play by ear really well.

TS: You mentioned being taken to Indian restaurants as a child. Did you have any interest in "exotica" or find yourself attracted to other cultures?

MT: I think jazz was, in a way, exotic for me. Also, when I was in high school, I took some extension courses on electronic music at the Manhattan School of Music and the New School, with Elias Tanenbaum and John Watts. I got into Cage and Stockhausen by babysitting for interesting upstairs neighbors in our apartment house and listening to their records.

College Life

I went to Yale in 1974, and my freshman year was a turning point. Two things happened. One was that the freshmen musicians around me were all classical performers. I was terribly intimidated by students who knew every Beethoven and Mozart opus number, and I became keen to assert a different kind of musical identity. The other thing was that I fell in with the Yale Jazz Ensemble. The ensemble's trap drummer, Frank Bennett, was married to a South Indian woman, Gita Ramanathan. Her father, S. Ramanathan, was an important South Indian musician and part of the nearby Wesleyan scene in the early '70s. Frank took me under his wing and said, "Let's listen to music together." I was seventeen or eighteen; he was probably thirty, doing his DMA in composition at Yale. (He eventually went into the film industry and is now an orchestrator in Hollywood.)

Frank took me to his house and picked out a reel-to-reel tape of *nagaswaram*. He said, "These people are coming for a house concert next week and you can come if you want." He put the tape on and said, "You hear that?" I said, "Yes," but of course, I didn't know what I was listening for. "You divide each beat into seven, you divide each seventh in two and then again in seven and you've got ninety-eight." I thought this was much cooler than anything else I was learning, so I went to the concert and sat as close to the *tavil* player as you and I are sitting right now. You know how Steve Reich says in his book that it's like having a tidal wave wash over you? That was the effect.

Frank was a great composer. He was composing big-band suites based strictly on South Indian *kriti* forms. That fall the ensemble played his "G-Song," a white-note, Mixolydian-mode piece, about half an hour long. It was an ecstatic concert! He also wrote a Karnatak violin concerto, which L. Subramaniam played when he came to New Haven in 1977. This was long before fusion became commonplace. It was a great time to be at Yale. All the composers were writing twelve-tone, super-modern dissonant music, but at home they were hanging out in kitchens with their friends, listening to world music and talking about it. That's the bug I caught.

TS: Were you listening to those old Nonesuch albums?

MT: Yes. These composers came out of the whole American experimentalist world music tradition: Henry Cowell and Lou Harrison. Even though my teachers didn't like Cowell or Harrison's music—it was too "washed out" for them—they were blown away by the system. You know how it is? Composers love systems—they love design, architecture, and all that stuff.

As a music major, I learned Western theory and history, the repertoire, and played Schumann and Bach on the piano. I did the whole music sequence and was completely hungry for musical intake. I spent all my time buying records, listening for hours every night, lights out. One day, at the end of my second year, I ran into David Lopato, the former pianist of the jazz ensemble. He had graduated the previous year and gone to CalArts, where he played in the gamelan. He used to date my cousin, so we were sort of friends. He started talking to me about gamelan. It was only a two-minute conversation in which he said, "It's really great; you have to check it out some time," but being the kind of person I was, I went immediately to a record store, and bought a gamelan recording. It turned out to be a Balinese gamelan record, the Nonesuch LP *Golden Rain*, with *kecak* on one side and "Hudjan Mas" and "Oleg Tumbelilingan" on the other [Lewiston 1969]. I still have my original copy. I went back to my room, opened the shrink wrap, put the record on, and two minutes later I said, "This is it; I want to do that."

TS: What was it about Balinese gamelan that turned you on?

MT: It was just brilliant, dynamic, breathless, precise. Even though at the time I didn't know anything and didn't have the words, now I know what the words are. First, I heard a tight organization of people. It takes so much work to play music that tightly. I loved the discipline and order. At some level, I knew it was there and it was compelling. And second, it stimulated my compositional imagination. It was like orchestral music, but *hot*.

TS: Do you remember when you first heard the word "ethnomusicology"?

MT: It was probably in my third year, when Mantle Hood came as a visiting professor. Hood had recently left UCLA and was freelancing, teaching seminars at Yale and Wesleyan. I don't remember having heard the word before then. Apart from me, the seminar was all graduate students. I was quite a bit younger than everyone else. It was very emotional for me somehow. I was a crazy kid, surrounded by grad students who were scared to show too much of themselves and felt nervous that they were going to be judged. But I was very vocal in class and caught Hood's attention. During the term, he took us up the road to Wesleyan, where we had a gamelan lesson with the Javanese musician Sumarsam, who had arrived not long before.

I had never seen or played a Balinese instrument, but I was completely determined to go to Bali. Mantle Hood ultimately helped me make contacts in Bali. So did another professor at Yale, Willie Ruff, the French hornist, who had been there. By this time I had gotten Colin McPhee's book, *Music in Bali* [1966]. I was completely hooked, so I applied for a Yale summer traveling fellowship. I wrote a proposal, did my legwork, and got someone in Bali to write a letter of invitation. I received the fellowship and, as soon as my third year finished, went to Bali. I was nineteen going on twenty.

That was 1977. It was my first time abroad. I traveled all around the island—in those days there weren't many foreigners there—and studied music like crazy. I didn't have any consciousness of research or anything except to learn to play. I had two main teachers, Nyoman Sumandhi in Denpasar and Wayan Gandera in Peliatan. I played music, all day every day, and learned to speak Indonesian. I had enough credits at Yale to take the fall semester off and still graduate on time. After six months in Bali, I went back to New Haven in time for my final semester. I finished that spring and applied for another traveling award that was available for seniors. The grant was something that still exists, a Watson Fellowship, though it had a different name at Yale. I was successful, so after I graduated I went back to Bali for a full year.

In the meantime I had applied to grad school in composition at Berkeley and was accepted for fall 1978. When I went back to Bali, I deferred my admission for a year. The whole other part of my life was my very close relationship with my composition professors. I loved music theory and all my classes. I was writing chamber music and getting it performed; my first orchestral composition was played in my senior year.

TS: Was it Balinese influenced?

MT: That piece, not really. But during my first stay in Bali, I sat up at night and composed a jazz big-band arrangement of Thelonious Monk's "Epistrophy" with a Balinese orchestration. I wrote interlocking parts to accompany the melody and used many other techniques. That was also performed in my senior year. I consistently used Balinese ideas in my music for some time after that.

I went back to Bali for the year, from the fall of '78 through the summer of '79, and started getting seriously into drumming. During that time I turned twenty-one and inherited a small trust fund—about three thousand dollars—and decided to use it to buy some gamelan instruments. I didn't really know what I was doing, but felt that I had to have instruments, so I ordered some—this must have been the late fall of 1978—and asked my parents to cable the money to the bank in Bali. I just ordered a few because that was all I could afford. One day I got a message that the money had arrived at the bank, and when I got there, the place was in chaos. Some kind of financial panic had occurred. I went in and discovered that just ten minutes before, the *rupiah* had been devalued by 200 percent. My money had quadrupled. By acting quickly, before inflation hit, I was able to buy a whole gamelan. That's how I got a gamelan.

OLABODE (BODE) OMOJOLA

In conversation with Margaret Sarkissian, March 4, 2013, Northampton, Massachusetts

Early Life

BO: I was born in Ado-Ekiti in Western Nigeria in June 1958. Now it's a big city and the capital of its state, but back then it was a relatively small town. I grew up like a normal Yoruba child. I followed masquerades—ancestral venerating masks—singing behind them or running after them. I took part in annual yam-eating ceremonies and also in little moonlight games within my compound in the evenings. The elders would gather us together and narrate folktales, which usually go with music. These were my childhood experiences, which speak to how I was taking an active role in musical activities around me.

My family was relatively privileged. Not that my parents were rich, but they had enough to send me to a good high school and a prestigious university. My father was a tailor, and my mother worked in a textile factory. My father was eager to make me go to school and have the proper education he never had. Whatever resources he had, he expended them on my education. On a typical day I would go to school, come back in the afternoon, go to my father's shop and help with tailoring activities like fitting buttons and so on. Then we would go back home in the evening, and if there was moonlight, we would take part in some musical activities and listen to our parents tell us stories and make us sing. There was traditional music all around me. My mother is a beautiful singer, so on many such occasions she was the one leading the folktale narration.

Things began to change when was I about ten and finishing my primary schooling. Both my parents were strong Christians, so I encountered another kind of music, missionary church music. I joined the choir and was exposed to Western hymns, Protestant hymns, and to compositions by Nigerian composers who were trying to make Christian religious music more relevant to the people. These two traditions were very strong in the church—Nigerian-type and British-type Christian religious music. We did things like Handel's *Messiah* when I was in the church choir. And that continued when I went to a high school run by Anglican missionaries.

MS: When you were learning these choral pieces, did you have instrumental accompaniment as well?

BO: No, only piano and organ. That was actually how I started playing the organ, because there was an organ in the school chapel that no one was playing. I had been exposed to that kind of music a few years before and was lucky to meet some seniors from the upper classes who taught me to read Western staff notation. I began to play hymns at the high school, and by the time I finished high school, I could play the "Hallelujah Chorus"! The Anglican bishop lived in our school compound. One day he was passing the chapel and heard someone playing the organ. He came in and he said, "Oh! I didn't know we had such talented kids in this school." I said, "Well, my Lord Bishop, I'm just learning," and he replied, "What you know is *more* than enough to come out and play for evening services at the Cathedral." That was how I started playing for evening services when I was about thirteen or fourteen. I would spend the entire week learning two hymns to be played on Sunday!

College Life

When people ask, "How did you become an ethnomusicologist?" it's hard to explain that it came from my study of Western classical music. By the time I was finishing high school, it was clear in my mind that I wanted to study music. When you studied music in Nigeria in those days, you studied Western classical music because Nigerian universities were modeled after British universities. So I went to the University of Nigeria for my undergraduate study, a BA in music. It was basically BA in Western music, although we did have one or two traditional ensembles come to campus to make us learn how to play traditional instruments.

MS: Did your parents have any objection to your intention to study music?

BO: Very strong ones! They wanted me to study medicine, law, or engineering because those were—according to them—more fee-paying jobs. And education in Nigeria—I believe maybe all over the world—is a means for attaining upward social mobility. When I entered the university, my parents' idea was for me to study something that could give me economic power when I graduated. So when I said I was going to study music, they were very shocked. My father said, "Music? Look at that guy out there who plays the guitar. He can't even feed himself! He can't feed his wife!" But my mother said, "Look, if they are studying music in the university, then it must be something important because universities are important." It's a kind of naïve philosophy, but one that has some profundity: to go to the university to study music must mean that music is important and also that there must be some kind of hope for jobs when I graduated.

So I went to the University of Nigeria, located in a town called Nsukka. It's the second-oldest university in Nigeria, founded in 1960. I studied music—things like Tonal Harmony, History of Western Music, Keyboard Harmony. We even had an orchestra. I started playing the violin in the orchestra, and I played the piano. It was Western music, pure and simple.

MS: Was there any sense that studying Western music in Nigeria was in some way "weird"?

BO: No, because it represented a modern kind of life, you know? You felt proud that you had some kind of association with famous people around the world: famous conductors, famous pianists, famous composers. You felt connected to this kind of metropolitan culture. You felt proud that you were part of this elite group; it didn't feel strange.

MS: So it was cultural capital in a way?

BO: Exactly! Especially for someone like me who also knew traditional music—during holidays I was still part of the traditional festivals. That always continued. I think the problem we had in Nigeria was that the planners of the musical curricula, who were trained by the British, did not think that traditional music should be incorporated into the curriculum. That has changed now.

MS: So for you at that point, was it like having two separate parts of your musical identity?

BO: It was. Both geographically as well as culturally, because when you go to the university campus, it's a different site, a modern cultural site. The music is different, the culture is different; it's the culture of academics with strong Western ways of doing things. And when I went home, it was a different atmosphere; traditional culture was quite buoyant and lively. So it was like traveling between two different spaces.

It was a four-year program at the university and then you had to go for a mandatory national service. You could work in a village to help build a hospital or teach in a village school that normally would not have a university graduate. That was the point at which I began to re-assess my strong interest in Western classical music. I went to teach in a school where we had some traditional musicians coming to perform on a regular basis, and I began to ask myself, "Why can't one study African music?" That was when I decided to move closer to African music. So when I went for my master's degree, it was in ethnomusicology and African music.

MS: Do you remember the first time you heard the word, "ethnomusicology?" What did it mean to you at the time?

BO: The first time was actually when I was an undergraduate. We had a teacher whose name was Wilberforce Echezona. He had just returned from Michigan State University with a PhD in ethnomusicology and came to teach at my university. He was the first African, I believe, to hold a PhD, but he was a minority: all the other professors were British and Americans teaching Western instruments. We related more to his Western training than the African side of things, but that was the first time I heard the word "ethnomusicology." I only heard it though—it went in through my left ear and came out from my right one.

MS: So the idea was floating around, and then you went off to do your national service.

BO: Exactly, floating around! I began reading literature by some African scholars, and I actually met Mosun Omibiyi-Obidike, a woman who did a PhD in ethnomusicology at UCLA. She was saying things like, "You know, one should study his or her own music." She was one of the people who encouraged me to start thinking about studying African music.

Sean Williams

In conversation with Ted Solís, March 21, 2008, Seattle, Washington

Early Life

SW: I was born in Berkeley, California, in 1959 to an architect and a housewife. I'm the youngest of two; my older brother became an English teacher in Spain. My parents had a house full of Japanese art and a *kabuki* record when I was growing up; I'm sure that was really fundamental to my love of Japan. We used to play the LP when we decorated the Christmas tree. It was a family ritual. You've got to remember, I grew up in Berkeley; they do things differently there.

TS: Do you remember whether it was the Lyrichord or Nonesuch recording?

SW: I think it was actually from Japan, because my parents had been to Japan a bunch of times while my dad was in Korea after the war. When I was four or five, my parents took me to hear Ravi Shankar with tabla player Alla Rakha when they came to Berkeley in 1964. I remember that very clearly; it's one of my earliest memories.

TS: Can you tell me about other childhood musical memories?

SW: When I was three years old, I was in daycare, and a man came in. I'll remember this for the rest of my life; he started playing ragtime on a big upright piano. I *ran* to the piano, pinned my body to it, embraced it, and felt the vibration through my entire body. I felt it all the way down to my feet, which were touching the piano. I don't think I've had that particular sensation since. I came home from daycare and said, "We heard something called the piano today. I want to do that, and I'll do *anything*, Mom and Dad, if you get a piano and let me take lessons." And they said, "Ugh! We don't want to hear anyone practicing; forget it. If you want to play piano, save up your money, and buy yourself a piano." They gave me a guitar for Christmas when I was thirteen, but no piano. From the time I started receiving an allowance, I started saving my dimes and nickels, and Tooth Fairy money, and when I was preteen I started doing little gardening jobs and babysitting jobs. By the time I was fifteen, I had enough money to buy a piano. My parents still didn't want to listen to me practice piano, but at that point I couldn't afford lessons, so I sort of picked away and did my best. I've been very lucky in my music learning in that I pick things up extremely quickly, but I still can't really play the piano.

In my first year at high school I saw some kids playing folk music in a certain place, so I started sitting closer and closer to them. I'd bring my guitar, just to have it in the case next to them. Finally one day, the guitarist was missing, and they said, "Hey, can you play?" And I said, "Yes, I can." At that point I'd memorized all the songs they'd been playing, so I just absorbed myself into their group. It was a folk-revival group, but then we moved into bluegrass. The banjo player turned out to be a flake, so I bought a banjo and started learning to play it. Pretty soon I was the banjo player. So I was in an all-girl bluegrass band and the school's madrigal singers. I sang tenor, alto, soprano, whatever they needed. Around that time there was a Renaissance fair in Marin County (we had moved there when I was in eighth grade) and that was when I first heard live Scottish bagpipes and Irish music. That began my lifelong love of those musics. I was about fifteen at that point, right about when I got the piano.

College Life

By the time I was seventeen and applying to colleges, I had started taking classical guitar lessons, mostly to please my father, who liked classical guitar. I got into UC Berkeley as a classical guitar performance major, even though I'd only been playing for a year and wasn't very good yet. When I got there, I joined the mariachi ensemble, playing *vihuela* and the Javanese gamelan, which was led by Jody Diamond and Pak Cokro. He was already old at that point, but still very dynamic.

TS: Were there any languages in your life during this period?

SW: I had studied French in high school for three years. When I got to college, I studied Irish Gaelic and Old Irish (a much older version of Irish Gaelic) for several years.

I was completely surrounded by music, from the first moment of being at college. At this point I'd added Appalachian dulcimer; I built a hammered dulcimer and taught myself how to play it. I was playing mandolin and had bought a four-string banjo from a boyfriend, so I was playing Irish music on that at open mics; I was also playing Javanese gamelan and still being a classical guitar major. I worked summers at Glacier National Park, where there was a lodge that hired only musicians, dancers, and theater artists. There was a Dishwashers' Chorus and a Bellman's String Quartet, and I was in a girl-group singing quartet called The Magnettes. I worked in the employee cafeteria and was in the house bluegrass band, playing banjo and singing. It was another hothouse environment; we'd get off work and instantly start rehearsing or go hiking. It taught me how to be at ease in performance. I'd say that the stage was set for me to do some kind of work in music. I seriously considered being a professional classical guitarist, but there was another woman classical guitarist at the time, Liona Boyd.

TS: Were you thinking of that as a limited niche?

SW: Exactly—she looked *precisely* like me, and I thought, "I can't do this." Of course, it was very shortsighted, but in a giant school like UC Berkeley you don't have anyone giving you career advice as an undergrad. You're sort of thrown to the wolves. I stumbled onto Alan Dundes, the professor of folklore; he's the one who first said the word "ethnomusicology" to me. This was 1980, right after Merriam died. The thing is, I was already taking world music classes because I loved the music, but no one had said the word "ethnomusicology." I had a meeting with Alan Dundes, because I was thinking of going into folklore, and he said, "Oh, you know, I'm really sorry for all of you ethnomusicologists; you must be in deep mourning over Merriam's death." I hadn't heard of Merriam or ethnomusicology, so I said, "Oh, yes, it's a shame." And he said, "You know, all the ethnomusicologists must be calling each other up"—because, of course, there was no e-mail back then—"and talking about this." And I thought, "All of us whats?" He said, "Ethnomusicology" and "ethnomusicologists"; I just scribbled, "Look up 'ethnomusicology.'" I hadn't heard the word until that moment and wondered why no one in music ever bothered to say "ethnomusicology." It was probably because I was on a classical music track. So I looked it up and thought, "Oh my god, this is who I am! Why did it take a folklorist to tell me that this is my field?"

TS: What was it about that word? What did it represent to you at that moment?

SW: I saw it as a place where I would not be sneered at for being passionate about music, a place where there was room for somebody like me, who hadn't been a violin player from the age of four. I could be a "bluegrass girl" *and* a professional academic.

TS: Where did you get the idea that it had to do with "musical passion"?

SW: What I saw at UC Berkeley among the classical professors and students was a sense of one-upmanship—"my music is better than yours." I didn't see a space for myself in that world, because I didn't respond to that kind of "put-down" learning style. What I saw in Alan Dundes was someone with generosity of spirit. When he said, "You must all be calling each other up," I felt that ethnomusicologists were the kind of people who would call each other up when someone passed away. From the very moment I heard the word, I had an implicit belief about who we are, and it was modeled for me by a folklorist, who himself was the most caring, generous-spirited professor I ever met.

TS: What about the "passionate about musical stuff" idea and the diversity of musical instruments? For some reason, that seemed to be an avenue for you.

SW: Yes. I came to it as a player. But remember, I was a player who had not been allowed to play piano as a kid by my parents. So each time I gained more autonomy, I bought another instrument. And *then* I took Bonnie Wade's "Music of India" course and Bill Malm's courses on Japanese music (he was a visiting professor at UC Berkeley just then). My father is a Japanophile in addition to being an architect, so he had set me up for adoring Japanese music, Buddhism, art, architecture, cherry blossoms in spring—you name it—the whole Japanese scene. So when I hit Bill Malm's class, I thought, "Oh, yeah; this is it!" And I knew, based on how wildly passionate he was about Japan—and he was just crazy about it—that it matched what I felt about music. So I studied with Bonnie Wade and Bill Malm and had already joined the Central Javanese gamelan with Jody Diamond and Pak Cokro. While all this was happening, I was still taking Gaelic language (I'm using "Irish" and "Gaelic" interchangeably here) and still very interested in Irish music. Ethnomusicology allowed me to feel joy, passion, commitment, and deep dedication in a way that the classical music classes did not seem to support or encourage.

Nineteen Sixties

Ethnomusicologists of the late 1920s and 1930s generation are now well into established careers; those of the 1940s generation are entering graduate school and getting jobs.

Soviet Cosmonaut Yuri Gagarin is first to orbit the Earth in 1961. Most remaining French and British African colonies celebrate independence in the early 1960s. American "advisors" to Vietnam increase in number after the 1964 Gulf of Tonkin incident; the Tet Offensive (1968) turns the tide of American public opinion against the Vietnam War. This, plus the assassinations of JFK, Robert Kennedy, and Martin Luther King further erode American 1950s' complacency and faith in government. The Arab-Israeli Six-Day War (1967) exacerbates Middle East political/religious tension; the Chinese Cultural Revolution rages from 1966 to 1976; the Civil Rights Act passes in 1964; the Hollywood Code breaks down by 1968; Mantle Hood introduces the term "bi-musicality" in 1960; the UNESCO Collection of Traditional Music is initiated in 1961; Frank Harrison, Mantle Hood, and Claude Palisca's 1963 volume *Musicology* advocates for a more holistic, less elitist, less stratified musicology of all musics; Bruno Nettl's *Theory and Method in Ethnomusicology* and Alan P. Merriam's *The Anthropology of Music* appear in 1964 (Merriam famously defining ethnomusicology as "the study of music in culture"); Nettl's *Folk and Traditional Music of the Western Continents* (1965) and William P. Malm's *Music Cultures of the Pacific, the Near East, and Asia* (1967), both published by Prentice-Hall, divide the world in the first widely distributed "world music text" survey series; Alan Lomax publishes *Folk Song Style and Culture* (1968), which expounds on his Cantometrics system.

SVANIBOR PETTAN

In conversation with Ted Solís, October 28, 2008, Columbus, Ohio

Early Life

SP: I was born in Zagreb, the capital of Croatia—Yugoslavia at that time—in February 1960. My father, Hubert Pettan [1912–1989], was a music historian, composer, and music educator. He was best known for his research in opera. As a composer, he was known for his art songs, though he also composed an opera and much chamber music. My mother Jagoda was a music teacher. As a family of musicians, we enjoyed playing music together. I remember, for example, at Christmas, my grandmother would play piano, my father violin, my mother recorder, and I played cello. Toward the end of my primary-general and music-school education, I also performed in a pop band with some classmates.

TS: What languages did you know as a child?

SP: My family has mixed origins—Croatian, Slovenian, Austrian, Italian, and Polish. We spoke Croatian at home, but I also used to practice German and Italian with my grandmother and French with my mother, while my multilingual father spoke some Slovene because his father was Slovenian. My grandmother came from the Istrian peninsula, a multiethnic area close to Italy. It was part of the Austro-Hungarian Empire, so German was an official language. Her husband was an officer in the Austro-Hungarian army, and German was clearly a marker of their elite status at that time. She was proud that she never had to work in her life; she just played piano and sewed. I always found that strange.

TS: Did you study German and Italian or just pick them up at home?

SP: German was my first foreign language in primary and secondary school. In secondary school, I added English and later studied Italian for two years as part of my university-level education.

TS: Was Russian common in the former Yugoslavia at that time?

SP: That's an interesting question. At public schools we could choose from four foreign languages—English, French, German, and Russian. At that time, at least in Zagreb and elsewhere in the western part of what was Yugoslavia, many parents took their children out of Russian classes for various reasons, preferring any of the other three languages. Today the tourist industry motivates people to learn Russian because the Russians are common and gracious guests.

College Life

I entered the University of Zagreb in 1978, first the Faculty of Law and, a year later, the Music Academy. After two years, I left law and decided to focus on music. I felt much more comfortable in musicology than in law. Why musicology? Maybe it was related to my father's interest in writing about music. I was not a first-class musician. My instrument in primary and secondary school was cello; I also played French horn for some time. I liked chamber music but never liked playing in orchestras because I couldn't express my own creativity. So I continued playing chamber music and playing other instruments at home. I have a big collection of musical instruments.

TS: Can you remember when you first heard the word "ethnomusicology"?

SP: As a part of my study of musicology there was one class in ethnomusicology, basically Croatian folk music and folk musics of Yugoslavia. At that time I could only find three books dealing with "other" faraway musics in the Music Academy's library: Olga Boone's *Les Tambours du Congo Belge et du Ruanda-Urundi* [1959]; Eta Harich-Schneider's *A History of Japanese Music* [1973]; and Mark Slobin's *Music in the Culture of Northern Afghanistan* [1976]. We also had some early issues of *the world of music* journal and a growing body of publications at the Institute of (Ethnology and) Folklore Research. I gradually began to realize that ethnomusicology was much more than domestic folk music research.

Yugoslavia was a non-aligned country, so many students came from Africa, Asia, and Latin America. I had many friends among them, so I thought, "Why don't I do my bachelor's thesis about African music?" I told my mentor Jerko Bezić that I would like to do fieldwork in Zanzibar. He said, "Well, I never did anything about African music, but my colleague Ankica Petrović, professor in Sarajevo, got her dissertation at Queen's University in Belfast under the guidance of John Blacking." She sent me some materials and remained supportive of my intention to broaden the scope of the discipline in Yugoslavia. I did fieldwork in Zanzibar in 1982 and defended my bachelor's thesis the following year.

Inspired by my experience in a faraway place, I made an exploratory trip, from the very south to the north of Yugoslavia, from Macedonia all the way to Slovenia. At some point during the trip I stopped in a city called Prizren in Kosovo and was amazed to discover that each ethnic community had its own cultural club: Albanians, Serbians, Turks, and Romanies (Gypsies). I instantly fell in love with Prizren.

At that point, I had to do the obligatory one-year military service. This was 1983–84, before my master's thesis. Most of my friends used all sorts of tricks to avoid this service, but I'm very happy that I did it. I went to the officer-in-charge in Zagreb and asked, "If I have to serve in the army, please send me to Prizren." The officer was surprised and demanded an explanation because Kosovo was already a hotspot politically and my request was in a sharp contrast to the mothers who were usually begging her, "Please don't send my son to Kosovo; they will kill him there." So I told her about the culture clubs and the next week I was in the army, soon afterward serving as an instructor for cultural affairs. It was perfect. I established a choir in which the soldiers sang together with local girls. That gave me contact with the civilian domain. Whenever I heard music coming from outside the military barracks, I took the military tape recorder and did research. This was the basis of everything I achieved later in Kosovo.

As a soldier, I got to know many Romany performers in a town quarter that was known for music, and I kept coming back for years after I finished my military service. At some point an old, very respected musician told me, "You're so interested in our music, why don't you come and live with us?" This sounded like a dream, and this dream later came true!

Tomie Hahn

In conversation with Ted Solís, April 18, 2008, Urbana, Illinois

Early Life

TH: I was born in 1960 in Mount Kisco, New York, but spent some of my childhood in Tokyo. My parents were both visual artists. My mother was Japanese American; my father was German American, although he was a specialist in Asian art. My father wanted to study in Tokyo, so the whole family went, from when I was four to maybe about six. My parents put me in public school, but after school, they had me take Japanese traditional dance, *Nihon buyo*. When we came back to the States, they found a teacher who taught Japanese dance at the Buddhist Temple in New York City. I still go there every Saturday, like I did as a child. Every weekend they would drive us to New York City and I would take language at the Japanese language school with all the other kids. I learned calligraphy from Shunshin Kan. He was amazing, both as the minister of the temple and a fencing black-belt instructor! We had all these weekend activities and Japanese dance was pretty much in my life from the beginning. During the weekdays I was in public school at Pleasantville, New York (an hour north of the city), where I was considered to be *the* minority, believe it or not (it was *not* a diverse community!). But when I went to New York City and was around all the Japanese Americans, then I was white. I'm always the opposite of whatever the larger group is, although I was lucky, because in Japanese school I had a best friend who was also biracial.

Music started for me pretty typically in fourth or fifth grade. In band we were asked what instrument we wanted to play, and I chose the flute. I played first chair flute all through middle and high school. I was very competitive. I took lessons with the first chair of the New York Philharmonic. Eventually I went to Bloomington, Indiana, as a flute player.

College Life

When I went to Indiana University in 1977, my cultural side was a void. I immersed myself in the whole machine of learning flute for orchestra, which really wasn't what I wanted to do but was sort of logical. I was not aware of anything else that was going on around me. Now I'm so bummed out about that, but at the time I just didn't know. For example, I passed the folklore building every day but had no idea what folklore was. I took an anthropology class, but all they taught us was how to measure skulls and things like that. Looking back, I could have really started that whole love of culture and its relationship with the arts so much earlier.

TS: Were you doing any kind of dance at that time?

TH: I was doing some contemporary dance with people I met—performance art, improv, happenings, and those kinds of things—not classes. It was pretty weird to do that in Bloomington in the '70s and '80s.

TS: Did you play in any ensembles as a music major at Bloomington?

TH: Yes, we had orchestras and bands and things there. I picked up playing Renaissance and Baroque music in an early music ensemble. It seemed more interesting to me than being lost in the middle of an orchestra or a band. Looking back, I don't know why I didn't connect with Japanese things at Bloomington. It's the largest chunk of time in my life where that aspect of me wasn't there at all. I just didn't seek it out. I was very lonely in Bloomington, and I learned a very deep lesson: there are many people in the world who want to play flute in the Philadelphia Orchestra. But it was so clear to me when I left: "I know that this is not what I want to do." I loved the music, but it was not attractive as a job or something that I would want to jump out of bed to do. I can't even give you a good reason. Maybe it was the factory aspect, having to play the same excerpts week after week and not knowing the larger scope of where that fit into the orchestra. I really don't know. I never analyzed it!

TS: Well, one of the things that sealed it for me was the fact that in ethnomusicology I could find more ways to be myself than almost any other way I could imagine. There are so many angles, so many points of view, and so many ways of expressing yourself.

TH: Yes, I think you nailed it. I only applied to two schools, which was probably not the brightest thing in the world, the University of Michigan and Indiana University. It was a pity that I didn't go to Michigan, because I would have probably met Bill Malm there. When I finally met him in 1989, I realized, "Gosh, if I had actually gone to Michigan instead of IU, we could have met." But who knows what would've happened? Maybe I would not have been interested in *sankyoku* then?

I graduated in 1982 and went back to New York. My family was in New York and my sister was living in New York City, so I went to the city and immediately started back with Japanese dance. I was also doing contemporary dance. I took various jobs during the day and danced at night. Two or three jobs really stick out from this chapter in my life. I was the company director of the Asian American Dance Theatre, based in Chinatown. That ended up being the rebirth of, "Oh, I know how to do this traditional stuff." By that time I had started going to the Buddhist Temple again to take class, and Sahomi Tachibana, my childhood teacher, was still there. The Asian American Dance Theatre was a very interesting, eclectic group that had dancers from all over Asia. They went on the road and performed at universities or colleges and museums all over the place. In addition to traditional dances, they also performed newly choreographed Asian and Asian American pieces. This was something really new to me. I entered into the very deeply political scene of Asian American organizations. I also worked at Asian CineVision, another strong political group in Chinatown. So, I was back dancing and doing a lot of performances because every week the group would be on tour. *That's* how I learned so much about other Asian cultures. We were literally backstage, dressing together, completely naked! I'd look over and see the *Bharata Natyam* dancer putting on her bells or bangles, while I was taking off my jewelry. It taught me a lot about the differences in the body and culture. In Japanese dance you never wear bangles because they would make sound and get in your sleeves. I learned a lot, though I had *no* idea what ethnomusicology was. Or dance scholarship.

Then I got a better job. I was still performing, but because I knew how to do architectural drafting, I got a job at an architectural firm. My father taught me how to draft when I was in seventh grade. So I worked in an architect's loft during the day and danced at night. One night I was having dinner with some friends: Jamie Pritchett, musicologist and John Cage scholar, and Frances White and my husband, Curtis Bahn, both composers of computer music. We were hanging out, and Jamie said, "You know what? There's a field that combines what you already do. It's called ethnomusicology." At the time he was a PhD candidate at NYU. He said, "You know what, you should meet Kay Shelemay; she teaches ethnomusicology at NYU." And I said, "Really? There's something that people do that combines all the things I'm doing?"

Virginia (Gini) Gorlinski

In conversation with Ted Solís and Margaret Sarkissian, October 26, 2007, Columbus, Ohio

Early Life

GG: I was born in May 1961, in Sacramento, California. If I think about it, the tendency to be involved in other cultural stuff has been there since I was born. My dad was career military and served in Vietnam twice. He sent back movies, and my mom would show them. He didn't send back scary things for the kids, just pictures of the market, stuff like that. I remember Vietnamese women washing clothes in the river.

Little did I know that twenty-five years later I'd be washing my clothes in the river in Borneo! Even at that time it fascinated me. I saw these ladies washing their clothes in the river; I was five and I went off and did my thing. My mom was terrified because she couldn't find me. In the end she found me by a little creek near the house, washing my new pink coat in the river. She said, "What are you doing?" I said, "I'm washing my coat in the river like the Vietnamese ladies do." I haven't forgotten that! And I remember my dad took pictures of the market and I saw women wearing *Ào dài*—the Vietnamese long dresses. My dad sent me a doll with a green dress. I didn't know it at the time, but I saw a purple one in one of these movies and said, "Ooh, I like the purple one." My mom must have told him, because I think they wrote every day, so he went back to the market and got a purple one. I really believe those sorts of things are directly connected to what I do now.

I grew up mostly in the Washington, DC, area, where I was in a high school that was remarkably diverse. It pulled from very affluent communities and also from communities that struggled. I started playing classical piano when I was about seven. I got a lot out of it. I don't regret it at all, although I think, in terms of my personality, it might not have been the best route! But eventually—in 1978, my junior/senior year in high school—I bought with my own money a Fender Rhodes eighty-eight-key electric piano (which I still have) and a Fender Twin Reverb guitar amp to go with it, used, out of the classifieds. I was really into that. I played in an all-girl band. We were *good*. I was in another band with guys, but I quit because they didn't know how to practice—they were mad! And then, at a show, the all-girl band blew them off the stage (from our perspective, at least). That was fun, one of those fond high-school memories.

College Life

I was always interested in different kinds of music and wanted to go into music as a university student. I really wasn't very good, but in 1979 I went to the University of the Pacific in Stockton, California, as a theory/composition major. After a year, I knew it wasn't the right match for me and decided to withdraw and move to San Francisco. My father had his last tour in the military at the Presidio, so I lived there for a few months. When he retired, my folks moved up to northern California. I stayed in San Francisco and rented an apartment with a friend on Larkin and Vallejo. I supported myself at first by demonstrating automated tellers for Bank of America and then as a file clerk in an insurance company, while I practiced like a fiend on the Fender Rhodes and took piano lessons down in the Castro [District] with Ron Gipson, a teacher who was recommended to me by my teacher at University of the Pacific. I studied with him, prepared audition tapes, applied to other schools, and wound up going to Michigan, Ann Arbor.

TS: Why Michigan? What was it about that particular place?

GG: I wanted to be a piano major—at least, that's what I thought I wanted to be. We all talked about "back East" on the West Coast—and considered the music schools there more rigorous. I wanted to see if I could hack it. I was trying to find my niche. So when I went to Ann Arbor my first semester as a piano major, boy did I have a bomb of a GPA—it was terrible! I was in the wrong field, but I still loved music. It's getting a little better now, but at that time, if you went into music in higher education, the only option you knew about was performance; you didn't know that anything else existed, except perhaps music education, but that's what pretty much everybody did. It's still like that to a large extent.

I went back to California for the winter break and saw one of my friends from University of the Pacific, who said, "You have a Javanese gamelan at your school." I said, "A what?" She said, "A Javanese gamelan. Come on, let's go to the music library and I'll play you a record." She played me a record of Javanese gamelan, and I remember thinking, this is nice, but how does it stop? That's what I wondered—how does it stop—because if you don't know anything about it, there's nothing for you to latch on to. So I went back to Michigan for the second semester and enrolled in Javanese gamelan because I wanted to know. Playing and listening to that record opened a door I didn't even know was there.

TS: Do you remember what record your friend played?

GG: I have no idea, but it might have been the one UCLA put out.

TS: *Music of the Venerable Dark Cloud* [Hood and Susilo 1967]?

GG: Yes, I think that was it. Before that, in November of my first semester, I had gone to an informational session for junior year abroad in Germany and thought, wouldn't that be cool? So the next year, I went to Germany and thought, well, that's the end of Javanese gamelan. But no! Dieter Mack and Danker Schaareman in Freiburg had a Balinese gamelan, so I enrolled in the academic class. Dieter said, "Now, one of the requirements of this class is that you also participate." So every Thursday we went to play Balinese gamelan *kebyar*. It was wonderful. We played in Basel and took the whole group (instruments and performers) to spend a weekend in a farmhouse on a hillside in French-speaking Switzerland. We did a lot of playing and I still remember in my hands, and in my ears, too, a lot of those interlocking parts. I got even more entrenched in music and culture because I took Southeast Asian culture classes in Germany, too. I also had to keep up with my piano lessons because I still needed it for University of Michigan, so I studied piano with Helmut Meyer-Eggen.

I came back to Michigan and enrolled in Indonesian language class with Pete [Alton L.] Becker [Judith Becker's husband], who taught us through pop songs. It was an interesting approach to language learning. I still remember a lot of the songs because he made us sing them through then go home and listen to the tape. It brought me even more into the Southeast Asian arts and studies circle. Judith Becker was very influential. She was gone the first year I started gamelan and Alan Feinstein led the group. Judith Becker was wonderfully encouraging. She inspired me in so many ways, as a teacher and as a musician. By that time, I was also getting deeper and deeper into the Indonesian language. After I graduated from Michigan I did the Southeast Asian Studies Summer Institute [SEASSI], which was at Michigan that year, so I just kept right on and did my second year of Indonesian there in the summer. And meanwhile, I applied to graduate programs in ethnomusicology and wound up going to Hawai'i in 1984.

TS: Before you go off to Hawai'i, can I ask if you remember anything about the first time you heard the term "ethnomusicology?" What did it mean to you?

GG: I think I became aware of the term through gamelan. I remember, too, that the graduate students would invite different faculty to talk about how they wound up doing what they're doing, and I went to Judith Becker's talk. So, it was definitely at Michigan that I heard it first. And then I sat in on Bill Malm's "Musics of Asia" class. I sat in because I couldn't fit the credits into my schedule, but I was very interested. I remember one of the most moving lectures Bill Malm gave was a slide show of Angkor Wat in Cambodia and other temples and artifacts. He showed some of the reliefs there and said, "And they stop here." I think it was Angkor Wat—maybe it was another temple—but he said, "They stop here. Nobody knows what happened; maybe they moved, maybe they died." And he also made me aware for the first time of the tragedy that happened in Cambodia, so that was a memorable moment.

Laudan Nooshin

In conversation with Ted Solís, July 9, 2007, Vienna, Austria

Early Life

LN: I was born in London in June 1963. My parents are both from Iran. They came as students in the late 1950s, early '60s. When my father first arrived, there were about thirty Iranians resident in the entire country, so most people knew each other. They used to have occasional get-togethers, and that's how my parents met. My father is an academic, an engineer. He got a post in a university town called Guildford, about twenty-five miles southwest of London, so we moved out there when I was about five. Guildford was an extremely mono-cultural, white, and fairly affluent place, so for a long time I was the only "brown" child in the whole school. I was brought up in an environment in which I always thought myself to be different. I used to play on my difference a lot at school; it was almost expected of me, but I always had a longing to belong to something, to not be different. I guess all of this is relevant, because it pushed me toward studying something for reasons that I was unaware of at the time.

At the same time, I had inclinations toward music from a very young age. My father tells me that when I was about three, he found me sitting in a corner of the room crying to music. He asked me what was wrong, and I said, "It was so beautiful." Music moved me, but I didn't come from a musical family, so I didn't have the opportunity to study music from a young age. I played the recorder, and when I started secondary school I started learning clarinet. I taught myself the piano and gradually became more involved in music making—Western classical music—at school and eventually studied music at university.

There was music at home, but not a great deal, and especially not a great deal of Iranian music. My first introduction to non-Western music was Latin American music. My French teacher in sixth form (sixteen to eighteen years) had lived in Chile and had close Chilean friends who were refugees and musicians. A group of us from school would go and spend time with them. That was my first experience of the way in which a music about which I knew nothing—and I didn't speak the language—completely grabbed me. That music drew me to ethnomusicology in the first place.

College Life

I graduated from high school and went to the University of Leeds in 1981 to study (classical) music. I was in the Latin American Society in the Student Union and used to organize Latin American concerts by some of the refugee groups of the New Age *canción* type. I was involved in the Chilean Solidarity Group and did some voluntary work for them.

When it came to my final-year dissertation—in the UK at that time all students had to write a ten-thousand-to-twelve-thousand-word paper—I decided to do mine on Iranian music, even though I knew nothing about it. It was a fairly basic undergraduate-level study. I found whatever texts I could and wrote about the *radif* and the *dastgahs*. I wasn't really encouraged by the department because nobody had done anything like that before. At most, someone had written about "Britten and Gamelan" or something like that. I was much more inclined to write about Latin America, except I didn't have the Spanish. I could read Farsi a bit, not very well, and could speak the language colloquially. In the process of writing the dissertation, I encountered very preliminary readings in ethnomusicology and became interested in it, so when I graduated that's what I wanted to do.

TS: What were some of those preliminary readings?

LN: I think Blacking's *How Musical Is Man?* [1973] was one of the things I looked at. I was at Leeds in the early 1980s and there weren't many ethnomusicology programs in the UK. In the summer of my second year, when I was preparing for my finals in the third year, I spent some time in the library at SOAS [School of Oriental and African Studies] as an external visitor, finding out what I could about Iranian music.

TS: So you grew up speaking colloquial Farsi, but you had no reading knowledge?

LN: I'm bilingual, but English is definitely my first language. My Farsi education was quite haphazard. I started learning from school textbooks, several times, but stopped. At one point I did have lessons with a tutor. I had a very ambiguous relationship with Farsi until I went to university, made Iranian friends of my own age, and suddenly had a motivation to speak the language. When I started my postgraduate studies, I took it much more seriously and went to language classes at SOAS. So my education in Farsi is actually partly a result of becoming an ethnomusicologist.

TS: Did you visit Iran as a child?

LN: I went to Iran once when I was about five. After that, I didn't go to Iran until 1999, almost thirty years later. In the 1980s, which would have been a logical time for me to go since I was working on my PhD thesis, the war with Iraq was on and music was highly problematical anyhow. It was just a bad time. And then other life circumstances meant that I couldn't go until 1999.

NIKHIL DALLY

In conversation with Ted Solís, July 5, 2007, Egham, England

Early Life

ND: I was born in Singapore in 1965. My mother, a Hindu Bengali whose family was from what had once been East Bengal (part of British India, now Bangladesh), was born in Kelantan (now part of Malaysia), and ended up in Singapore. My father was British but spent most of his adult life traveling around the British Empire working for various companies. He was with British American Tobacco in Singapore when he met my mother. When I was five, he was posted to Jakarta, where we lived for several years, and, apart from a brief stay in Korea in the middle, my parents stayed in Jakarta until they retired many years later. I did most of my schooling in the American-dominated Jakarta International School. When I was sixteen or seventeen, I came to the UK to finish my schooling at the United World College, an international sixth-form college in South Wales. After finishing school I spent another year back in Jakarta with my parents and then three years at Cambridge University doing music. So my upbringing was fairly international. After that I went to Solo to study gamelan for a year and then came back to this country, where I've been ever since.

TS: Did you have any experience with gamelan while you lived in Indonesia?

ND: Not actively. I'd been to *wayangs* and performances of dance—you can't avoid gamelan in Indonesia, even in Jakarta; it's all over the place. We had visited Solo, Yogya, and Bali. We'd been to Prambanan and watched the Ramayana. I loved it, but had never taken it seriously because I was "British." I was living as an expatriate in Indonesia and studying classical piano. I didn't look down on gamelan; I knew it was great music and I loved the sound of it, but I had never thought it appropriate for me to learn.

TS: So instead you studied piano in Jakarta.

ND: Yes, from Edith Knauer, an American lady. She had been a brilliant concert pianist in her time and had taught on the faculty of the University of Texas at Austin. At some point she had married and followed her husband, who was working for an oil company.

TS: So you were embedded in a Western musical world in Jakarta? Did you learn to speak Indonesian?

ND: Yes, but not very well, to be frank. I picked it up. We had servants, and when we went out shopping, eating, or whatever, we spoke it. And of course I had grown up in Singapore, where people spoke Malay. I think that having grown up in a place like Singapore, where everyone speaks three or four languages badly, I never felt there was an obligation to learn this language fluently. You learned what you needed to get by.

TS: Did you have any particular experience with, attachment to, or connection with your Indian background at all?

ND: Absolutely. My mother is Bengali, and we have Bengali relatives all over the place: Malaysia, Singapore, and India, so we visited them. My grandmother lived in Singapore for many years, even after we left. Many relatives ended up in the States, and my grandmother eventually went back to India.

TS: And how about music—did your mother play Indian classical music, or *Rabindra Sangeet*, or things like that?

ND: Oh yes, absolutely. One of my aunts was a classical Indian dancer, so the sound of Indian music was around.

College Life

I studied music at Cambridge from 1985–88. In those days the program was very rigid and academic. It was possible to choose instrumental performance as an option in the final year, but I didn't. We studied analysis, history, theory, harmony, and counterpoint. The course was designed to produce the next generation of musicologists, to sort the wheat from the chaff, as it were. At the end of it, a couple of the Fellows said, "I say, you should go into research, young man." By then, though, I was so utterly sick of academia that I said, "No, I want to go and be a real musician." So I went out to Solo, because that was my antidote to Cambridge.

TS: What did you mean by "sick of academia"?

ND: I had done so much of it and, in the process, became aware of the hypocrisies lying deep at the roots of the whole notion of studying *about* music without actually playing it, and writing papers on music about which one did not know the answers, dressing up one's surmises in the conventional language and thought of the time. I don't think there's anything wrong in writing about music—it's fascinating—but it did seem to me that so many things stated as being factual and obvious were merely current, conventional ways of thinking about x, y, or z. And despite the fact that people trumpeted the virtues of academic rigor and open-mindedness—testing everything against reality, always being critical, and all those great academic virtues—I felt that thinking outside the box was never taken seriously. There were so many other questions that I sometimes asked, but sometimes didn't bother to ask, where the answer I was given wasn't really satisfactory.

TS: Can you give me an example?

ND: OK, take the performance of medieval chansons by Machaut, for example. In the 1960s and '70s there had been a convention of performing such music with a lot of added instrumentation. Often the scholarship leading to those decisions was somewhat spurious; there was no clear evidence that these chansons were ever performed with such instrumentation. By the time I got to university the orthodoxy had shifted, and groups like the Gothic Voices and the Hilliard Ensemble started to perform this music entirely vocally. A lot of scholarship was unearthed to suggest this was the right way to do it. That was great. I liked the sound this new orthodoxy was creating, and the scholarship behind it was very convincing. But when one asked questions, there was more ridicule directed at ensembles that performed the old way than serious scholarly criticism. I thought that was wrong.

For me, gamelan was the antidote. Gamelan was not included in the curriculum at all, despite the fact that the Music Department owned a gamelan. The gamelan, presented by the Indonesian embassy, sat in the lobby of the library. (Can you imagine a worse place to put a gamelan?) The Music Department was not much interested, so it was up to a bunch of students and townspeople to organize their own gamelan society, collect subscriptions, and pay for visiting teachers. The way we learned gamelan was so obviously different from the academic rigor that was applied to Western music.

TS: Who was "we" and how did you get involved?

ND: "We" being the Cambridge Gamelan Society. There were two postgraduate students teaching at that time, Anthony Milton and Peter Lillington, who had been in Cambridge since their undergraduate days. They had learned from Alec Roth and Dave Posnett. In the early days of English gamelan, you went to *anybody* who came back from Java with any kind of information and said, "Teach me! What have you got?" They taught in a rote-learning sort of way. The whole notion of learning music in a completely different way was nice. I wasn't studying; I was just playing.

After my first year of studying gamelan, I went back to Jakarta to visit my parents during the holidays and took lessons there. In my second year, I took over teaching the beginners' group. Simon Cook was back from Java, so we got him to come from London every week to teach the advanced group.

TS: So, little by little, you became aware of the gamelan and somehow gravitated to it. Did you play most of the time you were at Cambridge?

ND: Yes, it was a simultaneous but growing antidote. For me, part of it was the whole expatriate search for identity. When I was in Indonesia, my identity was English. But when I came to England and looked around, I thought, "Oh, boy, I'm not really English. I'm not at home here; I don't get these people—help!" So I started gravitating toward things Indonesian, Singaporean, and even Indian—anything that would provide an antidote.

TS: So in your second year, you started teaching gamelan. Then what?

ND: I went on from there. I loved it. Perhaps "antidote" is a negative way of putting it; maybe "balance" is nicer. It depends on what mood you're in; sometimes you need an antidote, sometimes you need a balance.

MARIA MENDONÇA

In conversation with Ted Solís, October 27, 2007, Columbus, Ohio

Early Life

MM: I was born in London in January 1966. My family comes from very diverse ethnic backgrounds. My dad is Goan, which goes back to a Portuguese/Indian connection. My mother's family is a mixture of everything: my grandfather was Scottish and my grandmother's family hailed partly from the Spanish Philippines; there's also some German in the background, some Irish—you name it! And of course the Indian bit, which in the Anglo-Indian ethnic group is often sort of hard to trace, makes it even more diverse. I think of myself as very English because I was born and grew up in England. I've always thought of Britain as a profoundly multicultural country, and I usually identify as English or British because I think the challenge is that "English" or "British" can mean seventy different things.

I finally realized a few years ago that I have chosen these odd topics to explore—the ways gamelan has developed outside of Indonesia—*because* my background is profoundly about that. My dad's a jazz musician who grew up in India and Pakistan; there's no particular reason why jazz should be his thing. It's all this mixing and moving and immigration. Music has an affinity-type connection in my family. I think that's why I was gravitating to the "gamelan outside of Indonesia" thing, because it's so unrelated to notions of diaspora and music making in a conventional way. I like when music and ethnicity fall in the cracks and are hard to figure out. I think that's because of my family background, actually.

TS: You like it when music and ethnicity fall through the cracks—the little secret spaces. Can I clarify: Was your language background from childhood entirely in English? Or was Portuguese, for example, around in any form? Did you hear foreign languages at all or study any in school?

MM: English, definitely; no Portuguese at all, though occasionally Mum and Dad spoke to each other in Hindustani (a kind of bazaar language), but that was so they could talk privately in front of us! I studied French (seven years), German (three years), and a smattering of Latin (one year) at school. And later, Indonesian.

TS: And how about music?

MM: As I said, my father is a jazz musician. I always had jazz and all sorts of music going on in the background. Quite early on I knew I wanted to do something with music. My father wanted me to be a jazz musician, but I did all sorts of music. I played all sorts of instruments—classical guitar, piano, and violin, and I was always very interested in composition.

College Life

I had a scholarship to a music college—Trinity College of Music—on Saturdays for four or five years, when I was in high school. I remember going up to York University for an interview and my whole approach was quite straight, meaning "Western classical." So I went to the interview and they showed a video about the Music Department. One of the things in it was the Javanese gamelan ensemble. I looked at it and said to the person sitting next to me, "You'll never catch me doing that!" And she said, "How do you know? I've heard it's good; you should keep your mind open." We were both accepted at York.

I started at York in 1984. When I got there, I thought, "Well, this gamelan thing, this is one of the few places I'm going to encounter it, so I might as well do it to broaden my mind." I remember hearing gamelan and I wasn't too impressed by the sound. But as part of the "Music in Java and Bali" project that Neil Sorrell ran, we ended up playing gamelan a lot. As a multi-instrumentalist myself, I just loved the idea that I needed to be a multi-instrumentalist in order to play gamelan. That really clicked with me more than anything—having a go at everything and piecing things together in my head. It turned out that the gamelan people were the most interesting in the Music Department. Every one of the real oddballs, the ones who didn't fit in, was in the gamelan.

In my second year, 1985, I did an exchange program at UC–San Diego, specifically to study classical guitar and composition, which I did, but as part of that, in the beginning just for fun, I started going to San Diego State to join their gamelan. Bob Brown was teaching, and it was the beginning of Midiyanto's introduction to the US.

I came back to York, continued with gamelan, and finished up my degree. I was very interested in doing music theory and composition at graduate school but decided to take a year off. I was working as a receptionist in London, just at the point when everything started up at the South Bank. The Indonesian Embassy had donated a gamelan and there were classes, so in my spare time I ended up doing an awful lot of gamelan. And, during the year, I went to Indonesia for the first time, for a holiday.

Renata Pasternak-Mazur

In conversation with Ted Solís, October 27, 2007, Columbus, Ohio

Early Life

RPM: I was born in Olkusz, Poland, in June 1968. My parents are from the working class, but they both came from the same village. My grandparents met in a church choir and fell in love, but there was a social difference between them and they couldn't consider getting married until the war, when such matters were not as important. My father also sang in a church choir and my mother danced in a folk ensemble. I was involved in choirs for as long as I can remember: different choirs—church choirs, children's choirs, and school choirs—with different repertoires. My father loved accordion. He bought one when he worked in Germany and wanted me to start playing it when I went to the music school audition. I don't know whether you are familiar with the school system in Poland under socialism? It was very structured. There were state music schools at the primary and secondary levels, and getting into them was competitive. There were auditions, and you had to pass an entrance exam that tested your musical aptitude. Even if you passed the audition, acceptance depended on how many other candidates they had. At the audition, the director of the school advised my parents to send me for voice instead of accordion, which I actually liked better.

TS: Did you play the accordion well?

RPM: No, I had no professional instruction. Before I started formal education, I also learned guitar. My mom worked with the wife of one of the teachers from the music school. I was very excited about getting guitar instruction, so she arranged for me to have private lessons with him for a year. He was one of the people who pushed me to apply to the music school, set up my exam, and arranged a meeting with a voice teacher.

College Life

I started pursuing my music education at a state music school concurrently with my regular education. When I was in the third year of the music school, I was encouraged to enter what was called *Olimpiada Artystyczna, Sekcja Muzyki* (Olympic Games in Arts, Music Section), and I went to the national level. It was a competition that went from the school level to the national level. You worked on a topic of your choice and wrote some essays; there were quizzes, listening sections, and concerts, after which you were supposed to write a review. I was one of the winners and was offered free entry into a program in musicology, cultural studies, or art history at the university of my choice. I didn't hesitate a minute. I knew what I wanted to do—pursue my master's degree in musicology at the Jagiellonian University of Kraków.

I was originally interested in math, but when I was sent out as a substitute teacher, I knew I could not imagine myself as a math teacher at any level. I was fascinated by music. When I sang in the church ensemble, we won a festival of sacred music in Nowa Huta. After the concert, we were waiting for transportation. It was a very cold and gloomy night in November. We were exhausted. It was about 1 A.M. and we had had nothing to eat or drink. The atmosphere in the room was terrible. The director of the ensemble took his guitar and started to sing. People started to join in one by one, until finally everybody was singing with him. Music transformed the atmosphere in the room to something that was bearable, even enjoyable. It was unbelievable how our perception of the situation changed, even though the situation itself didn't.

That was the moment when I decided I wanted to be involved with music for the rest of my life. I saw the power of music. So for me, musicology was something that allowed me to combine my love of math with music. I was fascinated by the way music was perceived as a mathematical science for quite a long time. That was what originally attracted me to musicology. Later I went into twentieth-century musicology because I wanted to do something contemporary.

CHRISTOPHER J. MILLER

In conversation with Margaret Sarkissian, June 22, 2008, Northampton, Massachusetts

Early Life

CM: I was born in June 1969 in Victoria, British Columbia. I think my musical interest comes from my dad. He's quite musical, though he never pursued it. He's one of those people who hears something on the radio and, a half an hour later, is still whistling it. He's a dentist, so a professional, but his own family background was blue collar—his father was an electrician at a steel mill in Ontario. My dad had some interest in jazz and acquired some of the cultural capital of classical music—he had a few items in his record collection—but he didn't have much use for art. I remember his reaction to a sculpture at the Canadian Pavilion at Expo '86. Seeing that it was funded by the Canada Council for the Arts, he grumbled about it being a waste of taxpayer's money. So while my parents generously supported my interest in music—they bought a piano after seeing how much I liked to play—my dad did not encourage my interest in new music composition. I learned after getting involved in gamelan that I have relatives on my mom's side—she's Dutch, born in The Hague—who lived in the East Indies. I don't know the details.

My early musical training was not particularly conventional. I studied briefly with someone at the Victoria Conservatory who was supposed to be good with "creative students," but all that meant was playing arrangements of pop songs in addition to the Royal Conservatory of Toronto's graded repertory. I wasn't particularly motivated. I switched to a teacher a friend of my dad knew about, George Essihos, who taught a little bit of jazz and classical but mostly focused on playing by ear and improvisation.

College Life

It was a given in my family that I would go to university, and wanting to pursue music, I auditioned for the School of Music at the University of Victoria. I was accepted, and I started in 1987 as a composition major—they told me I would not have been accepted as a pianist. After two years, there was something of an exodus of composers—some grad students finished and others left, and, most important, Rudolf Komorous, the preeminent composer on faculty, took a position at Simon Fraser University. I decided to follow him. When I got to SFU, I discovered they had a gamelan.

MS: Was that your first encounter with Indonesian music?

CM: I think it was. I went a couple of times to Expo '86, which I later learned was the venue for the First International Gamelan Festival. I was interested in percussion—I remember happening upon some kind of Afro-Cuban thing. I also remember going into the Indonesian pavilion but just missing a performance.

I was vaguely aware of gamelan while at UVic, but the first time I saw gamelan instruments up close was at SFU, when I visited to see about transferring. A roommate who played encouraged me to take the course, so I did, at the first opportunity, in the spring of 1990.

My first teacher was the composer and *dhalang* Blacius Subono from STSI (now ISI) Solo [Sekolah Tinggi Seni Indonesia, now Insitut Seni Indonesia]. I liked it so much I came back to Vancouver for the summer intensive course. Pak Cokro, the legendary teacher from CalArts, used to come up every year, but that year he had had a stroke. Pak Hardja Susilo, from the University of Hawai'i, came instead.

I continued taking gamelan after that. I became good friends with a grad student, Kenneth Newby, who was the teaching assistant. He had just come back from a year in Indonesia, doing research—not as an ethnomusicologist, but to support his project as a composer. There was one summer where I met with him almost every afternoon to learn Balinese *gender wayang*, which really engaged learning by ear.

MS: Do you remember your first impression of gamelan music?

CM: One memory is the first concert I heard by the community group in Vancouver, which played on SFU's instruments. They opened with a *gangsaran*, going to "Roning Tawang." Hearing all that bronze, the sonority of it—there was an instant rush of excitement. Another really strong memory was a sense I got from learning the overture to the *wayang* at my first summer intensive—not the whole thing, but starting with *Ladrang* "Sri Katon," going into "Suksma Ilang," and then the *Ayak-ayakan*, *Srepegan*, and *Sampak* in *slendro manyura*. I was really struck by this almost visceral sense of moving through time with the tempo transitions. I remember almost visualizing flying through clouds. From that point on, I was hooked.

My first foray into composing for gamelan came from an invitation from an MFA choreographer. He was doing a piece that was a kind of critique of figures like Nijinsky and the impresario Diaghilev, through reenacting parts of "Afternoon of a Faun." The Debussy connection suggested gamelan. The community group, which I had just joined, agreed to play the music I wrote. I realized only in retrospect how lucky I was to be able to draw on a whole group like that.

Another important thing was hearing a group from ISI Solo that came through Vancouver as part of the Festival of Indonesia in the fall of 1991. They played a full-length program of new compositions, billed as "New Music Indonesia." I was blown away, really taken by it, and very curious about how they came to compose such music. I got a sense of how they composed pieces, by working with A. L. Suwardi, who returned to Vancouver after the tour for a one-month residency at the Western Front, an artist-run center in Vancouver. Three of us collaborated with him—he led us through his way of creating a piece. It was my first encounter with *komposisi baru* or *musik kontemporer*, which eventually became my dissertation research topic.

I graduated from SFU in 1992. Then, in October '93, I went to Indonesia for the first time and stayed until May 1995, for about twenty months. I followed a path that had been well established by others in Vancouver, going to Solo on the Indonesian government's Darmasiswa program. That's when I really learned to play. I had already learned a couple of pieces on *gendèr* by rote, one I transcribed actually, one or two pieces on *rebab*, and one or two pieces on *ciblon*. I had the basic technique down on those instruments, so I could really dig in right away.

MS: What did you do after you returned?

CM: I was back in Vancouver, involved with gamelan and with the new music scene. I worked in arts administration for some new music organizations. I realize in retrospect—and I've kicked myself many times for this—that while I was in Solo, even though I learned Indonesian, saw a lot of stuff, and got a really good feel for things, I didn't have any discipline about fieldwork. I didn't take notes! I have programs and some things like that, but when I think back, I ask myself, "Why didn't I write down the date of this or that?" It didn't occur to me at the time. At SFU the gamelan was not part of any ethnomusicology program. It was just there because there was a composer who was interested in it.

MS: Did you have any particular role models prior to starting grad school?

CM: One big one was Martin Bartlett, the professor at SFU, who was the de facto leader of the community group. What most impressed me was his intellect. It was very important for him to be a thoughtful composer, to really think about what he was doing and what it meant. It wasn't just about the craft of the music. He's one of a handful of composers in Canada who have strong connections to the American experimental tradition. He had studied in the Bay Area, worked with Pauline Oliveros, and studied Hindustani music with Pandit Pran Nath, like Terry Riley and some of those people. He had heard gamelan and gotten to know Pak Cokro when he was there. I remember a talk Martin gave at my first summer intensive. One of his big interests was tuning systems. He talked about equal temperament being a confining sort of thing. I can't remember exactly how he phrased it, but he held up a piece of staff paper and said something like, "The system of music is a jail and these are the bars on the windows!" He made very bold statements like that, but if you actually talked to him, he was always questioning and really encouraged dialogue and critical thinking. So although he had very strong opinions, there was something about the way he presented them that made it clear they were always evolving through critical dialogue with others.

Another person who really impressed me a lot at that summer intensive was George Lewis, a trombonist, who does computer music stuff. He was one of the younger members of the original Association for the Advancement of Creative Music, the same group Braxton was part of in Chicago. Lewis is now at Columbia. He was another person who was creatively engaged but also a very sharp critical thinker. They were both big role models for me. I think they probably helped push me toward finding a balance between scholarship and creative work.

MS: What was your initial perception of the field of ethnomusicology? You came at it from a slightly different background than many other people.

CM: Yes. It was one particular type of world music that brought me into the field, rather than the field exposing me to the music. Ethnomusicology clearly played a role in the presence of gamelan in Vancouver. Pak Cokro taught at the intensives because Bob Brown, one of Mantle Hood's students at UCLA, brought him to CalArts. Bob Brown also had much to do with the gamelan activity that Martin Bartlett would have encountered in the Bay Area. But there wasn't any ethnomusicology program at SFU when I was a student there. It was an unusual program, "interdisciplinary" in its own way, straddling the line between artistic and scholarly disciplines. There were courses like "The Arts in Context," which all Fine and Performing Arts students had to take. The course had a strong emphasis on trying to understand the relationship of the arts to society and culture. It took a cultural studies sort of approach. I remember being assigned some readings by Susan McClary and getting turned on to "new musicology," as they called it then, and all the French theory stuff. Not in a rigorous way, of course, but indirectly. We looked at postmodern theory from an arts angle. I remember coming across a little book that had a bunch of really influential essays in it by Frederic Jameson and Baudrillard. So indirectly, I was exposed to Roland Barthes and Foucault a little, but I didn't take any courses in which I dealt rigorously with any of that work. I do remember thinking, "Oh, this is the way to study the arts."

MADE MANTLE HOOD

In conversation with Margaret Sarkissian, June 13, 2010, Singapore

Early Life

MMH: I was born in Pacific Palisades, California, in September 1969. One of my earliest musical memories comes from when I was about six or seven. I remember a long thumbnail standing out as very unusual in the living room of our house in Honolulu, a place called Hawai'i Kai, with the distinct sounds of a *gender wayang* quartet in the living room and Persian rugs laid on the floor. I believe it was New Year's Day or something like that. And in the household I always remember various faces—a Ghanaian, someone from Indonesia, a Chinese. Growing up in Hawai'i, of course, that sort of diversity was not a surprise, but to have it in our house and to have so many people making different sounds, whether *gender wayang* or drumming, I remember it being very much a part of what Dad did, which I didn't really understand at that time.

I grew up in multiple places. I was born in California, reared in Hawai'i until around the third grade, when my father did a sabbatical, during the 1978 blizzard of Bloomington, Indiana. He replaced Alan Merriam for a year while Alan was on sabbatical. Later, we moved from Hawai'i to the East Coast, where I went to middle and high school. I think growing up in so many different places, you lose a sense of your roots, and friendships suffer. But automatically you revert to becoming a little bit more tightknit with your siblings and parents.

MS: We've asked everyone about their parents. Obviously, we know what your dad, Mantle Hood, did. How about your mom?

MMH: If we need to set the record books straight, I think one of the unsung heroes in the golden age of ethnomusicology is its intense collaboration with theater and dance. My mother, Hazel Chung Hood, had a wonderful role to play in that. The two of them, of course, were a pair in the productions they put on, the artists they worked with, and the details they learned in order to put on their productions. It's always a communication process between musicians, dancers, and theater people and how to communicate those elements of cross-cultural music performance. Mom had a big role to play in that, although under-researched in my opinion. I'm waiting for a dance ethnologist or a historian to look at some of those aspects.

My mother grew up in the West Indies and moved to Erie, Pennsylvania, at the age of ten or eleven, to stay with a great aunt who enabled her to go to school. Her family didn't have enough money to send her to school at home. She went on to study at Juilliard and did very well. She pursued ballet, but being Eurasian and not the right height, body build, or skin color, she realized she couldn't be successful in ballet. So she moved toward Broadway and eventually to modern dance with Martha Graham. Later in her career she toured with Yul Brynner in *The King and I* and then made her way to Indonesia, where she was one of the first to do an intense two-year study of ethnic dance, sponsored by the Ford Foundation. Mom and Dad were in Indonesia doing the same thing at the same time, but they didn't know one another. It was only after they got back that the Ford Foundation's advisory board said, "What do we do with this Hazel Chung? She's done all this training and that's wonderful, but where do we place her?" And so Mantle Hood actually wrote a letter that said, "Hazel Chung, would you come out here? I think you'd be interested in working with our program." And one thing led to another! Of course, it was a professional relationship in the beginning.

MS: That's a great story! And your siblings?

MMH: There are four of us altogether, four brothers. The oldest is my stepbrother, Marlowe, from my father's first marriage, and then three of us: Maiyo, Mitro, and Made. We were called the M-Brothers. And then there was Mantle and, of course, Mommy. All Ms.

MS: You're the youngest? I thought that with the Balinese name Made, you'd be second in order?

MMH: I'm named after Prof. Dr. I Made Bandem, who was studying with my father at UCLA at the time I was born. Hardja Susilo, who also studied with my father, named my brother Mitro after his brother in Java.

MS: Can you tell me how your own musical journey began?

MMH: The first time I got interested in playing music was in middle school. I came home after seeing someone who brought a beautiful tenor saxophone along with other instruments for a new concert band they were starting. That's when I knew I'd love to play music. So I went to Dad and said, "Dad, I'd love to rent an instrument for a year." He said, "All right, we'll give it a go." At the same time we also had students coming home on Monday nights to play *angklung*. So, during middle school I began to delve into both. That was how I entered the world of music.

MS: So you played saxophone and *angklung* at the same time?

MMH: Yes. I think starting with saxophone, really having fun with that, and then realizing, oh, Dad plays music and has these students. I took an interest in that, too. When I was around fifteen, I played in a garage band. We were listening to Flock of Seagulls, Oingo Boingo. My brother had an interest in the punk movement. Later, we got into heavy metal. We were interested in virtuosic heavy metal—Iron Maiden, Black Sabbath, and that kind of thing. It was a phase!

MS: Do you see these as threads that gradually made you who you are?

MMH: Not at that time, but as I look back on it, I feel thankful that I had this insider's perspective into becoming an ethnomusicologist. For me, it was a natural progression to move in that direction. It wasn't so much a career choice. There was a period of time when I rejected a lot of that. In my teens, I wasn't so interested in the experiences with Javanese music. I moved toward Balinese music, I think, largely because Dad was doing Javanese, and I loved, let's say, the rock-and-roll side of it, which I was also playing at that time. When I was eighteen, I went to Bali to live for a year. That really changed my whole perspective on music and its context, whereas prior to that, I was just fascinated by the music. After spending a year learning language, getting to know my host family and the village I lived in, and coming back with that experience, then I knew it was something I'd do at the undergraduate level and later at the graduate level.

MS: Was this some kind of a program? You mentioned a host family. How did you get connected?

MMH: Long story short, I had just finished one year of community college and then went to Bali with the whole family for a month-long vacation. After that I applied for a Darmasiswa scholarship, stayed on for a year with I Made Bandem and his family, and studied at the conservatory, ASTI [Akademi Seni Tari Indonesia], as it was called at that time.

College Life

I probably *heard* the word "ethnomusicology" many, many times while growing up. *Comprehended* it? Probably not till my second year of high school, when I really got a grasp of what my father did as a profession. It really didn't mean much to me at that point. It was only after returning from my experience of living abroad for a year, understanding the music in its context, that I came back with heaps of questions about *Semar Pegulingan*, for example, the seven-tone gamelan orchestra I was studying. I wanted to learn a lot more about its history, its background, and the resurgence of interest in it. This was an ensemble that my father acquired and used at UMBC, University of Maryland at Baltimore County. So, while I was gone for a year, Ketut Gede Asnawa—who was doing his master's degree in ethnomusicology at UMBC—said, "Please learn as much as you can about *Semar Pegulingan*." I got back full of questions, so it was really in my undergraduate years that I was hungry for learning much more broadly about the music that I had studied through my childhood.

MS: So you did your undergraduate work at UMBC. Where did you go from there?

MMH: After that, I applied for a scholarship, once again the Darmasiswa program, and got that for two years. From '92 to '94 I returned to Bali for two more years of study. I had lots of questions about Balinese music that I wanted to get into much deeper at the academic level, and when I got back I was very keen to do that. My grades were piss poor in high school, though. After I returned, I had a very sharp focus. I knew what I wanted to do, and I had three years to finish my undergraduate degree. I really flip-flopped in terms of my attitude toward study and studying music. I played quite a bit all throughout my middle- and high-school years, but it was only after I got back from Bali that I started to take music seriously from an academic standpoint.

MS: What kind of classes were you taking when you experienced that change?

MMH: It was a BA in the music program at UMBC. You could study musicology, performance, and also ethnomusicology, so I took many seminar classes with my father.

MS: How do you take the step from there to becoming an ethnomusicologist?

MMH: I admit it wasn't immediate. After returning from the two years in Bali, I came back in '94 and said, "OK, what do I do now?" Dad said, "Why don't you go to graduate school and get a master's? You never know—you can always fall back on it." But I spent two or three years working in the school systems in the Tri-State area: Maryland, Virginia, and Pennsylvania. I worked with a nonprofit organization called Nada-Brahma, and we developed a curriculum for introducing world music in the school systems. The partner that I had, Tim Gregory, is still very active in Nada-Brahma. He was a great mentor because he was a fantastic communicator, fantastic teacher, and we were keen to collaborate not only on introducing world music programs to K–5, but also collaborating musically, taking a lot of the music I'd learned in Bali to the stage. We even produced a CD called *Dance Your Dance*. For me it was a creative time, and I wanted to assimilate other elements I had learned.

Nineteen Seventies

Ethnomusicologists of the late 1920s and 1930s generation are now senior scholars; those of the 1940s and 1950s generations are completing graduate school and entering long-term employment.

East Pakistan breaks free from Pakistan in a bloody civil war, resulting in the creation of Bangladesh in 1971; China and the United States restore relations after President Richard Nixon's 1972 visit; Nixon resigns (1974) following the Watergate investigation. Chile, Argentina, Uruguay, and Brazil carry out anticommunist military coups and violent repression from 1973; the Vietnam War ends in 1975; António de Oliveira Salazar's *Estado Novo* comes to an end in Portugal, 1974; Angola and Mozambique gain independence from Portugal in 1975, all but ending European colonialism in Africa; the Khmer Rouge establish a brutal utopian regime, 1975–79; the Soviets invade Afghanistan in 1979. The Iranian Revolution of 1979 sets the stage for a worldwide Islamic resurgence. Mantle Hood's *The Ethnomusicologist* is published in 1971; John Blacking's *How Musical Is Man*, an argument against elitism in musical taste and participation, appears in 1973, the same year as anthropologist Clifford Geertz's *The Interpretation of Cultures*, a monument of symbolic anthropology; Paul Berliner's 1975 *The Soul of Mbira* emphasizes the complicity of the researcher in the study of musical performance; In *Outline of a Theory of Practice* (English translated title, 1977) Pierre Bourdieu expounds on "habitus." Edward Said's *Orientalism*, a widely cited indictment of colonial and postcolonial sociopolitical and artistic gaze, appears in 1978.

Jan Mrázek

In conversation with Ted Solís, July 7, 2007, Vienna, Austria

Early Life

JM: I was born in February 1972 in Prague, Czech Republic. No one in my family is a professional musician, though my mother plays piano seriously and everyone likes music. I started to play violin when I was about four. I liked Western classical music and was very serious about it. It was possible in Prague to hear very good performances, sometimes every day. I used to bribe the usher to get in to concerts. I decided to be a professional violinist and went to the Prague Conservatory when I was fourteen. It was a prestigious school, but the training was narrowly focused on performance. We had to practice for five, six hours a day. No one cared if you knew anything else, as long as you were a good musician. I was there for two years and then I went to America with my parents.

Before I went to conservatory, when I was about ten or twelve, I began listening to different kinds of music, including gamelan. I had some LPs of Javanese and Balinese gamelan that were published in the Czech Republic, and I began to read about Asian music. One reason for my connection with Indonesian music is that my father, Rudolf Mrázek, is a scholar of Indonesian political history. Various people came from the United States to see him because it was the Communist era and he couldn't easily get out. When I was about twelve, Audrey Kahin (the wife of George Kahin [an American scholar of Southeast Asian history and politics]) saw that that I was interested in Asian music but had few resources. She talked to Marty Hatch, who was then editor of *Asian Music*, and Marty sent me a box of back issues of the journal. So for the next few years, I read one *Asian Music* article after another. In some ways, this was an underground activity, something that would not be appreciated at the conservatory. Then, when I was sixteen, my father got a Rockefeller Fellowship to go to Cornell for a year, and I went with him. I convinced my parents that there was no point for me to go to school if I could learn gamelan. They agreed, and so I stopped school and spent that whole year—eight, ten hours a day—learning gamelan.

TS: Who did you study with at Cornell?

JM: There were a few teachers: John Pemberton, Philip Yampolsky, and Marty Hatch. Sumarsam was also there, working on his PhD and going back and forth between Cornell and Wesleyan. I had a lot of lessons with him. There was also a huge collection of recordings at Cornell made by John Pemberton and others of master musicians from the generation of the '70s: Martopangrawit, Tjakrowasito, Sabtosurwarno, and others. I learned from Pak Sumarsam, Pak Harjito, and from listening to the tapes.

College Life

My father's fellowship was originally for just one year, but it was extended, and then he got a job at Michigan. He has been teaching there for about seventeen years and is now close to retirement. I went to Michigan when I was eighteen, in 1990, and did my BA there. They had a gamelan, too, and people who were very skillful, like Judith Becker, René Lysloff, and Pak Trustho, who was a visiting artist. I studied a lot with him. I had been to Java and studied gamelan there for a number of months and already knew Indonesian when I went to America.

TS: How did you learn Indonesian?

JM: I learned by myself in Prague. I had an instruction book, no tapes. There weren't many Indonesians in Prague, so I only began speaking when I went to Cornell and met Indonesians, including Pak Sumarsam. I also went to SEASSI at Cornell in either 1989 or 1990. I wasn't supposed to be there, because I was a high-school student, but I knew John Wolff and said, "I want to learn Javanese," and he made it possible for me to join. So when I went to Java for the first time, I knew Indonesian and Javanese. I went to study gamelan, but also other Javanese things, like batik. Then I went on to my BA at Michigan.

TS: What year did you finish your BA?

JM: 1993, in three years. I planned to major in music and philosophy. I went to music and philosophy lectures, but didn't like either, so I ended up majoring in art history and Japanese language and literature. I never thought, "Oh, I'm not interested in music or philosophy." It was more, "Maybe this is not what I want to study here." I was still reading a lot. When I talked to students in America and mentioned any nice book I liked, they would say, "Oh, I read it for this or that class." And I said, "Why," because I didn't read books for classes. I was used to doing things I really liked outside school. I never thought I would stop playing or thinking about music; I just decided not to do it in school.

JULIE STRAND

In conversation with Ted Solís, July 5, 2010, on Skype

Early Life

JS: I was born in Baltimore, Maryland, in July 1972. We moved to Grand Rapids, Michigan, when I was less than a year old and I went through K–12 there. My dad was an oral surgeon. My mom started law school when I was eight and eventually became a lawyer. They got divorced when I was five, and my two brothers and I lived with my mom. Neither of my parents was musical, so there wasn't much music around the house. We had a piano and I played around with it, had piano lessons a bit, but never became a pianist. My mom also had an old clarinet, and I played around with that, too. I started playing it formally in the sixth-grade school band. As a single parent, my mom was very protective, and I rebelled against that. I also reacted against the homogeneity of the white, suburban, upper-class, midwestern community we lived in. Although we didn't have a lot of money ourselves, it did set me apart. I went to school with lots of spoiled rich kids who had everything they wanted.

I hung out mostly with musicians in high school. I thought it would be social suicide to get into music when I started high school, but I found most of my friends there. I was good at clarinet, so played in band, orchestra, and outside community ensembles. I was also good in math, physics, and advanced calculus, so I thought I might go into engineering, but I had advisors who gave me the "follow your passion" idea. I applied to colleges in both engineering and music, but I liked my musical persona better, so I ended up majoring in music.

College Life

I went to the University of Michigan to major in clarinet performance. My parents had been to Albion College, but it had to be a state school for me because of the money—my brother was in college, too. You couldn't really have a minor at U of M, and anyway, the music major had so many requirements that I didn't really have room for a minor.

TS: Did you consider getting a BA instead of a BM?

JS: You couldn't do that at U of M, but you could get something called a BMA, bachelor of musical arts, in which you could take fewer performance courses and more outside courses. I went for the BMA, but I was still playing a lot, which led to a musical crisis. I got tendonitis and had to rest my hands, so I couldn't practice as much as I needed to be a full-time musician. That crisis eventually helped lead me in the direction of ethnomusicology. In my first year, I had taken a freshman-required world music course, the first course in the history sequence, taught by Bill Malm. We learned about all these different cultures: "This is the kind of music they make in this culture; this is what they do with it; this is what it sounds like." Up to that point I'd never even heard of ethnomusicology. As a result of the course, I played in Malm's Japanese ensemble: *noh, kabuki, taiko,* and so forth. That was really hard, sitting on my knees for three hours! Oddly, Malm was the only ethnomusicologist I knew at Michigan. I was still heavily involved with Western music, so I never got to know Judith Becker or play in the gamelan. Around the time of my tendonitis, some friends came back from Ghana. They had learned to play the *gyl* xylophone of the Dagari from northwest Ghana and southern Burkina. That really turned me on.

I took an extra semester at U of M and graduated in December 1994. I stayed in Ann Arbor and worked for a while, until my aunt and uncle—who had a place on

Lake Michigan—invited my brother and me to live with them. I wanted to get out of Ann Arbor, so I joined them. It was only about an hour from Chicago, so I started going to Chicago and played with a new music/improv group called Ensemble No Amnesia, directed by Gene Coleman. Through them I got to know an Argentine composer, Guillermo Gregorio, and began playing for him. Although I was heavily involved with these groups, I thought, "I've got to go to Africa." I'd never been any place before, apart from Windsor, Ontario (just across the Canadian border from Detroit), and family trips to the Caribbean. But in 1997 I went backpacking to Ghana, Burkina Faso, and Mali for three months, February through May. All I had was a *Rough Guide to West Africa*. I couldn't speak any local languages—I went to these French-speaking countries and didn't even know any French! I discovered I had a relative, David P. Rawson, who was actually an ambassador [from 1995 to 1999] and had a house in Bamako, Mali, so I showed up there. It had been really rough going because I didn't have a lot of money and traveled very cheap. It was great to be able to stay in a nice place with air conditioning and such. We went down to Sikasso in southern Mali. I also went to Bobo-Dioulasso (the second city of Burkina), and heard this great xylophone playing, the main thing in that area.

TS: Did you have any percussion background before this other than playing in Malm's Japanese ensemble?

JS: No, never, but I grew up with two brothers who were drummers. I knew before I went to Africa that I wanted to study ethnomusicology, but I wanted to take a trip to see things for myself and find things I could maybe use later for research. I remember very early on that I was in a village and a guy playing a talking drum came over, sat down next to me, and started playing at me. He'd play something and they'd all laugh and he'd play something else. I knew he was saying something, but I of course didn't understand it, and that really fascinated me.

Katherine Butler Schofield

In conversation with Ted Solís, July 9, 2007, Vienna, Austria

Early Life

KBS: I was born in Brisbane, Australia, in early 1974. Both my parents are schoolteachers. My mother teaches English and history. She's now the headmistress of a large independent school in Australia. My dad is a science teacher, though recently he's become a kind of religious studies guru. My family is involved in the Lutheran Church in Australia, though my mother's father was a Presbyterian minister. I grew up with a very strong extended family culture of music; there was always lots of enthusiastic singing. What made my own nuclear family distinctive, however, was that both my parents were good amateur folk singers. They toured Southeast Asia with a folk group during the folk revival of the late '60s and early '70s. So we grew up—there are four of us, I'm the eldest—singing folk music. According to family legend, I could sing before I could speak, and I could sing harmony from the age of two. We sang as a family, a bit like the Von Trapp Family Singers.

TS: What kind of folk music was it?

KBS: Mostly English, Irish, Scottish, some American old time, and also country-gospel. My dad was also involved in outdoor education, so we lived in the Australian bush at an outdoor education center for a few years when I was growing up. Dad did a lot of playing for bush bands—the Australian version of *ceilidh* bands—and square dancing. When I was seven, Dad decided he wanted a fiddle in his band, so I started having violin lessons. Of course, when you're in urban Australia (we were back in Brisbane by then), you learn classical. So I did Suzuki violin.

College Life

I didn't intend to study music at university. I wanted to do law, psychology, or history— I've always had a historian's mindset. But when I got to the age when I had to make a decision, I felt that if I stopped playing violin, I would die. In Australia at that time, there was not much amateur classical music making beyond school level, so either I went to the conservatory to study performance, or I would have to stop playing. So I went to the Queensland Conservatorium of Music when I was sixteen. Fairly rapidly, I found that—to me, at least—it was not a very intellectual place. The program was half academic and half performance oriented, so we did do history and theory of music and things like that. That contributed to the bifurcation in my identity: I've got my performer's side and I've got my academic side. I studied viola, not violin, and got a job in a chamber orchestra when I was nineteen. That was the summit of my ambitions, so I quit my degree.

After a few months, I realized I hated the job. It was incredibly stressful. We played music up to Beethoven and then nothing until very contemporary works. It wasn't stimulating enough for a whole career, so I quit. I went back to finish my degree and continued playing casually for the orchestra, partly to fund my degree. When I went back to conservatory, I had a very intense personal identity crisis. I didn't know who I was. It was quite traumatic and took me about seven years to get over because I felt like I had failed as a performer. I survived the rest of my degree by singing jazz with a pianist friend. This got me into improvisation, and I really enjoyed that. At that point I was thinking, "What can I do with a degree in performance? I'm going to have to go down the academic route." That was when I started getting into musicology.

TS: Tell me more about how singing jazz saved you?

KBS: I think it was a restoration of the kind of music making I did as a child. I had all this ability in singing non-operatic styles and improvising harmonies because the music we did as a family was entirely improvised. I was listening to a lot of jazz—big band, swing, that kind of thing—and Ella Fitzgerald and other torch singers. I had a friend, Ian Reid, who was doing a law degree but had done a music degree. We loved the same kind of music, from the '30s, '40s, and early '50s, so we sang and played a lot together. Around that time, I got involved with a group of friends who had grown up in India and Bangladesh. Through them I became interested in India and Indo-Islamic culture and started listening to North Indian classical music. Somewhere along the line I realized that it was an incredibly complex, difficult, virtuosic system that is both elite and classical, and at the same time it's the performer, improvising or spontaneously composing, who is in charge of the work. It appealed to both the performance and the academic sides of me.

When I went back, I had two years left. The final year of a four-year degree in Australia is what's known as an honors year. You can leave after three years, or you can do an optional fourth year, in which you have to do a Research Methods course and a dissertation. The guy who ran our Research Methods course was Gregg Howard, an ethnomusicologist, who worked on Buddhist music in Japan and Southeast Asia. He was a nice man, very meticulous. This was the mid-1990s, when new musicology was starting to explode and penetrate what we were learning. I found the way we studied Western art music to be somewhat dull. It was basically a three-year succession of dead white men. In many ways, I'm grateful for that training, because I do have a very solid background in Western art music. On the other hand, I found new musicology, especially work like Susan McClary's, unconvincing. I had issues with McClary's fairly speculative understanding of sonata form and its meaning. For me, it didn't bear much relation to reality. It was interesting but didn't make sense to me. I was much more interested in why people liked music, what music meant to them, and why music was different in different cultures. I was becoming interested in India and in Islam, and at one point I started thinking it would be cool to look at medieval chant in Spain and the different interminglings of Andalusian music, to see how the music of al-Andalus coming up from Morocco influenced medieval chant. It was a pragmatic interest in what works, rooting music to reality rather than a philosophical speculation about its meaning.

Jonathan Dueck

In conversation with Margaret Sarkissian, October 27, 2007, Columbus, Ohio

Early Life

JD: I was born in Goshen, Indiana, in July 1974, Watergate year. My dad was an English and Mennonite Studies professor at a small Mennonite college in Kansas. My mom took a theology degree and then stayed home with us, so I had two highly interpretive parents who were really interested in literature. They're also very performative people, especially my mother. So that kind of interpretive environment and being part of a relatively elite church community was part of my life, even as a kid.

We moved from Kansas to Gretna in southern Manitoba when I was six. The name comes from Gretna Green, because of all the Scots who came to Manitoba. That was a real turning point for me, because the Mennonites where I lived in Kansas were mostly Anglo-assimilated. There were all kinds of distinctive things about the Kansas community, but it looked a lot like other small-town communities. In Manitoba, though, there was a strong sense of ethnicity in the Mennonite community. Immigration happened later, and even the children in the playground spoke Low German, a language I'd never heard before. So it wasn't only moving to Canada, another country, it was also moving to another area of the world in a pretty strong way. I think that early experience of difference within a people that I identified as my own, but which had a whole different language, folkways, food, and music, was a way into this for me. It was something I had to work on, rather than something that was self-evident.

MS: Were you aware of this cultural difference at the time, or are you reflecting in retrospect?

JD: I don't know if I would have consciously called it "culture shock," but I didn't understand the world around me. It took a long time. I think that shift made me very self-conscious about music because music was central in the community. I couldn't get the Low German jokes (all I know to this day is the swear words), but I could become part of the musical structures, and I found I was good at it.

MS: So music was the way you learned to socialize?

JD: Yes, music was my most successful entry into the culture that I would call my own. My dad taught English and Mennonite Studies at a little high school, the Mennonite Collegiate Institute. It's the oldest Mennonite school in Canada, and it had a remarkable choral music tradition. I'm literally a product of that institution.

College Life

I went to every college or university in Winnipeg and did my undergrad in between them! I have two degrees. One is a bachelor of church music from the Canadian Mennonite Bible College, a college of the University of Manitoba. It's not quite an English model, but the big public universities have smaller religious colleges that offer things like music and theology as part of the larger university. I also went across town to another Mennonite college, Concord College. This was a college of the University of Winnipeg, a competing and quite liberal institution, which had a Chair in Mennonite Studies. It had a formal insider's study, an ethnic studies tradition, and also a great literary tradition. So I went to the University of Manitoba, the University of Winnipeg, CMBC, and Concord College, and I took a couple of other courses by correspondence from different places.

MS: What kind of courses were you taking?

JD: The bachelor of church music was essentially a classical music degree. I took some courses in church music but also studied conducting—instrumental and choral—and took voice lessons. I was a voice major. I started in a School of Music but moved to CMBC because at the School of Music all my courses were programmed and none were interpretive. They were history and theory courses from a very applied sense. Not that they weren't smart—they were—but they weren't meaning-making courses. The Bible College really appealed to me because it was an academic institution, teaching academic theology. Its graduates went on in theology and philosophy. It provided the sort of framework for the Bible and theology courses that really interested me.

MS: At that point, where did you envision going with that?

JD: I wanted to be an opera singer, but at the end of the degree, I concluded that classical music was too conservative for me. I remember doing juries and singing a song a certain way. I'd studied it and had an idea of the way I wanted to sing it, but I was told, "That's not the way it's done." I didn't like the idea that I'd be constantly subjected to those pressures, not to interpret, but to perform in a way that conformed to some norm. And I really wanted to be writing things, so I took a degree in religion and music. I studied both an interpretive tradition as well as an applied tradition of performance. I think the writing tradition won out in the end. The other thing I realized was that local relationships are really important to me. I had friends who were singers who traveled quite a bit. I saw their relationships falling apart, and I saw the difficulty of maintaining home relationships when you're rarely at home. I wanted to make sure that as a scholar I could still have a good relationship with my spouse and have a good community of friends in an area.

Late Nineteen Seventies and Nineteen Eighties

Many from the late 1920s and 1930s generations are retiring or contemplating doing so; those of the 1940s and the older among the 1950s generation are now, if academics, senior scholars; those from the 1960s are in tenured or long-term employment.

Reagan/Thatcher austerity policies result in weakened unions and social safety nets, increasing wage disparities. The US Religious Right becomes a potent political force. IBM introduces the personal computer in 1981, the same year that MTV and CDs appear. Apple introduces the Macintosh computer in 1984; Microsoft introduces the Windows operating system for PCs in 1985. Chernobyl nuclear disaster occurs in 1986. The AIDS crisis rages into the 1990s. The Soviet Union, with its domination of Warsaw Pact countries, is on its way toward dissolution. Television viewing becomes widespread in the non-Western world. The *New Grove Dictionary of Music and Musicians* (edited by Stanley Sadie), with greatly expanded coverage of non-Western European art music (WEAM) subject matter, appears in twenty volumes in 1980. The International Folk Music Council (IFMC) changes its name to the International Council for Traditional Music (ICTM), 1981. Steven Feld publishes *Sound and Sentiment* (1982). Benedict Anderson publishes *Imagined Communities* (1983). Gerard Béhague publishes *Performance Practice: Ethnomusicological Perspectives* (1984). Anthony Seeger explores the relationship of sound and social structure in *Why Suyá Sing*, 1987, the same year Timothy Rice re-examines Merriam's 1964 models in the *Ethnomusicology* article "Toward the Remodeling of Ethnomusicology." Richard Schechner publishes the interdisciplinary performance studies monument *Performance Theory*, 1988. Ellen Koskoff's 1989 *Women and Music in Cross-Cultural Perspective* is an ethnomusicological landmark in its attention to gender issues. The University of Chicago Press initiates the *Chicago Studies in Ethnomusicology*, 1990.

W. F. Umi Hsu

In video conversation with Margaret Sarkissian, October 6, 2017

Early Life

UH: I'm Umi, formerly known as Wendy, Hsu. My pronouns are they/them, and I'm located in Los Angeles, where I live and work. I was born in August 1978 in Taipei, Taiwan. I spent the first twelve years of my life there, though my family always had the idea of moving to the United States. We moved to Virginia in 1991, where I spent the next twenty years.

My mom worked on the Taiwan side of a transnational import/export business started by our relatives in Virginia. They imported and exported Chinese cloissoné-style fashion jewelry. My dad's a dentist. The transition was hard on him because he would have to go back to dental school in order to become a licensed dentist in the US. He wasn't interested in that, so after three or four years, he moved back to Taiwan to continue his practice. I have one brother who's three years younger than me.

I've been a music junkie ever since I was a little kid. My mom had read about the effects of classical music on the brain, so she played a lot of music, especially Mozart. I responded to music kinesthetically—I remember dancing wildly to Mozart—so my mom put me through classical music training camp, Suzuki-style. We followed the Yamaha model, so at a pretty young age I was exposed to keyboard skills, ear training, and all those layers of classical musical education. Even then, though, I was also interested in pop music and collecting cassettes. My paternal grandmother sang lots of beautiful tunes from her era. She was a professor of flower arranging in the Japanese *ikebana* tradition and liked to hum Taiwanese and Japanese *enka* while doing flower arrangements or watering her plants. I got immersed in that sound world of Taiwanese old tunes (*laoge* 老歌) inspired by enka and original enka in Japanese growing up.

MS: What kinds of popular music were you listening to back then? Was it mostly Taiwanese?

UH: Yes. In the '80s, Taiwan was the center of Mandopop and exported music to Chinese-speaking communities, including Hong Kong, Singapore, Vietnam, Thailand, and definitely the PRC, once that market opened up. Mandopop shaped lots of other popular music forms of the time. I listened to enka because it was part of my personal aural history. *Enka* influenced Taiwanese music (which was not the same as Mandopop), and Taiwanese enka further articulated the sorrow and melancholic aspects of Japanese enka. I also listened to lots of folk opera (*gezaixi* 歌仔戲) that had been brought to Taiwan by people who immigrated from southern China from the seventeenth century on. I'd watch it on television with my grandparents. I was always next to them when they enjoyed their music.

MS: As a child, then, you responded favorably to Chinese opera, as opposed to thinking of it as "boring grandma stuff"?

UH: Absolutely. That's how I learned the Taiwanese language, which is very similar to the Hokkien dialect from Fujian Province in China. There was also an interesting gender element of the tradition that I was really drawn to. Southern-style Chinese opera had female cast members who played different kinds of gender types and gender roles. I always thought it interesting that there was a space in performance for gender fluidity. Even among the fans there were women who were in love with a particular character who was male on stage but everyone knew was played by a female-bodied performer. The fans were clued-in to this gender fluidity, and the disjuncture between the physical body of the performer versus the enacted body was central to being the object of infatuation.

In Taiwan there's a kind of neutral sex (*zhong xing* 中性) as a gender expression that's more than subcultural. If somebody happens to look more androgynous, people say, "Ok, you're more neutral than male or female." This expression also manifests in pop culture. For singers who appear to be gender neutral, that's part of their expression and identity as performers. I was always drawn to that. It was difficult for me to move to Virginia, where the gender dichotomy was really entrenched.

MS: How did your musical experience change when you moved to Virginia?

UH: My brother and I were both immersed in Western classical music in Taiwan. After moving to Virginia we became really active in the orchestra—he played cello and I played viola. We expressed ourselves in that world because in some ways it was easier: it was nonverbal, and there were things we could do musically that didn't involve putting ourselves out there ethnically and linguistically, which was a bit of a challenge initially. In Virginia the stereotype of the perpetual foreigner was rampant and we fought very hard against that, but in musical situations we were able to be ourselves.

This was also when I reclaimed and rediscovered my love for playing piano. As a kid, I had a hard time with piano. It was something I had to do but never felt that classical music made sense to me in terms of playing what had been written already. After I moved to Virginia I needed something to express my own feelings, so I played piano quite often.

MS: Were you playing a different kind of repertory at this point?

UH: I was starting to branch out from the center of classical music to the periphery, playing older works like Bach, but I also found early-twentieth-century work like

Shostakovich and Schoenberg interesting. In eighth grade my school district started a summer institute for kids who exhibited an interest in the arts, so I was invited to apply. I got in and then spent summers at camps with other kids who wanted to delve deeper into music. I learned some jazz, some blues, music history and theory, and got to hang out with college professors who were interested in extending the curricular reach to K–12 kids.

MS: What was your hometown, by the way?

UH: Newport News. It's between Colonial Williamsburg, the heart of Virginia's history, Richmond, the capital of the Confederacy, and Hampton, where a lot of athletes and rappers come from, and next to Norfolk, where there's a large naval base and a shipyard. It was a crazy cosmopolitan space with a military industrial complex and American southern heritage. I saw lots of military families and their kids, who had international experience, but through the lens of the US military. And then there was the Virginian experience in the suburbs, where black-white racial tension has always been part of the way people organize and see themselves and their spaces. It was *classic* in a sense, with a little bit of everything—symbolic of the new American South.

MS: And, in the middle of all this, you and your brother played viola and cello?

UH: Yes, we played as a duet that we called "the Hsuette," a play on words from our last name. People had a hard time pronouncing our last name so we reclaimed it in the musical context. We were both in the orchestra and realized that we loved playing music in front of people. Our mom became a kind of booking agent, getting us gigs at retirement homes and communities that were interested in having young people coming into their living spaces to play music for them. We played film scores, folk and traditional tunes, early American and Irish ballads—anything that had been curated and arranged for piano and cello. People loved it, and it was a way for us not only to be ourselves but also to do so in front of people who normally wouldn't know us as a family in a place where we were the only Taiwanese family. It was a good way to connect with people.

MS: When you went into these communities, did people sing along with you?

UH: Yes, they totally did! Any time we played a number from *The Sound of Music*, people would shout "again!" For some reason, "Climb Every Mountain" would bring people to tears, so it was always our epic ending. They'd clap and sing along. Sometimes people in the retirement home who had a hard time socializing would even start talking. I guess it was rare for some of them to talk, so our music would bring out a side of them that was more social.

MS: That's very cool. Did your musical activities continue through high school?

UH: Yes, I played in the orchestra, and then some friends and I started a string quartet. We took wedding gigs and parties as a way to get outside our comfort zone and make some money on the side. Two of our quartet members were composers, so we played some original music too.

College Life

UH: I joined a ska band when I started at Virginia Commonwealth University. The sound of first- and second-wave ska—earlier Jamaican-style ska—reminded me of some of the pickup bands I heard as a kid growing up in Taiwan. These bands played *nakashi*, a street music style originally from Japan that has become an object of fascination for me as a researcher. *Nakashi* originally means "flow" or "fashionable" and has been popular in Taiwan since the Japanese Occupation era of the 1930s. The pickup musicians are like song machines and can recall thousands of popular songs of their time. They play, typically, at tea parlors in hot springs, resorts, hotels, subway stations, and places like that, usually on guitar and accordion. Some of the comping styles on guitars and keyboard instruments sound very similar to early ska, so I made that connection in my head and always liked that.

MS: Being Taiwanese in a part of the country where you stood out as different, was music a way for you to fit in and find community? Did you imagine that you would pursue music at college?

UH: When I started to attend the summer camps as a thirteen- and fourteen-year-old, I decided that I was going to play music for the rest of my life, but in terms of professional aspirations, there were lots of strictures upon ideas about success and economic mobility. As an immigrant, I had to reconcile that with my own self and with my family. So when I started college, I majored in biology and pre-med. At some point I picked up music as a second major. I went through the whole pre-med education and even applied for and got into med school, but I still wanted to play music. In the end I had to come out to my mom and tell her that I didn't actually want to go to med school.

MS: How did your mom take that?

UH: Oh, she was really upset. She took it personally. She felt that music was not going to be a viable path, economically, so I had to tell her that, actually, I wanted to study music as a scholar. That was way outside her framework. It was difficult to reconcile different parts of me with what she thought I was going to become. I dropped the bio but maintained the pre-med and ended up pursuing a dual degree in music and religious studies. I think at the time I was having an identity crisis, and religious studies provided a creative and philosophical space in which I could explore my identity through the lens of Eastern thought and religions. I ended up studying the history and cultural context of Buddhism and American manifestations of East Asian religions—Zen and its creative offshoots in experimental modern music. I was fascinated by 1950s American experimentalism—John Cage, La Monte Young, Fluxus—and the intersecting points between Eastern notions and how they were manifesting in an increasingly globalized Western art world.

MS: At what point did you discover ethnomusicology? Do you remember when you first heard the term and what it meant to you at that moment?

UH: I think I heard it way early on, when I was in school in Taiwan, but I heard it in Chinese, so I didn't realize what it was until later. I grew up in the part of Taipei next to National Taiwan Normal University, a teachers' college with a well-known ethnomusicology program. But it was really in college where I was exposed to world music. I took an Intro to World Music course, loved it, and felt like it was a teaser.

Jason Busniewski

In conversation with Ted Solís and Margaret Sarkissian, October 27, 2007, Columbus, Ohio

Early Life

JB: I was born in August 1985, in Waukesha, Wisconsin. I've been a nerd all my life. I've always been fascinated by other parts of the world. I used to sit around as a kid reading an encyclopedia in my room. I started playing viola the summer after my fourth grade year, stopped for a while when I changed schools, and picked it up again in the middle of sixth grade. I've been playing ever since. When I was in high school, I was really into politics and was invited to go to the National Youth Leadership Forum on Defense, Intelligence, and Diplomacy.

College Life

I started at [the University of] Oklahoma as a political science and European studies major. To be honest, it was the last place I wanted to be. I got into Boston College but was offered very little financial aid. On paper it looked like my parents were making a decent amount of money, but having to pay almost all of it in bills and for our house, we couldn't manage. Oklahoma sent me a letter saying, "We'll give you this ridiculous National Merit Scholarship if you come to our school." My parents pretty much made me go. But being there has been great, because Zoe Sherinian is there and I've gotten a chance to study with her for four years now. I did music all through middle school and high school. I liked it a lot, but it wasn't really something I thought of as a career.

MS: How did you move toward thinking about it as a career?

JB: I was going along as a political science major in my freshman year of college—I've been a fairly devout Christian for a long time, since I was a little kid, and grew up in a Christian home—when I suddenly felt like I was being called to music. It was really weird, because it was never something I'd considered. So I auditioned for the School of Music and barely got in. At the time, I was involved with some people who were doing missionary work, and they made a point about how much the Christian gospel has been associated with Western colonialism and cultural imperialism. I learned from them to appreciate other peoples' cultures, not like situations you hear about with missionaries destroying cultures—that's kind of a stereotype. I think I learned more about appreciating other cultures from those missionaries than from anyone in the Anthropology Department or the Music Department.

MS: Were they other students?

JB: Yes, mostly students. There's a Christian belief that people are made in the image of God and that God is a creative God, so when people create beautiful works of art, they're reflecting the image of God. So all these different cultures in the world are fundamentally valuable because they're people reflecting the image of God. That's been a powerful idea for me. I ended up wanting to be involved with making Christianity a culturally appropriate thing. I mean, take India, for example: you have a number of churches where people are singing four-part harmony, or hymns in English, or even English hymns translated into Tamil or Telugu or something. It doesn't bear a whole lot of relation to the modes of spiritual expression and communication that the people in their culture have. That was a big thing in nineteenth- and twentieth-century mission work, this "civilizing the savages." I don't really know that people need all that much civilizing; it's just not necessary. Jesus was not a post-Enlightenment white guy and neither should his followers have to be. It's okay to be a Greek Christian or a Latin Christian, or whatever. It's fine to be an Indian Christian or a Japanese Christian, you know? It's something that's open to all cultures. At least, that's what I believe. I'm interested in it as a side-benefit of doing research, of being able to take away a Western cultural barrier from people if they want to investigate Christianity.

But to get back to my freshman and sophomore years of college. I was at a Christian concert with a friend of mine, a group called Caedmon's Call, who had gone to India with a group called the Dalit Freedom Network, a Christian human rights group that works with the Untouchables. They were singing about God's love for India and sharing videos of little kids running around the streets, and I just felt a pull on my heart. After that I found out that Zoe Sherinian was working on indigenization of Christianity in South India, which was maybe a coincidence, maybe not, depending on your take on things of that nature.

MS: Did you follow up on this burgeoning interest and take a class with Zoe?

JB: Well, I was a music major, and in your second semester as a music major at OU you take World Music. So I was thinking, how can I study Indian music? Ah, ethnomusicology—all right! How can I do this stuff with Christianity and music? So I fell into it, and I just absolutely love it. It's not something I planned to do at all, but I really enjoy it. I still get my social politics and stuff, but I love music. So I took the World Music class, and Professor Paula Conlon—she specializes in Native American music—introduced me to Dr. Sherinian. We talked, and the next year I took a class of hers, "Music and the Politics of Nation from the Middle East to South Asia." We looked at the cultural politics of music in *Bharata Natyam* dance in Tamil Nadu; music in Afghanistan (she brought in John Baily to talk and show a film); and Virginia Danielson came to talk about Umm Kulthum and *A Voice Like Egypt* [Goldman 1996]. I also took a graduate ethnomusicology seminar with Dr. Sherinian and some anthropology classes. I went on independent study and had an undergraduate research grant from our university this spring to attend the Heartland Seminar on Arabic Music in Racine, Wisconsin. I also wrote a paper on Bedrich Smetana's *Má Vlast*, a cycle of six symphonic poems that was essentially a Czech nationalist work. Mark Slobin's work has been really influential—his subculture/superculture theory is probably the single most influential theoretical concept. I also researched Hindu devotional music. I live in an apartment building with a lot of students from India, and there's a devotional meeting called a *satsang* that meets in the apartment above mine. Every Saturday night, I hear bells and cymbals and singing. So I went up and joined them and learned some *bhajan* singing, which is a simple devotional song.

TS: You sang along with them?

JB: Yes. I'm not really that interested in worshipping any deities, but it's participant observation.

TS: It's interesting that you were willing to do that as a devout Christian, because I've occasionally had Christian students in my classes who, when they were asked to learn a *kriti*, refused to do it, saying "No, I can't sing to a false God. Jesus is a jealous God, I can't do that."

JB: If you think about it and the commitments that are involved, it is a potentially hairy issue in maintaining personal integrity. But as a Christian, it's something I've prayed about and I view it as participant observation. There's no really good way to learn the music unless you do it. I was taking Karnatak violin lessons in India this summer, and I encountered the same thing. Being taught a *kriti*—it's what I have to do to be able to learn the music. Actually, it was interesting because in the *satsang*, there's the *aarti*, the sacred flame, and an image of Durga, and everyone went over there, said a prayer, and wafted the smoke over themselves. I drew the line at that. It was enough for me to observe my neighbors and friends doing it. And they were perfectly okay with me being there and doing some stuff and not doing other stuff. But I did eat the *prasad*. I viewed it as, "My friends are offering me food, okay." It was an interesting negotiation between me as the researcher, trying to participate and still maintain my own personal religious integrity while trying to respect the people that I'm with.

TS: So where are you now in your program?

JB: I'm about to finish my fifth and final year as an undergrad! I'm looking at grad schools. I went to India this summer with the Dalit Freedom Network.

MS: Was this your first visit to India?

JB: Yes, I went with the Dalit Freedom Network to see some of the things that they're doing with schools in the slums in Mumbai. It was a fantastic experience for me because I've had this long-standing desire to fight poverty. I started a student organization on my campus because there wasn't a lot of stuff going on for developing countries when I was a freshman. I tried to get some like-minded students to figure out what college students could do; it only costs a dollar a day for the anti-retrovirals to keep somebody with AIDS alive. I spend more money on coffee than most people in the world make in a given day. We like to think of ourselves as "poor college students," but we have *so incredibly much* potential. And as a Christian—yeah, yeah, everything goes back to this with me—one of the greatest commandments in the Bible is supposed to be "Love your neighbor as yourself." I do all of these things for myself, and if I'm supposed to love my neighbor in the same way, then I ought to try and secure these things for other people, no matter where they live.

TS: Have you had any chance to learn any Indian language yet?

JB: I haven't, unfortunately. That's definitely something I want to do down the line. This summer was a really good opportunity to see, one, what people are doing about poverty, because it's a passion of mine. I'd like to use music to somehow help with this. I was talking to Anthony Seeger about that the other night, and I think he's got some good ideas. I should probably e-mail him when I leave. Two, I was able to take Karnatak violin lessons with Ananda Raman, a local performer in a neighborhood called Nerul. And three, I was able to do some fieldwork at the church that was affiliated with the school. I'd go, with my tape recorder, and record the Sunday service, Bible studies, and music, and ask questions of people. It was a good chance to get some experience as to what to watch out for in future fieldwork—like needing to be really tenacious with questions. Not to the point of being obnoxious, but I have a tendency to stand back and observe and not necessarily ask all the questions that maybe I should. I think—and maybe I'm wrong on this—but it seems that in India you have to ask more than once. And not pry necessarily, but really be tenacious with your questioning. And I learned about scheduling, taking notes, things about recording. It was a really good opportunity to get some of that stuff out of the way now so that when I have a long-term research project, then I'll know what I'm doing.

PART 2

Career Trajectories

Many assume that teaching and research in a tenured college or university position—"professorial academia" or (more commonly) "the professoriat"—are the ne plus ultra of all who enter graduate school. Many others, however, feel that their interests are best served outside of that world, and they either leave or avoid it altogether. Reasons commonly expressed include: a general distaste for formal classroom teaching or "professing"; perceptions of "publishing or perishing" pressures; a desire to avoid "departmental politics" (presumably seeking a "politics-free" environment); and the idea that one can have a greater impact on society outside the professoriat.

As we see in this chapter on career trajectories, however, these stark differences tend to be overstated. Most of our interlocutors, regardless of employment status, do research of some sort, which they channel into varieties of teaching through their professional activities: university teaching, delivering public lectures, composing, concertizing, designing library programs and collections, museum curating, transmitting digital knowledge, editorial publishing, recording production, participating in NGO activism, and so on. By virtue of this teaching, most ethnomusicologists engage in "applied ethnomusicology," with impacts upon the community at large. They all passionately advocate for intercultural respect and understanding, and the preservation of cultural traditions they have researched. They bring to these activities competencies (linguistic, observational/analytical, trans- and inter-disciplinary, organizational, intangible "people skills," and others) acquired through informal and formal education and honed in the crucibles of fieldwork and dissertation writing. They have utilized this versatility differently, according to employment context (size of the institution, for instance) and epoch. In the late 1940s and early 1950s, for example, even a large school of music might have only one person who taught every-thing required, musicologically speaking: music appreciation, a freshman course on music literature, a music history survey, some period courses, a specialized seminar. With few ethnomusicological specialists active (and far fewer historical musicolo-gists than today), in a large music unit one might find a "seminar in musicology," including a week or two on "folk music," or "comparative musicology," or perhaps "ethnomusicology" (but not "world music," a term which would not appear until some thirty years later). Unless a given music department included on its faculty one of the few active ethnomusicologists, one was likely to get a broad overview of the still-wide-open field, which displayed the nearly limitless possibilities for those entering it. William P. Malm's classic *Japanese Music and Musical Instruments* (1959) was an example of the very broad approach still possible in scholarly monographs, before increasing numbers of graduate students in search of new territory began, as it were, to "slice the pie" more thinly. As Ricardo Trimillos notes, however, due to the general acceptance of global and multicultural subject matter, we may be entering (in some ways re-entering) an era in which an ability to teach some aspect of "world music" is not limited in music departments to ethnomusicologists. This tendency, and its obvious threat to the employment prospects of professionally trained ethnomusicologists, has been the subject of a number of twenty-first-century conference round tables.

Our interlocutors have typically entered ethnomusicology in two ways. Young people who began by studying or working in assorted areas relating to ethnic, cultural, and geographic diversity may have subsequently found or re-embraced music, been struck by the convergence of their cultural and musical interests in ethnomusicology, and thus turned in that direction. Conversely, they may already have been involved in some area of music, having had their interest in "the other" ignited or re-ignited by something. Among our interlocutors, the second way clearly predominates, although perhaps somewhat less during the late 1980s and '90s, when many ethnomusicologists were less concerned with sound per se than the social ramifications of those sounds. Once one is a musician in some capacity (in the broad, rather than elite and profes-sional sense), one has some tools with which to pursue a second, third, fourth musical area or expressive language if sufficiently motivated. On the other hand, discovering or newly pursuing music as a preoccupation, or as a confident competency, would appear a much more formidable step. While not by any means were all enrolled or engaged in formal academic music programs when ethnomusicology came into their lives, most were actively engaged in music. What was then required was some spark to activate the process of coalescence. In "Career Trajectories" we observe these "sparks" and the many ways ethnomusicologists have reconciled them with the realities of their working worlds.

Updates

The first interview for *Living Ethnomusicology* took place in Egham, England, in July 2007, and the last via Skype in October 2017. Considering the considerable time elapsed in many cases (one of our interviewees was an undergraduate at the time of his interview, and is now, fieldwork completed, finishing his doctoral dissertation!), we thought updates would appropriately serve our goal of outlining career trajectories.

Much can change rapidly for graduate students and junior faculty as they explore their field and take a variety of temporary work assignments while seeking more permanent footing. At that stage many accept employment related to aspects of their background they may not have thought of as their primary strength—part of the strategy of casting the widest net possible (see "Of Course I'm the Person for the Job" in the introduction). The job often involves teaching or supervisory duties in new areas; these may be inherited from a predecessor in the position or reflect developing unit initiatives. Anything coming to the department head's attention that seems exotic, folky, or non-WEAM (Western European art music) will quickly arrive in the ethnomusicologist's inbox. (Message: "Are you interested in this note from the African Studies Department?") Such circumstances may simply be a distraction, but they can also lead to a second or third research area. After moving past the pre-tenure potential pitfalls of divided research energies, some explore new or latent interests such as more performing, exploring new cultures, and the like. At any rate, much can happen in nine or ten years, as our interviewees attest.

Careers outside "Professorial Academia" / "The Professoriat"

(Positions at time of interview)

ARCHIVES/INSTITUTES

Shubha Chaudhuri (October 28, 2007)

PhD, Jawaharlal Nehru University (Linguistics)
Director
Archives and Research Centre for Ethnomusicology of the American Institute
of Indian Studies (ARCE)
American Institute of Indian Studies, Delhi

Graduate Studies

SC: Jawahral Nehru University was a very political campus, very different from the rest of Delhi. By the time I finished my PhD [1981] I was greatly disillusioned with academia. Not with the academic part of it—I loved teaching. I liked my research, too, but I was getting very disillusioned about what universities were about. I wanted to be in academia, but I didn't want to be in a university. I dearly would have liked to go and live in the hills and write papers on linguistics, but that was not an option, so I did a couple of projects where I could just be a research assistant and a research associate. For a couple of years I had that kind of involvement, doing the odd assignment and some little research jobs.

Building a Career

When ARCE was starting, Nazir Jairazbhoy and Daniel Neuman were looking for staff, and I kept bumping into people who had met them. A couple of my friends said it sounded like a good opportunity for me. I said, "What? Ethnomusicology, that's not my discipline; I'm a linguist." But then I thought, "OK, why don't I just go and see them." The front office was going to be in Delhi, and there was a position for someone who could take in collections, help organize them, and move them on to the archive, which was going to be in Poona. They were looking for somebody who could do that and also handle the publications, write the newsletter, be able to talk to scholars, and understand what the material was about. I later heard that Dan thought a linguist would have a good sense of methodology. It's quite a related discipline in some ways. And I had my Oxford University Press background for the publishing part of the job. That was how I got in.

MS: So you got in right at the beginning, when the archives started.

SC: Yes, September 1982. I thought I'd try it out. It's a nice job, and I can do my own academic work. I wasn't sure I wanted to do it for a career, because it was all so new. There wasn't even a physical space—we had to do everything, even ordering furniture and shelving. It was interesting to have that kind of challenge, and everyone I talked to told me how ethnomusicology had a lot of connections with linguistics as a discipline. It did feel very familiar as I tried to read about it. It was like linguistics some years before transformational grammar really hit—descriptive, talking about field methods, diachronic and synchronic research, and all those kinds of things.

MS: Was this the first time you heard about ethnomusicology? Do you remember any readings or role models who were inspirational at that early stage?

SC: I said, "Look, this is a new field for me, and if I'm to meet scholars and know who's what, I need to know a little more." So I would sit and talk to Nazir and Dan. I asked for a list of books I should read, and somebody made a list of ten books for me. At that point it was not so important that I should learn ethnomusicology but that the archive should have the materials that people interested in the field would need. I made sure we had the basic books and journals. And just through handling all those things, I got sucked in without realizing it.

Nazir had been talking about ARCE at SEM, so people knew this place was starting. Even in the early days, when we had nothing but a desk, two chairs, a sofa, and twenty tapes, people were getting in touch. I had to meet these people, talk about the place, find out what they were doing and what we could do for them, because there was no archive yet. They were not all ethnomusicologists. There were also people working in Indian folk performance—whether from theater or comparative religion—and with performance in other fields. Till today I enjoy that part very much: talking to people about their research, taking in their collections, and trying to understand them so that I could supervise the cataloging of it properly and send it on to the archives. It was a kind of vicarious research for many years.

MS: Is the Center affiliated with a university, or is it totally independent?

SC: It's totally independent. It's part of the American Institute of Indian Studies (AIIS), but we still have to raise funding. The AIIS is largely a fellowship-giving body. It's one of the major sources—together with Fulbright—for research in India, but we weren't tied up with the fellowship program. It sometimes seems funny that an ethnomusicologist can come on an institute fellowship and not even know that the archive's there!

At the beginning, Ashok Ranade, a well-known musicologist, was the director. He knew the discipline of ethnomusicology but decided to leave after the first few years. There was a funding crisis and all kinds of things going on. Those were the Cold War years, and this was an American organization. Suddenly it was 1985, he was leaving, and they asked if I would take over. I said, "I don't know the subject, I'm not a musicologist." They said, "But you can run an archive." They asked me to try it for a year and see if I could make a go of it. That was when I had to make a decision. Up to then, I was half playing at it. I kept saying, "This is not really my life. I'm a linguist, you know." The first time I came to an SEM meeting, Bonnie Wade laughed and said, "I'll always remember you saying, 'I'm a linguist, not an ethnomusicologist.'" They remember my underlining that all the time. Now suddenly there was a challenge to make a go of the place. I felt like I should try, not just let it go under. That meant a commitment, no fooling around, so I thought I'd better figure out what this discipline is and try and make a go of it. I was made director in 1986.

MS: What are your resources now?

SC: It's a very big archive now. We've got about twenty thousand hours of recordings. And what's been great for me was being in at the beginning and being able to invent it. We had a committee of ethnomusicologists for the most part, appointed by the American Institute of Indian Studies. Nazir Jairazbhoy was the founding chair, and Daniel Neuman was the second person to come on board as chair. We (Umashankar, who is chief technician, and I) set up a vault, and I learned whatever I could from wherever as we tried to create this archive. It was only in 1985 that I traveled outside India for the first time and went to see other archives. I went on a grand tour, to London and to my first SEM meeting in Vancouver. Then I visited other archives: Seattle, LA, Syracuse, and Indiana. Tony Seeger, who was at Indiana then, was on our committee, so I had two weeks at Indiana, taking notes and thinking about how we were going to develop our databases. It was amazing to see all the archives and realize, "They're just like us! We did this right!" I didn't know we did it right, but we were probably doing better than a lot of other archives because we were so scared of doing the wrong thing that we were bigger sticklers about standards than anybody else.

There wasn't ever any intention of having a major library, but we were always going to have books that backed up the collections. I felt that people who were interested in ethnomusicology would come because there was no university course, nothing. Now we have a pretty big library—about ten thousand books and all the major journals. So whether you are an ethnomusicologist or a student, you can find the basic texts and major works. At the beginning it was just an India collection, but a few years later I started broadening the scope. I still remember seeing Feld's book on the Kaluli [1982] and saying that we should have it because it was an important book. Encouraged by Dan Neuman, we made a new policy to say what's important in ethnomusicology, regardless of what part of the world it focuses on, should be part of our collection. For India we are really oriented to the field researcher and have basic journals, ethnographies, gazetteers, works on performing arts, folklore, religion, whatever—everything that an ethnomusicologist would want to look at for every part of India. We also have a big collection of offprints and a collection of newspaper cuttings from about the late '80s. We started that as a minor project, putting clippings up on boards for the scholars who come through. It felt like a pity to throw them away, so we filed them; people said it was a great resource, so we kept doing it. Now, it's a big project. We have eighty-five-thousand-plus cuttings, and we're doing a joint project with the Library of Congress to microfilm them. So all these resources have grown.

We also started buying commercial recordings, initially to back up the collections. We have recordings from 78s to CDs. There again sometime in the mid-90s, we made a decision that we should take in commercial recordings of world music. This happened because a few people would come in expecting an ethnomusicology archive to have Greek music or Native American music, which we didn't have. Although we can't start being an archive of all these musics, we can at least buy commercial recordings. So we put out a request for donations in our newsletter and we now have these resources, too. We have fairly state-of-the-art preservation facilities and a very good audio-visual lab, and we're now very much involved in digitizing our recordings.

I haven't been to SEM much recently, partly because I became very active in IASAA, the International Association of Sound and Audio-Visual Archives. This year the IMS [Indian Musicological Society] was accepted as the national committee for ICTM, and I'm the national representative. That was the final straw—I'm the funny linguist who's now on the IMS board! Now I've even done some small bits of fieldwork and one major field project in West Rajasthan with Dan Neuman in 1989–90 [Neuman and Chaudhuri 2006]. That's become my field area, and I've continued working in Rajasthan.

MS: So you've become a card-carrying, practicing ethnomusicologist!

SC: Yes, I guess I grew into it! Initially I would just go along, thinking that if this is an ARCE project that Dan is leading, I should know what is going on. But I got involved, and my role in the project kept changing. Finally, by the time it was being written up, I was a co-author. But I do feel hesitant to call myself an ethnomusicologist. I am more comfortable being an ethnomusicology archivist!

In the last few years I decided to keep up some fieldwork in Rajasthan. I find it's good for me to do that. I've just written a grant for the Ford Foundation, to do a project in Goa and Rajasthan called the "Archive and Community Partnership." We're looking at documentation not as a top down thing but having musicians identify what they think needs to be documented. We'll also work on model rights as part of this project, sharing rights, materials, and all revenue that come out of this project. We can't change all the twenty thousand hours in the archives and the kind of permissions we have, but at least for this project the materials will be shared. It's a pilot project to see how we can do this work with syncretic traditions, pluralism, and all these things. Tourism is also a major thing in both areas and creates certain demands of the musicians.

MS: You're the head of a successful archive, you've admitted you're an ethnomusicologist, and you're now doing your own field research. What do you see, looking back?

SC: I've seen the field change from being a very small group of people who all tended to know each other, a bit like a club! Although it's really grown, it's retained that closeness. It was always very hard to explain to people what this field was because it didn't have textbooks in those days. It's also remained very interdisciplinary, which is good for me and was very attractive. There are still people working on it more from a musicological side and other people still working from a very ethnographic perspective.

In India, it's still difficult because you have people who trained in ethnomusicology elsewhere and came back to India, and you have people in Madras trying to do things, but a lot of people just continued working in performance. There was some talk of various departments wanting to introduce ethnomusicology, but so far it has remained largely outside the university system. There are various people who have done PhDs, but they've either been absorbed in the West somewhere or are doing other things. We've been able to host workshops at ARCE. I did a very successful one in '93 for which I brought Tony Seeger out to talk about ethnography of musical performance. The workshop brought in people with an ethnographic bias who were already working in music. It was very good, because these are people who would benefit from being exposed to the field. A couple of them went on to study ethnomusicology outside India. Universities here have been having their funding reduced over the last so many years. I don't feel very hopeful that somebody will be able to come out with a department. But there are a lot of people interested now and trying to work with this kind of orientation, so I feel in some way that we provide a rallying point for them.

Update: June 28, 2016

I continue to be the director of the Archives and Research Centre for Ethnomusicology. In the past few years I have been doing more fieldwork than I had at the time I was interviewed. I have also been more involved with the idea of community archives.

Clara Henderson (October 28, 2007)

PhD, Indiana University (Folklore, Ethnomusicology)
Associate Director
Institute for Digital Arts and Humanities, Indiana University

Building a Career and Graduate Studies

CH: After I graduated in '78, I went traveling for a while in Europe but came back to York University to be Trichy Sankaran's assistant. It was around then that I thought, "Maybe I will study ethnomusicology." I hadn't really looked into the requirements at Wesleyan, but I figured that since I wasn't a music major, they'd want me to know music theory and everything. So, I took some music theory courses at York and started to play Western percussion—timpani and that kind of stuff.

But just then the Presbyterian Church in Canada approached me. They had a partnership with the Church of Malawi, which had sent a request for someone to come and start a music department. The reason they thought of me was that my music education was so different from what my parents' music education had been. Everyone in my family knew I liked different types of music. My sister, who worked in the head office of the Presbyterian Church, heard about the request and said, "Oh, my sister might be interested in that." At one point, I had thought it would be great to go to Ghana and study drumming, but when I realized they were asking *me*, I started thinking about all the problems. I didn't even know where Malawi was. I had to go home and look it up in the encyclopedia. But I knew, right from the start, that I would go because it interested me and because I was involved in the church. I had a desire to use my talents in some way. It never occurred to me that I would be able to use them in an African context. I ended up going to Malawi in February 1982. I was in my early twenties and worked with a committee of older Malawian men, most of whom were over sixty, to organize music workshops.

TS: What did they want you to do?

CH: Well, the church committee didn't exactly get what they had envisioned! Their vision was of an established male theologian-musician who would work with them to develop a music department. What they thought it meant was to train people in Scottish Presbyterian hymns and the Presbyterian Order of Service. Church music in Malawi had been developing for years, and people had been creating their own music, based on what they had learned from Scottish Presbyterian missionaries.

TS: And you were supposed to coordinate that?

CH: Yes, but there were really two traditions going on there. A lot of the work I had to do was teaching music reading. But what I did not do—which a lot of people in the Presbyterian Church in Canada, even to this day, think I did—was teach Malawians how to use their music for worship. Somehow that gets ingrained in people's heads, and that's what they thought I was doing. But it wasn't! There was tons of Malawian music in the church already, so I didn't need to do anything to stimulate the development of Malawian music. There was lots of room, however, for creating a forum for everybody who was interested in music to be able to come together.

TS: How long were you there?

CH: I started in 1982, and we got study leaves after every five years. I took one study leave in '87 and had another one coming up in '93. Before that second leave I met some people from Indiana University who had come to Malawi to establish a link between the two universities. Ron Smith came in 1989 and talked about the ethnomusicology program at Indiana, and Mellonee Burnim came twice, in 1990 and '91, to do choral workshops at the university. Mellonee and I became very good friends, and she told me more about the ethno program at IU. So I thought, "When I take my study leave, why don't I just take some courses at Indiana University?" I was scared of graduate school, unsure if I could handle it—I go into everything with a little tentativeness!—but I ended up going to IU for my master's thesis, from 1993 to '95. The study leave was a year. I took an additional year's leave to complete the master's. At first, I was just seeing if I could handle it, but then I realized, "I can handle it, so let me finish." I was able to get an assistantship at IU, which is how I supported myself during the leave of absence. I went back to Malawi in '95 to keep working. In the back of my mind, I thought I might come back for the PhD program at some point, which I eventually did in 2000.

TS: Did you acquire language skills while you were in Malawi?

CH: Yes, Chichewa. As soon as I got there, I realized that if I wanted to understand what was going on, even though so many people spoke English (especially in towns), I had to learn the language. So I poured myself into doing that right from the start. It really helped me. I do all my teaching in Chichewa.

TS: I think of you as a dance ethnologist, so I find it interesting that you've only mentioned the word "dance" once so far in this conversation, and that was in connection with Ghanaian dance.

CH: Yes! Well, one of the things that attracted me to work in the Church of Malawi was that I've always been interested in connecting body movement and worship. My stereotypical image of Africa was of women singing and dancing in the context of a church. So I thought, "Maybe when I go to Malawi, I'll learn how to free myself in that way." I was really attracted to the disconnect I saw between what bodies do in church and what minds, spirits, and souls do.

I had always taken Scottish dancing when I was a kid. Later, people would ask me, "Are you a dancer?" I'd say, "No, not really." But then someone said to me, "Yes you are; think of all the dance you've done all your life. Just because it isn't ballet doesn't mean it isn't dance." I have always struggled with that stupid stereotype.

TS: Do you consider yourself a dance ethnologist or ethnomusicologist?

CH: Now I see myself as an ethnomusicologist who is a dance scholar. I say ethnomusicologist because that's where my training is. I haven't studied dance scholarship from anyone in particular, except that at IU I took an independent study with Anya Peterson Royce. I got more into dance scholarship under the rubric of ethnomusicology when I took a course—I think it was "History of Ethnomusicology"—and did a project on dance within the Society for Ethnomusicology. I confined it to SEM, instead of getting into ICTM and other groups to keep it contained. What I started to uncover was really fascinating to me; all through our history people have been mentioning dance here and there. Dance has always been just under the radar of a lot of what we do, yet there have been people working really hard, right from the beginning of our discipline, to bring the interconnections between music and dance to the attention of the members of SEM.

I noticed at yesterday's [2007] Seeger Lecture, for example, Bill Ivey talked about the notion of having vouchers for the arts and listed visual arts, music, and some other things, but he didn't mention dance. Now, granted, Bill Ivey is a folklorist,[1] so he doesn't necessarily figure in the history of ethnomusicology, but he also mentioned a meeting at Purdue in 1954. He talked about Merriam being there and listed off other names, but the name he forgot was Gertrude Kurath. When I did my research, I discovered she was there right from the start. I was surprised by her influence and her impact on the early history of our Society. People like Charlotte Frisbie mention her, but what really impressed me at the 2001 SEM meeting in Detroit was when Bruno Nettl, Joann Kealiinohomoku, Nadia Chilkovsky Nahumck, Bill Malm, and Judith Vander presented a panel titled "The Gertrude Kurath Legacy for the 21st Century: Reawakening Sensitivity to the Dance-Music Interdependence." Maybe I'd heard some of that before, but when I went to their panel, I felt I was hearing about it for the first time. It made me go back and look at more things, and other tidbits popped up. For example, a couple of years after that 1954 meeting—in '56, I think—Willard Rhodes told Society members that "we need to remember to include popular music and dance within the purview of ethnomusicology."

These threads have always been there. People like Gertrude Kurath did a lot of good work. For about fifteen years she was called the "dance editor" for *Ethnomusicology*—the journal actually had a "dance editor"! She was always sharing information about what was going on in dance scholarship. Nadia Chilkovsky Nahumck, another early presence, attended meetings and tried to raise awareness about intersections between music and dance. Klaus Wachsmann made a speech—I think in 1968 to the SEM board of directors—in which he said, "Ethnomusicology is a centrifugal subject; we need to be interdisciplinary, we need to include linguistics and psychology." He listed off a bunch of other things, before finally saying, "and dance, for God's sake!" To me, that little quip says, "Dance has been there right from the beginning; we can't forget dance; dance, for God's sake!"

That's why, after I did all that research and was so surprised by the work that people like Joann Kealiinohomoku and Adrienne Kaeppler did right from the beginning, I thought, "Maybe we could start a dance section within the society to raise awareness about dance scholarship and give people who are interested in it a home." Back then they came to the society because they were finding a home for their interest in dance scholarship. Some of them were trained in anthropology so, while they weren't specifically studying ethnomusicology, they were from the same kind of background. Maybe a dance section would get us back above the radar.

TS: When did you start the dance section?

CH: We had our first section meeting in 2002 at the meeting in Estes Park, Colorado. I wrote a tiny blurb in the *SEM Newsletter*, quoting Rhodes and Wachsmann. I thought, "Isn't it time we did something about dance?" So we started the dance section.

TS: To go back to your current status, you came back to Indiana in 2000 to begin your PhD studies, and you're still on extended leave with the church. Have you maintained that official connection?

CH: Yes, I'm on the overseas staff of the Presbyterian Church in Canada (it's only people in the local churches who call you a "missionary"). Next year I'll have to decide whether or not I'm going back.

TS: Have you been teaching or doing something else as a graduate student?

CH: You mean, how have I been paying my rent? I've had graduate assistantships all the way through. I worked at the Archives of Traditional Music for a few years, and now I'm with the EVIA Digital Archive Project.

Update: July 4, 2016

In 2000 I took a leave of absence from my work in Malawi to begin PhD studies in folklore and ethnomusicology at Indiana University Bloomington (IUB). My goal was to work with the video and audio recordings, interviews, photographs, archival research, and field notes I had collected over eighteen years of fieldwork in Malawi, and to write about and analyze what I had been experiencing and learning. I also wanted to study theory and methodology in ethnomusicology—to understand the history of the field, where my research was situated in the discipline, and how I could contribute to the dialogue.

In 2007, when I was interviewed for this book, I was in the middle of writing my dissertation. On completion, I fully expected to return to Malawi to resume my previous work and to begin teaching music at the University of Malawi. These plans changed dramatically one day in 2009, when I was invited to apply for a position in the newly formed Institute for Digital Arts and Humanities (IDAH) at IUB, to work with faculty, technologists, archivists, and librarians developing digital collections, tools, and methods for research and creative activity. Throughout my graduate career I had been working with this same group of experts within the EVIA Digital Archive Project creating a digital archive of annotated ethnographic field video. So, working with IDAH seemed like a natural fit. I became IDAH's associate director, and oversight of the EVIA project was eventually shared between our institute and the Archives of Traditional Music.

My actual job title is associate director for Digital Arts and Humanities Projects, Institute for Digital Arts and Humanities. It's a full-time position. Ruth Stone is the director (it's one-third time for her), and Alan Burdette is the associate director for Digital Arts and Humanities Infrastructure (it's part time for him, as he is also director of the Archives of Traditional Music). We're a newly formed institute (came into being in late 2007) within the IU infrastructure. We deal with research in the arts and humanities on projects with an information technology or digital component. We offer faculty two-year fellowships to create a prototype for a research project involving digital initiatives with the intent that within the two years, they submit a proposal along with the prototype to a granting agency. We are hoping that the two-year fellowship to help them prepare the grant proposal will ensure successful applications.

Our EVIA (Ethnographic Video for Instruction and Analysis) Digital Archive Project also falls under the umbrella of IDAH projects. We have a lot of ethnomusicological field video (as well as field video from folklorists, anthropologists, and dance scholars) that has been extensively annotated by the collector using software created by our project. The projects are peer reviewed and published online and will be available through our search and browse website (www.eviada.org). The website will be freely available to SEM members and members of Indiana University and the University of Michigan initially; then we plan to make it freely available to other institutions as well (with some institutions paying for certain facilities such as higher quality video streams and the like). Our search and browse is like a high quality YouTube where the videos are good streaming quality and all have rich annotation to accompany them. We will also have persistent URLs.

(Clara passed away on October 2, 2016, in Bloomington, Indiana.)

Postscript, by Alan Burdette (director, Archives of Traditional Music, University of Indiana)

Clara submitted her update just a few weeks before she was diagnosed with an aggressive form of cancer, and two months later she was gone. At the time of her death, she was actively working to turn her award-winning dissertation, "Dance Discourse in the Music and Lives of Presbyterian Mvano Women in Southern Malawi" [Henderson 2009], into a book. She was also preparing her field recordings for deposit in the Archives of Traditional Music. In Clara's obituary, the Very Rev. Professor Silas Ncosana of Blantyre Synod, Malawi, wrote, "Clara, like no other missionary from overseas, entered into Malawian culture through local languages and music. She knew what *ziphwidzi* were and even ate them. Clara loved our people, ate with them, danced with them, prayed with them, laughed with them, and cried with them. She matured in Malawi, becoming truly one of us."

Clara was the daughter of a Presbyterian minister, and she maintained strong connections to her extended family with whom she kept close through stories and holiday visits to the family cottage on Lake Huron. For the entirety of her life she was devoted to the Presbyterian Church. She was a church elder, a Sunday school teacher, an overseas educator, and a performer. She brought that same devotion to the Society for Ethnomusicology, which became another sort of church for Clara, and for which she was a staunch servant. She was the founding member of the SEM Section on Dance in 2002 while she was still a graduate student, and she was its chair for many years, building it into a vibrant subcommunity within the academic society. The regular dance panels, workshops, and dance events held at every SEM conference were usually in part or in total the work of Clara and the dance section. As in every other arena in her life, she worked tirelessly to help others do their best work and to develop the bonds of a community in action.

She loved to sing, and she had a remarkable ear for adapting her voice to different styles. She possessed an innate musicality and fearlessness about trying new musics. She played with Indiana University's Mbira Queens, led by the Zimbabwean virtuoso Sheasby Matiure, during his residency at IU, and for several years she played with Bloomington's Women of Mass Percussion, led by Colleen Haas. She performed in innumerable ensembles put together for special occasions, and one of her prized possessions was a baby grand piano that she played and sang at for an hour every evening.

When she started on her path in ethnomusicology, she worked at the Archives of Traditional Music as a graduate assistant and later with the EVIA Digital Archive Project. [Because Clara was] an avid chronicler of her own family history, this work resonated with her inclinations toward the preservation of cultural documentation, and she became committed to the efforts of archival preservation and access. She worked tirelessly for the EVIA Project (an initiative focused on ethnographic video preservation and annotation) for fifteen years, first as a student assistant and later as its co-director. This project brought together scholars from diverse corners of the ethnographic disciplines for two weeklong intensive summer institutes. Indeed, it was Clara, during the early years of the project, who, more than anyone, fostered the feelings of community, family, and "summer camp for scholars" that affected nearly all of the ethnographers who participated.

Clara excelled at the kind of organization that brought people together for work or for fun. One of my favorite photographs of Clara is not so much a photograph of Clara but rather of a group of ethnomusicologists standing around her with their heads thrown back, laughing hysterically. Anyone who worked with Clara for more than a little while encountered her deep playfulness and love of laughter. Play—whether through joking, singing, dance, or games—was one of the ways she asserted her family history, her desire to connect to other people, and her love for the diverse poetics of this world and her fundamental faith in the world's fleeting nature.

Laurel Sercombe (March 22, 2008)

PhD, University of Washington (Ethnomusicology)
Archivist
Ethnomusicology Archives, University of Washington

Graduate Studies

LS: At that point [1975] I was almost twenty-five and realized that I was getting too old to be not as good as I wanted to be on the violin. I needed to do something else. That's when I realized there was a library school at the University of Washington and I thought, "That sounds so much easier than being a musician." Being a musician began to seem like the hardest work in the world to me. I ended up going to library school. I thought being a music librarian sounded like a way I could keep close to music, but wouldn't have to go to nighttime rehearsals, to auditions, and all that crap. For me it was a really good decision, though I had some musician friends who thought if you weren't going to do music—I still know people who feel this way—it's a total copout. It was a good decision for me: I ended up working here in the university music library for about three years after I'd done my library degree. I worked in the public library first, and then got the job here on campus in the music library.

Building a Career

I got my master of librarianship degree at the University of Washington in 1977; there wasn't a way to specialize in music. After three years of working in the UW music library (from 1979 to 1982), I thought, "It's probably time to look for something else." At that very moment Dan Neuman and Robert Garfias walked into the music library together and said, "Why don't you apply for our job?" I said, "What job?" They answered, "The job downstairs, in the Ethnomusicology Archives." I asked, "Why would I apply for your job?" Dan's wife was working in the library administration and for some reason thought I had experience in ethnomusicology. It was a total mistake, but that's how I was on their radar. I thought, "Well, it'd be really bizarre to go downstairs and work for Ethnomusicology," so I applied for the job. Honestly, I think they hired me because I *wasn't* an ethnomusicologist and they didn't want to have somebody come in with any kind of baggage about their own particular area. I think they liked the idea that I had been in the professional library scene—I was already here, I was cheap, and I could walk into the job—but I really had no idea what I was doing when I came downstairs. It turned out to be a great break for me. I think I had a latent interest in all kinds of music, and so it seemed to be a natural thing for me to move into ethnomusicology. It was a fabulous opportunity. That was 1982. I was deeply involved in antinuclear politics at that point. I can't believe I've been here ever since!

After a while I decided that since I was here anyway and didn't have any plans to leave the archive, I might as well go into the PhD program in ethnomusicology. So, in 1990 I started taking graduate courses. I had no intention of getting involved in Native American music, but while I was still in the music library, I met the native elder Vi Hilbert and got hooked on the idea of old recordings of elders and the treasures they contained. By the time I started taking course work, I found myself interested in George Herzog and the work he had done. I got really excited about working with local sound collections.

TS: Which Native American group are we talking about?

LS: "Coast Salish" is the best thing to call the Puget Sound area people. The elder I was working with, Vi Hilbert, identifies herself as "Upper Skagit." The Skagit is a river, so basically it has to do with their position on the river. Upper Skagit is a Coast Salish group, and the language that they speak in the Puget Sound area is called Lushootseed. It combined well with my archive work because I was just as interested in researching recordings as I was in developing relationships with a consultant. I did both, but I've probably used a lot more recordings in my research than most people I know in the field.

TS: Who made these recordings of the elders?

LS: Leon Metcalf, a non-academic music teacher in town, recorded a number of local elders in the early 1950s. They're good recordings, housed at the Burke Museum of Natural History and Culture here on campus. Melville Jacobs was an anthropologist on this campus for many years; his collection is in the UW Libraries, Special Collections. A linguist named Tom Hess, whom I got to know over the years, gave me all his recordings, so I've got them in the Ethnomusicology Archives. And then a few years ago Vi Hilbert decided to turn over her huge research collection to me, so now I've got thousands of recordings of local Native American songs, stories, and local events.

TS: Was Vi Hilbert an academically trained person?

LS: No, she's a very bright woman whose parents wanted her to become a modern person. She didn't live on the Rez but became interested in recording in the 1960s when she realized there were very few speakers of Lushootseed left. She had a hair-dressing business and didn't have any particular aspirations to do anything besides casual recording, but Tom Hess met her, and realized her tremendous talent and competency. So, basically, he tricked her into becoming a university language teacher, and she taught on campus. I'm not a very "woo-woo" kind of person, but when I started working with Vi, I really felt I was making a contribution, especially when I chose my dissertation topic, which has to do with the songs within the stories of the Coast Salish. The title of the dissertation is "And Then It Rained: Power and Song in Western Washington Coast Salish Myth Narratives" [Sercombe 2001].

That feeling of making a contribution is really important. I had a phone call a couple of weeks ago from a fellow at one of the local Indian reservations. He told me that, in the last year, he's gotten back into his traditional training, had an Indian name given to him, and has been doing sweat house work. One night, after a sweat, he had a dream that somebody walked up to him—a man in a cream-colored suit and a fedora—and gave him a piece of paper. He looked at the piece of paper and it had a number on it. When he woke up, he googled the number, and discovered it was an index number to a tape in my collection that has his granduncle on it! He asked if he could get a copy of it. Of course! My goodness. I said, "I know exactly what you're talking about. I can put it on a CD and send it to you." He said, "No, I'll come down and get it." So he and his wife drove down and were so excited to get the recording, but they also told me a lot about the family, and all the names that I know of local people in the recording.

Last week he came back down with four drummers. They stood in the little seminar room across the way and, in exchange for these recordings, they wanted to give us their songs, to thank us for the work. I invited Ter Ellingson and a couple of other people who were around to come in and they blessed us with these songs, these gifts. It just went kapow!—right into us. We felt the power. It was such an intense interaction. I love it, and I get to do this every day, my god!

Update: June 16, 2016

I've now been the archivist for the University of Washington Ethnomusicology Program for nearly thirty-four years. I never expected to stay in one job this long, but I got hooked—on the university environment, on the students, on the music, on the network of fellow archivists, on the smart and crazy people who populate the ethnomusicology profession. So I stayed, got a PhD along the way, published a little, got appointed affiliate assistant professor and sat on a couple of doctoral committees, reluctantly left the analog world behind and tried to make friends with all things digital. But enough is enough—as of June 30, 2016, I'm retired, just from the job though, not from all the rest of it!

Philip Yampolsky (March 23, 2008)

PhD, University of Washington (Ethnomusicology)
Director
Center for World Music, University of Illinois

Graduate Studies

PY: I went to Washington [in the fall of 1976] to learn new stuff. The problems that had plagued me in college, the feeling that I didn't know enough to say anything and therefore couldn't turn in papers, went away because in Seattle I did know something. I knew something about Ewe music and about Javanese and Balinese music. I've been this way all my life—I need a body of knowledge under my belt before I can speak.

Then I went into the field. I thought I had a beautifully designed topic about Javanese drumming and its connections to prostitute dancing: that the *ciblon* style of Javanese drumming actually came from street dancing and disreputable dance parties. It was a good topic, but an Indonesian scholar's topic, and I didn't get either of the grants I applied for. Instead, since I didn't have any training in the Indonesian language at the time, I got a FLAS (Foreign Language and Areas Studies) Scholarship to the intensive Indonesian language program at Cornell. That was in 1978–79. I took intensive language in the FALCON program and rewrote the grants.

Instead of making my project sound like something that would only be of interest to scholars of Java, I made it sound like it was of earth-shaking significance for understanding the relationships between center and periphery, village and town, or village and court. I got the grants and went to Java in January 1980. I think I had a Boasian notion of fieldwork: one should go and immerse oneself in it and be there for as long as possible. But in the process, I lost confidence in my topic. I came back after three years in order to write, but didn't feel I had gathered enough good material. Maybe I should have done what everybody else does and somehow make a dissertation out of the material I had. But I was faced with the same old problem—if I feel I don't know enough, I can't do much.

Building a Career

Providentially, after I returned home to Connecticut—Christmas 1982—the Ford Foundation in Jakarta called and said, "We're starting an ethnomusicology program at the University of North Sumatra and are looking for somebody who can teach in Indonesian, design a curriculum, and set up the program. Would you like to do it?" I said yes.

My interest in this project went back to a key moment in 1979. I had just completed the intensive language program at Cornell and was taking a follow-up summer program in Malang (East Java). Still influenced by Bob Brown, I was totally committed to Central Javanese court gamelan, but I was also increasingly influenced by Robert Garfias and trying to connect gamelan to the villages, through dance drumming. In Malang, I wandered into a cassette store and heard a cassette of violin, Javanese singing, drums, and a few gongs bong-ing in the background. My understanding of Indonesia was entirely based on Central Javanese court music and Balinese temple music, but here was this stuff with violins and a female singer. It turned out to be *Gandrung Banyuwangi*, so I took a side trip to Banyuwangi to find out more. It was news to me—there was something out there that didn't fit into the gamelan framework.

When I went to North Sumatra in 1983, there was no gamelan there. I was already dissatisfied with my dissertation research, so I was looking for a new topic and wondering whether there was any way I could connect North Sumatra with Java and Bali. I became interested in the question of the representation of music in Indonesia. Why was Javanese music so prestigious and North Sumatran music so un-prestigious? Toward the end of my fieldwork in Java I had become interested in recordings as documents. I spent a lot of time working in the offices of the national record company, Lokananta, and made a complete discography, which was eventually published, of everything they had recorded and published [Yampolsky 1987].

One of the things that struck me was that over thirty-five years or so, Lokananta had only published one record of Balinese music (recorded in Yogyakarta, Central Java) [I Nengah Sumerti 1959] and some popular music; everything else was Javanese. There was nothing from other islands, except a lot of stuff called "Regional Entertainment Music," tunes from South Sumatra, Sulawesi, or elsewhere, played on piano, bass, and drums, in a souped-up, harmonized style. There was nothing traditional. I became interested in the question of representation, or rather the lack of representation, of the huge variety of Indonesian music in the recorded media. So I began to study the local cassette industry in North Sumatra, what was represented, and what was not. Essentially, I was exploring the cultural politics of the media. As a result of this, I became aware of the role the media play in constructing one's image and understanding of what exists in the world. I gathered a lot of material about the recording industry and talked the Ford Foundation into giving me money to travel around Indonesia and collect cassette recordings for an ethno-library they were setting up at STSI [Sekolah Tinggi Seni Indonesia, now ISI, Institut Seni Indonesia] Solo. At the same time, I did my own study of the cassette producers, and of the kinds of music that were recorded in all those different places. As a result of all this, I began to make the study of Indonesia as a whole my trademark, rather than the concentrated study of Java, Sunda, or Bali, that most other ethnomusicology students were doing.

I came home in the summer of 1984. My parents were ill, so I relocated to Connecticut, with the intention of writing my dissertation. I kept myself alive as a temporary typist; I even became "Kelly Employee of the Month" at one point! I got a side gig from the University of Wisconsin to go back to Indonesia and build another collection of books and cassettes for their library, which helped further my study of the cassette industry. The University of Wisconsin agreed to publish my discography of the national record company, so after I returned to Connecticut, I typed up the huge discography and raised the question, "Why is the national record company only recording Java?" I made some lovely graphs and charts showing how much music from each area, how much music from each genre, and introduced a notion, which has continued to figure in my own thinking about Indonesia, of the government pushing respectability.

In the fall of 1986 I got an offer from Marty Hatch to teach gamelan at Cornell. I did that for three semesters. I started making use of the Cornell library to pursue the question of media and recordings of music and used microfilm newspapers from before the war to study the 78 RPM record industry in Indonesia. I also became friendly with the anthropologists, and my ideas were quite influenced by Cornell's radical, highly skeptical approach to the New Order in Indonesia. While at Cornell, I brought my wife, Tinuk, over from Java. I had met her in 1984 in Solo, but didn't have the money to bring her to the United States. But by 1987, with the job at Cornell, I was able to bring her. She came in the summer of '87 and we were married in October. Later, Tinuk was offered a job teaching Indonesian language at Yale, so we moved to New Haven. I had no job and was trying to write while dealing with my dying parents. That's when the Smithsonian made its first whispers.

The Ford Foundation was trying to promote awareness of Indonesia in the United States. Alan Feinstein, their arts and culture program officer, approached Smithsonian Folkways and asked if they'd like to do something on Indonesia. They said they would be interested but didn't have anyone who knew about Indonesia. Alan told them, "If you want somebody who has a grasp of Indonesia as a whole, talk to Philip." When Smithsonian asked if I'd be interested in doing two CDs on Indonesia, I said I'd be more interested in doing a multivolume anthology. I wrote up a proposal and Ford agreed to fund it, because it wasn't just the recordings, it was a big project with a training component. Smithsonian agreed to a pilot project, so I did three records in the first year, 1990. Published in time for the 1991 Folklife Festival, they were considered a success, and the rest of the project was funded [Yampolsky 1991–1999]. At the outset, I didn't know anything about sound recording, so I asked NPR (National Public Radio) and they recommended an engineer named Paul Blakemore. Paul designed a wonderful digital recording packet and came to Indonesia to do a workshop for me and Indonesian team members. I learned everything I know about sound recording from him, plus seven years of practice in the field.

The basic approach for the series came out of my studies with Robert Garfias. Instead of looking at the most refined, complicated, and prestigious art musics, we aimed for a sense of the entire musical culture: popular, folk, village, religious, and art music. We didn't know beforehand where we would go or what genres we would finally present in the series. The main island groups and cultural groups were obvious: Sumatra, Java, Bali, Kalimantan, Sulawesi, Irian Jaya. Then there was Maluku and the smaller islands. It took me a while to realize that I didn't have to do Javanese and Balinese gamelan, since there were already so many good recordings. I also decided we were going to aim at the opened-minded, non-specialist listener instead of catering to ethnomusicologists, who always wanted to hear the most obscure instruments and would be happy to hear the three surviving slabs of an eight-tone lithophone, if I could find it.

When the project finished in 1999, the Ford Foundation had an opening in the Indonesia office for an arts and cultural program officer. They already knew me, so I became program officer in 2000 until 2006. A main focus of the Ford program was on efforts to revitalize traditional music and other arts through the school system. Rather than teach anything about Indonesia, the schools taught Western art music, and did so very badly. We tried to subvert that, using the Smithsonian series as one of our key sources. We developed a big project with Endo Suanda and others to replace the existing Western-oriented teaching materials with new textbooks that would get Indonesian arts into the schools.

TS: Were you still doing this when you got the call from the University of Illinois to direct their Center for World Music?

PY: Yes. Illinois was proposed as a home for Robert Brown's collections in 2005. Bob Brown proposed my name because he knew I understood him and his Center [for World Music at California Institute for the Arts, and later in Berkeley]. It seems to me that if you are going to design anything—whether a program, like the ethnomusicology program at the University of North Sumatra, or an anthology, like the Smithsonian collection, or the Robert E. Brown Center for World Music at Illinois—you have to have some principles, some aims, and some canons. The basic canon I work with is "representative inclusiveness." You can't include everything, so you have to select, to represent large classes of things by specific instances, but the aim is to represent all of the major categories of something. So what I have to do at Illinois is create a World Music Performance Program that dovetails with the university's other offerings. I think university students have a lot of knowledge about popular music and possibly some about Western classical music, but they don't have much knowledge about musics that are not part of that system—music that doesn't use harmony, that doesn't use scores, that is improvised, that is oral, or that uses different scales. That's what we have to bring into a performance program. That's what I do at the Robert E. Brown Center for World Music: I bring challenging, difficult musics that are outside the normal experience of American college students.

Update: June 30, 2016

A financial crisis hit the University of Illinois around 2010. The Robert E. Brown Center for World Music was closed at the end of 2011 and the director position was eliminated. Though a disappointing end to a promising project, and an end that put me out of a job, this was liberating for me. At last I had time to finish my doctoral dissertation [2013], only thirty-five years late, and to write and publish several articles; I was free to apply for research grants. Beginning in 2012, I have been able to devote a lot of time to fieldwork and recording on a new topic, group singing in rural communities, in a place that has interested me for decades, the island of Timor.

ARTS MANAGEMENT

Lois Wilcken (October 28, 2007)

PhD, Columbia University (Ethnomusicology)
Manager
"Makandal" Haitian Dance Troupe, New Jersey

Graduate Studies

LW: I finished my degree and was working at home on the synthesizer and realized that I needed more work on rhythm. It occurred to me that ethnomusicology might help because it seemed that rhythm was a more developed element of music in other cultures. I thought I should look at African music more closely. So [in spring of 1979] I went back to Hunter College—I lived in Manhattan through the '70s until 1982, which was very convenient—and started taking ethnomusicology courses with Rose Brandel. Rose was trying to return to teaching after a stroke, but she couldn't and eventually was talked into retirement. Until Hunter hired a replacement, they kept the program going by inviting people like Kay Shelemay and Dieter Christensen to come in from other programs in New York.

I didn't think I was going to do another degree; I just wanted to take courses. The first course I took with Rose was "Music in the Arab World." The next semester—fall of 1979—Dieter Christensen taught a course about ethnomusicology and invited Adelaida Reyes-Schramm to talk about urban ethnomusicology. She had just finished a dissertation on music in New York City, and the whole urban ethnomusicology thing was blossoming. Bruno Nettl had just published his book [*Eight Urban Musical Cultures*, 1978], so that was something that we focused a lot on in that course. The next semester—spring of '80—I took "Music in Africa" with Kay Shelemay. Barbara Hampton was finally hired in the fall of 1980. By this time, I'd been inspired by Dieter's class and had fallen in love with the discipline. I got so caught up in ethnomusicology that I never really went back to composition.

TS: What was so inspiring about Dieter's class, by the way?

LW: I always felt that the grand ideas in ethnomusicology were his forte; that's what turned me on. I saw that ethnomusicology wasn't simply about studying exotic cultures. So I started another master's degree, this time in ethnomusicology, with Barbara Hampton. She came back to urban ethnomusicology and said, "You're going to do fieldwork in New York and write it up at the end of the semester." The previous spring I had met a guy named Ray Joseph, who is now the Haitian ambassador to the United States [2005–2010]; back then he was a reporter working for *The Wall Street Journal*. I was taking Kay Shelemay's course on African music and was very interested in spirit possession. I asked Joseph if it would be possible to see a Vodou ceremony in New York. He said, "Well, they do happen in New York, but are not open to outsiders." This turned out to be false, but I didn't know that at the time. So when Barbara told us to go into a community and do a term project, I thought about Haitians and contacted Joseph again. This time he said, "Well, I can bring you to the next best thing," and he connected me with a group called the Ibo Dancers. I hung out with this dance company for a while and eventually, through them, met Frisner Augustin. In January 1981, I went to my first ceremony.

Building a Career

Around that time Makandal came to New York. It was a troupe of about thirty-five people, mostly poor kids, put together by a couple of Tonton Macoutes (a special force within the Haitian paramilitary under the Duvalier dictatorship) to get to New York. Everyone was trying to get out of Haiti back then, so what they did was get a few artists who could do enough to convince the US Embassy that this was a real group. The artists carried the group, convinced the embassy, and got free passage; others had to pay a couple of thousand dollars to get out of Haiti. That's how Makandal got to New York. Before they left Haiti, someone said, "When you get to New York, look up Frisner Augustin, because he can help you." Makandal just showed up and wanted his help in staying together as a group. Frisner had come earlier with a different company but wanted to have his own group, so he helped them. I was already Frisner's student, and because I was the only one who had skills in English, I fell into the position of being what they called a "manager." My official title with the company was "executive director." I found it fascinating!

TS: I know some of this was in your book, *The Drums of Vodou* [Wilcken and Augustin 1992], but Frisner was a Vodou drummer and had been teaching in New York, no?

LW: Yes, he came to New York in 1972 with Jazz De Jeunes, a big band that used Vodou drums, and decided to stay. He did factory jobs off and on, gave drum classes, and played with various companies: Ibo Dancers, Troupe Shango, Louinès Louinis,

Jean-Louis Destiné. All of them had left Haiti, come to New York, and re-grouped into new companies that mostly played for Haitian community festivals in Brooklyn.

I had met Frisner in November 1980 at a Thanksgiving Day Haitian spectacle at Brooklyn College. Two folklore groups were hired to play: Shango and Ibo Dancers. Frisner was playing with Shango and I was hanging out backstage with the Ibo Dancers. I was planning to record the concert with a little Uher tape recorder left over from my electronic music work. One of the people in Ibo Dancers introduced me to Frisner, but we didn't really sit down and talk. Later, I was having dinner at the apartment of one of the Ibo Dancers when another guest said, "Oh, you should be taking classes with Frisner Augustin" and set up my first drum class right there. I went the next day—January 3, 1981. I remember the date because I was taking notes for my class with Barbara, which was just about over by then, but I anticipated it continuing into the next semester.

TS: Were you beginning to think about learning Creole at all?

LW: Yes. There were a few books—not like the number of books and tapes you can find today—but I mostly learned by being around people and trying out my Creole. I had studied French in high school with a very bad French teacher. I had to redo it in graduate school because there was a language requirement. French helped in reading the literature, but hardly anyone I knew spoke French. The vocabulary helps with Creole but it's totally different grammar, so you really have to learn Creole separately from French.

TS: Was it a pretty straight trajectory from taking drum classes with Frisner to running the group?

LW: Yes. Do you know Verna Gillis? She made lots of recordings and had a performance loft called Soundscape on the West Side in Hell's Kitchen, which was famous for her Cuban music nights. I had heard her give a talk at Hunter College. I took Frisner up there, just before Makandal came to New York in the summer of 1981, and introduced her to him. She asked him to make a recording of Haitian music for her. She said, "Bring me a cassette. I want to hear what they sound like, and we'll talk." Well, he didn't have a group at the time, but Makandal arrived right after that, so one of their first projects was to make a recording. The recording process was very long, but we finally got a cassette ready by October '82. Frisner made a copy for me, which I took to Verna's place and left for her. She called me early next morning and said, "I've been listening to it all night; when can we do a gig?" We arranged a series of staged ceremonies at Soundscape. Makandal had never done that before, but they were capable of it because the kids really knew Vodou in and out. They had grown up in Vodou houses and all got the spirits. By the way, the LP was called *Trip to Voodoo* when it was finally released [La Troupe Makandal 1982].

TS: What kinds of music did Makandal play before that?

LW: They did what most troupes did: choreographed pieces based on Vodou dances. They didn't stage ceremonies, but that's what Verna wanted. We came up with a suite of dances based on Vodou dances. At first, they were at a loss to know what to do. They only had a couple of hours to perform, but the ceremony takes about six to seven hours to get through all the spirits who are supposed to be saluted. So that was the first concern: Who do we leave out? What if that spirit isn't happy about being left out? People who ask for a staged ceremony don't realize what problems might be caused. Some of the people who came to those performances were very influential, like Robert Baron of the New York State Council on the Arts. He approached me because every time someone asked Verna, "Where's the manager of the group?" she pointed to me. That's pretty much how I became the manager. Baron said, "We want to fund the Haitian group, but you've got to get them incorporated as a 501c3 nonprofit organization." He told me about "Volunteer Lawyers for the Arts," and so we paid fifty dollars for a lawyer to do the whole thing for us.

It took a couple of years, but when we got everything set up, we went back to the New York State Council on the Arts with a proposal. By this time, though, the group had changed a bit and Frisner had a couple of white drummers and some jazz instruments—he was very interested in bringing in horns and electric bass—but this was frowned on by folk arts programs: it wasn't "authentic" any more. They made a big issue out of it, and I couldn't seem to convince them that it was only one thing we did: if they wanted us to stage ceremonies, we could do that, too. But a rumor went around that Makandal was no longer doing authentic Haitian music. In time, we worked that out and did eventually get funding. I went to work for City Lore and the people there encouraged me to keep these issues about authenticity alive. We always got grants from the Brooklyn Arts Council because they were not so concerned about such issues. We also got lots of contracts, and that was mostly what we did for a number of years: people would hire us to do a program at a college or sometimes a club. Frisner liked to do club gigs because of his interest in jazz. The group he came up with—Jazz Des Jeunes—was considered a Vodou-jazz group.

TS: Are you still involved with City Lore?

LW: Yes, I've worked at City Lore for thirteen years. I get my health insurance and other benefits from City Lore, but I keep the job part time, so I have time for Makandal. Makandal has grown, because when I went to work for City Lore, I went through yet another education, in applied ethnomusicology and public-sector work, and I learned how to manage a nonprofit arts organization!

TS: What's your job description at City Lore?

LW: Originally, they brought me in because they had an emergency need for a book-keeper, but they also wanted somebody who knew something about their field. They thought I must know bookkeeping because I worked with Makandal, though at that point Makandal was still very small and I really only kept records. I didn't know anything about bookkeeping principles, but I quickly learned. As time went on, I did other work, such as grant reporting, and gradually learned how to write grants.

Update: August 12, 2016

The transition from where I was in 2007 to where I am now has been dramatic, although I continue my work in a similar vein. In late 2011 I left my job at City Lore to work with my partner in La Troupe Makandal, Master Drummer Frisner Augustin, to change the primary activities of our company from performance to documentation. We planned a book and recordings. In late December we left for a two-month trip to Haiti to explore the possibility of living there. Near the end of February 2012, Mr. Augustin suffered a massive stroke and died four days later in his hometown. In the more than four years since, I have won NEA funding for a memorial project. The Frisner Augustin Memorial Project holds an annual drum festival—three so far—in his name in New York, and they are creating an online archive of his life and work. The archive will provide materials for a biography. In Haiti, I am researching two families in the rural southeast who practice family-based Vodou. Jazz in Haiti has also caught my interest, and no ethnomusicologist to date has explored it. For fun, I'm studying the trumpet, which I was surprised and delighted to find in Mr. Augustin's instrument closet after his passing.

FREELANCE COMPOSING

Barbara Benary (August 24, 2010)

PhD, Wesleyan University (Ethnomusicology)
Freelance composer
Composers' gamelan director

Graduate Studies

BB: I graduated in the summer of '68 and started at Wesleyan in the fall. In between, I traveled to California and visited CalArts. Some of the Wesleyan people were teaching there—Viswanathan, the flutist, Ranganathan, the *mrdangam* player, and Tyagarajan, the violinist. It was like a little family.

TS: Who were your mentors or most important influences at Wesleyan?

BB: Everybody! The graduate program had some fascinating people. Whatever we were learning got shared around. We taught each other. I learned about *mbira* from

Paul Berliner and Japanese folk song from Patia Isaku. I put composing aside for those years. It was more important to take things in than to assimilate and put new things out. My only link to new music was as a performer with Philip Glass's band.

TS: How did you decide what you were going to do as an MA subject?

BB: I was working on violin and Tyagarajan encouraged me to do fieldwork. I didn't have to do fieldwork for my MA, but I did. My thesis was called "The Violin in South India" [Benary 1971]. When I went to India, I wanted to find out everything about people besides my teacher and his family, the context, and the history. It was wonderful. There's such a strong music culture in Madras. If you have a teacher, that's your credentials; you can go and visit any other musician, and they'd be happy to talk to you.

TS: Did you have a fellowship to go to Madras?

BB: I had a graduate assistantship. I talked Wesleyan into letting me use the whole year's worth to travel to India. It's hard to imagine today, but this was the affluent '60s, and there was comfortable money in being a grad student. Everyone in my graduate program was paid to be there by Wesleyan. The first year I did busy work like helping the Javanese teachers organize their music, handing out notations, and stuff like that. Later, I did teach an introductory course.

TS: Who were the Javanese teachers at Wesleyan?

BB: Prawotosaputro from Solo. I think Sumarsam came later.

TS: Is that when you were turned on by Javanese gamelan?

BB: Yes. I walked into a room and there was this beautiful, shiny kitchen full of pots and pans; it sounded very pretty. Actually, a year before that, when I was still at Sarah Lawrence, I went to a Javanese concert at Wesleyan. I borrowed a tape recorder and recorded some pieces; they were very beautiful. I fooled around with some of the ideas and some Indian ideas in my last year as a composition student, but I never ended up using any of that in my theater music.

TS: When did you go to India?

BB: I went to Madras in the fall of 1969 and was there for about nine months. There was an option of going on for the doctoral program, so I decided to gather enough material to do both.

I visited all the violinists I could find, assembled any writings I could find about them, and talked to people. The musicians talked about the history of their *guru-shishya parampara* [a given tradition of gurus and their disciples] and who was related to whom. They were pretty good about not bad-mouthing each other. Some were obviously friends, even though they came from different families and sometimes even different castes.

I was curious about what constituted a musical tradition. That became my doctoral dissertation [1973]. Looking back, it was very amorphous. It was just various ways of looking at the tradition: What's it like to be a composer? What's it like to be a performer? Where does music theory come from? Where does musical vocabulary come from?

TS: After nine months in India, did you return to Wesleyan to write up?

BB: Yes. I had a bunch of handwritten notebooks and a typewriter. It was smooth sailing, and the faculty was extremely encouraging. They wanted students to succeed and couldn't wait to get somebody through the door with a PhD. They'd had the program for ten years and nobody had actually finished! I figured that if I didn't do it in a year, I wouldn't get it done. So I got a Woodrow Wilson dissertation fellowship for a year, holed up in my apartment with my boyfriend, and we both wrote our dissertations.

Building a Career

BB: I never would have left Wesleyan, except that I needed a job. I liked the community of the Music Department, which was diverse and quite fascinating. I was used to the town, but the problem was, anything I'd learned that could earn me a living, everybody else in town knew too. I couldn't get a job there. In 1973 Rutgers contacted Wesleyan and asked, "Who's just graduated and might be looking for a job?" They interviewed two of us, George Mgrdichian, the *'ūd* player, and me. Rutgers had three colleges: the original Rutgers, Douglas College (an affiliated women's college, which was run like a conservatory), and Livingston College. Livingston was founded after riots in Newark during the '60s and was supposed to be social progress oriented. The music faculty at Livingston College voted to hire me; they thought having ethnomusicology would cater to diversity.

TS: What made you start a gamelan in the first place?

BB: In the course of interviewing, I said I could teach "Music of India" and "Music of Indonesia" because those were the things I'd studied. I figured gamelan was more accessible than Karnatak music. If you have the instruments, you can get impressive results on a superficial level pretty fast. I offered to build a gamelan for a world music course, which would save them the five thousand dollars or so it would cost to import one. I spent my first summers in New Jersey learning to become a carpenter and instrument builder and communicating with homemade gamelan builders around the country. I formed Gamelan Son of Lion, and we performed at the college and other colleges in New York City.

TS: What was the response at Rutgers?

BB: It was all politics. I was a compromise candidate between the academic faction at Rutgers and the Livingston College faction, which comprised two new music

Careers outside "Professorial Academia"/"The Professoriat"

composers and two people doing jazz. Some were superficially interested in ethno-musicology and others were not in the least bit interested. The students, who were studying in both programs, didn't see a distinction at all. They took jazz, they took ethno, and were perfectly happy doing either. I never officially taught composing, but I composed and performed with students and faculty.

TS: Was performance curricular or extracurricular?

BB: Being in gamelan was part of the course, but it wasn't restricted to the course, and performance sessions were separate from the academic sessions. I was at Rutgers from 1973 to 1980. Two three-year contracts and then I had to do the tenure thing. That was an unpleasant experience and became very political. My co-founders of Gamelan Son of Lion, Philip Corner and Daniel Goode, both went through the tenure process before I did. Daniel went through it first. They turned him down, so he initiated a grievance procedure and fought them tooth and nail. Eventually they went to arbitration, which conceded that the evaluation had been prejudicial and gave him his job back. The next year Philip had to go through the same thing and they threw *him* out. They could not understand his concept of music theory, which was that music history should be taught starting with the present and going backward. That was way too radical for them. But because his case was essentially the same as Daniel's, they conceded pretty quickly and gave him tenure.

The following year it was my turn, but this time the administration had a tough new lawyer. Same result. I won the arbitration, but the lawyer argued that they were not going to honor arbitrations any more. By that time it was up to the union to do something. Unfortunately, the union attached my case to a class-action suit involving a number of women who were not tenured. The whole thing dragged on for ten years and I lost everything.

TS: All three of you were attacked on tenure? What was the issue, do you think?

BB: That's a good question. Although I had my assemblage of publications and presentations, I committed the ultimate sin of not publishing my dissertation. I didn't particularly want to publish it; it was a good dissertation, but in the course of writing it, I had exhausted my curiosity. There were so many other things I wanted to do instead, such as compose and play music. I became a pawn in an interdepartmental war between the staid composers of the main Rutgers department, who claimed they had hired me to be an academic, and those of my Livingston College department, who had hired me because I was also a composer. My compositions and concerts were of importance to the latter, but the Old Boys (whom I could never join anyway, on account of being a girl) decided that they were irrelevant.

TS: How did you maintain your gamelan?

BB: Philip Corner was a big factor in that. He said, "Let's move the gamelan out of Rutgers to my house in New York. I'll get all my new music composer friends to play in it." He rounded up a whole crew of composers who were associated with the Downtown Movement and we told Rutgers students, "You're welcome to come; just get on the train and come to New York." Three or four of them did, though over the years it dwindled to one former student who's still in the gamelan. Gamelan Son of Lion has been based in Philip Corner and Daniel Goode's loft since 1976!

TS: What has your career been like since then?

BB: I applied for ethnomusicology jobs elsewhere while this dragged on. I was a finalist for three jobs, but there was always another agenda. I had been living in New Jersey, near Rutgers, but moved to where my husband-to-be was, Stony Point, New York. We were married in 1977, had a daughter, and bought a house. I got back to classical music—string quartets, orchestra music, and that kind of stuff. I had played a lot of early music with my husband and was involved with folk music, which I had picked up at Wesleyan. I also got involved with the New England Old Time Fiddling movement and Sacred Harp singing.

I had all these musical hobbies—that's how I amused myself. I didn't make a living at it; I made my living doing all kinds of strange jobs. For a while I was a printer's devil, then I was a tofu maker, and eventually, when my child reached school age, I ended up teaching at her private school, the Rockland Project School. At first I taught music, social studies, and computer, because they didn't have anyone else. They figured I could teach social studies because I knew about other cultures. They had no Theater Department, so I combined social studies and theater by having the kids do a lot of historical plays, which they made up. I did that until the school dissolved. At that point, I decided I'd better get certification to teach in the public schools, which I was able to do by simply taking a couple of tests. I talked the New York State Board of Regents into believing I knew what I was doing.

TS: You should be proud of yourself; a lot of people would like to do that but can't! Were you able to make any money out of the gamelan stuff?

BB: No, I was lucky if I could make commuting money! I had an income until a few years ago. After teaching in public schools, I went into a music agency for a while. I had started looking for jobs and saw an ad for a music agency that wanted a bookkeeper. I wrote and said, "I don't know a thing about bookkeeping except I have run a gamelan as a non-profit for fifteen or twenty years and keep the books and write grants for that." It turned out that the son of the woman who ran the agency played gamelan! She said, "I've heard of your group and the fact is we don't really want to hire a bookkeeper; we want to hire a musician who can do the bookkeeping." I fit the bill. It was a very nice family business. I'd go over to their house, have lunch, sit down at the typewriter, and get on the telephone; the bookkeeping part of the job was pretty mindless. These days I just do private violin lessons. I could have done that when I was 18 years old! I always figured if all else fails, I can always teach violin or go busking in the New York subways. I had a little annuity from my Rutgers days, and I'm almost old enough for Social Security.

Other things just popped up from time to time. The whole Japan project was a surprise. Just after 9/11, I met Tomoko, a young Japanese housewife who had just come to the United States with her husband. She had studied Balinese dance in Bali and looked me up because she wanted to join a gamelan. She played with us for a while, but new music was a little stressful for her, so she joined the New York Balinese Gamelan. We stayed friends and talked about gamelan groups in Japan. I told her about the gamelan directory I had started in 1983 now housed on the American Gamelan Institute site. Jody Diamond was trying to broaden it and expand it to other parts of the world, but nobody knew anything about gamelans in Japan. So Tomoko decided we should do it. She started making a list and found some good connections. The networking thing was a lot of fun. She did all the corresponding in Japanese, and I did the writing. First, we put out a directory list, and then we decided to carry it a step further, go to Japan, and meet everybody on our list. I wanted to go to Japan with somebody Japanese because I don't speak Japanese and was jumping into it cold. So I went with her; we spent a week in the Osaka area and a week in the Tokyo area. I wrote down everything and we interviewed everybody we possibly could.

TS: Did you ever do any traditional Javanese music in your gamelan, or was it always a composers' gamelan?

BB: We always tried to have some percentage of Javanese pieces and a lot more Balinese. In my first year at Livingston College, I went to the 1974 ASEA (American Society for Eastern Arts) Summer School, where I fell in love with Balinese *gamelan angklung*. I recorded everything and made notations of what they were doing. When I got back I built a set of *angklung* instruments. That's been a great thing for me because I still use them. When people ask, "Can you do a workshop?" I ask, "Can you hire instruments for the workshop?" They answer no, and so I say, "Well, you can hire me and I'll bring the gamelan." Then I stuff all the instruments in the back of my car and bring them along.

TS: Do you think that if you had heard Balinese gamelan before Javanese, you might have gone in that direction?

BB: In a way, I went in both directions. I still like Balinese music; I just don't like it as much. I love *gamelan angklung* and the slower genres—*lelambatans*—that are not quite at the speed of light. I find *gamelan gong kebyar* a little overwhelming.

TS: Do you conceive of your ensemble, Gamelan Son of Lion, as a Javanese ensemble?

BB: Yes, the instruments follow the regular standard Javanese *karawitan* style, including the tuning (and having a wacky tuning is extremely important). There's no reason I can think of, however, why they would have to stay that way. Last year, a chamber music series asked us to perform a traditional piece, so I pulled something I loved out of my hat, "Gendhing Babar Layar." I sat down with a recording and Pak Harjito, Wesleyan's Javanese instructor—he's a lovely man—and worked out an arrangement that my group could learn. Gamelan Son of Lion is a composers' band, but if there's a gig, they'll buckle down and learn the music. Sometimes we play Lou Harrison pieces to represent traditional music, because they're almost traditional.

Update: July 2, 2016

Presently I do not teach ethnomusicology very much, other than occasional seminars. I've neglected the scholastic side of the field. However, since I am a hands-on ethnomusicologist, I continue to perform with my ensemble Gamelan Son of Lion, though I am easing off on my participation. The obvious change here is that I much prefer playing music to talking about it, and in my semi-retired state, I have happily let the latter aspect slide.

(Barbara passed away on March 17, 2019.)

FREELANCE PERFORMING/PEDAGOGY

Nikhil Dally (July 5, 2007)

BA, Music, University of Cambridge
Freelance performer/pedagogue
Gamelan teacher/piano freelancer

Further Studies

ND: By the time I got to the end of my course at Cambridge [in 1988] I had worked *ever* so hard. I had studied endlessly and did very well; I got a very good degree. By that time an increasing number of people [from the UK] had spent a year or longer in Central Java doing nothing but learning gamelan, people like Alec Roth, Simon Cook, and Jenny Heaton. They were coming back and starting to *teach* gamelan to the likes of us. So I thought, "Well, I'm fairly unemployable already, and I like this." My parents were still living in Jakarta, so I thought I could get a visa with no problem, rent a room somewhere in Central Java, and visit my parents every few months. So that's what I did. In 1988 I went to Jakarta, took a train out to Solo, and walked through the front gate of STSI [Sekolah Tinggi Seni Indonesia] (ASKI [Akademi Seni Karawitan Indonesia] at the time). People from England who'd been in Java told me, "Go and talk to Pak Hastanto and Pak A. L. Suwardi—they can help you." I went to them and said, "I want to stay in Solo for a year and take lessons." So I did. It was fantastic. I learned so much and played a lot.

In retrospect, I think the British folks who go out to Java now gain so much more than I did because they have been able to learn more before going. When I went, as I said, there were only two people in the country who played *gambang*, probably two who played *gendèr*, and maybe two who played any *kendhang ciblon*. I'd learned everything there was to learn in England, and it wasn't much at the time. I was starting from scratch and struggling through the basic technique of *gendèr*. These days, a British person wouldn't have to do that because he could reach a very high standard before going out. As a consequence, I don't think I "*masuk*-ed" much during that year. (Do you know that word? It means "to enter"; the Javanese talk about this a lot. You have to "enter" the music and feel with your heart.)

I didn't even begin to approach that while I was there. I was still very much at the stage where I had to record everything and transcribe it assiduously. I didn't have the ear to hear what was going on. When I attempted to play with ensembles, I inevitably got completely lost. I was learning a lot, but my musicianship had not matured. Intense gamelan learning can teach you some things, but there are other things that just take time, and I hadn't had that time. Some people need more time than others. I needed a lot!

Building a Career

TS: How did you start making a living out of gamelan?

ND: That started after I came back. I did a postgraduate course in composition with Robert Saxton at the Guildhall School of Music. I took the course because I couldn't think of what else to do, and my parents said, "We'll help you out and support you," which was wonderful. It was great and I loved it, but at the end of the year it was time to stop playing and start working. By then Alec Roth had set up the South Bank gamelan program—in 1990, I think. I came back from Java and was fortunate to be asked to teach one of the evening beginners' classes. They also had a program of daytime workshops for schools, so I started to do other work for the South Bank Centre [an arts complex in London]. At the same time, I did all sorts of freelance work, piecing together a living as best as I could. This included playing piano for dance schools, some of them very small and others quite prestigious, and for musicals and so on. I was also doing a lot of composing for theater companies. Gradually, I built a broad portfolio of work in the process of extracting myself from the rigidly "Western" way of thinking about music and launching myself into this very different, very aural world of gamelan.

To be honest, I think the gamelan would have ended up being a back-burner thing, and I would have continued being a pianist and musical director for theater shows. That was where the jobs were, but then I started to turn them down because I fell in love, got married, and started a family. That kind of life was just not compatible; I was asked to go on tour for four months around Europe when my wife was pregnant, and I thought, "No, I don't want to do this." Then I was asked to play for a show at the Royal Shakespeare Company—a plum job, except that I'd already arranged that we were going to Indonesia for Christmas. When you start to turn down jobs, people stop offering them to you, so that kind of work dwindled.

I had to shift my focus toward trying to earn a living that was sufficient to support a family and would have a timetable compatible with staying married! So a lot more teaching and gamelan workshop stuff came out of that. I was asked to start a gamelan program by a brilliant lady called Sylvia Downes, who was music principal for North Hertfordshire. Hertfordshire was one of the first counties to get its own gamelan. That was very exciting, partly because Sylvia was a brilliant manager, musician, and teacher. She ran a County Music Centre when she contacted me and said, "Nikhil, I want you to set up our gamelan program; how can we do it?" It was fantastic; we bought a gamelan from Suhirdjan in Yogya, and she gave me free rein in setting up the program. That was the first program. Since then I have moved from one gamelan thing to another, and now I have an arrangement with Berkshire Young Musicians' Trust. My portfolio shifted away from piano performance and toward the teaching of gamelan because of my circumstances.

I set up my own music school here in Egham because I thought, "Bloody hell, I need more work to support my growing family." I went on a Kodály musicianship course in London and signed up for the school-age teaching course, but met Helga Dietrich, an educator from Hungary, who was teaching the "early childhood" course, about preschool music teaching. I thought she was brilliant! I wanted to learn from her, so I switched to her course and then thought, "Gosh, I could do this." The whole idea of teaching, bringing out, and supporting musicianship in little children—helping them to really "*masuk*" the music rather than just play notes—is where it all begins. The thought was exciting because the great challenge when you're teaching adults, or teenagers, or even older children is that if their musicianship and musicality were supported and nurtured through their early years through a sound pedagogical process, then they would have a great advantage when learning piano, gamelan, or whatever later.

Musical backgrounds are increasingly hard to find these days in this country, even in contexts that are supposed to be musical. It need not be a rigorous musical education, but sadly, unless the person overseeing the situation has some idea of what making music "soundly" really is, it often ends up degenerating, stopping the child from hearing, listening, and singing in tune and moving in time. Pedagogy matters!

TS: So you started a school of musicianship. Do you focus on gamelan or Western musicianship?

ND: My object is to teach skills—processes, rather than products. In group musicianship classes I use a lot of ideas I've got from Kodály, from Colourstrings, from

Dalcroze, and from an absolutely brilliant dance teacher I worked with for many years who had studied developmental movement with Nancy Topf. I've also obviously learned a lot about musical priorities from gamelan. So I designed my own curriculum that combines all of the above in, I hope, a coherent manner.

TS: Do you have a website?

ND: Yes, dally.org.uk. Most of my work is connected with the music school, but another major component is teaching gamelan. I'm now teaching in Reading, Berkshire, where I have my own gamelan, which I acquired about ten years ago.

TS: This relates to a completely different question. I don't know whether you have any practical experience with Balinese gamelan, but do you have any thoughts about Balinese versus Javanese gamelan?

ND: To my embarrassment, I'm almost totally ignorant of Balinese gamelan. I don't really know how to listen to Balinese music because I've not spent time learning to listen to it. So my initial impression is "This is fast, this is exciting, this is noisy, but what's the point?" But that is almost certainly a total travesty.

TS: Why a travesty? People have different reactions. Some people hear it for the first time and fall in love with it.

ND: So the fact that I didn't fall in love with Balinese music tells you more about me than it does about Balinese music. If I took the time to learn to listen to it, I might learn to love it. It always interests me how the Javanese can find Western classical music boring, and how Western classical musicians can find gamelan boring. When you ask them about it, whether you're a Western classical musician or a Javanese gamelan musician, generally speaking they both say, "It sounds like the same thing over and over again." In a sense they're right, because all music is "the same thing over and over again," otherwise it wouldn't have coherence, but it's also different things happening, otherwise it wouldn't have variety. Great music has that balance right, between coherence and variety.

TS: You said that when you hear Balinese music you don't know what the point is. What do you think the "point" is in Javanese music?

ND: I don't know if there's a single word for it. In Western music the "single word" is possibly "tonality," which in its various implications and ramifications covers everything. I guess maybe in Javanese music: "*pathet*." Except that, again, it's a matter of definition, isn't it? Some people think that tonality is just about what key you're in, and some people think *pathet* is just about what *pathet* you're in, what gong note it is, but actually, it's to do with relationships, directions, movements, and shapes.

TS: For me the difference is between the *garapping* [realizing] and the not-*garapping*, and having to listen to people, and having to work your way through stuff to realize the music.

ND: Yes, *garap* and *pathet* are two parts of the same thing for me. A lot of Javanese complain that *Western* music doesn't have *garap*. If *garap* purely means the ability of the final *performer* to alter the text, then OK, maybe it doesn't have very much *garap*. But in Western music the *garap* is at a different place; it's actually further back in the chain. It's more in the lines of what the composer or arranger is choosing to do, so it's all a matter of definitions, isn't it? Where does *komposisi* end and *garap* begin? And where do you put that?

Update: August 14, 2017

The only significant development in my career since we last spoke is that I have become heavily involved in teacher training. Music education in this country has become increasingly underfunded and undervalued. Without a clear sense of good pedagogy, the result is all too often a confused scattergun approach that tries to produce quick and easy results but in fact betrays our students in the long run. (I found one website that described gamelan as "easy to play, easy to teach"! Can you imagine a more nonsensical statement?) Running my teachers' courses may, I hope, help to stem the decline.

Independent Research

Alex Dea (July 13, 2010)

PhD, Wesleyan University (Ethnomusicology)
Independent researcher, Java, Indonesia

Graduate Studies

AD: I went to Middletown, Connecticut, in 1973 and was there until 1980, with two years in Java for my fieldwork. Middletown turned out to be the hippie place of the East Coast—more trouble!

MS: Who were some of your role models as you were starting out?

AD: David McAllester, my counselor, was great, but he was an anthropologist, not a musician. We heard about Mantle Hood because of the gamelan, and we read Nettl and Merriam, which I liked a lot. It turned out that I was, in a way, more interested in the anthropological side of things. But my masters, the teachers I looked up to, were all performers. Sumarsam was there; we had some great Indian masters, we had Japanese music. I played *shakuhachi*.

MS: Do you think of yourself as part of any kind of scholarly lineage?

AD: Yes, because there are two things that I always remember. One was David McAllester. Although I never took a course from him, his aura and his approach and the few things that he said opened my eyes to the possibility that things could be different from how they looked. For instance, he said, "If I were in Indonesia, I would study popular music" at a time when I was trying desperately to be a classical gamelan musician. The other thing was when I was in junior high school I used to spend a lot of time in the public library, trying to get myself educated so I could be as American as possible. I found Colin McPhee's book, *Music in Bali* [1966]. I couldn't read it because my English wasn't good enough, but in the back were photographs of all those strange-looking people with their big eyes and Mario dancing with his funny crazed look and his skinny body. They were so intense! I kept the book on loan for about a year. So when you ask what the thread is, I always go back to Colin McPhee. He always talked about the notes, not about anthropology or abstractions or postmodernism, or any of the "-isms" that became popular in American ethnomusicology. It's come back around now with Michael Tenzer's work.

Building a Career

AD: I wanted to follow the academic path, but there were about ten of us looking for a job and only one job going. Where was it? College Park, Maryland. Who got it? Mantle Hood. Of course, they wanted a senior person, but they didn't tell us that, so we all tried for the job. I wanted to be an ethnomusicologist. I didn't know that I didn't want to be a teacher. I knew you had to be one, but I didn't know I didn't *want* to be one. I was still struggling with that when Cathleen Read (David Locke's wife, a *koto* master with a title) gave up and got a computer job at John Hancock Insurance Company in Boston. She said, "Why don't you get a job with us?" So that's what I did. That's how I got started in IT. At first, I was sad that I wasn't going to be playing gamelan, but I thought I'd try it for six months, and if I didn't like it I'd try for another job. I had enjoyed taking a programming course in college in the days when there was no such thing as a screen to write on! Everything was in punch cards. It was a bit more advanced now, but it turned out that I liked it. I liked working at the John Hancock Insurance Company, too. You have to remember, we were hippies and came from a very different mindset. To go into the Babylon of the "real world" was really different. But what I found out—big surprise—was that when we did well, we were praised and given bonuses. This was very different from what we'd learned in academia, where everybody was protective, not telling secrets, in case they lost their chance at a job—all the stuff that's not talked about in the Ivory Tower. I discovered it was much more unsavory in academia than in what I thought was the Babylon. In business, they were much more straightforward. So I decided to stay.

MS: How many years did you stay in that job?

AD: From 1980 until 1992. I stayed in Boston for about four years because they were very good at training us, but finally I said, "I have to go back to California, where the real people are." All my family was there, and I felt badly that I couldn't see them. I tested the waters and called a headhunter. I got a call from a bank that said, "We'll move you, give you a bonus for the first three months, and put you into an apartment." And they raised my salary. It was the worst thing I ever did, because Californian banks are terrible. Poisonous. I was there for two years and it almost killed me. So I quit and moved to a technology company. It was great for hippies: we could go to the office in shorts; we stayed late, but we could come in late; and they served great coffee for our breaks! I stayed with them a couple of years and learned a lot of technological stuff. But the company was too small. I decided to try for something bigger and ended up in a beautiful Silicon Valley company called Tandem. Subsequently, Tandem merged into Compaq and later into HP, so now I work with HP as a freelance consultant in the professional curriculum.

MS: You said that you decided to live in Java in 1992. How did that come about?

AD: I was hoping to do something with my Javanese recordings—I had recorded a lot in the two years of fieldwork when I was there. I was still very interested in Javanese music, so much so that I had my own ensemble in San Francisco. I picked the best players and we practiced at my home. We'd even play the occasional concert. Pak Cokro, one of the greatest masters of Javanese music of all time, was in residence at CalArts. He was my guru, so my wife (who was also a very good singer) and I would go down there to participate when they had concerts. By then, Pak Cokro was over eighty and had been teaching in America for about twenty years. The night before a concert, he had a serious heart attack. It happened overnight, so even the students were just finding out. I went directly to the hospital. He was lying on the bed, not in a coma, but in no condition to stand up. So I helped out, translating insurance and hospital things for the family. His daughter and son-in-law were both teachers at CalArts, so he had a lot of family support. I stayed maybe a week to help out and kept coming back to look after them. The family decided that when he got well enough, he should go back to Indonesia. At that point, I was going back to Indonesia every year to meet with my old masters. I realized that I had to go back with Pak Cokro.

He went back in summer of '92, and I followed about two weeks later, in August. I never went back. I stayed at his house in Yogyakarta because his family wanted me to keep him interested in music and be a companion, which was fine with me. Indonesia does not have a master-disciple tradition like India, but I was used to the idea from my Indian experience.

MS: Did you take your job with you?

AD: No, but Tandem was a very forward-looking company. They gave three-month sabbaticals for every seven years of work. I had done very well in the company and they didn't want me to leave, so it wasn't a problem to leave for a year. My wife had decided to leave me a year earlier. I had no wife, a house that I could leave, and my guru was going away, so I said, "I'm leaving, now." I had a good time for a year, getting back with all my masters—there were about ten of them still alive, but after a year, I realized I'd have to get a job. Tandem knew I was in Southeast Asia and they wanted me to take over some projects in Singapore, but I said, "I don't want a full-time job." I applied to the Asian Cultural Council for a grant to do video, which helped for another year. And in that time, Tandem got me interested in teaching. So I would go—mainly to Singapore, a little bit to Kuala Lumpur—to teach four, five, six times a year. That gave me about fourteen, fifteen thousand dollars, which is plenty over there. That's what I've done ever since. So I got to be a teacher after all—without having to do any grading!

MS: If you hadn't done that, what do you think you might have done?

AD: It's hard to say, because all the time I was in America, working in IT, having my gamelan friends, and managing a small gamelan, I was also composing, mostly rock 'n' roll, with a very good writer by the name of Stephen Policoff. He teaches at NYU. He's written some novels, but he was basically a scriptwriter. We loved the same things: Bob Dylan's poetry; Lou Reed's inability to sing in tune; Van Morrison's blues; and John Lennon's great tunes. I was composing all that time. I didn't want to be in a band any more, I just wanted to get rich writing songs for other bands to play. So if I didn't have anything to do, I might've gone back to work in IT and concentrated on getting the songs to work.

MS: Are you still active as an ethnomusicologist?

AD: I'm still interested in explicating systems of music. I've been writing all along, thoughts about the composition of Javanese music, the meaning of how Javanese play, a lot of things that Sumarsam talks about and is trying to articulate. We're actually in the same space, but coming from two different directions. Now that my masters are all dead, I have time to devote to my writing.

Over here in Indonesia, "ethnomusicology" means "survey of world music." They don't really do fieldwork. They do the performing part as learning, but they don't take the extra step that Mantle Hood advocated, that you talk about the theory based on your emotional knowledge. I'm still interested in that. They have a Department of Ethnomusicology at ISI, the University of Arts [as well as] Dance, Western Music, Gamelan, and *Wayang Kulit* Departments. What do they do [in the Department of Ethnomusicology]? A little bit of ethnomusicology as we think of it, a little bit of survey, but mostly they learn how to play the music outside of Java. They play Balinese music, they play Sumatran, they go to Flores or Sulawesi and other places, but they're not very disciplined in their approach. "Whatever is different, that's ethno. And you can learn it." And when you learn it, they expect you to perform it, make compositions, and do shows. [After some initial doubts] I realized, "This is really great," because they're actually learning how to do music that is not their own. They're actually doing world music.

So, back to your question: I want to go back to what I thought I should do in terms of writing. It's important to write. I've done so many videos, and I think that's also very important. I guess I do three things: ethnography, composition, and performance. I want to transmit the knowledge that has been given to me, because it's been a gift.

Update: June 25, 2016

Since our last interview, I am happy to say that almost 99 percent of my one thousand videos, more than that of audios, and photos and slides have been transferred to hard disc. Finally, I have time and access to see the content of the work I have done. When I was recording, there was only time to shoot and move on to the next project or event. I am ever conscious of the importance to create a channel for access to anyone and everyone interested.

Veronica Doubleday (March 5, 2010)

MA, University of Sussex (English)
Independent researcher, England

Building a Career

VD: When I finished my master's in 1970, I had to get a job to support myself. I wanted to write a book, a sort of autobiographical exploration, quite formless and very introspective. That's when I met John [Baily]. He had the "allure of the East" about him because he had just come back from Nepal and was interested in Buddhism. I liked the music he played, but I was most interested in his travels. Another attraction was that he wanted to study music in Afghanistan—I thought that sounded great. I'd traveled a bit in Europe but no farther. I would have loved the idea before, but I hadn't thought how to do it. I was really interested in writing my book and being in Brighton, but then I thought, "Oh, I could get away from all this." It was the right timing for me. When he played old recordings of music from Afghanistan and I looked at the record sleeves, I saw these desolate-looking hills and domed roofs that seemed to merge into the landscape, and I thought it looked like a fantastic place to visit. I was all for that idea.

We set off in the autumn of 1972. My parents weren't very keen at all. They didn't see it as a very stable prospect for me to go off with this penniless musician. But really, what could they do? They couldn't stop me. We took the Orient Express! We spent a week in Istanbul and then took a train from Istanbul to Tehran. I was bowled over by the landscape. I had never seen such, frankly, lunar-like wastes. I enjoyed it fantastically. We lived in Tehran for eight months and got work very quickly, teaching English. I worked for the oil company. I only had to work four afternoons a week and made masses of money. I earned enough to save some money and support John, because he didn't get paid immediately by his employers, the National University.

We went to Afghanistan with a couple of friends from Sussex University who were living in Tehran. We met them when they were visiting Brighton and stayed with them when we first arrived. They'd been to Herat quite a few times and wanted to visit again, so we went together. John had been to Afghanistan before. I hadn't. Even though we had been in Iran for a while and had learned Persian by then, it was a big contrast. I really wasn't acclimatized in some ways.

MS: We have a pretty good sense of your life in Herat because you write about it so eloquently in *Three Women of Herat* [Doubleday 1988], but how about the career aspect of it? You didn't go in intending to do research. Rather, you decided along the way to help John with his project and everything took off from there. At what point did you develop a sense of ownership, that this was your thing, as opposed to being part of what John was doing?

VD: I definitely developed that sense. When we first went to Afghanistan, I had carte blanche to do what I wanted. I was officially his research assistant and wanted to study miniature painting. I found a teacher and went to his studio for lessons. I wrote an account of my lessons, describing what I'd done and how I felt about it. I was writing "field notes" about everything I thought was interesting, families I met, and so on. I got into that very early on. John said it would be good to keep a record, like a diary, so I did, using a typewriter and carbon paper. I was quite disciplined, but didn't consider I was doing anything with his research. It was my own thing. I knew at that stage I wanted to write a book about women. So, in my mind, I had two projects: studying miniature painting and collecting material for a book about women in these very secluded circumstances. I also wanted to do a lot of photography, so to support John's project I was the photographer. I photographed hand movements on *dutars* as well as landscapes and tile work and things that linked up with my miniature painting studies.

Another thing I did was actually much more closely linked up with John's work. We had Persian lessons with a schoolteacher called Fata Khan Baburi. He helped John find *dutar* players to start with. John asked him to transcribe the texts of songs he was starting to record. So Fata Khan Baburi used to come to our house quite regularly, and I would work with him on song texts that we transliterated and romanized. He would dictate the words, which he'd already written down in Farsi, and then give a translation. I would say, "What does that mean?" and he would explain some of the poetry and its symbolism. This was important for me later, for my singing, because I became familiar with a lot of melodies and songs. I ended up doing a lot to help John in his work. I would type out all the song texts and, later, when we were in Belfast, I helped him write and edit his report. I also did a lot of cataloging of material as well. By the end of that first year, I had a lot of field notes, a lot of friends, and information about women and their customs. I'd become quite familiar with the music and had attended a lot of musical events. I knew quite a lot about music in Herat.

MS: Can I pause to ask if you remember when you first heard the word "ethnomusicology"? Because that's what you were doing by then, wasn't it? What did you think it meant at that time?

VD: I didn't have a particular "DUH! Ethnomusicology" moment! When John decided to do this research in Herat, it was in experimental psychology, so there wasn't the idea that "we're going off to be ethnomusicologists." How did I feel about the idea of ethnomusicology when I first came across it? I thought it sounded fascinating but felt a bit embarrassed when people said, "What are you doing?" It was a headache because you had to explain to people what it meant. It wasn't like saying, "I'm studying law." I had to say, "Oh, I'm with my boyfriend and he's doing ethnomusicology." "Oh, what's that?" "Well it's a bit like the anthropology of music." It wasn't this wonderful, alluring thing. I couldn't say "ethnomusicology" and immediately have a sense of positivity about it. But now it's fine—I can tell anybody, "I do ethnomusicology," and they don't need much of an explanation. They've heard the word.

After Herat we went back to live in Belfast. I was extremely reluctant to go there; it was such a difficult time. It was not a town you could wander around and explore. But John Blacking was very generous in that he let me attend seminars, classes, and everything that was going on. So I went along to all that stuff and really enjoyed the performance classes. He also had a lot of interesting visitors, so it was very exciting. By then I was definitely getting interested in ethnomusicology.

MS: So you began to learn about the theory and methods of ethnomusicology, but you did it outside the formal structure of a program?

VD: Yes, I was never a student, though I was welcomed and fitted in. I followed my own course of reading, especially ethnographies of women—whatever I could find in the library—things like Marjorie Shostak's *Nisa: The Life and Words of a !Kung Woman* [1981] and Elizabeth Fernea's *Guests of the Sheik* [1969], about women in Iraq. She was like me in that she went with her husband, an anthropologist, and described living in an Iraqi village, the friendships she made, the outings, and negotiations. John Blacking's Ethnomusicology Department was vibrant. I got on very well with the students, and we had plenty of musical interests in common.

MS: At that time, did you ever think about having a career of your own?

VD: No, actually I resisted it. John Blacking asked me if I would like to do a PhD, but it wasn't something I wanted to do. I wanted to keep my options open.

We went back to Afghanistan for six weeks in the summer of 1975 and that was when I decided to have my own project. I'd already been studying women, making friends, and thinking about writing, but after all that exposure in Belfast, I realized that I could do my own recordings. So I made some recordings of weddings in people's houses and cataloged them. After the summer of 1975 we went back to Belfast and stayed until autumn '76. I gave a talk about women's music in Afghanistan in the Wednesday afternoon seminar series. I had more material than I could get through in the allotted time, and Blacking said, "Oh, that's really good stuff. Next week, we'll carry on with your work." That was very encouraging. I don't remember when I first gave presentations at IFMC [International Folk Music Council, now ICTM, International Council for Traditional Music] meetings and such, but it was probably around then, too. I already had my own style. There was a meeting in Oxford, quite early on, and Henry Stobart likes telling the story that as an aspiring ethnomusicologist he went to that meeting and found it deadly boring until I took off my shoes and sat up on a table, got my drum, and started singing. Then he thought, "Oh, that's a bit different. Thank goodness for that." I firmly believe that if you're going to talk about music, you should actually listen to music, either recordings or, even better, live music because of its immediacy. There's so much information that to theorize about music and give a whole presentation without any music seemed that the values were all wrong. That was my approach.

MS: In a field in which having an academic position is part of the currency, you've charted a very independent course. Did you ever feel devalued in any way?

VD: That was an issue, you're absolutely right. I realized quite early on that there was no point in trying to have a parallel career in ethnomusicology. I don't know that I really wanted it, but I knew that for practical reasons, it would be difficult to get jobs in the same place. After we left Afghanistan in 1977, I really wanted to have children. I'd been very influenced by the way Afghan women think and I'd been ridiculed for not having children for so long. I wanted children and I wanted to write my book, so I wasn't interested in getting a job or teaching. The book took me years to write! I was slow, partly because I had two children and we lived between Belfast and Brighton until 1983.

MS: Looking at your career from this vantage point: you've become a successful author and you have your own reputation within the field. Can you reflect on that for a moment?

VD: Obviously, there's still the fact that we've been a husband and wife team and we've shared our data, so that puts me into an unusual position in a sense. I'm fine about being marginal in ethnomusicology because I've had a rich experience doing things I wanted to do. I wanted time to be creative, have various projects, and do my own reading. I've had that freedom. People have to work so hard if they've got a job teaching ethnomusicology and having a career like that. I've chosen not to be on that path for the freedom of doing my own projects.

MS: And you've also had the performing part of your life, too. That's a substantial part of who you are, isn't it?

VD: Yes, performance-wise, I hope things will continue to develop. John has been a great motivation for that, and I enjoy performance very much. I always feel validated after a concert because it usually has such a good response. I went to Delphi a few years ago with some friends. There's a cave you can only get to by going along a track; most people don't know about it. We went thinking we'd try to get an oracle. There wasn't anything like smoke or priestesses, but in my mind a very clear message formed that said, "Use all your gifts." I had a question: "What should I concentrate on, singing or writing?" The answer was, don't choose between them. Do it all and try to use all your gifts. If that involves doing research in Afghanistan, "Yes!" If it involves singing Afghan music, "Yes." Or writing or working on poetry, that's the path I want to try to get things out into the world.

Update: August 20, 2016

Ethnomusicology entered my life in 1972, with the beginning of my relationship with my husband-to-be, John Baily. It was not long before I became immersed in music research in Afghanistan, in the city of Herat. Then, in Belfast, I entered the heady intellectual atmosphere of John Blacking's Department of Social Anthropology at the Queen's University, which offered me an extraordinarily privileged access to music and dance cultures of many areas of the world. Hearing about other people's fieldwork encounters and friendships was exciting and inspiring.

Since that period (in the 1970s) my intellectual and creative path has been somewhat idiosyncratic. I have not pursued a career in ethnomusicology—but I have sought to make a contribution. My narrative ethnography *Three Women of Herat* (1988) was many years in the making, based on detailed fieldwork but seeking to go beyond the confines of conventional ethnomusicology. I aimed to convey how women in Herat lived and expressed themselves—not only through music but in every conceivable way. I enjoy interdisciplinary approaches, as in more recent publications combining photographic images with Persian-language folk quatrains, such as *I Cried on the Mountain Top* [Doubleday 2010]. I will soon be finalizing my latest publication, on lullaby singing in Afghanistan (and beyond) for a forthcoming volume, *Music and Spirituality in Central Asia* (Brill, edited by Giovanni De Zorzi and Alexandre Papas). This combines my interests in spirituality (in this case, Sufism) with women's expressive culture. Cultural meanings associated with musical instruments are also an enduring fascination, and I am slowly and enjoyably preparing a multifaceted publication around that topic, in part drawing on material collected by ethnomusicologists—but seeking to address a wider public.

LIBRARIES

Virginia (Ginny) Danielson (September 22, 2010)

PhD, University of Illinois (Ethnomusicology)
Richard F. French Librarian
Loeb Music Library, Harvard University

Graduate Studies

GD: [After four years of schoolteaching] I had become very interested in what constituted the music of people's everyday lives—whether it was popular music, Jewish music, or whatever was beyond the classical existence. So I thought, "Well, let's look at musicology." I wrote to a number of places that had programs in musicology and said I was interested in Jewish music. I was consistently referred to the University of Illinois, where Alex Ringer taught. That's how I ended up there, in 1975, if I remember correctly. I didn't know about ethnomusicology, but it was an academic moment when one was encouraged to look at contexts outside the United States. In those days, you had to go somewhere exotic, learn about it, and then come back and teach. And there were fellowships to do that.

MS: Do you remember the first time you heard the word "ethnomusicology" or learned about it as a discipline? What did you think it meant at the time?

GD: One of my undergraduate colleagues was already at the University of Illinois, and I went down to visit, to see what the place was like. I'm sure he talked to me about ethnomusicology. I think my understanding was that it was the study of folk and non-Western music. That understanding was pretty common for the time.

MS: Do you remember any of the early readings that made a big impression on you?

GD: I read a lot in German—those were the days when *everyone* at grad school was required to pass a German test. There were some wonderful scholars in Europe like [Erich von] Hornbostel and Robert Lachmann. Hornbostel's article "Melodie und Skala" [1913], which basically theorized melody, and the work Lachmann did with Jewish communities and communities of World War I prisoners made big impressions. They had that wonderful German clarity of thought. The whole teaching of musicology and ethnomusicology at the University of Illinois worked with the grand old men and women of the field—scholars like Frances Densmore and Franz Boas. The way in which introductory classes were taught was often chronological, from Guido Adler forward. So, one had more than a grasp of contemporary issues because the teaching and reading had to do with one's predecessors. In terms of thinking about my own scholarship, Alan Merriam's work was fundamental.

MS: Who were your ethnomusicological role models at that point?

GD: First, Steve Blum. He has been a mentor to me all along. One of his remarkable traits—which I don't think anyone will ever surpass—is his omnivorous grasp of music. He could move from talking about how Mozart used the key of D major to *bakhshī* in Iran in a millisecond. And his interest in both subjects was genuine. To him, it was all people making music. I don't know that I intended to learn this, but I certainly did learn from him, attention to detail of the musical performance, not just the tonal or rhythmic characteristics, but the overall timbre and construction of a musical performance.

MS: Was he on the faculty at Illinois when you were a student?

GD: Yes, for my first three or four years, then he went to York University in Canada. When I told him I was interested in the Middle East, he was the one who said, "Well, if you're serious, you'd better learn a language because you'll need it and they're all hard." So I picked Arabic, rationalizing that most people in the Middle East spoke Arabic. It *was* really hard. I started Arabic in my mid-twenties, which isn't really advisable.

Another role model was Charlotte Frisbie. She was around off and on, because she worked nearby in Carbondale, Illinois, and was friends with Bruno Nettl. Also fairly early on, I met Kristina Nelson and Salwa El-Shawan. I remember Bonnie Wade, too, but I think I was older at the time. Bonnie can walk into any room, however hostile, with a smile on her face. And I thought, "That's the way to do it." I knew some of the environments she faced were challenging, so I thought, "OK, duly noted. That's how to do things."

MS: Can you reflect on the process of transformation from somebody who entered the program cold and then developed an interest in Arabic and in the Middle East—the process that turned you from a graduate student into an ethnomusicologist embarking on fieldwork? That must have been a big step for you, coming from suburban Milwaukee?

GD: My father was a good model for me. He wasn't fearless, certainly, but it looked like he was. He was a great one for new experiences—going somewhere new, trying something new, doing something different. And, of course, Illinois was a large program; there was a huge cohort about to undertake fieldwork or who had done fieldwork, so I don't think anybody was particularly fearful about it. Preparing for fieldwork was something we talked about a lot. I think the faculty wondered whether I could do this, because they weren't accustomed to admitting schoolteachers. The academic world can be quite biased against schoolteachers. Those who teach in universities often think that people who teach in lower levels are somehow intellectually inferior. But my experience was that teaching was teaching, no matter where you did it. The task remained just about the same. My first trip to Cairo was on a language program.

MS: Why did you decide to focus on Egypt in particular? Was it because of that language program?

GD: Well, it might have been. I had done—in the way one did back then—a "state of research" paper on music in the Middle East. That tends to focus one's attention on Egypt because there's quite a bit of work done there. Bruno probably encouraged it because Jihad Racy was just finishing up his dissertation and had worked in a very lively music scene there [Racy 1977]. I foolishly thought I would have trouble as a female in the Middle East. Of course, that proved to be ridiculous. I settled on Umm Kulthum because I had a very naïve question of how someone could become *so* famous, and so [relatively unknown] in the West at the same time. I was, of course, proceeding from the assumption that any performer wanted to go global. I thought, "She's a female singer, so I'll spend a lot of time with women"—another ridiculous assumption, because, of course, her entire cohort was male. But one lives and learns. So when I went to Cairo on the language fellowship, I was already interested in her and basically did the preliminary work that one would have to do to do work on her. [See Danielson 1997 for one product of this research.] And her base was Cairo.

So, it was an amalgamation of things. I don't remember, for example, being as interested in Lebanon as I am now. A lot of us still labor under the assumption that most of the music of the region comes from the eastern Mediterranean crescent: Lebanon, Syria, Palestine, and Egypt. Of course, that's not true at all. It's just that the exposure of most North Americans is to that particular repertory. There were a lot of things I didn't know. And it was probably just as well, because it would have been very hard to even get permission to go to Iraq, Syria, or some of the places that one might now consider as good places. And I knew that the dialects in North Africa were very different from the one I'd been studying, so that seemed impractical.

Over the subsequent years, as it happened, I spent quite a lot of time in Egypt—in a provincial town in Upper Egypt for a couple of years, in Alexandria, and, of course, in Cairo. These experiences in Egypt, and in the Middle East and the Arab world more generally, became such an important part of the professional I became. First, ethnography remains the best training and experience ever for practically any job that involves human beings. My language skills, both from grad school and from practical experience in the Middle East, became critical to the jobs I was later able to get. And my own research experience led to the opportunities I've had in research universities, which depend, more than anything else, on a deep understanding, one way or another, of the research world. This connection to the Middle East led to a postdoc and to all sorts of opportunities not just in university libraries but across university departments and institutes as well.

MS: Reflecting a little more on the graduate school experience and where that took you, do you think of yourself as part of any kind of lineage?

GD: Yes, since you ask! One of the characteristics of the University of Illinois was a very broad-based training in music history and ethnomusicology. Let's use a real example: Vicki Levine was doing her work on Native American music and, simultaneously, one of her last classes was a seminar on nineteenth-century piano concerto cadenzas with Nicholas Temperley. We all did that. The faculty at the time—Herb Kellman, Bruno Nettl, Nicholas Temperley, Alex Ringer, Steve Blum—created a program that compelled all of us to look at a wide variety of music. When I see younger people coming out of programs now and all they've had is one or the other, or maybe a course here, or a dabble there, I think that the learning curve in their professional life is going to be very high. I'm particularly concerned about programs where the Ethnomusicology and Historical Musicology Departments are actually separate from each other. That's a lost opportunity to me. I feel very affected by that aspect of my lineage, even though at this point, I would no more publish or teach a topic in historical musicology than I would fly! But somehow or other, the awareness is there. I have been very grateful for that.

Building a Career

MS: How did you make the transition into library work?

GD: One of the things I talked to Bruno about early on is that I wasn't necessarily aimed for the professoriat. I have applied for jobs in teaching, but only when I had to have a job the next year. I enjoy teaching, but for me to make a living as a teacher implies a redundancy that I can't live with. I mean, if it's September, I have to be doing syllabi; if it's December, I have to grade papers—every year, same schedule. While I have obligations to the teaching enterprise during the semester, whether I'm teaching or not, I can be more creative with my schedule, and this suits me better. Part of it was just plain practical because it was becoming more difficult to get university jobs, and I wasn't sure I wanted to junket around doing a year here and a year there. *That* was not worth it to me in order to get a teaching job. Bruno suggested publishing, and of course he has good contacts in that area, so I looked into it, but there wasn't anything persuasive.

What I actually had was some experience of working in libraries, which I got as a grad student. We all picked up work here and there while we were grad students. So when my husband and I came back from the Middle East one time, we landed in Boston and I hadn't finished my dissertation. It was getting embarrassing. So I thought, "All I need is a job to provide a little income and I will sit and get this done." Somebody said, "Go to Harvard because they always have grant projects going." I did and got hired very quickly in what was really a scut job, but it did what I needed it to do, and I got promoted. In the succession of promotions, the succession of opportunities became increasingly interesting. So I stayed. Aside from a few leaves, I've been at Harvard for all these many years. It defies a career path—one can't invent these successions. My tendency has always been to take the next good opportunity that comes along. When people ask, I often say, "Mine was an apprenticeship—I never did get a library degree!"

MS: So where was your first real library job?

GD: In the rare book room of the Harvard Music Library! Until I arrived, the position had always been held by an eighteenth-century scholar. I was the first ethnomusicologist brought in because the department had finally made a senior appointment in ethnomusicology and needed somebody who could deal with relevant resources on the library side. It was a funny experience because at one point, my assistant looked at my desk and said, "Do you know you've got Chinese music on top of that C. P. E. Bach score?" It was exactly the environment I was trying to create!

Now I'm the director of the Harvard Music Library. It's an endowed position: the Richard F. French Librarianship in the Eda Kuhn Loeb Library. My current occupation is highly administrative. The library has a staff of twenty-two, so just keeping everybody going is more or less a full-time job. I do a fair amount of high-end selection for the library on the rare book market and also a lot in the recordings market in ethnomusicology. I also do a lot of work with audio archiving, which I started learning about at the University of Illinois. Occasionally, I teach Middle Eastern music in the Music Department at Harvard, and lately, I've done a lot of student advising. I've had a couple of master's advisees and senior thesis advisees in the last couple of years. Of course, enrollments in Arabic have gone up, and as kids become more interested in Arabic culture, it spins off to people like me. I teach by invitation of the Music Department. That's worked out extremely well, as I'm not beholden to them to do anything in particular, and they're not beholden to me. It's been a warm and gentle relationship in that regard. I also work with the Middle East Center and the Islamic Studies Program on an as-needed basis, and occasionally I do some outreach for them. There's an "Islam through the Arts" class that's very big at Harvard right now, and I teach in that. The downside of administrative work is that it is twelve months a year. It's very hard to get a leave, especially if you have any grant-funded projects going, because they have deadlines. It's hard to find time to do your own work. In fact, when I took my first permanent library job, I said, "I want two things: research leave and a flexible schedule." The person who hired me said "fine" to both, I think, laughing to himself because he knew that it would be impossible to get either one!

Update: August 13, 2016

By 2011, I had been in my position for twelve years, and it was time to move on. Leaving a good situation is never easy, and I still miss my old colleagues. Having held a complex position at Harvard that involved significant financial responsibilities, fundraising, grant administration, staff development, collections, multimedia preservation technologies, and other library technical services—as well as instruction—I was looking for another interesting position in library or archival leadership. My husband and I (whom I met in Cairo) had been looking for ways to return to the Middle East, and when the position of director of a new library at NYU in Abu Dhabi became available, it provided the right opportunity, especially as NYU hired both of us.

Helping to build a library in the Middle East, in a place with the resources to do a good job of it, seems to me a way to repay the people in this region from whom I have learned (and continue to learn) so very much. I consider myself a steward of their resources. This position has stretched my abilities while allowing me a place in the fold of an excellent music and ethnomusicology program and a wonderful Middle East studies program. I have reoriented myself intellectually, so to speak, as the historic concerns of my new home tend more toward the Indian Ocean than the Mediterranean. I struggle with a new dialect and different customs and learn once again to appreciate help.

Museums

Adrienne Kaeppler (October 28, 2007)

PhD, University of Hawai'i (Anthropology)
Pacific Curator, Smithsonian Institution

Graduate Studies

AK: After I finished my BA I continued into the MA program at the University of Hawai'i.

TS: Why did you make that switch to anthropology?

AK: I was always interested in dance, music, and the visual arts and in understanding other cultures. I took classes in anthropology, including one that was called at that time "Primitive Art." There were also many classes in dance in the Music Department—Barbara Smith was there by that time. I took Korean dance, Filipino dance and music, and Japanese music. I was one of the first people to take *gagaku* from Rev. Shamoto when he started to teach at UH. I was also interested in *shamisen*, so Barbara Smith sent me to Bando Mikayoshi and I entered the Bando School for *nagauta* [voice and shamisen lute-based music important in kabuki theater]. This was an outside group, not part of UH. I took shamisen for some time and then our teacher, Bando

Mikayoshi, whose [non-professional] name was Yoshiko Hara, wanted us to do not just one thing but two. You either had to take shamisen and singing, or singing and dancing, or shamisen and dancing, so I started taking Japanese dance, *Nihon buyo*. I did that for quite some time and kept taking whatever kind of music and dance ensembles they offered in the Music Department. Any movement traditions that were going, I tried to learn them.

I finished my master's degree in anthropology, with a thesis on Melanesian masks, and started my PhD. I was interested in doing Pacific rather than Asian anthropology and decided to go to Tonga to do my research. I really wanted to go to New Guinea, but it was right after Michael Rockefeller had been killed in New Guinea, so it didn't seem like a good place to go. Instead, I decided to go to the least-known Polynesian place: Tonga. I made the right choice, because hardly anyone had done research in Tonga. My project was "The Aesthetics of Tonga," because I'm one of these broad people. When I got to Tonga and started doing my research, I found that the most widespread art was Tongan dance. Because I already had a lot of background in dance, I didn't have to think, "Oh, I don't really know anything about dance." Many ethnomusicologists disregard movement traditions, but I already knew about dancing and how to move so I just joined in and started learning Tongan dance. In my first three months I learned a number of dance traditions that were still alive in Tonga. I lived with a Tongan family and started learning Tongan language. I went back to UH for the final year of what I had to do before my year of fieldwork and then returned to Tonga.

I planned to focus on Tongan music and dance. I got there in July or August 1965 and Queen Sālote died in December, which meant that all music and dance was stopped for a year. I'm a social anthropologist—it really doesn't matter *what* you study!—so I studied Tongan funeral ceremonies, social organizations, and social structure. All of my earliest articles are on social rank and Tongan funerals, but because I was still working on the dance part, it was actually very interesting. People couldn't dance, but they could talk about it. I ended up breaking down the structure of Tongan dance using linguistic analogies. I'd ask, "Is this movement the same as *this* movement?" And if they answered, "Now, do that again? Hmm . . . OK. Yes." It's like doing phonetics and phonemics in linguistics, "Is this the same as *this*?" And they answered, "Ah, noooo." "But is *this* the same as *this*?" "Yes." That is, I did the sort of analysis with movement that linguists would do with language. My dissertation ended up being on the "Structure of Tongan Dance" [1967]. It was a combination of knowing how to move and knowing how to ask linguistic questions that led to my PhD.

MS: Were you in anthropology because there was no PhD in ethnomusicology at Hawaiʻi at the time?

AK: I wouldn't have gone into ethnomusicology, because I was trying to understand the whole broad spectrum of the culture by looking at music, dance, and visual arts. I am still, I think, more a visual arts person than I am in either music or dance, although you probably know me from music and dance. But visual arts and dance go together; dance is a visual art.

TS: Do you remember the first time you heard the word "ethnomusicology"?

AK: I probably heard it when I was in the original group of people that Barbara had in her first ethnomusicology seminar, which was taught by David McAllester. I don't think I ever heard the word before Barbara.

MS: Were you already at a point where you realized that ethnomusicology was too limited a discipline for you?

AK: Yes, I was interested in music and dance, but never as a profession. Although I did opera, piano, and violin, these were just things I liked to do. I liked to tap dance, I liked to do baton twirling. My parents sent me to school to learn this and learn that if I wanted to. But it was never, "You have to practice your piano tonight"; there was never any of that!

Building a Career

AK: I finished my PhD on "The Structure of Tongan Dance" in 1967. I was the first PhD in anthropology at UH. I had been interested in museums since I was a young child, so I went to work in the Anthropology Department at the Bishop Museum. I worked on exhibitions and did research on various things such as objects from Cook's voyages, which took me all over the world to look at collections in other museums. I did a really big exhibition on Cook's Voyages at the Bishop Museum in 1978. I'm still sort of an authority on Cook's voyages.

One of my dear friends at the Bishop Museum, Pat Bacon, is Kawena Pukui's *hānai*[2] daughter. Pat said, "You know, you shouldn't just be working on Tongan dance material; you should be working on Hawaiian dance too. Come over to my house on Wednesday and Kawena and I will start to teach you something about Hawaiian dance." I said, "OK," although I didn't really know much about Kawena Pukui, who it turned out was *the* major person in the Hawaiian tradition. I went to Pat Bacon's house every Wednesday night for a long time and they taught me my first hula material. Then I did research with other people and became really interested in *Hula Pahu*, the oldest form done with a membranophone. I worked with three very important people who represented the three big schools of *Hula Pahu*, and wrote my book called *Hula Pahu* [1993].

TS: When did you leave the Bishop Museum for the Smithsonian?

AK: Sometime around 1980, the Smithsonian advertised for a curator for the Pacific. Somebody sent me a letter saying, "We'd really like you to apply for this job." I said, "Why not?" I applied and got the job. Although I moved from the Bishop Museum to the Smithsonian in 1980, I've gone back to Hawai'i every year at least once or twice. A lot of people still think I live in Hawai'i or do Hawaiian things! Every year I go to the Merrie Monarch Festival, the big hula competition. That's how I keep my hand in the Hawaiian and hula spheres: looking at how hula is portrayed on stage, how it's represented by Hawaiians themselves, and how it's changed from an observer's point of view. Hula continues to engage me.

MS: Could you tell us a little about what you do at the Smithsonian?

AK: I'm the curator of Oceanic Ethnology. Curators at the Smithsonian are primarily research people. We can do research on anything we want that is associated with our region—because we're region specific—although we can go outside our region if we want to. Since my focus is supposed to be within the Pacific, I've continued to do research on social structure, funerals, music, dance, performance, and visual arts. I just finished writing a book on the arts of Polynesia/Micronesia for the Oxford University Press series [Kaeppler 2008]. I continue to work on those subjects, but being a curator at the Smithsonian also involves speaking for your collection. Anything that comes in, we have to approve, or we can look for things to become part of a collection. We also give approval to things that are lent out and to all the exhibits in our field that are put on in the Smithsonian.

MS: So it's like having an academic position without having to teach?

AK: Actually it *is* an academic position. It's exactly the same as in a university and we're judged in the same way. We have annual performance evaluations, and every five or seven years—depending on where you are in the hierarchy—we have reviews, just like your tenure and promotion reviews, when we are evaluated for the next level. We're all academics; we just don't teach. But at various times I have taught classes at the University of Maryland and at other places—the Music and Anthropology Departments at the University of Hawai'i, at Johns Hopkins, UCLA, and Queen's University, Belfast (when John Blacking was there).

MS: So you can get a teaching fix every time you want one, without having a long-term commitment to a university?

AK: Right! And because we don't have to teach, I don't have to teach the same classes every time. Most people have a series of classes that they teach. That would bore me to death! At the University of Hawai'i, I taught Introduction to Anthropology, Cultural Anthropology, Pacific Culture, Hawaiian Culture. And in the Music Department, I taught Music of the Pacific and a class on Polynesian Dance. But every time I taught, I did a different class. At the University of Maryland, I've taught the Anthropology of Dance in the Music Department three or four times when one of the Music Department professors was going on sabbatical.

TS: How do you get release time to go and teach courses in other places?

AK: I use my annual leave to do it.

Update: August 12, 2016

Since our 2007 conversation, I continue along the same tracks. That is, I continue as curator of Oceanic Ethnology at the Smithsonian Institution, as well as continuing research, giving papers at conferences, and publishing. I have completed my second term as president of ICTM [International Council for Traditional Music] and am happy with my efforts to continue to expand the international flavor of the society by adding board members from additional parts of the world and holding meetings in such places as South Africa and Kazakhstan.

In addition to my research on music and dance, which was primarily in Tonga and Hawai'i, I have added research in Rapa Nui (Easter Island), including my recent publication of a case study of Rapa Nui performances at the Festivals of Pacific Art (as well as other studies, including Rapa Nui tattoos) [Van Tilburg et al. 2008]. Also, I continue to attend the Merrie Monarch Festival in Hawai'i each year, and the Festivals of Pacific Art every four years. At the last festival in Guam in May 2016, I gave two papers, one of which was on Tongan Brass Bands.

I also continue my interest in the UNESCO program on Intangible Cultural Heritage, having worked with the Tongans on "The Tongan Lakalaka: Sung Speeches with Choreographed Movements," which was declared a Masterpiece of the Oral and Intangible Heritage of Humanity in 2003, and published a book on the subject in 2012.

Jennifer Post (August 12, 2011)

PhD, University of Minnesota (Ethnomusicology)
Asia/Pacific Curator, Musical Instrument Museum

Graduate Studies

JP: While I was in Maharastra [in 1971] as an undergraduate, I lived with a musician family and spent a lot of time with musicologist Vamanrao Deshpande and some of the great singers and musicians, such as Mogubai Kurdikar. It was a phenomenal experience: I was a twenty-something imagining I could write sensibly about the theoretical structure of North Indian Music. Through the program I had an opportunity to meet Ram Dayal Munda, who worked at the University of Minnesota, and decided I wanted to work with Mundari music. So I went to Minnesota to continue composition with Dominick Argento and to study ethnomusicology with Alan Kagan and Maharashtrian language, history and music with Ram Dayal Munda. As I became more involved with Mundari music, it became clear that it would be problematic for me to go in that direction for a dissertation. In the US, Munda was my only source for musical information and language study, and it became increasingly clear that I would have trouble getting a visa to do long-term fieldwork in the then-troubled tribal areas of Bihar. Ultimately, my committee, made up of music and South Asian languages faculty at the university, turned down my proposal. My classmate Carol Babiracki, being a little younger, was luckier. She left Minnesota for Illinois and was later able to go to Munda's village to do fieldwork.

MS: What did you do at that point?

JP: Most of my master's work was focused on Hindustani music, South Asian languages, and South Asian studies. I started working with Indian miniature painting and exploring their inner connections to music. I had already studied Persian music with Hormoz Farhat at a Harvard summer program and was fascinated by these connections. My master's focused on how women were presented visually in relation to the artistic tradition and to instrumental performance. This was well before Bonnie Wade's study *Imaging Sound: An Ethnomusicological Study of Music, Art, and Culture in Mughal India* [1999].

I finished my master's in '74 and then stepped away. I spent about two-thirds of a year working at Cornell, taking courses, and playing in Marty Hatch's gamelan. I took some Indonesian language and played with the idea of going to Java. In early '75 I went back to continue my work at Minnesota. I stayed there for two more years, conducting fieldwork in 1976 and '77. I didn't actually finish my dissertation until 1982, because I had two children, in '76 and '78, which slowed me down a bit.

The dissertation was on "Marathi- and Konkani-Speaking Women in Hindustani Music" [Post 1982]. Initially, I worked with Mogubai Kurdikar, her daughter Kishori Amonkar, some other relatively young musicians. As I got deeper into the subject, I was confronted with how problematic my research was and decided to adjust my topic to look more historically at the women's musical practices. I sensed Kishori felt she was being used to expose a history that her community was not prepared to share.

TS: You adjusted your topic so that it was less socially controversial and more historical?

JP: Yes, it became a real ethical dilemma in terms of my relationships to the people because they were expressing such concern about what I might write. They could say whatever they wanted, and everybody knew their history, but they said, "We don't want to see this in writing." It really gave me pause. When you're in the midst of something like that and your life is wild and crazy anyway, it's not always the perfect time to reflect on what you're doing. If I had the opportunity to do it again and could have stepped away for a couple of months, I might have done something different. But I hit a bad moment. It took another generation before Amie Maciszewski and others were able to get some of the women to tell their stories. Amie has written about Girija Devi, but as I said, it took a generation.

TS: Were there any readings that were particularly influential as you were getting into the field?

JP: Definitely! Nettl's *Eight Urban Musical Cultures* [1978] was really important to me, as was Dan Neuman's book *The Life of Music in North India* [1980]. When Mantle Hood's *The Ethnomusicologist* [1971] came out, I was fascinated by his work on organology and by the systems he put forth. I also admired Elizabeth May's book *Musics of Many Cultures* [1980].

Building a Career

JP: I moved to Middlebury, Vermont, in 1979. I was married at the time, and my husband made Irish bagpipes. We had two very young children and wanted to live in a small town. I got involved at Middlebury College and ended up teaching there before I finished my dissertation, beginning around 1981.

MS: Were you employed as an adjunct?

JP: Yes, but I was also working with the Helen Hartness Flanders Ballad Collection. Helen Flanders was a wealthy Vermonter who got involved with collecting in the 1930s, mentored by the New England ballad collector Phillips Barry. She put together a phenomenal collection of hundreds of old ballads and a lot of fiddle tunes and dance tunes. The archive had been stuffed in a closet in the library until I found it. It had nothing to do with anything I'd ever worked with before, but it became a fascination and also a source of income. I was connected to the library and had a regular income. I was on the staff and also had opportunities to teach.

TS: Were there any recordings in the collection?

JP: Yes, cylinders and disks. Some had been transferred to tape at the Library of Congress, but I had to transfer others. I worked on cataloguing, classifying, and making them accessible, and then started traveling to the north country to interview relatives of the performers. I published a book on this: *Music in Rural New England Family and Community Life, 1870–1940* [2004b]. I worked with lumbering families in Maine, New Hampshire, and Vermont, and focused especially on a little town, Pittsburg, New Hampshire (population 780), right at the Canadian border. It was a fascinating project, all about the old songs and tunes, the collectors (Helen Hartness Flanders, Philips Barry, and others), and what the collectors of the '30s, '40s, and '50s missed.

Working at the library made sense, given my complicated personal situation: by then I was a single parent and one of my children had serious difficulties. At one point there was an opportunity for me to do a leave replacement at Dartmouth, which might have started me on an academic journey toward a tenure-track job, but it became clear I couldn't do it the way my personal life was going. So I said, "OK, I'll do this library thing for a while." I didn't have a library degree, so I spent 1986 commuting to Boston to get my MS in library science from Simmons College.

MS: Is that when you started doing the SEM bibliography?

JP: Oh yes, that started in the late '80s. I knew Joe Hickerson because I was working with traditional American music at the time. He must have asked, "Do you want to do this?" I was interested in the challenge, so I said yes.

MS: Had you been a member of the Society for Ethnomusicology before that?

JP: I joined SEM in 1977. I would have joined earlier but didn't have any money. I was so poor that a friend from grad school gave me my first membership. I gave my first SEM paper in the early '80s. I probably read one or two papers on my dissertation material but then started reading papers on the New England material as well.

TS: You were working in the library and teaching regularly at Middlebury, is that right?

JP: Yes, although there was a period during the early to mid-'90s when I didn't do any teaching in the Music Department. The Music Department had a long history of problems. I didn't want to get into it at the time—I had already observed it for twenty years and seen other people leave in frustration or lose their jobs. No faculty who dealt with music in social contexts had made it through! Then, in 1997, they advertised a tenure-track position. I didn't apply and the search was unsuccessful. The second time around, I was invited to apply but instead negotiated a position as half-time regular music faculty and half-time working with the archives. The following year, they invited me to apply for a full-time position again, so I did. When I was offered the position in '99, I remember taking long walks and asking myself, "Do I want to take this risk?"

TS: You mean you could have stayed at the library?

JP: Yes, but I loved teaching. I felt I was good at it and really connected with the students, despite the fact that I'm not the most outgoing person in the world. I don't regret those years, not for a second. I was bored out of my mind in the library by then, but I never, ever got bored teaching.

MS: Did you go through the whole six-year tenure cycle?

JP: Yes, I had two-year, four-year, and then tenure reviews. There were no issues in my two-year or four-year reviews. I published three books as I was leading up to my tenure review (*Music in Rural New England Family and Community Life, 1870–1940* [2004b], *Ethnomusicology: A Research and Information Guide* [2004a], and *Ethnomusicology: A Contemporary Reader* [2006]) and had just gotten a second Mellon grant. They had no questions for me during the process. And yet they denied me tenure in 2006.

Do you know what happens when the rug is pulled out like that? I didn't see it coming at all. I was so well covered; there was no chance that was going to happen. Then panic set in—who's going to hire somebody in their mid-fifties when there are so many new graduates? I took the terminal year and left Middlebury in 2007. I found a library job at Mansfield State College in Northern Pennsylvania, where I was nonteaching faculty.

TS: If there was no teaching and it was another library job, why did you leave Middlebury?

JP: Oh, God, I was so ashamed. What happens when someone doesn't get tenure? People don't want to talk to you; it's like you're sick. You lose everything. You lose your friends, because they don't know what to say. People I knew in the Anthropology Department didn't know what to say either, because nobody knew why it happened. They were ashamed, too. I had to get out.

I went to Mansfield State College in the fall of 2007, but almost immediately I heard about the job at the Musical Instrument Museum. People from the museum were at the 2007 SEM meeting in Columbus. I met them there, applied for the job, and was offered it in the early spring. I left Mansfield in the middle of the year and started at MIM in the spring of 2008.

MS: What's your job like at MIM?

JP: It's very different from academia; it's a high-pressure job. The standards, values, lifestyle, and goals are all corporate. It's a nonprofit, but one that needs to appeal to a certain kind of audience that is connected to money, to famous people, and that kind of thing. It's very strange for me, having been in the academic world as long as I have and done as much traveling as I have. An awful lot of the work I've done is with music in everyday life, with very small traditions, and with people who are not necessarily well known or famous. In the Musical Instrument Museum it's the total opposite. My job is to populate, document, produce (or find) video, and be involved in the designing of exhibits for all of Asia, North Africa and the Middle East, and the Pacific. Before the opening, I was responsible for over ninety exhibits. It's a fascinating challenge from a research point of view. I've given a couple of papers at conferences, but I'm not publishing because there isn't time to finish anything off, though I have found ways to gather data by being engaged in mini field projects as I document musical practices. I've also been working with eco-musicology.

TS: Eco-musicology?

JP: Yes, it happened naturally. As a researcher, I worked with Mongolian Kazakh herders who sang phrases in their songs such as, "Why is the snow going away, why are my fields no longer green." I started looking at musical instruments and recognizing what was happening to the woods and other materials. Traveling for the MIM I'm also able to gather data, especially in reference to environmental degradation and musical instrument construction.

TS: Have you worked on Mongolian language?

JP: I'm actually working with Kazakh people in Mongolia, so I work with Kazakh language. I've been learning in the field, not by taking classes. I studied Hindi and Marathi, but this has been the biggest challenge and most humbling linguistic experience for me. I've spent a lot of time in China and Xinjiang with the Uyghurs and in Mongolia and Kazakhstan. There are many languages and language families to keep track of during my travels.

TS: How did you get to Kazakhstan?

JP: In 2004 I had a Mellon Grant to travel with a group of faculty along the Silk Road. I went to Tashkent, Kyrgyzstan, and China with the group and then—to my amazement—they all went home. I carried on into Mongolia (with Middlebury College support), went on a road trip with colleague and Mongolian music scholar Peter Marsh, and ended up in the Altai mountains in Bayan Ölgii province, where the population is over 80 percent Kazakh. That's the music I fell in love with and became fascinated by. The Kazakhs in Mongolia have had opportunities that people in the former Soviet Republics have not had to maintain certain aspects of their musics and other cultural expressions. I felt I couldn't leave it, so I went back every year, and got another Mellon, a two-year grant, to continue that work.

Update: July 16, 2016

I was interviewed for this project during a three-and-a-half-year period I spent as a founding curator for the Musical Instrument Museum (2008–2011). In that position, I had a chance to interact with many people inside and outside of academia who contributed in valuable ways to the collections at the museum. The experience also provided opportunities for me to engage in small fieldwork projects in Asia and the Pacific, and to explore new ways to communicate as an educator. I left the museum in 2011 and taught ethnomusicology for a year at the New Zealand School of Music at Victoria University in Wellington and spent the following year at University of Western Australia in Perth working with the John Blacking Papers as archivist and researcher in the School of Music's Callaway Archives. In early 2014 I returned to the United States and began to teach ethnomusicology at the University of Arizona, where I continue to teach today. I currently hold positions as honorary senior research fellow at the University of Western Australia, and as senior lecturer at the University of Arizona.

I continue to work with Kazakh mobile pastoralists in Mongolia and have regularly spent summers in the field since 2010. This work is contributing to several writing projects; my primary focus at this time is on ecology and music. I am especially interested in documenting issues related to climate change and other causes of environmental degradation and their impact on music and sound production in Mongolia and regions of Central and East Asia. This work looks at how songs and narrative melodies are used to express mobile pastoralists' ecological knowledge and also how climate change is impacting musical instrument production throughout the region.

Public Sector

W. F. Umi Hsu (October 6, 2017)

PhD, University of Virginia (Critical and Comparative Studies)
Department of Cultural Affairs, City of Los Angeles

Graduate Studies

UH: I didn't know you could actually go on and pursue graduate work in ethnomusicology until I got to graduate school. In 2002 I went to the University of Virginia to pursue a master's in East Asian studies. I started taking classes in the Music Department, and that's where I met Michelle Kisliuk, who ended up being my advisor. I took classes with Michelle and just fell in love. I basically never left. I think she was teaching a class called "Performing Antiquities and Modernities." The course was about the re-performance of history, so we got into early music performance practice, historical reenactment, and even into Civil War reenactment and the ideologies around that. At the same time, we also explored some of the 1990s performances of "Pygmy" and Central African music in the style of pop music. The class was basically about performing different temporalities through aesthetic practices of our time and looking at that through the lens of representational and cultural politics. I enrolled in the PhD program in the Music Department in 2004 and spent seven years in the PhD program. I ended up writing a dissertation on the Asian American musical experience, specifically focusing on independent rock music. I did my fieldwork in East Coast cities, like DC, New York, Boston, and Philadelphia, meeting and hanging out with musicians in bars and performance venues.

MS: What did the field of ethnomusicology mean to you by that point, as an advanced graduate student?

UH: I always saw it as a critical exploration of music cultures. There was an attention to the sonic materials of music as well as an interaction with the cultural context of lived experience. Ethnographic methodology was in the forefront of Michelle's work and her pedagogy, so I really took to that and ran with it.

Building a Career

MS: You've obviously worked closely with Michelle. Do you see yourself as part of any broader lineage within the field?

UH: Lineage—that's an interesting word. Are you talking in terms of the transmission of knowledge or institution? Well, I can't stop being an ethnomusicologist: that's who I am and how I relate to the world. Even as a kid in different cultural or musical settings, I was always asking questions I'm still asking. So, in terms of the professional institution of ethnomusicology, I feel a bit of ambivalence. The institutional form is so narrowly defined as the academic path with the trajectory of becoming tenured faculty. That's not what I do, and I'm not sure it would be the right path for me because I'm interested in so many things. I'm interested in being exposed to lots of areas of music and turning what I know into actionable knowledge. Sometimes that means curatorial work, sometimes archival work and policy research, and sometimes it manifests in other ways, like in my own performance practice. For example, I'm still actively performing. I feel like the institutional path is too narrow.

MS: This segues beautifully into my next question. How did your career develop? How did you take that next step and what was it?

UH: While I was in graduate school, I became interested in digital humanities. I was a part of a nascent digital humanities incubator, the Scholar's Lab at the University of Virginia. This sort of graduate professional development program as an intervention of humanities advanced-degree program then became a national model. In the Scholar's Lab I saw that there were different ways I could express scholarship and deploy it in more actionable and engagement formats, working outside the traditional university setting. That was the link for me.

Within the context of the Graduate Fellowship in Digital Humanities, I designed a project for my dissertation on the social and musical experience of Asian American musicians. I noticed that almost all the musicians I was interviewing had a really active online digital life—at that time it was Myspace—so I came up with a data extraction project. I wrote a computer script to scrape information from the profile pages of the musicians I was studying, as well as from their friends' networks around the world on Myspace. I found not only that digital spaces were critical to their networking as musicians, but also that this networking was central to their identity formation. The social geography they produced exceeded national and regional borders and had an international and transnational context, even when most of the musicians were born in the US and had grown up as Americans. I found that interesting, so I extracted the data and then mapped it. I was able to see that these patterns interacted globally. It was an exercise in simply asking the question, "What is the geography of the social world in which these musicians are playing and forging their communities?" Through this work, I was able to locate the notion of transnationalism within the empirical observations of a networked sociality. This allowed me to ask further questions about the feelings of being in and actively making a digital diaspora and what it meant to have friends in specific locales discovered through this digital project.

I explored this emerging methodology within the context of ethnomusicology. I presented papers at SEM to introduce this way of thinking and research and to nuance the definition of multi-sited ethnography by introducing the digital as a theoretical and methodological consideration. My work was well received, but there was a bit of a barrier: some people felt it required too much technical knowledge. Now though, the technology has advanced to the degree that we don't actually need to have that knowledge in order to do the work. There are programming recipes that you can use without knowing a scripting language. I was really into this work and believe in its implications for making scholarship more relevant, so I ended up taking a postdoc fellowship in digital humanities at Occidental College. I spent two years (2011–13) there teaching classes on digital music cultures and offering project-based courses like digital design and website production. I also got outside the classroom and developed public-oriented work and community-based learning projects. For example, I led a project called "Sounds of Learning," in which we took our field recording techniques and technology outside our classroom and collaborated with a local elementary school. I paired my students up with sixth-graders and taught them how to do field record-ing. The sixth-graders went out and recorded sounds that were meaningful to their learning experience as a way to reflect on their years of elementary school. Finally, we co-produced audio pieces that ranged from storytelling pieces and reflective composi-tions to pop remixes expressive of a shared sensibility.

As I was finishing my postdoc in 2013, the ACLS Public Fellowship Program announced openings for another grant period. There were twenty opportunities with different nonprofits and public agencies, one of which was in the City of Los Angeles Department of Cultural Affairs. I was interested in working in public-sector arts admin-istration, so I applied and got the job. At the time, the agency was interested in having somebody who could help them with digital projects leading to a website redesign and coming up with a social media strategy within the context of municipal government.

I was there for two years and worked on web design and social media projects and then got into the world of data. "Data" is such a buzzword now, in both the government and private tech sectors. There are lots of conversations about "knowledge creation"— data as a raw form of knowledge—but in the business world, there's also the idea of "business intelligence," and "data analytics." So I became the person to figure out how to implement a data agenda, or what I'd like to call a "knowledge architecture" at the agency. I took a seven-month break after my fellowship and came back full time in my current position, as a digital strategist. I picked up all the work that I left off, but with a new focus on data and knowledge creation. That's what I'm doing now.

MS: How does your ethnomusicologist persona navigate this job?

UH: I would say that the focus of my attention on music cultures is now a broader focus on culture, on knowledge transmission, and on Foucauldian ideas about knowledge, power, and governmentality. The core theoretical stuff I was studying is still applicable, but I apply it outside the musical scope. Ethnography as a discipline is still central to my method. For example, I'm helping to design a cultural-asset-mapping project within an area of Los Angeles that was designated as a part of the Promise Zone economic development program by the Obama Administration. The goal is to use arts as a community inquiry and engagement strategy to elevate economic opportunities that are meaningful to the communities. We're working with local nonprofits, including LA Commons and folklorist Amy Kitchener, the executive director of the Alliance for California Traditional Arts. ACTA does folklore and fieldwork, so we're partnering with them to do field research within the vastly multiethnic microcommunities in LA to learn about cultural assets identified by the communities themselves.

MS: So this job gives you the opportunity to do both activist work and digital work?

UH: Absolutely. And I think activism means a certain thing within the public sector. Public sector work is often playing the role of the regulator—"You can't do x, y, or z"—and often that means doing work while considering the public interests and not acting on behalf of private interest, such as pro-commerce policies. But for me, a lot of the community knowledge work I'm doing has a stronger focus in giving voice to the community. It is ethnographic in the sense that we are out in communities to find out how people are experiencing their culture and valuing culture as assets. We ask questions like, "Are there any cultural treasures that have vanished in your neighborhood?" and "What does that look like?" I find the qualitative answers to be even more fascinating—mom-and-pop businesses that disappear because of gentrification, for example. So with this project we are building a website with a research database that will have all of the raw research data as well as a map of the cultural assets, digital storytelling media objects like photos and video recordings.

MS: That sounds amazing! Are you still playing music, by the way?

UH: I am! I've got a band called Bitter Party. We celebrate the melancholy of life, a sensibility from many of the songs originated in East and Southeast Asia. I'm writing a lot of songs for it. These songs belong to a genre that I'm calling "ghost pop" for animating marginalized voices and song materials from my personal stories, memories of my family, and research of Taiwanese music from the 1930s to the 1980s—unleashing and re-embodying the ghosts in the cannon that were previously unheard. I'm taking one lyric, a riff, or a rhythm at a time and pulling it out of its original context and then rebuilding in a whole new song compositionally for a five-piece band. For instance, taking a rhythmic pattern from the Hakka mountain songs that I've been learning (because one side of my family has a Hakka heritage) and integrating with a new-wave drum and bass section for a song about my grandmother living through the world wars from a small Hakka village migrating to cosmopolitan Taipei. So, yes, I'm playing a lot, collaborating with artists who are interested in exploring decolonizing practices, Asian American, and queer gender expressions within the LA arts context. It's been really life giving.

MS: Would you say that you are finding all sorts of other ways in tandem with your job to keep your ethnomusicological research going?

UH: In tandem in the sense that if I can't have a music focus here, I'll keep music going somewhere else, right? If my day job doesn't give me time for the sound-specific focus, then I'll do it elsewhere. Absolutely. I've got another project called *LA Listens* where I'm implementing ethnography and sound-based organizing strategy, working with community organizers in different parts of LA. Right now, we're focusing on the neighborhoods we know better—like East LA—to listen to and record sounds to document neighborhood change. We're also listening to community dissent. These communities are changing economically, gentrification and displacement is happening, so we're trying to find a way to engage sonically through oral history and field recordings. I'm using sound ethnography and practice as a framework to explore community dynamics and instigate positive change. It caught the interest of other groups, including the MIT School of Architecture and Planning, so through a collaboration with MIT we were able to get a design grant with NEA [to develop] a series of sound-based organizing and research strategies. We have produced a collaborative conference for planners, community organizers, sound researchers, and arts practitioners. And we are currently developing a toolkit that will increase the knowledge of sound-based research strategies as a way to make positive community change.

MS: Do you spend much time going out into the community and doing this kind of work on the ground, or are you mostly in your office coordinating people who do the work for you?

UH: I'm in the office more than I'd like, away from working with community groups that are doing the actual community work. I do the design and strategy thinking work from the office—coordinating, planning, managing, and sometimes fundraising. When I develop a project, I have to work with our grant writer to turn these projects into proposals, but honestly, I'd like to spend more time in the field.

MS: It sounds like a very practical or active kind of public-sector job—is that a fair assessment?

UH: Once I freed myself from the idea of having to work with sound as a subject, I turned the music and all the creative or critical frameworks into principals of practice and everything else that I do. So, yes, it is practical in the sense that I'm doing the kinds of things that I want to do within the broader disciplinary scope of engagement that I have. I miss dealing with sound and music, and I don't think I'll ever stop doing that work, even if I have to shift my focus to doing it on the side, as a side hustle or a night job. But there are jobs out there—not necessarily music jobs—that people with an ethnomusicological background can explore. That's something good to be mindful of.

MS: It's great to have somebody like you give insight into these career paths because, as you obviously know, there are so many people coming out of graduate school thinking, "What's the next step? How do I keep a roof over my head?" Anything that opens up conversations about the kinds of jobs we can have with the skills that ethnomusicologists have is incredibly valuable.

UH: Yes, I spent a ton of time trying to figure that out myself. The best moments have been when I feel like I'm still learning, as if I'm actually out in the field. I feel like my day job is my fieldwork. I'm always maintaining that critical curiosity, learning as I go, participating, and observing. That has been a really nourishing part of my experience.

MS: A couple of other people have said much the same thing: that as ethnomusicologists we have skills—especially people skills, because that's central to the work we do—that can be applied in many other domains.

UH: Absolutely. In addition, the interpersonal, the "people skills," include our ways of thinking collectively about people as groups. I think the sociological and anthropological ways of thinking are very applicable in different sectoral work, and we have the sensitivity to social dynamics and cultural meanings and can *listen* to and intuit dynamic patterns as changes occur. I think that's a huge asset.

I'm also currently an adjunct at two universities. I teach a graduate-level class on digital analytics strategy to master of science students in business analytics at the USC Marshall School of Business. I'm teaching the business students critical and design approaches to researching the digital in the current economy. My emphasis has been on research ethics, broadening their horizons so they can think systemically and ecologically about the multiple forces within society, not just through the lens of markets and economy. In addition, I'm an adjunct thesis advisor for the MFA program of Media Design Practices at the ArtCenter College of Design. I see my role there as a scholar-professional who can challenge design students to identify a practical and intellectual site of interrogation where design can influence positive societal change. It's neat to see that what I do resonates with the business-analytics and design-research professional communities. These are not the intellectual communities I thought I would contribute to when I was in grad school. I feel honored to be a part of these professional worlds.

Virginia (Gini) Gorlinski (October 26, 2007)

PhD, University of Wisconsin (Ethnomusicology)
Assistant Editor, Encyclopedia Britannica

Graduate Studies

GG: I didn't spend two consecutive years at the same undergraduate institution, with the same major, but I still got through. I used to tell that to students who were concerned about changing their major. I guess I liked having different perspectives. So I went off to Hawai'i in 1984. I was lucky to get FLAS funding at Hawai'i—that's how I was able to go. I was a normal, non–East-West Center music student with FLAS funding for Indonesian language study. I enrolled in intensive Indonesian language study with Professor Jim Collins. He was a remarkable influence, too, in what I've done. He arrived in Hawai'i the same year I did, so he was new faculty. David Harnish and I were the two students in the accelerated Indonesian class. Jim encouraged me to do the COTIM program. (It was COTI at that time: Consortium for the Teaching of Indonesian. Now it's Consortium for the Teaching of Indonesian and Malay). I went to Malang, East Java, for the first time in 1985 on that program.

This was 1985, but when I was still at Michigan, I worked with Jim Borders, the musicologist. He was my undergrad adviser with a project in the Stearns Collection of Musical Instruments. They had a bunch of gongs from all over the place, gong sets, individual gongs, and I did an independent study with Jim Borders on these gongs. I found out we had a gong set from Brunei, but that we don't know anything about the music of that huge island, Borneo, the biggest island in the South China Sea. That stirred me. I also had a good buddy, an anthropologist who now teaches at University of Georgia, who was getting ready to go to Borneo. And, by chance, Bernard Sellato, a visiting anthropologist, came through and gave a presentation on Borneo. So I was already intrigued with the place.

So in 1985, I went to the COTI language program in Malang and made more connections. It turned out there was a hostel for East Kalimantan (Eastern Indonesian Borneo) students in Malang. They heard about me, and I got a telephone call from someone who said, "We heard that you want to go to East Kalimantan." And I said, "Yes, I do." And they said, "Well you can't go there unless you come here first." Their hostel was right down the street, so I went, and one of the young men there was the son of a family that ran a hotel in Samarinda, which later became one of my adopted families. Basically, that community of students set me up. I also wrote to some officials, letting them know that I was coming and what I would like to do. And I went to visit during a nine-day COTI break. They arranged a guide for me to go upriver to visit a village and talk to people. Of course, I was late getting back to the language program and got chewed out. I finished the program, went back to Hawai'i, wrote up a Fulbright application—and got it!

The next year I went back to that same village and stayed there for about four months, until I had to leave because the Indonesian government was having a general election and prohibited research in rural areas during the campaign. I wrote to my friend, the anthropologist from Michigan who was now in Sarawak, Malaysia, and said, "What am I going to do?" Well, to make a long story a little bit shorter, for six months during the election campaign I went across the border to Sarawak. I had been working with Kenyah in the village in East Kalimantan. The museum people installed me in a Kayan village to study *sapé'* (a plucked lute). I was also studying Kenyah music, a shared tradition between Kayan and Kenyah. I practiced sapé' like a fiend with this Kayan plucked-lute community. What was interesting about them was that they said, "We don't want to speak Malay with you. You speak Kayan." And that's when I realized what every nonnative speaker of English who comes to this country knows: when you're thrown into a context where you have no recourse to other languages but the one that is used there, you learn fast. After the election, I went back to (Indonesian) East Kalimantan and finished up there for another eight months or so. Long Segar was the name of the community in Kalimantan where I worked for the most part and Uma Apan was the Kayan community in Sarawak where I stayed. It's now vacant, if not gone, as everybody moved out because of the Bakun Hydro-Electric Dam. So I went back to Hawai'i and wrote. I was done with my course work, so I got a job. At first I got temp jobs; some were good and some were crummy. Finally, I got a longer-term temp job at Prime Computer in Honolulu.

TS: Who were you working with at Hawai'i?

GG: That's an interesting story, because when I got there, Pak Sus (Hardja Susilo) and Ric Trimillos were both away. That's how I knew you, Ted, I was in your class. You taught a terribly named class in 1985, "Music of Non-Literate Peoples." We all laughed and called it "Music of the Illiterates."

TS: Yes, I was visiting for a semester and taught that preexisting, prenamed course. Titles like that were common and considered acceptable in those days!

GG: That was my first year. Ric Trimillos was my thesis adviser, but I really didn't work with him until I came back. Let's see, Pak Sus came back my second year. I had a number of courses with Byong Won Lee. I was enigmatic, though, in the Music Department, because I hung out over in Indo-Pacific languages. I had a key to their offices. I didn't have a computer, and they'd all leave at five. I'd look around the corner, and when it was empty I'd go in and write my thesis on their computers.

I got back from Kalimantan in March 1988, so I was away a year and a half. By then I knew I still wanted to work with Kenyah, but for my doctoral work I wanted to focus on a vocal tradition (I had worked with sapé' instrumental music before). When I came back from Sarawak after being shooed away during the election campaign and the Kayan wouldn't speak Malay with me, I went back to the Kenyah and said, "I don't want to speak Indonesian any more." So for the next eight months, it was Kenyah only. I got a pretty good foundation, and that's what gave me the guts to do a project based on vocal music, because of the language. I went back, but I wanted to go on the Sarawak side and work with a different Kenyah community because there are administrative differences and national differences in the way that governments operate. And they are very different places. So I went and was sponsored once again by the Sarawak Museum, by then under Peter Kedit. He's now retired.

TS: By now you've moved on to a PhD program at Wisconsin, right?

GG: Yes. Why did I pick Wisconsin? It came down to going back to Michigan or going to Wisconsin. I knew both Judith Becker and Andy Sutton, through gamelan and Southeast Asia connections. I like and respect and thought I could work with both of them. What it came down to was the requirements for the PhD. At that time at Michigan, ethnomusicology PhD students had to go through musicology and music theory exams, and I was not prepared to do that. On the other hand, Wisconsin had what seemed a brutal language requirement: three languages and a test. They required French, German, and a field language. Well I had the German and I had the Indonesian, so what was left was French. That didn't seem so bad.

Building a Career

GG: My first gig out of grad school was very common, a one-year replacement position at the College of William and Mary (1995–96). It was a wonderful teaching experience. At the time, William and Mary was also the home of the Borneo Research Council, under Vinson Sutlive. The following year ('96–97), I got a job at Cal State University San Marcos, near Escondido. I taught in an undergraduate visual and performing arts department. But, just like my freshman-year experience, after a semester I knew I was the wrong person for that position. So I looked around and applied to places I thought might match me better. That's how I wound up at Northwestern in 1997.

It was a tenure-track position in the School of Music. As is the case in many departments, ethnomusicologists are often the ones expected to have material that is accessible to the general student. We're often asked—I think more than a music theorist would be, for instance—to do classes for general students. I did a lot of them, and it was a very rewarding experience. You get such an interesting batch of people. Well, tenure time came up and I wasn't really looking for a job, but I remember saying to a friend that the only reason I'd leave would be for a Southeast Asian center, because Asian studies at Northwestern was not strong and I felt a sort of void. Just then a position was announced in interdisciplinary arts at Ohio University, which has a very strong Southeast Asia center. So I applied, got it, and decided to take the risk.

At Ohio they wanted me to re-form the core curriculum. They had "Introduction to the Arts I" and "Introduction to the Arts II," the first being a prerequisite for the second. I changed them into "Arts and Politics" and "Arts and Spirituality," two classes (with no prerequisites) that had integrity unto themselves. I went up for tenure early, after a year. I got through the department stage but was denied at the college level. I found out on the day that I was supposed to go to the Midwest Chapter ethno meeting. Well, at least I had a nice long drive to think about it. It hurt. How can it not hurt? It's hard. You know how the tenure thing works—I'd obviously been declared to be inadequate or whatever—so I resigned. I didn't stay the last year. I had always said to myself, if this doesn't happen, for whatever reason, I want to try something else.

I've always firmly believed that we have skills that are needed and marketable in areas outside the academy, but our programs deny it. We are systematically tracked into the university faculty position as the only legitimate position to come out of our training, which I think is sad. I had some savings I lived off while I applied for jobs outside the academy. It took me a year, because although we have great experience as academics, when that sort of experience is not coupled with administrative skills, proven administrative experience, marketing, or something to do with the business end, it's very difficult. And people don't want to hire someone who's been a university professor for ten years into an entry-level position.

I decided to go back to Chicago, and I was lucky to get a job as an editor at *Encyclopedia Britannica*. I've always enjoyed editing—helping people make their work comprehensible to a general reader. I've always valued that, and it was one of the frustrations I had with the academy. What is acknowledged and given points in the academy is accessible only to a thin stratum of the population. We all know how difficult it is to find introductory materials or materials that are accessible to people who aren't specialists on something like the music of Borneo or its interesting social dynamics. They're all so heavily theory laden. I'm not anti-theory—I mean, I love a good conversation about a question that has no answer—but at the same time, we want to pull people in, just like listening to that gamelan record did for me. *Britannica* is for educated nonspecialists. I'm a geography editor and have supportive and wonderful colleagues. I feel like I'm living testimony that there are fulfilling options outside the academy. It doesn't mean you're not worked to death. We're worked to death in the academy, and *Britannica* is very demanding, too, but there are fulfilling, legitimate options that are involved in education and cross-cultural stuff outside of a faculty position.

Update: July 18, 2016

During the nearly ten years since our conversation my professional life has taken a few more turns. In spring 2009 I shifted from geography editor to arts-and-culture (primarily music) editor at *Encyclopedia Britannica*. Later that year I tapped my ethnomusicological training as well as my editorial experience to help the Musical Instrument Museum prepare for its grand opening in April 2010 in Phoenix, Arizona. In 2012, intrigued by the explosion of MOOCs (massive open online courses) and the transformation of higher education through digital technology, I began to explore instructional design, first by taking a MOOC ("Surviving Disruptive Technologies") and then by completing a graduate certificate program in the field entirely online. In mid-2013 I left *Encyclopedia Britannica* to take a position designing online courses, primarily at the graduate level, for Pearson North America.

Although no longer the focus of my "day gig," music and ethnomusicology continue to shape my activities and my identity. Aside from my work at Pearson, I am currently designing an online certification program for piano soundboard technicians (bellymen) with Ken Eschete, a respected piano technician and instrument restorer. I am also writing a couple of articles for upcoming publications, and I look forward to returning to Malaysia this year (2016) to deliver a paper at an ethnomusicology conference, attend performances of contemporary sapé music at the Rainforest World Music Festival, and exchange field recordings of Kenyah music with local performers. Through such ongoing academic and practical engagement with scholars, enthusiasts, and performers of music—especially that of Borneo—I remain an active ethnomusicologist.

Judith (Judy) McCulloh (March 24, 2009)

PhD, Indiana University (Folklore)
Editor Emerita, University of Illinois Press

Graduate Studies

JMcC: After I got my bachelor's in English I went down the road to Ohio State and started a PhD in English.

MS: Did your interest in folk songs continue?

JMcC: Oh yes. I got a big old clunky box of a phonograph—I'm sure the needle wore out very quickly—and started buying recordings. I had a lot of the Folkways stuff, including some of the overseas stuff, and things that Kenny Goldstein was issuing. I got a bunch of revival stuff—The New Lost City Ramblers when they came around. I heard a pretty good variety of music at Ohio Wesleyan, and by the time I went to Ohio State, I was more seriously interested in folk music. Even at Wesleyan, I knew enough to give a talk about British and Anglo-American folk song. I knew about Child Ballads and stuff like that and could play examples and so forth. When I got to Ohio State, I did some work with Fran Utley, who was the main folklorist there. I had one quarter with him and became his assistant for a while. I took a class with

Claude Simpson on the broadside ballad, so I got some of the written older British tradition that way. But mainly I was working in medieval studies, Old English and Middle English, that kind of thing with Morton Bloomfield.

MS: So you were finding your way into folk-song studies through English departments rather than music departments at that time.

JMcC: Yes, Morton Bloomfield decided that if I was going to work in that area, I needed to know Sanskrit. Where should I go study Sanskrit? There was a wonderful professor at the Free University of Brussels in Belgium, so I applied for a Fulbright and got it. I went off to Belgium in '58, but the professor died while I was on the boat going over there. Eventually, they found a native speaker of Flemish to teach the course in French. I knew a little French, and somehow I got through the year. I sat in on some other courses and went folk dancing with some Flemish people from the countryside. You could make out basic stuff in Flemish if you knew German, so that was no big deal. We spent weekends learning traditional dances from the countryside.

The spring before I went to Belgium Fran Utley was involved in hosting a meeting of the Ohio Folklore Society at Ohio State. Richard Dorson came over from Indiana to give a talk, and he brought with him a trio of students who sang and played instruments. At the end, Dorson issued an open invitation to the every-four-years Folklore Institute at Indiana University, which would run for six or eight weeks that summer. I expressed some interest, and he said, "Well, come on over." I went to Indiana for the summer and took a couple of courses from Archer Taylor, the great Germanic riddle and proverbs scholar. There were a lot of people there and many of them sang and played: Kenny Goldstein, Ellen Steckert, and Joe Hickerson, as well as some other people who've since dropped by the wayside. There was music all over the place, and it was one big family. There was no class distinction, as it were, between established scholar and neophyte folknik. It was the most magical experience I ever had.

I went off to Belgium and got to thinking, "Do I really want to go back into English and do a dissertation on some exceedingly narrow topic?" I had done my master's thesis on some uses of the conjunction "and" in Middle English as exemplified principally in Chaucer's *Canterbury Tales*, Fragment 1. The thought of doing something like that as my life's work, as it were, was not appealing. Between that and this utterly open-ended field called folklore, there was no question, so instead of going back to Ohio State, I applied to Indiana, got in, and went there when I came back from Belgium. I never went back to Ohio State.

When I got there, I discovered that although Dorson was chair of the department, it was really nothing like it was that summer. It wasn't quite truth in advertising, except for the summer institute, which happened again in '62. It was at Indiana that I first heard about ethnomusicology, because I worked with George List, who had gotten his degree on Mozart. I sat in on one or two of George Herzog's classes, but he was very ill at the time and would show up for class later and later. He couldn't get himself together, though when he did, he was absolutely brilliant. George List was assigned to take over the archive, which was still the Archives of Folk and Primitive Music at that point, and started teaching classes in transcription and analysis, which I took. So it would have been from Herzog or List that I first heard the term "ethnomusicology," but I can't tell you which.

MS: What years were you at Indiana?

JMcC: I went there in the fall of '59 and was there for three years. Leon and I got married in '61. The closest job he could get to Indiana was at Illinois, in mathematics. I had one required course left to do, so the first year we were married, I stayed in Indiana and Leon was here in Urbana. We commuted every weekend. I moved to Urbana in the fall of '62, after the summer Folklore Institute. Aside from going off on sabbaticals a few times with Leon, we've been here in this same house ever since.

MS: How did you meet Leon?

JMcC: I first met him when I was at Cottey. I had a friend named Mary Thormeyer who lived in Worthington, Ohio, and I went home with her a couple of times on holidays. She and Leon knew each other from high school and had gone out. I guess he came over to say hello; they weren't dating at that point. When I went to Ohio Wesleyan, he was a year ahead of me and we bumped into each other. Then he went to Ohio State in math and I followed a little later. We kept running into each other and finally decided it was a good thing! So we made it permanent.

MS: When you were at Indiana studying with some of the founders of ethnomusicology, did you have any conception of the field as it was at that time? Or how it differed from or related to what you were doing in folklore?

JMcC: Not in any deep way. I knew there were anthropologists who were interested in this, because when Merriam arrived, I helped him do some stuff in the archives. I remember asking him about the *Anthropology of Music* because it seemed odd that there was no musical notation in it. He said (as he probably said many times to many other people), "I wanted to show it's possible to write about music without having transcriptions." I thought, "That's an eye opener." It was like that legitimized doing cultural commentary.

MS: What was your PhD topic in the end?

JMcC: I wrote about a hillbilly song called "In the Pines." Bill Monroe had a big hit with it under that title, and Leadbelly had a big hit with it under the title "Black Girl" or "Black Gal." I found about 160 variants of it (remember, this was pre-computer!), transcribed the music and words for every verse, and did a text-tune analysis. I sorted them out on the floor, right here; everything was fastened together with Scotch Tape. That's how we did it in the old days. You youngsters have no concept!

MS: We still have Scotch Tape!

JMcC: Yes, but you don't write one sentence of your dissertation, then tape on another sentence, and maybe three more sentences, until you have a string of little fringe-y paper trails.

MS: True. Who were your role models at that point? Who inspired you?

JMcC: George List was a taskmaster and, although he gave me a rough time and I gave him a rough time back, he said later, "We're both very stubborn people." That reinforced whatever sense I had of trying to be meticulous and getting my evidence all lined up, organized, and sensible. He would have reinforced that and set very high standards. I didn't always agree with him, but I could see why he wanted something done, and that was good.

In terms of life-long inspiration, the one person I should mention is Archie Green, who came through Indiana when he was working on *Only a Miner* [1972]. He was just meeting people and stayed at the cottage that Ellen Steckert and I had. He slept on the floor there for a bit and then went on his way. In terms of vision, imagination, and getting people to do things, he inspired so many people, and I happened to be one of the lucky ones. At the time, I was working on a comparison of Finnish and Finnish-American fiddle tunes at Indiana. I'd started a dissertation on that and studied Finnish for a couple of years. I even went to Columbia and took beginning and intermediate Finnish at the same time (which was most interesting) with Elli Köngäs Maranda, so I could understand the interviews on field tapes she had made with another Indiana University grad student, Meri Lehtinen. My project got bogged down for one reason or another; it wasn't going anywhere, and Archie said, "You know, there's this song that's really interesting. Somebody needs to write about it." That's typical Archie. I looked into it and it got more and more interesting. That's what I wound up writing about. List went for it, but because it was music, Dorson hated it. Dorson was not musical; he did not understand music and could see no value in it whatsoever. Anybody in the Folklore Program who had a musical interest was in bad shape. So, I did that study, and I have to say I still like the song.

MS: Do you think of yourself as being part of any kind of lineage in an academic sense?

JMcC: I'd say more Archie than anything, although I never formally studied with him. Many people who would say the same thing never formally studied with him. He was somebody who would give guidance and encouragement; he had the right approach to the world. When I worked at the press, I was always asking people to say, "OK, so what?" What does that mean? And once you figure that out, what's the bigger context? Somebody who sees the world through small bits; yes, I would say Archie was my role model.

Building a Career

JMcC: I finished the coursework for my PhD in '62, but there were some complications and I only finished the degree in 1970.

MS: When and how did you get your job at the University of Illinois Press?

JMcC: Archie had got a library degree at Illinois and then a job as the labor librarian in ILIR, the Institute for Labor and Industrial Relations (it has a slightly different name now, I think). He also had a joint appointment with the English Department and taught courses like "The Radical Novel" and "Folk Song and Ballad." I became his assistant for the folk song and ballad course. I made demo tapes for him and helped grade papers. I also helped him with some projects at the Labor Institute.

Around that time, Dick Wentworth was appointed associate director at the press. He came here from LSU Press, looked around the way an editor looks around, and said, "Nobody's covering American music in all its breadth." So he proposed a new series to the then-director, a Mr. Muntyan. Archie claims he named it *Music in American Life.* What do you do when you start a series? You go out and sign up a bunch of books, then you announce it with a big fanfare, and with luck other people will submit their manuscripts. Manuscripts started to come in, and Wentworth realized he needed help. Archie said, "Oh, I know the perfect person. She just got her degree, so get her before somebody else does." Well, I had no prospects of getting a job, so when Wentworth asked if I'd be interested in developing books in folklore and music—as calmly as I could—I said, "I'll try anything once." I had done a little work for Archie: I transcribed his original tunes for *Only a Miner,* and when he added a chapter or two for the book, I transcribed those. I did that at Cecil Sharp House in London. In those days they didn't have earphones over there, so I was playing those race and hillbilly records out into the room, and the very proper librarians at Cecil Sharp House couldn't quite grasp why this was worth listening to. I could tell by their faces! I also did the index for *Only a Miner.* So they knew me at the press from those ancillary things.

Not too long after that, a half-time copyeditor left, so they hired me in the early part of '72. I'd never done any copyediting as such, so I read the *Chicago Manual,* watched how other people marked manuscripts, and did it, no big deal. Eventually some other half-time person left, and I became full time. I remember the first manuscript I looked at. Wentworth gave it to me and said, "Write up some comments on this." It was Jeff Titon's *Early Down Home Blues* [1977]. I went through the manuscript pretty carefully, sat there typing away, and wrote about ten or twelve single-spaced pages. I gave it to Wentworth and he sent it right off to Jeff! I said, "That wasn't for his eyes." He said, "You've gotta learn, it's always for somebody else's eyes." Luckily, Jeff and I are still friends. The first book I actually copyedited was Glen Ohrlin's *The Hell-Bound Train* [1973]. In time, I became a full-time acquisitions editor. Then you came along at some point, which was nice.

MS: Yes, I was your assistant from '91 to '93. You were a great mentor for me and for so many people. *Music in American Life* has been a hugely influential series on American music. You had a role in shaping that whole field.

JMcC: Without bragging, I think it has made a difference. I was at the press for thirty-five years and there were 130-some titles out by the time I left. I wanted to get an overview or a snapshot coverage of American music—classical, folk, early and later, and all the ethnic groups—such that, if all the libraries in the world went down and all we had left was the series, people could get a pretty representative look at what was going on musically in this country from the beginning up to the time the ship went down. We got reasonably good coverage, although there's plenty to do, heaven knows, but there were three areas I think still need to be developed. One is the sacred area, which some people find a little too delicate to deal with, because it gets so personal, although there's more of that being done now. Second is, as you would expect, the whole ethnic range of music. Even if you had one book for every ethnic group in this country, that would be a lot, but there would still be more to do within each group. The third area that just cries out for attention is the business of music. In the old days, people would hear music in the home and the community and the worksite. They'd hear it directly or maybe on phonograph records. Now everything is so commodified. You hear it on your iPod or maybe on a CD, if that doesn't go out of fashion; but how does the music get from the hands and mouth of the performer into our ears. There are so many stages in between—decisions being made all along the line, whether aesthetic or marketing or legal, like what are the copyright issues, which are a can of worms. There are so many people and dynamics involved that we just don't see as consumers. We need to understand that much better than we do.

MS: When I worked for you, I was impressed that you knew *everybody*. You'd see something and you'd say, "Oh, so-and-so is working on this project, maybe they haven't seen this little newspaper item," and then you'd send it to them. You had an enormous network.

JMcC: Well, that was fun; it was one of perks of being an editor. You're mission control in a way, and it was a way of seeing projects develop. It was creative in that sense. I enjoyed working closely with people. I remember after I went to work at the press, I was at a folklore meeting and one of my fellow folklorists said, "What are you doing? I haven't seen you since graduate school." I said, "Oh, I'm an editor at the University of Illinois Press." "Oh, it's too bad you couldn't get a real job!" But a few years later, when the job market was not so good, people would start sidling up and asking, "How did you ever get that neat job in publishing?" They'd say, "It's too bad you're not teaching," because that's a stereotypical thing PhDs do. That did bother me because editors teach one on one. We just have a different venue for our classroom.

Addendum to the interview: I (Margaret) interviewed Judy in the front room of her Urbana home. As our conversation drew to a close, the phone rang in another room. Judy answered, and I could hear her talking about Archie Green. It was only later that I realized Judy had been talking to someone who was preparing an appreciation of Archie for National Public Radio (which aired the following day, March 25). On reflection, it seems all the more poignant that she knew of Archie's death when talking about him, but never let on that he had just passed away two days earlier.

(Judy passed away on July 13, 2014, in Urbana, Illinois.)

Postscript, by Margo Chaney (Exhibits Manager, University of Illinois Press)

Judy McCulloh hired me as her acquisitions assistant at the University of Illinois Press in November of 1994. From the beginning, I was struck by Judy's work ethic—not just the focus and the quantity of hours she worked in a day, but the breadth of her interests and application of her amazing energy. After she retired, she continued to attend professional conferences and bluegrass festivals at her own expense, and she set up her own small business as a book vendor. She read manuscripts for presses, continued to serve on various committees of the American Folklore Society, the Society for American Music, the Society for Ethnomusicology, and the American Musicological Society. Her husband, Leon, says that when she received the NEA Bess Lomax Hawes Award in 2010 for the preservation and awareness of cultural heritage, she was very honored but perhaps more excited at the opportunity to meet the other recipients at the award ceremony. In 2010 she also received a National Heritage Fellowship.

Judy loved introducing the people she loved to other people or music that she loved. Through all the years I worked with her, through her retirement, and even after her death, she remains a wonderful, strong, and gracious role model.

RECORD COMPANIES

Bernard Kleikamp (October 12, 2010)

Doctorandus (MA), University of Amsterdam (Drama)
President, PAN Records

Graduate Studies

BK: I got my candidate's degree, a three-year program like a bachelor's, and after that I studied drama, with extended side courses in ethnomusicology. Maybe I should explain the then-existing university system. After the candidate's degree, you could go on to the master's, which takes another three years, during which you take two side courses in any subject. Instead of two side courses, I decided to take one extended course in ethnomusicology. I'd done my research—I've always been very thorough in finding out about things I wanted to do. The decision was based on my prior involvement with traditional music and my education as one of the last people from a living tradition in the Netherlands, because living traditions don't exist anymore. I shouldn't say that because my youngest son is also a singer, and I educated him the same way that my mother educated me, by singing all the time. It didn't catch on with my other sons, but when the youngest son heard a song, he would say, "Sing it again, Daddy. Sing it again!" After the second time, he could sing it pitch-perfect.

TS: When you took this course, did you think about what you might do with the training?

BK: Yes, I knew that it would be the specialization of teachers, which didn't interest me very much, but I also knew that I would get an education in research. If I wanted to do my own research later, I would know how to set it up. For me, that was the most important thing to learn.

TS: Are you saying that you wanted to get some methodological training in how to preserve the culture you felt was disappearing?

BK: Yes, for me that was the most important thing.

MS: Did you study with Ernst Heins?

BK: Yes, there was a department called "Ethnomusicological Center 'Jaap Kunst.'" It was founded by Jaap Kunst in the late 1950s and still followed his program. It's now all changed with the restructuring of our university system, some ten or fifteen years ago.

MS: Did you have a conception of the broader field of ethnomusicology at that time, or were you just interested in your own projects?

BK: I got a good education in ethnomusicology. One of the subjects I remember quite well was the listening exam. We had to go to the studio of the Ethnomusicological Center, where there was a collection of tapes—some three or four hundred pieces of music from all over the world—and listen to them. We had to memorize the music and know its background, where it was from, the style, and basic things like that.

TS: Can you remember any of the things you read that made an impression on you?

BK: The way the education system worked we didn't read many books. We got a course packet that included chapters or extracts from books. Back then, you could copy anything and present it to your students—there wasn't really a problem with copyright. There were a few books that I remember: Bruno Nettl's *Folk and Traditional Music of the Western Continents* [1965] and Malm's *Music Cultures of the Pacific, the Near East, and Asia* [1967]. I still have those books.

TS: Did you enjoy the ethnomusicology courses?

BK: Yes, it was fun, because at that time I had already started my business as a concert agent. I took a course from an assistant who was working on his PhD on folk music in the Netherlands. It was an ongoing project in which the students participated, so I was not only a student, I was also an informant. I had a double role, which I enjoyed tremendously. That student assistant is still a friend of mine. He got his PhD and is now a professional musician. I produce his CDs. Later on, I also made some CDs of Ernst Heins's fieldwork.

Building a Career

I was about twenty-seven or twenty-eight and the publicity man for a local folk club. I was always a bit sore at the way musicians presented their publicity to me. One day a group challenged me and said, "Well, if you think you can do better, then why don't you become our manager?" I thought about it and said, "Why not?" I gave myself six months. From one performance a month, they went to six to eight performances a month. The band was happy and word spread. Other bands started asking me if I would be their manager and I said, "Oh, sure, I can do that." Suddenly I had a concert agency, Paradox. I kept it up for about twenty-five years and only stopped in 2003. The paradox was that in my early days as a student folk-club organizer, there was an anti-commercial tendency. We wanted to have a low threshold between musicians and audience. The musicians would ask very little for the performance, and entrance at the door would be very low. So when I started to promote events, it was against my original principles. That's why I named my agency Paradox.

TS: What kinds of bands were they typically?

BK: The musicians were all Dutch and mostly based in or around Leiden. One group played Romanian folk music and other groups played South American, Celtic, and Dutch-language cabaret-style music. I've always been broad-minded about music, even though I myself preferred traditional repertoire from the Netherlands.

MS: How did you take the step from being a concert promoter to having your own record company?

BK: At that time it was very rare for a folk band to have an LP. There weren't any small record companies, and the majors weren't interested in local folk music. So King's Galliard, one of the groups I worked with, decided to start its own record company, PAN Records. Their business model was to make an LP and then sell as many copies as necessary to pay for the next one. After a couple of years the band members decided they didn't want to be involved in running the company, they just wanted to be musicians. They asked me to take care of the business side of things, so I proposed a buyout. They agreed. That was the mid-1980s. Since then I've been the sole owner of PAN Records. I changed the approach immediately, from a company that promoted local and regional artists to a company that supported international artists and had an international distribution. In a way, I've been lucky, because just a couple years after that the CD arrived and there was so much interest in music that people would buy *anything*!

MS: What was your first CD?

BK: My first release was a Tuvan recording, *Tuva: Voices from the Land of the Eagles* [1991]. It's still my bestselling CD. The Tuva Ensemble was on tour in the Netherlands. On one of their days off I invited them to a studio and gave them an afternoon of recording time. From a very early stage, I began to approach ethnomusicologists and anthropologists about publishing their fieldwork on PAN Records if they had good recordings. Between 1990 and 2000 I had really good sales, so I could afford to finance projects. I can't do that anymore—it's impossible. My turnover is now maybe 10 percent of what is was ten years ago.

TS: Why do you think that is?

BK: Three reasons: saturation of the market, the economic crisis, and the illegal copies and downloads that started about ten to twelve years ago. That's really been the death of the CD business. I was lucky to set up my company in the good years. I was educated with the Bible and was always told that in the good years you have to save for the bad years, so in the good years, I invested for the future. I made so many recordings between 1990 and 2000 that I still have maybe thirty or forty CDs on the shelf. I've paid for the production, paid the artists, and have the liner notes, so with very little effort, I can continue releasing CDs. In the good years, I put out twenty to twenty-five releases a year because I wanted to build up a large catalog as quickly as possible. Now I'm doing six to eight, maybe ten releases a year.

TS: Why did you want to build up a large catalog as quickly as possible?

BK: Because I discovered that it was very hard to get distribution in other territories if your catalog was too small. Early on, I went to Midem (a yearly meeting of the music industry held in Cannes, France) with my catalog, which was then eight CDs, and approached various distributors. They said, "What are we to do with eight CDs?" So I thought, "OK, I'll come back in a couple of years with more discs." So I came with a catalog of seventy-five CDs, and then I could deal with international distributors.

TS: Are there ways in which your ethnomusicological training has helped you in this business?

BK: First of all, because of my training, I got to know releases of various companies in other parts of the world, which were examples to me of how *not* to do an ethnomusicological production. That got me to thinking, "How do I want to do it?" I wanted to have well-documented CDs, which, at that time, I could only find in Folkways. Folkways' documentation was adequate, but no more than that. To me, it usually lacked a lot of basic information. So I thought, "I can use Folkways as an example, but improve the model." And second, I wanted to have a good body of collaborators, musicologists who could give substance to the release plan of PAN Records. When I'd made my business plan and found good collaborators, I started releasing the Ethnic Series. My company was the first to pay active scholarly attention to brass-band traditions around the world. Now you see that *everybody's* doing it. The same goes for overtone music and throat singing—the Tuvans and the Mongolians. There may have been isolated releases of such music before, but at PAN Records, we did it systematically.

TS: Do you do ethnomusicological research yourself?

BK: Yes, I've been doing research and continue to record traditional music in the Netherlands. I've also made several field trips to Hungary and one to Cyprus to document a tradition that happens during the Orthodox Lent. Sadly, it turned out to be a touristic tradition, not a real tradition. I've also done fieldwork among ethnic groups in China, in Yunnan and Guizhou in the southwest, and also in Tibet.

TS: How did you pick these places to do research? Hungary, Cyprus, China, Tibet—it's kind of difficult to become an expert on so many places!

BK: Yes, I know! I got interested in Cyprus and did a lot of research there, but that turned out to be a dead end. Hungary was because I worked with Hungarian traditional groups. Some of the band members were musicologists and they invited me to go with them on field trips. I did that for a couple of years but discovered that the Hungarian musicologists were much better equipped than I was. Although that was another a dead end, I had a fascinating time.

With PAN Records, I've always wanted to document traditions that, first of all, were not covered by other companies, and second, were living as opposed to dying traditions. I didn't want my company to release the last surviving Tierra del Fuego singer, who at eighty-five was singing the songs of her youth. That's for other companies to do. I think music is an organic thing and it keeps on developing. Even though people tell you what they sing is traditional because their father or their grandfather sang it, there are always differences. Music always adapts to the flow of time. That's what I find most interesting, and that's what I aim to document.

I made an inventory of areas in the world that I thought deserved documentation but hadn't yet been studied. Then I looked at the list and I thought, "What would I want to do myself?" I thought, "China, but not the Han Chinese. How about the other fifty-five ethnic groups?" So I made a very ambitious plan to have *all* fifty-five ethnic groups covered with releases. I started with an anthology of music from China, and now I'm at number seven or eight. I know that was too ambitious, but I've been to China and found Chinese musicologists who can do it much better than I could, so I've done a couple of releases with Zhang Xingrong and Tian Liantao. Still, I've made some interesting recordings, and there will eventually be a couple of my own releases.

MS: How do you see your business developing in the future?

BK: I'm not only an ethnomusicologist, I'm first and foremost a businessman. I have been forced to keep adapting to the demands of the music-buying audience. In the mid- to late-1980s the demand was CDs, not LPs, so we had to change. The second change was to DVD, which many people thought would be the new CD, but eventually didn't prove to be so. Now there's the challenge of selling your music in the digital world because the CD is almost dead. That's always the challenge—adapt to the times and make music available in whatever way possible.

I realized that it's not enough to release good music; you have to own the rights, so I've been careful to make good contracts. If the musicians I worked with had composed their stuff (so it wasn't public domain), I'd always insist they sign a contract with my music-publishing company. I became a music publisher in the early-1990s and have always been interested in anything to do with copyright, especially copyright in relation to traditional music. I own the publishing rights to at least half of our releases. That provides a substantial extra source of income. Without that, I probably wouldn't be able to survive in this time of digital sales and digital downloads.

TS: So, diversification is always the key?

BK: Yes. I deal in rights, but I also think it's important to pay your artists, so I keep good track of royalties and things like that.

Update: August 5, 2016

When we talked in 2010, I had just started as a student again at Leiden University in Indian and Tibetan studies. I had done fieldwork among Tibetans in the mid-1990s and got stuck in working out the material. Musicologically I could cope, but I didn't understand Tibetan culture, where everything is connected to everything: religion, politics, culture, and social life. I needed to get an education in this and, right next door at Leiden University, there were the specialists who could teach me. I had time on my hands, as the crisis in the music industry left me with one day a week of work.

I needed to find something to occupy myself, so I embarked on an education in Tibetan culture and religion.

I studied on and off while continuing to run PAN Records. I stopped studying for a while after I had an aorta dissection in September 2013, which I barely survived and from which I had to recover for over a year. At the time of writing, all I need to do is to finish my master's thesis and I will have completed the degree. I continue with PAN Records, releasing the occasional CD but also releasing more and more digital-only downloads. The recordings, with cover and mp3s, are available on iTunes with full PDF liner notes on the PAN Records website.

If there's one thing in the past six years I've experienced, it's that I've been confronted with my own mortality and that of others. I'm beginning to worry how research results can be stored for future generations. I've seen archives closed down and dispersed for lack of funding. I've lost a couple of valued colleagues who made CDs for PAN Records—Jack Body and Wouter Swets. Vyacheslav Mikhalovych Shurov, who made over twenty discs for me, recently wrote that he's not well. We need a new generation to succeed us. I expect to be around for ten, maybe fifteen years more before I retire; I need to make sure that PAN Records and its archives survive me.

Daniel Atesh Sonneborn (October 28, 2007)

PhD, UCLA (Ethnomusicology)
Associate Director, Smithsonian-Folkways

Graduate Studies

AS: Eventually I reached a point where I saw that I could not progress in the kinds of work I liked to do without academic credentials. So I decided, "OK, what really makes sense, now that I know who I am and how I move in the world, is to do that more gracefully. To act as a composer who draws on resources from other cultures, I need to study ethnomusicology." I remember thinking, "I don't want to hang somebody else's god upside down over the mantle." I looked around to see who did ethnomusicology. I'd worked in the UCLA Ethnomusicology Archive when I was looking for Vietnamese music for *XA: A Vietnam Primer*, but I couldn't go there yet because I didn't even have a bachelor's degree.

So I went west again in 1975. My folks and my sister had moved to the West Coast. I drove a taxi for a while and produced things, wrote music for things, and tried to figure out how to make my way back to the academic scene. In 1979 I enrolled in a junior college because it seemed like the best way to do what I wanted, to get a doctorate in ethnomusicology. I thought of it as a way to enhance my cover story so that I could be me in the world, meet interesting people, and be involved in music in many ways. The junior college experience was great. I knew enough of what I wanted that I could make it into a great educational experience. By 1980 I had finished my sophomore year, which enabled me to enter the University of California system. I went to UC Santa Cruz and earned a BA in music composition. That's where I took my first formal courses in ethnomusicology, with David Kilpatrick.

At UC Santa Cruz I also encountered twentieth-century art music, something that held little attraction for me. I wanted to know, "What is this? Music is so important to me, but music of my own time is not doing it." So I decided to go to UC San Diego for my master's. I had a hard time there because of its art music orientation (as opposed to my tonal and neo-tonal polyrhythmic world-influenced stuff), but I made it through and did a master's thesis on corporeality in the music theater of Harry Partch. For that research I went back to the University of Illinois to talk to Ben Johnston, who had worked with Partch.

While I was at UC San Diego (1982–84), I took a seminar at San Diego State with Bob Brown and another one with Lewis Peterman. These seminars confirmed for me that this was the field I wanted to study. Bob Brown suggested that Jihad Racy at UCLA might be a good mentor for me, so I went up to meet him. He welcomed me as a colleague from the first moment. I was very excited when I started at UCLA in the fall of '84. I decided to live in the international graduate students' dorm, right on campus, so I didn't have to think about cooking, shopping, washing dishes, or commuting. I could be there because I knew why I was there. At that point it was so clear, and I wanted to drink at the spring of whatever they knew! I was like a duck in water, it was *so* much fun. I'm still grateful for that period.

From 1984 to '87 I was at UCLA, did my exams, and proposed a dissertation on Sufi music in Islam. There were several stops along the way. In 1979, when I first went back to school, I thought I would study Sufi music in the Wakhan Peninsula of Afghanistan, but the Soviets invaded and it became impossible. Early in my time at UCLA I thought, "OK, I'll study Sufi music in Sudan," based on a great BBC film I saw, and then they had a right-wing revolution and it didn't look too good. A little later I heard Nusrat Fateh Ali Khan's *qawwali* and thought, "Sufi Music in Pakistan: *that* could work." I proposed it and then they had a right-wing revolution. So I decided, "OK, why don't I just study the Sufi tradition in the United States; they probably won't have a right-wing revolution"—though now I'm not so sure! I proposed a dissertation on exactly that topic: musical change in Sufism as it moved from South Asia to the West over the last century.

Building a Career

I worked in a Sufi community in the San Francisco area and became the accompanist to their Thursday night *zikr* ritual. I did that for seven years while doing a lot of other things, including writing a book called *Planet Drum* with Mickey Hart and Fred Lieberman [1991]. I also worked on *Drumming at the Edge of Magic* (Hart's autobiographical project [1990]) and a number of Mickey Hart's *The World* series projects.

The CDs associated with *Planet Drum* won the first-ever GRAMMY Award for world music [in 1991]. After these projects finished, in 1991 or '92, I went back to writing my dissertation. I finished it, defended it, and then—in my own mind—sat down to wait, because I wanted to fulfill my original vision to get into something that engaged all that I am. After three years, I got a call from Mark DeWitt, who said, "There's a job at the Smithsonian that might interest you." It was interesting, but I was doing well financially, managing Hamza and doing consulting work. Finally, my wife said, "Look at your résumé and look at this job description!" It called for everything I'd ever done, except writing music. So I had to apply. Smithsonian offered me the job in June 1998 and I started in October. Now I'm the associate director of Smithsonian Folkways Recordings and the acquisitions manager for Smithsonian Global Sound. I've been at the Smithsonian for a little over nine years.

Update: August 7, 2016

In my mid-sixties now, I hold the same job title at the US national museum's nonprofit record label. New collection acquisitions, intellectual property issues concerning law and artists' rights, developing new concepts for engagement with our "encyclopedia of sound," and ongoing efforts to align with best practices fill my days. My writing is less reliant on theoretical ethnomusicology and more on storytelling. I spend time mentoring younger staff and interns, welcoming invitations to meet, lecture, and present wherever they may come from. With students considering a career in this field, we explore possible future paths and discuss how to achieve personal goals.

In 2007 downloading was moving toward dominance, mobile music delivery was expanding, CD sales diminishing. In 2016 free audio streaming rules, digital downloading is dropping precipitously, and CD sales continue their two-decade downward slide toward what may well be a cliff. Meanwhile, vinyl LPs are making a notable comeback. And it seems that more live-music festivals are happening—all over the world. As I regard the problems of our time, I hope ethnomusicology will engage more in those of the world's musics that are directly, implicitly, or philosophically concerned with resolving social injustices, economic inequalities, and other critical issues facing communities, nations, and the global environment.

NOTES

1. Bill Ivey studied ethnomusicology at Indiana University, though his work has straddled the domains of both fields.
2. In Hawaiian culture, adopted child, or so close as to be a virtual family member.

Careers within "The Professoriat"

(Positions at time of interview)

Undergraduate Student

Jason Busniewski (October 27, 2007)

Undergraduate student, University of Oklahoma

Building a Career

TS: What are you planning on doing next? Graduate school?

JB: Yes, I'm looking at Wisconsin, Columbia, Wesleyan, Santa Barbara, UCLA, maybe Harvard or Berkeley.

TS: Are you aware of people at any of those places that might be supportive of the different kinds of things you're interested in?

JB: Yes. I went to the Arabic Music Seminar this spring and Scott Marcus was there, which was great. I obviously dabble a little bit in Arabic music, so the chance to study Indian and Arabic music with him at UC Santa Barbara would be really great, although I'm almost afraid I'll get sucked more into Arabic music if I study there. UCLA is just an all-around good program. Wisconsin has a fantastic South Asian Studies program and a program for Indian languages that would be really helpful. Wesleyan also has a good Ethno program. I've been influenced theoretically by Mark Slobin, so I would like to work with him. Columbia has a strong program with crossover with anthropology. One of our new Ethno professors, Amanda Minks, has recently graduated from Columbia, so I've heard good things about them.

MS: What do you see as your trajectory? As somebody who's just starting out, what do you imagine your future will be?

JB: Well, I have a pending Fulbright application. If I get it, I'll be going to Chennai for nine months to look at film music and Christian music as two examples of India's cultural interaction with the West. That was going to be the tentative topic for my honors research, but we kind of pared it down to just the Christian music because that's where Dr. Sherinian has connections. If I do that, I will be looking at Karnatak music and how it's been incorporated into the Christian liturgy and issues of cultural identity. After that, I definitely want to stick with India. I don't want to commit to doing Christian music all the time—I'm partially motivated by being a Christian—but I want to study all kinds of things. I'd like to continue violin studies. I've ended up doing Karnatak music because of Dr. Sherinian's connections, but I'm also interested in North India, especially the cultural interaction that it's had with Central Asia. North India is a place of cultural mixture. The South is slightly more homogeneous, or at least slightly less influenced by Muslim and Persian culture. It's not something I know as much about, but I am interested in that. I don't know if that'll pan out as an actual course of research or not, I suppose it will depend on where I go for school and who's there.

TS: It's amazing talking to an undergraduate who has had all this experience in this field already. When I was your age, there was not even a *hint* of anything like this. It's quite remarkable. You're an impressive guy, Jason. It's quite rare for undergraduates to come to the national meeting.

Update: July 12, 2016

When I was first interviewed for this project, I was an undergraduate attending the Society for Ethnomusicology annual meeting in hope of meeting possible graduate advisors. As I write this now, I'm writing my PhD dissertation at the University of California, Santa Barbara, and turning my sights to the academic job market, which gives me pause to consider who I am as an ethnomusicologist and who I would like to become.

GRADUATE STUDENT

Renata Pasternak-Mazur (October 27, 2007)

PhD in progress at Rutgers University

Graduate Studies

RPM: I began my master's degree studies at the Jagiellonian University of Kraków in the fall of 1987. The musicology program involved two years of ethnomusicology;

the first year was "world music," the second year, Polish folk music. There were also classes in advanced harmony, including enharmonic modulations and that sort of stuff. In order to get into the program you had to pass a lot of exams. There were special musical exams: playing a piece—a Mozart sonata or something similar—harmonizing bass, harmonizing soprano, and an ear-training exam. I didn't need to go through these entrance exams because of the Olympic competition.

There was really no chance of developing an ethnomusicological career in Kraków, especially in the area of world music. We had only one professor dealing with ethnomusicology; she focused on Polish musical topics. World music was covered by Professor Jan Stęszewski, the head of the Musicology Department at the University of Adam Mickiewicz in Poznan. Initially, the Polish universities focused on different areas: Poznan, ethnomusicology; Warsaw, contemporary twentieth-century music; and Kraków, early music. However, later on it got mixed up, and when I was a student there, the distinction wasn't clear.

TS: Who were the ethnomusicologists in Poland?

RPM: Professor Stęszewski was at Poznan and Professor Anna Czekanowska was at Warsaw. They are the two most distinguished Polish ethnomusicologists. In Kraków there is nobody of that rank. In Poland the professorship is an academic rank, unlike here, where it's a functional rank.

TS: What does that mean?

RPM: In the US, the PhD is the highest degree you can get. In Poland, after your PhD you have to go on to another formal stage in your career, the Docentoga. You become a docent and no longer a doctor. Professor is not a functional title, as it is in the States, but a title that is given by the government. It takes a long time to reach the professorship stage. There are few people with that rank. In ethnomusicology there are only two, as far as I know, Professors Stęszewski and Czekanowska. It's like this in several other European countries. It's a result of the Communist approach, when they gave PhDs away for no significant academic contribution. So academia wanted to establish a further recognition of academic achievement. There is some discussion now about liquidating the Docentoga.

TS: Do you remember the first time you heard the word "ethnomusicology"?

RPM: I think it was when I entered the Jagiellonian University. In Polish, the word is Etnomuzykologia; it's very similar. It's still very difficult to get access to "world music," so we were very excited about the course and everybody enjoyed it.

TS: Tell me about the course; what did you learn?

RPM: We learned some theory of anthropology; we read some [works by] Polish anthropologists (Malinowski, for example) and other books that were available in

Polish. We covered different cultures, depending on what recordings were available in the department. They had the series of LPs published by UNESCO, so that was part of the instruction. Professor Stęszewski also gave a series of special-topic lectures, such as Eskimo music and *Noh* theater.

TS: Did you have to write a master's thesis?

RPM: Yes, but not in ethnomusicology. I presented my work on the Polish composer Witold Lutosławski.

TS: So, you went there to study musicology in general. You were interested in contemporary musicology and, as part of the program, you were required to take some ethnomusicological work. Is that right?

RPM: Yes, 100 percent of the students took it. It was something new to us, and we were very excited. Some students considered writing a master's thesis on folk music, but it was technically difficult. They needed to sponsor their own fieldwork, which was too expensive for them.

TS: Their own fieldwork on Polish things?

RPM: Yes, because at that time—at least in my university—we were unable to work on topics outside Poland for financial reasons, visas, and that sort of stuff. Toward the end of my studies, in 1991, I got a scholarship to attend the University College Cork in Ireland for a semester. I took courses in Irish music, learned to play the tin whistle, and took a workshop on set dancing. I was also involved in their African ensemble and took a course on African music.

TS: Who was teaching there?

RPM: Mel Mercier. I had a TEMPUS (Trans-European Mobility Programme for University Studies) Scholarship, an exchange that allowed students from Eastern Europe to go to Western universities. Because I was quite advanced in my master's thesis, I had my topic and worked on that. I was very excited to be sent to Ireland because many people wanted to go there. On my first day, I was told that I had an Irish sense of humor! There's also a kind of mental bond between Polish and Irish people, probably because of our histories. During the nineteenth century, Poland was divided between Russia, Prussia, and Austria, and Irish history was kind of similar.

TS: Was your English already pretty good by that time?

RPM: Yes, I had some English in high school, but not much. The really good instruction started at the university level in Kraków.

Building a Career

After five months in Ireland, I went back to the Jagiellonian University. I finished my thesis on Witold Lutosławski and his *Piano Concerto* and graduated in 1993. After graduating, I started work at PWM Edition, a music publisher in Poland. For a long time it was the only music publisher in Poland and functioned as an art institute, sponsoring research as well as publishing scholarly books. I was originally responsible for the export division, which also involved foreign music. Two years later, I started writing about music for *Gazeta Wyborcza*, one of the most important newspapers in Poland. In my final year (before coming to the US) I worked as a music teacher at the International School in Kraków. This school followed the British curriculum. Instruction was in English but because the students were children of foreigners from all over the world, they came with many different levels of English-language proficiency.

TS: How did you end up coming to the United States?

RPM: I met my husband and he had a job offer here. He had already signed a contract for a job in New Jersey before we met, so I agreed to come with him.

TS: What's his name and what does he do?

RPM: Paweł Mazur. Mazur means "Mazurka," so I have a very musical husband! He's a software developer, but music is an important part of his life. He liked that I was the music critic of the *Gazeta Wyborcza*. It was an interesting job, and he could impress his friends! We came in 1998, but we are seriously considering returning to Poland. We intended to come to the US for two or three years, but we had kids. I told him I cannot be a housewife! I was considering a PhD for a long time, but I wanted to taste some real life first. I had met so many professors and other people in academia who had never been outside academia, so they were completely detached from the real world. I didn't want to be like that. When I got my papers, a friend from the Jagiellonian University who got his PhD from Boston University, inspired me to go for a PhD.

TS: So, now you're a PhD student at Rutgers? When did you start?

RPM: In 2004. I was interested in music cognition and in the relationship between music and language, but I didn't get any encouragement in that direction. Instead, Professor Nanette de Jong (who is now at the University of Newcastle) asked me to prepare a lecture on Polish hip-hop for her class, "Introduction to Music." The students were extremely interested and she was surprised that there were so many interesting things going on, so she encouraged me to work on this topic further. As I worked on it, the idea of music in the context of socialism seemed to be a good match for me, with my background. The topic for my dissertation is music in Poland in a postsocialist context. In particular, I look at the hierarchy of genres from the very top (classical music) to genres that are perceived as "low," like Polish hip-hop. This year I presented on *disco polo*, a symbol of the "lowest" music in Poland. Folk music is a very special case that I will also work on.

TS: Did you have any background with hip-hop?

RPM: No, it was the first time I ever listened to hip-hop. Working with Professor de Jong was so inspiring for me that I decided it would be great to combine ethnomusicology and musicology. I wish I could go completely into ethnomusicology, but the way the program is structured it's not possible.

TS: What do you hope to do in future? How do you imagine your career?

RPM: I have a family and have taken a break from academia, but I'd like to go back to that world. I don't see myself in the "Ivory Tower," but still connected to real life. I'd like to teach at the college level. I still write about music; I write as a music critic for the Polish daily newspaper *Nowy Dziennik* in New York.

Update: March 24, 2017

I completed my PhD in January 2017. Because of family obligations and moving back to Poland, where my husband has an interesting job opportunity, my own professional development has become complicated. Still, I've published four articles/chapters based on my dissertation research (on Polish hip-hop, on the meaning of folk music in socialist Poland, on sacred music in the marketplace in postsocialist Poland, and on *disco polo*) and am currently working on a book chapter on cultural politics of the People's Republic of Poland.

With voice being my primary instrument, I've been involved in choral music as a singer in American and Polish choirs and as a church music director. In Kraków, I serve as a program advisor and marketing manager at a collegiate choir. In addition, I work as a volunteer for PAL (*program aktywności lokalnej*) educational programs aimed at social exclusion prevention and local community building.

I have been applying for teaching positions at local colleges, but so far nothing has materialized. It probably looks like I'm in permanent transition, and, while my final destination is unclear, recent serious orthopedic problems have prevented me from any new professional moves. I hope to fully recover soon and am working hard on it.

Contingent Faculty
(Adjuncts/Short-Term Positions/Postdocs)

Jonathan Dueck (October 27, 2007)

PhD, University of Alberta (Music)
Visiting Assistant Professor, University of Maryland

Graduate Studies

MS: How did you make the transition from opera singer to ethnomusicologist?

JD: I had no idea what ethnomusicology was. I wrote interview papers, even within music courses. In music theory papers, I'd analyze the structure of a pop song and then contact the guy and do an interview with him. Right from the start, I wanted to talk to people. I applied to six or seven musicology programs. I was pretty naïve. I knew there were scholars I wanted to work with, but I didn't really understand how programs were ranked. I ended up at Alberta because Wesley Berg was there and I knew I wanted to study Mennonites. I thought I would be studying musicology. I had no idea what ethnomusicology was, but Regula Qureshi called me one day, talked to me for ten minutes, and said, "You're an ethnomusicologist!" I was seized by the lapels, as it were, and decided *this* is the person I've got to study with.

MS: How did she come to that conclusion? Had you taken any classes with her?

JD: I'd never met her. Applying to Alberta was almost an afterthought. A good friend of mine said, "You really should apply there, they're interested in the things you're interested in."

MS: Was that the first time you'd heard the word "ethnomusicology"?

JD: Quite possibly. It was a crash course! I got into the PhD program on a music theory scholarship. I was interested in atonal and pop music theory, so I had submitted two sample papers on that. But Edmonton's a neat program; you're required to take courses in music theory, musicology, and ethnomusicology. Everybody is on the left end of academia, and they agree that critical studies, Marxism, and critical theory are a common core for these various disciplines. It had a small group of faculty, and there was a great emphasis on team teaching. One course had three fascinating faculty members—a musicologist, a music theorist, and an ethnomusicologist—for myself and one other student! I don't think it gave me a very bounded idea of the discipline, more like a hodgepodge of things that seemed useful and had some common critical core. But essentially it had to do with Regula expressing personal interest in me and in my topic. Several other programs to which I'd applied looked at my project and said, "We're really interested in you, your academic background looks great, your writing looks good," and so forth, and when they met me, they put effort into recruiting me. But in almost every case when they looked at my proposed project (an ethnographic study of Mennonites), they said things like, "Ethnography? We're not interested in interviews and that sort of thing"; "What a thoroughly marginal group to study"; or even, "You're a great candidate, but you really need to study Brahms or Sibelius." But Regula said, "I'm very interested in Mennonites. I want you to write about them, and I'm going to work with you." It was that personal interest and openness that drew me in.

MS: At this early stage, were there any role models who really influenced the direction you took?

JD: Mostly they were people I accessed as writers. Of course, Regula was a huge influence. I would also say Jeff Titon. He was a strong influence on how I think and write. And besides that, there are lots of ethnomusicologists who've been role models for me, just because of the people they are. But in terms of people I read, some of the more interesting are symbolic interactionist theorists. Mennonite studies is sociological, so I had a good background in sociology, and I think sociologically. My mother took a sociology major, so even at home, we had this kind of analysis. Thinking back, she really influenced me in that way. I read a lot of Howie Becker and have continued thinking in a symbolic interactionist way. Jeff Titon and Howie Becker have both influenced me because they're very smart theorists, but they're plain talkers and people never disappear from what they do. To me, those are important values. That's why I didn't go into musicology: I was interested in people.

Building a Career

JD: When I finished my PhD, I taught for a year at Alberta. Michael Frishkopf (who was on my committee and was a great advisor and mentor) went to Egypt for a year, so I filled in for him. It was both a marvelous and terrible year, in the way that first teaching years often are. The two years before that, I had lived in Atlanta while I wrote my dissertation, because my wife went to grad school there. I found Tong Soon Lee [then at Emory University] through the *SEM Newsletter*. He adopted and mentored me—it was incredibly kind of him to take on an advisee for nothing. He read my drafts and took me out for coffee—it was neat. It was through him that I connected with Maryland after teaching at Alberta for a year.

MS: Tell me about the Maryland job.

JD: It's a really interesting job. I got it at the last minute. Carolina Robertson had just gone to South America and left all her advisees behind. They needed somebody who could teach the graduate courses she normally offered and advise her students. They wanted somebody who was really interested in writing and knew something about ethnographic methods. I was visiting my parents-in-law in Virginia when I got an email from Tong Soon to say that I should drop by Maryland. I canceled everything and went to Maryland to meet Rob Provine. Shortly thereafter, they offered me the job.

That was July 2004; in August I moved to Maryland and started teaching! The position is not tenure track. It's called a "visiting assistant professor" position and has a one-year contract. Each semester I teach a "big money" undergraduate course called "Music in Society" with 225 students and three TAs. In addition, I teach three graduate courses. Every year so far, one of those has been a two-semester fieldwork sequence. One is required for the MA; both are required for the PhD. I also teach a graduate seminar every year, the topic of which changes. I've taught things like "The Internet, Intellectual Property, and Ethnographic Representation" or "Popular Music and Social Theories of Community, Memory, and Nostalgia." They're all pretty theory-driven courses that tie into what I'm trying to write at the time. On top of that, I advise. Being non-tenure track, I would normally teach a 3-3 load, but I get a one-course reduction because I've got something like eighteen advisees! I've already graduated seven MA theses, so it's been a totally exceptional opportunity for this sort of a job.

MS: Do you have any sense of job security, or are you always looking elsewhere?

JD: Pragmatically I do, because they need more faculty lines for the number of graduate students they have. In an ideal situation, the advising load would be less and another faculty line or two would be helpful. So, pragmatically my job is quite secure: I provide a graduate faculty member who functions as such, I'm less expensive than if I were tenure-track faculty, and they don't have to go through the normal channels to get a faculty line.

MS: Do you get the same benefits—sabbaticals, retirement savings—as regular faculty?

JD: No, I don't even get travel money or access to some campus services. Those are down sides. The biggest downside for me is just that the job is somewhat secure and yet it certainly is not as secure as tenure and it doesn't offer the advancement that tenure would offer. So, while I love the job and students, I like my colleagues, and it's a very good environment, I can't put down roots in the community.

MS: In a practical sense, then, your job is basically a string of one-year positions, except that they're all in the same place. Do you still have the hope that there will be a tenure-track position at the end of it all, either at Maryland or elsewhere?

JD: Yes, that's the goal. I apply for everything that moves! I'm working at writing and going to all the conferences I can.

I first became interested in music after moving to Manitoba as a child because I had problems placing myself in a social space and had to figure out some way to do so in terms of what existed. That's true for ethno, too. I came to ethno with my own set of questions, and I wanted to use ethno as a way to address those questions. I still approach it that way; I'm very question driven. I'm interested in understanding the social world that I interact with. And I'm a theoretical thinker, or at least I'm interested in engaging with social theory and with contributing something that's quite new, not only something that uses social theory, but something that other social theorists might be able to use.

MS: How do you negotiate being a relatively liberal Christian with your professional life, especially when the subject of what you study is your own community, in a sense?

JD: Ellen Koskoff has been a big influence on me because the way she studies Judaism gives me a lot of things to work with on Mennonites. There are a lot of parallels. Reading her Lubavitcher book and looking at how she put herself into that story and the way she related to the community is part of the answer to how I work with the Christian thing. You're somewhat of an insider and an outsider at once.

MS: Doing fieldwork within the boundaries of the place you live also makes your work a little different. Traditionally, at least, ethnomusicologists go "over there." It doesn't surprise me that you mention Ellen as an influence.

JD: Yes, as well as admiring her writing greatly. I've also been trying to find all the ways in which my community is not my community. So, for instance, one jumping-off point for me has been shape-note music. There's a tradition of shape-note music that you find in the rural South. The first time I heard it, my hair stood on end and I said, "I must go study that." And then I found there were other traditions. I was living in Atlanta, so I could connect to the shape-note singers in that area, and found that I'd accidentally arrived in the heartland! And then in Virginia, where my wife is from, there's an older shape-note tradition that has not circulated the way that Sacred Harp has. It's a Mennonite tradition, and I knew the songs from that tradition, even though nobody outside the area sings them. I knew them from Manitoba and from Kansas. They were songs that had circulated into hymnals—only Mennonite hymnals in some cases—not elsewhere. So I've been working on this comparative case, attending shape-note singings. I try to maintain what I see as the value of the kind of work I'm doing: accountability and face-to-face connections, identification with people that's going to continue after I write. Perforce, I can't get away from it. I like that accountability and I like the kind of feeling-ful connection that I have with the community. But the community is not singular, and it gives me lots of interesting jumping-off places to other places and communities.

But placing myself is tricky: what I'm most interested in does not fit very well into a rubric of area studies. I've been told on occasion, "You write great stuff, but your data isn't interesting." Why are they not interesting? Well, they're white, mainstream

Christians. It's not exotic enough! So, when people ask me, "What do you do, what do you study?" I say something like, "Well, I'm interested in religious identity and trans-nationalism," or—more abstractly—"I'm interested in the hinge between discourse and practice," which is really what I'm interested in. Then they'll say, "So what area do you study?" And I'm always torn! Do I say Mennonites? I study American folk music, I study popular music, I study shape-note music, I study Korean music—which of these places should I use? So I've settled on "Well, I study North American music and I've also studied African music, so I have these two areas, but ultimately, I'm more interested in studying the connections between those places."

Update: March 15, 2017

I'm still an ethnomusicologist, but I am also a scholar, teacher, and administrator in a second field, and I am just about to begin a new position primarily as an administrator. I was in a non-tenure-track position when we first talked, at a good US state university, at which I understood I had a good chance at a tenure-track job in ethnomusicology when the line was approved. However, though I was a finalist for the position, it went to a senior candidate, as the position had been categorized "open rank" and a strong senior candidate was interested. After asking around on faculty, I learned that a competitive offer was one way to begin a discussion toward a tenure-track position at one's "home" institution.

I obtained an outside offer for a long-term interdisciplinary fellowship and, when it became clear that the university, due to budget constraints, could not make a retention offer, I moved to the postdoc [in the Thompson Writing Program at Duke University]. The postdoc immersed me in a second field, writing studies, which I found satisfying—especially since the ways ethnomusicology draws on both social scientific and humanist/critical traditions were valued. I continued to work toward an ethnomusicology position and received a number of interviews and a good tenure-track offer, which I received while a finalist for another job and which, due to my inexperience in negotiating this lucky but tricky circumstance, fell through. I had continued to work and publish in ethnomusicology, developing three book projects, the first of which (a collection) has recently been published, the second of which is in press, and the last of which is under contract. After another year on the job market, during which I applied both in ethnomusicology and writing studies, I had one finalist visit in eth-nomusicology and four job offers in my new field. I rejected three of these offers and took the fourth, which meant cutting short the process of being under consideration for the ethnomusicology position. But having lost a job previously due to being a less savvy negotiator than I should've been, that was the course I decided to take.

Since then I have mostly been working happily in my new position [in the University Writing Program at George Washington University], which is constructed in an interdisciplinary way, just as the postdoc was. It has offered some marvelous lateral freedom in comparison to my experiences in music departments, where canons, both ethnomusicological and musicological, are still so much of a part of what we do. The main challenge of a position like this has been establishing myself in two fields at once, which I've found stimulating but also time consuming and travel heavy (going, for example, to two sets of conferences, to say nothing of publishing in two fields).

And just this spring I am entering a new chapter. I was up for promotion in my writing studies position and had been growing into my role as an administrator as well as learning a lot through service work with SEM. A new administrative position [as vice president academic and academic dean at the Canadian Mennonite University] came across my desk—home, for me—and I decided to apply for it. The breadth of experience that ethnomusicology positioned me for, in ways I certainly hadn't anticipated, and that writing studies particularly developed, turned out, I think, to be good preparation for me to begin to think about administrative work as a meaningful way to collaborate across disciplines and communities. In the end, I was offered the position and am now preparing for it, as I teach my last seminars at my current institution and wrap up administrative work for the year. I am thrilled at the possibilities of my new position and at the same time, of course, sad to leave my colleagues, students, and friends.

Summing this up, my experience has pushed me toward a critical consciousness of the role of canonical musics, sites, and subjects in ethnomusicology and toward a critical understanding of the university as an *economic* player and the academic job market as, presently, a buyer's market (despite the very good intentions and hard work of faculty on hiring committees and senior colleagues). And it has prompted me to understand academe as a place that is in a real and deep transition in which, I think, ethnomusicology has important roles to play.

Christopher J. Miller (June 22, 2008)

PhD, Wesleyan University (Ethnomusicology)
Lecturer, Cornell University

Graduate Studies

CM: I started at Wesleyan University in the fall of 1998. I was drawn by the program's distinctive combination of experimental music composition and "world music," and the very strong offerings in gamelan in particular, with not one but two Javanese musicians on the faculty, Pak Sumarsam and Pak Harjito. I wanted to continue with composition, for my MA, but went in with the idea of continuing in ethnomusicology for my PhD, which is what I did. It was at Wesleyan that I first encountered the field of ethnomusicology in a serious way.

Prior passing exposure to ethnomusicology led me to think of it as a bit stuffy or stodgy. My first seminars were with Eric Charry, who has somewhat of a no-nonsense approach and an emphasis on solid ethnographic data for research. At first I felt some friction rubbing up against that approach, but now I really appreciate it. I guess I came to Wesleyan with a general intellectual orientation, but without having a rigorous grounding in theory as an undergraduate.

MS: So you thought ethnomusicology was "stuffy"?

CM: A little bit, yes. I think in part it was a reaction against having to become more disciplined. I remember having a transcription assignment. I had done lots of transcription as a student of gamelan and had figured out my own way of doing it. I had learned gamelan notation and I followed that model, especially for transcribing *kendhangan* drum parts. I used to record my teacher, transcribe after the fact, and study through a combination of my transcriptions and the recordings. So for my assignment, I had the idea of trying to transcribe the change in tempo. I ended up with a spiral kind of thing. You travel along the line at the same rate, so a smaller circle would take less time to go around than a bigger circle. I thought of this as a way of mapping how a piece slows down. I took a particular recording of "Gambir Sawit" and tried to transcribe it. I remember Eric Charry asking, "Where did you get the melody?" I said, "Well, it's 'Gambir Sawit.'" Eric asked, "Yes, but what's your source for it?" I answered, "It's a piece everybody knows, what do you mean, what's my source for it?" He used that as an occasion to teach me about the discipline of documentation and the importance of sources, which *now* I totally appreciate.

Building a Career

MS: You're now at a point in your career where you are finishing your dissertation at Wesleyan and just about to start your first job at Cornell University? How do you feel about that? What do you see as your trajectory from here?

CM: Well, one thing I've thought about is how where you end up can determine certain directions you might go. For example, that Hampshire College job had the promise of a job-related reason to develop my creative side. That might be there at Cornell, but not in the same way, because I won't be teaching. They have composition teachers already. There is the potential to make connections with composers and with the percussion ensemble. The percussion teacher there is into improvised and contemporary music. Marty Hatch wants to make gamelan relevant to the department to try to increase the odds of them making an effort to keep it (and keep a teacher). The other attraction of Cornell, of course, is the very strong Southeast Asia program, especially the Indonesia program. A lot of major Indonesia scholars have gone through Cornell. They have huge resources at the library and in the collections there. I wouldn't necessarily have sought out area studies as a basis for further scholarly work, but being at Cornell, I can take advantage of that.

I've imagined a second research project being something on contemporary art music, possibly in North America, for practical reasons like being closer to home and not needing *another* language. My project overlaps the margins of ethnomusicology and musicology. I feel I have intellectual interests in common with people on the musicology end who are interested in ethnomusicology and in a more culturally grounded approach to music scholarship. A bunch of these people are starting to come to the ethnomusicology meetings rather than, or in addition to, going to the musicology meetings. I'm interested in trying to position myself somewhere between the two. But at the same time, I'm struck by where my first job will be. There might not be immediate opportunities to pursue this at Cornell; instead, there will be other opportunities to pursue, so I'll have to take advantage of that.

MS: Are you saying that you see yourself as existing on the cusp of ethnomusicology and musicology? Is that where you see a niche for yourself?

CM: Yes. I used to joke that the way that I felt about ethnomusicology is kind of the way I feel about being Canadian. That is, it's a great country, there are a lot of great things about it—like universal healthcare, social programs, and such—but I don't want to limit myself to it. Similarly with ethnomusicology, there's a lot that I really appreciate about it—like ethnography and the idea that music is about people making music rather than an object that you study on a piece of paper—but as a composer, there's also a sense that world musics offer us sonic models, instruments to use, or musical ideas to borrow. That was another thing about both George Lewis and Martin Bartlett: though they both thought about the relationship of music to the social, they were also very committed to experimental music that wasn't populist.

MS: I remember hearing you talk at Hampshire College, and you quoted Clifford Geertz's comment, "We're not there to mimic," and then you said, "But wait a minute— that *is* what I'm doing." That struck me as an interesting predicament for somebody who calls himself an ethnomusicologist.

CM: Well, of course, that is another part of my professional and musical identity that I sometimes take a bit for granted: a performer of gamelan. I can take it for granted in the Northeast because there are enough opportunities for it to be a part of my life and part of my work. I'm sure that will change depending on where I am. Sometimes I worry that I rest on my laurels and am not developing as a performer. I don't spend time studying new pieces. I maintain the level that I've got to through playing at *klenengan*. I'm pretty good at bluffing my way through stuff, which is a recognized skill, but it's one notch down as a legitimate way to actually know pieces. That's a bit of a tangent to the question about mimicking, but when I referred to that Geertz quote, I was thinking about the predicament of being a performer of a music that has a tenuous existence in the cultural context of North America. It's closer to being possible for gamelan than it is for a lot of musics, but it's still not really possible to be a full-time professional performer of gamelan. So what does it mean, then, to put so much energy into it? That's part of the reason that I don't put more energy into it than I do, because I've gotten to a level that I still get hired for gigs to play *suling*. If there is a piece I need to know, then I'll just brush up on it.

Update: July 19, 2016

When Margaret interviewed me for this book, in June 2008, I was preparing to move to Ithaca, New York, for a one-year contract as a two-thirds-time lecturer in music at Cornell University. Eight years later, I am still at Cornell. I am now a senior lecturer, and full time, after having added steel band to an assignment that has otherwise been focused squarely on Indonesian music. More specifically, I have, every semester since I started, directed the gamelan ensemble and taught an introductory-level course that combines hands-on study of gamelan with a seminar component that examines the broader range of music in contemporary Indonesia. This past spring (2017) I taught a new course I developed, called "Music in and of East Asia."

Ruby Ornstein (October 24, 2008)

PhD, UCLA (Ethnomusicology)
Adjunct Assistant Professor, College of Staten Island, CUNY

Graduate Studies

RO: I went to UCLA in the fall of '59 because they gave me the biggest fellowship. I planned to get a master's degree in music theory, return to New York, and teach in the city schools. I started taking the required courses and seminars and met students who were studying "ethnomusicology," a thing I had never heard of before. I became very good friends with one of them, Lois Anderson, a girl from Brainerd, Minnesota. Lois was there to study African music, which I thought was pretty weird.

I went to some Javanese gamelan concerts at Schoenberg Hall and found that fascinating. One night in my second year, I stopped in at a Balinese gamelan rehearsal. Mantle Hood had arranged for two Balinese drummers to teach at UCLA. I walked into the small room and there was a tremendous noise. It sounded like cacophony to me. They were missing a *klentong* player, so I sat down. I had no idea what I was doing, but one of the drummers pointed to me every time we got to the middle of the *gongan* and I hit the gong. And that was it! I started going to rehearsals regularly. Lois and I played interlocking parts together. I remember going to a party—the ethno people always had a lot of parties with great food—and Mantle sat down on the floor next to me and started to talk about changing my major. I told him, "You should let me make up my own mind. If it's a mistake, it'll be my mistake, but if it's the right track, I'll have made the decision." He said, "OK." So I made up my mind that this was what I wanted to do.

It was the Balinese music that absolutely grabbed me. I had no idea what was going on, but I was mesmerized. At the first sound, I just drowned in it. I took a course with Colin McPhee and spent a lot of time talking with him. I was lucky to have done that because he died while I was away. And, as they say, the rest is history. They gave me a fellowship, called the Fellowship for Study of Music of the Orient, or something like that.

Graduate student life at UCLA was a wonderful experience. We had various study groups and what we then called "native informants" for each of them. I didn't join all of them, but I did join the Javanese gamelan and the group from Ghana. We learned West African drumming and played at the Monterey Jazz Festival. That was some experience—the Modern Jazz Quartet and Thelonious Monk were on the same program! When the Africans arrived—one from Ghana, one from Nigeria—and needed a place to stay, I took them around. That's when I discovered how unwelcome they were in West Los Angeles. People would not rent to them. In fact, my roommate and I were asked to move by our landlady in Brentwood because she didn't like the color of our friends' skin. She said we gave the place "a bad tone."

TS: Who were some of the people in your cohort?

RO: Lois Anderson, Sarah Stalder, and Max Harrell. Max was in charge of maintaining the instruments, so Mantle Hood wouldn't let him leave, and it took him forever to finish his dissertation research. Then there was David Morton, who went to Thailand, and Donn Borcherdt, who went to Mexico. We had the greatest parties at Donn's house! He was a promising guy, but he died while doing his fieldwork.

TS: How did you conceive of what you were going to do in Bali?

RO: I talked to Colin McPhee about what to study. He was always concerned that the old music was going to disappear. I wanted to study *angklung* music, but he pooh-poohed that idea. I stuck with it as it was in my proposal, but once I got there, I changed my mind. I don't think anyone really cared.

I was in Bali from the end of '63 to the middle of '66. I went there as a fellow of the Institute of Ethnomusicology, so they gave me beautiful business cards with a logo and my name. Everywhere I went, I handed out those cards, and people gave me their cards in return. I started out in San Francisco at the consulate and got letters of introduction. You have no idea how far I got with those letters! In Jakarta I met someone from the Sukawati family. He and his wife owned a house in Ubud in the palace compound, but they didn't live there because he was with the Foreign Office in Jakarta. So that's where I lived—Puri Kantor, in Ubud. I had my own house in the palace compound. His uncle introduced me everywhere as his daughter. It was an entrée I couldn't have gotten any other way. When I finally arrived in Bali, the chief of protocol was there to meet me, because he was also a member of the family. The mother of the man whose house I was renting didn't speak any Indonesian at all, just Balinese, and when she opened her mouth, it was all red. I thought to myself, "This woman is bleeding to death! Why isn't someone taking her to the hospital? She's going to die right in front of me!" Of course, I didn't know about betel then.

The two wonderful Balinese I had gotten to know so well at UCLA were now back home. Tjokorda Mas was a minor member of the Sukawati family, and Wayan Gandera was principal drummer of the gamelan at Peliatan and son of Madé Lebah, who had worked with Colin McPhee. Because of these connections, I went to Peliatan to study. They didn't have the name Gunung Sari yet; that came later. When I heard them play for the first time, my jaw dropped and I realized what duds we were in Los Angeles!

TS: You said you were interested in angklung at the outset. How did the change in your topic come about?

RO: I realized angklung was old music. *Kebyar*, in contrast, was the music of the moment. I could actually record music that had been recently composed, especially in the north. No one had ever recorded that music. One of the composers, Merdana, was killed in 1965—because he was a Communist, they said. He wrote *Kebyar Teruna Jaya*, a dance piece that Wayan Gandera learned. Gedé Manik wrote an entirely different piece with the same name that everyone plays and dances; but Gandera learned Merdana's and taught it to Çudamani something like forty years later, almost from his deathbed. It's remarkable that he remembered the piece. When I listened to the Çudamani version and compared it to my recording, it was almost identical. He really had an ear!

I was *so* fortunate. They took me in at Peliatan, even though I was a foreign woman. Anak Agung Gedé Mandera—in whose palace compound they practiced and performed—treated me like a daughter. I started out learning their current repertoire, and when I was good enough, they invited me to become a member of the group. To have that experience was priceless. The only time I couldn't play with them was when they played for Sukarno at the palace in Tampaksiring, because he didn't like Americans. Ordinary people wouldn't believe I was there to study gamelan, because women didn't play gamelan. Eventually, I asked what the word was for a gamelan in Balinese; when I said "*magambel*," *then* they got it, but they were stunned that a woman was studying music. The local people all came to see.

When I arrived, schools like KOKAR (Konservatori Karawitan) were just starting. They tried to get Madé Lebah to teach there, but he wasn't interested in doing that. He was a really remarkable person. In those days, musicians didn't travel outside their milieu, but he always knew where the best groups were. I was his first student after Colin McPhee. I traveled around and made a lot of recordings with him. I was very fortunate, just as Colin McPhee was very fortunate. McPhee did not give enough credit to Madé Lebah when he wrote his books.

TS: McPhee didn't give enough credit to a lot of people—like his wife, for example.

RO: True. Did you ever meet Jane Belo? I had tea with her once in New York. I copy-edited the Balinese words for her book *Traditional Balinese Culture* [Belo 1970]. I had a friend who was with the Indonesian mission to the UN, Anak Agung Istri Muter, who was from the ruling family of Gianyar. Muter introduced me to Jane Belo, who asked, "Did you know that I was there with Colin?"

TS: Who would know that from reading his work?

RO: Right! McPhee also demeaned Lebah's contribution to his work; he spoke of him as his chauffeur. He gave a lot of credit to Wayan Lotring as a composer, but not enough to Lebah. While it's true that Lebah did drive him around, he also *taught* him. Colin McPhee was a very interesting man and a fabulous cook. He was also a great drinker, which is what killed him in the end. He had a lot of trouble finishing *Music in Bali* [1966]. He got a residency one summer from the Huntington Hartford Foundation—I drove him there. In the end it was a pity he wasn't alive when that book was published. No one will *ever* write a book like that book. It's the Bible for Balinese music. In class he gave out little snippets of old compositions that I still have. I'm sure everyone who took his classes has them too.

TS: Did Madé Lebah play the interlocking parts with you?

RO: Yes, we played whatever I wanted. That's why he was so wonderful. After I made recordings, I would transcribe them and then check the transcription, often with Gandera, because he had a really remarkable ear. (I recently wrote an article about Gandera for *Asian Music* [2006]. I probably knew him better than anybody else because I knew him when he was young.)

TS: Were you in Bali through the anticommunist killings of 1965?

RO: Yes. I saw some horrible things. When I first got there, I went up to see the devastation from the volcanic eruption of Gunung Agung. Houses were buried up to the roofs. It was terrible. And, in 1965, I went back to that same area. I went back to look at the rivers. The water ran red. People were taken away and you never saw them again.

TS: You stayed until '66. How did you finish your stay there?

RO: At a certain point, people were so frightened, they were not playing gamelan. There wasn't any point staying, as I couldn't make any more recordings. The situation was so bad that you couldn't get kerosene for cook stoves; people were using wood. After a while, there wasn't enough wood, so people were burning other things, like garbage. It was not possible to do any work, so in March or April I thought I should leave. I had done enough, so I packed up and distributed everything I owned to the people who worked for me. I had a big send-off and we went down to the airport and waited for the plane. In typical Indonesian fashion, it didn't arrive, so I went back and had to do it all over again later. I had two leave-takings.

I went to Jakarta but left when a friend of mine (the Sukawati in the Foreign Office) told me that it would be a good time to leave. There were a lot of trials going on then. I flew back via Singapore, Bangkok, and Holland, where I met Ernst Heins and did some research before I finally came home.

Building a Career

TS: Did you go back to Los Angeles?

RO: No, I went to New York because I was offered a position at Queens College and had family in New York. I started teaching at Queens in 1966. Ultimately, I would say, it was an unpleasant, unfriendly, and hostile-to-ethnomusicology situation. They thought ethnomusicology was silly. It was also hostile to me as a woman, even though I was a graduate. There were other women on the faculty, and they weren't treated nicely either. I liked the students, but I didn't care for the way I was treated.

I went to Brown University in 1969. It wasn't a very big program back then, though they had a *gamelan angklung*. It didn't work out well for me, but I finished my dissertation not long after I left.

TS: How long were you at Brown?

RO: I was there for two years, until '71. After that I came back to New York. I was a visiting lecturer at Yale for a year. I had to make a choice at that point: stay on the East Coast or move for an academic position. I chose to stay and get married. I never regretted that choice. I married a man who read and understood my dissertation. I'm not saying he understood all the technicalities of it, but he understood a hell of a lot. I never bothered to try and get another job. We raised two children in New York. Our daughter went to Yale, did her graduate work at the University of Chicago, and is an editor. She's married with two children. Our son went to Wesleyan and played in the Javanese gamelan. He lived in Chicago for ten years and played in the Javanese group Friends of the Gamelan. He and his wife are now at Yale, where he is a graduate student at the School of Forestry and Environmental Science (Yale also has a Javanese gamelan).

TS: What connection have you maintained to ethnomusicology over the years? It seems like you started writing articles again in the last couple of years.

RO: I didn't maintain any formal connection, but I kept up and I listened. I made a recording when I first came back for Lyrichord [Ornstein 1967]. It's still available—it was released first as an LP, then as a cassette, and now it's available on CD, number

7179, with detailed notes. Now I'm doing a new CD for the Smithsonian. It will have very good notes that will be available online. I want to do another CD, particularly of the North Balinese kebyar music that I recorded.

TS: Do you feel about your stuff the way I feel about the stuff I did in India around the same time? Hearing the old singers, who are all gone? Nobody cares about that style anymore. They all want snazzy sitar and *sarod* playing now. The vocal stuff I heard and recorded has all gone.

RO: People like us are almost historical ethnomusicologists. The kind of kebyar music that's being composed today is not terribly interesting to me. I wanted to know how they did it, not how they're going to do it. Because every time someone comes along, I hope he's going to do it differently. In the past, I think what they've done is to look at older pieces and pick out pieces and say, "Yes, I like that, I'll use that, but I'll change that, and I'll fix that," and make a new piece.

I was there at an interesting time and I was fortunate enough to meet interesting people. For instance, I met a Dutchman named Bernard IJzerdraat, who was known in Indonesia as Suryabrata. He was a graduate student of Jaap Kunst in Holland at the same time as Mantle Hood. In fact, they were rivals. IJzerdraat went to Indonesia, married a Sundanese woman, and stayed there. He lived in Jakarta with his wife, children, and a Sundanese gamelan. He started a foundation that gave awards to Claire Holt and myself. She got the highest award for her book and I got the next award for my record. We went to the embassy in Washington to receive them. He was a wonderful man.

TS: It seems that you have gotten the urge to get involved again?

RO: Well, I started teaching again. My husband, Robert Ludwig, has been at the College of Staten Island, one of the CUNY colleges, for many years. He teaches portrait drawing as an adjunct in the Department of Performing and Creative Arts. A couple of years ago, we invited the chair of his department to our annual tree-trimming party. She looked at our bookcases and asked, "Who is the ethnomusicologist here?" We talked and she ended up asking if I'd like to teach a course; now I'm teaching world music there.

TS: When did you start doing that?

RO: In 2007. This was my second year. Bob and I go out there every Monday evening. It's an undergraduate course that students can take to fulfill a humanities requirement. I get a really interesting mixed bag of students. They come in the evening after they've worked all day. The school has nothing—no films, no CDs—so I have to borrow everything from the library at the Lincoln Center for the Performing Arts. Next year I'll probably teach one or two more sections during the day.

Update: June 26, 2016

I am still teaching at the College of Staten Island. My students now come from even more diverse backgrounds. I have completed the CD of gamelan angklung for Smithsonian [Ornstein 2011]. I chose the music from field recordings I made in 1963–66. The CD includes extensive liner and track notes (*From Kuno to Kebyar: Balinese Gamelan Angklung*, SFW 50411). I am preparing a paper about an influential Balinese composer named Ketut Merdana, who was murdered in the aftermath of the 1965 coup in Indonesia. Owing to a recent change in the Balinese political climate, I can write frankly about him for the first time.

Marcello Sorce Keller (October 25, 2007)

PhD, University of Illinois (Ethnomusicology)
Serial Visiting Professor

Graduate Studies

MSK: I applied to and was accepted by the University of Illinois at Champaign-Urbana in 1974. I also obtained a Fulbright travel grant, inclusive of an orientation program at Indiana University. My parents were relieved that I was on my way to becoming a professor—a much more dignified profession, in their eyes, than arranging popular music.

MS: When you did your research on American programs, did you have much sense of what ethnomusicology was at the time?

MSK: I didn't have a clear idea about the field in all its articulations, but I did have a sense there were major differences among institutions where ethnomusicology was practiced. I had a sense that, for instance, studying ethnomusicology at Illinois or UCLA might have been a very different experience. However, my major preoccupation was to be accepted at one of the good institutions of the time. I was accepted at both the University of Michigan and the University of Illinois. At Illinois financial support was also available. I later discovered that Gerard Béhague had played a role in getting me accepted. He particularly liked, as he told me later, my double background. And, when I arrived, it was a welcome surprise to be able to speak French with an American professor, especially since initially I felt rather insecure about my English.

I enormously enjoyed campus life at Illinois; in particular, the high concentration of so many brilliant people in such a small place. The courses I took with Bruno Nettl, Charles Hamm, Lawrence Gushee, and Alexander Ringer fundamentally changed my attitude toward music, even beyond what I could have imagined. I was very fortunate to have, from the very beginning, a part-time assistantship that provided tuition, fee waiver, and a small salary so that I could survive economically.

Once my course work was finished, another fortunate turn occurred: sociologist Luigi Del Grosso Destreri hired me at the University of Trento in Italy. In addition to some teaching duties, there was the possibility of doing fieldwork in the Alpine area, part of which could be turned into my dissertation. The project was rather fuzzily defined at the outset. I only knew I was going to find in the Trento area a thriving oral tradition and an equally thriving tradition of choral groups called "Alpine choirs." Some kind of interaction was bound to exist between those two environments, living side by side. The Sociology Department wanted someone to document the oral tradition for some future use to be decided at a later time. For the purpose of my dissertation I obviously needed more than just song collections.

TS: Alpine choirs? Tell us more about what they are.

MSK: Alpine choirs are semi-professional groups that perform four-part arrangements of traditional songs, songs (or new pieces imitating their style) that circulate across the greater Alpine area, from France to Italy, Switzerland, Austria, and Slovenia. It became apparent to me that when such choirs take their tunes from the oral environment, they by necessity adapt them to their performing format. When that happens, people in the countryside or in the mountains, the original carriers of the repertoire, at some point get to relearn their own songs from the choral versions they hear in live performance, through recordings, or on the radio. In the process, a considerable amount of change occurs. My dissertation was therefore a study of this sort of ongoing feedback relationship, between the "oral" and the "choral" environments.

Building a Career

MSK: At the outset, there seemed to be the possibility of a long-term job at the University of Trento. This did not materialize, so once my fieldwork was completed, I returned to the US, defended my dissertation, obtained my PhD, and began looking for a job there. So I landed a couple of temporary positions. The first was at Northwestern University in Evanston, Illinois, replacing Paul Berliner, who was on sabbatical in Africa. The second was at the University of Illinois at Chicago, where I replaced Philip Bohlman while actively looking for the next position.

At that point I realized that my parents had aged considerably and needed my help. They were living in Bergamo, Italy, and I had no choice but to leave the States and look for a job somewhere in their vicinity. The Milan Conservatory had just opened a musicology program, and I was happy to join the faculty there. It entailed teaching more than full time: music history courses for general music students and ethnomusicology for musicology majors. It was a pretty heavy load. I was there from 1986 to 1993.

Shortly after my father died, I started wondering whether I really wanted to spend the rest of my professional life in Milan and felt a growing wish to reconnect with Switzerland.

So I conceived the adventurous plan of resigning from the Milan Conservatory and moving to Lugano in Switzerland (not much farther away from where my mother lived than Milan). She was delighted about my decision. However, the adventurous part of the decision consisted in retiring from regular, full-time work. I moved to Lugano in 1993 and, luckily, never regretted it, because new opportunities arose. I started making radio programs for Swiss Radio, where I had a weekly hour for some ten years, and did some music history teaching in a nearby school of music. Finally, around 2000—better late than never—I discovered my true avocation: "professional visiting professor/scholar"! A visiting professor does not need to bother with local problems and is only concerned with teaching and research. I love that! So I spent a few years visiting Australia, the United States, Malta, and the UK.

TS: Can you compare the experience of teaching and being a professor of ethnomusicology in Italy, and in the various places that you've been, with your experiences in the United States?

MSK: It may be an overgeneralization, but I feel a professor of ethnomusicology feels better supported and understood in the US than in continental Europe. That is simply because in the US, ethnomusicology is better established academically. In Western Europe, with the notable exception of the UK and Ireland, it gained relatively little space in academia. Even in Germany, where according to the official history, ethnomusicology was originally born as *vergleichende Musikwissenschaft* (comparative musicology), a history Germans are proud to tell, professorships are very few. In Europe, even more than in the US, the field of music studies remains strongly in the hands of historical musicologists—hard to believe in this day and age. In Austria, and Vienna in particular, ethnomusicology has developed much better. In Switzerland we only have at the moment one university chair for ethnomusicology, in Bern, occupied by Britta Sweers. One single chair is hardly adequate for an entire country—admittedly a small one—that comprises three language culture areas. Whenever a position is available, departments usually like to fill it with a historical musicologist, especially so if they already have a "token" ethnomusicologist.

TS: How about Slovenia, Croatia, and other countries in the region?

MSK: I do not know too much about what happens in that area by direct experience, but I get the sense that things are moving and growing there considerably faster than in Western Europe. For instance, in Ljubljana, Svanibor Pettan finally brought the official seat of the ICTM back to good old Europe! What I lament about Central and Western Europe is that ethnomusicology is seldom considered of equal importance with the other branches of music studies dealing with Bach and Beethoven (even when scholarly papers, with footnotes and all, concern themselves with how many times those great composers got the flu). Such extreme focus on the Western literate tradition makes it difficult to fight old stereotypes, and it is not unusual to come across doctoral students who ignore that "music" is no universal concept, that polyphony was not invented in the West, and that music does not necessarily need to be "artistic" in order to be "good." A "token ethnomusicologist" here and there is not enough to make the general public realize that conservatories of "music" actually deal with less than 1 percent of the musics that were made and are being made on this planet of ours, and there is so much more out there to explore.

TS: And how do you feel about developments that have taken place in ethnomusicology since the days when we were students?

MSK: So much has changed! The idea that cultural traits and musical traditions may be neatly distributed on the map and color-coded for convenience (like George P. Murdock once did with his *Ethnographic Atlas* [1967], and later Lomax still implied with his Cantometrics [1968]) has revealed all its limitations. We have also learned how unsatisfactory it is to study traditional musics without taking into consideration how they merge with popular repertoires, and how constantly they are being translated into new different frames of meaning. When we were students we saw the beginnings of urban ethnomusicology; later we were witness to, or even took part in the development of, themes such as "gender," "identity," and "conflict and war." To be sure, ethnomusicologists today can no longer be defined by the geographic area they study but rather, also, by the processes they investigate.

There is, however, one development that makes me uncomfortable. I see ethnomusicology losing ground that it could legitimately claim as its own. [There was a time when] the accepted wisdom was that historical musicology deals with the literate tradition of the West, while "all the rest" is for ethnomusicologists to have (without even ruling out entirely the possibility that an ethnomusicology of Western music could be developed). What actually happened is that other "musicologies," new ones, developed independently from ethnomusicology. Popular music studies have grown enormously over the last twenty years or so, and even though many ethnomusicologists deal with popular musics, most popular music scholars (I think of Richard Middleton, Philip Tagg, or Franco Fabbri, for example) do not claim to be ethnomusicologists at all. Other fields have developed as well—cultural musicology, sound studies, ecomusicology, "zoo-musicology," for example. There is, in my view, a danger that these might develop in total independence, further increasing the fragmentation of music studies. Today, music scholarship is even more diversified and fragmented than it ever was—I am tempted to say that we live in the "age of musicologies," and it is very hard to imagine where this proliferation will lead.

TS: Of all the "musicologies" you mentioned "zoo-musicology" is possibly the one that fewest people are aware of. Tell us something more about it.

MSK: Some one hundred years ago, scholars of the Hornbostel generation had such a broad view of music that they even asked themselves whether human beings really are the only living creatures producing meaningful sound. That question was related to the other question they were trying to answer, that of the origins of music. If we consider the evolutionistic outlook of the time, it makes sense to look for its origins among "primitive" people and even further among nonhuman animals. Over the past thirty years or so, scholars in the area of animal behavior have been bringing up new information that is extraordinarily exciting and, at this point, it seems imperative to study nonhuman musicality if we wish to understand what, if anything, makes human musicality special. The result of this imperative is that "bio-musicology" and "zoo-musicology" are rapidly developing as independent fields. I do not like that too much.

I personally look at zoo-musicology as an area conceptually part of ethnomusicology. Marine biologists tell us that humpback whales produce organized sounds over a long span of time and these sounds are highly structured, idiosyncratic to single populations within the same species (and therefore "cultural"), and are structurally variable in some of their segments and not in others, according to rules that can be extrapolated from practice; when they add that humpbacks from one population may learn a song from another group and adapt it the way they like it, that is what in ethnomusicology we call "oral process."

Update: June 23, 2016

Over the past few years I have become more sedentary. I am officially retired, delighted to keep in touch with academia as an adjunct in the Musicology Institute at the University of Bern. I still occasionally make radio or TV programs, continue to do research, and publish. It is a rather congenial mix of things for me, and I wish myself more of the same.

Julie Strand (July 5, 2010)

PhD, Wesleyan University (Ethnomusicology)
Serial temporary positions
Postdoc at Northeastern University

Graduate Studies

It was four years before I finally went to grad school. During the fall of 1997 I took French at a community college. I applied to the University of Wisconsin, where I might have studied with Lois Anderson, who did work on Ganda xylophones, but ended up choosing to go to Arizona State University because they offered me money. I liked ASU because the website described the program as emphasizing fieldwork, and I knew I wanted to go outside the country for fieldwork. I started in the summer of 1998.

TS: You knew this was a stepping-stone to a PhD and that we didn't have a PhD program at ASU, right?

JS: I had no intention of doing a PhD at that point. I just wanted to get an MA. I still had a bit of a bad taste from being in college. I didn't even know what ethnomusicologists actually did. As a matter of fact, you and Rich Haefer took us grad students out for pizza, and that's how we learned about professional things. In 1999 and 2000 I went to Senegal and the Gambia with Mark Sunkett as part of his "Drums of Senegal" project, an ongoing research project on *sabar* and other Senegambian drum traditions. He went every summer and hosted a group of students and other interested folks for drum and dance lessons and an amazing cultural experience. I went off by myself and studied *balafon* for a week in Gambia with a Guinean musician. That was the basis for my master's thesis, "Style and Substance: Improvisational Trends in Mandinka Balafon Music" [Strand 2000].

TS: Since you had no intention of going on for a PhD when you came to ASU, what changed your mind?

JS: I found I really enjoyed it, and, to be honest, I think I was pretty good at it. You all encouraged me to continue, so in the spring of 2000 I applied to programs at Wesleyan, UCLA, Texas, Washington, and the University of Michigan. Wesleyan had Eric Charry (who was, of course, working in an area close to what I wanted) and Anthony Braxton. I loved it there. The only music PhDs were in ethnomusicology or composition, and I loved that everyone was an active musician. Ethnomusicologists are often more into social theory than the music itself and don't play enough. You can't forget the music. I did a lot of playing, including Javanese gamelan for the first time.

TS: What were you thinking about for field research?

JS: My main ideas were Burkina Faso and language-music connections. I was really interested in surrogate musical languages. Luckily for me, things worked out really well. It happened that there was an amateur ethnomusicologist in Vienna, Andreas Szabo, who had gotten very interested in the music of the Sambla people of Burkina Faso and had adopted a boy, Mamadou Diabate, from a *jeli* [hereditary professional musician] family. The Sambla are members of the northwest Mande ethnolinguistic group, and while they bear common Mande jeli surnames (Diabate and Konate), their language is not understood by anyone outside the Sambla community. Szabo had read Charry's book, *Mande Music* [2000], and wrote to him to say how much he enjoyed it. In the e-mail he mentioned Mamadou and Sambla music, hoping Eric or someone he knew would be interested in doing research on the Sambla. Eric told me about Andreas's idea. I applied for, and got, a Fulbright, so in the fall of 2002 I went to Paris to meet with Patrick Royer, a French anthropologist who was at the time the only other scholar who had written a dissertation on the Sambla. After meeting him,

I swung by the Musée de l'Homme and met with Hugo Zemp, who had also worked with xylophone music in Cote d'Ivoire and later produced a documentary on it. Then I went to Vienna to meet Andreas and Mamadou, and finally on to Burkina Faso.

TS: How were your language skills by that time?

JS: I had taken four semesters of Bamana over two summers in the SCALI (Summer Cooperative African Language Institute) program, in 2001 at the University of Wisconsin and 2002 at Michigan State University. I studied Bamana because Jula is the trade-language version of Bamana and is spoken as a lingua franca in the western part of Burkina Faso. The Mossi are the largest single ethnic group in Burkina, but they live mainly on the central plateau of Burkina, which surrounds the capital, Ouagadougou. Mooré (the Mossi language) is from the Gur ethnolinguistic family, which is culturally and linguistically quite distant from Sambla and other Mande language groups.

I was there for eighteen months, from October 2002 to May 2004. My Fulbright was for a year, but I stayed eighteen months. I lived in Bobo (Dioulasso) and used that as my center of operations. From there I would motorbike around to the Sambla villages in the western part of Burkina Faso. I had to live in Bobo because they had electricity there, which I needed for my batteries and so forth. There were fourteen Sambla villages, about twenty-five thousand people in all. Their music emphasizes a large, three-person xylophone called the *baan*. It's some of the most incredible music I've ever heard.

The work was very demanding, and the language problem was considerable. I mostly depended on Jula, which has two tones. I found Sambla, which has three tones, to be very difficult. I was of course interested in music and surrogate languages, and the jelis would laugh when I told them that. They'd say, "We've been spending our whole lives learning and dealing with this; you think you can just come and learn it in a year?" Then, the ideas they had about me were a problem: first of all I was thirty and single. I was constantly dealing with misunderstanding and misapprehensions of what I was trying to do. From their perspective, as a single woman, my main objective *had* to be to find a husband and have children. So they would make up stories about me. And as a white woman, who obviously had to be rich, and who—of course—had a house full of black servants back home, I was always a spectacle wherever I went. I wished I could just take a walk someplace without having someone yell, *Toubabu* ("White person") at me. I went weeks and months without seeing another white face and without hearing or speaking any English. It was isolating for sure. I was very lucky with my teacher Sadama Diabate, though. There was never any sexual tension there, unlike some other researchers I knew who might be told by someone, "Ok, I'll be your teacher, but you have to sleep with me." I gave money to his family to build a house, as a form of payment.

TS: Did you have problems of access?

JS: Not much. The main problem was that I couldn't go into cemeteries, where some ceremonies took place, because women in general were prohibited from ceremonies during the burial process. No one ever explained why, but those were the rules, so I obeyed them. And sometimes they didn't tell me about things. They'd say, "We just had a big celebration of (whatever)," and I'd say, "Oh, why didn't you tell me?" Also the living situation in Bobo was difficult because I lived in a compound with a lot of other people in the family and had virtually no privacy. I had my own room, but my teacher was in the next room and others were always around. They thought nothing of coming into your room at 5 A.M., making noise, and so forth. I had a terrible time sleeping. I had insomnia for a long time, not to mention bad amoebic dysentery (three times!). I finally had to rent my own house to get some privacy so I could work and sleep. And then they would ask, "What did we do to displease you?" It's not normal to live by yourself over there, of course.

TS: Did you hire a cook or were you eating *to* [millet porridge]?

JS: No, I did my own cooking but was often served *to* and other local staples when I was in the villages or at someone else's house for dinner. I did hire a night guard, which was necessary for security. He would watch over the house at night and go home during the day.

TS: Who would you say have been the most influential people for you in ethno-musicology?

JS: Oh, Eric Charry, for sure. He was great to work with and kept me honest, helping me stay on track. Mark Slobin, too. He would do what we called "dropping the bomb." It would just be a little sentence in which he would ask about something, and I would think, "Omigod, I've got to completely rethink this." Mark Sunkett is another big influence. I was inspired by the true passion he had for what he was doing, and I would think, "Yeah, that's why I do this!"

TS: How about others who might not have been your direct teachers?

JS: Michael Veal at Yale (whom I've been friends with since Wesleyan) gave me good feedback and practical advice. I like his writing. He writes very accessibly for those who are not necessarily ethnomusicologists. The idea is to "translate your personal experiences and let the passion show through." I've always respected Bruno Nettl, who can write elegantly and profoundly, but still clearly and simply. Also, Steve Feld, who zeroes in on the music and says we should go "into the music; don't be separated from the music."

Building a Career

I came back to the US in May 2004. In 2004–05 I taught steel band at Wesleyan and started teaching lots of places. I taught "American Popular Music" in fall 2005 at Trinity College in Hartford, Connecticut, and "World Music" and "Film Music in Cross-Cultural Perspective" in fall 2006 at Emerson College in Boston. The film music course was an ethnomusicology-based approach to the subject, different from the usual film music courses. I'd had some contact with that approach through Mark Slobin, whose book *Global Soundtracks* is now out [Slobin 2008]. At both Trinity and Emerson I was what they called a "visiting lecturer" and was paid by the course. In the spring of 2007 I went on the Semester at Sea. I took some African xylophones and had a xylophone ensemble on board. From June to July 2007 I taught in Ghana for Lewis and Clark College, for my friend Franya Berkman. I taught about expressive culture and ethnic groups in Ghana; we'd go different places like Ewe country, Ashanti, and so on.

TS: Can I ask whether you had any health insurance during this time?

JS: I kept my student status at Wesleyan until I finished my PhD, so I had some kind of TA insurance, which would pay some hospitalization if I needed it.

TS: Were you paying into Social Security?

JS: At Wesleyan grad students were exempt from paying Social Security. I moved to Boston in the fall of 2007 and had one class on African American music at Tufts University. In the spring of 2008 I gave courses at Brandeis University ("World Music Survey"), Northeastern University ("World Music"), and Tufts ("History of Rock and Roll"). I was also tutoring for SATs throughout this time. In the summer of 2008 I taught "World Music" at Tufts. The next academic year, 2008–09, I taught two classes per semester at Tufts and felt like a grownup for the first time because I actually had benefits! I also taught a course at Northeastern, filling in for Steve Cornelius in the spring of 2009. I was essentially for hire; people would e-mail me and ask, "Can you teach this or that course?"

TS: Were you doing any playing?

JS: I hadn't played my clarinet since I'd gone on field research, and I was really sorry about that. I joined a Balinese gamelan gong kebyar at MIT. I'd heard Gamelan Galak Tika, directed by Evan Ziporyn, so I contacted him and said, "Can I play with you?" In 2009–10 I taught at MIT, partly filling in for Patty Tang, who was out on sabbatical and then family leave. I had benefits there and taught "Intro to World Music" for two semesters and "Popular Musics of the World." I also had one class at Boston University during the fall of 2009, a graduate ethnomusicology class about fieldwork. The problem with all this teaching is that I've had no time to publish. I didn't even manage to finish my dissertation and graduate until May 2009. (My dissertation, "The Sambla Xylophone: Tradition and Identity in Burkina Faso" [2009], can be accessed, with audio examples, at http://wesscholar.wesleyan.edu/etd_diss/3.) I was way too busy preparing courses and looking for the next gig. At least I've had some interviews, which I can't say everyone has had, and they were instructive.

Update: August 14, 2016

In the six years since my interview, quite a bit has changed in my life. As I progressed through a postdoctoral position at Northeastern University in Boston, I craved more interaction with the world I taught about in the classroom, so I turned my focus to study abroad. I developed my own summer program to Bali through Northeastern, which I ran from 2011 to 2013, not only teaching students about music and culture in Bali but also about how to take advantage of their time there to interact meaningfully with the environment for a true cultural exchange. Our goal was not just to acquire knowledge but also to leave parts of ourselves behind, sharing our culture with them as the Balinese did with us, a positive legacy of our presence that built bridges and created opportunities for further growth on all sides. These concepts also held true through my further experiences teaching with Semester at Sea, where I came to appreciate the value of ethnomusicology for young people, as music provides an accessible and attractive entrée into deeper intercultural exchange and understanding.

Over time, I yearned to make a broader impact beyond the undergraduate population. After teaching my last semester in fall 2013, I began the lengthy process of pursuing a career in public diplomacy for the US Foreign Service. There I hope to capitalize on the skills I gained in my education, experiences abroad, and teaching career to promote cultural exchange across nations in a world that is becoming alarmingly fragmented, misinformed, and afraid of one another, all while modern technology is ostensibly helping to bring us closer together. Here the focus isn't necessarily music per se, but to find common ground as human beings who share similar motivations and goals in life—yet to find vastly different creative avenues to express them. In my experience, misunderstanding differences breeds fear and separatism, while understanding motivations behind those differences makes them fade and facilitates working relationships.

Assistant Professors

Maria Mendonça (October 27, 2007)

PhD, Wesleyan University (Ethnomusicology)
Assistant Professor, Kenyon College

Graduate Studies

I went to the States to look at grad schools. I started on the West Coast and went to Berkeley to have a look at the composition and theory program. I looked at some other places, like Penn, and ended up at Wesleyan, simply to visit someone I knew from York. I thought I'd say hello to Sumarsam because Neil [Sorrell] had told me to. So I went and chatted with him, it must have been a long time—hours. At the end of it, *he* had decided that I was going to do ethnomusicology and come to Wesleyan. I went downstairs and met Mark Slobin in the hallway and we chatted about it, and then I went to gamelan that evening. I came away from my trip to America thinking, "Yeah, I'm not going to apply for music theory and composition. I'm just going to apply to Wesleyan to do gamelan and ethnomusicology." And that's what I did!

TS: Why were you looking at the United States? Was that an inevitable thing for you? Wasn't there anything in the UK that would give you what you wanted?

MM: I was really impressed by my year at UC San Diego. I really had one of the most stimulating years musically I've ever had. What I really liked about the States was that if you were doing ethnomusicology, you were pushed into all these taught classes, something we don't have in the British system. I didn't know what I wanted to do, but I really wanted to learn, and this seemed ideal for me. I really wanted to be stretched. I'd always thought ethnomusicology was a fascinating subject, from my exposure to Neil Sorrell at York University. That's why I came to the States. And also, financially, I got more support in the States.

TS: Do you think it's changing in the UK at all?

MM: Certainly master's degrees are very different these days. There are more taught classes, but not in the PhD system, as far as I know. There are some seminars, but the whole idea is to have an idea and do it. The PhD is very fast in Britain—three years.

TS: So, you came to Wesleyan in 1988, and you were offered pretty good financial assistance?

MM: They were very good to foreign students if they accepted them. They realized that we couldn't work. My wonderful job was to be the assistant to Sumarsam and Harjito for gamelan. I learned so much from watching them teach; it was extraordinary.

TS: Did you have any Indonesian language at that point?

MM: I'd been to Indonesia the summer before, so I'd done a little home study. Then I went to the SEASSI (Southeast Asian Studies Summer Institute) program in Hawai'i at the end of the first year of my MA.

The courses at Wesleyan were great, absolutely great. I started studying the soft instruments from the gamelan in depth. I knew all about the amazing gamelan players and scholars who had come out of Wesleyan—and there's a real host of them—but when I got there, I was the only grad student who was doing gamelan in any particular way. Initially, I was a little disappointed, but what it meant was that if they needed a *gendèr* player, or needed a *gambang* player, or something, they'd say "Oh, give Maria a few lessons!" So it was wonderful. And I also found that I really enjoyed ethno-musicology—even from my undergrad days—because it picked at the foundations of what I really believed in musically. It always made me question things. The funny thing is that as an undergraduate, I probably got the lowest marks for my essays in ethnomusicology, because I found it very challenging.

TS: Do you remember the first time you heard the word "ethnomusicology"?

MM: It must have been when I was an undergrad, studying with Neil. It was probably in a "Music of Java and Bali" course, where we did a lot of stuff about "What is music? What is musicianship?" That fascinated me.

TS: What did "ethnomusicology" mean to you at that point?

MM: I encountered it in a department where experimental music was very strong. I thought it was a fascinating field because there were connections—or possible connections—with experimental music. The York gamelan is quite an unusual beast, because there are lots of composers in it who used to compose pieces for gamelan, and there was a real emphasis on that. So I associated ethnomusicology with unconventional ways of looking at music in general. That's what really appealed to me about the discipline; it challenged basic notions of what music was, what music could be, and I loved the fact that it approached it from a variety of different cultural angles.

TS: What happened next at Wesleyan? You started thinking about a PhD?

MM: I wrote my MA thesis on *pathet* because it was something I really wanted to figure out; that was the motivation. It wasn't as if I had any answers; I wanted to figure out what was written about it and what I understood about it. Then it came to the PhD program, and I realized I really wanted to stay at Wesleyan, and everything was beginning to tick. While trying to think of a topic, I sat down with Neil Sorrell (who was on sabbatical there at the time), and he asked, "What do you find interesting about gamelan?" I said, "It's fascinating—I can go to Solo and chat with people from America, from England, from Czechoslovakia. We're in Java, and we're all connected by gamelan. There are gamelans all over the place—why doesn't anyone ever talk about this?" And I thought, "Oh, good, that's going to be my topic for my disserta-tion." When it came time to do fieldwork and I didn't get any grants, I returned to Britain and decided eventually, after some years of doing research in Britain, just to focus on gamelan in Britain.

TS: Are you working on turning your PhD dissertation [Mendonça 2002] into a book?

MM: Yes, I'm working on it at the moment: "Gamelan and Globalization." I'm tak-ing a step back and looking more generally at issues. I'm interested in the cultural globalization issue. I think gamelan is very interesting *because* it has all these issues of "falling in the cracks." The majority of gamelan activity outside Indonesia is not motivated by migration of Javanese, or Indonesians, or anything like that, though this has often followed the initial interest. People are attracted to it for such diverse reasons, and it develops in such different ways in different parts of the world.

TS: How did you do your fieldwork?

MM: When I finished my coursework at Wesleyan in '92, I went back to Britain and immediately was employed as a gamelan musician in a production of *A Midsummer Night's Dream* at the National Theatre, which was directed by the Canadian director Robert Lepage with music by Adrian Lee and Peter Salem. Their idea was that gamelan was an important focus. It was an interesting project and ran for quite a while. After that, various teaching opportunities came my way, and I started doing lots of freelance workshop stuff at the South Bank Centre.

I ended up taking on the gamelans at City University and Oxford. I did that for a year, juggling things, and then I got a post at the Halle in Manchester. The Halle Orchestra had bought a gamelan and needed to hire a gamelan coordinator to do education work. The idea was that you designed the whole program, taught it, and helped with fundraising. It was the first gamelan education job in Britain. I applied for it and got it. I used to go up to Manchester and do a lot of workshops and projects of my own design with schoolchildren and community groups. We had an interesting collaboration with the Royal Schools for the Deaf in Manchester. I also did lots of collaborative projects with different artists in the region—I worked with a storyteller, a poet, a puppet company—not necessarily artists who had any background in Indonesia. I had that job for two years.

Building a Career

I finished my dissertation in 2002. I was very long in finishing up because I got so involved in all this freelance gamelan work. I was trying to document bits of it at the same time, but it was very hard. I still wanted to do the multisite comparison and was saving up to do it. I went to the Netherlands and did some research on the first gamelan group outside of Indonesia, Babar Layar, which was active during the Second World War. I also interviewed lots of Dutch gamelan players. I had all these jobs going on and then I got a job at *Grove Dictionary of Music*, as an editor. I hoped that would give me more substantive space to do my dissertation, so I began working on it, interviewing people, and that kind of stuff. Eventually, I went freelance at Grove, and *then* I used my savings and went off and did my fieldwork. I went to a program in Hertfordshire. I used to go every week and be assistant teacher to Nikhil Dally so I could observe. That was the whole idea. I did that for a long time, a year or so, and meantime, if there was a project, a recording session, or something, I'd go along and try to interview people. I did lots of different things—Metalworks Gamelan, based outside Oxford, was another case study.

One thing that's been interesting to me is that my way of earning a living by being a gamelan person has often coincided with my fieldwork. It was very hard to draw the line sometimes. I would do all these projects and then go away and write a lot of notes. When observing and interviewing others, I ended up sort of acting it out, if you like, through my career possibilities. I used to set up different programs, like the one in Cardiff. Occasionally I'd go abroad and do a week of teaching somewhere. It was very piecemeal for some years.

TS: I also interviewed Nikhil and Pete Smith for this project when I was in London last summer. They're gamelan gigging musicians, among other things—a whole kind of profession that doesn't exist in the United States.

MM: I'm in the same groups with them—I did a lot of performing. In the end, I cut down on my commitments and wrote my dissertation, finally, and submitted it in 2002. I was still doing a lot of gamelan teaching and consultancy work in the UK. Then I was lucky enough to get a postdoc at the University of Chicago in 2004–05. That was a great experience for a year. Next I taught for a year at Bowling Green State University. And then in 2006 I got a tenure-track job at Kenyon College in Ohio. The position was initially funded by the Luce Foundation. I have a two-thirds commitment to the Music Department and one-third to the Anthropology Department.

TS: What do you do for the Anthropology Department?

MM: I teach an "Intro to Cultural Anthropology" course, but they also encourage me to devise my own courses for them, on the stuff I do that they don't do. I want to do one on performativity in general—nobody seems to cover that in our department— or stuff to do with Southeast Asia and Indonesia. So far I've only done the Intro to Cultural courses, but next year I'll have to devise some new courses.

TS: Are you teaching gamelan there?

MM: Yes, I'm teaching the *degung* [Sundanese gamelan of West Java].

TS: Why did they have a degung gamelan? Who was there before you?

MM: Henry Spiller. He actually taught with his own instruments, initially, and then they acquired one through Tony Lydgate, a gamelan benefactor who lives in Kauai. He gave five sets of degung to five different institutions, including Kenyon.

TS: How did you learn how to teach degung?

MM: In my last year in London, I did a project with Simon Cook. I was teaching at Bath Spa University—one of my many freelance gigs—where they had a Javanese set.

I spoke to Simon and he said, "Oh, wouldn't it be lovely to get the degung there and then they could have a workshop on each other's gamelan and we could do a joint performance?" I'd done a little bit of *kechapi-suling* before and was really interested in degung, so that last year I joined Simon's group. I didn't expect to activate that experience as a teacher so soon after.

TS: It seems like degung is very appealing these days.

MM: Yes, there's quite a lot of literature and quite a lot of freedom in terms of the improvisation. It's a kind of freedom that takes a long, long time to achieve in Javanese music, if you're talking about the soft instruments. It's also a chamber gamelan, which I really enjoy.

TS: What are you working on now?

MM: I did some research on the "gamelan in prisons" project that has been going on in Britain. I'm writing that up for publication at the moment. Then there's the "Gamelan and Globalization" book project.

TS: How often do you get back to Indonesia?

MM: Not enormously often. I went when I finished my dissertation in 2002. Then this summer I went to Sunda for a month, basically to learn a lot of Sundanese music in order to teach the ensemble at Kenyon.

TS: How do you compare your fieldwork in Sunda with your work in Central Java in terms of personal response and comfort zone?

MM: I'm so used to Central Java, it was very strange to be in Indonesia and not go to Central Java. But there are so many different things about Sundanese culture that I enjoy as well. It was sort of field research, but it was very music focused. I had all these music skills I wanted to get under my belt by the end of the month, so I'm afraid I was a real gamelan nerd. I woke up, I ate, I practiced, I had lessons, I practiced some more. I didn't really do any field research as such. It was all based on the acquisition of practical gamelan skills.

TS: Who are your ethnomusicological role models? Who inspired you most? Do you think of yourself as part of any kind of lineage?

MM: That's an interesting question. I think I'd have to say there's a kind of "Wesleyan connection," obviously, through Neil Sorrell. He's had an interest in transplanted gamelan. I probably developed that through the experience of being at York. I was always very inspired by Mark Slobin's work—an ethnomusicologist who moved from area to area. It was great to see somebody have so many diverse interests. I enjoyed being a graduate student in his seminars very much. And Sumarsam—there's another inspiring figure. He's an amazing player and an amazing ethnomusicologist. That's quite an extraordinary achievement.

Update: July 15, 2016

Since our initial conversation, I've remained in the same departments (Anthropology and Music) at the same institution (Kenyon College) but increased my interdisciplinary involvements to include Islamic studies and civilizations as well as Asian studies (one of the perks of teaching at a liberal arts college is this kind of cross-disciplinary involvement!). I was tenured in 2012, and following this I had a year's sabbatical leave in 2013–14, which I spent in the UK, pursuing my interests in documentary filmmaking. That was followed by a one-year appointment as Valentine Visiting Associate Professor in the Music Department at Amherst College (2014–15).

In 2007 I was writing on gamelan in prisons in England and Scotland, which I subsequently published. I followed up this interest in music and the prison context in the US as well, by participating in the instructor training for the Inside-Out Prison Exchange Program, the collaborative education program that "brings college students together with incarcerated men and women to study as peers in a seminar behind prison walls." (http://www.insideoutcenter.org/index.html). I have a longer-term goal of running this type of course at Kenyon in collaboration with a local prison. I hope to realize this goal in the next few years, teaching either a music course (preferably a performance course) or "Introduction to Cultural Anthropology" (another core course I teach at Kenyon).

In 2012 I participated in Filmmaking for Fieldwork at the Granada Centre for Visual Anthropology at the University of Manchester, a truly inspirational course, which helped me to activate a longstanding ambition of immersing myself in documentary and ethnographic filmmaking. The following year (2013) I was fortunate to receive a grant from the Great Lakes College Association New Directions Initiative, a midcareer grant funded by the Andrew W. Mellon Foundation, which enabled me to enroll in further training (editing courses and sound for documentary film courses) as well as purchase some equipment. During my sabbatical year in the UK, I shot my first film, about gamelan in Britain, a process I found completely engrossing: I've enjoyed the steep learning curve of being a self-shooter/editor immensely. More generally speaking, it's been very stimulating to think about ethnomusicology's relationship to the audio-visual, not only technically (in terms of the practice of filming) but also theoretically, and I'm looking forward to developing more of my own research/writing on the topic. I recently (July 2016) returned from Filmmaking for Fieldwork's Advanced Course, where I worked on the editing of my current film project, *Gamelan Encounters*. Film has also made its way into my teaching: documentary and, more generally, music and film has made its way into my course offerings, and my departments have been very supportive, which has been great!

Jan Mrázek (July 7, 2007)

PhD, Cornell University (Art History)
Assistant Professor, Asian Research Institute
National University of Singapore

Graduate Studies

I went straight to Cornell for my MA and PhD in art history. Ethnomusicology was my minor. My committee was Stanley O'Connor (supervisor, art history), Marty Hatch (ethnomusicology), and Jim Siegel (anthropology). The thing about Cornell that distinguishes it from lots of other places is that you have a lot of freedom. I wasn't really bound by any discipline. My study was in art history, and I did my PhD on Javanese shadow puppet theatre [1998].

TS: Is your book [Mrázek 2002] essentially your PhD dissertation?

JM: Yes, it's quite close to it. One point to note: it's on theater, although there's one long chapter about music. Music is important, but it's not a pure ethnomusicological work. I've never really thought about myself as being simply an ethnomusicologist, even though I was interested in music since I was very little.

Building a Career

JM: While I was doing my PhD at Cornell, I made some money by teaching gamelan. The Cornell Gamelan Ensemble is not really a class; it includes community members and some students. Marty Hatch let me take over the rehearsals while he went on sabbatical. He also gave me a big project: to make a catalog of the collection of Javanese recordings. I got paid five dollars per hour to listen to gamelan music!

I finished my PhD in 1998 and taught as a visiting lecturer at Cornell for one semester. After that, I got several job offers but decided to go to Leiden for a postdoc. So in 1999 I went to the Netherlands for three and a half years and worked on a project organized by Ben Arps called "Verbal Art in Audio-Visual Media in Indonesia." My project was on interaction—I'm still finishing a book about it—between Javanese theatre and television. My interest in *wayang* had started long before, but television was also a small part of my dissertation. I saw that television was very important, and Ben's project encouraged me to focus more on that. During my time in Leiden (1999 to 2002) I married Nunuk, a Javanese dancer I had met in Solo, Java. We worked together a lot because I was playing drum for her when she danced. I went to her dance lessons, dance rehearsals, dance performances, and she helped me to understand Javanese culture.

After I finished the postdoc, I got a job in the Art History Department at the University of Washington in Seattle. I mostly taught courses in art history: ancient temples, Indian art, and so on. I convinced my head of department to let me teach a course on Javanese dance in the Dance Department with my wife. I worked very closely there with Jarrad Powell, a composer who directs Gamelan Pacifica. We did two performances of wayang, and I was the puppeteer. It's very interesting: in each place the dynamics of the gamelan group is different. In Seattle, the members weren't particularly interested in Indonesia, but they were all very good musicians.

TS: What was your status in Seattle? Was it a tenure-track job or not?

JM: No, it was called "acting assistant professor"—a very ugly name. I had to renew my contract every year, which is one reason why I looked for other positions. I got offered a job in Singapore four years ago; that is where I am now.

TS: So you've been in Singapore since 2003. Can you tell me a little about the job?

JM: The job was in Media and Popular Culture in Southeast Asia, so there was nothing about music, art history, or traditional things when I was hired. The [department] head at the time didn't like traditional things! Luckily for me, they changed the head to Reynaldo Ileto, a historian from the Philippines. He encouraged me to do things I liked—art history and music. So now I'm mostly teaching visual and performing arts. I'm in the Southeast Asian Studies Department, which I quite enjoy. It's very interdisciplinary and I can teach courses that combine visual arts, dance, and music. I have very good graduate students who do all kinds of things, not just music or art history. I never feel comfortable in any single discipline.

TS: Are your students mostly Singaporean, or do they come from Southeast Asia, or beyond?

JM: The undergraduates are mostly from Singapore, though some come from elsewhere in Southeast Asia. There are quite a few exchange students from Europe and America who come for a year. The graduate program is very international.

I also teach gamelan and take care of the Thai Music Ensemble. When I came, there was no gamelan or other Asian music in the university. With the help of Rey Ileto, who is my close friend, I slowly convinced people that we should get a gamelan. Now I'm using the gamelan as a part of my courses, "Old and New Music in Southeast Asia" and "Arts of Southeast Asia." The dynamics of teaching gamelan in Singapore are very interesting. In Europe there is still the idea that there are two worlds. In Singapore, it's more complicated. There are Malays, who consider themselves to have Javanese heritage, so they study gamelan, and you have a Czech person teaching Southeast Asian music. Also, I began to work with a Thai language program here. The Thai embassy was very proactive and the Thai royal family gave us a set of Thai instruments. We had an intensive workshop, and then a teacher from Thailand came for half a semester. The next year they sent a different teacher for half a semester. In the meantime, whenever I have time, I have been going to Thailand to study with Thai teachers.

TS: Have you studied Thai language?

JM: Yes, here at the National University of Singapore and in Thailand. I started four years ago, so I'm still an intermediate beginner. One of the reasons I took the job here in Singapore was that I would be in Southeast Asia and could explore these other things. I know much less about Thai music than about gamelan, but I know enough to teach. Teaching Thai music is very different from teaching gamelan. It's more difficult to attract students, and you need students who are much more dedicated. But it's fun. The social dynamics are different in Singapore; you don't have the tradition that you have with gamelan. You don't have the sense of Malay or Islamic heritage. It's connected to Buddhism, and a lot of people in Singapore are either quite strongly Muslim or extremely strongly Christian and don't want to do things that challenge their beliefs.

Update: September 4, 2016

At about the same time I began to teach at NUS, the Filipino historian Reynaldo Ileto became the coordinator of what was then the Southeast Asian Studies Programme. In his vision of a Southeast Asian studies program in Southeast Asia—to oversimplify for the sake of brevity—we should not look at our region through the lenses of disciplines and theories developed in Europe and America, from above or from a distance. His untheoretical answer was to make the program into a meeting space for students and professors from different countries and different disciplinary backgrounds—many, not all, from different parts of Southeast Asia, but all with a long-term experience of living in the region and knowing at least one Southeast Asian language, often several; a space for a very diverse group of people to share views, experiences, and to learn to know and be with each other.

That might already sound like an allegory of gamelan playing; in any case, purchasing a gamelan set became one of the cheerful projects I initiated and Ileto passionately supported. The great thing about Javanese gamelan is that it is rewarding not only for those who study it seriously for years and decades, but it is also a friendly, welcoming musical culture for beginners or for people for whom socializing is at least as important as the quality of music. And so gamelan music and gamelan socializing became easily part of the learning space. Performances became—and of course this is typical rather than unique to our case—as much celebrations and social occasions as musical productions. If it is important that this was fun, it is equally important that this was part of a vision-put-into-practice of scholarship, teaching, and learning; it was fun that freed learning from various academic and other imperialisms (including that of disciplinary universals). This is only a quick, poor sketch of what playing, learning, and teaching music has been for me in Singapore, and why I have continued to be an ethnomusicologist.

To turn to the question of development and my present position: while something of what I have described above continues today, and our gamelan rehearsals and performances especially are very much fun, they are not quite part of the same larger learning environment. What is now the Department of Southeast Asian Studies has changed and moved in new directions, generally following or being pressured to follow what is perceived as American models and standards, and in other ways as well "globalizing"—we have now "Global Asian Studies." In practice at least, "Global Asia" feels qualitatively different from our Southeast Asian learning-meeting spaces that felt like a lively neighborhood.

Katherine Butler Schofield (July 9, 2007)

PhD, SOAS, University of London (Ethnomusicology)
Assistant Professor, King's College, London

Graduate Studies

While I was at the Queensland Conservatorium, I met my husband (who is now my ex-husband) and moved to England. He was one of the circle of friends who had grown up in India. He did his undergraduate degree at Cambridge and came to Australia for a year to catch up with old friends who had gone to the international school with him in South India. Probably that's how my interest in India began—you fall in love with something exotic because you're falling in love with a person.

TS: Was he from India?

KBS: No, he went to live in Bangladesh with his parents when he was two, so he'd grown up with a kind of third culture. I found that really appealing. When we decided to move to England, a mutual friend and academic historian said, "When you go to do your graduate studies, you *have* to go to SOAS." So I came to England in 1996 and found that SOAS had a Center of Music Studies. They didn't have a Department of Music yet. Because of visa issues, I entered as a spouse and wasn't able to start my course until '97. I was in the master's program, part time, from '97 to '99. Richard Widdess was my master's dissertation supervisor. As soon as I arrived at SOAS, I felt like I'd come home. It has a fantastic master's program in the theory and method of ethnomusicology that gave me a solid grounding in basic theory and method—the canon of ethnomusicology, if you like. It explored all the important issues, beginning with comparative musicology and going right up to globalization and identity and all those things we're talking about now. I felt that, academically, ethnomusicology was what I really wanted to do because of its emphasis on what people really think and say about music, as opposed to the speculative, subjective philosophizing in one's own head about the music. I got sidetracked into the subfield of historical ethnomusicology, partly because of my particular interests in Indo-Islamic history and partly because Richard himself has such strong historical interests. I loved SOAS. I finished my master's and then did a PhD there from 1999 to 2003.

One great thing about SOAS is that it's full of people who are working in your area but not in your discipline. There's so much fruitful interdisciplinary crossover. For example, my internal examiner was a historian of Islamic India. I also had quite a bit to do with the History and Language Departments. You can learn pretty much any African or Asian language, so I took Sanskrit as part of my master's degree. I loved how deep the language was. And when I started my PhD, I decided to learn Persian because I was going to be looking at a historical topic. I was able to take the first year of the Persian undergraduate degree as part of my PhD.

I developed a historical topic, partly because of Richard Widdess but also because I was already interested in the fact that all the great hereditary families of Indian musicians of the past were Muslim. I became intrigued by their stories about their *gharanas* and their family heritage, which could be taken back generations to the reign of Akbar. I went to India for the first time in 1997, just for a month, mostly to hang out. Then I went back to do my fieldwork for six months at the end of 2000 through the beginning of 2001. This meant going to archives and looking at Persian manuscript sources. I recently had another six-month stint from the end of 2004, and I'm hoping to go back more regularly for shorter visits in future, rather than having these long stints that don't really fit into the academic year once you have a full-time job.

TS: Then what language did you speak with people?

KBS: I had no spoken Indian languages, only Sanskrit and Persian, both classical languages. When I went back in 2004, I decided I needed to learn Hindustani (Hindi/Urdu), so I went to the Landour Language School in Mussoorie for six weeks and did an Intensive Hindi program. After some practice my spoken Hindi is better than my spoken Persian, for sure. I can read and understand basic Hindi and basic Urdu because they are basically the same language and I've got both scripts. One of my real aims is to improve my spoken Hindi and Urdu over the next ten years or so.

TS: Let me ask: If you had not been an ethnomusicologist, what might you have done instead? Is performance still part of your life?

KBS: Oh yes, it's still a big part. I've continued to perform throughout. I still got paid to play in orchestras until 2000, when I spent six months in India without practicing the viola. Basically, I never played the viola again, because the idea of trying to get back what I lost in six months of not playing was just too depressing. I started playing fiddle in a folk band in Cambridge and singing backing vocals. It's a return to my folk roots.

Building a Career

KBS: I finished my PhD at SOAS in 2003, and my first job was as a research fellow at Cambridge. I was there for three years. Actually I lived in Cambridge the whole time

I was at SOAS and commuted down to London. It's only forty-five minutes on the train. After that, I got a permanent job at the University of Leeds.

TS: Did you have any real conception of what an academic life as an ethnomusicologist would be like when you were a student?

KBS: I wanted to be an academic from the word "go," really. What I didn't realize until this year was just how heavy the workload can be in terms of teaching. It's partly because it's my first year but also partly because the University of Leeds has a good reputation, but one of the worst staff-to-student ratios in the country. My sense of it is that this has all come about in the last three years: our programs have not adjusted to a trebling in student numbers and a slight decline in staff numbers. It's been very hard and I have thought several times this year about quitting academia altogether.

TS: What is your load like?

KBS: I'm teaching the full-time equivalent of six courses over the year, but given that many are co-taught, I actually teach on twelve different courses. Teaching six courses of my own would probably be easier than co-teaching twelve because they would be more cohesive and coherent from my perspective. There have been weeks in the last year when I only had a total of fourteen hours sleep in a week because I had so much preparation to do. And, of course, you still want to keep up a decent amount of research time. The department has been having crisis meetings because they've recognized it's a serious problem. I'm going to give it another year and see how it goes. As a friend of mine says, "No matter what happens, keep publishing."

Update: July 26, 2016

ICTM, Vienna, in July 2007 feels like a million years ago in life and career terms. If you will excuse a digression into the personal, I was right in the middle of getting divorced and had simultaneously just finished the first year of my first tenure-track-equivalent job—an exhausting and disorienting time by anyone's estimation. At the time, these two things were certainly skewing temporarily who I thought I was and where I should be going, squeezing me into shoes I would never quite fit. Leeds was, in the end, not for me, and in January 2009 I took up a faculty position at King's College London, where I have been ever since, and I am now senior lecturer (associate professor) in the Department of Music and an affiliate of the King's India Institute. In the same year, I moved back to live in Cambridge, remarried, and within a single week in July 2010 gave birth to my son and was awarded a major European Research Council Grant for €1.2M over five years, to study interregionally the ways in which music and dance in North India and the Malay world were transformed from late-precolonial to colonial regimes circa 1750–1900. My family and my grant have consumed all my time since then until the present day and together have definitively shaped who I am now.

Tomie Hahn (April 18, 2008)

PhD, Wesleyan University (Ethnomusicology)
Associate Professor, Rensselaer Polytechnic Institute

Graduate Studies

TH: That was 1989. Just then I got a really strange gig—but that's what my life was like then—with a men's fashion show. I would wear a *kurogo* outfit (the black clothes and hood that *Bunraku* puppeteers wear) and "puppet" the men or the props on the catwalk. It paid a lot of money. This is not so important to know, except what it led me to. We went to rehearsals, we did the show, and during the show, I heard *shakuhachi*. It reminded me that I'd heard shakuhachi when I was growing up and how much I loved it. I heard the sound, looked off the catwalk, and saw Ralph Samuelson playing *sankyoku*. The minute I got off the catwalk, I went down and said, "Who are you? What do you do?" And Ralph said this word, "ethnomusicology," again. The next week, I had a shakuhachi lesson. Because I had been playing flute since I was seven or eight years old, I had the embouchure and the breathing, everything was more or less there. It was basically just learning the other side of what shakuhachi's all about. I realized, "OK, *this* is the instrument for me." So I started taking very serious lessons. It was right about the same time that I asked the architect I was working for to give me an afternoon off each week for a semester so that I could take a seminar in ethnomusicology with Professor Kay Shelemay.

As I was finishing my MA at NYU, Professor Shelemay took a job at Wesleyan University. The next semester I followed her there to work on my doctorate. I was at Wesleyan for a couple years and finished my PhD coursework about the same time Curtis went to Princeton for electronic music. I went off to Japan, and when I came back, I lived at Princeton and used the library there.

TS: Where did you meet your husband, by the way?

TH: We were both at Indiana University at the same time but didn't really get to know each other until he finished and came to New York City to play in jazz clubs. At that time he was primarily a jazz bass player. We hung out and started collaborating on contemporary performances combining live music, electronics, and dance.

Building a Career

TH: In our early collaborations, I danced, sometimes incorporating friends and colleagues from other dance groups, and Curtis created electronic tapes based on his work at the Center for Computer Music at Brooklyn College, where he worked with composer Charles Dodge. The performances were experimental and wild—it was really fun. We continue to collaborate, even now, and have performed and presented our work internationally. We both finished our PhDs in the same year, 1997. And then in '98 we both got jobs. He started teaching interactive computer music composition at Rensselaer Polytechnic Institute in Troy, New York, and I started teaching ethnomusicology at Tufts, near Boston. We lived in Sturbridge, Massachusetts. I would commute to Tufts in Medford, and he would commute to Rensselaer.

TS: What were you teaching at Tufts?

TH: "World Music" was the bread-and-butter course, and "Introduction to Asian Music." I found a new love when I was there: teaching First Year Studies courses designed specifically for nonmajor freshmen. It was really interesting to explore new areas, to learn more about what the student body was like, and to grab hold of students basically out of high school. They're really young and it was important to have a safe space for them to talk about whatever the issues were. The first one I offered was a course on being multiracial. It was really exciting for me because it was one of the first times that I felt like *I* was even talking with a lot of multiracial kids.

At Tufts so many kids started to come into my office and plop down on my couch and say, "I heard from so-and-so that you self-identify as biracial. I am too!" And often they would start crying. So a bunch of students started a biracial club and I was one of the faculty facilitators. That was very exciting for me. It was a new opening into an area that I hadn't quite considered exploring. So this theme was also folded into my book, which is an exploration that interrogates my own background and identity. It came out of not only the Chinatown Asian American political movement I had been around, but also this biracial exploration group.

When Curtis and I were completing our dissertations we heard horror stories about two-scholar families. Both of us were saying, "You finish your dissertation and get the job, and I'll do whatever I can." But that year we both finished, we both got jobs. It was somewhat deal-able for us to manage long commutes for a while, but after four or five years, that gets old. Perhaps we'd even still be commuting if I hadn't had a car accident in 2001. That changed our lives, so there's a blessing in there somewhere. It's a long story, but we got through it. We continued to teach that semester, but the accident woke us up. We started telling everybody—and this was prior to either of us receiving tenure, so it was a bold-out-of-desperation moment—"Look, we both want to be teaching in the same place. Somebody has to take both of us." In four months, I signed a contract at Rensselaer. I'm not sure I would recommend this path to junior colleagues today, though, as the economic, scholarly, and political climates have shifted over time. We were desperate and fortunate to have supporters.

Rensselaer is a *very* unusual school. I'm in an Arts Department, which is fascinating and also quite challenging. There are other ethnographers in the school—anthropologists, sociologists—but I'm the only ethnomusicologist. There's no Music Department;

it's an integrated Electronic Arts Department. It's a very tech-oriented school. I've had to translate what I know and teach to a wide range of students and dream up new classes and ways of teaching. One thing I really love is that I teach fieldwork methodology for artists *and* anthropologists. I have anthropologists from other departments—including grad students—who are mixed in with artists. The artists are not really interested in becoming card-carrying anthropologists, but they want to make art that's influenced by collecting data: interviewing people, making a radio show, collecting images or whatever, and making an installation or a documentary. I think the anthropologists learn a great deal about, "What do you do with this stuff called 'data'?" Because the creative artists in there are saying, "Oh! I could do this, I could do that, I could make a video or make a website that does this." And meanwhile, the artists are learning from the anthropologists about ethics and so on.

TS: That's wonderful. We don't see many confluences like that in other programs, at least not in my world.

TH: No, it's an oddity that I've grown to understand. After about two years at Rensselaer, I had to really think hard, "Why am I here? Where do I fit? How can I take what I love to do, my passion for why I get up in the morning, and find a fit for this school?"

TS: What would you put your finger on as the passion that makes you get up in the morning? Can you narrow it down to something?

TH: It's this combination of being an artist and a creative, expressive person, both as an artist and as an ethnographer, and finding ways that these two *can* overlap. So, wearing two different hats like that, to me, is not so different than being biracial, because I flip between different communities. I act differently when I'm in different communities. We all do, but for me, being biracial is a dichotomy that's embodied, so it's different than just a hat switch.

I'm fascinated to learn from the students in these classes. How are they going to use the information they learned from a fireman or from whomever they interviewed? And they'll find something really interesting to do with the information that I would never have thought of, coming from a background of straightforward ethnography. It was hard for me in the first couple of years to figure out why I was there. I had to look inside myself and actually ask myself what you just asked me: "What's the passion? Why do I get up in the morning?" I had to say, "Well, if we're teaching what we love, then we have to understand what that is before we start." I had to do a little soul searching. I do agree with your point about ethnomusicology offering an outlet for doing what *you* want to do, in combining the various things.

It's exciting. And dance scholarship is different, too. I walk the circle of performance studies and dance scholarship, and it's very different than ethnomusicology. I tend to go between these, but I feel as though ethnomusicologists are more inclusive of dance now, but dance isn't necessarily going into the sort of deeper musicological analysis. I think we're finally getting to a point where there's more cross-fertilization between dance scholarship and music. From my perspective, it's really nice to see the Dance Section growing in SEM. There are other scholars who are walking between two places. They're going to the Congress on Research in Dance or to Performance Studies International conferences. That's very healthy. It wasn't always like that.

TS: When did you get into all the electronic strapping-on and cyborgian kinds of things? How did that come about?

TH: In 1998 or '99, when Curtis and I were still living in Princeton, perhaps even before that, working with Perry Cook, a professor of music and computer science at Princeton. Curtis and his friends were starting to experiment with putting sensors on their instruments (this was many years before the Nintendo Wii was released, by the way). They put them on coffee cups, cat's tails; finally, one day Curtis gasped and looked over at me. "You're a dancer *and* a musician! Wow, let's make an interface for you." So he made the first interface for me that incorporated gestural sensors on my hands and stereo body-mounted speakers on my arms. We evolved a gestural language that allowed me to improvise with the computer, and we ended up loving to work that way. And for me it was wonderful, too, because it extended culture, which was what I was writing about in my dissertation. The thing was, in my straight ethno research I was talking about the senses and the body and how we embody cultural knowledge. And then here were the sensors, on my body, tapping into embodied cultural knowledge. Ask the simple question, "Why does my hand know how to do something like this?" Well, because it has been trained since it was four years old to do that, right? But I don't do ballet hands, so that's an embodied cultural sensibility. And then we realize, "Well, how do we tap into embodied culture with sensors?" It was a challenge.

Curtis mapped my body into the algorithms, into the programs, so it revealed something. Because otherwise you could have a ballet dancer sitting right next to me, moving her hand palm-up, palm-down, and it would be the same numbers. How do we tweak the system for cultural sensibilities? That became a real fascination for us. Not just as an "On/Off" button and a gimmick, but how to use technology to extend the body and extend culture. That was a really important thing for us: idiosyncratic technological interfaces. Not just, "OK, here's a mouse, use it to connect to your computer." Everybody has a mouse, everybody has a touchpad—it's sort of a universal. For us it was more, "No, this interface will be idiosyncratic for what you do, for your particular biracial-ness."

TS: The idiosyncratic part of it comes in the particular equipment, the particular setting, or what?

TH: All of it. For a while, we put sensors on my feet or different other parts of my body. Curtis basically asked me, "Where do you want a sensor?" Actually Joe Paradiso, a friend and well-known researcher at MIT Labs, puts sensors into sneakers for dancers. I realized, as a performer of Japanese dance, that I don't use my feet like that, but modern dancers do. So this fascinated me because it meant that—literally—the shoe can be worn by different people of different cultural backgrounds, but how it's used is particular, not only to the person but also to their cultural embodiment. That fascinated me.

Update: February 19, 2017

Since we talked in 2007 (and the publication of *Sensational Knowledge* [2007]), my research expanded dramatically from sound and movement to other sensory modalities. My research now locates the senses as vehicles for embodied transmission; an observation of which sensory modes are prioritized in transmission is shaped by the predilections of that culture. Historically, increased specialization separated research into individual sensory modes in academic disciplines, often occluding the multimodal dynamic of a fully embodied sensory transmission. For example, music studies focus on oral transmission, dance scholarship on enactive transmission, and visual art scholarship on vision-centered transmission systems. This construct literally divides the body by discipline. In addition, campuses have historically segregated the mind from these already compartmentalized sensory-centric modalities. In my interdisciplinary writings, conference presentations, and performances I assert that it is essential that research take into account the entire sensate body in order to understand embodied knowledge, expressivity, and what it is to be human. In a sense, by reconstructing the body, interdisciplinary exchanges in the arts and sciences have the potential to reveal new insights into relationships between body, mind, culture, and creativity. I have been collaborating on several projects with cognitive scientists regarding aspects of embodied cognition, the idea that the brain and the body shape human cognition.

When I came to RPI the composer Pauline Oliveros was one of my colleagues in the department, and we quickly became close. In 2014 I became the director [and promoted to professor in 2017] of the Center for Deep Listening at Rensselaer, a center that furthers the work of Pauline Oliveros and the practice she created, called Deep Listening.

Made Mantle Hood (June 13, 2010)

PhD, Universität zu Köln (Ethnomusicology)
Associate Professor, Monash University, Australia

Graduate Studies

MMH: In '95 I took two courses at West Virginia University and one at College Park. Dad was always in the background saying, "Hey, what about that degree?" Finally, in '98 I decided OK, let's go and find a master's degree program. I applied to two or three different places and ended up at the University of Hawai'i for two years. I did my master's there [M. Hood 2001] and then a PhD at the Universität zu Köln in Germany [2005].

MS: Why did you make that move? That seems an unusual career choice for most people who train in ethnomusicology in America.

MMH: There are probably a number of people to thank for that decision, one of whom is my mentor, Ric Trimillos, at the University of Hawai'i. He advised, "You can stay here in beautiful Hawai'i and do your PhD, but you really want to go to the person who can best advise the project you want to undertake. And an added bonus is, of course, to diversify your training, so that you're not staying at the same institution for an MA and PhD." I'd met Rudiger Schumacher, who became my Doktervater for my PhD, at a conference in Rotterdam. He's a specialist in the philosophical side of Balinese music and has transliterated and translated a very important manuscript on the topic that I was interested in, peeling back the layers of temple music and its practice in Bali. It was really a question of finding the right person, and that meant testing it out first. In 2001 I got a Fulbright to try a year in Germany, learn the language, and get a feel for what was going on there. Then I applied for a DAAD scholarship and got that for another two years, and then had a final year with the DFG [Deutsche Forschungsgemeinschaft], for a research project with the Berlin Phonogram Archiv. I just kept hopping to different continents and had a nice four-year experience in German culture. I completed my PhD in 2005.

Building a Career

MMH: About a year before I was finished, I got my first job. As we all do, we knock on doors, go to conferences, and ask what's going on in various places. I applied for four or five positions that were being advertised and got a few interviews, but I decided that the best place to go was Australia, the primary reason being that my wife is from Bali (she's the niece of I Made Bandem, so the family ties are further cemented there), and there's a big Indonesian population in Melbourne, so I went to Monash University.

MS: We've touched a little on this question already, but who were some of your role models in ethnomusicology? The people who inspired you?

MMH: At the top of the list has to be my father. First that's for family reasons, but it's also for a lot of the ideologies, the outlook, and the methodologies that influenced me. John Blacking would be another. He represents the European approach to ethnomusicology. We have a very strong American ethnomusicology in today's discourse, but I think we should remember some of the European discourses that were going on during Blacking's time. I'll be honest, I Made Bandem is a great hero of mine as well. I've grown up in his family and I've had a lot of his mentorship along the way. And, of course, [there is] my mentor, the late Rudiger Schumacher, who has passed away, for his work and its level of detail and specificity.

MS: Do you see yourself as part of a lineage?

MMH: Yes, in certain ways. I think "lineage" denotes a line or continuation of something. I view where I am more as the beginning of something that has many lines sprouting out of where I've come from. My father blazed a trail that was fast and furious and his own, but I think, from that experience, I'll draw my own line. I'm staying true to myself, so to speak, in career choice and career path. Whatever I've absorbed during that experience, I can only reflect. Based on where I am now, my path is something I've yet to blaze. Creating my own line, if you will, in the lineage.

MS: From the paper you gave at the conference yesterday, in which you talked about working on your father's recordings, you seem to feel a sense of obligation to his material and to preserving it as part of your work. Would that be fair?

MMH: Absolutely! I mean, one half of my goal in that paper was to preserve and publish some of the recordings, but as I got into the *Lestari: The Hood Collection* project [various artists, 2007], I realized that simply producing a CD was doing little or nothing to serve the communities of musicians. For me, that has always been a big interest. How can Hood's collection of field recordings from late 1950s Central Java help fuel an interest so that local archives in Indonesia can be empowered? So I took that on. That's been a research agenda for me for a few years now—local empowerment and negotiating tradition. It seemed like a natural project to take on and push to a level where there's an area of need—an applied ethnomusicology approach. So, yes, I am continuing the line but drawing new ones and, hopefully, creating a nice picture.

MS: In a practical sense, what is your career like at this point? What's your life like at Monash?

MMH: When I started at Monash, I was half time in [the] Music [Department] and half time teaching Indonesian languages. I did that for two years. I've been full time in Music for three years. Now it's all about the publication record. I've got an article that just came out this month. I have a book that I'm publishing with LitVerlag Press based on my dissertation. I just finished my sabbatical, and I'm preparing a report to my arts faculty. I've written two more articles during that time. So for me now, to balance out the training that I've had in teaching and administration, it's all about publication.

MS: Do they have an equivalent of tenure at Monash?

MMH: Yes. Even though I was two years in Indonesian, you're only eligible for tenure after three years of full-time status. I presented my case about three and one-half years into full-time employment with Monash and was tenured in 2009.

Update: July 19, 2016

Shortly after our conversation at the 2010 inaugural ICTM PASEA [Performing Arts of Southeast Asia] symposium in Singapore, LitVerlag Press published my book *Triguna:*

A Hindu-Balinese Philosophy for Gamelan Gong Gede Music [2010]. Also during this time I was elected Secretary of ICTM PASEA, and this would turn out to be a fortuitous assignment. Were it not for Ric Trimillos encouraging me to join PASEA, I would not have strengthened my network with some of the most important scholars in Southeast Asia. This networking would eventually land me a position in Malaysia.

My transition from Australia to Malaysia in 2012 was a strategic turning point in my career. After six years as lecturer in ethnomusicology at Monash University, corporate downsizing saw hundreds of staff, including myself, accept voluntary redundancy packages. I then moved over to Melbourne University for eighteen months, working closely with Cathy Falk before moving to Kuala Lumpur to take up my current associate professor position in ethnomusicology at Universiti Putra Malaysia. Had I not attended PASEA in Singapore, I might not have met many of my dear colleagues here in Malaysia. My earlier experience living and working in Indonesia since 1988, my ability to speak fluent *Bahasa*, and my sensitivity to *budaya Melayu [Malay culture]*, proved to be an excellent foundation for my current post.

Inna Naroditskaya (October 26, 2007)

PhD, University of Michigan (Ethnomusicology)
Associate Professor, Northwestern University

Graduate Studies

IN: When the problem happened with my hand [in 1994 or '95], I applied to three graduate programs in musicology. I went to visit the University of Michigan and met the department chair, Judith Becker. We had a half-hour conversation, and she asked me what I would like to do there. I said I had two options: Russian music or Azerbaijani music. She said, "If you do Russian music, I can't help you, but we have a good faculty; if you do Azerbaijani music, you'll be an ethnomusicologist and, most likely, I will be your advisor." I thought about how many people write about Russian music, so I said, "Sure, I'll go for ethnomusicology." I liked Judith a lot from the conversation. She became my advisor—she is divine! As soon as I left that meeting, I went right over to the Rackham Graduate Library and looked up the word "ethnomusicology." The first thing I ran across was Bruno Nettl's book on ethnomusicology. I went back to Flint and got all of his books because he seemed to be the one at the time who dealt with definitions. That was how I began to read. I had good musicology training, so once I was on a track, I could find my way.

TS: Then what happened? Did you get a fellowship or a teaching assistantship?

IN: Not the first year, no. Actually, I was blessed in the first year. I didn't know this at the time, but if you worked in the University of Michigan system, you could get free, or partly free, tuition. In the second year I got an assistantship. I worked with the medieval musicologist James Borders, and the Russian musicologist John Wiley. I loved Michigan, but there were big challenges there because they didn't know how to relate to me. I was a professional musician with a musicological background, and they couldn't turn me around. At the first meeting, for example, Jim Borders said, "Of course, you can't explain medieval notation because you're an ethnomusicologist." I said, "I can't because I have forgotten this; we used to study it in the sixth grade." He has a good sense of humor, so he got the message.

TS: Once you got into Azeri music, how did you proceed from there?

IN: I did coursework. I wrote a paper comparing carpets and *mugham* in Iran. That also came from my experience in Flint. I had been asked to give a lecture about the history of carpets in the Art Institute and thought the best way to explain carpets was through sound and visual patterns.

TS: Was this your thesis?

IN: Yes, I didn't have a master's degree from America, so I had to submit an extended master's-level piece of writing in my first year. I finally published it in *Ethnomusicology Forum* a year or two ago in a much-revised version [2005], but the idea was still a social and structural comparison of mugham and carpets. When I finished my coursework, I went back to Azerbaijan and had to revisit everything because from such a distance—geographical, temporal, and scholarly—many things looked extremely different. I had also taken a gender course with Ingrid Monson, who was teaching at Michigan for a year. At first, I was very opposed to the whole concept. In my culture, the rules seemed to be "natural." It was only when I stepped outside—although you can never totally step outside—and established some distance, that I could see gender from a different perspective. At the beginning of the course I was extremely resentful, but by the end of the semester I was her biggest convert. The next year, I actually taught this class, and ever since it has been one of my major courses—thanks to Ingrid!

TS: So, you went back to Azerbaijan to do PhD research?

IN: Yes, because I hadn't done much Azerbaijani music research when I lived there. We had classes in Azerbaijani music, but it was a very different process of study, so I had to go and do sociological interviews and so forth. I went twice while I was doing my dissertation. My Azerbaijani colleagues—the late Elkhan Babayev, Hajar Babayeva, Rena Mamedova, Aytach Rahimova, Alla Bayramova, and others—provided extraordinary help.

TS: What was the eventual title of your dissertation?

IN: "Continuity and Change in *Mugham* during the Last 100 Years" [1999]. I took one mugham mode and traced it from the introduction of the Soviet Union and the revolution afterward. I showed how mugham became associated with national identity in the early twentieth century and then traced it through symphonic works, showing how that led to the creation of composing schools and how it was adapted to the written Western European genre. I also traced the development of a jazz scene and showed how, as the socialist system faded at the end of the century, a kind of reversal began to occur, leading to interesting combinations of composed and improvised music. Mugham was the common denominator for everything. Also, since Ingrid indoctrinated me into gender studies, I started publishing articles about Azerbaijani female performers.

TS: Is that something you had experienced earlier? You mentioned that it was difficult to be a pianist and a woman with a child.

IN: You have to imagine that in a socialistic Azerbaijan, striking as it seems—and I'm speaking about urban culture here—it was gender-complex in ways that were beneficial to women. You could go both ways; you could expect to be provided for.

Building a Career

IN: I completed my research in Azerbaijan, finished my dissertation in 1999, and Michigan hired me as a lecturer. It wasn't a permanent position because Michigan doesn't hire its own people. I taught very interesting courses, including "Music and Orientalism," which combined my knowledge of Western musical literature and ethnomusicological methods and theory.

The following year, 2000, I got a tenure-track faculty position at Northwestern University. I taught a pro-seminar in ethnomusicology, ethnomusicology methods, and "Music and Gender in Non-Western Societies." I also taught "Ethnic Neighborhoods in Chicago" and an ethnographic course on ethnic weddings in the Chicago area. I continued to teach "Music and Orientalism," which proved to be a very successful class and could be taught at various levels—for graduates, undergraduates, or even nonmajors. I've also taught a course called "Russian Fairytale and Russian Opera"; it's not a particularly musicological class, but the methods look beyond traditional historical musicology. This is my eighth year at Northwestern. I got tenure about a year and a half ago. I was very lucky and had no problems; my book on Azerbaijani mugham was published [2003], I had two co-edited books [Hemetek et al. 2004; Naroditskaya and Austern 2006], and I'd gotten a research grant from Harvard to work on another subject.

TS: May I ask who has been most influential to you in ethnomusicology?

IN: There have been so many important people at Michigan—Judith Becker, Bill Malm (even though he wasn't teaching when I was there), Joseph Lam, and Amy Stillman. I'm also grateful to my musicological colleagues, especially Rich Crawford (an Americanist who crosses borders in interesting ways) and, of course, Ingrid Monson.

Update: June 26, 2016

Since 2007 I have been researching in several directions. First, questions about how diaspora enacts itself musically in the US. For me, a refugee from Soviet Azerbaijan, this has involved fieldwork in multiple places: Azerbaijan, the United States, Odessa, and Moscow. Azerbaijan has transformed its identity in terms of politics, statehood, religion, language, and aspirations. Many people left the country, and others migrated from the periphery to the urban center. The United States is a nation whose citizenship I value deeply and whose cultural patterns I am still discovering. In the no-longer-existing Soviet Union, I have begun researching and writing about Odessa (a Russian-speaking Ukrainian city), whose music lingua, language, theater, and overall cultural scene are intimately familiar, even though I never lived in the city. And Moscow, where I lived for one winter as a student, is a cultural center to which I gravitated while growing up, studying, performing, and visiting.

Two Russian capitals also are the cultural frames of my volume, *Bewitching Russian Opera: The Tsarina from State to Stage* [2012]. This volume came out after our original conversation and reflects my longstanding belief that ethnomusicology should not limit itself to studying the current scene; its analytical methods apply to historical as well as current repertoire. In that book, I researched operas created by one of the most powerful figures in the history of the Russian empire, Catherine the Great. Ethnomusicological lenses led me to ask what it meant when operas were created by an absolute monarch. How did these operas function, and how should they be perceived in historical contexts brushed over by nationalism, gender biases, and political twists?

Recently I became a full professor, which gives me great personal satisfaction when I think that twenty-six years ago I left my former homeland with my young son and two pieces of luggage. My son, now thirty-one, has completed his MA, worked for several years in Washington, DC, and was recently in Moscow on a fellowship. Life is full of surprises. Most recently, I finished an edited volume on weddings in diaspora (forthcoming, Indiana University Press). By teaming with an outstanding group of fellow ethnomusicologists, I also attempted to make sense of my professional and personal diasporic journey over a quarter century in America.

Laudan Nooshin (July 9, 2007)

PhD, Goldsmiths, University of London (Ethnomusicology)
Associate Professor, City, University of London

Graduate Studies

LN: When I graduated, I wanted to do a master's in ethnomusicology, and at that time there were only two places in the UK you could do that: Belfast, with John Blacking, or Goldsmiths, University of London. I decided to go to Goldsmiths and did a part-time two-year master's in ethnomusicology between 1984 and 1986.

TS: What did you emphasize in your MA?

LN: Iranian music. My master's thesis was on improvisation in *dastgah Mahour* (my PhD was on *dastgah Segah*). I transcribed and compared a number of performances. It was highly analytical, what I now regard as very structuralist. When I did my master's, I didn't have any funding, so I worked in various capacities, from McDonald's to piano teaching. I also worked in the Music Department office at Goldsmiths for about a year and a half. After I finished, I wanted to get into the "real world," so I continued working there. I really wanted to work somewhere like the South Bank Centre (an arts complex in London), in the education section, doing outreach work in schools. I had various ideas, but while I was working in the department office, everyone was made redundant and had to reapply for their jobs. This coincided with the deadline for postgraduate funding from the British Academy, which used to administer these things in the UK. My head of department said, "Why don't you put in a proposal for PhD research?" So I did. I got the funding and I also got my job back.

I had intended to go to SOAS for my PhD but decided to stay at Goldsmiths because there was no Music Department at SOAS at that time. Goldsmiths had a Music Department that had Western music as well, and Stanley Glasser, the head of the department, was building up ethnomusicology.

TS: You mention wanting to be in the real world, but was there something about academia that repelled you, something you were ambiguous about?

LN: Whether right or not, I did feel that academia was slightly disconnected from what I perceived to be the "real world." When I was doing my PhD, I got excited about some ideas then current in the UK—the whole debate about multicultural education in state-sector schools. I even had discussions with assorted people about setting up an organization to go into schools and run workshops. At that time—1988, I think—there were discussions happening around the proposed National Curriculum for Music. It included "world music," but many teachers felt ill equipped to deal with this. I went into schools and played some *setar*.

Another thing that would have been my dream at that time was to work at the BBC. I actually had my eye out for jobs in broadcasting or in publishing. Those were the areas I thought I would really enjoy. The mid-'80s was a pretty bad time in the UK: the Thatcher period, high unemployment, cuts in public-sector spending. It was not a good time to be trying to get into creative jobs.

TS: Did you ever think about the security of academia as a platform from which you could do these kinds of things?

LN: When I started my PhD, I never imagined I would be able to get a job, actually, because in those days there were only a handful of places that had ethnomusicology positions—Durham, York, Cambridge, Edinburgh, SOAS, Goldsmiths, and Belfast—and they each had one or, at most, two people. I had no conception that it would expand exponentially in the way it has over the last fifteen years. I didn't think I would ever end up having a job teaching. Having said that, one of the great things about Goldsmiths was that they gave their graduate students opportunities to do bits and pieces of teaching. So when I started my PhD, I went straight into doing the odd lecture here and there, which I really enjoyed. I was new and inexperienced, and yet, wow, the buzz and the interest I got from the students! That started me thinking that maybe this wasn't such a bad place to be after all.

TS: It's interesting that you say graduate students had no conception of what it would be like to work as an ethnomusicologist at that time. It's quite different now because there's more emphasis on graduate-student publishing.

LN: It's very different now because the "research assessment exercise" that we have in the UK means that if you apply for a job, you more or less have to have publications before you finish your PhD. In my very unstructured, unstrategic career, I wasn't aware of that at all. I thought I had to write the best PhD ever, and I took a long time to finish it. I wasn't aware of what was really involved: the need to publish.

TS: It's really interesting to hear how things have changed in the UK. By the way, you said you played some setar. How did that come about?

LN: I got the funding to start my PhD in 1987, which was about the worst time to be doing research on Iranian music. I couldn't go to Iran because of the war with Iraq, very few musicians were coming from Iran, and there weren't many diaspora musicians outside Iran. But I was doing a project on improvisation in Iranian music, and I needed to be able to back up my transcription and analysis by working with musicians. I had a setar, so I started learning with a teacher in London. The lessons were quite mixed, really; I spent quite a bit of time going through recordings with him, identifying *gushehs* and *dastgahs*. He did some teaching as well, but it was very difficult, not least because he lived a long way from me.

It was a big problem not to be able to study with an instrumentalist and also not to be able to go to Iran. Instead, I spent a week with Bruno Nettl in Urbana, Illinois, and stayed with Margaret Sarkissian, who generously let me crash at her house. Bruno was amazing and literally let me loose on his archive of recordings from his time in Iran. But performing was a way of adding another dimension to my research and trying to come to some understanding of the improvisational process.

TS: How far did you get in your performing?

LN: Not very far! I'm not a professional player. Plus, I just didn't have the expertise available when I needed it.

TS: Forty-five years ago, if you'd said, "I don't play," that would have been a plus! So now you play in a sort of pan–Middle Eastern ensemble?

LN: Yes, we have an ensemble that's been running for about two years. We call it "Middle Eastern," but it's really Iranian with a bit of Kurdish. I play *daff* and the students play various Middle Eastern percussion instruments and arrangements of pieces on their own instruments.

Building a Career

When my three years of PhD funding finished, I moved to Canada for personal reasons. I hadn't finished my PhD when I went. It didn't work out, and after a year I came back and started looking for work. After six months of applying for things and not finding anything, I started a PGCE (Post-Graduate Certificate in Education) course, a one-year teacher-training course that qualifies you to teach in primary or secondary schools. I started with the full intention of going into secondary-school music teaching. We did teaching practice with kids from eleven to eighteen, and I was glad to be able to use my knowledge of ethnomusicology.

Halfway through the course, I saw an ethnomusicology position advertised at the West London Institute of Higher Education. I applied for the job and got it. When I started, in 1993, it was more a teaching college than a research place, and there wasn't much postgraduate work. In addition to a degree program, we ran a Foundation Course, a "pre-degree" course, so I was teaching sixteen- to eighteen-year-olds, mainly rock guitarists, who came in not reading music but who wanted to go on to a degree. We also had a lot of mature students. So I went into an institution where I was literally in the classroom eighteen hours a week; it was a very heavy teaching schedule. On top of that, I was still trying to finish the PhD, and my older son was just eighteen months old.

I desperately wanted to carry on with my research, but I was glad to have a job. What I really liked about the place, though, was the then-head of music, Derek Scott (now at Leeds); he was very keen to expand into ethnomusicology. He's what you'd call a "new musicologist" and was teaching music and gender before anyone else in the UK. I replaced a composer. My first teaching responsibilities included a second-year world music survey course.

I was there for eleven years (until I went to City in 2004), and during that time the nature of the institution changed. When I started, the degrees were validated by Brunel University. Eventually, we were assimilated into Brunel University and moved to their main campus in Uxbridge, West London. The whole nature of my teaching also changed, and we became more research focused; the graduate provision increased, as did ethnomusicology to some extent. For the world music survey I was able to get in people to do workshops for us. Henry Stobart got us some panpipes, and I ran a Bolivian group for a while. We also took students to the South Bank Centre to play gamelan.

TS: Can you tell me about your first research trip to Iran in 1999?

LN: I had a sabbatical in 1998–99, a whole year off teaching. I'd started some fieldwork with the Iranian diaspora in London, something I'd gotten more interested in after I finished my PhD. I did two months of fieldwork, but it became increasingly difficult for me. I felt quite out of sympathy with some of the people I was interviewing, mostly expatriates who had very negative views about contemporary Iran. I'd gone in with a preconceived, essentialized notion about music and identity: "Iranians listen to Iranian music, and it plays a very important role in their cultural identity." I didn't know how to make sense of my own feelings, so I stopped working on that project because I had another piece of writing I had to finish.

Two months later I went to Iran with my husband and two children. I didn't really know what to expect. A lot of people had said to me, "It won't be what you think; you were brought up in Britain, you're British really." I'd always had this dream, from my childhood, of walking down the street and not being "different." I would look the same as other people. I'd always thought of Iran as "home," even though I'd only been once, as a child. It was probably something I needed to feel, because I'd never really felt at home in the UK.

When I went in 1999, I absolutely fell in love with the country. I felt like I'd come home. I was bowled over by all the music, particularly the popular music that had become legal again after Khatami was elected in 1997. I thought, "If I have a platform to write about Iranian music, I should be writing about what's happening in Iran now, because people don't know much about this." So I shelved all my diaspora stuff. I still haven't published it! I just felt a responsibility to let people outside know the richness and complexity of what was happening in Iran. I've been back many times since then. I would have spent more time there if I could; children make it complicated.

TS: How did you respond to the obvious gender restrictions?

LN: Well, women actually have a great deal of freedom, though legally, of course, there are many restrictions. In many ways, I wouldn't say that women are disempowered. You go into any family and it's the women who are the stronger. Iranian women are very strong and active. In the public sphere women are everywhere; they push at the restrictions. I arrived in Iran with a headscarf down to here, and immediately my sister-in-law pushed it back and said, "What do you think you're doing?" It's much more complex than simply saying, "Women are oppressed." Women do have a voice. I have an aunt who is a well-known filmmaker in Iran. She deals a lot with women's issues in her films and has won many international awards. She plays on these complexities. Personally, I didn't have restrictions in terms of where I could go. In fact, I arguably had more freedom than men, because I could go to mixed gatherings and I had access to all-female gatherings as well.

Update: July 16, 2016

In some ways not a great deal has changed since I was interviewed in 2007. I am at the same institution, still teaching, researching and doing more administration than I would like. At the time of the interview I was about to become co-editor of *Ethnomusicology Forum*, which took up much of my time in the four years that followed. It was a good experience, great for networking and getting to know a wide range of ethnomusicologists and others. And it meant I read everything that was published in the journal! But it was perhaps not the best move at that stage in my career, in that it took a phenomenal amount of time away from my own research at a time when I should have been building up my own publications. In the context of the UK periodic cycle of research assessment, this meant that prospects for promotion or moving to a new post were impacted negatively. Unfortunately, the role of journal editors is not sufficiently recognized in research assessment exercises of the kind we have in the UK, not only in supporting, promoting, and quite frankly improving the work of other scholars, but also in helping to shape discussion in the field of study.

In my time as co-editor, one of my "missions" was to cut across sub/disciplinary boundaries by commissioning or leading special issues, such as "the ethnomusicology of western art music" or "ethnomusicological approaches to screen music studies." Challenging what I find to be increasingly meaningless (and unhelpful) boundaries has been a constant theme through my career, both in my research and teaching. If I dig down deep enough, this is probably rooted in having grown up as an "ethnic" Other in a largely "white" suburban town and having spent many years challenging these kind of identity boundaries as well as the idea that identities have to be singular (see below).

In any case, I am definitely older and hopefully a little wiser than in 2007. I have seen through several large publication projects, including two edited volumes and a monograph [2009, 2014, 2015]. And I was recently promoted to reader, which in the UK is the level below full professor. I have also had major course directorship responsibilities in recent years, including for our PhD, DMA, and MA programs, which has been hard work, but I have really enjoyed working closely with the students. And I have also had a number of PhD students complete—it's always great to see these students move on and develop within or beyond academia. In terms of my research direction, having worked mainly on Iranian classical and popular music for many years, I'm excited now to be moving in new directions, exploring urban soundscapes—specifically the sounds of Tehran—and music in Iranian cinema.

Update: August 11, 2017

In September 2016 City University became part of the federal University of London, so it is now known as City, University of London. In May 2017 I assumed the role of head of the Music Department at City, University of London.

Olabode (Bode) Omojola (March 4, 2013)

PhD, University of Leicester (Ethnomusicology)
Associate Professor, Mount Holyoke College and The Five Colleges

Graduate Studies

BO: I felt like a door had opened. In spite of my love for Western classical music, I began to feel that I could study my own music and that the experiences I was having could actually become part of my academic world. And, at that same time, Omibiyi started a new program in ethnomusicology and African music at the University of Ibadan, the oldest university in Nigeria. It was founded in 1948. I was among the very first to enroll in the Institute of African Studies. We had two people teaching us ethnomusicology: Mosun Omibiyi-Obidike and Samuel Akpabot. Samuel Akpabot had studied at the same university as [Wilberforce] Echezona—Michigan State. He has a well-known book called *Ibibio Music in Nigerian Culture* [Akpabot 1975]. We also took courses in anthropology, fieldwork methods, history, archaeology, et cetera.

As I was finishing, Samuel Akpabot encouraged me to go for my PhD. There were two choices: the US or the UK. We didn't think highly of American education at that time, perhaps because we knew students who couldn't get into Nigerian universities but went to the US and came back three years later with a degree! We asked, "How did he do it? He couldn't even pass his O-levels here in Nigeria." We were biased against the US, so I went to the UK to study. Now, I realize that those people must have gone to low-rated colleges in the US.

I began to ask myself: "OK, so I did very traditional stuff in Ibadan. What shall I do for my PhD?" I decided to look at popular works by Nigerian composers that explored the issue of African identity. It was midway between what I was doing at Nsukka and what I was doing at Ibadan: Nsukka, Western music; Ibadan, traditional music; PhD, contemporary forms. I went to Leicester University in the East Midlands, UK, and spent four years there. I did coursework for the first year then went back to Nigeria for fieldwork. When I went back for my third and fourth years to write up and get my PhD, I ran into financial problems. I was on a federal scholarship when the Nigerian government decided that you couldn't go abroad to study any course that you could study in Nigeria. After I started at Leicester, they started a PhD program at Ibadan (where I did my MA). I didn't want to study in Nigeria. I wanted to travel. I got a scholarship and went to the UK. My first two years were fine, but by the third year the PhD program at Ibadan was fairly well established and music was added to the list of courses that you couldn't study abroad. The government stopped my scholarship. So what was I going to do? My supervisor, Anthony Pither, didn't want to me to go back. I was crying, and then Anthony said, "I know what we can do. The university regulations say that if you have reached what they call the 'writing-up status,' you do not need to pay the £3,500 school fees." And guess what, that meant you only had to pay £50! So he wrote to the university to let them know that I had reached the writing-up status. So after four years I got my PhD.

My defense brought me into contact with John Blacking. He was my external examiner. I was relatively young, about twenty-seven, when we met. I think he said I was the youngest doctoral student he had examined. He was very happy with my work. At the viva [orals], he said, "Look, I can speak to my friends to get you a job in the US." But I was eager to go back home because I wanted to develop Nigeria, so I went back.

Building a Career

MS: When you came back with a PhD, were your parents happy that you had studied music?

BO: Very happy! We had a car, we were living well, and they would come around to visit me. I went back to the University of Ilorin in 1988. They had started a new program called Performing Arts, which had music, dance, and drama. I headed the music unit and worked there. Eventually I became head of the department. From 1996 to 1998, I had an Alexander von Humboldt Foundation postgraduate fellowship. I worked with the late Professor Rudiger Schumacher, head of "Musikethnologie," the ethnomusicology unit at the University of Cologne. It's a fantastic fellowship. Once you are awarded the initial fellowship, you can always tell them, "I want to come over for three, six months to conduct research." That would soon become very important.

Everything was OK, normal life—until 2001. There's a lot of corruption in Nigeria. I didn't like that and wanted to do whatever I could to stop it. At the university level we had a vice chancellor (that's like the president) who had rather oily fingers, so to speak—stealing money and doing all sorts of horrible things. So we mobilized, and I became the vice chair of the university teachers' union. We publicized what this guy was doing, how he was stealing money, and mobilized our members to go on strike. The guy should have been removed, but we were the ones that got removed! We didn't know that he had such strong connections with the Nigerian government. So I lost my job in 2001. That marked a new phase in my life. I had gotten married some four, five years before.

Losing my job was a very painful thing for me. My papers had been sent out for promotion to associate professor, and when the reviewers wrote back, the vice chancellor sat on it. "You can't be troubling me if you want to become a professor here." So I got sacked and then I was at home, but I was not depressed. I was not happy that I lost my job, but I felt great at what I was doing. And I wasn't alone. We mobilized the university system to go on strike. Eventually, the university said, "OK, you have to go back to work." You know how union and employers fight. "And if you don't go back to work, you will lose your salary." So they started stopping people's salaries. And gradually our rank and file collapsed as people went back to work. But forty-nine of us remained; we said,

"Sack us, do whatever you want to do. We're not going to go back to work." We became known as the "Unilorin 49" (that's an abbreviation for University of Ilorin). I was busy doing my work as a scholar. I was able to go back to the University of Cologne in 2002 for another six months. I saved all my salary in Germany and took it back to Nigeria. While I was in Germany, I saw [information about] the Harvard-Radcliffe Fellowship. I applied and got it, which was what brought me to the US.

MS: So you had a one-year fellowship at Harvard and then, if I'm not mistaken, you went to Northeastern University?

BO: Yes, I was at Harvard from 2004 to 2005 and then taught as an adjunct at Northeastern from 2005 to 2006. And then in 2006 I came to Mount Holyoke College and the Five Colleges. Everything worked out well in the end. Two or three years ago we (the Unilorin 49) won our case. We kept fighting. We went to what they call the lower court and won. The university appealed to the appeals court and won. So we took it to the supreme court, and we won. The court ruled that they should pay us *all* our salary from 2001 to 2010. We all got a nice lump sum! It was a good struggle. I always tell people that whatever you believe in, go for it. If you are crushed, too bad, but you may not be crushed!

MS: Can you tell me what your career is like in a practical sense now?

BO: Well, I teach, and I write, I compose, and I try to do occasional major performances.

MS: You have a very unusual academic position, if I may say so. I don't think there can be many jobs like your Five College position. You are based at one institution, Mount Holyoke College, where you do half of your teaching; the other half of your teaching load is shared in rotation among the other four institutions in the consortium (Amherst, Hampshire, and Smith Colleges, and the University of Massachusetts at Amherst). How have you managed to navigate such a complex position?

BO: I would say, without trying to embarrass you, that people like you have made it very possible when there could have been challenges. There are challenges and there are certain schools that I love to teach at more than others, but when you have someone on the ground who does all sorts of bureaucratic navigation (if I may use your word) and deals with the logistics—which office am I going to use, what keys do I need—it makes it much easier. Arranging publicity is important because when you only teach on a campus once every two years, by the time you come back many of the students who knew you last time are gone. So when you have somebody who helps spread the word, it's not as challenging as it might otherwise be. Needless to say, each campus has its own academic culture and even climate and general ambience. So once I know this is my job, OK, this is what I signed for! I just keep doing it. But really, people like you have helped to make things easier on some campuses.

MS: To change the subject slightly, do you think of yourself as being part of any kind of lineage within the field of ethnomusicology?

BO: I would say the African lineage, if there is such a lineage, because from what you can see from my background, there's a strong Western cultural heritage influencing how we built up our careers. I think that is the way it is for most ethnomusicologists. But for African ethnomusicologists, Western music is foreign to them, and yet it was the academic foundation upon which they built their careers.

You may be aware of the high profile of Kofi Agawu, for example, who is more of a musicologist than an ethnomusicologist because he studied Western music in Ghana before going to England and the United States. The same thing for Akin Euba, who was exposed to Western music in Nigeria before studying in Europe and the United States. Euba, a strong advocate for African art music, is known for writing musical compositions that rely significantly on Western forms fused with indigenous African elements. I will say that I've been lucky here at Mount Holyoke and the Five Colleges, and that's why I like Linda Laderach, my colleague and former department chair. When I said, "Let's bring a high-life band!" she jumped at it, regardless of what people might think. So if I may refer to those African scholars as constituting a lineage, then I will say I belong to that group.

MS: Going back to when you first started out, before you went to do your master's degree, you said you began reading books about ethnomusicology. Do you remember what you were reading?

BO: Nketia, Akin Euba, and of course some Western scholars like A. M. Jones—the pioneering scholars of African music.

Update: July 8, 2016

I would say that there hasn't been much change since we talked in 2013. Apart from rising to the rank of full professor, I have continued to carry out my duties as a scholar working on Yoruba music traditions and practices in West Africa and their influences and re-interpretations in the black diaspora, mainly, Brazil, Cuba, and the United States.

Elizabeth Travassos Lins (July 11, 2007)

PhD, Museu Nacional do Universidade Federal do Estado do Rio de Janeiro (Anthropology)
Associate Professor, Universidade Federal do Estado do Rio de Janeiro

Graduate Studies

ETL: I became an intern at the Museu do Índio (Indian Museum) in Rio de Janeiro. It was a good experience for a student who liked anthropology. I went for the first time to an Indian village in the hinterlands of São Paulo with some colleagues from the museum. That was when I began to think of continuing to graduate studies in anthropology. I wanted to study a different society, not my society. Not peasants or Afro-Brazilian people from the cities, but a different social world.

I entered the graduate program in anthropology at the Museu Nacional in 1979 and met Anthony Seeger. He told me that anthropology and music were not radically separated, that there was something called "ethnomusicology," and that if you have a background in music, you can convert it into useful things in anthropology. So I began to read Tony Seeger's articles on Suyá music, and I said, "This is what I want to do." In Brazil at that time, if you told your professor of sociology, "I love Beethoven, I play the sonatas and I play Bach very well," he would say, "That's good, but you have to read Durkheim and Max Weber; Beethoven has nothing to do with it." Tony Seeger explained that these things could be related: my musical training could be useful to my anthropological and ethnological work. I was amazed to discover "anthropology of music," because I had never heard about it before. The field was nonexistent in Brazil. Tony Seeger was trying to establish something in Rio de Janeiro. At that time he was the sole ethnomusicologist in Brazil. While I was finishing my master's thesis [1984] with Tony Seeger, he left for Indiana University, so I was alone in Rio de Janeiro.

After finishing, I went to work at the Museu do Folclor (Folklore Museum) because they needed someone with training in both music and social sciences to take care of the archives and work there. It was there that I began to read Béla Bartók, Mario de Andrade, Carlos Vega, Isabel Aretz, Luis Felipe Ramón y Rivera, and Zóltan Kodály, and discovered that folklore and ethnomusicology had strong ties. There was a sort of denial of this heritage. In ethnomusicology in the '80s there was a strong criticism against folklore and comparative musicology, but the ties are very close. They are intimate enemies; they could be allies. But ethnomusicology was trying to define itself as a new field, so there was a sense that, "We are not practicing this old inventory of songs. We are analyzing structure. We are understanding music in context."

TS: Did you complete your PhD at the Museu Nacional?

ETL: Yes, but many years later, because I was working in the sound archive. I was so fascinated that I began to do more missions to collect folklore music among peasants in Brazil. I began to understand that folklore was a very interesting thing, and that musical folklore in Brazil was very important. Even though as an intellectual tradition it was considered minor, old, and archaic, it was still very interesting because we had a very important author/poet/writer/musicologist called Mario de Andrade [1893–1945], who was a brilliant man. When I was reading Alan Merriam or Bruno Nettl, for instance, I realized that Mario de Andrade had anticipated so many things. I discovered that maybe we *had* an ethnomusicology, an anthropology of music in Brazil, even though we didn't have a name for it. I decided to write my PhD on ethnography and another subject that began to be important to me, what I call the "ideology of autonomous art"—the particular ways Western societies understand art. Once you have worked with indigenous peoples outside Western societies—like Afro-Brazilian peoples, for example—you understand that art is something very particular. So I connected anthropology, folklore, and anthropology of music in my PhD dissertation [1996].

TS: Where were you doing field research at that point?

ETL: In Northeastern Brazil, among *cantadores de viola*, people who improvise verses with *viola* (a ten-string guitar) and sing *romances*, an important Iberian tradition that has survived in Brazil.

Building a Career

ETL: I worked in the sound archive of the Museu do Folclor for ten years, from 1983 to 1992. I left the archive in 1992 but stayed in the same institution as a researcher until 1996, when I left for the university. Now I am associate professor of anthropology and ethnomusicology, and I teach in the School of Music and the School of Drama. I like it, but I am the sole anthropologist in the whole school; that's a problem for me. I don't have many anthropologists as colleagues there.

TS: So you are not connected with the School of Anthropology or the School of Social Sciences? Do you feel isolated?

ETL: Isolated? Well, that's one side of the coin. The other side is that I feel I am in the right place because I like anthropology of music. I like anthropology, I like performance studies, and it's OK to write about musical expression because I am in the School of Music. If I were in a sociology department, they would ask, "Oh, is music really important? Perhaps it's not so important," and I would have to compete with sociologists writing about traditional things in sociology: modernization, globalization, et cetera.

TS: So, because you are the only person, you have more autonomy and more freedom to do what you want?

ETL: Exactly. I'm free! My colleagues say, "We have confidence in you; if you say this project is important, then go ahead."

TS: Do you teach any ensembles?

ETL: No, my colleagues wanted me to make an ensemble because they needed more teachers to lead chamber music and popular music ensembles. It's a large school with five hundred students, and they are overwhelmed, so they asked me, "Please, do an ensemble with folk music because the students want to play folk music." I told them, "I don't know how to do it. I'm not a folklore singer; what am I to do?" I tried. I formed an ensemble, but it gave me the opportunity to discover that the voice was crucial. We listened to the recordings, we transcribed, and we practiced. We could play the guitar, the drums, and everything, but when it came to singing like them, we just couldn't do it! So, I began to ask myself, what is the difference between the throat, lungs, stomach, and nose voice? It's very difficult to translate vocal style. So I'm now working on a research project called "Vocal Styles and Social Processes," and I'm trying to review the literature on voice in the social sciences and ethnomusicology, but this will take me many, many years.

(Elizabeth passed away on October 28, 2013, in Rio de Janeiro, Brazil.)

Update: August 15, 2017 (by Antônio José Pedral Sampaio Lins, edited by Anthony Seeger)

Following this interview, Elizabeth Travassos spent a postdoctoral year at the University of Belfast in Northern Ireland (2008) and was appointed associate professor at UNIRIO [Universidade Federal do Estado do Rio de Janeiro], where she taught until her death in 2013. She continued her involvement with vernacular music and published widely. She was active in several national and international professional organizations, was one of the founders of the Brazilian Association for Ethnomusicology (Associação Brasileira de Etnomusicologia—ABET), and served as secretary to the organization and as head of the program committee for its 2011 biannual meeting. With Cláudia Neiva de Matos, Fernanda Teixeira de Medeiros, and Liv Soldic she organized three international conferences on "sung speech" (*palavra cantada*) and edited the first two influential volumes from the conferences [Matos et al. 2001, 2008]. The third appeared posthumously [Matos et al. 2014]. She is survived by her husband of thirty-eight years, architect and urban planner Antônio José Pedral Sampaio Lins, and their son João Travassos Lins. Her early demise was mourned by all who knew her.

Postscript, by Anthony Seeger

Elizabeth Travassos Lins was an intellectually rigorous and courageous, warm, and supportive person whose work addressed many aspects of music in Brazil. She undertook field research among Indigenous and non-Indigenous communities, worked in a folklore museum and archive for years, and taught at the Brazilian Conservatory of Music and later at the University of Rio de Janeiro—UNIRIO. For her MA thesis on Kaiabí shamans' songs she did difficult fieldwork alone among the Kaiabí indigenous group in Mato Grosso, Brazil. She served as principal researcher of the audiovisual archive of the Folklore Museum (now National Center for Folklore and Popular Culture) and published audio recordings of Brazilian vernacular music as well as articles on regional vernacular music. Later, teaching at UNIRIO, she collaborated with scholars there and at other institutions to further the study of all forms of Brazilian music and to promote the methods and objectives of ethnomusicology. Her book *Os Mandarins Milagrosos: Arte e etnografia em Mario de Andrade e Béla Bartók* [1997] was based on her doctoral dissertation in anthropology and is a brilliant, sophisticated, and frequently cited discussion of the work and philosophy of the man who set the agenda for much of Brazilian music research, Mario de Andrade, and those of Béla Bartók—who did something similar in Europe. As her MA thesis supervisor and occasional mentor of her later activities, I valued most her ability to say "I don't agree with you at all, Tony, I think you are wrong" (and sometimes the opposite) without timidity or rancor. This intellectual rigor and honesty made her a wonderful advisor and an invaluable collaborator with many projects in Brazil during her busy career. Her originality and humanity infused everything she touched. Her research, career, and life were warmly supported by her husband Antônio Pedral Sampaio Lins, often with a quiet smile and a gentle stillness that opened ample space for her animation and humor.

PROFESSORS

Stephen Blum (October 28, 2007)

PhD, University of Illinois (Ethnomusicology)
Professor, CUNY Graduate Center

Graduate Studies

SB: I went straight from Oberlin to Illinois in 1964. I entered as a master's student in piano, but my hope was to study musicology. There were hardly any assistantships in musicology, and I doubt I could have qualified for one. There wasn't a separate program in ethnomusicology at that time. Bruno Nettl came as a visitor that same year, so I was in his first classes. I had no idea that he would stay, and was delighted when he did! The following year, I took Charles Hamm's "Introduction to Musicology" course.

TS: What courses did you take from Bruno?

SB: I took two in my first year, "Introduction to Music of the World's Peoples" in the fall and "European Folk Music," which I loved, in the spring. I had a bit of trouble getting into that class—when I told my advisor I wanted to take it, he said, "Well, that's for musicology students, not for the likes of you." So I went to Alex Ringer, who picked up the phone and worked it out. Both courses were wonderful with an interesting group of students, including James Dapogny (who made an edition of Jelly Roll Morton) and Jerry Graue. In the spring Bruno mentioned that he was going to be there permanently. In my third year, he had a thirteen-hour-per-week research assistantship for the first time, and I was the obvious choice because I had taken his courses.

TS: Do you remember the first time you heard the word "ethnomusicology"?

SB: It was probably the summer after I graduated from Oberlin; I stayed and worked at the library and saw Bruno Nettl's books. When I went to Illinois, I was surprised: "Oh, the author of these books has just come for a one-year guest visit, goodness me." And since I was interested in Asia, taking "Introduction to Music of the World's Peoples" was the obvious thing to do. We got along quite well, and I've known him for more than forty years.

TS: Did you have a particular interest in East Asia at that point? You had taken that East Asian history course at Oberlin.

SB: I'm not really sure why I chose East Asia. In those years, the CIC—the Big Ten and the University of Chicago—had an East Asian language program every summer funded by the federal government. Students were paid six hundred dollars for eight weeks. My assistantship at Illinois only paid eleven hundred dollars for the whole year, so I applied for it. The choices were Chinese or Japanese, and I chose Japanese, thinking it would be hard to go to China. That was shortsighted—this was 1965, and at the time I was more interested in Chinese culture—although I quickly became, and still am, fascinated by Japanese music. I started the second-year Japanese course, and the summer course at Ohio State was wonderful: it was the best language course I ever took. There were plenty of these six-hundred-dollar fellowships; it was easy to get them. All you needed was a letter from your advisor—Bruno wrote for me. It was good, and it got me more involved in Asian Studies. After my third year I had another summer fellowship to learn Persian. And in my fourth year I had a National Defense Foreign Language Fellowship to study Arabic.

TS: How did you make the transition from Japanese to Persian?

SB: I just got more interested in the Iranian area, I guess. Partly through literature. People, especially Iranians, are always asking me how I got interested in Iran, but I can't recall anything more specific. At the time, I was naïve and had no idea. I can't really imagine that professionally I could ever have competed with ethnomusicologists specializing in Japan—there are so many good ones.

TS: I forget when Bruno got interested in Iran. Did you get interested in Iran through him?

SB: It must have been somehow related to Bruno's interest. In my third year, when I was his research assistant, Peter Crossley-Holland came during the fall semester, and Bruno asked me to take care of him. I helped him make tapes for his lectures. Making a tape of one three-minute example with Peter Crossley-Holland took about thirty minutes. The next semester, [Nour-Ali] Boroumand, the great Persian musician, came. He had taught German at the University of Tehran and was also an amateur musician from a wealthy family. Bruno had come to know William Archer, a psycholinguist who was interested in ethnomusicology and had published a short piece, "On the Ecology of Music" in *Ethnomusicology* [1964]. Bruno and Dan Neuman went to Iran with Archer in the summer of 1966. That must have been when they arranged for Boroumand to come to Illinois. As I had with Crossley-Holland, I took care of Boroumand while he and his wife stayed at the Illini Union and made a lot of recordings of his *radif*. We had no idea at the time, but the versions I recorded turned out to be quite valuable. (Incidentally Mahour, an institute in Teheran, now wants to issue them on CD so that people can compare those performances with the official version he recorded later.)

TS: How about fieldwork?

SB: I did my fieldwork in Iran in 1968–69. When Bruno went to Iran with Dan Neuman and William Archer, they made a short trip to Khorasan, and Bruno thought it would be a good place for research. Archer wanted me to study the whole country, to see how it was modernizing. I didn't want to do that, so it became a violent argument. My original proposal had been accepted and funded; my view was that his unit was meant to administer the funds and that was that. But Archer kept prodding and pushing me harder, saying I should write about the situation in the whole country, especially in Tehran. He said, "Just as all the music of the United States is in New York, all the music of Iran is in Tehran." I knew perfectly well that all the music of the United States was not in New York, and you couldn't begin to get a sense of the regional differences by staying in New York. Iran is even more that way, since there are so many language groups and religious differences.

TS: What happened?

SB: I had taken two tape recorders so I could make copies of tapes. It took four months to get them out of customs and I was stuck in Tehran while I waited. I arrived at the end of August, but couldn't go to Khorasan until the end of December. That was good in many ways, as I had time to practice languages and visit homes where boys were learning Qur'an and different religious activities were going on.

I was only in Khorasan for about seven months. Mashhad, then the fourth largest city, is now favored by the religious regime because it is a religious center that draws thousands of pilgrims. There were lots of speakers of the Turkic language now called "Khorasani Turkish," but at the time, there hadn't been any fieldwork on the language. The first significant fieldwork was done in 1971, and the results were only published in the 1990s.

TS: But your lingua franca was Persian, no? How did you proceed with your fieldwork, then?

SB: Yes, Persian was the only language I used in speaking with musicians. I had met a high-school student from Bojnurd, one of the places I ended up studying, at the religious gatherings in Tehran. He had a friend (another high-school student) who was a native speaker of the Turkish of this area, the main language of Bojnurd. This student had a nice script, and everyone told him, "Oh, you write so beautifully, you could write the titles for movies." So he'd come to Tehran to do that, but his title writing services hadn't been needed. So, luckily for me, he was available to help me. I hired him and rented a house next to the governor general's house. Finding a house was hard because a lot of people wouldn't rent to me. I think that someone from SAVAK, the secret police, would follow me around and tell people not to rent to me. But eventually I rented this house and he lived in it, so when I was interviewing people, he would make notes and go over them with me later. He was indispensable. I didn't record many interviews—I didn't want to inhibit the speaker.

TS: How were you financing this; did you have a grant or fellowship?

SB: Yes, through MUCIA (the Midwest University Consortium for International Activities). The project was supposed to have something to do with modernization, so I wrote that into my proposal. Archer said I should be involved with how Iran is changing in the modern era, even though I wasn't interested in that. When I'd go with my assistant to a teahouse and ask people if they ever sang, some people would be offended: "Are you accusing *me* of *singing*!?" So I started telling people I was interested in languages, folklore, and religion. Eventually the secret police confronted me and said, "Look, you told this person you're studying religion, you told that one you're studying folklore, you told this one you're studying languages: what are you doing? You're a spy!" It's still the same today. I was back in Khorasan with Ameneh Youssefzadeh in January 2006, and she had an old torn letter of permission. The secret police came to our hotel and interrogated her about me and what was I doing. I didn't even see them.

Building a Career

I had to come back from Iran in the middle of March 1969 because my mother was ill. I came out to Illinois and was offered a job in music history at Western Illinois University. I went back to Iran for the rest of the summer, came back, and started teaching there in the fall of '69. I had a good group of colleagues, including Wendell Logan, and taught there for four years. Western Illinois was very good in terms of teaching, but over time I became fed up for all kinds of reasons.

I had bought a farmhouse out in the country and was so sick and tired of hearing the phone ring that I'd ripped it out of the wall. Some poor guy had to ride his bicycle out to my farmhouse with a telegram from Nicholas Temperley offering me a one-year job at the University of Illinois while they searched for a replacement for Henrietta Hock. Illinois was just starting to acquire its reputation when I was a graduate student. Alex Ringer had arrived in '62 or '63, Bruno Nettl came in '64, and Charles Hamm came around the same time. They were trying to make it a super department. So even though Illinois was only a one-year job, I quit Western Illinois and moved to Urbana in 1973. After that first year, Illinois offered me the job, so I stayed there another three years.

At that point York University in Toronto wanted to start a master's program in what they called "Musicology of Contemporary Cultures." I was close friends with Bob Witmer, who had arrived at Illinois in my second year as a grad student ('65–66), and had stayed in touch when he went off to York. In order to get permission for the program, they had to show it wasn't duplicating any other program. If you put "contemporary cultures" in the title, it was easy to show that, because none of the others emphasized contemporary cultures. It was meant to be a euphemism that would embrace musicology and ethnomusicology. I was hired as the founding director of the program "Musicology of Contemporary Cultures" in 1977 and was there for ten years, until '87. After that, I went to CUNY.

TS: How do you compare the teaching or the professional situation at York and CUNY?

SB: The basic constituency at York was students who had come up through the jazz program, so we had a strong North American emphasis. At CUNY I've also taught several jazz musicians with intellectual interests; three of the best came from Wendell Logan's program at Oberlin. Wendell had been my colleague at Western Illinois. We left at the same time, and he went to Oberlin to start a jazz program. The CUNY students remind me, up to a point, of the Toronto students, although, on the whole, they're more proficient because they survive in New York.

TS: Why was there such a jazz constituency at York University?

SB: When Sterling Beckwith set up the program, it was something of a contradiction. York was intended for students who weren't good enough to get into the University of Toronto, but it was also supposed to do things that the U of T didn't do, such as jazz, South Indian music, free improvisation, electronic music, and so on.

A big difference between York and CUNY was that at York, ethnomusicology was in the driver's seat. There were more ethnomusicologists than anyone else teaching in the undergraduate program. CUNY, however, has far more international students. Every class I have taught has had several students who aren't native speakers of English. At CUNY I had the opportunity to supervise dissertations on a wide range of topics. I taught an African music course once at York, and that was a fairly large part of my teaching at CUNY during the first ten years or so. I've stopped now, because I'd rather have Barbara Hampton teach the courses on Africa. Since then I've done more with Iran plus Central Asia to the east, or Iran plus Kurdistan and Turkey to the west. In 1995 I started teaching a research techniques course for our students, instead of the same course that other students take, because many of our students don't have a background in Western music history.

TS: Have you kept up your performing?

SB: I did at York, very much; that's another huge change. My aim was always to combine teaching, performance, and writing, but I couldn't do it at CUNY. I've always taken teaching very seriously; that's the main priority. But most of what I've written has been produced since I stopped practicing piano three or four hours a day. It's actually a miracle they hired me at CUNY with so few publications. Barry Brook was running the UNESCO World History of Music (initially called "Music in the Life of Man" and later changed to "The Universe of Musical History"), so the fact that I'm a dilettante and not a specialist in anything made me look appropriate to him for being associate editor of this project [International Music Council 1982]. That project (which ultimately failed) was a large reason why I was hired, but after two and a half years, in the fall of 1990, I quit. I was also hired to start the concentration in ethnomusicology. So in a sense I've founded two programs: the one at York and the one at CUNY.

Update: June 22, 2016

At present, almost nine years after our conversation and forty-seven years after I began teaching, I'm about to retire as a teacher of ethnomusicology, the music history of Europe and the USA, and to a lesser extent music theory. I continue to supervise several dissertations still in progress, but am able to devote most of my energy to writing without the obligation to teach four seminars a year while also supervising dissertations.

Salwa El-Shawan Castelo-Branco (October 26, 2007)

PhD, Columbia University (Ethnomusicology)
Professor, Universidade Nova de Lisboa

Graduate Studies

SCB: When Columbia University offered me a fellowship, I ended up going full force into ethnomusicology. I finished my master's in piano and started an MA in ethnomusicology at Columbia University in 1973. Dieter Christensen was my advisor.

MS: Were you one of his first students?

SCB: Yes, though Adelaida Reyes Schramm was his first PhD. I finished in '80. At that time, it was not required to do fieldwork for your master's at Columbia, so I did an annotated bibliography on Coptic music. After the master's, I decided to explore Arab music and what was conceptualized at the time by John Blacking and others as "musical change" for my PhD. Today I think of it as the invention of tradition, within the framework of nationalism, and modernity, but at the time, it was couched in other theoretical terms. My field research looked at musical change in Arab music between the late '20s and the late '70s. I went back to Egypt to carry out fieldwork for a year in 1977–78. Meanwhile, I met my Portuguese husband, Gustavo Castelo-Branco.

MS: You met him while you were at Columbia?

SCB: Yes, we met in New York, when I was living at International House and he was doing a PhD in particle physics. We got married in 1974, after my first year at Columbia and before I did my fieldwork. I realized early on that my fieldwork couldn't just be on Arab music; it had to be much more encompassing. It had to include cultural policy, the role of media (especially radio and the recording industry), and Western music, including the role of culture politicians in institutionalizing Western music, because all of these things were connected. It was quite challenging because my father was deeply involved in all of these processes as someone who defended Western music, so he had to be an object of study for me, which was awkward for us both. We mutually respected each other, even though by this point we had different ideologies and ideas. He was always honest about his perspectives, so I had some really wonderful interviews with him. Through him I got access to a lot of documentation, like the minutes of meetings in the Ministry of Culture, that led to the institutionalization of ensembles like the Arab Music Ensemble, which had introduced radical changes like replacing the solo singer with a chorus and so forth. This was very helpful. People knew me, either personally or through my father, as a Western musician. So when I went to interview musicians involved with Arab music, my relationship with them was initially conditioned by the way they perceived my father. They'd say, "What do you know about Arab music to write a doctoral thesis? Go and learn 'ūd, go learn qanun," which I did.

MS: It must have been very difficult for you to go back to Cairo, being well known as a Western musician and then to have to persuade all those people that you were interested in Arabic music?

SCB: Yes, it was very difficult.

MS: Did your husband go with you to Cairo?

SCB: No, he had his first postdoc in Bonn. I went back and forth: four months to Cairo, two months to Bonn, another three or four months to Cairo, and so forth.

MS: May I ask if you ever interviewed Umm Kulthum?

SCB: Yes, once. It was fantastic. Of course, she had a prepared speech. She didn't give this young person any importance, but for me, it was a memorable moment. I interviewed many historical figures, like Abdul Halim Nowera, conductor of the Arab Music Ensemble, who really created a new style and implemented many changes in Arab music performance that I wrote about. I also interviewed a lot of people who today have passed, like Tharwat Okasha, the influential minister of culture. I was able to make many of these connections through my father.

Building a Career

SCB: At the end of my graduate work, I started looking for a job. Until 1974, Portugal had a fascist regime, so we were looking for jobs in the US; but it was difficult for two academics to find a job in the same place. I got an assistant professor job at NYU in '79, even though I wasn't quite finished with my PhD, and my husband got his second postdoc at Carnegie Mellon University in Pittsburgh. Then he got offers from the University of Iowa and Virginia Tech in Blacksburg, but there were no prospects in either place for me and no prospects in theoretical physics in the New York area for him. It was a very difficult time for ethnomusicology in terms of jobs. My job at NYU was a tenure-track position to start an urban ethnomusicology program. I loved it and stayed for three years before moving to Portugal. Meanwhile, our daughter, Laila Maria, was born in New York in 1981.

By this point, with the establishment of democracy following the 25th of April revolution in 1974, things had improved in Portugal. My husband and I were offered positions with good prospects for getting tenure. So, in 1982, we took leaves of absence from our jobs in the US and decided to try living and teaching in Portugal for a year. My husband's Physics Department at the Technical University in Lisbon had a long trajectory, but the Musicology Department at the Faculty of Social Sciences and Humanities at the Nova University of Lisbon had only been founded in 1981. In 1984 the chair and founder of the department reached retirement age, and I was appointed chair. So, in a very short period of time, I learned Portuguese, took on a teaching and an administrative job, had a second child (Ricardo), and worked toward establishing ethnomusicology as a scholarly discipline in Portugal and consolidating the four-year undergraduate program in musicology at the Nova University of Lisbon. After a year, we decided to stay in Portugal.

It was very challenging for me at first. The courses I taught included an introduction to ethnomusicology, world music, and fieldwork, with the first semester to prepare a research project. Students, several of whom are my current colleagues, got interested in ethnomusicology through the courses on field research. It took eight years to start a master's program, which I established in 1990. Shortly thereafter, a doctoral program was launched, and in 1995 I founded the Institute of Ethnomusicology. This is a center that initially promoted research in ethnomusicology, congregating students and scholars. The institute gradually expanded the scope of its research to include cultural and historical studies in music and dance, performance, creation, education, and music in community. Several branches were founded at the Universities of Lisbon and Aveiro and the Polytechnic Institute of Porto.

MS: This move also had profound implications for your own fieldwork, did it not?

SCB: Yes, I finished my PhD in '80 and moved to Portugal in '82. So for several years I published articles that were basically spin-offs of my dissertation. I went back to Cairo in 1984–85, did a project on the cassette industry, on which I published an article in *the world of music* [1987]. I tried to keep going back in order to update my work on Arab music in Egypt. I gradually developed a new area of expertise in Portuguese music, which was very helpful for me to advise my students' work on Portuguese music. At that time, it was only possible to get research support if you worked on Portuguese or Portuguese-influenced musics.

MS: Is that still the case?

SCB: Less so. I organized an ICTM Colloquium in 1986 titled "Cross Cultural Processes in Music: The Role of Portugal in the World's Musics since the Fifteenth Century." It was a very important event for students and my colleagues in musicology, but also for university administrators, cultural politicians, and foundations. It helped the understanding of what modern ethnomusicology was about and my position within the international scholarly community. I started doing field research in southern Portugal in the region of Alentejo in 1986. My main focus was on the politics and aesthetics of two-part singing by formally structured choral groups both during the postrevolutionary period (since 1974) and the period that preceded it (1933–1974) in which Portugal was ruled by a totalitarian regime. In the 1990s I expanded this research to include migrant communities from the region of Alentejo in the metropolitan area of Lisbon. I have been revisiting the communities I worked with in Alentejo ever since. During the same decade, I expanded my research to include the folklore movement in Portugal more generally and began my work on fado in Lisbon, focusing especially on the instrumental accompaniment and the role of fado instrumentalists as composers and mentors for fado singers. In the 1990s I also carried out field research in Sohar, Oman with Dieter Christensen, which resulted in a jointly authored book and other publications [Christensen and Castelo-Branco 2009]. Since then I have continued my research on the politics of cultural heritage and musical nationalism in Portugal.

MS: Proving yourself seems to be a theme—first in Cairo and then in Portugal!

SCB: Yes. Portugal has a hierarchical class system and a very inbred academic culture. I'm still fighting hard to change that and to internationalize. This can be done now because there is a real structure.

MS: In the process, you had an opportunity that would have been unlikely had you stayed in New York, the opportunity to shape a field completely.

SCB: That's very true. When I look back, I'm pleased with the results. I institutionalized ethnomusicology in Portugal. I see all these former students who came into the field inspired by what I've been trying to do and are now doing good work themselves, not only within the framework of ethnomusicology but also in popular music studies. It's wonderful.

TS: Is Portugal more multicultural now than it was thirty years ago?

SCB: Oh, yes. Not only Africans from Portuguese-speaking countries but also Brazilians, Ukrainians and Rumanians, Hindu-Gujeratis, and Africans from non-Portuguese African countries, among others! It has been a very quick change.

TS: Has that resulted in more opportunities for your students to do fieldwork at home?

SCB: Yes, wonderful opportunities. We have students working on the Cape Verdean community, the Hindu-Gujerati community, and the Goanese community. And, of course, there are also the Timorese, African, and Brazilian communities, which have all grown over the last two decades.

Update: January 1, 2017

In the ten years that have elapsed since our conversation, I continued teaching, carrying out research, and directing the Institute of Ethnomusicology at the Nova University of Lisbon. My research has focused on cultural politics, musical nationalism, identity, the recording industry, heritage, and music and conflict. I was principal investigator of several research projects carried out in Portugal in collaboration with students, colleagues, and interlocutors in the field, resulting in many publications, of which the most significant is the *Encyclopedia of Music in Twentieth Century Portugal*, the first major reference work focusing on the country's music in the past century. Conceived from an ethnomusicological perspective, it was co-edited in collaboration with several graduate students, most of whom are now my colleagues, and published in four volumes in 2010.

During the same period, I was also elected or appointed to leadership positions both in Portugal and internationally: vice chancellor of the Universidade Nova de Lisboa (2005–2007), vice president of the Society for Ethnomusicology (2007–2009) and of the International Council for Traditional Music (ICTM, 2009–2013), and president of ICTM (since 2013). In addition, I was appointed by the Portuguese Ministries of Culture and Higher Education to evaluate music programs in higher education and research projects, as well as to institutionalize a national sound archive. During this period, the Institute of Ethnomusicology, Center for Studies in Music and Dance, became one of the leading centers for ethnomusicological research in Europe.

Frederick C. Lau (October 26, 2008)

DMA, University of Illinois
Professor, University of Hawai'i

Graduate Studies

FL: I knew I wasn't done studying music, but in Hong Kong in 1982 there was nowhere to go. I applied for a government scholarship to go to Guildhall School of Music in

London as a flute major and to schools in America, because they gave scholarships. I got into Yale, Toronto, and Illinois, but only Illinois gave me money. When the big scholarship to Guildhall came, I decided not to go to Illinois. It gave me plane tickets, book money, living allowance, concert money, everything and more. So I wrote to Alex Murray, the flute professor at Illinois, and said, "I got this scholarship, I want to study with Trevor Wye at the Guildhall. I'm not coming until I finish." I spent a year in London and was so into it that I thought, "I want to stick around." Trevor said, "OK, you can study with me at Northern [The Royal Northern School of Music] after Guildhall." But my scholarship wouldn't renew. So I wrote to Alex Murray and said, "I'm done here now." He said, "Yes, we're holding your TA, if you still want it."

I ended up in Illinois in 1983, a flute major, taking a master's degree and studying with Alex Murray. He was interested in a lot of things and even had some Indian flutes given to him by Pannalal Ghosh. I also studied composition with David Liptak and took music history classes. While I was in England, I had started to find studying performance a little boring. I was playing in six orchestras—but playing the same pieces all the time! I needed something more challenging. That's why I continued to compose, but composition was full of odd people writing weird music. I needed a different challenge. That's when I came across this "Anthropology of Music" class. I didn't know what it was, but it sounded interesting and I saw this guy—Bruno Nettl—walking up and down the hall, so I said, "I'll take a class from this guy." I thought, "This is so interesting because there's a personal human connection to the music." That was the first time I heard the word "ethnomusicology." That class opened up everything. It was the first time I had met people who spent time studying other kinds of music, not just the Western classical music I spent so much time trying to master. They looked at other music on an equal footing and equal value.

TS: Did that make you think about the music you had already rejected?

FL: That came much later. When I was choosing a topic for my dissertation, I never thought I would do Chinese music. Never in a million years! But when I talked to Alex about choosing a topic for my DMA thesis, he asked, "What do you know about your own flutes?" I said I didn't know anything about "my own" flutes. Alex said, "Why don't you learn something about your own culture? Look, Isabel Wong is down the hallway. She's Chinese, you're Chinese; why don't you go talk to her?" That's how I got into Chinese music, and that's how I became critically engaged in looking at myself! I began to realize that my attitude toward my own music was embarrassingly colonial. If I had known, I would have gotten a lot more out of CUHK. Look at Yu Siu Wah. He was three years ahead of me, studying Chinese music in the same environment in a major way, while I resisted the idea. Even when Larry Witzleben was there and we took classes together, he was more diligent and serious than us, because we rejected Chinese music.

TS: What did the traditional culture that you grew up with represent to you? You said, "junk grandmother stuff," but why were you feeling that way? We typically think about Chinese being very reverential about tradition and having respect for their grandparents.

FL: I'm very deferential to my grandparents. I just hated their stuff, right? On the radio you had a choice of Cantonese opera music or, at that time, Western pop. We tuned in to Western pop because the cool people spoke English; they dressed up to date and fashionable. I wanted to be like that.

I had finished my master's and thought I could do both a DMA and a PhD. I was naïve. Finally the graduate adviser told me the bad news: I couldn't do it. That's when Bruno said, "Well, there are two ways you can go. You could apply to Chicago, study with Phil Bohlman, and you get your degree there, or you could finish this quickly, get a grant, and write your dissertation. It's not required, but write a dissertation anyway, do your research, and keep publishing if you're interested in this field. Once you get a job, nobody will care what degree you have. They'll look at what you can do and who you are." I asked which he would recommend. He said, "Me? I'd finish as fast as I could and get a job. I finished at twenty-four—how old are you now?" I said, "Twenty-nine." I took his advice—do fieldwork and write a dissertation. I applied for the CACPRC grant—that was the former Fulbright for China. I got it and went to China to do fieldwork.

TS: On what topic?

FL: On Chinese flute music! I found my proposal recently—it was totally uninformed and naïve. I wouldn't give a grant to me if I saw it today. But I got the grant, went to China, and did fieldwork. The project was very naïve. Absolutely no theory—descriptive, simplistic! I came back and Bruno said, "Just write a twenty-page story about your fieldwork. That's the basis of your dissertation." After three months, he asked, "Where's your story?" I said, "Ah, I cannot write." He said "Why not?" I was taking this hegemony class with Tom Turino and sitting in a symbolic anthropology class with Ed Bruner. It was all backwards! I was looking at my stuff and thinking, "What the hell was I doing?" I didn't know anything. I went to do fieldwork; I came back and *now* I'm seeing all these frames. I couldn't hang any of my stuff on them! I was reading Clifford Geertz—the Balinese cockfight. I mean, what was that to do with flute music? Cockfight? I don't know! It took me a long time to write because I was not ready to do it at the time.

TS: Immobilized by theory!

FL: Yes. The thesis was called "The Music and Musicians of the Chinese Bamboo Flute in the Peoples' Republic of China." I'm still working on a book from that material. It'll be called "Red Bamboo." It's been another hang-up for me. I couldn't go back, it was so traumatic and theoretically challenged. I just couldn't get it to a point that I liked.

Building a Career

I finished in 1991 because I got an interview for my first job at CalPoly San Luis Obispo. I had a couple of sabbatical replacement/part-time jobs at Eau Claire (Wisconsin) and Millikin (Illinois), teaching flute and music appreciation. CalPoly was looking for an ethnomusicologist who could do other things. In the meantime, I was having an identity crisis! I told Bruno, "I have a problem. They won't hire me as a flute player because I do other things. And the musicologists see a guy who plays the flute, so he's not very serious about his studies." But Bruno kept saying, "Don't worry, it'll work out. If they fly you out for an interview, the first thing you need to do is have a draft of your dissertation." Lo and behold, I got an interview.

Bruno said, "When you go, take your draft with you, completed, in a box—a Kinko's box. Make sure it's a Kinko's box, with everything in it. Carry it with you." So, I carried the thing there and did my spiel. Then, in the last meeting with the search committee, the theory guy asked, "Where are you in your dissertation?" I said, "I'm so glad you asked. Here! I'm done. All I have to do is defend, that's all." I pulled the Kinko's box out of my bag and put it on the table. That was how I got my first job. I taught a flute studio, conducted an orchestra, and taught a world music class, music of Africa, music of Latin America, and a new course called "Cultural Concepts and Structure in Music" because the theory guy wanted some non-Western theory in the sequence. I couldn't do gamelan—I'd only been playing for a year or two and couldn't even play *bonang*—but I could do mbira and panpipes because we played panpipes at Illinois with Turino and I knew one mbira piece, "Nhemamusasa," So I started mbira and panpipe groups at CalPoly.

I taught there for nine years. I kept talking to Bruno, because the teaching load there was really hard. He said, "Well, whatever you do, keep publishing. If you want to go somewhere else, you can't slack off." So every summer I went to do fieldwork and branched off with new topics. I only had one interview, at Pomona, but the terms were not good. The next job that came up was the one at UH in 2000. That's where I am now.

MS: We've been asking how people's career trajectories have worked, and one of the things that seems to have shaped some of your recent choices is the academic couple thing. Can you talk about that a little?

FL: I wouldn't have been happy at CalPoly for a long time. I had funding to do things, but I always knew I didn't want to teach only undergraduates. I wanted a bit more involvement in ethno for myself. That meant I had to rebalance myself as I was still performing full time and doing ethno. I knew that if I want to get more into the ethno side, I had to do less performing. When the UH job came, I was gambling. I said, "OK, I still want to play, but it's going to be like this. When I have a gig, I'll practice like crazy, but other than that, I'll be full time ethno." That's what happened. At that time, personal life had very little to do with my choice. Now it's an issue, because my wife,

Heather Diamond, finished her PhD in American studies at UH, and she's teaching but hasn't been treated fairly. She has been doing really minimal stuff, so we're looking for a joint appointment, and that affects me. She said, "You're in your dream job." I said, "It may be my dream job, but if you're not settled, why should you be less than who you are?" So that's the problem we're encountering right now.

Update: June 29, 2016

I became the chair and professor of ethnomusicology at the University of Hawai'i at Mānoa in 2003. My specialization is Chinese and Asian music. I have been teaching classes in these areas in addition to teaching classes in world music and ethnomusicology. Beside my various roles in the department, such as being associate chair, member of personnel and search committees, I have been an active member of the Center for Chinese Studies, Center for Korean Studies, and Asian Studies Program outside Music.

In the fall of 2009 I was elected and appointed the director of the Center for Chinese Studies, a campus-wide unit that focuses on presenting research and overseeing programs related to all aspects of Chinese studies on campus. I transitioned from being academic teaching faculty to being a half-time administrator. Under my watch, I was involved in developing our Confucius Institute, which is housed under the Center. I have organized conferences and events and learned to write grants, which resulted in bringing in a substantial grant for the university. I worked to develop faculty and student exchanges with a large number of Chinese universities and became a regular visitor to many educational and academic conferences in China. This transition was important in my career because it has allowed me to develop skills in international education and exchange, skills I didn't think I had. As a result, I came into contact with a range of Chinese students, scholars, and officials. It was overall a fulfilling but unexpected career experience and transition.

Update: August 5, 2017

In January 2018, I will start a new position as senior professor of Ethnomusicology at CUHK, the school where I was once told I would never make it in music. I have come full circle in my career.

Peter Manuel (September 11, 2010)

PhD, UCLA (Ethnomusicology)
Professor, John Jay College and CUNY Graduate Center

Graduate Studies

PM: I continued seamlessly into the MA program [at UCLA]. I continued to study with Nazir and hang out with the ethno gang—Gordon Thompson, Jane Sugarman,

Paul Humphreys, Scott Marcus, Mikyung Park, Eddie Seroussi, Cindy Schmidt, Susan Asai, and others—going to their parties and all the terrific performances that were happening. I was interested in Urdu poetry, *ghazal*. In India I was in a Muslim, Urdu-speaking world, and I really loved that, so I wrote my MA thesis on ghazal-singing, about which nothing had really been written. I finished my thesis on "The Light Classical Urdu Ghazal Song" in '79 and moved into the PhD. program. I didn't want to write about playing sitar; there was enough of that out there, so I chose *thumri* as a topic, got an AIIS grant (American Institute of Indian Studies), and went back to India for the 1980–81 academic year. I continued my sitar studies with Kalyan [Mukherjea] (who had moved back to Delhi) while doing research on thumri. I probably should have stayed longer and done more, but I did the obligatory year. Of course, as soon as I got there, I found that an Indian, Shatrughan Shukla, had written a fat dissertation about thumri in Sanskritized Hindi. It was a solid study, later published as a book [1991], so I had to work around that, translate and re-present the parts that were particularly useful, and add my own perspectives [1989].

Building a Career

I finished my dissertation in the spring of '83: "Thumri in Historical and Stylistic Perspectives." Luckily for me, Lois Anderson was going on sabbatical from the University of Wisconsin, Madison. She called Jihad Racy to ask if he had anyone available to replace her in the fall, and he recommended me. It was just for one semester, but I'd applied for other jobs and hadn't gotten close to one. I put everything in my car, drove to Madison, rented a nondescript place, and discovered Andy Sutton and the gamelan scene. Madison was a wonderful, friendly community. I started playing gamelan. Andy was great—not only a chum but also another mentor figure. I have great respect and affection for him and learned a lot from him.

It was only a one-semester job, so in December I went back to LA, not knowing what I was going to do next. As soon as I had rented a place and settled in, Madison called and said, "We've got funding for you to come in the spring. Why don't you come back?" So I loaded up the car, went back, and taught for another semester. It was more of the same, except that this time I met Beth Robin, who became my wife. She was doing a piano DMA. That was the spring of '84. I had no further employment but stuck around because Beth and I were getting along nicely.

Then came SEM in Los Angeles in the fall of '84, the meeting at which Jim Koetting passed away. Lois Anderson said to me, "You're looking for a job? Why don't you write to Brown [University] and offer your services." I had nothing lined up, so I wrote to the chair of the department and said, "I'm terribly sorry to hear about Jim Koetting, but if you need someone to teach his classes in the spring, I'm available." He said, "Great, why don't you come?" This was the spring of '85. Brown was a difficult situation compounded by a lot of problematic dynamics that didn't involve me, but

I got some more teaching experience, and UCLA offered me a semester of teaching in the fall of that year. I was going back and forth across the country, loading up my sitars and all my LPs into the back of whatever vehicle I was driving. I ran through two transmissions and basically destroyed two cars.

Beth and I got married in the summer of '85. We went to UCLA and I taught there, but, again, it was just for one semester. I was still applying for tenure-track jobs but not getting anywhere. I was determined to stay in the field; if it meant going back and forth across the country and destroying transmissions, then so be it. With nothing else on the horizon, I did a Semester at Sea in the spring of '86. By this time I was working on *Popular Musics of the Non-Western World* [1988], so the Semester at Sea was a useful way to get to places like Sri Lanka, if only for three days.

Life was really semester-to-semester. I got back from the Semester at Sea not knowing what I'd be doing next when Columbia called and offered me a job. That really saved my ass! It wasn't a tenure-track job—they made that clear from the start—but it had some features of a tenure-track job in the sense that it could be held for seven years and included a sabbatical possibility. At that time the program was Dieter Christensen, Phil Schuyler, and me. Dely [Adelaida Reyes] Schramm was teaching occasionally on a course-by-course basis, and there was a small community of grad students.

TS: Was that when you first began to learn more social theory and anthropology?

PM: Yes, Dieter was strong on that. It was absolutely imperative that I learn who Clifford Geertz was—I could see there was a gap in my education that I had to fill. They had me doing a mixed bag of survey courses—some things I was prepared for, and some things I was not. At some point, Philip went to Maryland and there was a revolving door of junior people—Gage Averill, Sean Williams, Michael Largey—it was so fast, I couldn't keep up. It was difficult in some ways because I could see it wasn't going to be a lasting gig. I kept applying for real tenure-track jobs and was discouraged because I wasn't getting any, but in the meantime I had a stable base and was teaching and learning. I also had my first sabbatical and got a grant to go to India. That was '89–90. Beth and I had a baby and lived in Delhi for nine months or so while I did the research for *Cassette Culture*. We were very comfortable in Delhi. We rented a little flat in Defence Colony and a nanny to help us manage the baby. Kalyan was there, too.

In spring '92, I got the job at John Jay College of Criminal Justice. It was my last year at Columbia. I knew my clock was running out, and I don't think Dieter would have supported me for tenure, even if it had been an option. Columbia was a great place to be—terrific academic environment, sharp students, and a good strong South Asia Studies program outside music—but it was hard to get along with Dieter. John Jay is one of the twenty or so colleges in the CUNY system. Music is a service program, and there were just three people in the department: Dan Paget, Laura Greenberg, and Ray

Kennedy. Ray, who was retiring, had established a tradition of teaching a rock class. They were open minded enough to have one of the three positions be some sort of vernacular music. I had been teaching rock at Columbia, which was really annoying at the time because I hadn't listened to rock since 1970. Columbia needed a class that would attract students because no one was taking their classes. So they said, "Peter, you've got long hair, teach a rock class." That was maybe the hardest class of all.

I got the John Jay job, supposedly because I could teach rock, jazz, and Latin music; they weren't so interested in Indian music. But at CUNY, if the Grad Center wants you, they can engage you. Steve Blum had just started the graduate program. I didn't really know him, but at that point the program basically consisted of Steve with Barbara Hampton teaching an occasional course, so he was happy to have me come onboard. I started teaching a grad seminar every semester. So since I started in fall '93 I have spent half my time at the Grad Center, down by the Empire State Building. I didn't have to wait seven years for tenure because, by this time, I had a couple books out and I was an OK teacher. I think I got tenure around '98.

TS: I'm not exactly sure how to articulate it, but you always seem to be breaking new ground, finding some corner that really needs to be explored that people haven't thought of before.

PM: I like to publish and be productive for my own personal reasons. I'm not the most verbal person, so writing has always been a form of expression. I think some of the things I've been most interested in, I do them whether I think anyone will be interested or not. Let's take *Popular Musics of the Non-Western World*—I really hoped that would be something on every ethnomusicologist's shelf. And it got around; it served its purpose for a while. Now it's pretty obsolete! Some of the Indo-Caribbean stuff I do now, I almost don't care if other people read it or not; it's interesting to me.

TS: When did you first visit Cuba?

PM: I think it was around '84, when I was in Madison. Steve Loza had been there, but no one was going there ethnomusicologically. People weren't writing about Cuba; there was very little written about Latin music at all.

TS: Was your interest in flamenco a natural outgrowth of the Cuban stuff?

PM: In some ways it was. I started taking flamenco guitar lessons in New York. I was a beginner, and it's a difficult thing. I knew my way around the fret board, but the right hand techniques were completely new to me. I was never one of those people who would spend a year in Spain and party with the Gypsies, so I never got into it that deeply. At the same time, it was terrific music, and there was nothing in English (or European languages aside from Spanish) about it. There was a lot of stuff in Spanish, of course, but most of it was published in Spain, and you couldn't get those books here. It seemed like an interesting place to go and work on my Spanish at the same time, and it was closer than India. I saw an opening and developed it as a third area.

TS: That's what I'm saying—you had a certain instinct for that: for example, your article "The 'Guajira' between Cuba and Spain" [2004]. It's a wonderful subject and such a logical thing. I'm interested in those kinds of things, but I certainly don't write about them as much. It's exactly the kind of connection I would zero in on and find fascinating, but you actually made a big deal out of it. I really appreciate those kinds of things.

Update: July 8, 2016

Since our 2010 conversation, I conducted further fieldwork in India and the Caribbean, which generated some new publications and video documentaries [2010, 2011, 2014, 2015; Manuel and Largey 2016]. Though rewarding, the trips were also exhausting and difficult in their way, involving much spinning of wheels and changing from Plan A to Plan B and then Plan C. I like to always be actively engaged in a research project, as the mind is like a monkey in a cage, but as I turn sixty-four, I'm not sure how much more foreign fieldwork I will undertake. Perhaps none, though I am determined to remain productive.

Mohd. Anis Md. Nor (March 17, 2009)

PhD, University of Michigan (Asian Studies)
Professor, Universiti Malaya

Graduate Studies

MA: I went to the University of Hawaiʻi in 1980. I had finished at Universiti Malaya in 1978. I worked one year as a TA and spent one and a half years researching. By registering myself in Universiti Malaya while negotiating the UH scholarship, I was given a grant to conduct research. That's how I did an intensive year of research in Negri Sembilan [West Malaysia]. I drove every day, Monday to Friday, at 5 A.M. to Seremban and came home at 11–12 midnight. I befriended all of the artists, informants, and master teachers. I went to Jelebu and Lenggeng to work with one of the best-known *silat* [traditional Malay martial arts] masters, and I became a performer in the Negri Sembilan ensemble, Sri Minang. Halfway through the year they asked me to be the lead performer, the primo dancer.

I was learning all the Minangkabau styles: *caklempong* music, the dance motif movements, the *randai*, as well as *silat*, because I wanted to know as much as possible so that I could speak for the Negri Sembilan diaspora of the Minangkabau people. I realized that there was very little comparative knowledge of performative traditions in Negri Sembilan and West Sumatra. I thought that by doing a one-year immersion in Negri Sembilan I would be eloquently prepared when I went to West Sumatra. I was *so* wrong! When I got to the highlands, everything was new to me. It turned out that the Negri Sembilan dialect was actually a very low and crude kind of Minangkabau. I had to relearn the language, the behavior patterns, and everything! By the time I finished my studies in the Indonesian Arts Academy in Padang Panjang, West Sumatra, I had befriended all of the master teachers, had a very good rapport with everyone, and was ready to write my thesis.

Then Hawai'i came through, so I went with two heavy bags of raw field materials. I took everything with me—about thirty-five cassettes of recordings and interviews, about a dozen boxes of slides, and my transcriptions. I had no idea what Laban notation was, so I devised my own transcription as a memory tool. I brought transcriptions of the *caklempong* [bonang-like gong chimes] style that I played—what the left and the right hand played, in what speed, and what rhythm, and all that. Judy Van Zile asked me to see her with all my stuff. She had no idea what I'd brought! I said to myself, "How am I going to bring it? I have these two bags." She just said, "Bring everything you have." So I heaved it all the way from my house. When I got there, she was shocked! She said, "What's all that stuff, what are those huge bags?" I said, "My field materials." I unzipped the bags and took out everything. She looked at me and said, "My God, I never expected this." I said, "Well, I was one and a half years away from home in the field, you know. I want the tools now." She had the idea that you had to suffer the whole phase of going to the monastery before you could become a monk!

She had no idea about my background, that I'd been a performer for so many years doing all these things. She only came to know later, but it was too late. I was very careful. I took coursework that linked me to the ethnomusicology people—Barbara Smith, Ric Trimillos, and Byong Won Lee—and to Alice Dewey in the Anthropology Department. That's how I finished my entire work in two years, which was rare in Hawai'i. I went back to Minangkabau for about two months in between because I found out that I did lack certain things. I organized my writing, defended my thesis, and got my master's in twenty-three months. I was very insistent on finishing in two years because I had to. "If I don't go back by the twenty-fourth month, my contract will be finished and I'll have to pay back the government everything I spent studying here and will never be an academic." So I got back and started teaching in 1982.

MS: You started teaching immediately?

MA: Yes, because I was on a scholarship, I had to go back and teach. I got tenure in 1984 and was given a doctoral scholarship to complete my PhD. In 1986 I finally went to Michigan to work with Judith Becker. It was one of the most rewarding periods in my lifetime. I don't think it will ever recur again in any karmic cycle. I finished my doctoral program and defended in three years, eight months. I got the scholarship in '85, went to Michigan in '86, and finished in June 1990. That was when my dream of scholarship and fun really materialized. It was fun and it was scholarship!

MS: You've talked eloquently about Krishen Jit and Judith Becker. Were they your primary role models?

MA: Yes, definitely. I would not have enjoyed life as a scholar if the fun section were missing. I've seen a lot of my colleagues who don't have fun. What I saw in Krishen was a person who was bright and intelligent and yet so humble and friendly. Likewise, Judith Becker's way was accommodating, but also stern. She listens to you but then provides alternative answers or suggestions. All of her suggestions are so solid that you don't want to argue anymore. You just say, "Oh my God, give me some more!" These two people taught me a lot about being humble and being a good listener as well as being a good mentor.

MS: Do you see yourself as part of any kind of lineage?

MA: What lineage you are talking about? I don't have any lineage. I went to Hawai'i, so I'm the first Malaysian ethnochoreologist. Ethnochoreology or dance ethnology in America is very dysfunctional because American colleges don't provide avenues for ethnochoreologists to go as far as ethnomusicologists and pursue the highest levels of education. There are a lot of people like me who ended up having to go back into ethnomusicology and work with Asian studies to do things beyond conventional ethnomusicology. Michigan provided that avenue, but I ask myself why other American universities are unable to provide that kind of excellence for ethnochoreology, yet they do it so well in Europe. Look at the UK and Europe. Their training programs in dance anthropology are so superior. Look at their publications and their scholarship; nothing matches! What we have in America is a handful of people who were produced way back. But after them, there's nobody else. You have a few people, but where are the younger ones?

Alan Merriam inspired Gertrude Kurath. She was the first generation. Then you have Alice Dewey and the people at UCLA who followed her: Elsie Dunin and Allegra Fuller Snyder, top, top scholars who are all now retired. Who's left? Judy Mitoma, who's running her own act, and Judy Van Zile at Hawai'i. They could give you the best education to MA level but couldn't take you further. So people end up doing critical studies at places like Temple University. But this is performance-studies-oriented critical analysis, not ethnochoreology. It's not ethnological; I learned the difference very early.

If you have a dream but there's no scholarship for the following generation, then it stops short of being what Europe is producing—tremendous numbers of good young scholars. Adrienne Kaeppler is not a professor in the US; she is with Smithsonian. I had the top ethnochoreologists in America who were my mentors: Adrienne Kaeppler, Joann Kealiinohomoku, and Judy Van Zile. All of them belong to that same generation of people who trace their roots back to Kurath. So if you're talking about a generational line in ethnochoreology, then I fall into a category within the lineage of the Kurath line. In ethnomusicology, I'm under Judith Becker, so you read again all the way back to Mantle Hood—everybody ends up at UCLA again. That's the only generational lineage, but I never acknowledge it seriously.

Building a Career

MS: What is your career like in a practical sense?

MA: I consider myself the perpetual inventor, because no matter how good you are, it is very difficult to survive and make a niche for yourself in a country like Malaysia, where performing arts are of little concern. People who are in positions of power but have very little scholarship can feel very threatened if you start to embark upon serious scholarship. So I have to be careful. Talking to you like this right now in America would be impossible in Malaysia. So instead of making the people who are in positions of power feel threatened, I persuade them that I provide the missing link. I niche myself in a way that creates a certain amount of indispensability. To create and impart that element of indispensability, you have to invent it. You have to invent it so that the knowledge you carry, the mentoring you do, the number of students you have, the conferences you attend, the international tours you do, all add up to your being a person who should not be taken lightly by the bureaucrats and the people in power, including fellow scholars at my university. I know they would not be talking to me unless it was absolutely necessary. I love it that way. I am not a person you will find every day in a place like the faculty club. I don't mingle around; I don't go to formal functions. I want to keep whatever I can do in a twenty-four-hour period under control because I have a mission.

People are very envious of my achievements because I am not working through any connections. I work purely from the merit I have created—my connectivity and networking, international connections, and grants. This has to be continuously invented. You have to really be smart to bridge that in a way that will privilege you as an indispensable individual, not a threatening one. It's a very subtle way of diplomacy that is a third-world/first-world kind of thing.

MS: You have done this effectively, not only within the university context but also with your work with the Johor state government.

MA: Yes, precisely, and with the federal government. That's why, if you notice, my critical writings and my critical analytical presentations are all in English—not in Malay. And these are all published, not by Malaysian but by foreign publishers [1993, 1996, 2011, 2017]. My work is available for those scholars who want to read it, but the majority of people in Malaysia don't. So it's a safe niche for me. I can be very sharp and critical when I'm dealing with the global world as a global being in the medium of English. At the same time, I can be persuasive, diplomatic, and very suave in Malay, because you have to survive in that situation. I'm confessing this to you because it's the only way I can survive! These two worlds are such contrasting worlds, you know.

MS: One final, perhaps flippant, question. If you hadn't taken this career path and become a leader in dance ethnology in Malaysia, what might you have done?

MA: Oh, I'd have probably been a politician and become prime minister of Malaysia! Honestly, I've never given a thought to that because one thing I can tell you is that I'm truly happy in my life. I have wonderful parents, I have a wonderful family, and I have wonderful friends. I am so thankful. Maybe because I was given such a good way of looking at the world by my mentors that the greater the heights I reach, the more I'm humbled. I love that feeling. I mean, when people give me accolades, I'm more humbled and feel that there is a cycle, which to me is very spiritual. Because you care and you share, the door is opened up in front of you.

Update: July 15, 2016

My earliest introduction to academic ethno-performative discourses emerged from the days of my undergraduate years of active dancing and musicking in the University of Malaya Cultural Ensemble, culminating into serious endeavors of ethnographic "dialogics" with my master teachers to locate my personal interest in ethnomusicology and ethnochoreology, which at most times are interconnected and overlapping in my performance practices. Those formative years constantly remind me of my mission in endeavoring ethnomusicology/ethnochoreology in my professional career as a teacher-mentor-scholar. Midway through my academic career I became fascinated with esoteric and mystical musicking of the Muslim communities in Southeast Asia, which led me to interrogate the notion of performative Sufism among Sufi musicians and practitioners in insular Southeast Asia, which I find most challenging as I deal with the issue of Islam and the performing arts at this time of global Islamophobia.

Svanibor Pettan (October 28, 2007)

PhD, University of Maryland Baltimore County (Ethnomusicology)
Professor, University of Ljubljana

Graduate Studies

SP: My plan was to do a master's thesis on music in Egypt. Since the University of Zagreb had no graduate studies in ethnomusicology at the time, I turned to the University of Ljubljana, which was relatively close. Unfortunately, my supervisor there was not as open to novelties as Professor Bezić in Zagreb was. She said, "Well, it's nice that you're interested in Egyptian music, but what has that to do with us?" I argued, "Well, there's so much literature, and there are different ideas outside Yugoslavia about what ethnomusicology is," but she was convinced that national folk music research was the only way that was appropriate. I already had recommendations and a nice research plan for Egypt, so I was bitterly disappointed. Finally, I opted for a compromise and proposed a comparison between Egyptian folk dance music and music from Kosovo. Fortunately, Professor Bezić agreed to be my co-supervisor, so in the end it was possible to do this comparative study.

TS: So you went to Egypt for your fieldwork?

SP: Yes, I did fieldwork there from 1986–87. I defended my master's thesis, "Folk Dance Music in Egypt and Respective Phenomena in the Folk Music of Kosovo," in 1988. By that time I was ready to go to America for my PhD. With the help of Ankica Petrović I got in touch with Jozef Pacholczyk, founder and chair of the graduate ethnomusicology program at the University of Maryland Baltimore County. The other professors were Mantle Hood and Philip Schuyler. Karl Signell was an adjunct faculty member in charge of the Turkish Music Center. Pacholczyk's scholarly interest in Egypt made a natural connection between us. The motto of the program was "Music wherever, whenever," so I didn't have to trouble myself with the question of relevance.

TS: Did you get a fellowship?

SP: Yes, I was a teaching assistant. Soon after I arrived in 1988 I was given a music appreciation class for nonmajors, every Monday from 7 until 10 P.M. In the beginning, of course, it was a major challenge for me. I remember the chair of the department told me, "I know how people in Europe teach—you are a 'big professor' and students just sit there. You're not supposed to teach like that here." So I asked, "What should I do? Should I entertain the students?" And then, step by step, I understood what he meant; it was a very useful and positive experience. After that, I was in charge of a musicianship laboratory, and in that class I introduced Balkan rhythms and some other non-Western themes and approaches that were highly unusual for a solfège-like class but were very well received. In the end, I just supervised two other graduate students in the lab, which provided me with precious time to write my dissertation.

TS: What was the subject of your PhD dissertation?

SP: I had originally wanted to do my PhD research in Burma, but there was a war, and my supervisor advised me against the idea. Second on my list was Somalia. I went to the Somali embassy in Washington, DC, and started the process, but a civil war started there, so that was also out of the question. My third option was Kosovo, which I already knew from my master's thesis. In the end, my dissertation was about interaction and creativity related to Romany (Gypsy) musicianship in Kosovo. With its different ethnicities, religions, languages, and musics compared to Slovenia and Croatia, Kosovo positioned me more as a culturally challenged outsider than a Yugoslav insider. I did fieldwork during the summers of 1989, '90, and '91. As soon as the spring semester ended in Maryland, I flew to Kosovo and stayed there until September. The summer was the best time to do research because that's when they had weddings, circumcisions, and other major events. In 1991 the war started and I had to leave, but my research was done for the most part.

Building a Career

TS: So you finished your PhD at UMBC in 1992 [Pettan 1992]. What happened next?

SP: Well, after Burma, Somalia, and Kosovo some colleagues made jokes, "Please don't come to do research in my country, because wherever you plan to do research, there's a chance of war!" It's interesting that war became the topic of my further research [Pettan 1998]. In 1992, I returned to the now-independent but still war-torn Croatia and also got a job as adjunct faculty in Slovenia. For six years I worked full time in both countries. In Zagreb, Croatia, I was a researcher at the Institute of Ethnology and Folklore Research. I also taught classes at the University of Zagreb Music Academy and at the University of Ljubljana in Slovenia, where I taught ethnomusicology and music history. By changing the title of the course "music history" to "world music history," I created space for non-Western musics and laid foundations for later expansion of ethnomusicological views and practices

In 1998 I quit the job in Zagreb and continued to work in Slovenia. There were two reasons for this. First, I had married in 1992. My wife was Slovenian and I was Croatian; it was a question of "Where should we live?" She couldn't get a job in Croatia, while I already had a job in Slovenia. And second, the conditions for life and research were better in Slovenia. For example, I was able to get financial support to attend SEM conferences. That wasn't possible from Croatia at that time. I've been teaching at the University of Ljubljana ever since, but in different departments. First I was at the Music Academy, a conservatory-type institution. In 2003 I moved to the Faculty of Arts' Department of Ethnology and Cultural Anthropology, and two years later to its Department of Musicology, where we now have a program in ethnomusicology.

TS: You've seen a lot of places, so I assume you created the program the way you wanted it to be?

SP: It's on the way. I envision courses such as "Introduction to Ethnomusicology," "Musics of the World/Anthropology of Music," "Traditional Music of Slovenia," "Popular Music," "Selected Readings in Ethnomusicology," and "Applied Ethnomusicology." Participation in the Bologna Reforms, which aims for the compatibility of European university programs, enables much needed exchanges of professors, students, and ideas.

TS: Oh, that's very interesting: European Union university programs. Do you have a PhD program in musicology at Ljubljana with students from other parts of Europe?

SP: We welcome and already have European and other international students on all three levels (BA, MA, and PhD). I often teach bilingually in order to accommodate both domestic and foreign students.

TS: Do you teach music performance?

SP: This is planned and will hopefully be in effect in the future. It will largely depend on the human capacities and other resources we have. Much will be up to my new assistant, whom I expect to get this month. What we have at the moment is Slovenian traditional music. Are you familiar with the practice of Tánsházz? We transferred this practical learning method from neighboring Hungary and organize Slovenian (rather than Hungarian) folk-dance gatherings to live-music accompaniment on a regular basis. The dance teachers and musicians come from the Slovenian folk-music-revival movement. Theoretical knowledge that students get from me in the classroom is complemented by practical experiences outside the class. There will also be singing and traditional instrument-playing workshops, not exclusively Slovene in the ethnic sense, but also in cooperation with representatives of diverse minorities living in Slovenia.

Update: August 9, 2016

In 2011 I became secretary general of ICTM [the International Council for Traditional Music] and brought the council's office to Slovenia, the smallest country in its history, in which English is not an official language. It was a major challenge after Columbia, UCLA, and Australian National University, but the entirely positive results of the ICTM's stay at the University of Ljubljana has justified all the hardworking days and sleepless nights. It's interesting that professional associations like ICTM or SEM are essential in our lives in so many ways, but we usually write about them only at anniversaries. They enable firsthand sharing of knowledge and experiences on a global scale, presenting and exchanging theoretical and methodological tools to strengthen and improve the quality of our research work, and creating social networks that are often sustained over our entire careers. After five years of this service, I can say that I still enjoy contributing to the best of my capacities to intercultural dialogue, understanding, and appreciation across social, cultural, and political barriers.

Stephen Slawek (October 25, 2007)

PhD, University of Illinois (Ethnomusicology)
Professor, University of Texas

Graduate Studies

SS: After five years of struggling to survive in India without any outside support, studying the sitar and having achieved a certain level of competence in performance—I had performed on the radio and in various places in India from Calcutta to Kanpur to Gorakhpur and Banaras, Bhopal, Meerut, and Simla—I realized that I couldn't live in India forever and needed to come back to the United States. I had applied for graduate school in Asian Studies at the University of Pennsylvania, but Lewis Rowell suggested I consider ethnomusicology instead. He said the program at Hawaiʻi would be a good fit for me because there was a strong interest in performance, the location was great with so much Asian culture around, and the East-West Center would be a potential source of funding. So at the last minute I applied to the ethnomusicology program at Hawaiʻi, not knowing what I was getting into. I was just looking for a way to attach my India experience and my study of the sitar to something within the Western academic world where it would be of some value.

Before being trained to study culture, I absorbed it for five years. Maybe if I had gone to India first as a graduate student, having had some training, my perspective would've been different. But when I went to India, I had very little idea of what to expect and essentially fell into behavioral patterns on the basis of what I encountered. I don't know how that plays into things, other than being even stranger as a person by the time I got into ethnomusicology because I had become bicultural in my makeup.

I was accepted, got the East-West Center grant, and went to Hawaiʻi to learn about ethnomusicology. That was in the mid-1970s, so ethnomusicology was just about to undergo a sea change of focus. At the time, the Hawaiʻi program was a terminal master's program; there was no PhD. My mentor at Hawaiʻi was Professor Barbara Smith. She was extremely dedicated as a teacher and guide. Her perseverance in editing my master's thesis taught me a lot, not just about academic writing, but how to mentor students in the early stages of their graduate education. I happened to meet Bruno Nettl at the IFMC [International Folk Music Council, now ICTM, International Council for Traditional Music] conference in 1977, hosted that year by the University of Hawaiʻi. I had enjoyed reading his work in Barbara Smith's "Introduction to Ethnomusicology" course. He encouraged me to apply to the doctoral program in ethnomusicology at the University of Illinois at Urbana-Champaign. That was my trajectory and academic introduction to ethnomusicology. I entered through the back door. I didn't become an ethnomusicologist because I had a desire since age five to be an academic student of music; I became an ethnomusicologist because it looked like a place that my unconventional background might actually get some acceptance.

Shortly before meeting Bruno Nettl, I had spent six weeks studying with Pandit Ravi Shankar in Los Angeles. He had come to Honolulu in March 1977 to perform his first concerto with the Honolulu Symphony Orchestra. He remembered meeting me a year earlier in Banaras and accepted our invitation to have lunch in our miniscule apartment. He had me play for him and, subsequently, invited me to study under his guidance. The six weeks in Los Angeles was the beginning of a thirty-year period of receiving instruction from him.

MS: For somebody who trained in an Indian context, you must have a deep understanding of lineages. Do you see anything comparable in your ethnomusicological world?

SS: I studied with Harry Powers and have found his work to be exceptionally solid and rigorous. Back in the late '70s and early '80s his *Grove Dictionary* article on India [1980] was groundbreaking, incredible work. I always felt that in terms of musical analysis and history, his work was really inspiring. Harry Powers was one role model and Bruno Nettl was another. I was attracted to Bruno Nettl's work because, although he dealt specifically with the music, he also made direct ties between what was going on in the music and broader cultural processes and themes. That's what I felt ethnomusicology should be: there should always be a concern for the organization of sounds into culturally meaningful forms. If you couldn't show some sort of direct connection between those things, then for me it didn't hold a lot of interest.

TS: What was the program like at Illinois when you arrived?

SS: I started at Illinois in '78 and was there for two years of coursework. I was the last ethnomusicology PhD student who had to take two semesters of Notation History and two semesters of Introduction to Musicology! I sat in on a course with David Stigberg on Mexico, a course with Isabel Wong on China, and a couple of seminars, one on improvisation with Charlie Capwell and one on folk music with Bruno Nettl. Apart from that, 80 percent of my training at Illinois had more to do with historical musicology than ethnomusicology. In other words, although I mentioned the sea change in ethnomusicology—when anthropology suddenly became more predominant—I arrived just as that was beginning and went through the program on the older model. I went to India in September 1980 for my dissertation fieldwork, which had nothing to do with classical music—it was on Hindu popular devotional song. I came back to Illinois in January '82 and was there for another year and a half.

Building a Career

SS: By the time I got to the University of Texas, I felt—once again—that I was on the periphery. I didn't have an exceptionally weak background in anthropology, because I had taken some courses at Penn, including a course with David Sapir (the grandson of Edward Sapir) and done some reading on my own, but I didn't have seminars in anthropology. I had to pick that stuff up on my own. I had Steve Feld as a colleague for several years at UT and learned a lot from him, so that was good.

TS: What has your career been like in Texas in a practical sense? Has the program changed in important ways since you've been there?

SS: I started at UT Austin in 1983. Before I arrived, the program was small, just Gerard Béhague and one other person. I think I was the third person to come in on the line I occupy, and I'm still there. My first predecessor had been let go very early in the probationary period. The second, Kristina Nelson, decided to leave because she didn't like academia and wanted to make a bigger impact in the world. Two years ago, the

Institute for Latin American Studies gave us an extra faculty line. We hired Robin Moore, but then Gerard died, so we went from four down to three again. We kept his line and hired Josh Tucker, who does Peru. Then we got an additional line through a cooperative venture with the Center for Middle Eastern Studies and hired Sonia Seeman. So now there are five of us.

When I arrived, there wasn't anything on India in the Music Department, so I started the whole program of teaching sitar and tabla. It's been interesting to see the clientele change over time. In the early '80s it was your typical late-'70s hippie hang-overs and a few South Asians. By the mid-1990s, it was mainly children of South Asian immigrants; that trend has continued. Now I've got twenty-two students doing sitar and tabla. In 1999 I managed to get a gamelan, so that was a big change. We argued for somebody doing the Middle East; Africa with Veit Erlmann; Indonesia with the gamelan (and Veit Erlmann has also done some research there). And in terms of per-formance, we've been bringing Pak Rasito Purwopangrawit on and off since 1999. He's a fantastic teacher, so we've had a pretty good gamelan program, although it's always a struggle to get him funded. I don't know how many Indian musicians I've brought in to give concerts or talks, so there's been a pretty good South Asian ethnomusicology perspective since 1983. Some of my students—like Peter Kvetko, David Henderson, and Amie Maciszewski—are beginning to establish themselves around the country. So I would say that, in different ways, I've had an impact.

MS: You mentioned having students who are children of immigrants. Do you have much contact with the broader South Asian community in Austin?

SS: What happens—and I think other people who do South Asia would agree—is that when Indians reach a certain critical mass, they tend to split off into regional areas, like Bengalis and Marathis and South Indians, and then maybe even Telugu, Tamil, and Kannada speakers. I would say that until the early 1990s, I had more contact with local community organizations. And even in the famous tenure battle, a local Indian community organization wrote a very strong letter of support that went into my file. So I was pretty well connected at that time. But over the years it just got so big and things split off. I was trying to do certain things in the university, and other community organizations arose and wanted to be in charge of their own agenda. So I said, "Fine, that's good." Now I do concerts that are attended primar-ily by students. There must have been 350 to 400 people at the last concert, mostly students. Few audience members come from the community in general because there are now so many concerts of Indian classical music in Austin that the mar-ket's flooded. It's also a matter of having the time, between editing *Asian Music*, teaching sitar and tabla, teaching academic courses, and having a hand in running the program. As you get older, you're asked to do other things. I'm chairing the Ethnomusicology Committee of the American Institute of Indian Studies, which

Tony Seeger had done for eleven years. So I'm busy, and my engagement with the local community has dwindled.

TS: How does performing fit into the picture?

SS: Outside performing is not a big part of my income by any means—it's an occasional supplement that might buy groceries for a few weeks here and there, but it's not significant. If I perform, I usually want to make sure that the accompanist gets taken care of first; if my travel and expenses are covered and there's a little bit extra, that's fine. Within UT, I would say that a quarter to a third of what I do is based in performance. In terms of what I do professionally in ethnomusicology, I perform maybe three times a year, at most. So professionally, I think it would amount to less than 10 percent.

TS: How much do you still practice?

SS: It depends on whether I have concerts coming up! For example, in the last month, I had two concerts, so for the last two months, I've been trying to practice more. If I had a concert coming up, I used to practice up to four hours a day and I'd be up until 1:00 in the morning letting it all out. But now I'm getting older and my joints aren't taking it as well. I can't do it as much as I used to.

Update: July 11, 2016

My present career situation is very much like it was during our original conversation. I'm in the same position in the Butler School of Music as a professor of ethnomusicology. I spent the past six years as division head of Musicology/Ethnomusicology, which entailed a moderate amount of administrative work, and I also spent three years as faculty coordinator of a university partnership, funded by the US State Department, that paired the Butler School of Music with the National Academy of Performing Arts in Karachi, Pakistan. While I had become involved in Javanese gamelan performance practice some years before the original conversation, I have now become responsible for keeping our Javanese gamelan ensemble active, so I have spent quite a bit of time the last three years trying to improve my knowledge of *karawitan*.

My primary focus continues to be Hindustani music, and I have continued to give performances on the sitar. I was fortunate to have two opportunities to perform Ravi Shankar's Concerto No. 1 for Sitar and Orchestra, once with the Oakland–East Bay Symphony in March 2014 and again the following February with the UT Symphony. Another change that occurred in the interim is that my sitar guru, Ravi Shankar, passed away in December 2012. I had devoted a great deal of my professional energy and emotional life to maintaining my part of the *guru-shishya* relationship. With his passing, I have moved to another phase of that relationship.

Tan Sooi Beng (September 1, 2009)

PhD, Monash University (Ethnomusicology)
Professor, Universiti Sains Malaysia

Graduate Studies

TSB: When I went to America, I was quite open about not going back to Malaysia. Many of my Chinese friends were also running away from Malaysia because of the NEP [New Economic Policy], an affirmative-action policy that privileged indigenous people. This policy and its implementation created tensions between the different races in the country. The professors at Cornell taught me that it is possible to use one's research skills and knowledge to transform and create a better society. I made up my mind that I was going to go home to teach and develop peace-building music projects among students. However, I needed more exposure to non-Western music. That was when I applied to do my master's at Wesleyan. For the master's program, we had to take courses. I took African, Indian, and Japanese music courses, and I played in all the ensembles to get a good background in music outside of Southeast Asia, because we didn't have any of that at Cornell.

In my second year, I went back to conduct research in Malaysia and studied the *Phor-Tor* Festival, the seventh-month festival. The Chinese believe that ghosts are released from hell during this month and must be appeased with offerings of joss-sticks, food, puppet theater, and opera shows. The Chinese community in Penang made use of the festival to raise money to build their own schools—Chinese schools, which were not supported by the government—hospitals, a town hall, and so on. They also used the performance stages to talk about the rights of the Chinese—the right to study one's own language, to write, to practice one's own culture—because the new National Cultural Policy (that privileged indigenous culture) had just been implemented, and the Chinese felt that their own culture would disappear under the domination of Malay culture. Through my research, I was exposed to how minorities employed festivals and performances to raise awareness about their own rights and culture and to contest national policies.

MS: What was that like? You had grown up with the idea that it was all about Western music and now you were looking at Chinese traditional performing art forms. Do you remember how you felt at that time?

TSB: I had an identity crisis! I was Chinese, but I was also Malaysian, and I was very westernized. I was at a crossroads where I had to look for myself. So, while I was doing this research, I started learning some traditional instruments like *erhu* and I joined a Chinese orchestra. I grew up mixing with people who spoke English and who went to English schools. I didn't mix with people who spoke Mandarin or went to Chinese schools. There was a big divide between the English-educated and the

Chinese-educated. Many of the people who played in the Chinese orchestras came from very poor families that made herbal drinks and sold medicines by the roadside. I tried to learn how to speak with them, which I couldn't do at the beginning. I knew Hokkien, but these organizations were run using Mandarin. That was where I learned how to speak Mandarin; it was the turning point in my life. I tried to understand where they were coming from and to understand more about the working-class Chinese in Penang and in Malaysia.

MS: You've mentioned some of the people who were influential in getting you started, but were there other people who inspired you or were role models?

TSB: The person who influenced me most was Bell Yung. He introduced me to Chinese music and the functions that music played in the lives of ordinary people. And then my supervisors at Wesleyan were Mark Slobin and David McAllester. Mark taught me to be critical in ethnomusicology approaches and methodologies. David, in particular, was quite a role model—I was very political at that point, so he would try to moderate my ideas and make me more objective in my writing!

Building a Career

MS: After you finished your master's, you went back to Malaysia and started teaching at your hometown university, USM [Universiti Sains Malaysia], in Penang.

TSB: Yes, immediately. I was engaged as a lecturer in the Performing Arts Program at USM. I had no opportunity to teach the Chinese music that I had focused on for my MA research. Because of the National Cultural Policy, the only music courses the university supported in the performing arts were Malay. So I took the opportunity to learn with the local Malay musicians who were teaching courses on *makyong*, *wayang kulit*, and so on. I joined the groups, learned the music, and went into Malay music in a big way. Training in Chinese and Malay music not only helped in my teaching but also provided the skills for my future community-engagement projects with young people. During this time, I also had the opportunity to attend and learn from the methodology workshops on community theater run by PETA [Philippines Educational Theater Association] for empowering the marginalized children and communities in the Philippines.

After five years of teaching, USM requires you to do a PhD. I decided to do it in Australia because I had already taken enough coursework and just wanted to write the thesis. I got a scholarship to Monash University to study with Margaret Kartomi. The graduate students in the Music Department and the Center for Southeast Asian Studies at Monash provided camaraderie and frequent dialogues on the diverse approaches to the study of culture.

I wanted to work on a topic that could feed into my vision of using the arts to bring people of different ethnic backgrounds together. I chose to study *bangsawan* theater, a form that was popular among Malay and other communities who lived in the Malay Archipelago in the early twentieth century. By looking at old newspapers and record catalogs, interviewing veteran performers, learning drumming patterns, and performing with surviving troupes, I found that mixing cultures and languages was very common in the past. The popular music of bangsawan on old 78 RPM recordings clearly illustrated different routes to cultural interaction. Bangsawan of the past was a truly multiethnic form. It was later Malayized and reinvented by the nation-state in the implementation of the National Culture Policy. My pioneering diachronic study inspired younger scholars and policymakers in Malaysia to explore alternative histories in performance and film studies [Tan 1993].

MS: What is your career like now in a practical sense? You are teaching, of course, but I know you do a lot of other things outside the university. Can you describe some of those things?

TSB: When I finished my PhD, I wanted to work with young people. I thought many young people were like me. I knew a lot about Western classical music but nothing about my own traditions. In the national schools, children only sang, learned Western notation, and played the recorder during music lessons. It was important for me to try to introduce traditional music to them. I was instrumental in developing a music program for the national secondary school system in Malaysia. In this program, musics of Malaysia's diverse ethnic groups were included in music-appreciation classes and practical instruction in selected ensembles was introduced. I also ran workshops on the musics of Malaysia, Southeast Asia, and other parts of the world, and wrote textbooks for schoolteachers and students. At the university level, I set up the first music department in the country that incorporated both Western and non-Western music in its curriculum.

I started wondering how we could encourage young people of different ethnicities and religions to interact. That was when I got involved with Young Theatre Penang and began to work with children's-theater activist Janet Pillai, and a contemporary dancer, Aida Redza. We gathered a small group of young people of different races and social backgrounds, who ranged from ten to eighteen years old, and ran six-month projects. I would do the music, Janet the theater, and Aida the dance sections. Our projects included team- and skill-building games; at the end of the project, we would put on a play that was usually based on some story about the city the children had researched. We tried to combine Chinese, Malay, or Indian forms with modern dance and theater.

MS: What I find so special about your project is that you involve children from across the races and religions in a society where they don't otherwise mix much.

TSB: Yes, definitely, because if you're Indian, you would normally only be introduced to Indian culture—Bharata Natyam and all that. If you're Chinese, you would only play Chinese music, except for the richer children who can afford to play piano and learn Western classical music. Malay children would only be doing Malay music. Through our program, we introduce what we call "crossovers." We have Malays playing Chinese music and Chinese playing Indian music—same with dance and theater. By doing that, the children actually have to go out and observe what the other culture is like. Sometimes they even go and stay with each other. If you're studying about an Indian family, you go and interview the Indian family. At the end of the project there's so much crossover, they don't feel as though they are Malay, Chinese, or Indian any more. They are Malaysians. And they learn how to speak different languages, just a little. We always mix languages in our plays.

MS: Now that you've been doing this work for twenty years or so, do you see any results of this work in Penang? Does this make a positive difference?

TSB: Many of these kids are now in graduate school or finishing up their bachelor's degrees. Some continue to volunteer as facilitators or performers in present-day projects. A few have become dancers and theater practitioners. The majority of them are not, but they do appreciate other cultures and are more open-minded in their dealings with one another compared with kids who have not gone through our programs. They have friends who cut across races. We are trying to create "Malaysian culture" rather than "Malay, Chinese, Indian" culture, so that what is Malaysian will cut across races in terms of audience, performance, and language.

MS: In the process you've worked with some wonderful local musicians and given them a forum for their art—Cikgu Baha [Mohd. Bahroodin Ahmad] was the only one I was lucky enough to meet—but you've given them a special place, too.

TSB: Yes, many of the traditional musicians are invited to work with the children. Even the *dalang* [puppeteer] who just passed away, dalang Hamzah [Hamzah Awang Mat], used to come from Kelantan to teach the USM students, and then we would invite him to teach the children as well. Cikgu Baha and Mak Minah Alias used to teach the children Malay dance before they passed on. Presently, dalang Juffry from USM provides workshops on puppet making and music making, Che Mat, who specializes in Malay traditional music, offers classes in gamelan music, and Quah Beng Chai, the Chinese dragon dance master, teaches drumming to the young people. These workshops also provide opportunities for the musicians to mix with children of other races.

In the 1990s I moved on to community-engaged theater that emphasized the involvement of multiethnic communities and traditional artists in the research and creation of plays. The communities of different races provided the stories, issues of concern, and materials for the content of the plays; they also formed the audience for the performances.

Update: June 22, 2016

I am still professor of ethnomusicology at Universiti Sains Malaysia and actively engaged in educating young people and communities about their heritage and rights using the arts and music as tools. I am now more vocal about decolonizing research and bringing about social justice and change in the communities I work with. Toward this end, I am actively promoting activist research, which is participatory and collaborative, and engages academic university students, young people of the multiethnic communities, as well as tradition bearers in Penang to revitalize their musical cultures. An example is the rejuvenation of the endangered Hokkien Potehi glove-puppet theater of the state. The aim is to democratize research so that communities and young people are able to recover their histories that are not written in history textbooks, to revitalize minority cultures that have been marginalized, and to let communities have a voice in the processes of research and documentation of their cultures. By so doing, I acknowledge that the communities are sources of knowledge and that they engage in an ongoing analysis of their social and cultural processes. For cultural sustainability to take place, the communities and tradition bearers must take ownership of the research and documentation. Constant dialogue must take place among all collaborators in all aspects of the research process. I learned this from my long-term work using participatory methods to educate young people about their traditions.

Michael Tenzer (October 27, 2007)

PhD, University of California, Berkeley (Ethnomusicology)
Professor, University of British Columbia

Graduate Studies

MT: I was twenty-two. I had just bought a whole gong kebyar, shipped it back to the States, and moved to Berkeley in the fall of '79. With the few friends I knew there, I started Sekar Jaya.

TS: So the devaluation of the rupiah was indirectly responsible for the founding of Sekar Jaya? What's the word for that?

MT: *Kebetulan*, a serendipitous concordance of events. The instruments were still on the boat, and I didn't even know how I was going to pick them up or where I was going to put them. Two other people were especially crucial in starting Sekar Jaya: Rachel Cooper, a student of Balinese dance, and Wayan Suweca, a great Balinese drummer. Suweca was teaching a summer gamelan intensive at UCLA. We three had become friends in Bali the previous year, and they came up to visit Berkeley just as I was starting school. Neither of them had a job, and Suweca was overstaying his visa, but his commitment was remarkable. Suweca said, "Why don't we start a group?" Rachel

Careers within "The Professoriat"

knew lots of people in the area, I had the instruments, and soon I was introduced to a whole network of like-minded folks.

What happened next is actually a result of the whole Bob Brown Center for World Music scene, which was really big in the mid-1970s in Northern California. This was before my time, but many people were involved. In 1974 Sam Scripps, the newspaper magnate, had funded Bob Brown with hundreds of thousands of dollars to bring close to 150 major artists from around the world to Berkeley, including several from Bali. So many people were there to study that famous summer of '74, like Steve Reich and Philip Yampolsky. Bob Brown's enterprise eventually faltered, and he had to leave the Bay area. He moved to San Diego, probably a year before I got there, but that left a vacuum in which many people wanted to play Balinese music. So we had a group instantly.

We couldn't meet at UC Berkeley because there was no space. So we decided it was going to be a community gamelan, just like in Bali. Somehow—I forget exactly how—we contacted a woman who lived in a large home in the Berkeley Hills and who thought a gamelan would be "charming." She said, "You can rehearse in our living room." We brought the instruments over—of course, it was much more than she expected! When she heard the noise, it freaked her out because it was loud and we were still quite cacophonous. The next Tuesday when we went back, there was nobody home—a signal from her—but we heedlessly broke into the house. We climbed in through the window and went right ahead and had our rehearsal. We already had an intense group of people! Of course, we couldn't continue on at that location.

We rehearsed all through that fall, cramped in the house of some of the members. We didn't have any money, but everybody chipped in twenty bucks a month to give Suweca something to live on. He would sometimes busk on Telegraph Avenue to get a little extra money, but he stayed because we were hungry to learn. We decided to have our first concert at Fort Mason in San Francisco in February 1980. It was an old army barracks that had been converted for arts groups to use as a performance space. They published a monthly calendar and put us on that month's cover. It was a huge success. We had to turn away about four hundred people! Sekar Jaya went on to so many great things and is still going—2009 will be our thirtieth anniversary. It still functions the same way we set it up originally: it's a community; it's all done collectively. It's something I'm deeply proud of because Balinese equate Sekar Jaya with foreign interest in their music and dance, and people all over the world know about the group.

TS: Were you taking any ethnomusicology classes yet?

MT: I took one class with Bonnie Wade and wrote a paper about Balinese drumming, but I was much more into contemporary Western music and taking music-analysis courses. All through grad school I had a split life: I was doing composition at Berkeley and Sekar Jaya on the side. Eventually, some of us rented a house, moved the gamelan there, and had a whole communal living scene. Suweca stayed for the first two years but finally had to go home. After that, we started raising money to bring in other teachers.

TS: How long were you in the MA program?

MT: Two years; then I was awarded a Fulbright and went back to Bali for another year from the fall of '81 to the fall of '82. In the meantime, I was having difficulties with my composition. I don't think it's uncommon in grad school. I was having an artistic crisis in what I wanted to write, and I wasn't writing very much. I was concerned about that but was getting a lot of pleasure out of the gamelan and our strong community. Bali had changed me, of course. I was personally conflicted, because, to this day, composition is important to me, and I felt an inner struggle between loyalty to the aesthetics of musical modernism, which I hold dear, and the more participatory aspects of Balinese music making. I didn't want to give up my identity; I didn't want to *be* Balinese. I wanted to be an outsider *and* I wanted the respect of the Balinese. I was able to resolve these feelings in time, through composition and scholarship. But I'm always warning my students. I watch some of them get sucked into whatever cultural area they're doing, and I encourage them to hold on to part of themselves. They don't always listen to that; maybe not everyone needs to hear that, but to me it's really important.

The Fulbright year deepened the issues even more. I went to Bali totally free and unencumbered for a solid year. I found a great teacher, Wayan Tembres, who was brilliant, a musical powerhouse, fun, and open to anything. I was his sidekick. I played music thirteen, fourteen hours a day for a year. I'd get up in the morning, and by 7 A.M. I was off on my motorbike to Tembres's. I'd study for three or four hours, then we'd go to a rehearsal, and then I'd go to a performance. *All* the time, for a year. I focused on drumming. I wasn't thinking about scholarship or writing a dissertation. I hadn't read anything about ethnomusicology, nor did I care. In retrospect, I'm grateful that I wasn't under the gun of a dissertation and just pursued the music for its own allure.

That year, I composed my first pieces for gamelan with Tembres. That was huge for me: to have the experience of composing music, teaching it in the Balinese way, and having players, in this wonderful warm Balinese village atmosphere, playing the socks off my music in the way only they can play.

TS: And then you came back and started your PhD at Berkeley?

MT: Yes, I started my PhD in composition in January of 1983. I did my PhD in three and a half years, during which time Sekar Jaya continued. By then we had pretty steady grant support and always had a Balinese teacher in residence, so we hatched a project to perform in Bali. This was some time in '83. It took two years to make it happen. Nothing like that had been done at the time. You had individuals like Harold Powers and Jon Higgins who performed in India, but no gamelan had done that. Sekar Jaya went to Bali in 1985 and played all over the island, including a centerpiece concert at the annual Bali Arts Festival. We presented traditional repertoire and a piece I co-created with dancer/percussionist Keith Terry, which was a terrific success. It was one of those times when one feels one could have died right afterward! Life would have been enough because it was so rewarding—not only the kind of reception we got, but also the feeling that we had made a positive contribution to their world.

TS: What would you say was the positive contribution to their world?

MT: We showed how much we loved their music, and we did our best job to present it to them. The Balinese adored it. One of my drumming teachers described to me how he broke down in tears of joy watching us. We were on TV, and people came and embraced us in the streets. There's a film called *Kembali* that really captures it well [Mayer et al. 1991]. On top of that, there's the personal: the last person to join Sekar Jaya before we left was Pam Hetrick, the woman I ended up marrying. We got together during that trip. We got home and I blasted through my dissertation, a big symphonic piece, "Lelambatan," based on the eponymous Balinese classical genre.

Building a Career

I finished grad school in 1986 and began teaching at Yale. It was [an] extremely tearful [time], though, because I felt like I was wrenching myself away from Sekar Jaya. Yale hired me as a composer to teach the composition seminar and theory classes, but during the interviews I asked [musicologist] Claude Palisca, "Are you interested in the gamelan at all?" He said, very dryly, "We're interested in a *general* sort of way." I nonetheless brought the instruments with me, found an unused basement room, and started a gamelan right away. Sekar Jaya continued on, using a new set of instruments that Rachel Cooper had purchased.

After my first year of teaching (1986–87), I got a travel fellowship and went to Bali for several months during the summer. I studied hard and composed new pieces. Then in my third year ('88-'89), I was offered Yale's Morse Fellowship, a full-year leave for junior faculty. By that time Pam and I had married, so we took off together for the year. First we went to Spain and stayed for four months while I composed a Symphony for Strings. Then we did something I'd always wanted to do: go back to my roots with Frank Bennett, visit India, and study music with his family. We spent three months in Madras and I studied *mrdangam*. Finally we went to Bali, which was a turning point for me as a musician. Two things happened. First of all, Eric Oey, a publisher I had met casually, said, "Why don't you write a little book about Balinese music? I'd like to publish it." I had never written anything in my life other than mediocre papers in graduate school, but I sat in Bali for four months and wrote my little book about Balinese music [1991]. It was written by hand, in a notebook! It cracked open a really big egg for me, because I loved doing that and was ready to frame my experiences as a writer. And second, I broke out and began writing avant-garde Balinese music. I took what I learned in Madras and realized the principles involved for gamelan. I composed one piece in which I set full mrdangam-style patterns, orchestrated for the gamelan. That piece gave me something I could develop in my music, because up to that point I was still struggling with what I wanted to write. But now I had found something I knew I wanted to do—a modernist take on traditional music, a self-aware exploration of the sonic resources of their instruments.

When I went back to Yale, a colleague said, "Why don't you teach a world music course?" I thought it was a good idea, so that's when I started reading ethnomusicology. My book hadn't required any scholarly perspective; it just required me to pour out what I'd learned. But all of a sudden I was interested in writing and learning about everything! I was thirty-three or thirty-four years old when I began teaching myself ethnomusicology.

TS: What did you read? What turned you on?

MT: What blew my mind early on was Simha Arom's book that had just come out [*African Polyphony and Polyrhythm*, 1991]. I was not that engaged in the social-theory side of ethnomusicology until quite a bit later, although, because I knew Mantle Hood, I read Merriam, Hood, Nettl, Feld, and of course all the gamelan literature. I learned a lot, and I'm very grateful, but it didn't take hold of me; it was more like what I needed to know to do my job. Then, in 1990, Michael Friedmann, a Schoenberg specialist and close friend who had seen the manuscript of my little book, said, "That's not the book you can write; why don't you write 'the real one.'" So I resolved to do that.

TS: Do you mean the *Gong Kebyar* book [Tenzer 2000]?

MT: Yes, the rest is just academic career.

TS: Let me ask the big question: Do you call yourself or have you ever called yourself an ethnomusicologist?

MT: Naïvely, I always *did*! In grad school I thought, "I'm doing non-Western music, so I guess I'm an ethnomusicologist." But someone told me, "You're not an ethnomusicologist. The people doing scholarship and writing dissertations, they're ethnomusicologists." At first I thought, "Are you crazy?" For this person, as I saw it, it was all about credentials. If you're not writing scholarship, then you're not an ethnomusicologist; your credentials—not what you did—defined you. I was incapable of seeing the sense in that at that time. But now I do.

TS: You were at Yale for ten years, from 1986 to 1996. Did you get tenure?

MT: No. That's how it was then. They promote you to associate professor, but they don't tenure you, and after ten years, they say goodbye. I knew that would happen, so I was always looking for jobs. That was unpleasant—my family was starting and the kids were born. I got the job at the University of British Columbia in 1996. I love the job. I teach five courses per year, two and three, but two of them are gamelan ensemble, so it's really three academic courses a year. I *have* taught Western theory and composition, but mostly now I teach ethnomusicology because we have more grad students and need more ethno courses.

Update: June 1, 2016

Now (and possibly for the rest of my working life) my interests have turned toward the big picture—understanding Music (with a capital M) globally as structured sound in as many varieties as I can possibly comprehend and compare. I am a frustratingly slow learner, and what this has meant for me, especially in the past ten years, is that one of the most important principles of ethnomusicology is only now gradually working itself deep into my bones. The realization, so obvious to most, constantly stuns me. It is that music is an emic concept, so vast and varied that in its long history and at its horizons, it shades off into ritual, speech, work, technology, and other things we call "life."

Sean Williams (March 21, 2008)

PhD, University of Washington (Ethnomusicology)
Professor, Evergreen State College

Graduate Studies

SW: By that point I was dead certain that I was going to be an ethnomusicologist, so I applied to three graduate schools: Harvard in Celtic languages and literature; UCLA in folklore and mythology; and the University of Washington in ethnomusicology. I thought Harvard was a long shot because I had no family members who went there and I didn't think I was good enough. I applied to UCLA because I'd been so inspired by Alan Dundes and I knew they also had ethnomusicology and Celtic languages and literature programs. Finally, I applied to University of Washington because by that time I had met my then-husband, Cary, who was from Seattle. I got into UCLA and the University of Washington, so it was a matter of deciding where we wanted to live. I chose the University of Washington, partly for Cary, because I knew he'd be able to work there, but also because it had a fantastic visiting-artist program that allowed graduate students to study directly with musicians from all over the world. Instead of moving straight to Seattle after graduating from UC Berkeley in '81, I deferred my acceptance because I felt that, in order to be a good ethnomusicologist, I needed to get a life first. So we packed up our meager belongings, moved to Europe, and traveled around Europe and the Near East for a year. I heard live acoustic music everywhere I went, from a wedding in rural Egypt to a men's quartet in Bavaria, where I was working as a ski-lift operator for the winter.

We spent some time in Ireland as the culmination, at least for me, of this journey. I heard these guys singing in Gaelic and thought, "That's pretty wonderful." I asked them about it, and they said, "Oh, if you want to hear the real thing, you need to get yourself to the United States, where there's a singer named Joe Heaney. He's the guy who knows all the songs." So I took a note of his name and thought, "This sounds good, but he's probably living in New York City," which is about as far from Seattle as you can get. But when I got to Seattle to start the graduate program, someone said, "Oh, you like Irish music? Well, it's your lucky day, because we've just hired Joe Heaney to work here."

TS: Was it one of those University of Washington short-term visiting-artist positions?

SW: That's right, one- or two-year positions. I started working with him immediately. He found out right away that I had done two things that a lot of students hadn't: first, I had studied Gaelic for several years, and there are very few academics in the States who do that, and second, I'd been to Ireland. So he started giving me Irish-language songs. That was great; it really cemented what understanding I had of Gaelic at that point, because it was embedded in the songs. We worked all the time: I probably got more than two hundred songs from him during the several years I worked with him.

TS: What kind of songs were they?

SW: A lot of love songs and laments in Irish, and a bunch of English-language ballads and drinking songs. Any time he was annoyed with me—which was often—he'd make me memorize drinking songs. That was 1983–84. He had emphysema and died on May 1, 1984. It was the first time somebody very close to me had died, which messed me up, to the point that I delayed an extra year before I wrote my master's thesis on his singing, on variation, and on the difference between Irish-language and English-language singing.

TS: What's the official title of your thesis?

SW: "Language, Melody, and Ornamentation in the Connemara Singing of Joe Heaney." I finished it in 1985. I have to say it wasn't a very good master's thesis, but part of it was that I was so hacked about his death. There was such a sense of desperation as he was dying, that all those songs were going to go with him. That really marked off the master's thesis, my introduction to graduate school, ethnomusicology, and the professional world. I started going to conferences: 1984 was my first conference. It was the twenty-ninth annual SEM conference at Santa Monica. I got yelled at by John Blacking because I had asked him a question in a public forum along the lines of "What do you do when your informant"—I was still using the word "informant"—"disagrees with your analysis?" And he said something along the lines of, "That proves how stupid you are." There were about three hundred people in the audience, and I thought "OK, I'm just gonna die here." Of course, I was referring to Joe Heaney, because he constantly disagreed with me. I was just trying to figure out what the heck he was doing, but like any twenty-four-year-old, I was very naïve and made a lot of mistakes.

TS: Great question, though, just the kind of question people are asking today.

SW: Exactly. So, at that point—the mid-1980s—I was ready to come back to Indonesian music. I knew that I'd want to come back to it because of something that Jody Diamond said. She described an event in Java where she had been playing the *slenthem*. She described a waterfall, a valley, fireflies, and playing gamelan. It placed an image in my head. I'm very patient, so I just held the image in my mind, and thought, "I really want to do that; just not today." And then, when I was studying with Usopay Kadar, he played an example of a Central Javanese singer, Waldjinah. It was a very beautiful song, maybe *kroncong*, and I thought, "Wow, that's really pretty." I looked up more information and came across *kacapi-suling*. It sounded so much like Irish harp and wooden flute music that I thought, "OK, I definitely want to do this." So I studied Indonesian language on summer programs at Northern Illinois University and Ann Arbor and did the Southeast Asian studies track. I studied politics and Islam at the University of Washington, got a grant to study advanced Indonesian in Malang, East Java, and then got a Fulbright for two years to do my dissertation research in Sunda, West Java.

TS: Why did you choose Sunda? Everyone else was doing Central Java or Bali.

SW: I felt that both Central Java and Bali were dominated by guys, that Sundanese music was quite under-researched, and I wanted to do something different. Also, I had heard kacapi-suling and thought, "This is so irresistible that I really want to check it out." I finished my doctoral exams and left for Indonesia two weeks later, May 1987. After living three months in Malang, hearing lots of music and really enjoying myself—but not necessarily improving my language skills, because I was surrounded by American students and families who spoke only Javanese to each other—I moved to Bandung, West Java, where I was the only English speaker among the people I knew. I studied at a place called Jugala, which means "wealth"; it was run by the mercurial politician and *jaipongan* choreographer Gugum Gumbira and his wife, Euis Komariah, an amazing singer. She became my surrogate mother and central focus for two years, and I also studied jaipongan dance with him that whole time.

TS: How did you hook up with them?

SW: I had studied suling and kacapi with Burhan Sukarma, the suling player who was a visiting artist at the University of Washington in 1986–87. I was unbelievably lucky while I was at the University of Washington, between Joe Heaney and Burhan Sukarma! He and his wife, who is an American, were very kind and welcoming, so I studied with him while studying for my exams. When I went to Indonesia, Burhan was already back there; he was the one who told me to go to Jugala. He said, "Euis Komariah is the best singer; just go there." I went and said, "Burhan Sukarma told me to come here; I'd like to study with you." Euis Komariah said, "OK, why don't you sing something?" So I sang her an Irish song, and anytime there's something happening in Indonesia, you get a huge crowd; by the time I was done singing, there were about thirty people there. I sang a song from the *sean nós* tradition and translated it into Indonesian. They talked among themselves in very rapid Sundanese, which I didn't understand yet, and then she turned to me and said in Indonesian, "Oh, it's really the same! We have the same story, most of the ornaments are the same, and your voice—you're singing in tune. You may study with me; why don't you move your bags upstairs?" So I did, right away. I was overcome with gratitude then, and I remain overcome with gratitude now. I should say that in two years, she never once asked me for any money. When I got back and got a job, I started putting money away because I knew that someday she'd need it. Finally, a year ago, in 2007, I told her that I had saved this money and she said, "OK, now we need it." I sent her two thousand dollars, which was basically the cost of two years of lessons; it was so satisfying to be able to give something back for the fact that she basically gave me a career by spending all those hours, weeks, months, and years with me.

TS: I still have guilt pangs about those kinds of relationships, which I never even came close to repaying.

SW: Yes, you *cannot* pay any of these wonderful people back. But my book is also a kind of payback because I try to include photographs of the people I worked with. My Sundanese friends and teachers can't read much English, but they can see their photographs in the book and show it to their friends.

Building a Career

In February 1990, while I was finishing my dissertation, I got a call from Dieter Christensen. He said, "We'd like to hire you at Columbia University this fall; will you be done with your PhD?" I'd written one chapter at that point, and I said, "Oh, yes, I'll be done; I'm almost done now." I roared through my dissertation as fast as I could. I worked at Columbia for a year and loved it. I knew it was a one-year visiting position. Gage Averill had it before I did. He was one of my best buddies in graduate school, so when he left, he recommended me. He went from Columbia to Wesleyan, so I grabbed the Columbia job. A whole bunch of UW grads had held that position and gone on to other things. It was a great time to be in New York. I started looking for a permanent position and saw the opening at Evergreen State College in Washington State. Evergreen offered me the job, so I accepted it. I've been there ever since, except for a lively summer term teaching for the Semester at Sea. It's been a great place to be an ethnomusicologist, even though I'm the only one there.

TS: How have you managed to do your research when you're obviously teaching a lot?

SW: I have sixteen hours of contact time a week. That's one of the reasons it took ten years to turn my dissertation into a decent book [2001]. I wrote new chapters and did more research in Indonesia, but I also went back and forth between Irish and Indonesian music. I've been to Ireland many times now to do new research and take students there. I haven't been back to Indonesia much since I had a child in 1994, because once you have a family, you have to start thinking about three or four plane tickets to Indonesia—that's thousands of dollars. Who can afford that? When I went from Columbia to Evergreen, I took a one-third pay cut because I wanted a permanent job and a place to raise a kid. Going to Ireland was a lot cheaper—the airfares are still a lot cheaper. And I knew that in Ireland they don't cut the seat belts out of cars the way they do in Indonesia, so I was reasonably sure that if I got in a car accident in Ireland, my child would be safely belted in. So, for very practical reasons that had everything to do with my family, I expanded my research areas.

TS: It's funny how our lives revolve around seemingly little things. Let me ask you one thing. It seems to me that you encountered some negativity—especially early on—but you seem to have turned that negativity to positive energy.

SW: Yes, part of that is that I'm pretty optimistic, so I just make lemonade out of lemons. But the other thing is that I make decisions instantly. I heard the music of Waldjinah and decided, "Indonesia, that's it! That's where I'm going to do my dissertation." All that came from hearing one track.

My heart and soul is with live, acoustic music. I think there's a place for mediated and electronic music; it's just not for me. Part of it has to do with coming of age in the '70s and being told in high school that girls can't play electric guitar, can't play drums, and certainly can't play electric bass, because [those are] only for guys. For that matter, I was even told that girls shouldn't go to college, because they would take away a place intended for a young man who would do something important in the world. At that time, I loved rock and roll. I was listening to a lot of Led Zeppelin and Black Sabbath and really enjoyed that. I sure wish I'd had a musicologist sit me down and say, "You know what's really cool about the Led Zeppelin song 'Kashmir'? Let me tell you." I wish I could have just nailed the musical element, so I could figure out why I liked it.

In terms of the whole field, it is expanding as musical choices expand. I don't think this signals the death of ethnomusicology as we know it, though I've been hearing that since 1980. As soon as people began studying elite classical musics of Asia, you heard, "You're not good enough unless you live in a mud hut in West Africa and have spiders the size of small dogs crawling all over you at night!" There was a sense that "it was always better in the old days, back when we roughed it." And at conferences you'd hear someone saying, "Well, we had giant spiders and rats in my kitchen," and the next person says, "You had a kitchen?" It's actually very funny, but I think there's always a low level of concern that has gone through decades of ethnomusicology regarding where it's going next. "These young people today, studying electronic music: how dare they?" or "They're doing all their music on MTV: how dare they?" or "They'll never be as good as I was."

Update: October 4, 2017

I have become much more confident about myself as an ethnomusicologist. I wrote a textbook about Irish music [2009] for Routledge, and my long project of writing about my Irish singing teacher Joe Heaney came to a close with the completion of *Bright Star of the West: Joe Heaney, Irish Song Man*, which I co-wrote with Lillis Ó Laoire of the National University of Ireland at Galway [2011]. It won the Merriam Prize in 2012, and the completion of the two books went a long way toward my developing a sense of intellectual freedom to explore new subjects. I finished both of those books as my first marriage ended, both my father and my Sundanese mentor Euis Komariah died, and my daughter finished high school and entered college; there was so much closure and completion that I felt I could go in virtually any direction. I even (kind of) appeared in an Irish film, *Song of Granite*, written and directed by Pat Collins [2016]. It's about Joe Heaney's life and features a young ethnomusicologist who looks, acts, and talks just like I did when I worked with him. She is probably a composite of all of us who worked with him, but it was still startling to see and hear her. Editing both volumes of *The Ethnomusicologists' Cookbook* [2006, 2015] was also part of that exploration of new things; the cookbooks are relevant to our collective work, but they include more of an interdisciplinary approach to what we all love.

Professors (emeriti/retired)

John Baily (March 5, 2010)

DPhil, University of Sussex (Experimental Psychology)
PhD, Queen's University of Belfast (Social Anthropology)
Professor Emeritus, Goldsmiths, University of London

Graduate Studies

JB: I always intended to continue with postgraduate studies. One of my professors from Oxford had moved to the University of Sussex, and I became his research assistant in 1966. I was interested in human movement, spatial orientation, motor control, and sensory-motor skills. In about 1968 I made a significant discovery in the university library: Bruno Nettl's book *Theory and Method in Ethnomusicology* [1964]. This was the first time I encountered the word "ethnomusicology." Through Nettl's book I discovered Mantle Hood's article "The Challenge of Bi-musicality" [1960]. Ethnomusicology looked like a very interesting subject, and the idea that it also involved learning to play the music you were studying made it doubly attractive.

I completed my PhD in 1970, age twenty-six, and took to the road in another battered old vehicle, bound once more for Australia. I traveled again through Afghanistan, and this time I had a cassette tape recorder and made my first recordings of Afghan music, a *tanbur* player in Mazar-e-Sharif, up in the north. The musician was working in a barbershop, and I recorded a few tunes after he finished a customer's haircut. The significance of the barber-musician connection did not dawn on me until several years later.

I drove across North India and up to Kathmandu, where I stayed for seven months. It was getting on for Christmas when I arrived and got a week's engagement in a restaurant as a singer-guitarist with a small, local dance band. Through one of the band members, I met the Nepali tabla player Krishna Govinda, and through him the sitar player Narendra Bataju. They were about my age and had been together as a sitar-tabla duo since boyhood. They had scholarships to what was then the Maris College of Music in Lucknow. Narendra was blind from birth and Krishna looked after him through all those years in India.

I started taking tabla lessons with Govinda, which I eventually published in my first book, *Krishna Govinda's Rudiments of Tabla Playing* (Unicorn, 1976). It included diagrams of hand positions to explain the different tabla strokes and an accompanying audio cassette. I was fascinated by the generative rules that allowed one to expand compositions from sixteen to thirty-two and then to sixty-four *matras*. My lessons took place at Narendra's house in old Kathmandu. He heard me playing several of my modal guitar compositions and, having heard Ravi Shankar and Yehudi Menuhin's "East Meets West" pieces over BBC World Service, suggested we do something together. He called this our "East-West Mixup."

It became increasingly difficult to stay in Nepal (due to visa problems), so I went on to Australia. But things had changed, and the job I had been half-promised by George Singer was slow in materializing. I was yearning to have a career as a singer/songwriter and to develop the East-West Mixup when I was suddenly offered the opportunity to join a rock group in London, McGuinness-Flint. Sadly, the newly configured group was a flop, and after three months I was shown the door.

I had no job and little money saved from my brief encounter with the world of popular music. I went to stay with friends in Brighton, which is when I met Veronica [Doubleday]. Narendra and Govinda had arrived in Paris and came over to Brighton for a few days. We did some recordings for BBC Radio Brighton, with Veronica singing. Right from the start we performed as a duo, singing together with me playing guitar; she was very keen on the Narendra connection. Our best piece with Narendra and Govinda was a song called "New Day," which probably owed something unconsciously to Dylan's "New Morning," but the lyrics were all about Nepal.

By now I realized I did not have the talent or the inclination to make it as a professional musician, and my thoughts turned again to studying ethnomusicology, combining my interests in academe and music. I started inquiring about where one could study ethnomusicology in the UK, and somebody said, "This new man called Blacking has just arrived in Belfast. Why don't you contact him?" I went over to Belfast to see him—on what happened to be Bloody Friday (July 21, 1972). Nineteen car bombs, nine people killed, 130 injured; that was my first day in Belfast! Blacking had lots of ideas about the relationship between the human body and the musical instrument, but he didn't have the training in psychology and physiology that I had in order to understand what it actually involved at an ergonomic level. So we decided to put in for a Social Science Research Council [SSRC] grant.

[Veronica and I] had some friends who came over from Iran and said, "Come to Iran, there's loads of work there teaching English. You can make really good money in Iran." So we set out for Iran because it was next door to Afghanistan—and we could start learning Persian.

MS: Did you already have an idea about Afghanistan at this point?

JB: I did. I liked Afghanistan much more than Iran for various reasons. Iran was very westernized and modernized and Afghanistan wasn't. Afghan music was much more rhythmic and funkier and more engaging for me. So Blacking, bless him, bought me a tape recorder—a Sony TC-800B, the poor-man's Uher—and a stack of tapes. We finished our time in Iran, and then in July 1973 we went off to Afghanistan. The SSRC had rejected our original grant proposal but had thought the project was interesting and invited a resubmission. Bizarrely, they accepted the rewritten proposal: to compare the Herati *dutar* with the Irish fiddle! In the end, the Afghan *rubab* substituted for the fiddle.

A royal coup happened a week after we arrived in Afghanistan. Mohammad Daud booted out his brother-in-law and cousin, King Zahir. We were stuck in Kabul for six weeks or so, waiting to hear whether we would be allowed to do the research in Herat. While waiting, I became the student of a very famous Afghan rubab player, Ustad Mohammad Omar, which later became a great asset in my life as a rubab player. Eventually, I heard from Blacking that we had got the SSRC money, so in October '73 we took up residence in Herat, and I worked mainly on the fourteen-stringed Herati dutar, a newly invented instrument first described by Lorraine Sakata and Mark Slobin.

After a year, reality hit. We had to go back to Belfast in 1974. It was a difficult time to be English in Belfast, with bombs going off all over the place. We were there for two years, and that's when I learned about ethnomusicology in a formal sense. The anthropology and ethnomusicology seminars in particular were extremely important. Blacking invited some very interesting speakers, and some of the papers were published in the Queen's University Papers in Anthropology. From that I learned the

365

importance of a top-line research seminar, and during all the time I've taught, I've always tried to have a weekly seminar with visiting speakers.

I applied for another SSRC grant, a "Conversion Fellowship," intended to convert people in the natural sciences to social science. Imagine that! I got the grant and we went to Herat for another year, but this time did a much broader project on the anthropology of music in Herat. This is where Veronica's work with women became really invaluable, covering that side that I simply couldn't get to.

Building a Career

For the last year of my fellowship, we lived in Oxford so that we didn't have to return to Belfast, but in 1978 I got the newly created lectureship in ethnomusicology in Belfast and was there until 1984. Students came from all over to study with Blacking, but he was often away. So—with his help—I had to tailor courses to give "the Blacking line." I became "the voice of Blacking." Blacking never considered himself an ethnomusicologist; he always wanted to be known as a social anthropologist, even though the world of anthropology thought he was a bit wacky and didn't take him too seriously. Despite this, when he had a conference in 1975 on the anthropology of the body for the Association of Social Anthropologists, they all came to Belfast!

It was at Belfast that I started my work as a film maker, editing all the video footage I'd shot during my fieldwork, starting with hand movements and moving on to broader things. With the help of a staff assistant at Queen's new television center, I edited three films about Herat. When the Royal Anthropological Institution and Leverhulme Trust came up with a film training fellowship at our National Film and Television School, those films got me one of the two places on offer. Queen's wouldn't give me a year's unpaid leave, so I resigned my tenured position. A lot of people thought I was crazy to give up a tenured job to go to film school for a year, but we were keen to get out of Belfast by this time. And when the fellowship was re-advertised I won a second year. While at the NFTS, I directed my most successful film, *Amir: An Afghan Refugee Musician's Life in Peshawar, Pakistan* [1985].

After that, I was out of work for two years. I became a visiting research fellow at Sussex University, where the only thing I had to do was organize an ethnographic film series. In 1985 I started a business called "John Baily, Ethnomusicologist." In '87, with the help of friends in the US, I made a self-financed tour that started in Boston. I hauled myself around the country for a couple of weeks with two very heavy 16 mm films, a rubab, and a suitcase.

Some months later, Columbia invited me for an interview and offered me a job. In '88 we moved to New York. The kids were about eight and ten years old. It was very stimulating to work with Dieter Christensen. In my second year, he suggested that I teach a course on "visual ethnomusicology," as he dubbed it. It was extremely popular. The position, which was meant to be a tenure-track associate professorship, turned out to be a two-year visiting professorship. I must have made a good impression somewhere, because in the middle of my second year, Columbia relented and said that I could be transferred to tenure track. But because I had been a visitor, I hadn't paid any income tax, so I asked if I could go back to England for a year before continuing.

In 1990 we went back to the UK fully expecting to return to Columbia after a year, but no sooner was I back in England than the job at Goldsmiths came up. My sons were very unhappy in New York. I was astonished—I thought they'd love being in America, but they didn't. So I applied for the Goldsmiths job in London and got it. When I arrived, it was still a rather staid department, but now we have a strong program in popular music studies and we're a much more sexy place!

MS: You've already touched on this, but do you think of yourself as part of a scholarly lineage?

JB: Well, Blacking, of course. For a long time we were described as "the two Johns." I've tried to avoid overdoing the Blacking connection because I wanted to be recognized for myself, not just because I was a student of Blacking's. But all of my teaching was strongly influenced by the Blacking approach. People who came to study with me got the Blacking line. There were big photos of Blacking on the wall of my office just to remind them of where they were coming from. Blacking's name is not nearly as important today as it was twenty years ago, but at that time he was *the* man of the moment, and it was my wonderful good fortune to connect with him.

MS: Most ethnomusicologists learn to perform the music they study, but you've taken that to a level that not that many of us reach in terms of competence.

JB: Well, inside me is somebody who also wanted to be a musician, and I met the perfect partner to accompany me in this. I wouldn't be doing what I am doing without Veronica.

MS: Are you performing more now that you're retired?

JB: Yes, but I need management. I think I've found it in the form of Viram Jasani and the Asian Music Circuit in London. He's a successful Gujerati businessman and a very good sitar and tabla player. For twenty years he's run the Asian Music Circuit, a nonprofit organization that promotes Indian music in the UK. Last fall I did a series of rubab master classes at the Asian Music Center in Acton. He was very pleased and is beginning to get more interested in Asian music beyond India. He wants to promote Afghanistan, so we're working on a Herat festival next September.

In 2002, after 9/11 and the defeat of the Taliban, we set up the "Afghanistan Music Unit" at Goldsmiths to do two things: research the state of music in the post-Taliban era and set up educational programs. A few months later, I went to Kabul for the first time in many years and wrote a long report on what I found. My film *A Kabul*

Music Diary [2003] was a product of that visit. On the basis of those things, the Aga Khan Trust for Culture asked if I would set up a music school in Kabul. They have developed a culture bearers' program, which they had used successfully in Tajikistan and Uzbekistan, where you identify certain individuals as master musicians and pay them. You pay their students, too, not a lot, but enough to cover travel expenses and things like that.

I saw that Afghan popular music didn't need any support, but it was clear that art music did. So in 2003 I set up a program with four master musicians to train youngsters in the art of ghazal singing and in playing the instruments that accompany it, principally tabla, rubab, and *dilruba*. Led by Mirwaiss Sidiqi, the school has grown into a formidable institution with a lot of students and more teachers. They've opened up a second school in Herat and are planning others in Mazar-e-Sharif and Jalalabad, but with the present security problem, their efforts are a bit constrained. I'm extremely reluctant to go to Afghanistan at the moment; it's too dangerous, not just from bombs, but also from the danger of being kidnapped. And as I get older, I like traveling less.

In 1996 I had a grant from the Arts and Humanities Research Council: Diasporas, Migration, and Identities Program. That took me back to Kabul and is why I started this music-of-migration study, exploring how music flows and where the centers of creativity of new music are. That's why I'm hopping around the world looking at Afghan music in Australia, Toronto, California, Pakistan, Iran, London, Hamburg, and Dublin. We're beginning to see how the size and nature of the community and its ethnic mix are shaping the way music operates in particular diasporic situations. Everything has changed with the new communication systems—IT, mobile phones, social media. People can maintain contact with each other in ways that were previously just unimaginable. When we wrote our books, we never for a moment thought that anybody in Herat would ever read what we had written. And now the grandson of my teacher, Amir Jan Khoshnawaz, is the local stringer for *Voice of America* in Herat. That's amazing, isn't it? And my book, *Music of Afghanistan: Professional Musicians in the City of Herat* [1988], has been translated into Dari and is about to be published in Pakistan.

Currently, I hold a Leverhulme Emeritus Fellowship, so I'm reviewing all the data from my many short field trips from 1985 (when I made *Amir*) up to now, trying to read the field notes and catalog the materials if they're not already cataloged. I've got to the stage where "the Baily-Doubleday Collection" needs to be well documented because without documentation, the recordings are not very helpful. That will be AMU's next project.

Further than that, I've got two ideas, one wacky, the other not. The not-wacky idea is to set up a sort of virtual music center in Herat University. We need some way of video conferencing with people in the faculty of music so we can discuss Herati music every week for two hours via a video link. There's a lot of traditional music there that needs to be researched and recovered; they also need to research the present state of music making in Herat and then, in due course, to feed back as they digitize all the material about Herat for the university archive. But they don't have a department of music at the moment in Herat. My wacky idea is that there is a special dance that the Afghans do—it's their national dance, the *attan*. My dream is that certain units of the ISAF forces [International Security Assistance Force] should learn to perform the attan because they're meant to be engaging with Afghan culture and I believe in the role of music and dance in promoting reconciliation.

Update: June 22, 2016

Since my retirement in 2008 I have continued as head of the Afghanistan Music Unit at Goldsmiths. From 2009 I held a Leverhulme Emeritus Fellowship, which included a period of fieldwork on Afghan music in Australia. One outcome of my fellowship is the monograph *War, Exile and the Music of Afghanistan: The Ethnographer's Tale* (2015). This covers my work on Afghan music from 1985 to 2015 and comes with a DVD containing four of my films. In 2011 I visited the co-educational vocational music school in Kabul, the Afghanistan National Institute of Music (ANIM), and made a short film about the school, *Return of the Nightingales*, available from UCL Institute of Education, London University. In 2014 Veronica Doubleday and I were invited to participate in ANIM's Winter Gala in Kabul as performers and teachers. In preparation for the Research Excellence Framework 2014, in which the Afghanistan Music Unit was entered as an "Impact Case Study" by Goldsmiths, I created the online Afghan rubab tutor (www.oart.eu) in collaboration with Evangelos Himonides at the UCLA Institute of Education. This ICS was awarded a 4* grade by REF, the top mark.

Judith Becker (October 25, 2007)

PhD, University of Michigan (Ethnomusicology)
Professor Emerita, University of Michigan

Graduate Studies

JB: When we got back from Burma, my husband got a job teaching at the University of Michigan. We're in the 1960s now. Bill Malm was already at Michigan, and that's when I discovered that there was a thing called "ethnomusicology." I'd had this transformation, and the world was never going to be the same again. It wasn't for my husband, either—just as Burmese music was a revelation to me, Burmese language was a revelation to him. We both wanted to find out where each fit into the big picture—neither one of us had a clue! And so it started: first, he got his degree in linguistics, and then I got mine in ethnomusicology. That was the agreement! That's how I got started with this whole adventure. Of course, it took a little while because we had had three children in the meantime. We couldn't do it all at once, and we didn't have any money. Eventually, and bizarrely, we both got hired at Michigan.

MS: How did you get from Burma to Java?

JB: That was another kebetulan [lucky accident] you could say. I was a graduate student working on my PhD, one course at a time. I was at home eating a peanut-butter sandwich, and my husband called up and said, "The Ford Foundation has got a job opening at IKIP Malang [the state university in Malang, Java]. What would you think if we were to go to Java?" And I said, "Wow! Cool!!" So we took the family and went to Java in 1969. That's how I ended up in Indonesian music. I have to give my husband a lot of credit—he was the one who went to Burma, and he was the one who initially went to Java. I went along as the spouse. I was finishing up my coursework, so it was the right time to think about dissertation research. I decided that if I'm going to be in Java for two years, I might as well study Javanese music. I got to Java and got really interested in what was at that time modern gamelan music. Of course, it's very old fashioned now.

Building a Career

JB: When we came back in 1971, I wrote my dissertation, and I got my degree in 1972. That's when I was hired.

TS: Was teaching gamelan part of your job description?

JB: Yes, it was, but that had started when I was still a graduate student. Bill Malm bought the gamelan in 1967. He ran it for six months and decided it was too much, so he said, "You do it!" This was before I'd been to Java! I didn't know anything!! Do you remember that old UCLA recording, the one that had "Udan Mas" on it?

TS: *Music of the Venerable Dark Cloud* [Hood and Susilo 1967]?

JB: Yes! I had that recording. So I listened to it, read Jaap Kunst's *Music in Java* (1949), and tried to figure out what I was hearing. I figured out what I thought the various instruments were doing and taught the gamelan to do that. The following fall, 1968, we got enough money to bring Hardja Susilo from UCLA to the University of Michigan for three weeks. The point was for him to train me so that the gamelan could carry on, because I was hanging on by the tips of my fingers! When he first arrived he came into the gamelan room and said, "OK, play something for me!" So we played my version of "Udan Mas." After we finished playing there was this interminable silence. Finally Susilo said, "Well, there's Yogyakarta style. . . . And then there's Solo style. . . . You might even say there's Surabaya style. . . . And then there's Ann Arbor style!" That was the beginning of my learning about gamelan: Susilo. He stayed for three weeks and taught me some basic stuff. We worked intensively, eight hours or more each day,

PART 2 Career Trajectories

every day. And then he went back to UCLA, and I spent the whole rest of the year teaching the gamelan all the stuff he had taught me so intensively. He came back the following year, 1969, for another three-week intensive session and did the same thing. After that, I went to Java, and that's when I began to really find out what I was doing!

TS: Who were your role models?

JB: In terms of mentoring, Bill Malm was always a tremendous support. At that time he was the only ethnomusicologist at Michigan, and he had two students, Mark Slobin and me. I started taking courses in about '65 or '66, but only one course per semester because I had three little kids at the time. In terms of intellectual guides, I would certainly say Clifford Geertz, who, when I was a graduate student, I found inspirational; he later became a friend. Gregory Bateson was another big intellectual inspiration.

TS: It's interesting that you're mentioning anthropologists rather than other ethnomusicologists.

JB: I was also influenced by Charlie Seeger. I was smitten with structuralism for a while, and all his systematic grand schemes were very inspirational. Now I look at them and think, Eeewww, but at the time, the whole field was so exciting and magical to me. It was such a revelation—the idea that there was such a field and that people were seriously looking at all of these strange musical systems, which I had now come to realize were *incredible musics*.

MS: So you had a sense that there was a "field," even as you were getting into it?

JB: Oh yes, definitely. The national ethnomusicology meetings were small, and everybody knew everybody, but there was a feeling that we really were pioneers. It was vibrant and exciting.

TS: Did you have an expectation that you were going to get a job in this field? There weren't too many programs at that time.

JB: I didn't worry about having a job because this was still the '60s. It was just the beginning of the feminist movement. It seems so absurd now, when I think about it, but I fully expected to be supported my whole life! And my husband expected to support me, too. That was the way it was.

MS: Do you think in terms of lineages? You were William Malm's first student and then you taught alongside him for so many years. So many people have been through your program.

JB: I don't think lineages are very strong in our field. I certainly do notice that when I go to other places to speak, there's a definite culture to the school. And that culture is a reflection of the interaction of a set of professors and a set of students. Yes, I notice that. But once those students graduate and get a job, they begin to mold into the culture of their new institution. You get institutional cultures—I don't think there's anything bad about that. I don't think you get lineages because for a lineage to develop, all my students would have had to stay at Michigan and only talk to each other and to me, but they don't. They go out into the world and they're talking to another group of colleagues and another group of students.

TS: Do you think that your influence on the Michigan program has shaped or moved it in any particular directions?

JB: I don't think I've had any influence on the Michigan program. I've had an influence on my students, but not on the program. We're fighting the same fights we were fighting thirty years ago in the department, exactly the same. I learned early on to shelter myself from the politics of my musicology department and from the politics of the School of Music, which were not particularly welcoming to our field. But in a sense, who cares? It's the students that matter.

Update: July 17, 2016

No significant change in status.

William P. Malm (March 12, 2016)

PhD, UCLA (Ethnomusicology)
Professor Emeritus, University of Michigan

Graduate Studies

WM: I had applied for admission to NYU to study with [Curt] Sachs. I was admitted, but had fallen madly in love with a dancer over the summer. Not only was she beautiful, but she lived in California *and* had a car and a typewriter. It was all I wanted in life, so I didn't go back to New York. I left my apartment, took a train, and went to California. I went to UCLA because a man named Laurence Petran taught a course on folk music. I got there in about 1954 or '55, I think. Just after that, a guy who had been studying in Holland showed up. His name was Mantle Hood. Elizabeth May and I were the first two PhD's in Ethnomusicology from UCLA.

TS: You had already been taking courses with Petran when they hired Hood. Did that change things a lot for you?

WM: Of course! Hood just took over the program. He had a small gamelan in his apartment.

MS: What was that like? After being Devi Dja's one-man gamelan, what was it like to hear the real thing for the first time?

WM: It was a kick, and, of course, I was intrigued.

TS: What was it like working with Hood?

WM: Well, that's a tough question; I have to think how to answer that. He was OK, as long as you knew who was boss.

TS: Were you supported with any kind of assistantship at UCLA?

WM: I did TA there, but I went on the GI Bill. Very honestly—and this is quite true—I took a PhD because I was so angry for being taken away from my first job at Illinois. When I was at Northwestern and the GI's were coming back, every one of them was on the GI Bill, but my dad and I were paying for me. I can remember the only time in my life that my father ever cried was when I handed him the tuition bill for Northwestern. So when I got drafted, I thought, OK, I'll get a PhD at their expense.

MS: How did you get interested in Japanese music?

WM: Back in New York, when I lived above the Metropolitan Opera House, my older brother sent me a souvenir from Japan. I opened the package and there was a *shamisen*. It came with a whole book of notation, but I couldn't read it. That's what got me to Japanese music—I actually had a *nagauta shamisen*. When I got to LA, there were a lot more Japanese things than in New York. I got into Japanese music because I couldn't find a book that said what the hell it does. What does *noh* drama do? What does *kabuki* do? I knew none of the rules, except the *yo* and *in* scales. Well, that's like knowing *slendro* and *pelog*—it doesn't get you very far in gamelan. That's why I decided to go into Japanese music for a PhD.

TS: How was your research in Japan funded?

WM: I had a Ford Foundation grant. Ford had never given money for the arts, only for social sciences. So I proposed to study "Music as a Cultural Phenomenon in an Urban Area of Japan" and received a five-thousand-dollar grant. When I got to Japan, I studied kabuki music. The grant was for one year, but it was renewed, so I stayed for two years. Ford Foundation, though, was nothing like the Fulbright organization. That's really well organized. There's an officer in the embassy to help you, and you meet other Fulbright people. Ford just said, "Here's your money; report in six months." We had to find our own way around.

TS: How did you get to Japan?

WM: My wife and I took a Norwegian freight boat from Los Angeles to San Francisco to the Philippines to Hong Kong to Kobe—same boat, all the way. The passenger list consisted of my wife and me, a lady Philippine phys ed teacher, and a missionary, his wife, and two kids. That was it for twenty days on the ship. We finally got to the

Philippines, and the next day the captain said, "Oh, by the way, I read something in the paper about a music conference." Can you believe it? The only day I happen to be in Manila and they had a Southeast Asian music conference? I met a bunch of people who were in the business of being ethnomusicologists! It's insane some of the things that happened to me. It's been a lucky life!

MS: What was the date of that conference?

WM: Here it is in my diary: "August 30th 1955. It was their first meeting. I almost flipped when I found out about it. . . . We first met Professor Jose Maceda, a young man around my age, who had done some work on Philippine native music. He introduced us around to various delegates, to musicians from India, Pakistan, Thailand, Indonesia, Korea, Japan, China, and other places. I nearly went mad with excitement, for this was an opportunity of a lifetime. . . . Sambamurthy spoke first on Indian music and sang and played a few pieces." I'm so glad I kept track of that!

TS: Do you remember your first day in Japan?

WM: Oh yes, I remember that very well. First of all, arriving on a freight boat means you don't go to the harbor and dock. The boat stops in the middle of the water: a crane comes, gets the baggage out, and drops it on a barge. You go down a ladder to get onto the barge, and *then* you're taken into Kobe. There was nobody waiting for you with *leis*. I still remember our first meal. It was in a restaurant, I don't remember where, but the TV was showing a football game. I could hear, "I'm loyal to you Illinois," the fight song of the place I'd taught in for one semester. I couldn't believe it.

We finally got to Kyoto and found a nice *ryokan* [inn] with a beautiful view, *o furo* [Japanese bath], and everything. Next day, we took a steam train to Tokyo; I still remember the smoke coming in through the windows. I had almost no money, and a guy was going by selling ice creams, so we bought some. Of course, my wife got diarrhea by the time we arrived in Tokyo. The first word I learned in Tokyo was *geri*, the Japanese word for diarrhea! I learned Japanese very quickly that way. I found a drugstore and got some medicine.

Part of the problem was that we stayed in the only hotel we saw when we arrived in the dark. It was the Tokyo Station Hotel in Marunouchi, a business district like Wall Street. There was nothing there but buildings for office people—no restaurants! I didn't know that the other side of the station was like Fifth Avenue, full of shops and restaurants. I'd just walked in the wrong direction. That was my first Japanese experience. It was a "learning experience."

One of the first things I did was set out to find [the prominent musicologist] Shigeo Kishibe. I didn't know anybody else. I took a taxi and got close to his place. The first color picture in my book and the description of a festival in the prologue of the text are actually both from this moment when I was searching for Kishibe's house. I finally found his door and knocked. The maid answered and said he wasn't there. I couldn't do anything! All that time and suddenly to be at the doorstep of my only contact and I couldn't even leave a message. I just fell apart and cried.

Finally, I found a place to stay in Shibuya. It was a little house in the backyard of a bigger house, where the owner's mother had stayed. He divorced, and his mother moved back into the main house. So I got the little house with a garden—it was perfect. Once we had the little house, I began to wonder who else was around. With Fulbright you meet other Fulbright people, but that wasn't the case with Ford. So I wrote to the foundation back in the US and asked, "Who else is here on your money?" They sent me a list, and I invited them all to a dinner party. There were a lot of interesting people in Japan on Ford money. I went to buy a ticket for *bunraku* and got talking to a guy in front of me in line. He also turned out to be in Japan on a Ford: Jim [James] Abegglen, he did his PhD in sociology at Chicago and wrote a thesis on the Japanese businessman. After that party, the Ford Foundation secretary visited, and I met her. She was very impressed at how I got the group together, so I got a second year of the grant.

MS: It takes an ethnomusicologist to hold a party and get everybody together!

TS: Can you tell us about beginning your research? How did you start to take lessons, and what was the interaction like? You must have been one of the first foreigners to do that kind of thing. How did you make contact with your teachers?

WM: Through Kishibe. I wrote to him, and he picked my teachers. That's how I did it, because you had to have a go-between. You can't just go in, introduce yourself, and say give me lessons. You had to have somebody introduce you. The question is—how did I meet Kishibe? Neither he nor I have the foggiest notion of how we met! When I applied for the Ford Foundation grant, I needed a reference from Japan, but I had never been to Japan. I got Kishibe's name from someone at UCLA—I don't remember who—and wrote to ask him to do this for me. He didn't know me, but he wrote a positive letter. It was his first letter in English, so it was really funny. I think the committee gave me the funding because they were amused by the letter from Japan!

TS: How did you rationalize yourself to your teachers? Did they grasp what you wanted to do? Or did you even know exactly what you wanted to do?

WM: I wanted to learn the music well enough to write a thesis on nagauta. I took lessons with a shamisen teacher, and then I studied with a singing teacher, a drum teacher, and a flute teacher—I learned the whole thing! I couldn't be analyzing music unless I could play all the parts a little bit. After my first drum teacher, I studied with Tanaka Denzaemon XI, *iemoto* [leader of a professional lineage] of the Tanaka-*ryu*. He played in the kabuki theater. My teachers were professional performers. My voice teacher and shamisen teacher were both teaching at Geidai. You know where Geidai—the University of Fine Arts in Tokyo—is? Well, it's in Ueno. The original building was built back in the Meiji era and there was no place to practice, so we all sat in one room to practice. It was a very curious situation. Kishibe did me a great favor. Of course, dealing with traditional musicians meant dealing in Japanese. None of them spoke English. Backstage kabuki, forget it! It was all colloquial Japanese that doesn't show up in the textbooks.

TS: Did you learn by imitation?

WM: I got the shamisen notation way back in New York from my brother. And drum lessons don't use notation anyhow, ever. You learn how to do it, "*Chiri kara chiri popo*," you have to learn names for everything. You had to memorize the whole thing.

Remember, this was 1955, and the American Occupation Army was still there. People were very willing to do something for a foreigner, for an American. Tanaka Denzaemon XI was the iemoto, *the* number one. You can't get a professional name from the school without paying him. I wrote a whole chapter on lessons in my book *Six Hidden Views* [1986]. You come to the *genkan* and take your shoes off. First you say, "*Gomen nasai*" [excuse me], and then you go to the lesson room and sit down. You sit there until the teacher decides to come in. He always sits in the *tokonoma* area, and you sit on the other side for your lesson. He was very strict. If you were doing kabuki music, you really needed two drums, so another *deshi* had to be there to play the other half—*tsu ta pon, tsu ta tsu ta*. He's doing that while I'm doing the other part. That boy was as tight as the drum because if he made a mistake, the teacher had a *haraogi*, a fan wrapped in leather and kept in a box. He'd go *tsu ta pon, tsu ta tsu ta pon*; if you play it wrong *bang, bang*! He'd shout and bang the box. I got real Japanese lessons from him! Denzaemon was a great teacher.

TS: What did your wife do while you were taking your lessons?

WM: Well, what she had to do, poor thing, was study *koto* because Kishibe's wife was a koto teacher. But the major thing she wanted to do was study dance, and that came out beautifully. I don't remember how—again, probably through Kishibe—but we got a very good teacher, Tsuji Isami of the *Hanayagi-ryu* Japanese dance guild.

TS: Were you making recordings of performances and analyzing them as you did your research?

WM: I had a big and very heavy reel-to-reel recorder; it weighed a ton, but I didn't record much. I learned in the proper way; I took lessons. I learned to play the drum, I learned shamisen, I learned the vocal part, and I played the whole piece. I only did the analysis and wrote my thesis when I got back to Los Angeles.

Do you know what happened next? It's here in my diary: "January 9, 1956. Our evening was spent with Donald Richie [American scholar of Japanese culture] in the beautiful house of Tex Weatherbee. Between drinks, dinner, and music, Donald asked me if I was interested in writing a book on Japanese music for Tuttle. Needless to say, I was." Tex Weatherbee, Richie's partner, was an editor for Tuttle. So, here I was, a graduate student who came to Japan in September 1955, and by January 1956 I had an offer to write a book. So I said yes! It was an incredible opportunity. Fortunately, I had my wife's little portable typewriter. I took it to Japan and wrote the whole thing on it. I started writing in January '56 and finished in maybe eighteen months, never having written anything in my whole life. I handed in the manuscript in July '57 and then got the boat home in September.

That Tuttle book—*Japanese Music and Musical Instruments* [1959]—was not a scholarly book at all; it was a coffee-table book. Tuttle does books on flower arranging, judo, and things they sell to the tourist industry. That's how it got to be so spectacular—they didn't care about what I said, they wanted to see how it looked! I was so lucky to have that as my very first publication. It was the editor who said, "I think we should have drawings." Fantastic! We got all those wonderful drawings. And what's the dirtiest word in publication? Color. It was the editor who said we should have color pictures. And then I said, "Look, this book has got so many Japanese words, I think we should have an index." And the editor said, "OK, but I think we should have it in Japanese, too." And because it was printed in Japan, I got a bilingual index! That book stayed in print from 1959 to last year. But Tuttle was never going to change or do a second edition, even after so many years. So I finally took it away and got Kodansha to do a new edition.

MS: Here's a newspaper review, dated December 27, 1959. My goodness! It's a very long review by Henry Cowell. How did Mantle Hood react to that when you returned?

WM: Well, you see, I have said that two very aggressive men just don't make a good team in the context of thesis writing. It's natural that the methodology of the guiding professor tends to dominate. Under the guidance of Jaap Kunst in Holland, Hood analyzed Javanese *pathet* in a "scientific" style.

MS: You mean you had to analyze music his way?

WM: Yes, that's right. I had to create tables of how many times a note goes up or down. My part of the thesis dealt more with how the structure of the music was organized. Both systems have their value, but my interest was that of a composer. I think the tables in *Nagauta: The Heart of Kabuki Music* are basically useless, but the thesis won the Monograph Prize of the American Academy of Arts and Sciences in 1959 in the Field of Humanities, so I guess both methods have their place.

Building a Career

WM: So, it's 1959. Here I am, one book published, one book in press, a wife and a baby, and no job. I got a job offer from Michigan, so I left. When I was hired at Michigan, there was no ethnomusicology department; it was Music Literature and Musicology. On the musicology side was H. Wiley Hitchcock. I had met him on the beach when he was teaching summer school at UCLA. We got along well, and he knew I was looking for a job. They held interviews at the AMS Convention in Chicago. My wife was pregnant at the time, so I told her, "Don't have the baby until I get home." I got on the train, went to Chicago, and met H. Wiley Hitchcock and the other people in the department—Louise Cuyler and Hans David—and then went straight home. My wife had the baby the next day! Louise Cuyler was a tough cookie! She was hard on other people in the department but not on me, because I came in with a magic word: publications. I already had more publications than she had, so I was hired at the assistant-professor level, not lecturer. That was a pretty good start for a first job.

When I came to Michigan, the first things I taught were music appreciation classes and one class in music history, "Introduction to Music," that all music majors had to take. It started off with Greek modes, carried on to the Hours of the monastery, and all that stuff. I did it for one semester. The next year, I started to change it. "Introduction to Music" was the first course some students had in the University of Michigan, so I entered the class in full faculty robes and said "Welcome to the University of Michigan." I still get people who come up and say, "I remember that first lecture!" I used examples from all over the world and invaded the system. My colleagues didn't know, because they never dropped by to see what I was doing at nine o'clock in the morning. I had a lot of fun. Then in 1966 I got the Henry Russel Award for outstanding teaching and promise in research. None of those other musicologists had that!

MS: At what point did you start getting students coming to study ethnomusicology?

WM: In 1964 I went to a convention in Moscow, and after that I got on a book exchange, which was great, except that I don't read Russian. Some time, maybe '65, I gave a course on Western music, and a young man came in who was in violin and music criticism. He was trying to do a term paper, so I talked to him about it. I'm sitting at my desk and behind me are all these books in Russian, which I can't even read, but he does. His name was Mark Slobin. He was the first student, and Judith Becker was the next. They were our first ethnomusicology PhDs, so I got off to a good start! I started with two awesome students who were a pleasure to work with. If a student wanted to major in ethnomusicology they had get a master's degree first before they started a PhD. I was a one-man factory, so I could only take so many theses.

TS: Judith eventually went to Indonesia, which was, of course, an old interest of yours. Did you keep up some connection with Indonesian music?

WM: Well, my major field was Japan. I got a note from Mantle Hood saying that the New York World's Fair had a gamelan for sale. Now, you have to realize that when I came [to Ann Arbor], the University of Michigan had an awesome Japanese program because this is where we taught Japanese during the war. You go to the library and the books are from the Meiji Period, for Pete's sake. Japanese was already here. When I walked in the door, the Stearns Collection of Musical Instruments was just sitting here and there was also a Center for Southeast Asian Study. All these things were already here at the university; I didn't create any of them. I simply latched on!

TS: So Hood told you about the gamelan at the World's Fair in 1964, if I'm not mistaken?

WM: I had all these contacts with area studies, so I talked to Peter Gosling from the Southeast Asian Studies Center and to the provost and the dean of the School of Music, to get ten thousand dollars for a gamelan. I sent a deposit and then had to figure out where we were going to put the gamelan. I was lucky—the School of Music was just being built, so there were all these empty rooms in Burton Tower. I figured I'd put the gamelan there. I kept waiting for it to arrive, but it never showed up. Finally, I wrote; they said, "Gamelan? Oh we have no gamelan." And I said, "What do you mean, I put five hundred dollars down on that gamelan." That was my first white hair! I wasn't tenured yet, and I'd just wiped the university out of five hundred dollars. Later, I discovered that Wesleyan had got the gamelan somehow. For a while, there was only one word you couldn't say to me: gamelan!

A year or so later, I got home and found a letter that said, "Dear Sir, your gamelan has arrived in New York, please present $10,000." It was unbelievable, insane! I didn't want a damn gamelan, but there it was. By that time the provost had gone to Berkeley, and I had to start a whole new game. But the beautiful thing about the University of Michigan is that I got the money a second time. And then, I'm sitting in my office in Burton Tower, and a guy comes to my door and says, "Are you Professor Malm?" I said, "Yes." "Sign here, please." I came downstairs and there was a truck with a complete gamelan in boxes. He dumped it outside the Burton Tower elevator.

I went home, got a crowbar, and Mark Slobin, William Anderson, and I opened up the boxes. The whole gamelan was there, but no instructions for how to put it together. We had to put all the stuff into the elevator, take it up to the eighth floor of Burton Tower, take it out, put it in a room, and put it together. And then we had a gamelan. Of course, I only knew one piece, "Udan Mas," because I'd never played with a gamelan. I got it for the Stearns Collection, not in terms of starting a performance group as such.

TS: Can I ask about your teaching Japanese music at Michigan? How did that come about?

WM: Well, if you play nagauta, you can't play alone. You can't play it like shamisen. You need hayashi; you need the whole thing. The University of Michigan had a setup for Japanese studies, which had good money. Mitsubishi or somebody gave millions of dollars to ten universities, and Michigan was one. On one of my trips to Japan I wrote a letter back to the library listing fifteen books that they should order. I got a letter back, "Dear Sir, Thank you for the letter. We have ten of them; we'll buy the other five." There'd never been anybody here in music and yet that library had books—really impressive. So I went to the Japanese Center and asked how we could get instruments. When we got money to buy instruments, I went to a store in Japan and ordered them. We had one room on campus that had *tatami* mats, so we moved them to Burton Tower and set up a Japanese music room.

TS: Did you give lessons on all the instruments?

WM: Yes, and singing. Thursday was my Japanese day. I could sit in Japanese position for hours, giving drum lessons, shamisen lessons, voice lessons, flute lessons. I was the one-man band again. Here's a photograph of the first performance of the Kabuki Music Study Group. It's dated Monday, May 21, 1962.

MS: In your Seeger Lecture you mentioned that in 1965 you went to Malaysia to get real field experience but what you got was malaria. Can you tell us more about that?

WM: Well, I didn't have enough information on Malaysia when I wrote that first textbook with Prentice-Hall. It was a project that Bruno Nettl and I did. I was writing *Music Cultures of the Pacific, Near East, and Asia*, and Malaysia was the one part of the world I had no information on, so I got a grant from the Wenner-Gren Foundation and went there. I located a former English civil servant, Mubin Sheppard, had tea with him, and learned all I could about Malaysian music and drama.

MS: That's the first time you've mentioned Bruno Nettl. You're pretty close in age. At what point did you get to know each other?

WM: When I came to Michigan, he was the music librarian at Wayne State. We did those Prentice-Hall books together. They were doing a series of books on music history and wanted one book on world music, so they asked me. I wrote back saying, "Well, if the classical era of Western music that only lasts a few decades gets seventy-five thousand words, I think the world should get more." So they replied, "All right, who'll write it?" That's when I thought of Bruno. He was one guy who could write, so after some conference, he and I sat down and divided up the world! He wrote *Folk and Traditional Music of the Western Continents* [1965] and I wrote *Music Cultures of the Pacific, Near East, and Asia* [1967].

By the way, I also went to the Wenner-Gren conference in 1965. That was a great conference. The two giants—Hood and Merriam—were always at loggerheads. Oh it was terrible. And in the midst of them was a nice Quaker, David McAllester. He went to the Wenner-Gren Foundation and asked if we could have a conference to get more togetherness. We met in the Foundation's headquarters, which was very cold. You can see in all my pictures—everyone is standing by the fire to warm up! On top of being in that room, we were all in the same hotel. And the hotel had a hospitality room with free drinks. So, naturally, the conference continued into the night. That was the good news. It was going very well, Hood and Merriam were doing all right during the meetings, but during the social hour Dick Waterman insulted Hood, and the music/anthropology conflict was not resolved.

I respected Mantle Hood, but I recognized that he and I were both building empires. I did a pretty good job building mine here. I'm glad I did. It was a lot of work, a lot of fun, and a lot of power play.

MS: Earlier you mentioned your first students, Slobin and Becker. Judith Becker eventually joined you on the faculty at Michigan.

WM: Yes, she was my student. What happened was, her husband, a linguist, was already on the faculty. I don't believe in hiring our own students, but this was a special case because she was a very talented person who was trapped. On February 12, 1970, I fell down a staircase at my home, thirteen steps, right down to a cement floor. The thing that saved my life was the open metal door; I hit the door rather than the cement floor. I smashed my face and cut up all the muscles. My whole face was paralyzed. I was unconscious for a few weeks and they drilled out part of my skull to stop the bleeding. You can imagine I was not in too good a shape. I won't bother you with the details, but one was that I couldn't handle things emotionally. I'd listen to Bartók's *Concerto for Orchestra*, last movement, and just burst into tears. My courses in the winter term were taught by Mark Slobin. When Judith Becker came back from Indonesia, I moved that she be hired. The idea of hiring our own graduate student was unacceptable to some of my colleagues. On top of that, Judith was a woman *and* a woman who taught ethnomusicology. Of course, I had enough clout because I'd published more than the rest of them and had the—magic word—money. I pulled more grants than any of them. So I took a Valium and went to the department meeting. I wrote out what I was going to say and read it—as cold as steel. I went very slowly, not an emotional voice at all, because if I had gotten emotional, I'd fall apart. Actually, my colleagues had never heard me like that before. I was usually flamboyant, but here I was giving a very deliberate speech, and I got that job for her.

MS: Can you tell us about the University of Oklahoma film series that began in the late 1980s? I still use those films in class, and I know a lot of my colleagues do, too.

WM: I'm glad to hear that. Yes, that was a neat thing. Eugene Enrico put the whole thing together. He's a Michigan-trained musicologist who specializes in Renaissance music and was interested in court music. He wrote me to ask if there was any court music in Japan because he realized he could get a free trip to Japan that way. And of course there was, so he got the project going. The other professor in the films, Sidney Brown, was a Japanese historian at Oklahoma. Once we did that first film, *Gagaku: Court Music of Japan* [1989], we did six others: *Music of Bunraku* [1991], *Shinto Festival Music* [1993a], *Nagauta: The Heart of Kabuki Music* [1993b], *Music of Noh Drama* [1997], *Shakuhachi* [2002], and *Koto Music* [2004].

The films were all done amazingly well, but they were very compact: twenty-eight minutes or so to get across something you can use in class. As you know, I don't speak too clearly. I had a helluva time enunciating for all those films. In the *Gagaku* film, I was in the Imperial Palace—in my stocking feet—standing by that giant drum, making a long and complicated speech. I wrote the script but had to memorize it because there was no cheat sheet or anything. I tried so hard to enunciate every word, but each time I'd blow something and have to do it again. And when I got it absolutely perfect, somebody in the building flushed the john! I got extremely angry because we'd probably done it five times and my feet were cold.

We had a great time making those films. My favorite was the *Shinto* one. We went to my favorite area, Asakusa in Tokyo, and took my *matsuri-bayashi* teacher there and sat him on a stage. The least valuable was the *Noh* drama filmed outdoors at *Takigi Noh* in Kyoto. The film work in *Shakuhachi* is superb. You could almost learn to play the shakuhachi if you look at it carefully. And the *Bunraku* film was interesting because it was about theory. It's got great footage of Takemoto Sumitayu, the famous singer, and of a live play. We only had two cameras and one guy, so we shot that same play five days, although you don't see more than ten or fifteen minutes of the actual play.

TS: Do you feel that you were beholden to anybody or part of a lineage in terms of your approach or methodology?

WM: That's difficult to answer. Look, Hood and I were both very strong characters. I don't think he got that from Jaap Kunst; I think it was in his body. He grew up in California in the Douglas Fairbanks era. He wanted to be a swordsman! I don't think I owe much to him. I remember my piano teacher; I was very fond of him—he did help me a lot. And my *tsuzumi* teacher in Japan, Tanaka Denzaemon XI: I dedicated a book to him, but that's not what you're asking me exactly.

MS: How about you, do you feel that you created your own lineage?

WM: Well, sure. My lineage is my students: Slobin, Becker, Shelemay, Pat [Matusky] Yamaguchi, Hughes, plus thirty-four years of graduate and undergraduate students.

TS: To link this to something you said earlier: you said you were much more oriented toward theoretical underpinnings of music, but you did not try to force that on your own students. Mark Slobin, for example, does a lot of sociological stuff.

WM: I never told a student what to do in terms of topic. I only guided on method. That's the good news. The result was that I didn't have anybody doing Japanese music! Just when I was getting lonesome, I got David Hughes and finally had a student who worked on Japanese music. I was doing too perfect a job. I didn't want to force students to go into Japanese music just because it was my field.

Regula Burckhardt Qureshi (April 21, 2008; February 25, 2017)

PhD, University of Alberta (Anthropology)
Professor Emerita, University of Alberta

Graduate Studies

RQ: We went to India and Pakistan for a whole year (1968–69) as Saleem was doing research on Jinnah. I took *sarangi* lessons and started recording. I had an Uher tape recorder and went everywhere. I recorded a lot during Muharram: the Shi'a *majlis*, the chanting, which is so beautiful. I had the same sarangi teacher, but I was also able to go to Pandit Ram Narayan's house and study with him.

When we came back, I wanted to become a real student. An Indian colleague on the faculty told me about anthropology—I never knew about that field—so I took a course with a student of Margaret Mead's. That's when I wrote my first paper, a class paper on the chanting of poetry I had experienced in Pakistan. I started reading and found that nobody had ever written anything about this. Then I discovered there was a field called ethnomusicology and a book called *The Anthropology of Music* [Merriam 1964] and decided, "*This* is what I want to do."

TS: Was that the first time you heard the word "ethnomusicology"?

RQ: I don't remember where I heard it first. In the summers we used to drive down to Washington, DC, to stay with my parents. That's when I started looking for people. My father sent me a newspaper story about Bob Brown and his "Curry Concerts" at Wesleyan. Wesleyan was too far away, so I started looking for people who were closer and found Harold Powers in Philadelphia. I wrote and asked if I could visit. He welcomed me to his house. By that time I had gone beyond the anthropology course and had written my paper. At the time SEM's Jaap Kunst Prize was for non-Americans, so I submitted the paper and won the prize. That's how I published my first paper; I wasn't even a student yet.

TS: Was that the paper on sung poetry?

RQ: Yes, it came out in 1969 [Qureshi 1969]. Powers had just come back from Banaras and had brought Lalmani Misra, a professor from Banaras with him. He wanted me to play for Lalmani at his house, so I went there with my sarangi. I played my *khayal*, and after I finished, Lalmani and Harry looked at each other and said, "Where did you learn, and who taught you?" So I told them and they said, "Well, you learned from someone who doesn't really know the tradition." Lalmani said, "Muslim *ustads* don't really know *rags*. You played the *rag* wrong." I had a raised *ni* going up, and a lowered *ni* coming down; you don't do that in *Madhuvanti*. I was devastated. I had learned wrong. The encounter with Powers made all this real to me—the whole Brahminical scriptural thing and Muslim musicians. I started doing more work on Muslim stuff because I realized that nobody knew that it was there.

I went to my first SEM meeting in Chapel Hill, North Carolina, in 1971, where I presented a paper on the Shi'a *majlis*. I had a recording, and people were quite excited about it; they had never heard anything like this. For the first time, I met other ethnomusicologists who were also India people; it was a fantastic experience for me. First I met Nazir Jairazbhoy. I could relate to him immediately because he was Indian and knew Urdu. We became pals right away. Harry Powers was there—I already knew him—and Bonnie Wade, my great female colleague; Dan Neuman had just come back from a year in Delhi, where he did fieldwork for his dissertation. They all became lifelong friends.

TS: How did you get into an academic program?

RQ: I did a master's degree in music history at the University of Alberta and was allowed to write my thesis on the sarangi. I didn't know much, so it was very basic, but it allowed me to enter the PhD program in anthropology in 1974. That's when the real work began. I took everything from zero up. I didn't mind in those days because I wasn't raised to be a career-oriented person. I just wanted to be a scholar on my own. I made plans for my dissertation fieldwork—not on sarangi, which was my personal music and not in the academic picture at all, but on *qawwali*. I had been introduced to qawwali in '68–'69, when we were in Pakistan for the year. Nobody knew about qawwali in the West, but I thought it would be a good subject for a dissertation.

I had the good fortune to have two wonderful professors: Michael Asch, the only son of Moses Asch (who founded Folkways Records), had left the US before the Vietnam War and was very big in social structure and linguistic anthropology; and Regna Darnell, a linguistic anthropologist trained at Penn, who wrote the main biography of Edward Sapir. With their training, I constructed a theoretical question for my dissertation and began to apply for grants. The SSRC [Social Science Research Council] invited me for an interview in Chicago. They were impressed with my project and gave me money. It gave me a great boost that they liked the theoretical foundation, though I also did a wide-ranging ethnography. If I wanted to check the holistic paradigm of anthropology, I needed to look at everything: marriage, kinship, the economy, modes of subsistence, social structure, religion, ideology, et cetera. I had all that imprinted in my brain—they don't teach that way nowadays, but it was handy because it provided a bunch of tools.

TS: And so you went to India to do fieldwork. What year was that, by the way?

RQ: 1975–76. We drove from Paris to India in a Peugeot with our kids in '75. We did a bit of a road trip—through Italy, down the coast to Yugoslavia. Saleem had always wanted to see these places. In those days it wasn't easy to do car trips like that. We did it just in time, before all the revolutions. It was an unforgettable experience. I decided to do my research in Delhi at the Nizamuddin Shrine because there are no major shrines in Urdu-speaking areas of Pakistan; the major shrines are in the Punjab area and, not being a Punjabi speaker, I wouldn't have had access. I couldn't have done the work without Saleem. Coincidentally, it was the International Year of Women, so he said, "I'm donating my year to help you!" So when I walked into a shrine, I had him with me. Otherwise, it would have been difficult as a foreign woman.

TS: Saleem took off a year, too?

RQ: He had a sabbatical. He did his own work and he also did things with me. He could explain when we went to shrines or met anybody. People were either suspicious or they thought, "Oh, all Western women are you-know-what." He gave me an identity there and made it possible for me to record. I had my Uher reel-to-reel tape recorder and a Sony Walkman. I ordered a video recorder and eventually got it through customs. I felt that I had to be able to see what the listeners were doing when they were hearing. The video recorder was black and white; I couldn't afford the color tape.

We had rented an upstairs apartment in Nizamuddin West, near Humayun's Tomb, and along came two qawwals, one with a harmonium on his shoulder, the other with a *dholak*. My landlord freaked out, especially when they started playing! He said, "This can't happen here. People will see these unkempt, illiterate musicians coming, and they'll think this is some kind of bawdy house." These things were tough, but I continued having my lessons. I was totally immersed: I learned the repertoire, bought books, took Persian lessons—because so much of the most venerable poetry is in Persian—and talked to Sheikhs.

When I returned to Edmonton after that year, I had a real crisis. I had gotten to know the qawwals very well and could see how abject their poverty was. I came back and said, "What am I doing? This is totally callous. We go there and are well-to-do enough that we can go around with tape recorders." I had to rethink. I was paralyzed and couldn't do anything with the material. I went back to anthropology and took more courses. That was when the Marxist paradigm became prominent in anthropology. Michael Asch was very taken with looking at the mode of production. We were now looking at economic material foundations of inequality and of kinship. I came back in 1976, but I didn't get my dissertation written and defended until '81. Eventually, I felt I had the tools I needed and could begin to put a certain distance between myself and my experience and see it in terms of intellectual salvation. I was able to make peace with my situation and to see ways in which one could approach the study of music.

Building a Career

RQ: I finished, and then there was a big slump. Women were not doing well in academia in those days, so I became a sessional (adjunct lecturer) teaching anthropology at the French College in Edmonton. For a long time I thought, "Never mind, I don't need a career, I'll just learn from my teachers and publish things." I *was* publishing already, but it finally got to the point that I really wanted to teach and make a living of my own. I was lucky and got an amazing five-year postdoc in music (1983–88) at the University of Alberta. I brought the instruments that I had collected on trips, put them on a shelf in the hallway of the music department, and started an introductory course in ethnomusicology. The rest of my courses were in music history.

TS: How did this become a tenure-track ethnomusicology job?

RQ: One of my colleagues was Alfred Fisher, a composer and deeply musical person. When he became chair, he pushed for me to get a position at the very moment a female dean in the faculty of arts started to hire women. I was hired in 1988. My first and only position! I was older than most people at that stage, because I grew up in this sort of amateurish way. I started building ethnomusicology with a general introductory course. In the second year, I added a course that introduced the field itself: introduction to ethnomusicology. Next, I started a course on India, because playing music was really at the back of everything I did. That never stopped. I kept studying with gurus and collecting stuff.

TS: Was there any world music performance or ensemble component to your teaching?

RQ: That started because I realized I always had to have live music; I hated studying music on paper. I taught the way I was taught; first you learn how to sing. The students learned a small hymn to Ganesh or something easy. Then they learned Indian solfège and several different rags. It was a three-hour ensemble class, once a week. The first half of the class was vocal, and the second half was learning how to play an instrument. I had several sarangis and was able to get money to buy more instruments—sitars and tablas. I invited a friend from the community, an engineer, who was an excellent singer and played the harmonium. He helped me. So the students learned songs, everybody sang, everybody played, and it worked out well. Other people from the community taught sitar and tabla. The early immigrants—especially those who came in the '50s and early '60s—from India and Pakistan generally had music training.

TS: What was your working relationship like with other members of the department, those in "mainstream" music?

RQ: It worked well, because I played in the Edmonton Symphony Orchestra for almost ten years, and I'm just a person whose head is full of Western classical music. At home my dad always played the piano repertoire and my mother sang, so I belonged in the world of Western music. I have always had great relationships with Western musicians because that's my music, right? I think that was my advantage. Because I had [that background], I could enjoy it and share it with anyone in the world.

TS: So you've been doing that since 1988; when did you retire?

RQ: I retired in 2005 when retirement was still compulsory at sixty-five years. The law changed two years later—bad luck! But since the academic year starts on July 1, and my birthday is in mid-July, my sixty-five years were not complete until July 2005, which gave me another year of employment. I continued to get contracts from the dean of arts till 2015, first as director of folkwaysAlive!, and of the Canadian Centre for Ethnomusicology (which I had founded around 2003).

T. M. Scruggs (October 26, 2007)

PhD, University of Texas (Ethnomusicology)
Retired Professor, University of Iowa

Graduate Studies

I went to the University of Texas, Austin, in 1981. It was wonderful being back in school after working for so long. Whenever I have students who aren't sure if they should go to graduate school, I say, "Then don't go. Work for a while, then you'll be ready." I was surprised to find people my age at Texas: Larry Crook was coming in and Tom Turino was near finishing. I was a "nontraditional student." It was a little unfortunate for some of the other students in the graduate seminars, because we'd traveled, been places, and read a lot. It was an uneven match, but I really thrived being there.

MS: Who were the influential figures for you early on?

TMS: I'd heard of Mantle Hood because of his book *The Ethnomusicologist* [1971]. I remember being impressed that you could use all these different tools not only to learn about the people and the music but also to *play* the music. You would be recording the music, learning the technical knowledge that would make it successful, and making films. There's a whole chapter in *The Ethnomusicologist* about how he made films. That really stimulated me.

As far as role models went, Gerard Béhague was pretty difficult to view as one. On one hand, he had a lot of experience traveling around Latin America, and for my first couple of years, it was excellent. He challenged me and introduced me to so much. But on the other hand, he could be unfairly nasty to people and occasionally to me; I couldn't relate to that at all.

There wasn't anyone else around that made me think, "Wow, in my own unique way, I would like to be where that person is." In my first year, the SEM conference was in Hawai'i [1981], but I couldn't afford to go. Since then, though, I regularly made an annual pilgrimage to SEM meetings. It's surprising how many people we consider to be pretty good friends—even close friends—we've been meeting only once a year all our lives! I think [SEM] has a way of filtering people who are not only interested in music but are also the kind of people who are willing to invest so much time and effort into other cultures. It means that you are in a pool of people who can relate to each other on a lot of levels.

MS: True. Where did you end up doing your fieldwork?

TMS: When it came time to do my master's, I did it on Flaco Jiménez and *conjunto*, which was right there in Texas. I was able to drive to my fieldwork. I was in bars, taking notes under the table, and stuff like that. All the while I was thinking of going to Eritrea because of the Ethiopian connection. I had made a lot of friends from Eritrea in Chicago, and when I went backpacking around Europe in 1980 I made contact with people high up in the Eritrean resistance in Italy. I even went out to New York City to talk to Kay Shelemay. We decided that idea was crazy, because of the war. So, since I already spoke Spanish, I started thinking about Central America. I looked in the *New Grove Dictionary*, which had just come out in 1980, at the articles on Central America. Linda O'Brien did a good job on Guatemala, but there were only two paragraphs on three other countries—and now I can look back and see that half of *that* was wrong. I thought, "Well, this looks like it could be both a contribution to the field and something that fits my political background and interests." So, that's where I went to do my doctoral research. It was safe, for the most part. I went on several shorter trips before I got a Fulbright and lived down there from May 1987 to May 1989. During my two years there I learned to play *marimba de arco*.

Building a Career

TMS: While I was working on my dissertation, my girlfriend (now wife) got a job at Iowa. It was tough moving from Austin, Texas—"The Live Music Capital of the US"—to the sparse cultural pickin's of Eastern Iowa. I directed the Latin American Studies program and taught a class there, but then I got a job of my own at Florida International University in Miami. Around that time I developed severe back problems; it turned out I had a deformed spine, and I was fairly incapacitated for three years. It was tough because I came to Florida right after Hurricane Andrew, and what was supposed to be an easy commute turned into a very long commute, which was a real problem for my back. It was not such a great school, and Miami was disappointing because it was too dominated by two racist elites: the established local one and a new one that had been flown out of Cuba back in the early '60s. The well-off Cuban Americans pretty much controlled the Latin part of Miami. It doesn't reflect a lot of what the population was, and it certainly didn't reflect all the Nicaraguans and Mexicans and Salvadorans who were coming in. So, when they offered me a full-time job at Iowa—we also wanted to have children—I happily took that job. I started at Iowa in the fall of 1994. Our first child was born in April 1995. As soon as I signed the contract, we stopped the birth control!

I was the first trained ethnomusicologist among the several universities in Iowa. The School of Music, located too far from a major city to skate by with temporary instructors, had dozens of tenure-track positions in Euro-classical music, and then me and a new jazz professor. I wanted to diversify the university and local Iowa area with a student-based ensemble of some sort, even though it would be an overload. Earlier at FIU I had tried a *marimba de arco* trio but soon realized that the Nicaraguan marimba is too difficult a first step for an entry-level musical group. I brainstormed that steel pan would work well, and I was so lucky to find Dawn Batson's student group at the University of Miami, which she graciously let me join. It's funny, I thought there were hardly any pan ensembles nationwide because there was only a handful of ethnomusicologists who played it. Little did I realize that steel pan (shorn of much cultural context) had exploded within percussion departments after one percussion professor introduced his ensemble at their national conference. Creating a new group and playing was so rewarding, even if a bit of a time sink. The semester-end concerts grew until we had overflow crowds. It's a common ethnomusicologist's conundrum to balance actual performance and academic study of music, both personally and institutionally. Publishing was the only *real* criterion for promotion; my chair told me this kind of ensemble was looked on as a joke. Nice support, huh? Fortunately for my pursuit of tenure, a new percussion professor took the project off my hands.

Writing things out has never come easy to me, but a clicking tenure clock and a relative lack of distractions (besides busy little children) helped me get my research onto paper. It was around this time that a new inclusionary approach to reference publications generated expanded possibilities, like our first major reference work, the *Garland Encyclopedia* [*of World Musics*]. Unfortunately, these are not given appropriate credit for the level of mastery needed to create a substantial entry. Most *Garland* articles, for instance, involve a good deal of original research. It's satisfying that I was able to cover previously neglected parts of Central America for *Garland*, *MGG* [*Die Musik in Geschichte und Gegenwart*], [the New] *Grove II*, the [*Continuum*] *Encyclopedia of Popular Music* [*of the World*] and other reference works. I remember how around that time Bruno Nettl introduced me at SEM as "Mr. Central America." All the entries are practically book length when totaled up. These didn't count like they should have for tenure, but I had a 2000–01 grant for an updated book based on my dissertation. Two weeks before fall classes, when we were away, a huge lightning bolt struck our home and the slow-burning fire heavily smoked everything. It was declared a total loss. My research was damaged and scattered, we had to relocate to a rental house, and I had to devote my writing time to overseeing reconstruction. It took the wind out of my sails for a monograph; even today I haven't really recovered.

I changed course and wrote articles and chapters in edited volumes. Unfortunately, they don't travel in the ways a single book can. I still hope to produce one, especially something directed at Nicaraguan audiences.

I guess there's a bit of irony that a proud freethinker like myself ended up researching Catholic masses. The connecting thread comes from the social commitment of liberation theology and the best-known mass with these tenets, the Nicaraguan Misa Campesina by the country's leading singer-songwriter, Carlos Mejía Godoy, who's become a good friend through all these years. I pursued this theme of religious music and local agency within global belief systems and gathered some excellent contributions from fellow ethnomusicologists for a special issue of *the world of music* [2005]. I feel we have a moral obligation to return the fruits of our research back to where we originally obtained the data, the "field." I am working on versions in Spanish of already-published articles for Central American and internet journals, as well as original work, such as a study of song and violence in mid-Central America that was just published in the internet journal based in Spain called *Trans* [2006]. I still would like to publish more for a general-reader audience—a worthy goal, though more daunting than it first seemed.

The two articles, or I should say two article-length works, I've gotten the most feedback from are actually not on Central America. For a seminar paper in graduate school I went back to my late 1970s and early 1980s Chicago experiences and analyzed how master tenor saxophonist Von Freeman intertwines language and music in his performances. I shared it with some friends in Chicago and suddenly got a phone call from a free weekly that wanted to feature it. Lightly "de-academic-ized," it came out in 1987. I was so foolish not to drop everything and fly up from Austin: Von had the weekly stacked up at the club's door and talked about it all night. Oh well. I rewrote the piece to position it within jazz scholarship, which surprisingly had next to nothing about actual performance, and it appeared in *Current Musicology* [2002]. The other piece still awaits full publication. To recruit me to lead student trips, a Canadian company gave me a free trip to Santiago in eastern Cuba in spring 1997. This came out of the blue, and I was determined to relax and *not* do field work. That went out the window when I encountered a musically intense universe habitually ignored by both capital-centric, Havana-based Cubans and non-Cuban researchers. The main result of my attempt to not studiously document everything was that I never did get a photo of Compay Segundo and me laughing it up. Another "Oh well!" He and others had recorded *The Buena Vista Social Club*, and it came out later that year. After the movie followed, I gave multiple talks on this world music blockbuster, the reality on the island, and issues of global circulation and mediation. A short version exists in an edited volume published in the Dominican Republic that's hard to access, but when someone at NYU posted an unauthorized copy on the web, it went everywhere: "Buena Vista" was in the title and shows up early in Google searches. At least as vehicles for dissemination, the reach of the internet begins to raise the question of the utility of traditional publication venues: I still get requests for an article I have yet to officially publish.

Update: August 7, 2016

At the beginning of 2007, the year our conversation took place, my family and I returned from an awesome eighteen months in Venezuela, where my anthropologist wife, Laurie, and I taught and did research on Fulbrights. Our primary goal was to provide a good experience and language immersion for our two grade-school-aged boys, but I successfully delved into the music industry and gathered music that reflected the issues of that exciting time, especially the new impetus for more recognition and inclusion of *afrodescedientes* into the national arena. It is revealing how much my research methods differed from my doctoral work. "Gather" was the operative verb: in contrast to twenty years before in Nicaragua, the topic led me less to field recording and more to tracking down home-reproduced CDs from contacts or the street. The challenge to produce quality sound documents moved to accurately documenting the details of comparatively easily available sound objects: the who, when, and where of a blank home-industry produced CD, typically sleeved with an umpteenth-generation photocopy of an album cover, if that, and then attempting to locate the musicians. This was the opposite order of previous ethnomusicological methodology. Our field research increasingly entails encounters with mediated product due both to continuing urbanization and to the price and portability of quality recording equipment: people are recording themselves and do not need us to arrive to do it. While not all-encompassing by any means, a generational shift has moved our study-object from musical artifacts we helped create through our recording to music product that spans the range from professional studio to home-artist produced.

My own trajectory within the field changed soon after returning from Venezuela. I had a coveted tenured position but also had a second career running a nonprofit that had steadily increased its demands on my time. When I began graduate school in 1981, I also launched into trying to build a nonprofit able to support worthy social-justice projects. I was very private about this growing vocation, which led to a somewhat schizophrenic life for a good while. The nonprofit's success has helped fund some excellent progressive think tanks and media endeavors. Beyond the tedium and inherent isolation of the job, it has been rewarding intellectually to study such a divergent field as political economy, one that has helped me understand the major motor forces that undergird a modern society. Unlike my journey in the anthropology of music, however, I often found my deepening understanding of the workings of Finance (capital F) to be personally distressing as it revealed in greater detail the inherent immorality of the economic system we live in. I took an early retirement option that the University of Iowa offered and we relocated to my home, the San Francisco Bay Area.

After being the "token ethnomusicologist" at a major institution for a long time, it was an adjustment to become an autonomous anthromusicologist. My nonprofit work remains full time, especially involvement with TheRealNews.com, but I have served on doctoral committees and on *Ethnomusicology*'s editorial board, and I strive to continue research on which I give papers and talks. That part of our profession is mobile; teaching is not. Countless times I had reminded eager prospective graduate students of the specter of undesirable living situations in an academic career: one has to go where the job is, I counseled, so be prepared for an unanticipated home address. Like many others in our field, I came up against the other side of that coin: you can move to where you want to live, but you can't conjure up a job there. It is a situation that now confronts too many just entering the job market, regardless of their own geographical preferences: the unfortunate reality is that economic pressure has flipped the percentages in only two decades from 70 percent tenure track to, now, 70 percent contingent positions. This is a crisis in education in general that will take a major collective effort to address and turn around. I find the new option of online teaching alienating, and there are unanswered questions about how this new mode of instruction might undermine our position as employees of the corporations that universities are.

I have taught various individual classes and been able to fill in for colleagues and teach graduate seminars in ethnomusicology, first at UC Davis and then at Stanford. Ironically, only after leaving my tenured position of many years could I teach students pursuing degrees in my own field. It is a reminder that my joking "token ethnoid" appellation does, in fact, accurately describe the career path for the majority of our colleagues.

Ricardo Trimillos (August 1, 2016)

PhD, UCLA (Ethnomusicology)
Professor Emeritus, University of Hawai'i

Graduate Studies

RT: I was lucky that my introduction to ethnomusicology was in Hawai'i because it's so intercultural and Asian oriented. We were completely immersed in Pacific and Asian cultures, whereas growing up in California, we only saw other cultures at staged festivals. In Hawai'i it was a lived experience, which made so much more sense to me. I suddenly discovered that I fit in more here. For example, growing up in California, there were things that happened but couldn't be explained and so were considered "superstition" or "ghost stories." It was very much part of being Filipino, but hey, if you grew up in California, you were ashamed of that because you're not supposed to be superstitious. You're supposed to be modern. But in Hawai'i there's a lot of spirituality, so it was much more naturalized. I found that much more comfortable because you could talk about it and nobody thought you were crazy or "primitive."

MS: I find it fascinating that you went to Hawaiʻi for a master's program, discovered it felt so much more Asian centered, and yet the significant person for you was Barbara Smith.

RT: Yes, Barbara Smith was one of those "out of step" *haoles*, very aware of and sensitive to things Asian and Pacific. Barbara was—and remains—an extraordinary person. Ninety-five and still going strong! Originally from California (like me), she had gone to Eastman School of Music and was hired in music theory to teach the Eastman method to local kids. That's when she found out that there was all this other culture going on. Because she was extremely curious about other cultures and very open, she didn't fit into the music department, then a bastion of Western culture designed to "civilize the natives." It was sort of serendipity because she started the ethnomusicology program in 1960 and then we showed up in '62 as part of the first batch at the East-West Center.

MS: Who else was in your cohort?

RT: Fred Lieberman, Rebecca Stewart, Ranganayiki Ayangar, and Hoʻoulu Cambra (then known as Zaneta Richards). Carl Wolz, the dance ethnologist, was also part of the program because, at the time, ethnomusicology and dance ethnology were both in the music department.

MS: Do you feel part of any lineage?

RT: Absolutely! The lineage is what you always call the "Hawaiʻi Gang," and it goes back to Barbara Smith. She's legendary in terms of the rigor she expected out of students, and that has gone forward, particularly in the master's degree.

MS: Was there anyone else there, or did she run the program singlehandedly?

RT: She was the only one of the faculty who was really interested in ethnomusicology. She had help in the sense that there was one native Hawaiian faculty member, Dorothy [Kahananui] Gillett, in music education.

MS: In those early days at the East-West Center, what were you reading that influenced you?

RT: Our "text" was all the little articles in the back of Kunst's *Ethno-Musicology*. We also read some things that had been published in the *American Musicology* journal by Charlie Seeger and articles on American Indians—the Bella Coola Indians. Then, in our second year, the Prentice-Hall series came out—1964, I think—so we read those, but there really wasn't a lot. There were a lot of films and recordings, but not much literature, per se.

MS: Were you starting to think about fieldwork?

RT: Yes, because the American students in the first intake were guaranteed travel to Asia. It was assumed we would do fieldwork at the master's level. As it turned out, my experience was different from the rest of my cohort because I became part of a coordinated team research project to go to Sulu. A group of us—two anthropologists, a political scientist, a linguist, and I—used to go out drinking together. One of the anthropologists had already been to Sulu and done work with the Ateneo de Manila, a Jesuit university. He suggested we figure out something we could do there together. As luck would have it, one of his teachers from the Ateneo, Father Frank Lynch (a famous anthropologist), came and taught for one semester, so we all got to know him. That was when we hatched the idea to go to Sulu together. We sold it to the East-West Center as a coordinated project with Father Lynch as the advisor. I was the only heritage scholar in the group, all the rest were haoles.

The nice thing about the project for me was that we were all on different islands, so that when one of the others heard there was a wedding or something going on, they would send out word, "Hey there's something going in my community," and I would go and observe it. I was more or less centered on the main island of Jolo. At the time, the peace and order was really great, not like now. It was a bucolic and wonderful place to be, with natural beaches and a lively performance tradition—not just music, but dance and *daling-daling*, little troupes going around to every settlement.

MS: Was this your first visit to the Philippines?

RT: Yes. When we arrived in Manila, we did three weeks of orientation at the Ateneo de Manila. That was the first time I met many of my relatives, most of whom were in the north, the Christian part of the Philippines. I spent most of my research time in the south, but occasionally, once every six weeks or so, I would go up to Manila for R&R and I would see them again.

MS: How long was the field research?

RT: The whole program was two years. I started in '62 and finished in '64. The first year of the program was coursework. The summer and third semester were for fieldwork—about four months in all—and then we came back in the spring and wrote up. I finished but didn't make the deadline for depositing in the spring of '64. I deposited later, so my MA says 1965, but I was gone by then. In the fall of '64 I got a Fulbright to go back to Germany; that's when I went to Cologne.

MS: Why did you go back to Germany?

RT: The Fulbright opportunity came up, and Barbara said I should really study somewhere else to get more experience. I applied for the Fulbright, put down Germany again, and got it. I was still not completely committed to ethnomusicology per se, because I was still playing piano. My proposal was to study ethnomusicology with Marius Schneider and organ with Michael Schneider, the organist at Cologne Cathedral. I was still hedging my bets! When I arrived, the first person I met at the university—literally coming down the stairs as I was looking for the musicology department—was Robert Günther, who was assistant at the time (and later became professor). He befriended me, and that sort of sealed the deal. Marius Schneider was very interested in me; first of all, he thought I was Spanish because of my name! He had lived in Barcelona during the de-Nazification period. He had actually done some archival work on Filipino music, so he was very interested in the Philippines.

The Fulbright was just a year, but they asked me to stay another semester because we were working on a project that involved a lot of transcription. As luck would have it, I was already looking to come back to the States to start a PhD. I had applied for a doctoral grant from the Danforth Foundation (Danforth was a big newspaper family out of Illinois), which funded minorities and women to do doctorates in anything to increase the diversity pool. I was on a Fulbright from '64 to '65, then got the Danforth grant that funded the extra semester in Germany (fall of '65), and in January '66 I went to UCLA.

MS: Why did you choose UCLA for your PhD?

RT: I was thinking about staying on at Cologne and doing the doctoral program there, but Schneider was quite perceptive and asked me, "Where do you want to have your career? If you want a career in America, you need to go to an American university." And because he was pals with Jaap Kunst, he said, "There's this guy at UCLA who studied with Jaap Kunst—this Hood guy—so why don't you go there?" So I said, "OK, I'll apply there."

MS: What was the scene at UCLA like when you arrived?

RT: It was a very exciting scene because the semester before, Mantle Hood had just done the soundtrack for *Lord Jim* [in other words, provided gamelan color for Bronislaw Kaper's score]. He was a big star, hobnobbing with all these Hollywood types. It was like ethno showbiz—a really big deal! I arrived in the spring semester, when they had a series of ethnic concerts at Schoenberg Hall—mariachi, gamelan, and all that kind of stuff. I had studied koto and gagaku at Hawai'i, so I joined both the koto sankyoku group and the gagaku group. As it turned out, the koto teacher at UCLA was a Tenrikyo member. The gagaku in Hawai'i was also run by Tenrikyo people, so they knew each other. The koto teacher asked me to help teach beginning koto, which was fun for me. So, I jumped right in and was soon involved with the logistics and infrastructure of the institute.

There was a lot of money pouring in—from Rockefeller and from Ford—not that it was misused, but I must say we lived high on the hog! Anything you wanted, you could get. Charlie Seeger had been there a year and was working on his melograph, the automated transcription machine. People were giving him millions for that thing. Klaus Wachsmann joined the faculty the same semester I arrived. So the triumvirate—Hood, Wachsmann, and Seeger—were all there together. Again, for me, there was some serendipity involved—being at the right place at the right time. When I arrived, the chair of the Music Department was Walter Rubsamen, a historical musicologist and second-generation German. He was the bane of ethnomusicology students because he looked down on ethnomusicology—it wasn't real music—and thought all ethnomusicology students were stupid because they didn't know Western music. I had just come from Germany and spoke English with a German accent. (It was true: Sus [Susilo]—who was one of my first friends—made a recording of me to prove it!)

The musicology faculty always flunked the ethno candidates the first time around in their musicology exams—except for Bonnie Wade and me. Bonnie passed first time because she was really bright. With me it was because I had this German background: I told Rubsamen that it would be really difficult for me to write the acoustics exam because I had taken acoustics in Germany and didn't know the terms in English. He said, "Oh you can write it in German!" So I did and, of course, he loved that. I was the little guy who showed up and was the model kid. There were a lot of ways in which I was exotic and that helped me get through the exams the first time.

MS: Who else was in your cohort?

RT: The ones I actually studied with were Lois Anderson, Jim Koetting, David Kilpatrick, Dale Olsen, David Liang, and Fred Lieberman. Bonnie came the next semester; she was a master's student, so she was behind me. Those were the golden years! A couple of them have died: Donn Borcherdt, who did Mexican mariachi music, died in the field, and Max Harrell, who did Sundanese music. Susilo was there, too. He was an artist in residence but was working on a master's degree, so he sat in on coursework. There was also a big African contingent because of Wachsmann. If I think of my gang, we had a lot of parties! Of the hardcore ones, there were probably eighteen to twenty of us there at the same time. Some were master's students, but most of us were PhDs.

MS: How long did you stay at UCLA?

RT: I was there until the spring of '68. I went back to the Philippines for fieldwork. Because I got through the exams quickly, I didn't have too much to do. There were not a lot of required courses at UCLA, which was good, so I had about eight months of additional fieldwork and went back to Jolo, Sulu.

Building a Career

RT: I was ABD at UCLA by the spring of '68. That was when I got the offer to teach at Hawai'i. I started teaching there in the fall and, in a sense, never left, although I did teach elsewhere for a couple of years—a year at Santa Cruz and one semester at UCLA.

MS: Was the program just you and Barbara Smith, or was there anyone else around?

RT: No, Barbara and I built up the program. When I arrived, I said that every good ethno program needs a gamelan, so we arranged to get a gamelan, and the first faculty member I recruited was Susilo. Barbara was the "anonymous donor" who bankrolled the gamelan. She came from a wealthy family out of Ventura, California, so she just bought it. It was a beautiful palace gamelan, the "second gamelan" of some prince. He had sold it to a batik dealer, and it was just sitting at the dealer's house. I went to see it with Pak Cokro and Pak Soedarsono, and they said it looked really good, so we bought it. That was 1969. It arrived in '70, and Sus built up the gamelan program.

Those were the golden years of ethnomusicology at Hawai'i. We started an undergraduate program in ethnomusicology, called "World Music." A lot of our graduate students came out of that program. Both Barbara and I were very interested in the pedagogical part of music education—how to teach and how to get public-school teachers interested in ethnomusicology. We became very active in MENC [Music Educators National Conference] and the College Music Society, all those groups having to do with the pedagogical part.

I was in the Music Department until 1990, when I transferred to the Asian Studies Program as chair. I'm still active in Ethnomusicology, but it freed up a position for somebody else to come in. I retired in the spring of 2011. If I look back over my career, it's been atypical because I didn't jump around like everybody else did. I was very happy at Hawai'i, with the social and cultural environment of Hawai'i and how I fit in. I was never involved with the status thing of making more money by going to another school. I feel validated by that experience because I've been in the program for forty years and am trusted by the Hawaiian community; they know I'm there for the long haul. I'm often asked to be a spokesperson for Hawaiian music, as somebody from the outside who knows it and can talk to the haoles about it. I studied hula and the choral singing part—not to perform, just to do it—and I was also very active with the state arts agency, which gave out money to all these people, too.

MS: Going back to that question I asked earlier about lineage, you are now the head of a lineage with generations of students who went through your graduate program and have become influential elsewhere.

RT: Yes, I think the most satisfying accomplishment for Hawai'i is that our reach has been very international. I mean, if you look at whom we trained, many of them have gone back to their "own countries." Look at the whole Malaysia scene—all those guys there [Mohd. Anis Md. Nor, Made Hood, Clare Chan, Mayco Santaella]; look at Verne [La Verne de la Peña] and JoJo [Jose] Buenconsejo in the Philippines; and Sun Hee [Kim], who's now teaching in New Zealand. Our reach has been beyond just the United States. Our mission was one of empowering people—not just Americans—to go out and do this stuff.

MS: Your decision to retire was clearly not because you are slowing down—why did you decide to retire in 2011?

RT: Well, it's something I learned very early in life: don't wait until you can't do something to retire. I really wanted to be able to travel and do things long term where I don't have to rush back to the university. That's what decided it for me: I can still get around and am physically able to travel, which I really enjoy doing.

MS: Unlike some retired senior colleagues, you've remained unusually influential in the field.

RT: Yes. First of all, I've still got some doctoral students hanging over, which keeps me involved. And then Fred Lau asked me to stay on to support him. So I do the one-credit ethno forum course every spring, which means I'm still very much part of the faculty in terms of having a presence there. And for me, that's enough. The class meets every two weeks, so I can travel in between if I want. In terms of my own personal rhythm, I've been able to get back into better physical shape by not going to all these cocktail parties! I do a lot of physical exercise in the morning and feel much better. I'm finally at the point where there's a nice balance between my intellectual professional activity and just relaxing and hanging out.

Academic Administrator

Gage Averill (October 28, 2007)

PhD, University of Washington (Ethnomusicology)
Dean, Faculty of Arts, University of British Columbia

Graduate Studies

GA: I would have never been able to go on to graduate school, but Dan [Neuman] and Lorraine [Sakata] nominated me for a Mellon fellowship and I got it. Mellon would have liked me go to a different school, but I had just bought a house in Seattle and was going through back surgery at the time, which they accepted as a reasonable rationale to stay at UW. So one semester I wrapped up my undergraduate degree and the next semester I started a PhD program. Although they required everyone to go through an MA program at Washington, Mellon wouldn't allow it, so they waived the rule. I thought Mellon required that you finish your degree in five years from a BA, so I went full steam ahead to get the doctorate done quickly. I only found out years later at a Mellon conference that only two or three people had ever gotten through in that amount of time. But it was a good motivator, so I pushed on and got through with a lot of help from faculty there.

MS: At that point, did you have any particular role models in ethnomusicology?

GA: In school you see teaching, so I picked up on different teaching practices of my professors and modeled myself on them. Lorraine Sakata had done some extraordinary graduate seminars, so I modeled my graduate teaching on the informal and nurturing environment she created. Dan Neuman had the most brilliant command of English and exuded a sense that everything was easy. I looked up to Dan for a lot of modeling and, maybe eventually, administration. I was just an insecure kid, late to music, trying to stay afloat! Then they brought in Chris Waterman, and I watched him in front of classes of hundreds of people. I'd never seen anyone perform in a classroom as well as Chris. He would give students an immediate sense of contact, reach out to them, and engage them. I cobbled myself together, looking at everything they did—there was probably no single mentor.

MS: Why did you choose to do your research in the Caribbean?

GA: Well, getting back to what I was doing in Seattle, I'd started a couple of small bands and was playing in a few larger ones, largely within a Cuban and Brazilian musical framework. I put together an ensemble doing Brazilian pop, was in two different *escolas da samba*, and was learning *capoeira*. For a couple of years we had a Cuban carnival ensemble as well, a *comparsa*, and an informal kitchen rumba group. I found it a very profound encounter and wanted to work on that, but the word from everyone was that if you really wanted to do extended work in Cuba, you're SOL, "shit out of luck." The relationship between the US and Cuba at that point was so sour that there was essentially no regular traffic.

I had done a paper for Lorraine Sakata's transcription class and remembered a Verna Gillis recording of Haitian *rara* that I had played on the radio years ago (I eventually redid the liner notes for Smithsonian for that album). There was something about the music and its social and cultural meanings that really disturbed me. I was obsessed with it for a while, so I thought about working on *rara* in Haiti. I looked around; there was essentially no major work on it, simply short pieces in the existing literature, like Courlander's book [1960]. Those mentions were bafflingly contradictory, so it looked like no one really had a grip on what this music was about. I couldn't have chosen better, I think. At the time though, it was a retreat, a back door, from what I really wanted to do, which was to work in Cuba. But for a number of reasons, my dissertation research ended up focusing on Haitian pop music instead, working on power and issues of political economy.

Building a Career

I got my PhD in August 1989 and started teaching at Columbia that fall. I had gone down to Miami to work on a Haitian festival, and while I was there I got a call from the Smithsonian Festival of American Folklife. They wanted me to curate their festival on the Caribbean the following year. I suddenly had this possibility of directing the biggest folk festival in America. I had already spent five years running the Northwest Folklife Festival, so I decided to take the job. I went back to Washington State, but when I arrived, I got a phone call from Dieter Christensen saying that I was their preferred candidate for a job at Columbia. I hadn't applied for the job, but Dan Neuman had recommended me. Dieter asked if I would come and check out Columbia. So I did, and then I had to make a choice. I decided to go into academia and follow through on my Mellon commitment to teach for five years. I took a one-year replacement for Peter Manuel, which they would have converted into a three-year-and-see, but by that time I had an offer from Wesleyan.

MS: So you went to Wesleyan as an assistant professor?

GA: Yes, assistant, tenure track. I started in 1990. Wesleyan was rebuilding after the death of Jon Higgins and an external study of the graduate program. It was a period in which there was a danger that the graduate program would be ended. So they hired two of us, Kay Shelemay from NYU and me from Columbia. They were also looking for someone in jazz, and Anthony Braxton's name had come up. All three of us arrived in the same year.

MS: So you stood for and got tenure at Wesleyan, but relatively soon after you moved on. Why was that?

GA: Yes, the year before coming up for tenure—'95, I think—I had been asked to teach a course at NYU, which was having problems rebuilding in the post–Kay Shelemay era. I had done a one-semester stint there and hadn't alienated people too badly, so they asked me about coming in to be chair. They wanted me to spend three years trying to become full professor, which was necessary for the position. They made an offer and I went.

MS: You went up the steps of the academic ladder pretty quickly.

GA: Yes, it was pretty quick! The expectation of being chair was a great motivator for me to work on a second project—the Barbershop book [2003]. It was an incentive to get the book in shape within a couple of years for the next promotion. I was at NYU for seven years, from 1997 to 2004, and then in the summer of 2004 I went to the University of Toronto as dean.

MS: Was administration a track you were consciously working toward?

GA: It's largely no, but with a little yes—I'll explain that! When I got into graduate school at Washington, I also got a job running the Northwest Folklife Festival, which was at that point the largest folk and traditional festival in North America—four thousand performers over five days on twenty-four stages—a huge event with an extraordinary amount of preparation. I had been running tenant unions and drama productions throughout my life, so running a festival was another challenge, but one that involved some of the same management pieces—long-term planning, six-month goals, and objective planning. I realized I had some ability in these areas. Then, when I was in grad school, Dan Neuman asked me to run a festival of pianos. We brought in five international pianists from around the world and five reconditioned nineteenth-century pianos. I remember going to a party with University of Washington president [William P.] Gerberding. Dan introduced me, and Gerberding asked, "Why is it that ethnomusicologists make such great administrators?" Dan and I looked at each other and cobbled something together, "Well, we plan long-term fieldwork projects in distant places without typical support, so we have to be extremely well organized. And we engage in participant observation, which is essentially being with people, talking to them about their musicking and their lives, and learning from them. These are great planning as well as great social skills to be doing administration."

Dan always imagined me doing some administrative work—he actually said that in job letters later on. It was never on my mind, but when I arrived at Wesleyan, the department was at an arm's length from the university and desperately needed some administrative help. I started out as undergraduate coordinator and then the next year became graduate coordinator. It's mostly a graduate program, so the graduate coordinator in some ways functions as a stand-in chair. And linked to the university, I became head of the students' affairs committee, an advisory body to the dean. I was doing administration the whole time. That's what NYU was reading. In this game, it's typical to draw people for the next administrative level from the level below. I had not been thinking about trying to be a chair. What I do think, when I'm in situations—and this is a bit of hubris—I like to see things well run. For example, if I have to live in a department, I would rather have some control over how it's run than just carping from the sidelines. That's probably the character piece or the personality flaw that pushes me in that direction.

MS: You always had that "character piece." I remember the first time we met you were the chair of the SEM Student Concerns Committee. Even within the society you quickly scaled the ladder: Student Concerns Committee chair, student member on the council, council, board, and then, president!

GA: Yes. I like solving problems. A lot of my research work involves organizational challenges. It's a similar thing—connecting things or trying to imagine a flow diagram. I think of things in terms of flow. I really like puzzles, but also the sense that I can impact the world that I have to live in.

Update: July 8, 2016

At the time of our conversation, I had just left my job as dean of the Faculty of Music (and professor of ethnomusicology) at the University of Toronto and was appointed to be the vice principal academic and dean of the University of Toronto, Mississauga campus (UTM), a role equivalent to a provost for the campus of eleven thousand students. In July 2010, I became the dean of arts (social sciences, humanities, and the creative and performing arts) at the University of British Columbia, a faculty of nearly fifteen thousand undergraduate and graduate students. I have just completed my first six-year term and have been reappointed to a second term.

Before getting my doctorate in 1989, I had worked as a tenant/community organizer and a festival director of folk and traditional music (among others, the Northwest Folklife Festival in Seattle), along with always playing in bands, so I had spent my adult life running enterprises of different scale and complexity. As a result, academic administration came naturally to me, and my goal was always the same as with festivals and community organizing: to create and maintain the support structures that allow transformational magic to happen through education, the arts, and social change. My experience before ethnomusicology also led me always to engage in activities outside of the academy (music journalism, festivals, musical copyright trials, and so on), so I was always an engaged ethnomusicologist, even if I didn't always use the term.

PART 3
Self-Positioning in and Reflections on the Field

The word "ethnomusicology" means many things to many people: it can be fraught with emotional baggage: rejection by or of the field; confusion; a burden; gratitude (as expressed, for example, by Regula Qureshi and numerous others) for representing or encapsulating a long-sought professional or personal identity; or an important personal and professional tool (the late Clara Henderson felt ethnomusicology "sharpened [her] ethnographic and analytical lens for understanding new situations, social contexts, or employment opportunities"). Note: Charles Seeger's aphorism, often cited in our field, "Ethnomusicology is what ethnomusicologists do";[1] Mantle Hood's "[Ethnomusicology is] a field that has almost as many approaches and objectives as there are practitioners"; and another Hoodism, "There seems to be something about the term itself—'ethnomusicology'—that both repels and attracts" (Hood 1971, 1). A recent SEM listserv posting reinforces the ever-increasing difficulty in delineating ethnomusicology. Some consider this a strength; others, its principal weakness:

> Many of the changes that have occurred in our field [since the Previous Position Statement on Ethics] have a direct bearing on the statement and our work. Among these changes are: expanded and new notions of the field and fieldwork, expanded role of social media, increasingly contingent status of academic labor, expansion of IRBs, the increasing digitization of music and related issues of use, licensing and copyright, and many others. (McGraw 2017)

Salwa El-Shawan Castelo-Branco enumerates others, some of which, with critical numbers of interested scholars, have had meetings specifically devoted to them:

> conflict, social injustice . . . social and environmental change . . . civic engagement, collaborative paradigms, public sector, advocacy, outreach, music and public policy, music and conflict, human rights, social activism, music, war and reconciliation, music displacement and disaster, and dialogic knowledge–production.

A number of these subjects have become primary areas of investigation in their own right. They all retain the strong emphasis on the living human condition—"about the living," in the words of Jonathan Dueck—but can lack, for some of our co-conversationalists, the directness of what Fred Lau calls the "ineffable quality and affect" of music, which they consider essential. Within the past year we asked them all (long after their original interviews, typically) to situate themselves as ethnomusicologists and vis-à-vis the field. In this final section, we encounter a rich array of opinions on the subject, none of which "settles" the impossible questions of what ethnomusicology either "is" or "should be." Whether our *Living Ethnomusicology* colleagues advocate more or less attention to performance, or to sound, or to context, or social theory, ecology, social activism, and many other approaches, their wide-ranging and thoughtful answers exude the wonder and excitement that led us all to Ethnomusicology.

THE QUESTIONS

Question 1: What does calling yourself an "ethnomusicologist" connote? What kinds of personal self-image does it bring up for you?

Question 2: How does the field as you now see it relate to that self-image of yourself as an ethnomusicologist? Are we, as a "field" or "discipline" or "profession," doing or not doing the sorts of things that are consistent with this personal vision? Do you have any suggestions for how we as a field or society could?

Answers, contributed in 2016–17 (unless otherwise noted), are listed alphabetically.

GAGE AVERILL (B. 1954) ·

Q1: First of all, because I've been a chair and dean for fifteen years, calling myself an ethnomusicologist provides the comforting feeling that I maintain a (however tenuous) link to a distant life as a researcher-teacher. As a student of ethnomusicology, I worked primarily on popular music and developed a second area in something that would have been described as "ethnography at home" (barbershop harmony) [Averill 2003], and so I never felt any allegiance to the exoticized and traditionalist notions of ethnomusicology. Because I embraced an early affinity to cultural and critical studies, I found myself at home in performance studies, cultural anthropology or cultural geography, and so on. But there is only so much time for meetings, and because my core training was in ethnomusicology, I ended up consistently prioritizing ethnomusicological societies for my core service/participation and academic identity.

PART 3
Self-Positioning in and
Reflections on the Field

404

Q2: If anything, I think the conception of ethnomusicology I wanted to advance in the 1980s has been *too* successful. To oversimplify, I wanted to infuse ethnomusicology with the concerns for social differentia and contestation that were the basis of the cultural-studies turn, and I wanted to bring an awareness of the power of representation and the legacies of colonialism in the ethnographic disciplines. When I first started, this perspective was little represented in ethnomusicology, but in the last thirty years, it has become nearly hegemonic. But in the process, I feel we've lost opportunities to help people cope with the loss of cultural meaning under the impact of global modernity, in part by abandoning documentary and analytic methodologies. We have also failed to grasp the potential

Gage Averill at the 52nd Annual SEM Conference in Columbus, Ohio, October 2007. Photo by Margaret Sarkissian.

of massive computational and technological advances to readdress some of the abandoned questions from earlier paradigms of ethnomusicological history.

I think there's a potential new relationship between cultural anthropology and anthropology of the senses and ethnomusicology, on the one hand, and, on the other, technologies that allow massive crunching of numbers comparing cultural data around the world. They're doing this in linguistics, they're doing it in anthropology. We are allergic to it in ethnomusicology, but I think there are new possibilities with Information Technology to take a second look at some of that. At the same time, neuroimaging is providing new clues to the workings of the mind in real time.

JOHN BAILY (B. 1943)

Q1: I discovered ethnomusicology through Nettl's *Theory and Method* book [1964] while conducting my doctoral research in experimental psychology. The very word "ethnomusicology" seemed cool and sexy, and the subject somewhat more appealing than "experimental psychology." I later realized that "ethno" was short for "ethnography" and the participant-observation methodology of anthropology as applied to the study of music. I consider that ethnomusicology is the study of all kinds of music: as sonic structure, as cultural process, and as social act. I see myself as an academic with particular strengths in systematic research (arising from my training as a scientist), detailed documentation, and learning to perform as research. I also see myself as a semi-professional player of the Afghan *rubab* and Herati *dutar,* usually performing in conjunction with my wife Veronica Doubleday, singer of Herati traditional

PART 3
Self-Positioning in and
Reflections on the Field

John Baily in Geneva for a concert with Paul Grant, August 2011. Photo by Liliane de Toledo.

and popular music and player of the Afghan frame drum, *daireh*. I continue to be very interested in cognitive ethnomusicology. I come from a scientific background, and somewhere deep inside me there is still an experimental psychologist and an empiricist.

Q2: Ethnomusicology today has moved away from the Blacking paradigm of research, but there remains scope for the kind of ethnographic fieldwork he pioneered in the 1950s. The world is a much-less-safe place than it was fifty years ago, when I first visited Afghanistan, and extended periods of fieldwork in faraway places are more difficult to pursue. To that extent the musicological aspect of ethnomusicology has come to dominate, and, in the UK at least, most teaching and research positions are in departments of music, not of anthropology. Nevertheless, ethnomusicology remains a fascinating interdisciplinary field of study combining anthropology and musicology.

JUDITH BECKER (B. 1932)

Q1: For most of my career as an ethnomusicologist, dating from my days as a graduate student in the 1960s, I defined myself, in part, by what I was not. I was not a musicologist who exclusively studied high-status musics of European traditions. I was, in my mind, open to the beauties and mysteries of all peoples' musics. It was a position of moral superiority.

In the present context, that interpretation appears naïve. The distinction between musicology and ethnomusicology is no longer clear cut, as cultural context has become important to both fields, musicologists now study all manner of musics, music analysis no longer has national boundaries, and all the world's musics are readily available to all the world's peoples all of the time. The prejudices of Western music conservatories remain in place and remain a thorn in the butt for many of us, but the larger ideological struggle has been won.

Q2: As content as I am with my designation as an ethnomusicologist, one aspect of the field continues to be troublesome: the resistance of many ethnomusicologists to collaboration with colleagues in the sciences, particularly, neuroscientists and evolutionary biologists. In each generation there are particular academic disciplines

PART 3
Self-Positioning in and
Reflections on the Field

406

that become widely relevant, that become "core" because of the importance to scholars in related fields of the issues addressed, or by theoretical approaches, or the methodologies they bring forward. When I was a graduate student in the '60s, those of us studying ethnomusicology felt that we had to be cognizant of anthropology (because of its emphasis on cultural context) and linguistics (because of its structuralist analytic approaches). Today, to my thinking, core disciplines include neuroscience and evolutionary biology: neuroscience because of the widespread importance of studies of music and the brain, and evolutionary biol-

Judith Becker at the 52nd Annual SEM Conference in Columbus, Ohio, October 2007. Photo by Margaret Sarkissian.

ogy because of the interest of evolutionary biologists in the time-honored question as to why music is so important to peoples everywhere. Both include scholars, such as Aniruddh Patel, Steven Brown, Patrick Savage, and Tecumseh Fitch, who are deeply involved with musical studies. We should be paying attention.

Barbara Benary (1946–2019)

Q1: I would call myself a musician first, with ethnomusicologist as a modifying factor. I feel like I am still an ethnomusicologist because that's how I think. Ethnomusicology is like a set of sunglasses I put on, a perspective that colors my relationship to musical situations so that I think of them comparatively and in relation to a cultural context, which I always enjoy. I'm always interested in cultural relativism, new sounds, how they relate to things I know, and trying to work them into my head and into other creative things I do. The other area where I'm still an ethnomusicologist is through my composing. At

Barbara Benary, "Mother of Lion," being interviewed by New Music Box, June 2011.

this point, I can't say that I often sit down to write a piece based on a specific bit of world music; it's rather that everything I've heard is there in my head and comes out in the mix indirectly, if not specifically.

Q2: I think of myself as a kind of dropout from "the field"—at least the academic end of it. It brings to my mind a flock of scholars impressing each other with minutia in scholarly gatherings. Several decades ago when I was a youngster with a shiny new

PART 3
Self-Positioning in and
Reflections on the Field

PhD, I got annoyed at the Society for Ethnomusicology, where it seemed that academics had no interest in or respect for those who used ethnomusic creatively, at which point I stopped paying my SEM dues and decided to spend more time playing and listening to music. I tried, to no avail, to suggest that the journal include material of interest to performers as well as scholarly dissections. So many musicians who were not academics wanted to jump into learning ethnic performance practices. Though I haven't paid close note to it over the years, I think the field, along with academia, has loosened up a good bit with regard to allowing actual performance activity to be a valid form of scholarship.

STEPHEN BLUM (B. 1942)

Q1: I don't think I've ever thought of ethnomusicology as a clearly defined field, and I don't think it should be. I tell people, "Forget it; it's a nice umbrella that accommodates all sorts of things people wanted to do and couldn't do under the rubric of musicology," although that has changed to some extent. I'm grateful for so many opportunities to work and teach as an ethnomusicologist, though I like to think of myself as a teacher of music more generally, and as a musician who no longer performs but did so for much of his teaching career. My desire as a graduate student to engage in scholarly study of music as well as performance could only have been satisfied by a field of research open to the entire world. A self-image as an ethnomusicologist is deeply satisfying at the same time that it entails continual awareness of the harm done by my nation to so many others, not least Iran, where my work as an ethnomusicologist began. In my view, a self-image as an ethnomusicologist needs to include a willingness not to ignore the harm that has been and is being done to the weak by the strong: all the forms of murder, most of which are perfectly legal, as Brecht put it. No other area of musical research forces us to confront these realities on a daily basis and to think critically about our responsibilities as scholar-citizens engaged in the world.

Stephen Blum with Scheherazade Qassim Hassan, New York University Abu Dhabi, 2015.

Q2: I think of ethnomusicology more as a field of activity than as a "discipline" or "profession." I reject the specious distinction between "Western music" and "world music" (formerly "non-Western") and wish that the excellent work our colleagues in

PART 3
Self-Positioning in and
Reflections on the Field

408

the Society for Ethnomusicology are doing were not so often ignored or dismissed by music scholars and pedagogues who think of ethnomusicology as a profession with its own approved "methodology" (a pretentious word I've tried to avoid over the past forty-seven years). As more people start to see the need for a music pedagogy that would prepare students to understand and participate in diverse ways of making music, the field that's now called ethnomusicology may acquire a new identity and might even need to change its name. I would prefer "musicology," but then there are questions of organization. The American Musicological Society would not like lots of the things that we are doing at this meeting, so it wouldn't be practical to have one society.

JASON BUSNIEWSKI (B. 1985)

Q1: As an ethnomusicologist, I see myself as a musician, an interdisciplinary researcher, a writer, an educator, and a contributor to public discourse, among other things. Since the first time I visited India as a college student and saw the beautiful Anglo-Indian architectural syntheses and decaying colonial-era buildings of Mumbai, I've been fascinated with the colonial encounter as moment of great cultural production. Years later I'm writing about the place of the Scottish Great Highland bagpipe in the rural music of India's Garhwal Himalayas and how a very foreign instrument, introduced through military service, has become a strong local marker of indigeneity. In doing so, I hope to expand our thinking about colonialism in South Asia to give more attention to collaborative aspects of the colonial encounter and examine the colonial military as a space for musical production, an issue almost untouched by our field's current scholarship, as well as the shifting landscapes of indigenization and local identity.

Jason Busniewski, circa 2017. Photo by Erik Helgestad.

Q2: Over the course of my graduate career, I've also discovered a deep love for teaching. On a personal level, there's something wonderful about sharing my fascination with musics from around the world with my students, but I also view teaching ethnomusicology in the wider context of the humanities. By teaching students about ethnocentrism and reflexivity and introducing them to new people and cultural expressions from their own communities and around the world, we help them to develop the necessary habits of mind to think critically and empathetically about the world we live in. I have sometimes observed a sort of ambivalence toward teaching among ethnomusicologists, especially teaching undergraduates and nonmajors, but I find it a joy and an opportunity for me to personally contribute to society.

Salwa El-Shawan Castelo-Branco (b. 1950)

Salwa El-Shawan Castelo-Branco, 2010.

Q1: Calling myself an "ethnomusicologist" connotes a deep commitment to the understanding of human beings through music and other expressive practices. This entails producing and transmitting knowledge that is socially relevant. It also involves a responsibility toward society by engaging collaboratively with communities, institutions, and policymakers, especially in the areas of research, education, and heritage, and promoting the use of music in valuing cultural diversity, combating stereotypes and prejudices, contributing to resolving conflict, bringing about reconciliation, and nurturing dialogue. Being an ethnomusicologist also involves engaging in cultural diplomacy and building global networks that can improve communication and build partnerships among musicians, scholars, and community leaders that can contribute to the sustainability of music cultures across the globe. Finally, as a senior scholar and educator, I am committed to the future of young ethnomusicologists and have striven to create professional opportunities for them.

Q2: To a great extent, the vision I outlined above reflects some of the recent developments in the field of ethnomusicology. An increasing number of ethnomusicologists have been involved in carrying out collaborative research, engaging with musicians and communities, and addressing conflict, social injustice, and social and environmental change. In September 2015 I worked with Beverley Diamond in the organization of the first scholarly forum that involved our two largest scholarly organizations, the International Council for Traditional Music and the Society for Ethnomusicology, as well as the European Seminar in Ethnomusicology. Held in Limerick, Ireland, it focused on "Transforming Ethnomusicological Praxis through Activism and Community Engagement." I think there is a greater realization that not only should we be producing knowledge, but we also have a social responsibility; this is the kind of ethnomusicology I've been trying to promote in Portugal: both as a solid scholarly field, grounded in current social scientific perspectives with fieldwork as an indispensable methodology, and as a socially relevant field of action.

Shubha Chaudhuri (b. 1952)

Q1: I really don't call myself an ethnomusicologist. I'm very clear—I'll never be a musicologist. I'm not into the music, the analysis, but more into working on musicians and social organizations. I trained as a linguist, have no training in music (but found myself running an ethnomusicology archive for over thirty years now), and

PART 3
Self-Positioning in and
Reflections on the Field

410

worked in the area of ethnomusicology in one way or another. It is a field I have very much enjoyed being a part of, albeit on the fringes. My introduction to ethnomusicology was more about getting to know ethnomusicologists as a part of my work at ARCE. As a linguist, I found the literature of ethnomusicology surprisingly accessible and could see the connections between the fields.

As an archivist, I have enjoyed being able to work with culture and tradition on the one hand, and with cutting-edge technology on the other. There is a close-knit community of those who work in ethnomusicology archives, and that is the one I identify with. I think the reason I got into this job so happily was that my work and my PhD were totally theoretical and practically mathematical. And then I had this reaction, "Oh, enough of that! I want something down on the ground. I'm living in India with all these wonderful things around me, so much rich culture everywhere, and I'm trying to do this very rarified thing." Ethnomusicology gave me a way to engage with my culture in so many ways.

Shubha Chaudhuri, February 2018.

Q2: I do feel the field is changing, and, situated as I am in India, I do not perhaps have a picture that is comprehensive enough for me to stand in judgment. However, from my perspective I can say that I admired the generations of ethnomusicologists I saw, the deep engagement with fieldwork and with the people with whom they worked. One saw the years that they spent in India keeping up those connections and identifying with the culture. As director of ARCE, I had the benefit of interacting with many ethnomusicologists, and ARCE benefited from the support that we received, including the lengths to which people went to deposit their recordings in the archives.

I see that attitude changing, and as a result I feel more distanced from this community. Perhaps it is inevitable as a field or discipline grows and develops, losing the feel of a pioneering movement, which is what ethnomusicology felt like in the years when I first came in contact with it in the early 1980s. In India, ethnomusicology has come from being a very misunderstood discipline. It was like, "Oh, they want to call their music classical music, but our classical music is ethnomusicology!" But change is happening in India—ethnomusicology is not a bad word anymore. The term is now much better understood. Today the Indian Musicological Society has a bunch of ethnomusicologists on the board.

NIKHIL DALLY (B. 1965)

Q1: I am interested that Ted and Margaret have chosen to call me an "ethnomusicologist." I don't really know what an ethnomusicologist is. I am a musician and a teacher

PART 3
Self-Positioning in and
Reflections on the Field

of music and a trainer of music teachers. And one of the kinds of music I like playing and teaching and training others in is gamelan. About that subject—in other words, teaching gamelan—I do have a lot to say, much of which is embedded in my paper on the subject, "Kodály, Kinaesthetics and *Karawitan*," which you can find on my website, dally.org.uk.

In brief, however, karawitan is music that is fundamentally vocally conceived and spiritually underpinned. Therefore, by carefully harnessing concepts of music education that emphasize singing, movement, and the spiritual imagination in a rigorous but sensitive way, we can teach gamelan so as to truly renew our students' ways of hearing and understanding music and of relating to others. Gamelan, taught and learned well, can remind us that what really matters in life is something transcendent, something rooted beyond the visible world. Nothing we can do or make can express it, yet we must forever strive to represent it to ourselves: that is what music is for. To guide our students on that greater journey and to keep their eyes fixed not on transient goals but on an eternal process—that is the true privilege of being a gamelan teacher . . . and perhaps, even, an ethnomusicologist . . . ?

Nikhil Dally leading a workshop at St. Donat's Art Centre, Llantwit Major, Vale of Glamorgan, Wales, for students of Coety Primary School, Bridgend. Date unknown.

Q2: If academics could write in a way that laymen would listen, they could be out there changing the world, whether in music, education, science, or whatever. The world does not listen to academics because academics talk to themselves. Learning ought to be something that changes society. That's why I'm out there trying to change society by the way I teach gamelan or by the way I teach musicianship in my music school. I think it's great for anyone to learn as much as he can about any kind of music, whether "other" or not. I think there's obviously a danger with any kind of "-ology." We tend to think that for a piece of learning to be worth the title of "knowledge," it has to fit into a certain "box." It has to be something you can research and produce case studies about. Having evidence, research, and all that sort of thing is a very good thing; what I find a bit of a shame, though, is that some people go out there and gather the raw material—the fieldwork, the research, and the interviews—but because they want to be "-ologists," they won't say what they *think* about it. They don't dare to admit that their participation involves having opinions, feelings, passions, and ideas about it. But ideas and opinions and feelings and passions are what make the world go 'round.

PART 3
Self-Positioning in and
Reflections on the Field

Virginia (Ginny) Danielson (b. 1949)

Q1: The disciplines I learned as "ethnomusicology" continue to form the bedrock of my professional existence. Close listening (a favorite of one of my mentors, Steve Blum), whether to people, to sound arts, or to the aural artifacts of existence, remains central to my thinking, and I strive for it. My particular interest lies in music in society and its politics. In the world of sound studies and posthumanist scholarship, my interests occasionally strike me as passé—artifacts, perhaps, of twentieth-century scholarship. In many respects we are well past the era of area studies; yet language and history remain so very key to understanding (even in the Emirates, where English is the lingua franca). I watch new developments in our field and search for intersections with interest.

Ginny Danielson in Abu Dhabi, January 2018. Photo by Rebecca Pittam.

I am responsible for nearly fifty people, and ethnography may be the best organizational and management skill I have ever learned. And there is likely no better training than scholarly training for a position in university leadership.

Q2: Something that worries me a little bit is that one doesn't want to lose fieldwork and ethnography: there is no better skill for anything you do, any career that you're going to pursue, than ethnographic fieldwork. The ability to talk to people who don't necessarily know what you're talking about, to try to make yourself clear, to elicit information, to elicit points of view—those are skills that generalize to every walk of life.

I would also like to see graduate students given more time to work on things before they rush to publication and presentation. In some of the tenure files I've looked at, I've seen as many as ten versions of the same piece of work. It's the academic mill that makes people have to publish so much—one major article a year—but there's only so much thinking and thoughtful writing a person can do. We've got to slow this down a little bit to incubate things that are really worth reading.

Alex Dea (b. 1948)

Q1: When lay people ask me what I do, sometimes I do say I am an ethnomusicologist. However, since most people do not know this term, I use the term ethnographer. It is easier for them to understand that I make video and audio documentations of the old masters of classical Javanese music, dance, and theater. I am from the

PART 3
Self-Positioning in and
Reflections on the Field

"old school" of ethnography—document, contextualize history, illuminate cultural points of view pertaining to my material for the Javanese performing artists. It was only fortuitous that ethnomusicology was something I was interested in at all, because Jaap Kunst did that wonderful book on Javanese music. If he had done something on Greek or Egyptian music, I wouldn't be interested. It was sort of a trap! I went to Wesleyan because they had the gamelan, not because I wanted to do something with the theory of anthropology in music.

Alex Dea with Pak Cokro's gamelan in Yogyakarta, Indonesia, preparing for "Unmasked Rasa," a dance-theatre production that toured in Australia, Malaysia, and India with Malaysian dancer Ramli Ibrahim, 2008.

Q2: I feel that I am in a "field." Although trained, I am too undisciplined to be in a "discipline." My income and self-funded projects are not from the "profession" of ethnomusicology. I studied ethnomusicology because I was interested in world music in order to be a composer and a performer. Following Mantle Hood's concept of "bi-musicality," I have taken that to the extreme. I am actualizing what I thought at the beginning was my personal vision of three "Rs": Release (of my audio and videos), wRiting (contextualizing my treasure of documentations), and Re-inventing (composing and performing).

Now in the twenty-first century, we must get the facts, but we have to get close. In the twentieth century, you needed the distance, because there's a lot of doubt in the academic world that they are really doing something *true*, or not distant enough—the idea of the "scientific" approach. The idea *then* was that you had to be very clear. What you said had to be something that could stand on its own. I was taught that even though you learn, you have to be distant. You have to be academic. You have to write in a way that is distant. [But] I'm a performer and a composer, and from that I get research.

VERONICA DOUBLEDAY (B. 1948)

Q1: In the 1970s I hesitated to call myself an ethnomusicologist: the word was unfamiliar to the general public, and I wasn't sure I had earned the right to that label. Now, several decades on, I have embraced the field, but in some ways, I have begun to draw away; I enjoy going to occasional conferences, but I need to keep space for the important work of documenting Afghan music as it was in the 1970s, prior to the enormous upheavals of conflict, and as it continues to evolve. Performance of Afghan music (singing and

PART 3
Self-Positioning in and
Reflections on the Field

414

playing the frame drum) has come to the forefront of my ethnomusicological activities. With John [Baily] I have been invited to perform all over the world, and the task of fostering awareness and appreciation of Afghan music is ongoing—and always rewarding. For me this kind of activism is an important strand of ethnomusicological endeavor.

Q2: These days, I don't feel such a close connection with the field, although I've got a sense of responsibility to write and work on the Afghan material. I find ethnomusicology—the style of writing schol-

Veronica Doubleday with her teacher Zainab Herawi (on harmonium), singing and playing the daireh *drum. Zainab's house, Herat City, Afghanistan, 1977. Photo by Oliver Doubleday.*

arly articles—very constraining. I want to reach a broader audience. I've found a lot of interesting things and want to tell them in a story kind of way. For the layperson, you have to get behind things, amplify them, and bring them to life. I'm trying to communicate something about the Afghan sensibility, both to a broader audience and to Afghan people, using the poetry of the song texts I've been singing.

Jonathan Dueck (b. 1974)

Q1: I am happy to be an ethnomusicologist. Being an "ethnomusicologist," to me, is about the study of people and music. I usually tell people within academe that it is like being a cultural anthropologist of music. For people outside academe, I tell them that I study the musical practices of living people (though of course historical ethnomusicology—and really, all ethnomusicology—traces the traditions of past generations too, but I still think the field is about the living). The activity of paying close attention to musical practice is a way of paying close attention to other people, close and embodied attention—and there are few things that I think the world needs more, right now, than that kind of cultural work.

Q2: I think ethnomusicology needs scholars who collaborate with local groups, here at home (wherever that is). I think it's great to see people like Regula Qureshi, who are really involved with community institutions and not simply doing academic work. Regula is a real model for me, the way she interfaces with the community.

Also, in DC, every arts agency and every cultural policy group in North America has a presence. There are lots of international groups, too. We're producing people

Jonathan Dueck in Trinity Park,
Durham, North Carolina, February 2013.
Photo by Celia Mellinger.

who would be fantastic for these institutions, and many of our graduates go and work in them. What I think would be really neat is if we were to ask them, "Now, what didn't you get in the ethno program? How would you restructure a program to address nonprofits?"

I am concerned at the state of graduate education in ethnomusicology, where most graduates still do not have positions. We are producing far more PhDs than there are jobs [for them]. They're all very good candidates; they all have publications and grants and good references, and so forth. In one way, you can see it as very meritocratic, but in another way, it's also quite contingent. It depends on how the person has circulated. I think that very good people are selected—I have no qualms about that—but the process seems to me to be quite contingent.

VIRGINIA (GINI) GORLINSKI (B. 1961)

Q1: As I think about my own ethnomusicological activities and the identity of the field as a whole, I continually return to the idea of multiple personalities. Ethnomusicologists—especially those who do field research—necessarily have multiple personalities, each with allegiance to a different community. Those communities often have conflicting demands, expectations, and, ultimately, perceptions of the ethnomusicologist. For example, the academic community expects the ethnomusicologist to prioritize production of scholarly and, ideally, theoretical books, papers, and presentations. By contrast, the field community may expect a compendium of local stories and oral historical accounts to pass on to future generations. A government office may want transcriptions or arrangements of traditional music that can be incorporated into the public-school curriculum. Meanwhile, local, national, or international libraries may hope for establishment of a well-documented archive of field recordings. All such communities, with their associated personalities, products, and activities, are integral to the ethnomusicological identity. As ethnomusicologists, we need to ensure that the communities within which we operate are aware not only of the complexity of the ethnomusicological identity but also of the ever-shifting priorities that go along with it. Indeed, it is the ability to manage this chameleonic identity smoothly and equitably that, in my mind, is the mark of a fine ethnomusicologist.

Q2: I think it's important to recognize that there are lots of paths and lots of destinations. I wish the academy would think about its curriculum. Realistically, there are not as many positions for the types of scholars we're turning out as there are scholars to fill them. Let's acknowledge this and get our people out there into a variety of professions

PART 3
Self-Positioning in and
Reflections on the Field

where they can make a difference. The positions are there, but we have to start early. You can't just track someone through on a straight academic trajectory and expect them to be able to come out and take on an assistant directorship of, let's say, the Old Town School of Folk Music in Chicago, although these are the sorts of positions where they need people like us. I am reminded of a comment by Stanley Fish [1995, 2]: "If you want to send a message that will be heard beyond the academy, get out of it."

Gini Gorlinski in Evanston, Illinois, December 29, 2017.

Ethnomusicology students should be required to take courses in, say, music administration, or marketing, or business . . . and instructional design or instructional technology, because many graduates will likely become online faculty. In an era of accelerating adjunctification of the academy, when more than half of all university faculty positions are part time (in the US, at least), and when contingent (non-tenure-track) positions, which already amount to 70 percent of all faculty posts, are increasing, shouldn't the field strive to implement strategies both to exploit and to accessorize the multifaceted ethnomusicological identity so that its impact may be felt across professions?

Tomie Hahn (b. 1960)

Q1: The interdisciplinary inclusivity of our field since the 1990s has enabled me to be an ethnomusicologist while also a performer, visual artist, and sensory studies and dance scholar. I no longer shelter, or hyphenate, multiple identities. When asked what my profession is, I pause, knowing the blank stares and crossed eyes "ethnomusicologist" provokes. Yes, it'd be much easier to say I am a welder, but explaining what the heck "ethnomusicologists" do invites storytelling that is always enjoyable. In many ways I feel like I grew

Tomie Hahn with mask, 2015.

up and (fell) into Ethnomusicologyland. As a six-year-old, I was literally performing Japanese dance on top of conference tables for my father's lecture series, and, in my twenties, I was astonished that there was a field called "ethno-music-ology." It seemed like I'd been translating between cultures for a long time, to others and my (biracial) self. For me, "ethnomusicology" will always stand as a traditional *and* political term. We offer interdisciplinarity and difference. I am inspired to challenge the forms in which we display our knowledge—personally this would be to seek new avenues for displaying or imparting embodied cultural knowledge.

Q2: I'd like the senses to come back together in our canons. We've got to come back to our senses, literally! If I had to put it in a nutshell, we tend to specialize so clearly on a sensory parameter. People in music have great ears. People who are great eye people inhabit a building on the other side of campus that is for eye people—the art people. And dancers, people who move from the waist down, are relegated to work in some awful place on campus. This shows us a lot about the ivory tower and the history of the university, but it also tells us a lot about being human. We're fully unchallenged in sensory immersion as human beings. We taste, we feel, we smell on an everyday basis. But when we go to work, we focus so much—almost as if we have blinders on—on the sensory parameter of our particular art form. Ethnomusicology is great because it *does* include the wonderful thickness of culture. We talk about food. We talk about the visuals of a *wayang*. We talk about the look of the instrument, the sound of the instrument; the movement, maybe not as much. We're beginning to thicken our discussion, but I would like to see more of that, so much so that we break down the sensory walls between channels.

CLARA HENDERSON (1955–2016)

Clara Henderson at the 51st Annual SEM Conference in Honolulu, Hawai'i. November 2006. Photo by Alan R. Burdette.

Q1: Being an ethnomusicologist means I have a passion for all types of music, dance, and movement, from all cultures. It means I love striving to understand what music and movement mean to people; the role of music and movement in their lives; the impact music and movement have on their relationships, their society, politics, religion, and culture. Studying ethnomusicology has honed my intercultural competence and polished my ethnographic and analytical lens for understanding new situations, social contexts, or employment opportunities, by helping me discern how different infrastructures operate and how best I might navigate them.

Q2: Ethnomusicology as a field or discipline and ethnomusicology as an academic society have come to mean different things to me. The field/discipline encompasses ethnomusicologists working in academic institutions as well as those working in non-academic contexts (museums, arts centers, media, radio, television, public archives, festivals), while our academic society leans toward the involvement of those *conducting research* and *teaching* in academic institutions. Because of this perceived difference, I don't believe our academic society is an adequate reflection of the ethnomusicological endeavors taking place in the middle of our field, let alone the far-flung corners. Some studies claim that "only 30 percent of faculty are now on the tenure-track, while 70

PART 3
Self-Positioning in and
Reflections on the Field

418

percent are [adjunct or non-tenure-track faculty]," and that "recent graduates have less than a 50 percent chance of obtaining a tenure-track position" (*The Conversation* 2016).

These sobering statistics suggest that, apart from students, those who attend our society's annual meetings represent a low percentage of our ethnomusicology graduates and their work, particularly those employed outside of academia and non-tenure-track faculty without travel support. As an academic society, and as a field/discipline, therefore, ethnomusicology's challenge in the coming years is twofold: to develop a richer perspective of our field by creatively engaging the ethnomusicological outliers in our society and designing opportunities for them to showcase their research, work, and insights at our annual meetings, and to better prepare our students for the vocational realities of their ethnomusicological training and graduate degrees by developing courses and programs that expand their skill set and present tenure-track positions as just one in an array of employment opportunities available to them.

MADE MANTLE HOOD (B. 1969)

Q1: For me, as the son of the late Ki Mantle Hood, the first connotation associated with the title "ethnomusicologist" is almost always "lineage." I am very aware that I am a second-generation ethnomusicologist who descends from one of the pioneers of the field. This has never been a burden or a blessing. The "field" began so early in my life that ethnomusicology has never really been something to judge objectively from a distance. Rather, it has always been close to my heart, and if by some medical procedure it were removed, life would stop beating. My father gave me a childhood and teenage years surrounded by performing-arts graduate students from Ghana, Indonesia, Korea, Japan, and many other countries. Equally significant, my mother Hazel Chung, who

Made Mantle Hood and his father Ki Mantle Hood in the village of Singapadu, Bali, two months before Mantle passed away, May 2005.

paralleled the development of ethnomusicology by pioneering ethnic dance studies at the tertiary level, helped nurture in me an understanding of movement arts. My daughters Maile and Mahealani play gamelan, study dance, and speak three languages. I think they are off to a good start.

Stepping out beyond a person's national boundaries into a culture, into a new language that instills values and morals, is critical to what it means to be an ethnomusicologist. I speak four languages, have lived, worked, and studied in Europe, North

America, Australia, and Southeast Asia. More than half my life has been lived outside of my home country. For me, ethnomusicologists immerse themselves in other cultures as a critical methodological approach. An international ethnomusicologist must step beyond the confines of her/his own culture to gain consciousness and become deeply sympathetic of multiple ways of being, living, and experiencing the diversity of musics around the world.

Q2: Applied ethnomusicology is an exciting development as the merging of the cutting-edge theories of North American ethnomusicology, together with practical applications and methods from Europe and beyond, will provide much-needed strategies for empowering marginalized, traditional performing artists who strive to sustain their arts in the twenty-first century. I am glad to be positioned in the heart of Southeast Asia at this time because I think now, more than ever, is an exciting period in the field when ethnomusicologists will collaborate with multiple stakeholders to play a significant role in sustaining performing arts in the region. We need to empower ethnomusicologists to work collectively toward answering questions like what is Indonesian ethnomusicology, what is East Asian ethnomusicology, what is European ethnomusicology?

Umi Hsu, January 15, 2018. Photo by Clifford Pun Studio.

W. F. UMI HSU (B. 1978)

Q1: Being an ethnomusicologist is a way of life, a way of living and engaging in the world that is driven by curious, critical, and deep listening to the world. To me, the practice of ethnomusicology is a continuous encountering of the world while being enchanted by discovering new meanings of sounds and music. Sensing patterns of the forces of human emotions, values, and ideologies expressed sonically and being irresistibly moved by these forces, an ethnomusicologist cannot help but dance to the never-ending song of life. Through dancing and moving to sound, they unravel new knowledge about the humankind. That's how I feel as an ethnomusicologist. I cherish every moment that I get to be this person.

Q2: The professionalization of the field of ethnomusicology saddens me. The field's narrowing vision of what counts as knowledge and work has led to the creation of a system of credentialism that leaves out, in my opinion, some of the most creative and experimental practices of ethnomusicology. The preponderance of professional anxiety that has encouraged the growth of a society of careerists very concerned with lineage and the reproduction of the field. What if we as a field seek a balance in how we value printed and expressive matters? What if we listen to our world not competitively but compassionately and openly, even with one another? What if we co-explore with

PART 3
Self-Positioning in and
Reflections on the Field

420

colleagues outside of our discipline how a sounded perspective could transform lives? What if we celebrate the impact of music, not just among ourselves but with our practitioner colleagues who devote their lives to making social change? What if, instead of imagining a future without ethnomusicologists, we focus on building a world together where everyone can listen and dance to the world like an ethnomusicologist?

ADRIENNE KAEPPLER (B. 1935)

Q1: Actually, I do not call myself an ethnomusicologist. Rather, I am an anthropologist who uses music and dance to understand society and especially the relationships between the performing arts and social organization.

Q2: I continue to take a wider anthropological view of the world than many ethnomusicologists take. There is a lot about ethnomusicology that doesn't interest me in the least. I find the strictly musicological analyses uninteresting. I don't care for the analyses of sound. I find it boring, as it usually does not add to cultural understanding. By this, I mean the analysis of pitch levels, where they're moving to, the rhythm in which they're played, that sort of thing. I like

Adrienne Kaeppler and Hawaiian Associate Moana Eisele in the library at Grove Farm, Kauai. Photo by James Di Loreto, Smithsonian Institution.

the things that are more ethnologically oriented. I like the "ethno" part of it but get easily bored with the non-"ethno" part. Even within the narrower view of ethnomusicologists, I continue to be critical of those who only study sound and not the movement dimensions of how sound is made and how dance and other movements are such important parts of performance. That is, I would like to remind ethnomusicologists that music is also a visual art including the structured movement systems that go along with movement. For example, in *gagaku*, the sound of the *biwa* is really very minimal, but it's the whole movement system, the visual element of it as well, that is crucial. Nobody analyzes that! Or how you move your arms when you're playing drums. I think all of that is totally fascinating and very interesting, but hardly any ethnomusicologists are looking at it.

And finally, let me express again that in addition to a participant observer's point of view, there should also be a focus on the indigenous knowledge of socially constructed performance traditions, the activities that generate them, and how and by whom they are performed and judged. Only then will we be deserving of the prefix "ethno" in a globalized world.

PART 3
Self-Positioning in and
Reflections on the Field

Bernard Kleikamp (b. 1951)

Q1: By training I'm an ethnomusicologist, and by profession I'm a music publisher. I'm in the happy circumstance that I can combine these two in running PAN Records.

Bernard Kleikamp with Duan Yaocai, a blind musician and multi-instrumentalist from the Bai ethnic group, in the yard of Duan Yaocai's house in Shuang Yang village, near Dali, Yunnan, China, April 20, 2011. Photo by Yanghong.

The proceeds of PAN Records have also allowed me to fund my own (and sometimes others') fieldwork. I tend to think that being independent and not having to be responsible to any organization has given me a unique view on the field.

Q2: I've considered some ethnomusicologists a bit otherworldly, in the sense they don't seem interested in the reception of their research and its usefulness for other researchers. As an executive producer for a commercial record company, my first aim is to make a product that sells at least enough to break even and preferably make profit. In the past I've received many proposals for CD productions that didn't meet our standards. Sometimes the sound quality of the recordings was just not good enough. Often the liner notes needed editing or partially rewriting. Sometimes basic information was missing—Who? What? Where? When? Why? The five W's of ethnomusicology. Sometimes liner notes needed years to be written or eventually ended up not being written at all. Sometimes the proposed subject, bluntly speaking, was not interesting. PAN Records has always been interested in documenting living traditions, not dying traditions.

Frederick C. Lau (b. 1957)

Q1: An ethnomusicologist to me is someone who has a firm foundation in music but is also equipped with an interdisciplinary agenda and outlook. It is through music, its ineffable quality and affect, that ethnomusicologists make their impact. Taken as a whole, it is through their analysis, observations of performance, participation in music making, intense theorizing, intercultural understanding, and knowledge that we understand how different societies function and cultures are made. My image of an ethnomusicologist is someone who is open minded, inclusive, tolerant, kind, compassionate, and full of aloha!!

PART 3
Self-Positioning in and
Reflections on the Field

422

Q2: The field has changed quite a bit since I began over three decades ago. People are becoming more interested in contemporary issues—such as torture, war, nationalism—inspired by geocultural politics. Once a field that drew its strength from other disciplines and fields of study, ethnomusicology now seems to have become more narrowly focused on the "now" and its relevance and serviceability to people. Consequently, the scholar's purview has become more confined and not as inclusive and tolerant as before! The study of music has inadvertently been diminished in the process.

Fred Lau in concert at Orvis Auditorium, University of Hawaiʻi, Mānoa, Hawaiʻi, October 2016.

I think the field is a little imbalanced right now. When we were entering the field, people were doing descriptive stuff—very ethnographic, very data based. At that time, we wanted to move on to more theory-oriented stuff. I think now a portion of the younger generation seems to have lost track and has gone overboard. They are more theory heavy, but not as well rounded in terms of their training. They rejected Western music for various reasons—could be colonial, could be anything—but it is a functional language that we need to have. You don't have to embrace it as an ideological apparatus; it's a way to get through to your data. That's why, in my program, I continually insist on transcription and general knowledge of music and theory. We require it. We don't accept anyone without undergraduate training in music.

WILLIAM P. MALM (B. 1928)

William P. Malm playing shamisen *in the Japanese Music Room in Burton Tower, Ann Arbor, Michigan, circa 1976.*

Looking back over your career, do you have any retrospective sense of the field? You've seen so many different trends in ethnomusicology, were there any directions that were or weren't so interesting to you? What's your feeling about the field now?

Basically, I can say that I was never an ethnomusicologist, really. I never took an anthropology course in my life, not one. I had no concept of music in society from a sociological science point of view. I was very myopic; basically, I was interested in

PART 3
Self-Positioning in and
Reflections on the Field

how music worked. My thesis asked, What is it and how does it work? I don't have the qualifications to study the sociology of that material. I'm not equipped for it. I never had a course in sociology or in anthropology. I strictly learned to read music and I don't read it well, frankly. I learned to listen to music and to analyze it. I'm basically a music theorist more than a musicologist.

PETER MANUEL (B. 1952)

Q1: In "the field"—whether India, Spain, or elsewhere—I invariably introduce myself as a musicologist rather than an ethnomusicologist. Whatever the etymology of the word may be, it nevertheless implies, however incorrectly, the study of people who are "ethnic," and hence somehow exotic, curious, and marginal, as opposed to those such as myself who are not. I feel embarrassed by this connotation, although it does in fact cohere with my own intuitive self-image as someone who "has no ethnicity," having been raised in a white-bread, midwestern community and lacking the slightest interest in my relatively remote British Isles ancestry.

Peter Manuel, 2018.

Q2: As the fields of musicology and theory open up to accommodate non-Western and vernacular musics, the distinguishing features of "ethnomusicology" become ever less clear. I always resented the seemingly hegemonic notion of "music in culture," which implicitly excluded studies involving purely formal analysis (which now could be claimed by theory) and, conversely, would implicitly claim for ethnomusicology such things as a sociomusical study of Beethoven, the likes of which are now common in the field of historical musicology. And as we learn more about and extend our attention to the musics of birds, whales, and other creatures, even our supposed focus on music as "humanly organized sound" is undermined. I see no need for myself or anyone else to be crippled by this definitional dilemma. One of the great things about the field for me is that it's just such a great group of people. I love our conferences; the people are so creative. For me, that is one of the great delights of the profession.

When I was SEM journal editor, I was a little disappointed. Obviously, lots of people were doing good work, but for one reason or another they were publishing in other journals or books. I was a little surprised that it was sometimes tough to fill the journal with publishable copy. You would think that the flagship journal in our field would have a surfeit of really good publications. Maybe it's just a reflection of still being a small field.

PART 3
Self-Positioning in and
Reflections on the Field

424

There are so many people doing really solid and interesting work that there's a lot of diversity. I think there's a healthy practicality or pragmatism, which I like. The field is not slavishly following whatever trends emerge in literary theory or whatever, and yet there's a healthy interest in other fields.

Judith (Judy) McCulloh (1935–2014)

Judy passed away before we asked for formal reflections. These thoughts are drawn from her 2009 interview.

Q1/2: There's a great variety of work going on, and I guess what I'd like to see is what I'm most interested in myself, a cultural approach to music and to the people involved in it, rather than a very exquisite technical analysis. I see a lot bigger future in the broad view than in the narrow view. Even though there's a place for that narrow, focused view, it's nothing that turns me on. I never really encouraged that in any ethnomusicology or *Music in American Life* book I've done. I figure that Yale, Kent State, or other places can do that, and that's just fine. Or technical stuff can go into a MUSA Edition,[2] and the author can back off and write about the setting and what the music really means, what difference the music makes. Why should we care if that music is out there? That's the kind of question I'd rather see the field address more. Not a profound answer, but that's where it is.

Judy McCulloh in her garden, Urbana, Illinois, summer 2010. Photo by Mary E. Yeomans.

Maria Mendonça (b. 1966)

Q1: For me, the label "ethnomusicologist," flawed though it may be, connotes a particularly interdisciplinary approach to the study of music and sound, which I think is very important. As a person who grew up with a lot of music in my family (including a father who was a professional musician), music has always been the connective tissue for a whole range of life experiences. The way ethnomusicology highlighted and "validated" these connections was a large part of my attraction to ethnomusicology as an undergraduate. In other words, there were many disciplines and modes of thought that might have incredible insight into your work in music/sound if you were curious enough or committed enough to explore them. I think interdisciplinarity is an important part of what ethnomusicology contributes to the academy: this kind of interdisciplinary approach to studying sound/music is something that is not always celebrated to the same extent in other areas of music studies. Part of this is our discipline's connection to anthropology, which I've always

Maria Mendonça at COSI, Toledo, Ohio, November 2009. Photo by Allie Terry-Fritsch.

found inspiring and provocative, and not only because it's at the basis of my job description at Kenyon(!)

Q2: Every time I come to a conference and hear papers, I'm really excited by the new things that crop up. I would like to see more exploration of how ethnomusicology exists and grows in settings outside of academia, and in ways that explore the growth and resignification of the discipline rather than enforce boundaries between academia and other settings.

CHRISTOPHER J. MILLER (B. 1969)

Christopher J. Miller performing in Gamelan Madu Sari's production of "Semar's Journey," Roundhouse Community Arts and Recreation Centre, Vancouver, June 2007.

Q1: As I settle into a career that is aptly described as "hybrid"—the limited scope of my position has the upside of offering even greater flexibility to do what I want, with resources that make dealing with the perhaps more acutely felt differential of status and compensation that also come along with being at a Research 1 institution worth getting over—I am cognizant of just how profoundly ethnomusicology has shaped my outlook on all that I do. Ethnomusicology does not, for me, subsume playing gamelan, but it does make me aware that no music making is really an end in itself. I believe that musical traditions as distinctively different as gamelan are especially effective at disrupting the idea that there is one way to think musically and should thus continue to have a place in the academy. Even as I don my creative-musician hat, which I now mostly do as a member of a free-improvising trio with two fantastic like-minded colleagues—a type of music making that feeds my creative inclinations even better than composition, the focus of my studies prior to turning to ethnomusicology—I cannot escape the questioning perspective that that turn led to. I will never regain the innocence of certainty in my aesthetic biases. But I would not want to. The ability to recognize the value in all music is itself invaluable.

Q2: My position is not quite as limited as it was initially, but it still, at least in terms of official duties, offers less scope, challenge, and reward than a tenure-track job—which, despite now having my PhD in hand, I have made no headway trying to land. The

PART 3
Self-Positioning in and
Reflections on the Field

426

likelihood that I will spend the rest of my academic career pretty much exactly where I am now unavoidably shapes my sense of myself professionally as something other than what I think of as a capital-E Ethnomusicologist, responding to the demands of academic ladder-climbing with an overriding focus on the production of scholarship.

It is according to this logic that my better-paid professorial colleagues are discouraged from busying themselves with directing ensembles—an activity that increasingly seems ancillary to the field, but one that is my primary charge. Ethnomusicology's relationship to the performance of the musics that are, in part, its object of study has always been fundamentally tangential, the historical emphasis on performance at programs like the one I went through at Wesleyan notwithstanding. Though it is because of ethnomusicology that gamelan ensembles were first formed in North America, for most of the most accomplished players, whose relationship to ethnomusicology is tenuous to non-existent, playing gamelan is an end in itself. Performing alongside such colleagues, as well as having come to ethnomusicology through gamelan, and not the other way around, further contributes to my sense that "ethnomusicologist" accounts for only part of my professional identity.

MOHD. ANIS MD. NOR (B. 1955)

Q1: I would call myself an "interlocutor of emic musicking," which emanates from the desire to deliberate on emic interlocution of traditional musical discourses of maritime Southeast Asia within the linguistic arch of Austronesian-speaking people, sans contestations of political, nationalist, or religious hegemonies. I would see myself as the Southeast Asian man whose scholastic undertaking is to privilege knowledge of the "other and the familiar" in the context of world music.

Mohd. Anis Md. Nor at the International Symposium "Negotiating Intangible Cultural Heritage" in Osaka, Japan, November 2017. (Left to right) Eulogia N. de la Peña, Svanibor Pettan, Mohd. Anis Md. Nor, Verne de la Peña, and Shota Fukuoka. Photo by Yoshitaka Terada.

Q2: The combined fields of music and dance within the discourses of ethnomusicology and ethnochoreology have enabled me to appraise and revisit contemporary practices of "musicking" among indigenous maritime Southeast Asian communities from the perspectives of interdisciplinary discourses of music and dance as holistic entities of maritime Southeast Asian performing arts. Consistent to my endeavors to investigate, interrogate, and solicit emic and etic knowledge of traditional performance practices, I have now engaged my

PART 3
Self-Positioning in and
Reflections on the Field

studies into the combined fields of dance and music within the premise of "choreo-musicology," which I believe will provide a newer platform for ethnomusicological discourses in Southeast Asia and to other parts of the world that see the relevancy of this approach. Also, I oblige my students to employ critical theories and reflexivity, even when researching their own communities.

JAN MRÁZEK (B. 1972)

Q1: I'm still trying to understand it! When I was a graduate student at Cornell, I read a lot of ethnomusicology. Somehow, I never felt, "Oh, this is me." I could argue with

teachers. I liked the music. But I didn't like all the writings. They didn't appeal to me as much as some anthropological writings. I studied more by learning gamelan and talking to people in Java than by reading ethnomusicology. I never think of myself as an ethnomusicologist. I don't even feel very comfortable with the term "ethnomusicology." Perhaps it's in part because of who I am. When I came to America, people would say, "Oh, you are Czech. That's cool!"—you know, the "ethnic" thing. I feel that sometimes in ethnomusicology there is a similar kind of exoticizing of other things, rather than just taking it seriously and learning. I

Jan Mrázek with the servant/clown/god Semar and his grandchildren, after a Wayang Hip Hop performance at the National University of Singapore, Singapore, October 2016. Photo by Miguel Escobar Vallera.

prefer to think of myself as a musicologist, not an ethnomusicologist. I enjoy playing violin the same way I enjoy playing gamelan.

Q2: I don't like writings that are just about general theory. I feel that has been happening in ethnomusicology over the last ten or fifteen years. There's an emphasis on generalizing about things, like identity. I write about identity; obviously it's important, but it seems that now everything has to be studied in terms of something current, like transnational flows. An interesting political thing about Singapore is that people are looking toward America and American theory. If you publish in an American journal, you get so many points; if you publish in a Southeast Asian journal, you get maybe half the number of points. I feel that's a problem. I have a lot of very good friends, people I respect, from America. One of them came to Singapore and basically talked about Southeast Asia in the 1960s. He was criticizing Southeast Asia for having highrise buildings for people to live modern lives. Of course not everyone is like that, but I feel that sometimes there is a disconnection between people making theory in America and people who live in Southeast Asia.

PART 3
Self-Positioning in and
Reflections on the Field

428

I don't feel comfortable in any single discipline; I think it's important to study everything. Not just music, but art, visual art, language, society. If you study something like Javanese theater, you are forced to be interdisciplinary if you take it seriously. You have to study the visual aspect, the music, the social event, the story, and the literature—every aspect is important. If ethnomusicologists are too focused on the music, as happens in some cases, they can't fully understand, because music is part of the larger whole.

INNA NARODITSKAYA (B. 1955)

Q1: Although I trained as a concert pianist and also have special affection for libraries, I believe that I have always been an ethnomusicologist, curious to see what happens in someone's kitchen, typically venturing off the main street in some oblique path or yard. Mainly, I love learning from people. An ethnomusicologist, for me, is a person with complex interests, an open mind, who can listen carefully and not assume they know anything. I believe our wonderful colleague whom I greatly admire, Bruno Nettl, once wrote that who we are is defined by what we do. Perhaps I've rephrased his thought, or maybe it was not him.[3] I think ethnomusicology is all of the above—a scholarly field that deals with

Inna Naroditskaya with Felix Shinder, singer and leader of a well-known group Den'gi vpered/Money In-Advance in Odessa, Ukraine, May 2016.

music densely woven into the texture of life and thus wedded to other scholarly fields. It is a discipline that develops analytical methods, concepts, and knowledge. There is a place for applied ethnomusicologists—ethnomusicologists involved in musical management, journalism, performance, cultural diplomacy, as well as teaching in schools, giving public lectures, and consistently learning about music and about nonmusical elements of musical events.

Q2: First, I think very positively about what we're doing now, studying local and specific cultures, but I think at some point we need to step back. We often do such divided and far-ranging searches that someday we may lose common ground. Second, "comparative studies" was horrible when it became overwhelming and overpowering, but some types of comparison should be done and some comparative perspective should be kept. I believe that even though "diaspora" has become a magic word, we're still dealing with nationalism. Nationalism is a form of diaspora, and that could

PART 3
Self-Positioning in and
Reflections on the Field

429

become one of our common grounds. Ethnomusicology should be called "musicology" and then it would have to expand historically in a deep way, because as long as we remain rooted in "today," then five years from now we separate what we wrote from the readers for whom we wrote it. We embrace the notion that "everything is built on interviews," "everything is built on what happens today." We should forget about what happens today; it's important and has value, but we have to write not just for people who read it today. Our work has to have historical perspective; it's not just "dated" or "outdated." The danger comes when we write for ourselves, for our readers today.

LAUDAN NOOSHIN (B. 1963)

Laudan Nooshin in Kazbegi, Georgia, September 2017.

Q1: I have continued to call myself an ethnomusicologist but at the same time am ambivalent about the term and the ways it separates us from others in the music studies "family." In 2001 I suggested that we could usefully ditch the "ethno" and the "ology" and just have a broad field of music studies. Part of me feels quite strongly that the musicology/ ethnomusicology paradigm does not serve us well; for one thing, where does it leave all the other areas of music study, such as music psychology, music education, popular music studies, film music studies, and so on? I know that this paradigm is perhaps more relevant to the UK and that the landscape of music studies in the US is slightly different; and it is worth noting, of course, that the differing scholarly landscapes in different countries will have an impact on the answer to your questions. For instance, there are far more ethnomusicologists who come from a social science background in North America than in Europe and some other parts of the world. I have consciously sought to break down the [musicology/ ethnomusicology] "divide," both in my teaching and my research.

I have recently considered not calling myself an ethnomusicologist any longer but simply a music scholar. Still, in terms of my training, my lineage, and my scholarly friends, ethnomusicology is my "family." I don't think there is any doubt that what I do is "ethnomusicology," but whether I define myself solely as an "ethnomusicologist" is another matter.

Q2: Clearly there is enough that we share and hold in common to make us a unit of some kind, but whether that is a "field" in its own right or a subdiscipline of something

PART 3
Self-Positioning in and
Reflections on the Field

430

else, I'm not sure; and, of course, many ethnomusicologists will have different views on this. For myself, due to my training in Western art music, and partly due to the kinds of questions I ask in my research, I feel that my work, broadly speaking, is part of music studies (I am deliberately not using the term "musicology"). I don't tend to think of myself as a social scientist, but some of my work uses ideas from the social sciences and other areas, and I certainly engage with social scientists in various ways. I'm not sure how useful the notion of disciplines or fields is any longer. I would encourage us to think of the broad area of music studies less in terms of "discipline" and more as a network of people who have overlapping interests that draw on many different areas of study and methodologies but whose ultimate aim is to better understand music and music making and the place of music in people's lives. And for that purpose, I would challenge the idea that we all need to be one thing or have a single thing that defines us as "ethnomusicologists." I'm not sure that's even healthy in today's world.

Olabode (Bode) Omojola (b. 1958)

Q1: As an ethnomusicologist, I think of myself as someone constantly interested in understanding the various ways individuals and communities use music for self-expression and identification, community building, and social bonding, and in ways that engage the changes that constantly redefine or modify their social lives and cultural experiences.

Q2: The field of ethnomusicology, to my mind, is currently undergoing changes that call into question some of the assumptions about ethnomusicological work. For example, the increasing rise in the profile of "native eth-

Bode Omojola during his fieldwork in Sao Luis, Brazil, March 2014.

nomusicologists," those who are native to the cultures they study, has implications for how we define insider-outsider relationships. Also significant is the expanding scope of Africanist ethnomusicological research in ways that cover new music traditions—notably, the works of African composers of European-influenced art music, an idiom not hitherto considered to fit well within the scope of ethnomusicology, but whose cultural significance is beginning to gain the attention of scholars. We have people like Nketia and Akin Euba, whose view of African music is a lot wider than what non-African ethnomusicologists think about African music. I think most African ethnomusicologists would think the same way. We have a rather inclusive approach to the definition of African music.

PART 3
Self-Positioning in and
Reflections on the Field

431

Looking from another angle, at times I do wonder whether I am being caring enough, if I may use such a moralist terminology. You know, the kind of relationships that we forge with our so-called "informants," or I think there's a better word for it now—assistants. When I'm in front of a class talking about Yoruba drumming, there is all sorts of information that I learned from such people. I have built my career on other people's knowledge. Of course, we refine things, we theorize, but without what they are doing, or what they have done for us, we wouldn't be what we are. So, I wonder whether we are giving back enough to those people? I am connected with them even when I am in the US. I help them on the phone. I go to Nigeria every year for about six weeks, and five of those weeks are spent working with traditional musicians. Many of these people are very poor, so while they are happy that they have helped me, they are also wondering how they, too, could be helped. My Yoruba master drummer, for example, is always, always asking me, "Do it for us, too. We, too, want to travel." I would like to see more attention and perhaps more recognition given to such people. The Nigerian ethnomusicologist, Meki Nzewi, has decided that whatever he publishes, he will put his name and the names of his associates. So he will say, "an article by Meki Nzewi AND. . . ." That's the kind of thing that perhaps I, too, should be doing.

RUBY ORNSTEIN (B. 1939)

Ruby Ornstein in her study, New York, 2018.

Q1: I arrived in Bali not long after a serious volcanic eruption; I left having experienced the immediate aftershock of the failed coup of 1965. In between I learned two new languages, how to behave properly in a hierarchical culture, how to play kebyar music well enough to perform with a world-famous gamelan, and how to record gamelan music under conditions and using equipment that would now be considered archaic. When I think about myself as an ethnomusicologist, it brings up thoughts and feelings about my preparation for doing field work and experience as a fieldworker. It reminds me that the experience was life changing in ways I am still unable to express in words. I was the first woman to study Balinese gamelan. I still remember how astonished everyone was when I arrived and said I had come to study gamelan, because women did not play gamelan. The same people in the village where I lived and elsewhere accepted me. I, in turn, accepted the fact that I was a spectacle because I had white skin, red hair (attributes of a witch), and freckles. I remember with great joy the welcome I received from the musicians of Gunung Sari of Peliatan village. Charles Seeger, who was in residence at UCLA when I was there, said, "Well, Ruby, Bali will never be the same

PART 3
Self-Positioning in and
Reflections on the Field

once you've been there." But, actually, the opposite was what happened. *I* was never the same. All of these experiences led to a dissertation that for a long time I thought no one read. Only in the past few years have I discovered that other ethnomusicologists had not only read my dissertation but found it very valuable. That has been gratifying.

Q2: I don't have an opinion about the field as a whole, but I do have an opinion about what's going on in Bali. I think it's too bad that the conservatory has taken such a grip on music and that we're so concerned about what's going on in the conservatories. I think that ethnomusicologists who study Balinese music ought to be more concerned about the music that's going on outside the conservatory. Instead of going to Bali during your summer vacation and visiting the people at the conservatories in Denpasar, why not get on your motorcycle and go to more remote areas and find out what *they're* doing? Never mind the competitions and the yearly festivals. Anybody can go to them. Why not go where nobody else goes?

In *Staying Local in the Global Village* (Rubinstein and Connor 1999) somebody wrote about how poorly dance is taught in the conservatories. It's not one-on-one anymore, and I'm concerned about that.

In recent years Balinese scholars have been studying their own traditional music and other performing arts, but there is not enough exchange of ideas and research between them and Western scholars. I believe that an important role for ethnomusicology is not only to report on what there is but also to rediscover and encourage the reinvigoration of traditional music before it is lost. (Shades of Colin [McPhee]?) The field of ethnomusicology is uniquely placed to accomplish this goal.

Renata Pasternak-Mazur (b. 1968)

Renata Pasternak-Mazur at the Cherry Blossom Festival, Newark, New Jersey, April 2011. Photo by Paweł Mazur.

Q1: I'm not sure if I want to be called "ethnomusicologist" or would rather be called "musicologist" (if it meant somebody who studies music, any music in context of culture). My ideal discipline would study music regardless of its belonging to "my" culture or some "other" culture (within or outside "my" country), a discipline, which studies all music: the music labeled as classical, popular, and ethno/world, et cetera. Fortunately, both musicology and ethnomusicology have become more inclusive, and I hope they will finally merge one day.

Q2: I wish we actually listened more to the ideas that don't correspond to our own and disturb our discourse. We tend to treat our perspective and values as universal and try to push agendas, especially political ones, although it does not belong to our mission. Such "missionary" approach (which is not unique to ethnomusicology) does not help our scholarly mission, especially when we study cultures that don't share American values. Moreover, our interest in other cultures sometimes seems to be a tool for celebrating openness to cultural diversity more than anything else. I don't know if it can be changed, but I wish we would admit it, at least.

Svanibor Pettan (b. 1960)

Q1: As an undergraduate student in Yugoslavia in the 1980s, I started to cherish the world of music that was much broader than the scope of my university study of musicology, which to a considerable extent reflected the study of "dead, white,

male composers." For me, ethnomusicology became a window for broadening knowledge and deepening understanding of music in its widest sense, and at the same time for enriching my capacities as a researcher, pedagogue, and musician. Without the firsthand communication with fellow ethnomusicologists and musicians active in different geographical and cultural contexts, many of my perspectives would remain limited to a surface level. Ethnomusicology has marked both my professional and private life and has enabled me to experience positive

Svanibor Pettan in Brisbane, Australia, 2012. Three Secretary Generals of ICTM (left to right): Svanibor Pettan (2011–2017), Stephen Wild (2006–2011), and Anthony Seeger (2001–2005).

effects of the encounters with many interlocutors, students, and their environments on all continents. No doubt, living the life of an ethnomusicologist is a welcome responsibility, pleasure, and privilege.

Q2: Decades ago, it was essentially important for ethnomusicology to achieve legitimacy for the scholarly study of any music and to challenge the exclusivity of the top-bottom prescriptive attitudes based on the notions of authenticity and national relevance (folk music) and aesthetic and conceptual superiority (Western art music). In Europe, critiques of ethnomusicology used to come from two sources: folk music researchers and music historians. Both preferred to see ethnomusicology as the study of (national) folk music, but for different reasons.

Nowadays, after sounding achievements in postcolonial, gender, and minority studies, to mention just a few, applied ethnomusicology anticipates new broadening of our field, particularly in relation to ecology and engaged scholarship. Is the anthropological focus on humans still sufficient? I very much welcome the increased interest about the advances in biomusicology, ecomusicology, zoomusicology, and sound studies.

As a person and as a scholar, I'm interested in going beyond the broadening and deepening of knowledge, toward exploring how our knowledge and understanding of music and its life in different cultural contexts can change human conditions for better. I've worked with refugees and various minorities and have managed some projects that I hope did make a difference for these people. What followed was the foundation of the applied ethnomusicology study group at the 2007 ICTM conference in Vienna and its first symposium in Ljubljana in 2008. It is encouraging to see that engaged scholarship appeals to many of our colleagues, regardless of generational or territorial differences. We clearly want to give the discipline more relevance in a humanistic sense.

Jennifer Post (b. 1949)

Q1: While ethnomusicology still struggles to maintain its relevance in academic departments, and the use of the term "ethnomusicology" has been challenged in anthropological, musicological, and even ethnomusicological discourse, I maintain its use in my own vocabulary to describe "what I do." I believe ethnomusicology continues to identify the unique work we do as we develop an understanding of musical and sound-related practices and relationships with individuals and communities we work with in the field. As ethnomusicologists, we share the belief that the field is any location (real or virtual) that provides opportunities for people to engage with one

Jennifer Post with Köken's family, Qara Qatu in Tolbo, Bayan Ölgii Province, Mongolia, 2013.

another in mutually respectful ways. My identity as an ethnomusicologist is therefore wrapped up in the engagement with others—initially through music, but ultimately as humans who share interests in the arts—who provide social, emotional, and practical support for one another. As an ethnomusicologist I also believe I have a responsibility to work with students and others to underscore the importance of diversity, to communicate about the powerful ways that music has been used to inform about and combat injustice, and to bridge social and political differences.

PART 3
Self-Positioning in and
Reflections on the Field

435

Q2: I've seen incredible changes in ethnomusicology over many years, and, of course, I've documented some of it because I was a bibliographer. I have watched us go from a discipline with a relatively narrow to a dangerously broad view. I say "dangerously" because it is now so hard to define the discipline. Today students and professionals travel along multiple pathways populated with literature from very diverse fields. I don't know where to draw the boundaries any more. We've become more politicized; we have embraced so much more knowledge and theory. This frequently changing terrain creates both weakness and strength for all of us; it fractures our discipline and weakens our roles in the academic world, but it expands our collective knowledge and spreads our ideas about significant links between music/sound and human and nonhuman production and values. I'm working in geography and political ecology in my research, and I love it. I'm looking at ecology and sustainability in relation to practical issues such as "how dense is this wood, and what is the economic impact?" A generation ago, we weren't talking in the same way.

As I look at [SEM] and the discipline now, I'm feeling pretty good about where we are because I think we're on a really good track. I was on the SEM board when we spoke in 2011, and my fellow board members included Gage Averill (president), Pat Campbell, Suzanne Flandreau, Debbie Wong, and Tim Cooley, and Steve Stuempfle. Later, I shared board service with Harris Berger (president), Greg Barz, Anne Rasmussen, Jim Cowdery, Sandy Graham, and Bev Diamond. These diverse groups of people work in academia but also music education, libraries, and museums, and we all worked together to support the discipline. My view of the discipline has also become more global as I travel widely and meet colleagues in different locations around the world. The discipline is slowly evolving to embrace global rather than Euro-American-centered values in research and scholarship. It was not like this a generation ago.

REGULA BURCKHARDT QURESHI (B. 1939)

Q1: For me, ethnomusicology was like a beacon. Early on, I didn't know what it was. I married a guy from India and became culturally involved. When I discovered ethnomusicology, it became a home: a musical and professional home. It is an environment I can learn from, an amazing thing to be part of. To me, this kind of collegiality in a profession is an American thing. There wasn't much going on in Canada at that time. It was at SEM meetings that I connected with ethnomusicology. I love America because of this. I remember the first time I gave a paper: people were very excited about it because it was about a very beautiful Shi'a chant. People responded, and I made connections; it was all very collegial and human. That's what I like most about ethnomusicology; we still have that spirit, and it doesn't look like it's going away, even though we're becoming more scattered and more technological.

PART 3
Self-Positioning in and
Reflections on the Field

436

It's also important when you have students, especially in Canada, where we're not part of the mainstream, especially in outposts like Alberta. It's really important to teach these students how *they* can make connections. I tell them to go to the meetings; I take them around and introduce them to everybody so that they can connect with the people who wrote the books and the important works. It's a wonderful system. It's exciting, because everything comes to life. The one person who is a model

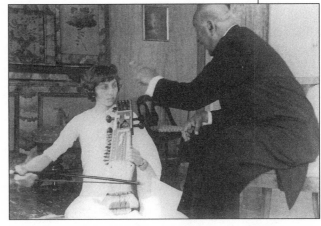

Regula Qureshi learning an Urdu song from Pir-o-Murshid Musharraf Khan. Washington, DC, May 1966.

for all this is Bruno Nettl. In the old days, wherever the meetings were, we would have morning coffee together in some nice place. He is the ultimate model for how you build students, all the way from his own writings, to writing with students, to working with other institutions: he's a master. Look how many students he has and where these people are. It's wonderful. In some ways there is an old-worldly student spirit in him.

Q2: If there's any kind of a criticism I have about the field, it is "How do we get together across the barriers of not only culture, but of race, of whatever is dividing us?" That was just my life, and it still is, in a way. But it seems to me that for many years I could count African American colleagues on one hand. I look at ethnomusicology, and it's so damn white! Why is that so? Maybe it has something to do with privilege, and maybe we have to do something special to make sure everyone has equal access. So, for me, changing that would be a priority.

KATHERINE BUTLER SCHOFIELD (B. 1974)

Q1: I no longer call myself an ethnomusicologist, if I ever did, although ethnomusicologists are my home and my beloved tribe and I masquerade as one institutionally when it comes to training future generations. The freedom King's College has given me to be myself—primarily, a historian—and study music and the people who make it in whatever way I desire has been utterly liberating. I am now recognized mainly as a historian of early-modern India; a cultural historian of the Mughal empire (1526–1858) who treats music and listening as endlessly revealing modes of examining Mughal and early colonial worlds as worlds unto themselves. I love the music, sure; but for all the periods I study, its sounds are inaccessible except through the testimony of

PART 3
Self-Positioning in and
Reflections on the Field

Katherine Schofield with Dan Neuman at the 51st Annual SEM Conference in Honolulu, Hawai'i, November 2006.

historical listeners. I am far more interested in what humanly significant sounds meant and did for those people, in that place, in that time: in writing through music histories of the ephemeral, the emotions, and the senses; and in writing auditory histories before the era of recorded sound. If, instead, I choose to locate myself within music studies, then I say, quite deliberately, that I'm a musicologist. The ethno bit does no useful work for me—I don't do ethnography; "ethno" others a major music system that is in no way lesser than Western art music; and doing "music in/as culture" has frankly never distinguished ethnomusicology anyway.

Q2: I think it is high time to provincialize, to decolonize, to reclaim the term "musicology" for the study of all the world's music and sound-making practices, across all timeframes, using whatever methodology is most apposite. The long-term collaborative project I'm involved in now is actively working across subdisciplinary fields—between WAM musicology, ethnomusicology, and history—to create a level playing field upon which we can write afresh a connected critical history of the world's music: one that provincializes Europe and even colonialism, and that pays attention to specificity, difference, and detail all the way down, while paying equal attention to the ways in which musical systems, people, and materials have always circulated and connected, and analyzing any wider historical patterns and processes that may become audible as a result.

T. M. Scruggs (b. 1951)

Q1: Outside academia's walls I am pleasantly surprised at the immediate positive reactions I get when I describe myself as an ethnomusicologist: so often people's faces light up at the mention of the field; apparently, we enjoy a positive image among the general public. John Santos is a master percussionist who lives in the San Francisco Bay Area and has done substantial research on African Caribbean music; at a community college he lists his degree as *de la calle* ("from the street"). He is a perfect example of our field's challenge to develop a more inclusive approach and engage with colleagues outside of formal academia. When we met, I presented myself as having *been* an ethnomusicologist, as I no longer had a paying position. John stated flatly: "Oh no—once you are an ethnomusicologist, you are *always* an ethnomusicologist."

Q2: We've made headway, but surprisingly little in the battle for the acceptance of other musics and cultures within what are called, after all, "Departments of *Music*" and

Part 3
Self-Positioning in and
Reflections on the Field

438

"Schools of *Music*," not "Conservatories of the European Classical Tradition." I give Ellen Koskoff primary credit for helping put the study of gender on the map in our field. We dropped the ball on that one, and it was picked up by musicology, which was looking around for some way to expand its canon.

In the same way, musicologists expanded their canon into popular music studies, especially in the United States. Ethnomusicology and the amorphous field of popular music studies have a funny history. As I went into graduate school, I was starting to think, "Is there going to be some kind of big *moment* when mass-mediated musics are considered worthy of study?" But I think everyone recognized that once half of Africa moved into urban environments in the 1970s, what else would you expect to study? So we have included popular music in our field without much controversy, but we haven't ended up carrying the banner. There are so many musicologists now doing popular music that musicology has tried to position itself as being classical music *and* popular music. It's not necessarily been the best for the field of popular music, which needs a good dose of anthropological and ethnographic methodology. And then we've had

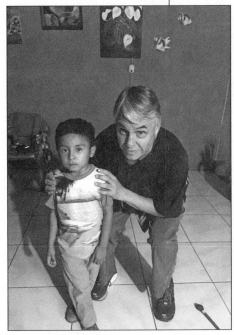

T. M. Scruggs with four-year-old marimba de arco *prodigy Samuelito, great grandson of Manuel Palacios who, with his brothers Carlos and Juan, formed a* marimba de arco *trio Scruggs recorded in 1985 for the 1988 album* Nicaraguan Folk Music from Masaya. *Monimbó, Masaya, Nicaragua, July 2017.*

people from cultural studies. So now, in popular music, we have people who don't know music who are writing about music. And they also don't know anthropology. It's disappointing to me that what the field of ethnomusicology has to offer hasn't made more of an impact.

Moving through the world without an official position has reinforced my feelings that the walls around institutions of higher learning would best be reduced to rubble. I welcome the recent turn within our field toward the value of public-sector work, and I hope for more integration of independent scholars and other people outside academia who do work that clearly falls under the title of ethno-musicology. We could learn from the Experience Music Project in Seattle that deliberately and productively integrates university-based and commercial world intellectual workers in their conferences on popular music. Relatedly, our field continues to suffer too much from a citation complex. Translation can be daunting, yet it does not explain nor excuse how often scholarship in the nation or region being investigated is ignored or only superficially mentioned and not substantively engaged; Raúl Romero's (2001) discussion of this issue remains relevant.

PART 3
Self-Positioning in and
Reflections on the Field

439

LAUREL SERCOMBE (B. 1950)

Q1: I think of myself as a sound archivist with a degree in ethnomusicology, but I do identify with the image (at least my image) of the ethnomusicologist—someone with an inclusive, wholehearted approach to the study of music. Ellen Koskoff is my ideal ethnomusicologist. I don't have theoretical chops, but I read and learn from those who do. And as my husband the scientist says, ethnomusicology parties are much more fun than science parties.

I take my role as a preservation person very seriously and do feel that based on my experience with Native American songs, there are a whole lot of reasons for preserving stuff, and we can't anticipate why we need to preserve it. When Metcalf, Jacobs, and Hess recorded stuff, they had no idea that two generations later, folks were going to be coming into my office saying, "I want to hear my grandfather's song."

Q2: Ethnomusicology now seems to be a bunch of smaller fields of study under one big umbrella. Once you find your niche and your little community of niche-ites, it's easy to feel you have little in common with all the other niches. The annual SEM conferences tend to reinforce those divisions, while at the same time identifying and exploring the larger issues facing the profession through program themes and plenaries. This seems healthy to me.

Laurel Sercombe on her Beatles pilgrimage in Abbey Road, London NW8, England, 2002.

I tend to see ethnomusicology through the lens of my Archives. It's been really interesting to see the change away from a geographic focus. When I first started working here, everything that came in was because somebody had gone somewhere, recorded a body of material, and brought it back to the archive. You figured out what geographical area it went under and you cataloged it. The change away from that has been gradual, but now we have people doing research in downtown Seattle, and they have to get permission before making any recordings. Sometimes the recordings are on the internet, and I have a lot of trouble grasping the "There is no there, there" when it comes to research documentation. So as an archivist, I'm finding it very challenging to deal with the change of focus, especially when the documentation is entirely virtual. I certainly have no dislike for this—I think it's fabulous that so many things have opened up and people are so creative in what they research, but as an archivist, I'm finding it difficult to adjust.

Stephen Slawek (b. 1949)

Q1: When I introduce myself as an ethnomusicologist, I usually follow up (in response to the quizzical expressions) with the explanation that ethnomusicology combines musicology and anthropology, and that most ethnomusicologists do research on music other than Western art music. However, I don't actually identify closely with a self-image as an anthropologist of music. My self-image fits closely with the designation "musician-scholar," a term that arose in the 1980s among European students of Hindustani music who developed academic research on Indian music in addition to their performance studies. I think of myself as a musician and scholar of music with special interests in South and Southeast Asian music and rock music. I would say that, for me, what appeals most is that grounded study that actually shows some sort of meaningful connection between the organization of sound and its being used within the culture in a certain way. I think there are many other ethnomusicologists who fit this particular brand of ethnomusicology.

Stephen Slawek performing at a concert arranged by the Surmandal Music Circle and Konkani Association of Hyderabad, India, July 2014.

Q2: While there are others who follow this approach to ethnomusicology, I can't say that it is the most prevalent type of ethnomusicology being done today. I feel that rather than asking "Why this particular style of music in this context?" more ethnomusicologists today ask, "What is this music doing for these people?" The concern becomes less to do with musical style and more to do with social action. The current interest in Latour's Actor Network Theory is exemplary. There isn't much need to be competent in musical performance in this approach. One's performance skill becomes more a utility of pedagogy, for example, to keep an ensemble functioning, rather than a key aspect of scholarly inquiry into what it is about musical style that helps to define a particular subculture's identity. On the other hand, ethnomusicology, at least as I understand it, has become so diffuse, ranging over so many different issues, concepts, and approaches, that it is inevitable that the prevalence of any one approach will diminish in size when attempting to view the field/discipline as a whole. Ultimately, I believe the integrity of the discipline is its inclusive nature that celebrates diversity, both of the subject matter it engages and of the approaches it takes in studying its subject.

Daniel Atesh Sonneborn (b. 1949)

Q1: From first entry into the community of ethnomusicologists, with very few exceptions, I was welcomed into the circle for my ideas and as a person. I am interested

PART 3
Self-Positioning in and
Reflections on the Field

Atesh Sonneborn celebrating (after a decade of work) the launch of 127 titles of the UNESCO Collection of Traditional Music at the Smithsonian Castle in Washington D.C., December 2015.

in people everywhere, their music, musical practices, and tastes. When someone asks, "What do you do for a living?" I tell them I'm an applied ethnomusicologist. For me that connotes a wide-ranging scope. Quite often the other person nods but looks bemused. The role has provided a marvelous cover story for unquenchable curiosity, allowing me to spend time getting to know people and explore musics. My professional role has afforded endless learning—in experiential, affective, embodied ways—about how others think and feel. Opportunities continually arise at Smithsonian Folkways to help build bridges of knowledge via new productions and acquisitions so that many more can gain deeper understanding about themselves and the rest of the world through music and its contexts. It has been and remains a magnificent honor.

Q2: Going forward, I hope more ethnomusicologists will engage as activists at the frontlines against ignorance on issues of importance to our society and the world. There is so much we still don't know. As an applied ethnomusicologist, I find most interesting the part of the field that fosters the transition from the mind world of the academy to "regular people" who are not in the academy. I think the field has burgeoned and gotten stronger and more thoughtful. There's a greater understanding, the most positive aspect being the shift from the culture of The Other of the 1960s or '70s to the concept of participant observation. Now it's a much more collaborative field. These are people you're going to build your career on, and you owe them a debt. The debt is a debt of relationship. That's probably the most positive thing I've seen.

My critique is that I think there are some people who would do well not to go right into college after high school, or graduate school after college. I have met academics who started school when they were five, and they're still in school. They're missing some pieces. It's not the fieldwork experience at the end of studies but in life throughout that makes for better understanding, I think.

MARCELLO SORCE KELLER (B. 1947)

In the absence of the usual two questions as to "identity as an ethnomusicologist" and "critique of the field," we present Marcello's "Reflections" section from the original 2007 interview, with answers to the two questions inextricably intermingled.

PART 3
Self-Positioning in and
Reflections on the Field

442

TS: Considering what you have said about the different areas of research you are attracted to, do you feel you are an ethnomusicologist after all? And if so, what is your position in relation to the field and its boundaries?

MSK: The short answer is that it is in the company of people who profess to be ethnomusicologists that I feel more comfortable. So, I guess, I belong to this group. And yet I am disturbed by the word "ethnomusicology," which I find both pompous and exceedingly unmusical. I wonder whether any label can ever be capable of describing all that we are interested in doing. Even speaking of our actions as a "field" is unnecessarily restrictive. After all, when Max Weber was once asked what his field was, reportedly he replied that he was not a donkey and therefore had no field. In other words, this is a personal malaise that not many scholars seem to share. Luckily, I can live with it.

Marcello Sorce Keller, 2006.

TS: Who are your role models in ethnomusicology? People that you think you've been most influenced or excited by?

MSK: I've been enormously influenced by Bruno Nettl. There is hardly anything I do or write about that is not in some way or another influenced by his teaching and his publications. If I ever did anything good at all, it is by pushing his ideas one or two steps further than he did—maybe to a point where he would possibly not agree with my doing so.

TS: If you were to describe a Bruno Nettl style or approach, what do you think that would be?

MSK: I think it has been very characteristic of him to let his students follow their own paths, according to their own inclination. That is why, fortunately, there is no "Nettl School." Look at his students, so very different from one another. There are no replicas of Bruno Nettl around, no "Nettls" on a smaller scale. It is also relevant to observe that in Nettl's work the anthropological and the historical dimensions always combine at some level and, explicitly or implicitly, his approach is always comparative. In his classroom teaching, comparisons would often come into consideration. That is how he has helped me look at the Western tradition with the eyes of the outsider. And that is how I could at some point comprehend what an anthropological singularity the Western way of making music represents, especially from the nineteenth century onward, when the concept of "classical music" was invented in Europe, and other cultures were forced to reclassify some of their repertoires as "classical" in order not to appear inferior.

PART 3
Self-Positioning in and
Reflections on the Field

443

Julie Strand (b. 1972)

Q1: Since I officially left academia, I've thought a lot about how being an ethnomusicologist still holds a place in my identity. In a field where the primary career track is teaching and publishing research, how does this identity inform the way I move through life, now that those are no longer my primary professional activities? Honestly, this has been a difficult question to answer, and it ties into my search for

Julie Strand at Pura Ulun Danun Bratan, Bedugul, Bali, Indonesia, on a Dialogue of Civilizations study abroad program, Northeastern University, with baby owls of unknown identity, June 2012.

a meaningful career that utilizes the skills and training I have as an ethnomusicologist within a nonacademic working environment. I do see it as an invaluable axis upon which I can relate to people, particularly those of different cultures. I see great potential for humanity to negotiate vast cultural divides by finding common themes through how we articulate culture through creative expression, whether it's music, visual art, literature, theater, even architecture and design. But how do we reach beyond the ivory tower, how do we make appreciable difference in this world through these finely honed yet largely esoteric skills? How do we help the world see the value of what we do beyond classrooms, journals, and conferences? For myself, the Foreign Service provides a meaningful outlet where I believe that I can make the greatest difference.

Q2: My concern is that we don't become so entrenched in our work as it relates to tenure cases, book awards, and personal achievement that we lose sight of how we can broaden our impact beyond higher education and into the world around us. I see great promise within the various threads of applied ethnomusicology, also in the importance placed on non-Western scholars working within their own cultures as we see how people represent themselves within a shared academic language. There's also great potential in collaborating with experts in other fields. Ethnomusicologists are working together with neuroscientists and psychologists to understand how music is perceived and processed by the brain, unleashing greater understanding of how music cognition interacts with other brain functions. Frustrated by the dearth of academic positions, some ethnomusicologists have chosen to utilize their skills and knowledge base to develop new generations of technology, while still others have chosen paths in intercultural communication, which intersects with almost any industry that involves people of different national and ethnic origins.

Part 3
Self-Positioning in and
Reflections on the Field

Tan Sooi Beng (b. 1955)

Q1: For me, being an ethnomusicologist means being an engaged activist researcher committed to social justice, equality, and social transformation. Not only do I write about how ordinary people use music and the arts to contest power structures and national ideologies, but I also advocate for change in the education and political system. I have devised methodologies and provided safe spaces for peace building among young people of different ages, races, religions, income levels, and gender. I do this through collaboration with artists of diverse ethnic backgrounds and tradition bearers, and by getting people of different races interested in diverse cultural forms (including marginalized forms). Dialogue and participatory methods are employed to encourage young people to conduct their own research with communities, learn different types of music, and recreate the forms themselves. They perform together for multicultural audiences.

Q2: The methods of documentation, recording, archiving music, performing, and teaching remain vital and are consistent with my personal vision. However, I strongly believe that we can no longer be neutral in our research and shy away from politics if our research subjects are being marginalized or are divided by race. Power relationships

Tan Sooi Beng playing multi-ethnic instruments, 1992.

within and outside the communities, between academia and community, and among researcher and researched should also be acknowledged. Collaborative research with our research subjects, constant dialogue between researchers and research subjects, and participatory processes can help to promote power sharing. Bringing the subject of power relationships and methods of participatory collaborative research to the classroom can help to decolonize ethnomusicology.

The Applied Ethnomusicology Sub-Study Group within the ICTM, started in 2007, has helped me connect with other colleagues who are engaging communities through music in other parts of the world. I think this is an important direction in which ethnomusicology should go.

Each year I have at least four or five students who take part in my community educational work. Many of them have since adapted the methodologies in the schools, teachers' training colleges, and universities where they teach. We also network with other groups in the Southeast Asian region. The seeds have been planted and are growing.

PART 3
Self-Positioning in and
Reflections on the Field

445

Michael Tenzer (b. 1957)

Q1: My view on this has evolved appropriate to my age and daily life. Before, it was fieldwork and exchange; now it's reading and reflection. It also means continuing to make music with my own hands so as never to cease obeisance to musicology's real master. But mostly it is teaching, where, in my own mind, I keep my happy memories of fieldwork in Bali as alive as I can. For undergraduate teaching, I prefer to sit on the floor with students rather than at a desk or lectern. I like to be among them rather than stand in front of them. My curiosity about them as individuals presents

Michael Tenzer, Paris, France, 2010.

difficulties because there is never enough time to reach out. I constantly remind myself that even though my job is to be a professor in a university, the university system is mainly antithetical to learning about music. I actually think of it as a kind of lie. Learning music is apprenticeship, companionship, communality—not testing, evaluation, and grades, and I consider that juxtaposition in itself an ethnomusicology lesson. Productive critique is a middle ground. Graduate advising is a total joy, I find—forming close bonds likely to last a lifetime, with people who share your passions, have much to teach you, and have placed themselves in your hands.

Q2: I can't decide if what I do is consistent with some notion of our "discipline." I never did an ethnomusicology degree, and at this point that feels liberating, because I feel strong in several perspectives. But the question does not provoke me much. What I am interested in is integration and transformation. In 1928 Oswald de Andrade told fellow Brazilians to cannibalize their oppressors—swallow and integrate the best of what had been imposed on them as a colony. That's how I see ethnomusicology vis-à-vis university music teaching as a whole. We need to gradually absorb European music and its practices, and eventually cease to see ourselves as separate from them. We have thrived on the idea of conflict between the West and the rest: it allowed us to portray ourselves as different and to argue, on the basis of much-needed diversity, that we should grow. But that it is ultimately divisive, and while it may not be time yet, our separate strands need to come together. I tell my students that I don't really believe in ethnomusicology (as a "faith"). I believe it exists, but I think it's a word that describes us all. We're all doing different things. I think there is a core set of issues defining the field, but I don't necessarily identity with them, even though I find them very interesting and love to read and learn about them.

PART 3
Self-Positioning in and
Reflections on the Field

446

Elizabeth Travassos Lins (1955–2013)

An anthropologist who never referred to herself as an ethno-musicologist, Elizabeth passed away before we asked for formal reflections. These thoughts are drawn from her 2007 interview.

TS: Do you have any critique of ethnomusicology as you see it today? Is it moving in the direction you like, or do you have any problems with the field of ethnomusicology?

ETL: I don't want to be unfair, but I feel that ethnomusicology is not properly an independent field, because all theorization comes from the social sciences. There are a few exceptions: John Blacking tried to formulate some new theories that arose from his musical experience (anthropology of the body, anthropology of performers); and Anthony Seeger wrote a musical anthropology of an Amazonian people. I feel there is an expectation that new ideas can arise from the musical experience and musical practice of many peoples and that

Elizabeth Travassos Lins in her office, circa 1997. Photo by Antônio José Pedral Sampaio Lins.

these can have an impact on the social sciences, but this has not happened yet. I don't know why, because music is very important. I'm saying the obvious thing, of course: music is very important to the human species, isn't it?

Let's forget the social sciences for a moment and think about biology and the evolution of the species. Hominids are defined by many things, but modern man, as we know him, is defined by language and music, so music must play a very important role. Then how is it possible that music can be considered an "art," an "expressive form," or something that we do when we are at leisure? This is a very particular understanding, derived from modern Western societies. The ethnomusicologist's experience with music in different cultures should have made a greater contribution to the anthropologist. And who did this? In fact, a few social scientists tried. I think of Lévi-Strauss; he tried to understand music among the human capacities—logic, myth, music, poetry—in *Tristes Tropiques* [1955]. It was a way of theorizing the role of music in human life, but I don't feel ethnomusicologists have had the courage to do this. Of course, in every textbook, they say, "Music is very important" and "Music is not only a reflection of social life; social life is a product of music," but I feel we are still waiting for a stronger statement.

Ricardo Trimillos (b. 1941)

Q1: What attracted me to the field, once I got into it, was the wide latitude of what you could do as an ethnomusicologist. There's a lot of flexibility: there are many things you can do and still be within the identity of the profession. That's what I really enjoyed

Ricardo Trimillos at the Hawai'i International Film Festival symposium at the East-West Center, Honolulu, Hawai'i, November 1983. (Left to right) Prof. Barbara B. Smith (University of Hawai'i at Mānoa), Ricardo Trimillos, and Dr. Wimal Dissanayake (East-West Center).

and feel satisfied about calling myself an ethnomusicologist; it allows you not to be a generalist but gives you the flexibility of looking at many things and not losing the identity of the profession you're involved with. So I'm still quite happy to be called an ethnomusicologist—and of course, that also always includes dance. We always understand the two together, even though the field is called ethno*music*ology. That goes back to my childhood cultural stuff, because we sang *and* danced. So yes, looking back on it, I think the label is still satisfactory and something I wouldn't want to change.

Q2: I think we've been through a period of identity crisis in the field where we've become so social-science oriented. I've always been concerned about the music part, but I see that coming back again. In the '80s and early '90s there was all this cultural theory, and people were not paying as much attention to the music as sound. I think that was partly because a number of the people who came into the field at that time were nonmusic people who didn't have any background in music, so it was hard for them to relate to things like transcription and analysis. So we became very social-science oriented. To me, that was to the detriment of music, because I kept asking, "What does ethnomusicology do that anthropologists can't do?" Our thing is that we can also talk about the sound. It's like a pendulum that swings back and forth. We're coming back to the point where sound is important again.

I find it interesting that ethnomusicology has been the touchstone for diversity. Now everybody is climbing aboard and getting diverse, which is good, but it has negatively impacted the ability of our students to get jobs. Now that we've told the music education people that they need to do something about world music and the musicologists that they need to know about other aspects of the world, they're the ones saying, "Oh yes, I can do the world music course *and trecento*." A lot of music departments don't want research in ethnomusicology, just somebody to teach the world music courses, so, of course, the people who can do that *and* do the "real stuff" are getting the jobs. I see that as a problem for further employment; a lot of our students are not getting jobs in academe and have to find other things to do. The Hawai'i program has been very successful in getting people into applied ethnomusicology of different kinds. We have people who are in museum studies, arts agencies, and things like that.

PART 3
Self-Positioning in and
Reflections on the Field

448

Lois Wilcken (b. 1949)

Q1: I find myself using "musicology" more than "ethnomusicology" to name my profession. I have long felt that the latter is the broader category. The prefix "ethno," moreover, carries too much negative baggage for my liking. I understand the historical reasons for the term, but we are long overdue in catching up with the evolution in thinking that has taken place. And of course, ethnic groups are no longer our only focus. Think of the focus on the individual that people like Tim Rice promote, which will guide me in my biography of Frisner Augustin. And so, I increasingly tell people that I am a musicologist. My family is particularly appreciative, as they can more easily remember what I do.

Q2: Most of my critiques are working themselves out. We have a huge applied ethnomusicology section now, and that was always a neglected part of the field. The membership of the applied section seems to grow by the day. I do primarily applied work, so I naturally want to see the development and expansion of this activism with the public. The perception that music can be a way of crossing social barriers and healing the divisions among many publics motivated my decision to

Lois Wilcken and Master Drummer Frisner Augustin (1948–2012) taking a break during a Haitian community festival at Clara Barton High School, Brooklyn, NY, November 1985. Photo by Chantal Regnault.

join the field in the early 1980s. Despite progress, however, our discipline needs to think even more seriously about applying the knowledge we gather as a way to address the very challenging social tensions we are now experiencing across the globe. I believe we have much to offer.

Sean Williams (b. 1959)

Q1: Being an ethnomusicologist—to me—is fourfold: one can simultaneously be a researcher, a musician, a writer, and a professor (or whatever career one has landed). Their respective order of importance shifts constantly, depending on necessities of opportunity, funding, time, and inclination. Even as I teach my Irish studies students about the *sean-nós* ("old style") singing tradition, I can see in my mind's eye two older gentlemen in Connemara grasping each other's hands as one of them sings; I teach my students the song he was singing, I read them the poem I wrote about the experience, and I look forward to seeing the singer again on my next field trip to Ireland.

Sean Williams, circa 2015.

I have songs and tunes from all over the world going through my head all the time, and I set aside one day each week during the school year just for writing down the results of my research and my new ideas. All of it is connected in the mind and body of this ethnomusicologist.

Q2: I see the field today as being richly diverse and far broader than the way it was presented to me in graduate school. I believe that the Old School format of academia was to produce an endless array of mini-me junior professors who would move through the same process as all the previous generations of professors. At this point, particularly because of the breathtakingly swift trend toward hiring mostly adjunct rather than full-time, tenure-track faculty, the field is quite appropriately branching out to include public-sector work as something to be proud of, rather than to be ashamed of. If we are serious about ethnomusicology, then fostering a culture of bringing all the world's music to *all the world's people*—not just to college students—is healthy, forward looking, and realistic. That is worthy of celebration.

PHILIP YAMPOLSKY (B. 1945)

Q1: I think ethnomusicologists should follow their musical interests wherever they lead. The entire world of musical activity is open to us. My own leanings are toward the "area scholar" approach, focusing on a region and drawing on ethnography, history, linguistics, agriculture, and any other relevant discipline to understand the nature, function, and development of music there. My topics have ranged from the study of classical Javanese gamelan music in court cities to discographical and archival research on the recording industry in Indonesia (thus involving a lot of urban popular music), plus a seven-year peripatetic survey of the music of Indonesia as a whole, and I am now happily working on sung poetry in rural communities in Timor. I have also practiced two kinds of applied ethnomusicology, doing foundation work to support traditional music in Indonesia and producing recordings to educate listeners about the diversity of Indonesia's music. One thing I regret is having had little chance to teach. All of this is ethnomusicology, as I see it, but my current research, involving settled fieldwork on a largely unknown music, comes closest to my ideal, because in addition to increasing knowledge of the world's music, it has the dimension of advocacy on behalf of a particular music and the culture that produces it.

Q2: I feel that ethnomusicology should be looking at the entire range of human musical activity. I have no quarrel with the study of popular and mass-mediated musics, and some of my own work has been concerned with them. But I believe the field

PART 3
Self-Positioning in and
Reflections on the Field

450

today is at fault in favoring them so lop-
sidedly. We largely ignore those musics
that are *not* popular, not mediated, not
globalized, not in diaspora—the rural
and marginal musics that are under the
radar and off the map. I am not abashed
to call these musics "traditional": by dis-
allowing that term we make it difficult
to even recognize that musics in distinctive, historically deep, highly local-
ized idioms still exist. They are indeed
waning in many places, as their elderly
practitioners die out and younger generations take up urban popular music
instead—but all the more reason for us
to document them while we still can.
They are irreplaceable, vanishing evidence of the astonishing multiplicity
of forms humans have developed for
expressing their thoughts and emotions.

Philip Yampolsky recording topeng Betawi *in Bekasi, West Java, Indonesia, in August 1990. To his left, wearing headphones, is Joko Kurnain (Institut Seni Budaya Indonesia, Bandung). Photo by Tinuk Yampolsky.*

And many of them are indeed vanishing, or changing radically. When people talk about tradition, they say, "Oh, tradition is always changing, art never stands still." While that of course is true in the long run, people use that idea to avoid any evaluation of the quality of change, accepting every change as equally valid. Whereas I see a lot of musics changing at an accelerated pace under external pressure, sometimes under coercion from government or religion, sometimes to conform to the demands of commercial media, or because of social aspirations to "modernity," many of these changes tend toward same-ness, erasing musical difference. (A concern for musical difference—which underlies my whole life in ethnomusicology—is often criticized today as Orientalist, or colonialist, or exoticist, or romantic, or nostalgic.) The trends of change are toward adding instru-ments and harmonies of global popular music, changing to media-friendly song forms and presentation, putting standardized, mechanical beats underneath, imposing a stage aesthetic that values virtuosity and spectacle and requires polished performance with neat beginnings and endings. The claim that all these changes are merely change as usual, organic developments of tradition, is, to my mind, facile and complacent.

NOTES

1. This has been attributed to others but may have first been delivered in a 1966 UCLA ethnomusicology graduate seminar (Trimillos 1993, 23n).
2. Music of the United States of America, a project of the American Musicological Society.
3. Probably actually Charles Seeger, as noted in the introduction to this section.

PART 3
Self-Positioning in and
Reflections on the Field

Postlude

"I know it when I see it"

It is now more than a decade since the idea for *Living Ethnomusicology* emerged at the 2006 Society for Ethnomusicology meeting, partly born of the plumeria-scented Waikiki-beachfront evening, the bewitching falsetto of the late Auntie Genoa Keawe in the rooftop bar, those *ono* mai-tais that first emerged in our Prelude, and the warm, stimulating fellowship of other Ethnos. In the course of our journey through the lives and careers of fifty fascinating ethnomusicologists and ethnomusicological fellow travelers, Margaret and I (*pace* the late Alan P. Merriam and his long, earnest pursuit of these questions) may not have settled anything about what ethnomusicology "should be." To dispel any such illusions, one need only scan the book's concluding section, in which our fifty contributors critique the field of ethnomusicology and where they fit therein. If anything, we have indeed encountered a "gaseous coalescence" of backgrounds and paths emerging from them.

However, in the many personal encounters, and during the years of transcribing and editing interviews and writing, we have felt strong resonances with aspects of our own lives, while noting the remarkable array of differences. No matter the many methodologies and interests that some may have considered an obstacle to a facile definition of "Ethnomusicology" (see Reyes 2009). No matter the mind-boggling variety of backgrounds, abilities, conditions of employment, creative media, and activist outlets that apply to our interlocutors. No matter: I would venture that they, we, and many of our readers share, at some point in most of these narratives, a sense of "Yes, that's me!!" "That's how *I* felt!" Like Supreme Court Justice Potter Stewart's memorable 1964 pronouncement on pornography: "[We] know it when [we] see it."

Jeff Titon's words, "I take people making music as my paradigm case of musical 'being in the world'" (2008, 31) apply to us, and it is clear and appropriate—and important—that we can add "a passion for *knowing* about people making music"—*living* people, for the most part. We can also safely say that the "knowing" almost always involves the emotionally charged processes of creating and maintaining exceptionally close and often lifelong connections with those same people. Many of us live with a sort of occupational guilt born of knowing that we cannot really compensate them for the worlds they have opened to us and the careers that we build in our shared, transplanted corners of those worlds. The synergy of bittersweet guilt, pleasure, deep personal relationships, and music is extraordinarily rich. In the words of Umi Hsu, "Sensing patterns of the forces of human emotions, values, and ideologies expressed sonically, and being irresistibly moved by these forces, [ethnomusicologists] unravel new knowledge about humankind."

This book integrally reflects these essentially defining features of our field. Deeply entwined with and grateful to our participants through our years of interactive interviews, we ourselves can hear their voices; in *Living Ethnomusicology* we strive to have you hear them too. We are proud to have collaborated with such an inspiring and fascinating group. Whatever aspirations we may have realistically had to unequivocally define and delineate the field of ethnomusicology have been in some ways superseded by the fascinations of participating in this journey with them. Most appropriately, then, it is the journey, and the people—those aspects of ethnomusicology that attracted most of us in the first place—we are proud to share with you here; we envy you that journey before you.

Ted Solís

Afterword

The people profiled in this book, including the authors, have come to ethnomusicology over three generations on several continents. Wrapping up their experience and emotions seems too tidy. But four threads shine through this tapestry, which I'll try to tug without unwinding the texture. Let's call it the Four A's of Ethnomusicology.

Attraction. The draw to the field can arrive so early, as with Hood's family legacy, that it can be a preexisting condition: "It has always been close to my heart, and if by some medical procedure it were removed, life would stop beating." Or it can come later in life as a guiding light. For Qureshi, "ethnomusicology was like a beacon," a strong metaphor suggesting a move away from shadow to light. It's hard and even unnecessary to analyze the many types of attraction, but Becker summarizes the magnetic power of the field eloquently: "I was, in my mind, open to the beauties and mysteries of all peoples' musics." Even more optically, Benary thinks of ethnomusicology as a way of sensing music vividly: "Ethnomusicology is like a set of sunglasses I put on, a perspective that colors my relationship to musical situations."

The coziness of the discipline helps support the attraction, as Manuel says: "One of the great things about the field for me is that it's just such a great group of people. I love our conferences; the people are so creative. For me that is one of the great delights of the profession." Lau locates his attraction in the virtues of an ideal practitioner: "My image of an ethnomusicologist is someone who is open minded, inclusive, tolerant, kind, compassionate, and full of aloha!" Who wouldn't be drawn to such a congenial interest group, rare not just in academia but also in the other bureaucracies that house ethnomusicologists?

Mark Slobin, 2018. Photo by Manny Parks.

Ambivalence. But the lenses are not so rosy. Becker follows her 1960s "beauties and mysteries of music" with this caveat: "It was a position of moral superiority. In the present context, that interpretation appears naïve." Always clear eyed and open eared, ethnomusicologists sense the dangers of the very attraction that drew them in. Blum spells it out: "A self-image as an ethnomusicologist needs to include a willingness not to ignore the harm that has been and is being done to the weak by the strong." Even the authors admit to a deep sense of ambivalence in their blend of pleasures, positive engagement, and perils of position: "The synergy of bittersweet guilt, pleasure, deep personal relationships, and music is extraordinarily rich."

Ambiguity. Partly, ambivalence comes from the inbuilt ambiguity of ethnomusicology itself. As Blum puts it, "I don't think I've ever thought of ethnomusicology as a clearly defined field, and I don't think it should be." Even those, like Nooshin, who say they "do" ethnomusicology don't necessarily want to be counted in the guild: "I don't think there is any doubt that what I do is 'ethnomusicology,' but whether I define myself solely as an 'ethnomusicologist' is another matter." No surprise: the field arose almost 150 years ago from very mixed motivations among Europeans busily cutting out disciplines from the rich fabric of natural philosophy, with its blend of scientific study and humanistic understanding of "mankind." It's a ragged robe to put on as your daily outfit. It doesn't help that lay people you meet don't really grasp what it is you do. And figuring out the right way to deal with the music and musicians you love gets harder when the world of work thinks you're a square peg in their round pigeonholes, as the writers above often remark.

Even intellectually, the constant drift of the discipline leaves some feeling unmoored, as Post complains: "I have watched us go from a discipline with a relatively narrow to a dangerously broad view. I say 'dangerously' because it is now so hard to define the discipline." But it always was, as the authors point out. Breadth is a blessing and a curse for ethnomusicology, it seems.

Action. Despite ambivalence and ambiguity, encountering the world of music provokes a commitment to the music community and a sense of urgency about constructive action. Tan stakes a strong claim: "Being an ethnomusicologist means being an engaged activist researcher committed to social justice, equality, and social transformation." Blum says this is only natural: "No other area of musical research forces us to confront these realities on a daily basis and to think critically about our responsibilities as scholar-citizens engaged in the world." Alas, "these realities" limit ethnomusicology's impact, as Scruggs laments: "It's disappointing to me that what the field of ethnomusicology has to offer hasn't made more of an impact." So there's a sense of dedication and struggle that runs through the pages herewith, where the personal and the professional mix awkwardly in two arenas of action: the expressive and messy sphere of music's daily life and the hardened zone of institutional possibility.

Ethnomusicology has widened its scope, broadened its membership, and deepened its engagement of the world's music dramatically since I began in 1965. Perhaps a sequel ten years down the line will reveal what the students and successors of this volume's contributors have made of a discipline that one hopes will remain creatively undisciplined.

Mark Slobin

Works Cited

Abu-Lughod, Lila. 1991. "Writing against Culture." In *Recapturing Anthropology: Working in the Present*, edited by Richard G. Fox, 137–62. Santa Fe, N.M.: School of American Research Press.

Adelson, Roger, ed. 1997. *Speaking of History: Conversations with Historians*. East Lansing: Michigan State University Press.

Akpabot, Samuel Ekpe. 1975. *Ibibio Music in Nigerian Culture*. East Lansing: Michigan State University Press.

Anderson, Benedict. 1983. *Imagined Communities: Reflections on the Origin and Spread of Nationalism*. London: Verso.

Archer, William. 1964. "On the Ecology of Music." *Ethnomusicology* 8 (1): 28–33.

Arom, Simha. 1991. *African Polyphony and Polyrhythm: Musical Structure and Methodology*. Cambridge: Cambridge University Press.

Averill, Gage. 2003. *Four Parts, No Waiting: A Social History of American Barbershop Harmony*. New York: Oxford University Press.

———. 2004. "'Where's One': Musical Encounters of the Ensemble Kind." In Solís 2004c, 93–111.

Babiracki, Carol M. 2008. "What's the Difference? Reflections on Gender and Research in Village India." In Barz and Cooley 2008, 167–82.

Baily, John. 1976. *Krishna Govinda's Rudiments of Tabla Playing*. Brighton, UK: Unicorn.

———. 1985. *Amir: An Afghan Refugee Musician's Life in Peshawar, Pakistan*. Film. London: Royal Anthropological Institute.

———. 1988. *Music of Afghanistan: Professional Musicians in the City of Herat*. Cambridge: Cambridge University Press.

———. 2003. *A Kabul Music Diary*. Film. London: Royal Anthropological Institute.

———. 2015. *War, Exile and the Music of Afghanistan: The Ethnographer's Tale*. Farnham, Surrey: Ashgate.

Baily, J. S., and G. Singer. 1967. "Behavioral Compensation through Informational Feedback and Transformed Visual Input." *Australian Journal of Psychology* 19 (1): 49–43.

Barret, Renaud, and Florent de La Tullaye, dir. 2005. *Jupiter's Dance/La Danse de Jupiter*. Film. France: Production Kinoise.

Barz, Gregory, and Timothy J. Cooley, eds. (1997) 2008. *Shadows in the Field: New Perspectives for Fieldwork in Ethnomusicology*. Oxford: Oxford University Press.

Beaudry, Nicole. 2008. "The Challenge of Human Relations in Ethnographic Inquiry: Examples from Arctic and Subarctic Fieldwork." In Barz and Cooley 2008, 224–45.

Becker, Judith. 1980. *Traditional Music in Modern Java: Gamelan in a Changing Society*. Honolulu: University Press of Hawaiʻi.

Béhague, Gerard, ed. 1984. *Performance Practice: Ethnomusicological Perspectives*. Westport, Conn.: Greenwood.

Belo, Jane. ed. 1970. *Traditional Balinese Culture*. New York: Columbia University Press.

Benary, Barbara Lynn. 1971. "The Violin in South India." Master's thesis, Wesleyan University.

———. 1973. "Within the Karnatic Tradition." PhD diss., Wesleyan University.

Berliner, Paul F. 1975. *The Soul of Mbira: Music and Traditions of the Shona People of Zimbabwe*. Chicago: University of Chicago Press.

Blacking, John. 1973. *How Musical Is Man?* Seattle: University of Washington Press.

Boone, Olga. 1959. *Les Tambours du Congo Belge et du Ruanda-Urundi*. 2 vols. Tervuren: Musée du Congo Belge, Annales du Musée Royal du Congo Belge.

Bourdieu, Pierre. 1977. *Outline of a Theory of Practice*. Cambridge: Cambridge University Press.

Burckhardt, Titus. 1951. *Du Soufisme*. Lyons: Derain.

Castelo-Branco, Salwa El-Shawan. 1987. "Some Aspects of the Cassette Industry in Egypt." *the world of music* 29 (2): 32–48.

———, ed. 2010. *Enciclopédia da Música em Portugal no Século XX*. 4 vols. Lisbon: Temas e Debate.

Charry, Eric. 2000. *Mande Music: Traditional and Modern Music of the Maninka and Mandinka of Western Africa*. Chicago: University of Chicago Press.

Chaudhuri, Shubha. 1981. "Deviance and Perception of Grammaticality." PhD diss., Jawaharlal Nehru University, New Delhi.

Christensen, Dieter, and Salwa El-Shawan Castelo-Branco. 2009. *Traditional Arts in Southern Arabia: Music and Society in Sohar, Sultanate of Oman*. Berlin: VWB.

Clifford, James. 1988. *The Predicament of Culture: Twentieth-Century Ethnography, Literature, and Art*. Cambridge, Mass.: Harvard University Press.

Collins, Pat. 2016. *Song of Granite*. Film. Amerique Film.

The Conversation. 2016. "Is It Time to Eliminate Tenure for Professors?" Editorial post dated June 28. Cambridge, Mass.: The Conversation, Inc. https://theconversation.com/is-it-time-to-eliminate-tenure-for-professors-59959.

Cook, Nicholas. 2008. "We Are All (Ethno)musicologists Now." In *The New (Ethno)musicologies*, edited by Henry Stobart, 48–70. Lanham, Md.: Scarecrow.

Cooley, Timothy J., and Gregory Barz. 2008. "Casting Shadows: Fieldwork Is Dead! Long Live Fieldwork!" In Barz and Cooley 2008, 3–24.

Cooley, Timothy J., Katherine Meisel, and Nasir Syed. 2008. "Virtual Fieldwork: Three Case Studies." In Barz and Cooley, 2008, 90–107.

Courlander, Harold. 1960. *The Drum and the Hoe: Life and Lore of the Haitian People*. Berkeley: University of California Press.

Courlander, Harold, and Maung Than Myint. 1953. *Burmese Folk and Traditional Music*. Recording. Folkways Records FW04436/FE4436.

Danielson, Virginia. 1997. *The Voice of Egypt: Umm Kulthum, Arabic Song, and Egyptian Society in the Twentieth Century*. Chicago: University of Chicago Press.

Davis, Martha Ellen. 1992. "Careers, 'Alternative Careers,' and the Unity between Theory and Practice in Ethnomusicology." *Ethnomusicology* 36 (3): 361–87.

De Zorzi, Giovanni, and Alexandre Papas, eds. Forthcoming. *Music and Spirituality in Central Asia*. Leiden: Brill.

Diamond, Beverley. 2006. "Canadian Reflections on Palindromes, Inversions, and Other Challenges to Ethnomusicology's Coherence." *Ethnomusicology* 50 (2): 324–36.

Doubleday, Veronica. 1988. *Three Women of Herat*. London: Cape.

———. 2010. *I Cried from the Mountain Top: Images from the Afghanaid Archive (1980–2010) with Traditional Afghan Poetry Selected and Translated by Veronica Doubleday*. London: Afghanaid.

El-Bakkar, Mohammed, et al. 1957. *Port Said: Music of the Middle East*. Vol. 1. Recording. New York: Audio Fidelity Records.

Feld, Steven. 1982. *Sound and Sentiment: Birds, Weeping, Poetics, and Song in Kaluli Expression*. Philadelphia: University of Pennsylvania Press.

Feltz, William. 1977. "Music for Multicultural Students." In *Culture Learning: Concepts, Applications, and Research*, edited by Richard W. Brislin, 89–94. Honolulu: East-West Center/ University Press of Hawai'i.

Fernea, Elizabeth Warnock. 1969. *Guests of the Sheik*. New York: Doubleday.

"Finding Paths on the Job Market." 2016. *SEM Student News* 12. http://c.ymcdn.com/sites/ www.ethnomusicology.org/resource/group/dc75b7e7-47d7-4d59-a660-19c3 e0f7c83e/ Publications/SEMSN12.pdf.

Fish, Stanley. 1995. *Professional Correctness: Literary Studies and Political Change*. Oxford: Clarendon.

Frisbie, Charlotte J., and David P. McAllester. (1978) 2003. *Navajo Blessingway Singer: Frank Mitchell, 1881–1967*. Tucson: University of Arizona Press.

Geertz, Clifford. 1973. *The Interpretation of Cultures*. New York: Basic.

———. 1988. *Works and Lives: The Anthropologist as Author*. Stanford, Calif.: Stanford University Press.

Goldman, Michal. 1996. *Umm Kulthum: A Voice Like Egypt*. Film. Arab Film Distribution.

Gourlay, Kenneth A. 1978. "Towards a Reassessment of the Ethnomusicologist's Role in Research." *Ethnomusicology* 22 (1): 1–36.

Green, Archie. 1972. *Only a Miner: Studies in Recorded Coal-Mining Songs*. Urbana: University of Illinois Press.

Hagedorn, Katherine J. 2001. *Divine Utterances: The Performance of Afro-Cuban Santería*. Washington: Smithsonian University Press.

———. 2002. "Sacred Secrets: Lessons with Francisco." In *Mementos, Artifacts, and Hallucinations from the Ethnographer's Tent*, edited by Ron Emoff and David Henderson, 31–44. New York: Routledge.

Hahn, Tomie. 2007. *Sensational Knowledge: Embodying Knowledge through Japanese Dance*. Middletown, Conn.: Wesleyan University Press.

Halliburton, Richard. 1929. *New Worlds to Conquer*. Garden City, N.Y.: Garden City Publishing.

———. 1932. *The Flying Carpet*. Indianapolis: Bobbs-Merrill.

Harich-Schneider, Eta. 1973. *A History of Japanese Music*. London: Oxford University Press.

Harnish, David. 2004. "No, Not 'Bali Hai'! Challenges of Adaptation and Orientalism in Performing and Teaching Balinese Gamelan." In Solís 2004c, 126–37.

Harrison, Frank Llewelyn, Claude V. Palisca, and Mantle Hood. 1963. *Musicology*. Englewood Cliffs, N.J.: Prentice-Hall.

Hart, Mickey. With Jay Stevens and Frederic Lieberman. 1990. *Drumming at the Edge of Magic: A Journey into the Spirit of Percussion*. San Francisco: HarperSanFrancisco.

Hart, Mickey, and Frederic Lieberman. With D. A. Sonneborn. 1991. *Planet Drum: A Celebration of Percussion and Rhythm*. San Francisco: HarperSanFrancisco.

Hemetek, Ursula, Anna Czekanowska, Gerda Lechleitner, and Inna Naroditskaya. 2004. *Manifold Identities: Studies on Music and Minorities*. Amersham: Cambridge Scholars.

Henderson, Clara. 2009. "Dance Discourse in the Music and Lives of Presbyterian Mvano Women in Southern Malawi." PhD diss., Indiana University.

Herskovits, Melville J. 1948. *Man and His Works*. New York: Knopf.

Herzog, George. 1945. "Drum-Signaling in a West African Tribe." *Word: Journal of the International Linguistic Association* 1:217–38.

Hood, Made Mantle. 2001. "The Kendang Arja: Improvised Paired Drumming in Balinese Music." Master's thesis, University of Hawai'i.

———. 2005. "Triguna: A Hindu-Javanese Philosophy for Gamelan Gong-Gede Music." PhD diss., University of Cologne.

———. 2010. *Triguna: A Hindu-Balinese Philosophy for Gamelan Gong Gede Music*. Münster, Germany: LIT.

Hood, Mantle. 1960. "The Challenge of Bi-Musicality." *Ethnomusicology* 4 (2): 55–59.

———. 1971. *The Ethnomusicologist*. New York: McGraw-Hill.

———. 2004. "Afterword: Some Closing Thoughts from the First Voice; Interview with Mantle Hood by Ricardo Trimillos." In Solís 2004c, 283–88.

Hood, Mantle, and Hardja Susilo. 1967. *Music of the Venerable Dark Cloud*. Recording. Los Angeles: Institute of Ethnomusicology, UCLA (with Columbia Records).

Hornbostel, Erich M. von. 1913. *Melodie und Skala*. Leipzig: Peters.

International Music Council. 1982. *Music in the Life of Man*. Paris: International Music Council, UNESCO.

Kaeppler, Adrienne L. 1967. "The Structure of Tongan Dance." PhD diss., University of Hawai'i.

———. 1993. *Hula Pahu: Hawaiian Drum Dances, Vol. 1: Ha'a and Hula Pahu, Sacred Movements*. Honolulu: Bishop Museum Press.

———. 2008. *The Pacific Arts of Polynesia and Micronesia*. Oxford: Oxford University Press.

———. 2012. *Lakalaka: A Tongan Masterpiece of Performing Arts*. Tonga: Vava'u.

Kippen, James. 2008. "Working with the Masters." In Barz and Cooley 2008, 125–40.

Kisliuk, Michelle, and Kelly Gross. 2004. "What's the 'It' That We Learn to Perform? Teaching BaAka Music and Dance." In Solís 2004c, 249–60.

Kleikamp, Bernard (producer). 1991. *Tuva: Voices from the Land of the Eagles*. Recording. PAN Records PAN2005CD.

Koskoff, Ellen. 1989. *Women and Music in Cross-Cultural Perspective*. Urbana: University of Illinois Press.

———. 2008. "Field Notes, Bali: May 4." Unpublished.

Kunst, Jaap. (1949) 1973. *Music in Java*. 2 vols. Edited by E. L. Heins. 3rd enlarged ed. The Hague: Nijhoff. (English edition of *De Toonkunst van Java*, 1934.)

La Troupe Makandal. 1982. *A Trip to Voodoo*. Recording. Brooklyn, N.Y.: Gayrleen Records 1374.

Leichtman, Ellen C., ed. 1994. *To the Four Corners: A Festschrift in Honor of Rose Brandel*. Warren, Mich.: Harmonie Park.

Lestari: The Hood Collection, Early Field Recordings from Java. Recording. 2007. Mainz: Wergo SM 1712–2.

Lévi-Strauss, Claude. 1955. *Tristes Tropiques*. Paris: Librairie Plon. First American edition translated by John and Doreen Weightman. New York: Atheneum, 1974.

Lewiston, David, et al. 1969. *Golden Rain: Balinese Gamelan Music*. Recording. New York: Nonesuch Records.

Locke, David. 2004. "The African Ensemble in America: Contradictions and Possibilities." In Solís 2004c, 168–88.

Lomax, Alan. 1968. *Folk Song Style and Culture*. New Brunswick, N.J.: Transaction.

———. (1950) 1993. *Mister Jelly Roll: The Fortunes of Jelly Roll Morton, the New Orleans Creole and "Inventor of Jazz."* New York: Pantheon.

Malm, William P. 1959. *Japanese Music and Musical Instruments.* Tokyo: Tuttle.

———. 1963. *Nagauta: The Heart of Kabuki Music.* Westport, Conn.: Greenwood.

———. 1967. *Music Cultures of the Pacific, The Near East, and Asia.* Englewood Cliffs, N.J.: Prentice-Hall.

———. 1986. *Six Hidden Views of Japanese Music.* Berkeley: University of California Press.

Malm, William P., Eugene Enrico, et al. 1989. *Gagaku: The Court Music of Japan.* Film. Norman: University of Oklahoma, Center for Music Television.

———. 1991. *Music of Bunraku.* Film. Norman: University of Oklahoma, Center for Music Television.

———. 1993a. *Shinto Festival Music.* Film. Norman: University of Oklahoma, Center for Music Television.

———. 1993b. *Nagauta: The Heart of Kabuki Music.* Film. Norman: University of Oklahoma, Center for Music Television.

———. 1997. *Music of Noh Drama.* Film. Norman: University of Oklahoma, Center for Music Television.

———. 2002. *Shakuhachi.* Film. Norman: University of Oklahoma, Center for Music Television.

———. 2004. *Koto Music.* Film. Norman: University of Oklahoma, Center for Music Television.

Manuel, Peter. 1988. *Popular Musics of the Non-Western World: An Introductory Survey.* New York: Oxford University Press.

———. 1989. *Thumri in Historical and Stylistic Perspectives.* New Delhi: Motilal Banarsidass.

———. 2004. "The 'Guajira' between Cuba and Spain: A Study in Continuity and Change." *Latin American Music Review/Revista de Música Latinoamerican* 25 (2): 137–62.

———. 2010. *Tassa Thunder: Folk Music from India to the Caribbean.* Film. New York: Peter Manuel.

———. 2011. *Creolizing Contradance in the Caribbean.* Philadelphia: Temple University Press.

———. 2014. *Drumming for Ganesh: Music at Pune's Ganpati Festival.* Film. https://www.youtube.com/watch?v=UPJyFltCpdU.

———. 2015. *Tales, Tunes, and Tassa Drums: Retention and Invention in Indo-Caribbean Music.* Urbana: University of Illinois Press.

Manuel, Peter, and Michael Largey. 2016. *Caribbean Currents: Caribbean Music from Rumba to Reggae.* Philadelphia: Temple University Press.

Marshall, Lorna J. 1976. *The !Kung of Nyae Nyae.* Cambridge, Mass.: Harvard University Press.

Matos, Cláudia, Elizabeth Travassos, Fernanda Teixeira de Medeiros, and Affonso Romano de Sant'Anna. 2001. *Ao encontro da palavra cantada: Poesia, música e voz.* Rio de Janeiro: 7Letras.

———. 2008. *Palavra cantada: Ensaios sobre poesia, musica e vos.* Rio de Janeiro: 7Letras.

———. 2014. *Palavra cantada: Estudos transdisciplinares.* Rio de Janeiro: EdUERJ Edição.

May, Elizabeth, ed. 1980. *Musics of Many Cultures.* Berkeley: University of California Press.

Mayer, Jim, Lynn Adler, and John Rogers. 1991. *Kembali: To Return.* Film. Berkeley, Calif.: Ideas in Motion.

McAllester, David P. 1986. "Autobiographical Sketch." In *Explorations in Ethnomusicology: Essays in Honor of David P. McAllester*, edited by Charlotte J. Frisbie, 199–216. Detroit: Information Coordinators.

McGraw, Andy. 2017. Post on the Society for Ethnomusicology Listserv (January 20) from SEM Ethics Committee Chair Andy McGraw (subject line [SEM-L] ETHICS and SEM from amcgraw@richmond.edu).

McLean, Mervyn. 2006. *Pioneers of Ethnomusicology.* Coral Springs, Fla.: Llumina.

McPhee, Colin. 1966. *Music in Bali.* New Haven, Conn.: Yale University Press.

Mendonça, Maria. 2002. "Javanese Gamelan in Britain: Communitas, Afinity, and Other Stories." PhD diss., Wesleyan University.

Merriam, Alan P. 1964. *The Anthropology of Music*. Evanston, Ill.: Northwestern University Press.

———. 1977. "Musical Change in a Basongye Village." *Anthropos* 72 (5–6): 837–46.

Mohd. Anis Md. Nor. 1993. *Zapin: Folk Dance of the Malay World*. Oxford: Oxford University Press.

———. 1996. *Regional Performance Tradition in Contemporary Thai Performing Arts*. Bangkok: Čhulālongkǫnmahāwitthayālai, Sathāban ʿĒchīasǔksā (Institute of Asian Studies, Chulalongkorn University).

Mohd. Anis Md. Nor, and Stephanie Burridge. 2011. *Sharing Identities: Celebrating Dance in Malaysia*. London: Routledge.

Mohd. Anis Md. Nor, and Kendra Stepputat. 2017. *Sounding the Dance, Moving the Music: Choreomusicology in Maritime Southeast Asia*. London: Routledge.

Mrázek, Jan. 2002. *Phenomenology of a Puppet Theatre: Contemplations on the Art of Javannese Wayang Kulit*. Leiden: KITLV (Koninklijk Instituut voor Taal-, Land-en Volkenkunde).

Murdock, George P. 1967. *Ethnographic Atlas*. Pittsburgh: University of Pittsburgh Press.

Naroditskaya, Inna. 1999. "Continuity and Change in *Mugham* during the Last 100 Years." PhD diss., University of Michigan.

———. 2003. *Song from the Land of Fire: Azerbaijanian Mugam in the Soviet and Post-Soviet Periods*. London: Routledge.

———. 2005. "Azerbaijani *Mugham* and Carpet: Cross-Domain Mapping." *Ethnomusicology Forum* 14 (1): 25–55.

———. 2012. *Bewitching Russian Opera: The Tsarina from State to Stage*. Oxford: Oxford University Press.

———, ed. Forthcoming. *Music in the American Diasporic Wedding*. Bloomington: Indiana University Press.

Naroditskaya, Inna, and Linda Phyllis Austern. 2006. *Music of the Sirens*. Bloomington: Indiana University Press.

Nettl, Bruno. 1956. *Music in Primitive Culture*. Cambridge, Mass.: Harvard University Press.

———. 1964. *Theory and Method in Ethnomusicology*. New York: Free Press.

———. 1965. *Folk and Traditional Music of the Western Continents*. Englewood Cliffs, N.J.: Prentice-Hall.

———, ed. 1978. *Eight Urban Musical Cultures*. Urbana: University of Illinois Press.

———. 1984. "In Honor of Our Principal Teachers." *Ethnomusicology* 28:173–85.

———. 1995. *Heartland Excursions: Ethnomusicological Reflections on Schools of Music*. Urbana: University of Illinois Press.

———. 2002. *Encounters in Ethnomusicology: A Memoir*. Warren, Mich.: Harmonie Park.

———. 2009. "Contemplating Musicology at Illinois and in the World." *Sonorities: The News Magazine of the University of Illinois School of Music*. Urbana: University of Illinois, School of Music. 19–23.

———. 2010. "Ethnomusicology Critiques Itself: Comments on the History of a Tradition." In *Music Traditions, Cultures, and Contexts*, edited by Robin Elliott and Gordon E. Smith, 85–100. Waterloo, Canada: Wilfrid Laurier University Press.

———. 2013. *Becoming an Ethnomusicologist: A Miscellany of Influences*. Lanham, Md.: Scarecrow.

———. 2014. "Second Thoughts: A Short Personal Anthology." In *College Music Symposium* 54, special issue: "Ethnomusicology Scholarship and Teaching: Then, Now, and into the Future." https://symposium.music.org/index.php?option=com_k2& view=item&id=10675:second-thoughts-a-short-personal-anthology& Itemid=128.

Neuman, Daniel M. 1980. *The Life of Music in North India: The Organization of an Artistic Tradition*. Detroit: Wayne State University Press.

Neuman, Daniel, and Shubha Chaudhuri. With Komal Kothari. 2006. *Bards, Ballads, and Boundaries: An Ethnographic Atlas of Music Traditions in West Rajasthan*. Calcutta: Seagull.

Nooshin, Laudan, ed. 2009. *Music and the Play of Power in the Middle East, North Africa, and Central Asia*. Burlington, Vt.: Ashgate.

———. 2014. *The Ethnomusicology of Western Art Music*. London: Routledge.

———. 2015. *Iranian Classical Music: The Discourses and Practice of Creativity*. Burlington, Vt.: Ashgate.

Ohrlin, Glenn. 1973. *The Hell-Bound Train: A Cowboy Songbook*. Urbana: University of Illinois Press.

Olatunji, Babatunde. 1960. *Drums of Passion*. Recording. Columbia/Legacy: CK 66011.

Orczy, Baroness "Emmuska." 1947. *Links in the Chain of Life*. London: Hutchinson.

Ornstein, Ruby. 1967. *Gamelan Music of Bali*. Recording. Lyrichord: 7179.

———. 2006. "Wayan Gandera Redux." *Asian Music* 37 (2): 141–46.

———. 2011. Liner notes to *From Kuno to Kebyar: Balinese Gamelan Angklung*. Smithsonian Folkways Recordings SFW 50411.

Pettan, Svanibor H. 1992. "Gypsy Music in Kosovo: Interaction and Creativity." PhD diss. University of Maryland, Baltimore County.

———, ed. 1998. *Music, Politics, and War: Views from Croatia*. Zagreb: Institute of Ethnology and Folklore Research.

Post, Jennifer C. 1982. "Marathi- and Konkani-Speaking Women in Hindustani Music." PhD diss., University of Minnesota.

———. 2004a. *Ethnomusicology: A Research and Information Guide*. New York: Routledge.

———. 2004b. *Music in Rural New England Family and Rural Life, 1870–1940*. Lebanon: University of New Hampshire Press.

———. 2006. *Ethnomusicology: A Contemporary Reader*. New York: Routledge.

Powers, Harold S. 1958. "The Background of the South Indian Raga System." PhD diss., Princeton University.

———. 1980. "Mode." In Sadie 1980, 376–450.

Powne, Michael. 1968. *Ethiopian Music, an Introduction: A Survey of Ecclesiastical and Secular Ethiopian Music and Instruments*. London: Oxford University Press.

Qureshi, Regula. 1969. "Tarannum: The Chanting of Urdu Poetry." *Ethnomusicology* 13 (3): 425–68.

Racy, Ali Jihad. 1977. "Musical Change and Commercial Recordings in Egypt, 1904–1932." PhD diss., University of Illinois at Urbana-Champaign.

Reyes, Adelaida. 2009. "What Do Ethnomusicologists Do? An Old Question for a New Century." *Ethnomusicology* 53 (1): 1–17.

Rice, Timothy. 1987. "Toward the Remodeling of Ethnomusicology." *Ethnomusicology* 31 (3): 469–88.

———. 2007. "Review of Mervyn McLean, *Pioneers of Ethnomusicology*." *Yearbook for Traditional Music* 39:164–70.

Romero, Raúl. 2001. "Tragedies and Celebrations: Imagining Foreign and Local Scholarships." *Latin American Music Review* 22 (1): 48–62.

Rubenstein, Raechelle, and Linda H. Connor. 1999. *Staying Local in the Global Village*. Honolulu: University of Hawai'i Press.

Sachs, Curt. 1962. *The Wellsprings of Music*. The Hague: Nijhoff.

Sadie, Stanley, ed. 1980. *The New Grove Dictionary of Music and Musicians*. London: Macmillan.

Said, Edward. 1978. *Orientalism*. New York: Pantheon.

Samuelson, Paul A., and William A. Barnett, eds. 2007. *Inside the Economist's Mind: Conversations with Eminent Economists*. Malden, Mass: Blackwell.

Sarkissian, Margaret. 2000. *D'Albuquerque's Children: Performing Tradition in Malaysia's Portuguese Settlement*. Chicago: University of Chicago Press.

Schechner, Richard. 1988. *Performance Theory*. Hoboken: Taylor and Francis.

Scruggs, T. M. 2002. "'Come on in North Side, You're Just in Time': Musical-Verbal Performance and the Negotiation of Ethnically Segregated Social Space." *Current Musicology* 71–73:179–99.

———, ed. 2005. "Musical Reverberations from the Encounter of Local and Global Belief Systems." Special issue of *the world of music* 47 (1).

———. 2006. Música y el legado de la violencia a finales del siglo XX en Centro América [Music and the Legacy of Violence in Late-Twentieth-Century Central America]. *Trans—Revista Transcultural de Música/Transcultural Music Review* 10. http://www.sibetrans .com/trans/articulo/144musica-y-el-legado-de-la-violencia-a-finales-del-siglo-xx-en -centro-america.

Seeger, Anthony. 1987. *Why Suyá Sing: A Musical Anthropology of an Amazonian People*. Cambridge: Cambridge University Press.

Sercombe, Laurel. 2001. "And Then It Rained: Power and Song in Western Washington Coast Salish Myth Narratives." PhD diss., University of Washington.

Shankar, Ravi. 1971. "Concerto for Sitar and Orchestra." Score. New York: Schirmer.

Shostak, Marjorie. 1981. *Nisa: The Life and Words of a !Kung Woman*. Cambridge, Mass.: Harvard University Press.

Shukla, Shatrughan. 1991. *The Origin, Development, and Style of Thumri*. Delhi: Hindi Madhyam Karyanvaya Nideshalaya.

Slawek, Stephen M. 2000. "The Classical Master-Disciple Tradition." In *The Garland Encyclopedia of World Music, Vol. 5: South Asia: The Indian Subcontinent*, edited by Alison Arnold, 457–67. New York: Garland.

Slobin, Mark. 1976. *Music in the Culture of Northern Afghanistan*. Tucson: University of Arizona Press.

———, ed. 2008. *Global Soundtracks: Worlds of Film Music*. Middletown, Conn.: Wesleyan University Press.

Smith, Barbara Barnard. 1987. "Variability, Change, and the Learning of Music." *Ethnomusicology* 31 (2): 201–20.

Solís, Ted. 2004a. "Community of Comfort: Negotiating a World of 'Latin Marimba.'" In Solís 2004c, 229–48.

———. 2004b. "Introduction. Teaching What Cannot Be Taught: An Optimistic Overview." In Solís 2004c, 1–19.

———, ed. 2004c. *Performing Ethnomusicology: Teaching and Representation in World Music Ensembles*. Berkeley: University of California Press.

———. 2014a. "Conserve, Adapt, and Reconverge: Rationalizing a Template in Hawai'i Puerto Rican Musical Performance." In *Soundscapes from the Americas: Ethnomusicological Essays on the Power, Poetics, and Ontology of Performance*, edited by Donna A. Buchanan, 61–85. Farnham, UK: Ashgate.

———. 2014b. "'The Song Is You': From External to Internal in Ethnomusicological Performance." In *College Music Forum* 54, special issue: "Ethnomusicology Scholarship and Teaching: Then, Now, and into the Future." http://symposium.music.org/ index.php?option=com_k2&view=item&id=10691:ethnomusicology-scholarship-and -teaching-then-now-and-into-the-future&Itemid=124.

Sonneborn, Barbara. 1998. *Regret to Inform*. Film. Berkeley, Calif.: Sun Fountain.

Stone, Ruth M. 2001. "The Ethnomusicologist at Work." In *The Garland Encyclopedia of World Music, Vol. 10: The World's Music: General Perspectives and Reference Tools*, 3–168. New York: Routledge.

Strand, Julie. 2000. "Style and Substance: Improvisational Trends in Mandinka Balafon Performance." Master's thesis, Arizona State University.

———. 2009. "The Sambla Xyophone: Tradition and Identity in Burkina Faso." PhD diss., Wesleyan University.

Sumarsam. 2004. "Opportunity and Interaction: The Gamelan from Java to Wesleyan." In Solís 2004c, 69–92.

Sumerti, I Nengah. 1959. *Keluarga Putera Bali Purantara Jogjakarta-Gamelan Bali*. Recording. Surakarta: Lokananta Records ARD038.

Susilo, Hardja. 2004. "'A Bridge to Java': Four Decades Teaching Gamelan in America; Interview with Hardja Susilo by David Harnish, Ted Solís, and J. Lawrence Witzleben." In Solís 2004c, 53–68.

Tan Sooi Beng. 1993. *Bangsawan: A Social and Stylistic History of Popular Malay Opera*. Singapore: Oxford University.

Tenzer, Michael. 1991. *Balinese Music*. Berkeley: Periplus.

———. 2000. *Gamelan Gong Kebyar: The Art of Twentieth-Century Balinese Music*. Chicago: University of Chicago Press.

Terkel, Louis "Studs." 1972. *Working*. New York: Avon.

———. (1993) 2006. *Division Street: America*. New York: New Press.

Titon, Jeff Todd. 1977. *Early Downhome Blues: A Musical and Cultural Analysis*. Urbana: University of Illinois Press.

———. 2008. "Knowing Fieldwork." In Barz and Cooley 2008, 25–41.

Travassos Lins, Elizabeth. 1984. "Xamanismo e musica entre os Kayabi do Parque do Xingu." Master's thesis, Federal University of Rio de Janeiro.

———. 1996. "Os Mandarins Milagrosos; Cancoes Ancoes do Povo e Ideologia da Arte." PhD diss., Federal University of Rio de Janeiro.

———. 1997. *Os Mandarins Milagrosos: Arte e etnografia em Mario de Andrade e Béla Bartók*. Rio de Janeiro: Zahar.

Trimillos, Ricardo D. 1993. "Philippine Music as Colonial Experience and National Culture." In *The Age of Discovery: Impact on Philippine Culture and Society*, edited by Belinda A. Aquino and Dean T. Alegado, 17–24. 2nd ed. Honolulu: University of Hawai'i at Mānoa, Center for Philippine Studies.

———. 2004. "Subject, Object, and the Ethnomusicology Ensemble: The Ethnomusicological 'We' and 'Them.'" In Solís 2004c, 23–52.

Tuhus-Dubrow, Rebecca. 2013. "The Repurposed PhD: Finding Life after Academia—and Not Feeling Bad about It." *New York Times*, November 1.

Turner, Victor. 1982. *From Ritual to Theater: The Human Seriousness of Play*. New York: Performing Arts Journal Publications.

Vander, Judith. 1988. *Songprints*. Urbana: University of Illinois Press.

Vandor, Ivan. 1973. Review of Mantle Hood's *The Ethnomusicologist*. *Nuova Rivista Musicale Italiana* 3–4:478–80.

Van Tilburg, Jo Anne, Adrienne L. Kaeppler, Marshall Weisler, Claudio Cristino, and Angela Spitzer. 2008. "Petrographic Analysis of Thin-Sections of Samples from Two Monolithic Statues (MOAI), Rapa Nui (Easter Island)." *Journal of the Polynesian Society* 117 (3): 297–300.

Vetter, Roger. 2004. "A Square Peg in a Round Hole: Teaching Javanese Gamelan in the Ensemble Paradigm of the Academy." In Solís 2004c, 115–25.

Veurman, Barend Willem Enno, and Dirk Bax. 1944. *Liederen and dansen uit West-Friesland.* The Hague: Nijhoff.

Wade, Bonnie C. 1999. *Imaging Sound: An Ethnomusicological Study of Music, Art, and Culture in Mughal India.* Chicago: University of Chicago Press.

Wilcken, Lois, and Frisner Augustin. 1992. *The Drums of Vodou.* Performance in World Music Series, no. 7. Tempe, Ariz.: White Cliffs.

Williams, Sean. 1985. "Language, Melody, and Ornamentation in the Connemara Singing of Joe Heaney." Master's thesis, University of Washington.

———. 2001. *The Sound of the Ancestral Ship: Highland Music of West Java.* Oxford: Oxford University Press.

———. 2006. *The Ethnomusicologists' Cookbook: Complete Meals from around the World.* London: Routledge.

———. 2009. *Irish Traditional Music.* London: Routledge.

———. 2015. *The Ethnomusicologists' Cookbook: Complete Meals from around the World.* Vol. 2. London: Routledge.

Williams, Sean, and Lillis Ó Laoire. 2011. *Bright Star of the West: Joe Heany, Irish Song-Man.* New York: Oxford University Press.

Witzleben, J. Lawrence. 1997. "Whose Ethnomusicology? Western Ethnomusicology and the Study of Asian Music." *Ethnomusicology* 41 (2): 220–42.

Yampolsky, Philip B. 1987. *Lokananta: A Discography of the National Recording Company of Indonesia 1957–1985.* Madison, Wisc.: Center for Southeast Asian Studies, University of Wisconsin.

———. 1991–1999. *Music of Indonesia.* 20 discs. Washington, DC: Smithsonian/Folkways Recordings SFW 40055–40447.

———. 2013. "Music and Media in the Dutch Indies: Gramophone Records and Radio in the Late Colonial Era, 1903–1942." PhD diss., University of Washington.

Youssefzadeh, Ameneh. 2010. "Une passion pour l'Iran: Entretien avec Stephen Blum." *Cahiers d'Ethnomusicologie* 23:231–48.

Zemp, Hugo. 2005. *Siaka: An African Musician.* Film. Watertown, Mass.: Documentary Educational.

Index

Abebe, Getamesay, 88
Abu-Lughod, Lila, 4
academic couples: Judith Becker, 4, 369–71, 381;
  Frederick C. Lau, 332–33; Judith McCulloh,
  241; Philip Yampolsky, 189; Regula Burckhardt
  Qureshi, 40–41; Ruby Ornstein, 274; Salwa El-
  Shawan Castelo-Branco, 325–27; T. M. Scruggs,
  388; Tomie Hahn, 130, 297–98; Veronica
  Doubleday and John Baily, 369–70, 209–14,
  365–69, 405–6, 414–15
Actor Network Theory, 441
Adelson, Roger, 8, 20
Adler, Guido, 215
Adorno, Theodor, 60
Adzenyah, Abraham, 106
Afghanistan National Institute of Music (ANIM),
  369
Aga Khan Trust for Culture, 368
Agawu, Kofi, 316
Akademi Seni Karawitan Indonesia (ASKI). *See*
  Sekolah Tinggi Seni Indonesia
Akademi Seni Tari Indonesia (ASTI), 147
Akpabot, Samuel, 313
Ali, Mirza Mahmud, 41–42
Alliance for California Traditional Arts (ACTA),
  232
All India Radio, 95
American Council of Learned Societies Public
  Fellowship Program (ACLS), 231
American Folklore Society, 245
American Institute of Indian Studies (AIIS), 173,
  175, 334, 347

American Musicological Society (AMS), 245, 378,
  409, 451n2
American Society for Eastern Arts (ASEA),
  55–56, 66, 200
Amiot, Jean Joseph Marie, 11
Amonkar, Kishori, 224
Anderson, Benedict, 101, 159
Anderson, Lois, 269, 270, 279, 334, 396
Anderson, Ruth, 70
The Anthropology of Music (Merriam), 125, 241, 383
Arab Music Ensemble (Cairo), 326
Archer, William, 321–22, 323
Archives and Research Centre for
  Ethnomusicology of the American Institute of
  Indian Studies (ARCE), 92, 173, 174, 176, 177,
  410, 411
Archives of Folk and Primitive Music (Indiana
  University Bloomington), 240
Archives of Traditional Music (Indiana
  University Bloomington), 181, 182, 183
Aretz, Isabel, 317
Arizona State University (ASU), 279–80
Arom, Simha, 357
Arps, Ben, 291
Arts and Humanities Research Council, 368
Asai, Susan, 334
Asch, Michael, 384, 385
Asch, Moses, 45, 384
Asian American Dance Theatre, 130
Asian Cultural Council, 208
Asian Music (journal), 150, 272, 347
Asian Music Circuit (UK), 367

Nahumck, Nadia Chilkovsky, 180
Narayan, Pandit Ram, 383
Naroditskaya, Inna, 103–5, 304–7, 429–30
Nath, Pandit Pran, 65–66, 144
National Association of Schools of Music
  (NASM), 18
National Curriculum for Music (UK), 308
National Defense Foreign Language Fellowship,
  321
National Endowment for the Arts (NEA), 195,
  233, 245
National Film and Television School (UK)
  (NFTS), 366
National Heritage Fellowship, 245
National Merit Scholarship, 164
National Public Radio (NPR), 1, 189, 245
National University of Singapore (NUS), 291, 293
Navy School of Music, 33
Ncosana, Silas, 183
Nelson, Kristina, 215, 346
Nessa, Chuck, 89
Nessa Records, 89
Nettl, Bruno: academic vs. performer dichotomy,
  16; debt to informants in ethnomusicology, 7,
  10, 11; *Eight Urban Musical Cultures* (1978), 191,
  225; *Encounters in Ethnomusicology* (2002), 19;
  ethnomusicology and musicology, 2; *Folk and
  Traditional Music of the Western Continents*
  (1965), 247; influence of, xx, 84, 101, 180, 205,
  215, 282, 304, 309, 317, 323, 345–46, 357, 380, 389,
  429, 437; *Music in Primitive Culture* (1956), 84;
  philosophy of ethnomusicology, 1, 5; refugees
  in the academy, 45; study under, 217, 275, 320,
  321–22, 330–32, 443; *Theory and Method in
  Ethnomusicology* (1964), 84, 125, 363, 405
Neuman, Daniel M.: influence of, 99, 174–76,
  184, 398–401; *The Life of Music in North India*
  (1980), 225; work in India, 174–76, 184; work in
  Iran, 322
Newby, Kenneth, 142
New Grove Dictionary of Music and Musicians
  (Sadie, ed.), 159, 388, 389
The New School for Social Research, 115, 116
New York State Council on the Arts, 194
New York University (NYU), 130, 208, 219
New York University, Abu Dhabi, 297, 327, 372,
  390, 400–401
New York World's Fair, 379
Nketia, Joseph Hanson Kwabena, 316, 431
Nonesuch Records, 4, 24n11, 34, 99, 116, 117, 122
Nooshin, Laudan, 133–35, 307–12, 430–31;
  ethnomusicology, identity within the field, 456
Northwestern University, 30–31, 32, 237, 276, 304,
  306, 373
Northwest Folklife Festival, 400, 402
Notoprojo, K. P. H. (Cokro, Pak), 66
Nowera, Abdul Halim, 326
Nzewi, Meki, 431

Oberlin College, 49–50, 320, 321, 324
Ohio State University, 239–40, 241, 321

Ohio University, 238
Ohio Wesleyan University, 39, 239, 241
Ó Laoire, Lillis, 363
Olatunji, Babatunde, 5, 80
Oliveros, Pauline, 144, 301
Olsen, Dale, 396
Omar, Ustad Mohammad, 365
Omibiyi-Obidike, Mosun, 121, 313
Omojola, Olabode "Bode," 118–21, 313–16,
  431–32; ethnomusicology's debt to informants,
  7, 10
Ornstein, Ruby, 42–43, 269–75, 432–33; study
  under, 94
Otto, Steven, 107
Oxford University, 62

Pacholczyk, Jozef, 342
Palisca, Claude V., 125, 356
PAN Records, 245, 247–48, 249, 251, 422
Paradox (concert agency), 247
Park Mikyung, 334
Parvez, Shahid, 96
Pasternak-Mazur, Renata, 140–41, 256–60, 433;
  influence of national origin upon fieldwork, 18
Patel, Aniruddh, 407
Peace Corps, xv, 88
Pemberton, John, 55, 66, 101, 150
performance studies, 5, 159, 299, 300, 317, 339, 404
Peterman, Lewis, 252
Petran, Laurence, 372
Petrović, Ankica, 127, 342
Pettan, Hubert, 126
Pettan, Svanibor, 126–28, 341–44, 434–35;
  biomusicology, ecomusicology, zoomusicology,
  13; influence of, 277; influence of national
  origin upon fieldwork, 18
Philanthropic Educational Organization (PEO),
  37, 43n1, 84
Philippines Educational Theater Association
  (PETA), 350
Phor-Tor Festival, 349
Pilates, Joseph, 31
Policoff, Stephen, 208
Pomona College, 17, 332
Post, Jennifer C., 72–74, 223–29, 435–36; thoughts
  on ethnomusicology, 456; museum work, 15
Powers, Harold S., influence of, 71, 355, 383–84;
  personal performance study, 24n8; study
  under, 72, 346
Prentice-Hall, 125, 380, 393
Princeton University, 297, 300
Pukui, Mary Kawena, 221
Purwopangrawit, Pak Rasito, 347

Queens College, 43, 273
Queensland Conservatorium of Music, 154, 294
Queen's University Belfast, 366; "scene" in 1970s,
  213
Qureshi, Regula Burckhardt, 39–42, 383–87,
  436–37; community outreach, 415; diversity
  in ethnomusicology, 11; study under, 261,

Margaret Sarkissian is a professor of music at Smith College. She is the author of *D'Albuquerque's Children: Performing Tradition in Malaysia's Portuguese Settlement.*

Ted Solís is a professor of music at Arizona State University. He is the editor of *Performing Ethnomusicology: Teaching and Representation in World Musics.*

The University of Illinois Press
is a founding member of the
Association of American University Presses.

Composed in 10.5/15 Minion Pro
with Centaur display
by Kirsten Dennison
at the University of Illinois Press
Cover designed by Jim Proefrock
Cover illustration: Image by Rob Russell (https://tinyurl.com/ycxg2mdw)
Manufactured by Sheridan Books, Inc.

University of Illinois Press
1325 South Oak Street
Champaign, IL 61820-6903
www.press.uillinois.edu